Antonio Gramsci

SELECTIONS FROM
POLITICAL WRITINGS
(1921–1926)

ANTONIO GRAMSCI

SELECTIONS FROM
POLITICAL WRITINGS
(1921–1926)

with additional texts by other Italian Communist leaders

translated and edited by
QUINTIN HOARE

LAWRENCE AND WISHART
LONDON

Lawrence and Wishart Ltd
39 Museum Street
London WC1

First published 1978
English translation
Copyright © Quintin Hoare, 1978

This book is sold subject to the condition that it shall not, by way of trade or otherwise, be lent, re-sold, hired out, or otherwise circulated without the publishers' prior consent in any form of binding or cover other than that in which it is published and without a similar condition including this condition being imposed on the subsequent purchaser

Printed in Great Britain at
The Camelot Press Ltd, Southampton

CONTENTS

	page
INTRODUCTION by Quintin Hoare	ix
OUTLINE CHRONOLOGY, 1921–1926	xxv

I SOCIALISM AND FASCISM

1 Caporetto and Vittorio Veneto	3
2 War is War	5
3 Workers' Control	10
4 The General Confederation of Labour	12
5 Real Dialectics	15
6 Officialdom	17
7 Unions and Councils	20
8 Italy and Spain	23
9 Socialists and Communists	25
10 England and Russia	27
11 The Italian Parliament	29
12 The Communists and the Elections	32
13 The Elections and Freedom	35
14 Elemental Forces	38
15 The Old Order in Turin	41
16 Socialists and Fascists	44
17 Reactionary Subversiveness	46
18 Referendum	48
19 Leaders and Masses	52
20 Bonomi	54
21 The "Arditi del Popolo"	56
22 The Development of Fascism	59
23 Against Terror	61
24 The Two Fascisms	63
25 The Agrarian Struggle in Italy	66
26 Those Mainly Responsible	68
27 Parties and Masses	71
28 Masses and Leaders	75

29 One Year	79
30 The "Alleanza del Lavoro"	83
31 A Crisis within the Crisis	85
32 Lessons	87

II THE ROME CONGRESS

33 Theses on Tactics of the PCI ("Rome Theses") – *Bordiga and Terracini*	93
34 Congress Interventions	118
35 Report on the National Congress to the Turin Communist Section	123

III TOWARDS A NEW LEADING GROUP

36 Origins of the Mussolini Cabinet	129
37 Togliatti to Gramsci (1 May 1923)	132
38 Gramsci to Togliatti (18 May 1923)	138
39 Report by the minority of the Italian delegation to the Enlarged Executive meeting of June 1923	143
40 What the relations should be between the PCI and the Comintern	154
41 Faction Meeting: Fragment of the minutes (12 July 1923)	157
42 Three fragments by Gramsci	159
43 Gramsci to the Executive Committee of the PCI	161
44 Our Trade-union Strategy	164
45 What is to be Done?	169
46 Gramsci to Scoccimarro (5 January 1924)	173
47 Gramsci to Terracini (12 January 1924)	177
48 Gramsci to Togliatti (27 January 1924)	182
49 Gramsci to Leonetti (28 January 1924)	188
50 Gramsci to Togliatti, Terracini and others (9 February 1924)	191

IV THE NEW ORIENTATION

51 Editorial: March 1924	207
52 "Leader"	209
53 Against Pessimism	213
54 Gramsci to Togliatti, Scoccimarro, Leonetti, etc. (21 March 1924)	218

CONTENTS

55	The Programme of *L'Ordine Nuovo*	224
56	Problems of Today and Tomorrow	229
57	Gramsci to Zino Zini (2 April 1924)	237
58	Gramsci to Togliatti, Scoccimarro, etc. (5 April 1924)	240
59	The Como Conference: Resolutions	243
60	Gramsci's Intervention at the Como Conference	250
61	The Italian Crisis	255
62	Democracy and Fascism	267
63	The Fall of Fascism	273
64	Report to the Central Committee: 6 February 1925	276
65	Introduction to the First Course of the Party School	285
66	The Internal Situation in our Party and the Tasks of the Forthcoming Congress	293
67	Elements of the Situation	306

V THE LYONS CONGRESS

68	Minutes of the Political Commission nominated by the Central Committee to finalize the Lyons Congress documents	313
69	The Italian Situation and the Tasks of the PCI ("Lyons Theses") – *Gramsci* and *Togliatti*	340

VI REARGUARD ACTION

70	The Party's First Five Years	379
71	A Study of the Italian Situation	400
72	The Peasants and the Dictatorship of the Proletariat	412
73	Once Again on the Organic Capacities of the Working Class	417
74	We and the Republican Concentration	422
75	On the Situation in the Bolshevik Party	
	I Gramsci to Togliatti	426
	II To the Central Committee of the Soviet Communist Party	426
	III Togliatti to Gramsci	432
	IV Gramsci to Togliatti	437
76	Some Aspects of the Southern Question	441
NOTES		463
INDEX		508

INTRODUCTION

This volume's predecessor, *Political Writings (1910–1920)* (SPW I), contained a selection from Gramsci's political journalism during the First World War and in the two stormy years of revolutionary upsurge in Italy which followed the War. It closed on the eve of the January 1921 founding congress of the Italian Communist Party (PCI) at Livorno, with Gramsci at the age of twenty-nine already a well-known figure on the revolutionary left in his country, through the key animating role which his weekly journal *L'Ordine Nuovo* had played in the factory-council movement in Turin – Italy's "Petrograd". The present volume (SPW II) spans the six brief years of the PCI's legal existence, before the Italian fascist dictatorship became total. The first piece translated here was written on the morrow of the Livorno Congress, the last a few days before Gramsci's own arrest and entry into the darkness of Mussolini's prisons, from which he was to be released eleven years later only in time to die – aged forty-six.

If the period covered by SPW I was the crucial political watershed of this century – encompassing the Great War, the October Revolution, the débâcle of the IInd International and the creation of the IIIrd – the years that followed were hardly less momentous. They saw the restabilization of the bourgeois order where it had been most threatened in the wake of the War, and a crushing succession of defeats for the forces of revolution. They saw a growing bureaucratic involution of the young Soviet régime, in the conditions so harshly imposed by foreign intervention, civil war and imperialist blockade; Stalin's increasing domination of the Bolshevik Party; and in turn the increasing domination of the latter over the Communist International as a whole. Finally, they saw the rise to State power of fascism, first and most notably in Italy – an ominous prelude to the black tide of the thirties and to the Second World War.

It was in late 1920 and early 1921 that sections of the Italian ruling class – first landowners in central and northern Italy, followed closely by powerful industrial and financial forces – began to turn to the hitherto insignificant fascists as an appropriate instrument with which to prosecute their class interests. Perhaps the foremost consideration which led them to do so was an awareness of the extreme weakness of the traditional State institutions and party-system created in the half-century since national unification. In Italy, by this time the revolutionary upsurge had already passed its peak, and the defeats inflicted upon the working class in April and September 1920 had been decisive ones; but this was not perceived to be the case by the Italian bourgeoisie and landowning classes as a whole. Even those who did grasp the significance of the victory that had been achieved in 1920 wished to ensure that the opportunity would now be seized to eliminate once and for all any possibility for their opponents to regroup for a new trial of strength.

So the fascist *squadristi* were financed and equipped for the task of destroying the material resources and the political morale accumulated in four decades of working-class struggle. They burned and looted, bludgeoned and killed; and the mass socialist and trade-union organizations put up no adequate defence. Fascism acquired mass proportions; it also took on a dynamic of its own, with a considerable degree of autonomy from those sections of the traditional political class and of the State apparatus who had encouraged and thought to use it. In October 1922, the March on Rome brought Mussolini to full governmental power. In the ensuing four years, the fascists perfected a novel type of bourgeois class rule, characterized by the following main elements: total destruction of all independent working-class institutions; permanent mobilization of a mass political base, initially at least of a predominantly petty-bourgeois nature: suppression of all independent forms of political organization, including of the ruling class itself, outside the fascist institutions; defence, rationalization and development of Italian capitalism, in harmony with the essential interests of big capital; a militarist and expansionist ideology, facilitating imperialist adventures.

The PCI too was founded after the revolutionary moment had passed. Although, on paper, it emerged from the Socialist Party (PSI) in January 1921 with 60,000 members – one third of the total – its real strength in 1921 was about 40,000. Moreover, its popular support, as reflected in electoral results, was far weaker in relation to that commanded by the PSI than the balance of forces at the latter's Livorno Congress had suggested. The Communist Party was, of course, from the beginning a prime target for fascist repression, and its membership figures reflect this: some 25,000 in late 1922; perhaps no more than 5,000 active members in early 1923; a slow build-up to around 8,500 in November of that year and to 12,000 in the spring of 1924 (with 5,000 more in the youth organization); expansion to 25,000 members by the end of 1924, in the less repressive conditions which followed the murder of the social-democratic deputy Matteotti, when the fascist leadership's confidence temporarily faltered in face of the upsurge of opposition which the crime provoked; 27,000 members at the end of 1925, despite renewed repression – a figure which probably did not alter much in the year that remained before the party was finally driven into total clandestinity in October 1926.

Thus the PCI, despite a significant implantation in the most combative sectors of the working class, was always a relatively small party prior to fascism – although, of course, the extent to which different policies might have changed this remains open to debate. Certainly, the party's refusal to accept the Comintern's united front policy elaborated in late 1921 – a refusal which was intransigent under its first leadership headed by Bordiga (see, e.g. Rome Theses, Part Two below), and which was only imperfectly rescinded under Gramsci's leadership in 1924–6 (see, e.g. Lyons Theses, Part Five below, especially pp. 338, 359 and 372–4) – was a grave handicap. The history of the party in the first six years of its existence was the history of a revolutionary organization of modest proportions, formed and initially led on an extremely sectarian basis, striving – in notably adverse conditions, dominated by a new form of reactionary violence at first countenanced by and subsequently mastering the Italian bourgeois state – to work out a strategy and tactics that would allow it to maintain and extend its mass base and mobilize against ascendant fascism a working class and peasantry dominated by other political forces (social and Christian democrats). These aims, of course, were tragically not to be achieved.

In this context, the coordinates governing the concerns of an Italian Communist leader such as Gramsci during this period were clearly defined: 1. the imperative need to analyse the novel form of reactionary organization that was fascism, and to find an adequate response to it; 2. the insertion of this theoretical and practical task into an international framework, in which the Comintern was seeking to assess the historical significance of social-democracy's continuing strength and of the ebbing of the post-war revolutionary upsurge (especially after October 1923) and to work out a line capable of meeting these unforeseen circumstances; 3. the complex relations with other political forces on the Italian left, above all the PSI, given the contradictory pressures of on the one hand the Comintern united front policy and on the other the

PCI's sectarian formation; 4. the intense inner-party struggle that was conditioned by the foregoing problems, as by more direct forms of Comintern intervention and by the course of events in the Soviet Union. These then provide the master themes of the present volume. What is fascism, what Italian historical specificity had produced it and how to combat it? How to defeat reformism and destroy its influence over the masses? What kind of revolutionary party could carry out these tasks, and how could it gain a mass implantation? How to evaluate and relate to events in the Soviet Union and the evolution of the Comintern?

When the Italian Communist Party was founded in January 1921, Gramsci – despite *L'Ordine Nuovo*'s earlier-mentioned key role in the central revolutionary experience of the post-war period – was in a totally isolated position on its first central committee. Bordiga had begun to organize a national communist faction within the PSI in the autumn of 1919 long before any of the *Ordine Nuovo* group recognized the need for an autonomous organization of communists. It was only in May 1920, after the defeat of the April general strike had exposed the PSI leadership's inability or unwillingness to take a revolutionary initiative in practice despite its fiery rhetoric, that Gramsci finally understood the need for such an organization. Then, however, he found himself unable to persuade Bordiga that parliamentary abstentionism should not be the programmatic basis for the faction, so could not join it. At the same time, he was forced to break with most of his *Ordine Nuovo* comrades – Tasca, Togliatti and Terracini foremost among them – since they had not yet drawn the same conclusions as he had from the PSI's passivity in April. Gramsci was thus almost entirely alone in the summer of 1920. And although by the autumn of that year the other members too of the original *Ordine Nuovo* group had come to accept the necessity of a new organization, and like Gramsci now joined Bordiga's national communist faction, by that time the unity of the group was shattered; indeed, Terracini and Togliatti fell for a time more completely under the political dominance of Bordiga than Gramsci was ever to do. The absence of any least element of the *Ordine Nuovo* thematic from the October 1920 manifesto of the communist faction was a clear enough reflection of the political basis upon which the embryonic Communist Party was being formed.

Thus Gramsci's articles of 1921 and 1922 (see Part One below) in the new daily *Ordine Nuovo*, now an official party organ, were written within considerable subjective and objective constraints. On the one hand, democratic centralist norms – as then interpreted, at least –

permitted only limited room for individual expression of views, certainly once a party line had been established. But more importantly, despite genuine differences which were indeed to grow throughout this period, and unlike Tasca who by the March 1922 Rome Congress had formed an opposition tendency based on the line of the International, Gramsci did not have an autonomous overall political outlook at the time, distinct from that of the Bordiga leadership. On the central question of policy towards the PSI – the question which was to govern the party leadership's refusal to apply the united front policy – Gramsci was at one with Bordiga. It was only years later (see p. 380 below) that he was to understand Lenin's dictum to Serrati: "Separate yourself from Turati, and then make an alliance with him." The sole – though crucially important – issue on which Gramsci began to develop specific and articulated disagreements with the party leadership in 1921 and 1922 was on the nature and significance of fascism, and to some extent – though less than was the case for Tasca – on the centrality for revolutionaries in such a situation of the struggle against fascism.

In May 1922, Gramsci went to Moscow as PCI delegate to the Comintern; he was to remain there for eighteen months. He was very ill for part of the time; he learnt Russian; he fell in love and married – an unhoped for experience movingly recounted in Fiori's biography; he attended the second Enlarged Executive meeting of the International in June 1922, the Fourth World Congress in November of the same year, and the third Enlarged Executive in June 1923. Beyond this, little is known about Gramsci's life in Moscow; his own writings are frustratingly uninformative on the subject. What is, at all events, clear is that he remained, at least until mid-1923, in substantive agreement with Bordiga on the main issue which divided the PCI from the Comintern Executive – the united front, and relations with the PSI – and only differed from him on tactical questions (though it is true Gramsci did subsequently on one occasion – see p. 196 and n. 112 below – claim already to have been "in favour of the united front right through to its normal conclusion in a worker's government" even at the time of the Rome Congress). Moreover, though such tactical differences on occasion took a sharp form – notably at the Fourth World Congress – Gramsci did not question Bordiga's leadership of the party as such at this time, despite quite explicit encouragement from Rakosi to do so with Comintern approval. (Nevertheless, though only Tasca and a relatively small minority around him opposed his leadership and line in this period, Bordiga did in fact begin to lose his grip on the party in

1923. This was partly due to his arrest and imprisonment for most of the year. It was partly a result of the fragmentation of his majority when some of its members were persuaded by Gramsci at the June 1923 Enlarged Executive meeting to participate in a provisional leadership against Bordiga's advice. But most of all it was because, in the long run, his intransigent policy — of principled non-participation in leading bodies, given his disagreement with the International line — precisely condemned him to passivity.)

It was only after Gramsci moved to Vienna at the end of 1923, as a first step towards his return to Italy, that he began — in a series of letters (see Part Three below) to former members of the original *Ordine Nuovo* group now belonging like himself to the Bordigan majority — to construct explicitly a potential alternative leadership. Although this involved breaking up the existing majority, it did not initially exclude reaching agreement with Bordiga on a new basis. For Gramsci was still far more hostile to Tasca and the Right, whom he viewed as tendentially liquidationist of the party that had been created at Livorno. But he was determined both to end the long conflict with the International and to combat the doctrinaire immobilism which characterized the party under Bordiga's guidance. In the event, predictably, these objectives led him inexorably towards a break with Bordiga. By the time of the consultative party conference which took place clandestinely near Como in May 1924 a few days after his return to Italy, Gramsci had welded together a Centre current with a slender majority over the Right in the central committee (the hard core of the Bordigan majority had followed their leader's advice and resigned from the body some months earlier) — though, of course, in the party apparatus and in the membership as a whole Bordiga's dominance was still overwhelming.

Gramsci led the party from May 1924 until his arrest in October 1926. Despite the hopes of 1924 itself, when the Matteotti Affair seemed to jeopardize the fascist hold on power and when the party was rebuilt to something approaching its strength prior to the violent repression of late 1922 and early 1923, the period as a whole formed a bleak prelude to the total dictatorship which Mussolini finally established at the end of 1926. The party's existence in 1925 and 1926 was at best semi-legal, subject to continual harassment and the arrest or assassination of its cadres, who were increasingly driven underground or forced into exile. In Gramsci's internal documents and newspaper articles of this period (see Parts Four, Five and Six below), historical analysis, and study of the internal contradictions of the ruling class in general and fascism in particular, more and more came to predominate over immediate strategic and tactical perspectives, other than of an essentially party-building kind. Such strategic perspectives as were developed – above all, the need to forge an alliance of Northern workers and Southern peasants – were of an "epochal" nature (though it is certainly true that the PCI did have some limited success in this period in creating base organizations in the factories and in its greatly intensified work among the peasants).

Perhaps not surprisingly, in this situation of growing impotence, under impossible conditions, the internal struggle which raged in the PCI in 1925 and 1926 – and which saw Bordiga's overwhelming domination in May 1924 at all levels below the Central Committee totally reversed within eighteen months – was hardly focused on the situation in the country at all. Instead, it was centred on "Bolshevization" and on relations with the Comintern (see especially Part Five below). At the same time, particularly after the Lyons Congress in January 1926, it is plain that Gramsci was increasingly concerned more with the future than with the present. The last thing he wrote before his arrest, following his famous letters on the situation in the CPSU (see pp. 426–40 below) – themselves notable for their freedom from tactical considerations, at such a moment – was the never-to-be-completed essay on "The Southern Question" which concludes this volume. It is hardly necessary to stress the extent of its detachment from a situation of the party which Gramsci was subsequently to liken to a shipwreck – with himself as the captain unable to leave while there were still passengers on board (see *Quaderni del Carcere* – QC – pp. 1762–4, quoted in the Introduction to *Selections from the Prison Notebooks* – SPN – p. lxxxvii).

The texts translated here represent perhaps one quarter of Gramsci's identified political writings and internal reports for the period 1921–6. Pending a critical edition at present in preparation under the auspices of the Instituto Gramsci, most of these can be found in the following collections: *Socialismo e fascismo: l'Ordine Nuovo 1921–2*, Turin, 1966; *La formazione del gruppo dirigente del PCI nel 1923–1924* (ed. Togliatti), Rome, 1962; *La costruzione del partito comunista: 1923–1926*, Turin, 1971; *Per la Verità*, Rome, 1974. Although the title of the present volume does not imply a similar restriction to that operating in SPW I, since all Gramsci's output during these years can be broadly classified as political, the selection is nevertheless once again not a *representative* one. First of all, it is unbalanced in favour of substantive texts. This has meant excluding from Part One virtually all Gramsci's numerous articles on international events and polemical pieces on the PSI and other left forces, and from Parts Four and Six most of his shorter contributions to the 1925–6 faction struggle, even though these categories account for a considerable proportion of his total production. Obviously, too, primarily literary or historiographical criteria would have resulted in a very different choice. But the present volume does contain as many as possible of Gramsci's considered political texts of the period, on the most important issues which faced him. Moreover, any reader will quickly discover that the writings included here deal with many of what continue to be central political questions today: organs of working-class power; bourgeois, parliamentary democracy and proletarian, soviet democracy; the revolutionary party, its nature and its functioning; proletarian internationalism and the evolution and nature of Soviet society; fascism and its specificity as a form of bourgeois class rule; the fight against reformism and at the same time for unity of the working class in action and hegemony over other oppressed layers; the nature of the epoch; and so on. At least, this conviction has fundamentally governed the selection made.

* * * *

In the fifteen months between June 1919 and September 1920, Gramsci and *L'Ordine Nuovo* established a uniquely dialectical and intimate relationship to the revolutionary Turin proletariat, theorizing its experience and at the same time stimulating and seeking to channel that experience by means of its own theoretical work. Gramsci's articles from this period, the most important of which are translated in SPW I, provide an unmatched record and systematization of, reflection upon, and set of programmatic prescriptions for emerging organs of proletarian power. The actual forms of such power, both prior to and succeeding the revolutionary seizure of power, have probably never been written about so concretely or with such force and passion. In addition, Gramsci began in this period to theorize the relationship between, on the one hand, "voluntary" organizations such as unions or parties and, on the other, councils which potentially could become organs of the whole working-class – indeed after the revolution the foundations of its state and instruments for the exercise of its class rule.

What is clear from the writings collected in the present volume is that there is a very great degree of continuity between the 1919–20 *Ordine Nuovo* and Gramsci's positions right up to the time of his arrest (see, for example, pp. 372, 393–4 and 410 below). Even some of the earlier debates with Bordiga and Tasca (see SPW I, pp. 199–236 and 239–98) were repeated at the Lyons Congress, with the same protagonists. But more importantly, the fundamental orientation of the PCI under Gramsci's leadership was towards the creation of autonomous class organs at the base: "workers' and peasants' committees", "agitational committees of proletarian unity", etc. Insofar indeed as Gramsci did come to accept the united front other than "from below" – and it was his misfortune to move in this direction only at the moment when the Comintern, under Zinoviev's erratic direction, was itself becoming increasingly ambiguous about what the united front really involved (the ill-starred formula of social-democracy being the left wing of the bourgeoisie, for instance, was consecrated by the Fifth World Congress in 1924) – he tended to see it as *based* on such grass-roots organizations (see, for instance, the PCI proposal in late 1926 of a "Republican assembly on the basis of workers' and peasants' committees"). At the same time, Gramsci was himself to emphasize, in the last piece he wrote before his arrest (see pp. 441–2 below), that the highly original and concrete approach to relations between workers and peasants in Italy that was so characteristic of the PCI under his leadership was demonstrably foreshadowed in the *Ordine Nuovo* positions of 1919–20.

However, just as Gramsci's positions in 1919–20 had been flawed by his failure to integrate within them any real conception of the role and nature of the revolutionary party, similarly – after the foundation of the Communist Party – it can be argued that any adequate articulation of the relation between party and organs of workers' power continued to elude Gramsci. In 1919, the mistake had been in effect to downgrade the central role of the party in making the revolution. Now, the error was to accept as generally valid the one-party system which had been arrived at pragmatically, and without conscious intention or accompanying theorization, under the force of circumstances in the Soviet Union (though Gramsci was, of course, never to formulate the notion of party/state fusion in practice or party pre-eminence as Bordiga had so crudely in 1920). This inevitably had its effect upon the fertile path of theorization of the nature of proletarian power which *L'Ordine Nuovo* had embarked on in 1919, and which Gramsci was to continue to tread until he died. As with the linked question of proletarian democracy, acceptance (however critical) of Soviet reality as a universal model, at least in this important respect, was to represent a real barrier – and the genuine anguish of Gramsci's writings on party unity, both here and in the Prison Notebooks, is related to his partial awareness of this. To say this, of course, is not at all to dismiss what Gramsci did write on the party, either before or after his arrest; but it does argue that, for all its originality and force, there was a crucial limitation to it.

The question of the Soviet model was, manifestly, at the very centre of what was termed the "Bolshevization" of communist parties called for by the Fifth World Congress in 1924 and applied throughout the International in the following year. This process – around which so much of the Italian inner-party struggle was to revolve – had two proclaimed objectives: to proletarianize the party, and to homogenize it. Both aims are in themselves valid enough, within carefully defined limits. Thus in the somewhat confusing debate between Gramsci and Bordiga (see Part Five below) on whether the party was an "organ" of the working class, as the latter argued, or a "part" of it as the former held, there was a substantive issue at stake on which Gramsci was entirely right; and the eloquent passages in the Lyons Theses on this subject are related immediately to Gramsci's subsequent preoccupation in prison with the formation of working-class intellectuals. Similarly, a concern to homogenize the political consciousness of the PCI, given its recent formation and disparate origins, was also legitimate; and the conception of an internal party school functioning by correspondence which Gramsci advanced in 1925 (see pp. 285–92 below) shows clearly that his own aim in this respect was far from being merely factional.

Nevertheless – and it is a major qualification – the Bolshevization campaign cannot possibly be interpreted *simply* as a process aimed at achieving more proletarian and more unified parties. It was evidently linked centrally with the Russian inner-party struggle, and with the elimination of international allies for the Russian opposition. After all, the Comintern had been dominated by Zinoviev organizationally since its foundation, while Trotsky and Radek had played central roles in its first congresses. Furthermore, all questions of inner-party functioning involve issues of principle which transcend the particular conjuncture in which they arise. Now it is undeniable that repressive conditions such as existed in Italy in 1924–6 rendered a flourishing inner-party democracy difficult to sustain, and that in fact, despite the bitterness of the faction fight and some undoubted centralist excesses, there was a remarkable degree of real discussion in the circumstances. However, just as measures which the Bolsheviks took under the pressure of circumstances in the Civil War became enshrined later after Lenin's death as permanent and unchallengeable aspects of Soviet party functioning, so too did the Bolshevization process introduce a qualitative change into the lives of the other Comintern parties (and one whose consequences remain to this day, to a greater or lesser degree, not just in the contemporary Communist Parties, but in all political organizations whose roots lie in the IIIrd International). Gramsci's acceptance of Bolshevization at face value was no doubt sincere; but it was to reinforce that aspect of his thought which was always to remain locked to the Soviet model – even at the very time when, in prison, he was developing a complex conception of the (different) relations between State and civil society in the West, and of the role of the party in the transition to communism, which departed radically from what he knew to be the course adopted in the USSR.

Something similar can be said more generally with respect to events in Russia and the evolution of the Comintern as a whole. After some initial sympathy with the Left Opposition in 1923–4 (see, for example, pp. 191–2 below), Gramsci aligned himself increasingly firmly with the majority in the CPSU from mid-1924 on. He was genuinely convinced by the charge levelled against the Opposition by Stalin and Bukharin that its positions neglected the peasants. Perhaps more importantly, he made repeated comparisons – from as early as May 1924 (see pp. 252–3 below) – between the danger to the unity of their respective parties represented, as he saw it, by Trotsky and by Bordiga. But aside from these two aspects of the inner-party struggle in the Soviet Union, themselves not in any substantive sense primary, Gramsci surprisingly does not seem to have concerned himself seriously with the full range of issues under discussion within the Russian party, or – despite his long stay in the Soviet Union and command of the Russian language – to have reflected critically, at least prior to his arrest, on the overall development of the Russian revolution. Yet the course of events in the USSR, of course, was of central importance for each and every party of the IIIrd International – and it is here alone, perhaps, that Bordiga showed a superior awareness to Gramsci in the mid-twenties.

It is difficult to avoid the judgement that from 1924 on Gramsci, confronting in exceptionally grave and difficult conditions the responsibility of leading his party, made an *a priori* choice of unconditional alignment with the Comintern leadership. As he said in January 1924, while still striving to construct a new leading group in the party: "I will ... take the doctrine and tactics of the Comintern as the basis for an action programme for our activity in the future." This choice was perhaps not surprising, since one of the principal motives which had impelled Gramsci to challenge Bordiga's leadership of the PCI was his determination to end the damaging conflict with the Comintern. (Moreover, Bordiga was in fact to align himself in 1925–6 with the Russian Opposition.) Nevertheless, it was to have serious consequences, even upon his writings in prison. For even then, although he was to move into clear opposition to the policies of the Third Period (as we know from his brother's testimony, and from the publication in 1964 by the PCI weekly *Rinascita* of a memoir by a communist fellow-prisoner, Athos Lisa, who unlike Gramsci had supported the line in 1931–2), he never went back to attempt any general analysis of the course of events in the Soviet Union which had made the Third Period possible – although it is certainly possible to interpret many individual passages in the Prison Notebooks as a critical reflection upon Soviet development.

Paradoxically, it was Gramsci's very qualities as a political leader, one might argue, which led him uncharacteristically astray on the crucial terrain of relations between Italian and Russian developments. He was right to be dismayed at the passivity of the Italian party's policies in its first years; right to see that these bore a heavy responsibility in weakening the working-class resistance to fascism; right to feel the urgency – as Bordiga certainly did not – of sinking roots in the working class, fighting in the front line with it around even partial demands, exploiting divisions within the ruling class. But precisely because he felt so strongly – and so correctly – that Bordiga's leadership was disastrous, and also because he certainly felt a considerable measure of co-responsibility for the policies of the first years and above all for the prolonged resistance to the united front, Gramsci swung over in 1924 to base his new orientation for the PCI on a full acceptance of Comintern policy – just as the latter was more and more coming to reflect primarily Soviet concerns and the Russian inner-party conflict.

On the question of fascism, the debate between Gramsci and Bordiga was equally fierce; but this time there can be no doubt of Gramsci's superiority. Even under Bordiga's leadership, his articles on fascism (see Part One below) – despite uncertainties of analysis which led him to emphasize now one aspect of the phenomenon, now another – were not only incomparably better than Bordiga's sublime lack of interest in the question at all (see, for example, the place accorded to fascism – two mentions! – in the Rome Theses), they also had a concreteness of analysis which gives them a greater permanent value than the more formally "correct" positions of Tasca (though the latter had the merit of understanding earlier and more consistently than Gramsci the need to fight fascism through united front tactics). In fact, Gramsci alone in the PCI was really interested at this time in the concrete study of fascism in all its dimensions and ramifications and internal contradictions. The debate continued up to Gramsci's arrest, in one form or another. Bordiga, as always, maintained a simple and inflexible stance (see pp. 322–3 below), whose inadequacy is not hard to discern. Light-years separated it from Gramsci's finely nuanced formulations in the Lyons Theses (see especially pp. 349–50 below).

There is an obvious connection between the assessment made of fascism and its significance and the strategy one adopts to fight it. Here, as already pointed out, Gramsci was to remain at one with Bordiga at least until mid-1923 in his resistance to the united front as proposed by the Comintern (i.e. "from above"). Indeed, his visceral hatred for, and unilateral analysis of, the maximalist PSI – which was for him certainly the main factor – meant that right up to the moment of his arrest Gramsci was not fully to grasp the true class coordinates of the united front strategy, continuing to see social democracy as the "left wing of the bourgeoisie". Nevertheless, despite this incomplete abandonment of old errors, his leadership of the PCI was characterized by a notable flexibility of tactics within a basically Leninist framework, and by a consistent attempt to arrive at a "concrete analysis of the concrete situation" – as the writings translated in this volume demonstrate, at times brilliantly. Above all, he understood – unlike Bordiga – the need to fight to win the majority of the working class.

It is important to appreciate that Gramsci, beyond the tactics of the united front, always posed the question of class unity and class alliance in specifically class and class-institutional rather than party terms. This is very clear in the Lyons Theses (see p. 357 below), where the fundamental task of the Communist Party is defined by Gramsci as having three aspects: "(a) to organize and unify the industrial and rural proletariat for the revolution; (b) to organize and mobilize around the proletariat all the forces necessary for the victory of the revolution and the foundation of the workers' State; (c) to place before the proletariat and its allies the problem of insurrection against the bourgeois State and of the struggle for proletarian dictatorship, and to guide them politically and materially towards their solution, through a series of partial struggles." Moreover, there is no real doubt that there is a substantive continuity between this position and Gramsci's later views in prison. The Athos Lisa report, alluded to earlier, recounts how Gramsci developed the following themes, *inter alia*, in the course of discussions with other communist prisoners: the need for a military organization capable of taking on the power of the bourgeois State – but a military organization conceived of not in narrowly technical terms, but in essentially political ones; the importance of the intermediate slogan of a "constituent assembly", first as a means of winning allies for the proletariat in its struggle against the ruling class and subsequently as a terrain on which to fight against all projects of peaceful reform, demonstrating to the Italian working class how the only possible solution in Italy resides in the proletarian revolution; the existence of all the objective conditions for a conquest of power by the proletariat, but the imperative urgency – as a precondition of such a conquest of power – of realizing the proletariat's hegemony over the peasantry.

What then, finally, was Gramscis' view on the "nature of the epoch" at the time of his arrest? What was his assessment of the degree of bourgeois restabilization which had taken place since the post-war revolutionary upsurge? What was the meaning of the famous passages in the Prison Notebooks on war of manœuvre and war of position? There is no place here either to attempt any full answer to this crucial question, nor to try to chart the elements of continuity and discontinuity between Gramsci's positions before and after his arrest. This essential task of textual analysis far transcends the limits of this introduction. But one thing can nevertheless be said. It is certainly necessary to give full weight to the passages translated in SPN on "passive revolution". Gramsci was prepared to look even the worst eventuality in the face. But there is no justification at all for concluding, as some have done, that Gramsci considered revolution to be no longer on the agenda, for a whole historical epoch; or that it involves only cultural and ideological activity; or that it no longer requires confronting in the final resort the repressive apparatus of the bourgeois State. (On these questions, there was no break in continuity between the writings collected in the present volume and the Prison Notebooks.)

What is true is that Gramsci – more than any other Marxist – was led by the working-class defeats of the early twenties to turn the focus of his attention to the specific ideological and institutional mechanisms whereby a ruling class seeks to secure and organize the consent of the exploited and oppressed masses to the existing order. This did not prevent him from perceiving clearly the dialectic of coercion and consent which characterizes all forms of class rule. He never neglected, for example, the role of violence in maintaining bourgeois dominance even under conditions of parliamentary democracy, or reciprocally the importance of means of ideological control even under a fascist dictatorship. But it is no doubt his unique preoccupation with the political and ideological hegemony over civil society which is the dominant mode of class rule under "normal" conditions of bourgeois democracy that in part explains Gramsci's compelling attraction for socialists of the most widely differing persuasions. Moreover, this emphasis long pre-dated his imprisonment. Even some of the most important theoretical formulations of the Prison Notebooks were essentially elaborations of conclusions he had reached in the period of his active involvement in the class struggle. A striking example is provided by the passages on pp. 199–200 and 408–9 below, in which Gramsci expresses in embryonic form the very ideas which were later to be so powerfully developed precisely in the momentous notes on "war of position".

The eloquent texts collected in the present volume, like the best of Gramsci's writings in prison, reveal at the same time – on almost every page – what it is that constitutes the other major factor in Gramsci's contemporary standing. Even today, when world capitalism appears more vulnerable – both in the imperialist heartlands themselves and in the former colonies of Asia and Africa – than for a long time, socialists have to contend not just with the present class enemy, but also with the legacy of past defeats. Gramsci lived a defeat for most of his adult life, from 1920 until his death in 1937. Yet in defeat, he neither abandoned hope, nor withdrew from struggle (militant organizational struggle until his arrest, militant intellectual struggle thereafter), nor ceased to think for himself. He turned defeat into a preparation for future victory – not his own as an individual, but that of the working class. Saved by a fascist prison from the terrible dilemma posed by Stalin's ascendancy for other communists of his generation; saved in that prison by his confidence – or rather determination – that black reaction would not last for ever, and that the proletarian revolution remained historically on the agenda, in an epochal sense; Antonio Gramsci can today be seen for what he was – the greatest Marxist Western Europe has produced in this century, and the one from whom there is most to be learned.

OUTLINE CHRONOLOGY, 1921–1926

1921
- January — PSI Livorno Congress; party splits when Serrati leadership, organized as "unitary communist faction", refuses to expel reformists; PCI founded.
L'Ordine Nuovo becomes a daily organ of the new party.
- March — *Märzaktion* in Germany.
Tenth Congress of Bolshevik Party.
- April — Gramsci seeks a meeting with D'Annunzio.
General elections, in which PCI wins 290,000 votes, PSI over a million and a half.
Arditi del Popolo begin to form, as fascist terror continues unabated.
- June — Giolitti government falls, Bonomi becomes prime minister.
Third World Congress of the Communist International.
- August — Conciliation Pact signed between PSI deputies and Fascists in parliament.
- September — Maffi and Lazzari form a "Third-internationalist" tendency, against the Serrati leadership of PSI.
- October — PSI Milan Congress; Serrati majority for withdrawal of application to join IIIrd International.
- December — Comintern Executive formulates the united front policy.

1922
- February — Bonomi resigns, Facta becomes prime minister.
Alleanza del Lavoro founded.
First Enlarged Executive meeting of the Comintern; Italian delegates vote against leadership on the United Front.
- March — USI Congress decides against joining the Red Trade-union International.
Second Congress of PCI at Rome; minority emerges, led by Tasca, to fight for acceptance of Comintern line.

April	Conference of the three Internationals in Berlin.
May	Gramsci goes to Moscow as delegate to Comintern.
June	Second Enlarged Executive meeting of Comintern.
July	Facta government falls; political crisis temporarily resolved by formation of new weak Facta administration.
August	Failure of the "legalitarian" general strike in Italy.
September	PSI holds Rome Congress, expels reformists who form Unitary Socialist Party (PSU), led by Turati, Momigliano and Matteotti.
October	March on Rome. Mussolini administration formed, with participation of individual right-wing *popolari* and Liberals.
November	Fourth World Congress of the Communist International; PCI delegates, under pressure from international leadership, accept principle of fusion with PSI.

1923

January	In PSI, former Republican Nenni forms National Committee of Socialist Defence, to fight against fusion with PCI, now favoured by Serrati as well as Maffi and Lazzari.
February	Bordiga arrested.
March	Comintern convenes European anti-fascist conference at Frankfurt.
April	Popular Party congress in Turin launches idea of "Freedom Blocs"; pro-fascist right wing breaks away. PSI congress in Milan produces a majority opposed to fusion. Twelfth Congress of the Bolshevik Party.
May	IInd and Two-and-a-half Internationals merge in Hamburg.
June	Third Enlarged Executive meeting of Comintern; this installs provisional "mixed" leadership of PCI majority and minority, following Bordiga's arrest.
July	PCI majority decides to form a faction.
September	Defeat in Bulgaria.
October	Platform of the Forty-Six issued in the Soviet Union. Defeat in Germany.
November	Gramsci moves to Vienna.

December	New Course discussion launched in Soviet Union.
1924	
January	Lenin dies.
February	*L'Unità* founded.
March	*L'Ordine Nuovo* relaunched as a fortnightly.
April	General elections, in which the PCI wins 270,000 votes, the PSI 340,000 and the PSU 415,000.
May	Thirteenth Congress of Bolshevik Party. Gramsci returns to Italy. Consultative conference of PCI near Como.
June	PSU deputy Matteotti murdered by high-up fascists; opposition parties secede from parliament to meet in a separate assembly on Aventine Hill in Rome. Fifth World Congress of the Communist International calls for "Bolshevization" of the communist parties.
July	Fourth Enlarged Executive meeting of Comintern.
August	Third-internationalists from PSI fuse with PCI.
September	PCI launches slogan of "Workers' and Peasants' Committees".
October	Trotsky publishes "Lessons of October".
November	Communist deputies leave Aventine, after refusal of other opposition parties to convert assembly into permanent "anti-parliament", and return to parliament. Amendola creates National Union of Democrats and Liberals.
December	Stalin launches attack on the theory of "permanent revolution".
1925	
January	Mussolini speech gives signal for fascist counter-attack which puts an end to the Matteotti crisis.
February	First discussion of the "Russian question" in the Central Committee of the PCI.
March	Fifth Enlarged Executive meeting of Comintern, which reviews the progress of the Bolshevization campaign.
April	PCI initiates correspondence school.
May	Anglo-Russian Trade-union Committee formed. Gramsci addresses parliament for the only time, on freemasonry. PCI opens pre-congress discussion.
June	Bordiga's supporters form the *Comitato d'Intesa*.

July	National Union holds its only congress; pro-fascist right wing breaks away. Popular Party expels left wing led by Miglioli. *Comitato d'Intesa* dissolved.
November	Attempt on Mussolini's life by former PSU deputy Zaniboni fails; fascist régime intensifies repression of opposition forces.
December	Fourteenth Congress of Bolshevik Party.

1926

January	Third Congress of PCI at Lyons.
February	Sixth Enlarged Executive meeting of Comintern; Bordiga main pole of opposition to leadership.
April	Joint Opposition begins to form in Soviet Union.
May	British General Strike. Pilsudski comes to power in Poland.
October	PCI Political Bureau sends letter to the Central Committee of the CPSU. Gramsci begins lengthy essay on "The Southern Question", but is arrested before it is completed. New attempt on Mussolini's life is taken as pretext for making fascist dictatorship total.

ABBREVIATIONS

CGL	Confederazione Generale del Lavoro (General Confederation of Labour)
USI	Unione Sindacale Italiana
PSU	Partito Socialista Unitario
PSI	Partito Socialista Italiano
UIL	Unione Italiana del Lavoro
PCI	Partito Comunista d'Italia (after 1943, Partito Comunista Italiano)
CPSU	Communist Party of the Soviet Union
PCF	Parti Communiste Français

I

Socialism and Fascism

1. CAPORETTO AND VITTORIO VENETO

The period we are passing through can be defined the Caporetto of Italian maximalism.[1] The Communist Party, which is born and has to organize itself in the travails and among the perils of this exceptionally difficult moment, must express the working class's precise, cold determination to have its battle on the Piave and its Vittorio Veneto. So our slogan can be this alone: organization, maximum effort of organization, maximum speed in ordering and organizing the fabric of the new party. Certainly, the existence of a strong political organism of the working class would have been necessary today. Certainly, it would have been necessary to be able already to speak of action, and no longer of preparation. But the birth of the Communist Party is precisely linked to the conviction which has taken root in the proletariat's most intelligent vanguard, that we would have arrived at the present situation inevitably, given the incapacity of the Socialist Party to carry out its historical task. And that it was therefore indispensable to change course, and to begin the positive and definitive work of preparation. The present situation thus causes no surprise or demoralization among the Communists. It does not cast them down, or make them regret the tactics they followed at the Livorno Congress.

Maximalism, which is today in full flight, indeed decomposing, applied in the civil war the same tactics which General Cadorna applied in the national war. It wasted the proletarian forces in a multiplicity of disorganized and chaotic actions; wore the masses out; deluded them about the ease and speed with which victory would come. Italian maximalism and General Cadorna had precursors: the Chinese Boxers, who thought they could dislodge the English and Germans from their forts by advancing against the machine-guns in a turbulent mob, preceded by paper banners on which horrible, frightening monsters were painted.

The central idea of maximalism was not that of the Communist International: i.e. that all the activity and effort of the proletariat should be turned and directed towards the conquest of political power and the foundation of the workers' State; that all the specific problems of the working class can be effectively solved through the solution of the first and most important problem – that of winning political power and having armed force in its own hands. The central idea of maximalism was given it by the reformists: to govern without having direct responsibility for government; to be the *éminence grise* of the bourgeois government; to compel the bourgeois government – through terror (the monsters of the Chinese Boxers) and through the strength of the unions and the parliamentary group – to implement *that limited degree of socialism which can be implemented in Italy, given the country's economic condition and the danger of a blockade.* This vulgar Machiavellianism has been the effective programme of Italian Maximalism, and has produced the present situation, the Caporetto of the working class. The hasty organization of a few thousand fascists was enough to knock down the castle that had been built with the revolutionary phraseology of the Bologna Congress.[2] And thus something recurred in twentieth-century Italy, after the cruel experiences of the War and the Russian, Hungarian, Bavarian and German revolutions, which had seemed only conceivable in the ... eighteenth century, when 45 Hungarian knights succeeded in dominating all of Flanders for six months, simply because the population did not succeed in arming itself and counterposing a defensive and offensive organization to that organization of 45 men.[3]

It is in such conditions of chaos and collapse that the Communist Party is born. Its militants must show that they are truly capable of dominating events; that they are truly capable of filling every hour and every minute with the activity which that hour and that minute require; that they are truly capable of welding together the links in the historical chain which must end with the victory of the proletariat. We are in the midst of the Caporetto of verbal, verbose revolutionism. The first link to be forged is the Communist Party. If our will is strongly dedicated to this patient work of organization, then we shall succeed also in forging and welding together the other links. And the working class will have its battle on the Piave; it will have its Vittorio Veneto.

Unsigned, *L'Ordine Nuovo*, 28 January 1921.

2. WAR IS WAR

Understanding and knowing how to assess accurately one's enemy means that one already possesses a necessary condition for victory. Understanding and knowing how to assess one's own forces and their position in the field of struggle means that one possesses another extremely important condition for victory.

In Turin too, the fascists clearly want to carry through the general plan of action which has secured easy triumphs in other cities. Contingents have been called in from outside – units from Bologna, picked troops, well-trained. Demonstrative parades have been stepped up, with the fascist forces organized and drawn up into columns in military fashion. Their supporters are continually assembled without warning, under orders to come to the meetings armed. This serves to create an expectation of mysterious events, and thus to create a war psychology. Alarmist rumours are spread in great profusion ("the first to be killed will be a socialist student, we will burn *L'Ordine Nuovo*, we will burn the Chamber of Labour, we will burn the Cooperative Alliance bookshop"). This expedient has two aims: to disintegrate the proletarian forces through panic and the unnerving uncertainty of the wait, and to familiarize the fascists with the objective to be achieved. Will the fascists have the easy triumph in Turin which they have had in other cities?

Let us first observe that to have asked for help from outside is a proof of the organic weakness of Turin fascism. In Turin the fascists base themselves upon – and can base themselves upon – only one category of the petty-bourgeois class: the category of shopkeepers, certainly not famous for its sublime martial qualities. The Turin working class is certainly morally superior to the fascists and knows that it is morally superior. The counter-revolutionaries of the General Confederation of Labour (in order to dishearten the masses and strip them of all capacity for attack or defence) are saying that the workers, since they did not fight in the war, cannot combat and defeat fascism on the terrain of armed violence. As far as Turin is concerned, this defeatist and counter-revolutionary assertion is objectively untrue. The Turin workers have had the following "war" experiences: general strike of May 1915, armed insurrection lasting five days in August 1917, manoeuvres involving broad masses on 2–3 December 1919, general strike with episodic use of Irish tactics and development of a unitary strategic plan in April 1920, occupation of the factories last September with the accumulation of a wealth of experience in the military sphere. Another incontestable fact: after August 1917, the workers most suspect of revolutionarism had their exemption lifted and were sent to the front in the most exposed positions. The Turin proletariat gave more soldiers to the trenches than any other, and from this point of view too has accumulated military experience which has already borne fruit, precisely during the occupation of the factories. The accusation of "peace-mongering"[4] is ridiculous and absurd if addressed to the Turin workers, who have shown, especially in August 1917, that they are not afraid of bullets or blood. The same cannot be said of the Turin fascists: despairingly called upon for help by D'Annunzio, they were characteristically stingy with their heroism – despite their claim to have organized themselves to save Italy from the dishonour of the "thick-lipped executioner."[5] They limited themselves to letting off a bomb under the windows of *La Stampa*. The fascists (especially those from Turin, who only fought the war in newspapers and offices) are aware of this inferiority of theirs, just as the workers are perfectly aware of their superiority.

These conditions of a psychological and moral nature are supplemented by others of a practical, organizational kind. What has been most painfully surprising, in the cities that have fallen prey to the fascists, has been the absence of any spirit of initiative among the mass of workers. In these cities, all revolutionary energy was concentrated in the offices of the Chamber of Labour. Once the Chamber of Labour was hit, the working class was decapitated and became incapable of any action. But in Turin, the very great centralization of the movement does not deprive the working class of its energy and capacity for action. Even during the War, the Internal Commissions had become the centre around which the revolutionary forces crystallized. They kept the class struggle going and preserved an unbroken spirit of autonomy and initiative even in the darkest periods of capitalist and state oppression, when the trade-union organizations joined committees of industrial mobilization and abdicated all freedom and independence. This meant that it was possible for the workers in August 1917, although the Chamber of Labour had been occupied by the police and the centres were all widely scattered, to maintain for five days a bitter struggle with arms in hand and more than once threaten conquest of the city's central points. It also made possible the admirable manoeuvres of 2–3 December 1919, when the working-class forces left the factories in order and under discipline, and like an immense converging rake swept the city from the outskirts to the centre. Again, during the occupation of the factories, it made possible the autonomous, yet unitary and naturally centralized development of a whole range of revolutionary actions and initiatives of incalculable and unpredictable scope.

The movement of factory councils and communist groups has perfected this articulation of the working-class movement in Turin, which can no longer be decapitated and paralysed by any reactionary gale. One may say this: while in the other industrial cities the working class has not yet gone beyond the stage of mass frontal attacks – the tactics of General Cadorna which led to Caporetto – in Turin this stage has been definitively left behind. In the campaign for the factory councils, the communists always reminded the Turin workers of what had happened in Barcelona.[6] They always spoke to the workers in the rough, sincere language which must be that of the revolutionary proletariat. They never hid the fact that perhaps Italy would pass through a period of reaction and that, as in Barcelona, the possibility was not excluded that the Chamber of Labour and trade unions would be dissolved or placed in conditions where they could not function. So it was necessary to multiply the revolutionary centres and organizations. So it was necessary to stimulate among the masses the spirit of initiative and autonomy; necessary to replace the bureaucratic and bestial centralization which characterized the trade unions by a democratic centralization, an agile and flexible articulation, that would allow the proletarian body to continue to live whatever blows might be inflicted either on it as a whole or on its individual members. This realistic propaganda was begun as early as 1919. At that time, the present repentant Magdalenes of maximalism called the Turin council movement "reformist", because it proposed to "qualify" and "instruct" the workers, while the maximalists merely preached great frontal actions and inserted the noun "violence" after every third word in their speeches. Today, one can see how necessary that propaganda was and how only through that work of preparation could the future of the proletariat truly be defended.

This objective presentation of the conditions in which the struggle will take place is in no way aimed at diminishing the gravity of the danger. The Turin working class certainly finds itself in a good war position; but no good position can, in itself, save an army from defeat. The good position must be exploited in all its possibilities. Woe to the working class if it even for a single instant permits the fascists to put their plan into execution in Turin, as they have done in other cities. The least weakness, the least hesitancy could be fatal. The first fascist attempt must be followed by a swift, decisive, pitiless response from the workers, and this response must be such that the memory of it will be handed down to the great-grandchildren of the capitalist gentlemen. When fighting a war one must act accordingly, and in war blows are not given by agreement. However, the Turin working class has already stated, in a resolution from its political party, that it considers the fascists to be merely the instruments of an action whose instigators and main principals are to be found in very different circles. *La Stampa* too wrote (on 27 January, just five days ago): "The present powerful organization [of the fascists] is encouraged by *businessmen, industrialists, farmers.*" In war and revolution, to take pity on ten means to be pitiless with a thousand. The Hungarian working class wanted to be gentle with its oppressors: today it is paying, and the women of the working class are paying and the children of the working class are paying, for its gentleness: pity for a few thousand has brought misery, grief, despair to millions of Hungarian proletarians.

Blows are not given by agreement. All the more implacable must the workers be, in that there is no comparison between the damage which the working class suffers and the damage which the capitalists suffer. The Chamber of Labour is the product of the efforts of many working-class generations. It cost hundreds and hundreds of thousands of workers sacrifice and privation, it is the sole property of a hundred thousand proletarian families. If it is destroyed, those efforts, those sacrifices, those privations, that property are annihilated. They want to destroy it in order to destroy organization, in order to take away from the worker the security of his bread, his roof, his clothes, to take away this security from the worker's wife and his child. Mortal danger to whoever touches the Chamber of Labour, mortal danger to whoever *encourages* and promotes the work of destruction! A hundred for one. All the houses of the industrialists and businessmen cannot save the casa del popolo [house of the people], because the people loses everything if it loses its house.

Mortal danger to whoever touches the worker's bread, or the bread of the worker's son. War is war: whoever seeks adventure must feel the iron jaws of the beast which he has let loose. All that the worker has created at the cost of his sacrifices, all that generations of workers have slowly and painfully wrought with blood and with sorrow, must be respected as something sacred. The tempest and the hurricane break when sacrilege is committed, and carry away the guilty like straws. Mortal danger to whoever touches the property of the worker, of the man condemned to have no property. War is war. Woe betide whoever unleashes it. A militant of the working class who has to pass into the next world, must have a first-class accompaniment on his journey. If fire dyes red the patch of sky over one street, the city must be provided with many braziers to warm the women and children of the workers who have gone to war. Woe betide whoever unleashes war. If Italy is not used to seriousness and responsibility, if Italy is not used to taking anyone seriously, if bourgeois Italy happens to have acquired the sweet and facile conviction that the Italian revolutionaries are not to be taken seriously either, let the die be cast: we are convinced that more than one fox will leave his tail and his cunning in the snare.

Unsigned, *L'Ordine Nuovo*, 31 January 1921.

3. WORKERS' CONTROL

Before we examine the configuration of the draft bill presented by Hon. Giolitti to the Chamber of Deputies, or the possibilities which it opens up, it is essential to establish the viewpoint from which the communists approach discussion of the problem.[7]

For the communists, tackling the problem of control means tackling the greatest problem of the present historical period; it means tackling the problem of workers' power over the means of production, and hence that of conquering State power. From this point of view, the presentation of a draft bill, its approval, and its execution within the framework of the bourgeois State, are events of secondary importance. Workers' power has, and can only have, its *raison d'être* and its source within the working class itself; in the political capacity of the working class; in the real power that the working class possesses, as an indispensable and irreplaceable factor of production and as an organization of political and military force. Any law in this respect which emanates from bourgeois power has just one significance and just one value: it means that in reality, and not just in words, the terrain of the class struggle has changed. And insofar as the bourgeoisie is compelled to make concessions and create new juridical institutions on the new terrain, it has the real value of demonstrating an organic weakness of the ruling class [*classe dominante*].[8]

To admit that entrepreneurial power in industry can be subjected to limitations, and that industrial autocracy can become "democracy" even of a formal kind, means to admit that the bourgeoisie has now effectively fallen from its historical position as the leading class [*classe dirigente*] and is effectively incapable of guaranteeing the popular masses their conditions of existence and development. In order to shed at least a part of its responsibilities and to create an alibi for itself, the bourgeoisie allows itself to be "controlled" and pretends to let itself be placed under supervision. It would certainly be very useful, for the purposes of bourgeois self-preservation, if a guarantor like the proletariat were to take upon itself to testify before the great mass of the population that nobody should be held responsible for the present economic ruin, but that everyone's duty is to suffer patiently and work tenaciously, while waiting for the present cracks to be repaired and for a new edifice to be built upon the present ruins.

The field of control is thus the field upon which bourgeoisie and proletariat struggle for class leadership over the great mass of the population. The field of control is thus the basis upon which the working class, when it has won the trust and consent of the great mass of the population, can construct its State, organize its governmental institutions with the participation of all the oppressed and exploited classes, and initiate the positive work of organizing the new economic and social system. Through the fight for control – which does not take place in Parliament, but is a revolutionary mass struggle and a propaganda and organizational activity of the historic party of the working class, the Communist Party – the working class must acquire, both spiritually and as an organization, awareness of its autonomy and historic personality. This is why the first phase of the struggle will present itself as the fight for a specific form of organization. This form of organization can only be the Factory Council, and the nationally centralized system of Factory Councils. The outcome of the struggle must be the constitution of a National Council of the working class, to be elected at all levels – from the Factory Councils to the City Councils and the National Council – by methods and according to a procedure determined by the working class itself, and not by the national Parliament or by bourgeois power. This struggle must be waged in such a way as to show the great mass of the population that all the existential problems of the present historical period – the problems of bread, housing, light, clothes – can be resolved only when all economic power, and hence all political power, has passed into the hands of the working class. In other words, it must be waged in such a way as to organize all the popular forces in revolt against the capitalist régime around the working class, so that the latter really becomes the leading class and guides all the productive forces to emancipate themselves by realizing the communist programme. This struggle must equip the working class to select the most able and energetic elements from its own ranks and make them into its new industrial leaders, its new guides in the work of economic reconstruction.

From this point of view, the draft bill presented to the Chamber of Deputies by Hon. Giolitti represents merely a means for agitation and propaganda. It must be studied by the communists in this light; for them, not only is it not a final goal, it is not even a point of departure or a launching-pad.

Unsigned, *L'Ordine Nuovo*, 10 February 1921.

4. THE GENERAL CONFEDERATION OF LABOUR

The communists will not have the majority at the Confederation's forthcoming congress at Livorno:[9] indeed it is almost certain that in spite of all their efforts of propaganda and organization, the communists will not have a majority at future congresses either. The situation presents itself in the following terms: to win a majority at a congress, the communists would have to be able to carry out a radical revision of the rules; but to change the rules, it is necessary already to have the majority. If the communists were to let themselves become bogged down in this vicious circle, they would play into the hands of the trade-union bureaucracy. It is therefore necessary for the opposition to have a precise approach and method capable of breaking the present state of affairs.

The General Confederation of Labour (in other countries there exists an identical situation to the Italian one) is a mechanism of government which cannot even be compared to the bourgeois parliamentary State. Its models can only be found in the ancient Assyrian and Babylonian State organizations or in the martial associations which still emerge and develop today in Mongolia and China. The explanation for this is a historical one. The masses entered the trade-union movement for fear of being crushed by an adversary whom they know to be very powerful [. . . phrase missing . . .] and whose blows and initiatives they are not able to foresee. Disturbed by their condition of absolute inferiority, lacking any constitutional education, the masses abdicated completely all sovereignty and all power. The organization became identified for them with the organizer as an individual, just as for an army in the field the individual commander becomes the protector of the safety of all, the guarantor of success and victory.

It should have been the task of the Socialist Party to give the proletarian masses the political preparation and constitutional education which they lacked. It should have been the task of the Socialist Party gradually to renew the organizational forms and transfer as much power as possible into the hands of the masses. The Party did nothing in this direction. The organization was left entirely at the mercy of a small group of officials, who carefully built up the machine which today gives them absolute power. Seven years without a congress have allowed even more: a whole swarm of officials has been echeloned in the most important positions, and a fortress has been constructed that cannot be taken or penetrated even by the most tenacious and willing. The Socialist Congress at Livorno can only be explained by this state of affairs which exists in the trade-union field. The Socialist Party has entirely fallen into the hands of the trade-union bureaucracy, whose human and organizational resources secured a majority for the unitary tendency. The Socialist Party has been reduced to the role of a janissary for the mandarins and *condottieri* who are at the head of the union federations and Confederation.

The Communists must recognize this state of affairs and act in consequence. The communists must consider the Confederation in the same light as the parliamentary State, i.e. as an organism whose conquest cannot take place by constitutional means. Moreover, in considering the question of the Confederation, the following postulates must also be borne in mind: that we want to achieve proletarian unity, and that we want to pose the problem of control of production in a revolutionary way. The field of activity of the Communist Party is the whole mass of workers and peasants. The Confederation is the scene of the greatest degree of propaganda and activity only because numerically it embraces most of the organized workers and peasants in Italy, i.e. of those who are most conscious and experienced.

We believe the struggle for the creation and development of factory and enterprise Councils to be the specific struggle of the Communist Party. It must enable the party to graft itself directly on to a centralized organization of the working-class masses, an organization which must be above all the other existing ones and which must be recognized by the masses as the only one competent and authorized to issue slogans for general action. Through the struggle for the Councils, it will be possible to win the majority of the Confederation in a stable and permanent fashion; thereafter, if not in the pre-revolutionary period then certainly in the post-revolutionary period, it will be possible also to win the leading positions. This process has already been seen in Russia; in the revolutionary days of November 1917, the proclamations and manifestoes of the Bolshevik Party did not carry the signature of the All-Russian Federation of Trade Unions, but that of the All-Russian Central Executive Committee of the Factory Councils.[10]

It is certainly important to have a strong communist minority, organized and centralized, within the Confederation. All our efforts of propaganda and activity must be directed to this end. But both historically and tactically it is more important that no effort should be spared to ensure that, immediately after the Congress at Livorno, it is possible to convene a congress of the Councils and Internal Commissions of all Italian factories and firms, and that a Centre is nominated by this congress that will embrace the entire proletarian mass within its organizational framework.

Unsigned, *L'Ordine Nuovo*, 25 February 1921.

5. REAL DIALECTICS

Events are the real dialectics of history. They transcend all arguments, all personal judgements, all vague and irresponsible wishes. Events, with the inexorable logic of their development, give the worker and peasant masses, who are conscious of their destiny, these lessons. The class struggle at a certain moment reaches a stage in which the proletariat no longer finds in bourgeois legality, i.e. in the bourgeois State apparatus (armed forces, courts, administration), the elementary guarantee and defence of its elementary right to life, to freedom, to personal safety, to daily bread. It is then forced to create its own legality, to create its own apparatus of resistance and defence. At certain moments in the life of the people, this is an absolute historical necessity, transcending every desire, every wish, every whim, every personal impulse. Events present themselves as a universal fatality, with the overwhelming momentum of natural phenomena. Men, as individuals and *en masse*, find themselves placed brutally before the following dilemma: chances of death one hundred, chances of life ten, a choice must be made. And men always choose the chances of life, even if these are slight, even if they only offer a wretched and exhausted life. They fight for these slight chances, and their vitality is such and their passion so great that they break every obstacle and sweep away even the most awesome apparatus of power.

This is the situation which the real dialectics of history creates for men at certain moments – the decisive moments in the painful and bloody development of mankind. No human will can create situations of this kind; no little man, even if he puffs out his cheeks and distils from his brain the words which most touch hearts and stir the blood, can create situations of this kind. They are the blazing brazier in which flow together all the passions and all the hatreds which only the sight of violent death can arouse in the masses. Only this can be considered as a revolutionary situation in this historical period, which has as its immediate past experience the deeds of the Spartacists, Hungary, Ireland, Bavaria. In this situation, there is no middle term to choose; and if one fights, it is necessary to win.

Today, we do not find ourselves in such a situation. Today, we can still choose with a certain freedom. The freedom of choice imposes certain duties upon us, absolute duties which concern the life of the people and are inherent in the future of the masses who suffer and hope. Today, there exists only one form of revolutionary solidarity: to win. It therefore demands of us that we should not neglect any single element that might put us in a condition to win. Today, there exists a party that truly expresses the interests of the proletariat; that expresses the interests not only of the Italian proletariat, but of the workers' International as a whole. Today, the workers must have and can have faith. The Italian workers, maintaining an iron discipline, without a single exception, in response to the slogans of the Communist Party, will finally show that they have emerged from the state of revolutionary infantilism in which their movement has hitherto floundered. They will show that they are worthy and capable of victory.

Unsigned, *L'Ordine Nuovo*, 3 March 1921.

6. OFFICIALDOM

The Confederation's Livorno Congress is finished. No new slogan, no line has come out of this congress. In vain have the broad masses of the Italian people waited for an orientation. In vain have they awaited a slogan that would enlighten them, that would succeed in calming their anguish and giving a form to their passion. The congress has not confronted or resolved a single one of the problems which are vital for the proletariat in the present historical period: neither the problem of emigration, nor the problem of unemployment, nor the problem of relations between workers and peasants, nor the problem of the institutions which can best contain the development of the class struggle, nor the problem of the material defence of working-class buildings and the personal safety of working-class militants. The sole concern of the majority at the congress was how to safeguard and guarantee the position and the power (powerless power) of the Socialist Party.

Our struggle against trade-union officialdom could not have been better justified. In many regions of Italy the workers had entered the field *en masse* to defend their elementary right to life, freedom of movement on the streets, freedom of association, freedom to hold meetings and to have their own premises for the purpose. The field of struggle swiftly became a tragic one: fire and flame, cannonades, machine-gun fire, many dozens killed. The majority of the congress was not moved by these events. The tragedy of the popular masses defending themselves desperately from cruel, implacable enemies was not able to render serious this majority made up of men with withered hearts and shrivelled brains, or inspire it with a sense of its own historical responsibilities. These men no longer live for the class struggle, no longer feel the same passions, the same desires, the same hopes as the masses. Between them and the masses an unbridgeable abyss has opened up. The only contact between them and the masses is the account-ledger and the membership file. These men no longer see the enemy in the bourgeoisie, they see him in the communists. They are afraid of competition; instead of leaders they have become bankers of men in a monopoly situation, and the least hint of competition makes them crazy with terror and despair.

The Confederal Congress at Livorno was an awesome experience for us; our pessimism was outstripped by this experience. We of *L'Ordine Nuovo* have always seen the trade-union problem, the problem of organizing the broad masses and selecting the leading personnel for their organization, as the central problem of the modern revolutionary movement. But never as today have we felt the full gravity and extent of the problem; never, as today, have we felt the full scale of the gangrene which is eating away at the movement. At the congress, the articles of *L'Ordine Nuovo* were read, annotated, commented on, they filled the hall with clamour and tumult. Yet these articles did not convey even the tenth part of our pessimistic judgement on the inadequacy of those men and institutions.

Moreover, this judgement has become still harsher since the congress. Yes, because while the workers were fighting in the streets and squares, while fire and flame were striking terror into the hearts of the people and driving them in despair to individual acts of fury and the most terrible reprisals, we could never have imagined that the so-called delegates of these popular masses would lose themselves in the swampy and miasmatic marshland of private feuds. The masses were spilling their blood in the streets and squares, cannon and machine-guns were appearing on the scene; and these leaders, these men at the top, these future administrators of society, raged and foamed because of a newspaper article, a caricature, a headline.

And they would like to convince us, these people, that we have done wrong; that we have committed a crime in separating ourselves from them. They would like to convince us that it is we who are light-minded, that it is we who are irresponsible, that it is we who seek "miracles", that it is we who are not capable of understanding and weighing the difficulties of historical situations and revolutionary movements. They would like us to become convinced that in them are realized the wisdom, the competence, the skill, the good sense, the political and administrative capability accumulated by the proletariat in the course of its struggles and historical experiences as a class. Come, away with them! The Confederal Congress rehabilitates Parliament, rehabilitates the worst assemblies of the classes which in the past have shown themselves most corrupt and putrefied.

Our pessimism has increased, our will has not diminished. The officials do not represent the base. The absolutist States were precisely officials' States, States of the bureaucracy. They did not represent the popular masses and were replaced by parliamentary States. The Confederation represents, in the historical development of the proletariat, what the absolute State represented in the historical development of the bourgeois classes. It will be replaced by the organization of the Councils, which are the working-class parliaments, which have the function of eating away bureaucratic sediments and transforming old organizational relations. Our pessimism has increased, but our motto is still alive and to the point: pessimism of the intelligence, optimism of the will.[11]

Unsigned, *L'Ordine Nuovo*, 4 March 1921.

7. UNIONS AND COUNCILS

The end of the CGL's Livorno congress opens a new period in the history of the Italian working class. A new system of forces has now been established: two conceptions are ranged against each other, embodied in two distinct parties, and each can only develop and consolidate itself at the other's expense. The new period will be one of bitter struggles and polemics, and one does not need to be a prophet to forsee that the biggest struggles and bitterest polemics will rage over the factory councils, and control of production.

The Communist Party of Italy has a body of political doctrine on these questions, and an immense store of historical experience. The very discussion which is taking place today in the Russian Communist Party, on the functions of trade unions in the period of the proletarian dictatorship, shows how the problem of union organization does not cease to be actual or important simply because the working class has become the ruling class; simply because, in its struggle against the national and international bourgeoisie, it has far stronger battle organs at its disposal, such as the Red Army and the Extraordinary Commission to Combat Counter-revolution.[12] The trade-union question continues to remain a central question for the workers' state. The greater or lesser solidity of the general organization of revolutionary forces – and hence, in the last analysis, the solidarity of the revolution itself – may depend upon the solutions which the Communist Party gives to it.

The theses of the Second Congress of the IIIrd International represent the body of doctrines specific to our party. These theses state that in this historical period a new problem faces the proletariat, the problem of control; and they state that the natural and specific organs of the struggle for control are the factory councils. The councils represent the only possible form of organization of the industrial proletarian vanguard. They stand in the same relation to the unions as does big industry to the capitalist economy in general. Hence, the councils are those most interested in control and in the nationalization of industry. They organize the mass of workers employed in the big plants, in the capitalist formations which represent the transitional phase between private property and communism, and it is they who most keenly feel the urgency of the historical thrust towards radical economic transformations. From the Marxist point of view, the factory councils are the new economic organization which presses at the flanks of the old organization, and which tends to break the latter's structures as it comes into being and develops.

The question of the councils interests the party at present not just as a new type of industrial organization, but also as a means of organizing the broad mass of workers directly creating a mechanism that can produce a new working-class leading stratum and train a new administrative personnel. Because they function as a selective mechanism in this way, the factory councils are especially disliked by the old union bureaucracy. Wherever the councils have emerged – in Italy, in Russia, in England, in the United States – the same phenomenon has occurred: in the councils, the working class always selects a predominantly revolutionary leading personnel, and supports the positions and the representatives of the Communist Party; by contrast, in the old union bodies, the positions and the representatives of reformism prevail. In October 1917 in Russia, the General Confederation of Labour was in the hands of the Mensheviks, the Central Executive Committee of the factory councils was in the hands of the Bolsheviks; the council organization provided the basis for the action of the Russian masses who followed Bolshevik slogans.

The factory councils must fuse with the unions, but the moment for this fusion cannot be fixed *a priori*. According to the theses of the Moscow congress, fusion must take place naturally, spontaneously, and the unions must base themselves firmly upon the councils, becoming the means for their centralization. A new type of trade organization will thus be created, specific to the period of the dictatorship and capable of fulfilling the tasks imposed by the needs of the workers' state. In Russia, the fusion of the unions with the factory councils took place about six months after the October Revolution. Today, after three years of the workers' state, there is a new discussion on whether the time has come to pay great attention once more to the councils, in order to prevent new forms of syndicalism and to combat the new bureaucratic sedimentations that have been forming for three years.

The Livorno congress makes it necessary for the Italian communists today to examine this question and study it deeply, so that communist sections and groups can carry out a really coordinated and centralized overall activity. For the broad mass of Italians, the problem is an almost entirely new one. It is vitally urgent today to find a solution to it quickly; however, this must be done without sacrificing revolutionary precision or wisdom.

Unsigned, *L'Ordine Nuovo*, 5 March 1921.

8. ITALY AND SPAIN

What is fascism, observed on an international scale? It is the attempt to resolve the problems of production and exchange with machine-guns and pistol-shots. The productive forces were ruined and dissipated in the imperialist war: twenty million men in the flower of their youth and energies were killed; another twenty million were left invalids.[13] The thousands upon thousands of bonds that united the various world markets were violently broken. The relations between city and countryside, between metropole and colonies, were overturned. The streams of emigration, which periodically re-established the balance between the excess population and the potential of the means of production in individual countries, were profoundly disturbed and no longer function normally. A unity and simultaneity of national crises was created, which precisely makes the general crisis acute and incurable. But there exists a stratum of the population in all countries – the petty and middle bourgeoisie – which thinks it can solve these gigantic problems with machine-guns and pistol-shots; and this stratum feeds fascism, provides fascism with its troops.

In Spain, the organization of the petty and middle bourgeoisie into armed groups occurred before it did in Italy; it had already begun in 1918 and 1919. The world war cast Spain into a terrible crisis before other countries: the Spanish capitalists had in fact already looted the country and sold all that was saleable in the first years of the conflagration. The Entente paid better than the poor Spanish consumers were able to do, so the owners sold all the wealth and goods which should have provided for the national population to the Entente. By 1916, Spain was already one of the richest European countries financially, but one of the poorest in goods and productive energies. The revolutionary movement surged forward; the unions organized almost the entirety of the industrial masses; strikes, lockouts, states of emergency, the dissolution of Chambers of Labour and peasant associations, massacres, street shootings, became the everyday stuff of political life. Anti-Bolshevik fasces (*somaten*) were formed. Initially, as in Italy, they were made up of military personnel, taken from the officers' clubs (*juntas*), but they swiftly enlarged their base until in

Barcelona, for example, they had recruited 40,000 armed men. They followed the same tactics as the fascists in Italy: attacks on trade-union leaders, violent opposition to strikes, terrorism against the masses, opposition to all forms of organization, help for the regular police in repressive activity and arrests, help for blacklegs in agitation involving strikes or lockouts. For the past three years Spain has floundered in this crisis: public freedom is suspended every fortnight, personal freedom has become a myth, the workers' unions to a great extent function clandestinely, the mass of workers is hungry and angry, the great mass of the people has been reduced to indescribable conditions of savagery and barbarism. Moreover, the crisis is intensifying, and the stage of individual assassination attempts has now been reached.

Spain is an exemplary country. It represents a phase through which all the countries of Western Europe will pass, if economic conditions continue as they are today, with the same tendencies as at present. In Italy, we are passing through the phase which Spain passed through in 1919: the phase of the arming of the middle classes and the introduction into the class struggle of military methods of assault and surprise-attack. In Italy too, the middle class thinks it can resolve economic problems by military violence. It thinks it can cure unemployment by pistol-shots; it thinks it can assuage hunger and dry the tears of the women of the people with bursts of machine-gun fire. Historical experience counts for nothing with petty bourgeois who do not know history. Similar phenomena are repeated and will continue to be repeated in other countries, apart from Italy. Has not the same process affected the Socialist Party in Italy, as had already occurred several years earlier in Austria, Hungary and Germany? Illusion is the most tenacious weed in the collective consciousness; history teaches, but it has no pupils.

Unsigned, *L'Ordine Nuovo*. 11 March 1921.

9. SOCIALISTS AND COMMUNISTS

Each successive event which occurs in the present period shows more clearly the features of the two parties which emerged from the Livorno Congress: communist and socialist. To many at the time, it appeared idle to distinguish between communists and socialists on the basis of their general statements. But unfolding historical events, in so far as they require a critical interpretation and oblige one to take up a clear and precise position towards them, have on the contrary highlighted the mutually opposed methods of the two parties. The Livorno split should have come about at least a year earlier, for the communists to have had the time to give the working class the organization required by the revolutionary period in which it is living. Many things, however, have happened since Livorno, things which are certainly serious and which have revealed clearly the substantive difference between communists and socialists.

The difference lies in their respective methods and in their interpretation of historical facts. The socialists have never understood the spirit of the period through which we are passing in the class struggle. They have not understood that the class struggle may be converted at any moment, at any provocation, into an open war which can only be concluded with the seizure of power by the proletariat. The fact that the socialists lack any method of orienting the working class and peasantry towards new forms of rule also derives from the fact that they have not understood the spirit of this historical period. The socialists believe that the terms of the struggle between the two classes are the same as before the War. For the socialists, the War and the Russian revolution have no value. They therefore continue to trust in their old methods and see socialism as a distant goal.

But there are, it is said, also communists inside the Socialist Party; there are those who assert that we are living in a revolutionary period. The communists – that is to say the former revolutionary maximalists – would indeed like to be the majority of the Socialist Party. But the difference is only one of words. In reality, they have shown that they are the same as the others. In reality, they have not been able to establish a method of their own, different from that of the non-communist socialists. The Socialist Party has moved steadily rightwards, in spite of all the generic revolutionary declarations which some of them still have the hypocrisy to make before the masses. The communists who have remained inside the Socialist Party have followed the right-wing current. No distinction can thus be made inside the Socialist Party. There are only two methods existing today: that of the communists in the Third International and that of the socialists.

The socialists, still face to face with history, have now confirmed their inability to organize the working class as a dominant class. The events of Emilia, Apulia, Tuscany and the most recent ones in the Casalese precisely make it clear that the socialists have entirely lost sight of the problems and needs of the workers.[14] They show that the socialists have a horror of civil war, as if one could reach socialism without civil war. The socialists still believe they can oppose the bourgeois class, which organizes and unleashes its violence everywhere, with protests in Parliament and resolutions deploring fascist barbarities.[15] Nor is it only in this sphere that the socialists are distant from the working class. In the life of the factories and trade unions things are no different.

The serious problem of the industrial crisis which threatens a lockout in every plant is also seen by the socialists with the mentality of before the War, i.e. with the mentality which leads them to think that one can continue with a policy of compromises and middle roads. Faced with the problem of power, as with that of production, the socialists are equally devoid of a method or a clear idea. It is for this reason that, where they still hold sway over the masses, the latter are as if disoriented and slow in finding the road to counter-attack. But there are responsibilities which must one day be paid for. There are problems which cannot always be postponed. History will in the end pass sentence on the inept and the errors they have committed. Under the pressure of events, the masses will one day see that they have been betrayed, and will in the end orient themselves towards the historical party, the Communist Party. Provided, however, it is not already too late. . . .

Unsigned, *L'Ordine Nuovo*, 12 March 1921.

10. ENGLAND AND RUSSIA

The trade agreement between England and Soviet Russia, considering the moment in which it has been concluded, represents an undoubted political victory for the Moscow workers' government.[16] The Kronstadt revolt, staged by international reaction to wreck the negotiations, failed to induce Lloyd George's government to change direction. The Soviet State has been recognized by England as the sole legitimate authority, alone capable of giving permanent guarantees for the fulfilment of international contracts. But this political victory of our Russian comrades must not encourage over-rosy illusions or engender indolence. It is not international communism which stands to gain by this agreement, but capitalism and imperialism.

The fact that England recognizes politically the stability of the workers' government, and comes to accept the idea of trading with it, is an event in the realm of common sense; but it does not change by one hair's breadth the existing economic relations between communism and capitalism. England, an eminently industrial nation, maintains its superiority over Russia, an eminently agricultural nation. The peasant class in Russia will indeed be enabled to restore its economy, ruined by six years of war and destruction. But it will not be the Russian proletariat which offers the peasants the possibility of restoring production; it will be capitalism – and a foreign capitalism at that. The very foundations of the workers' State are damaged and corroded by this fact, and the Russian comrades do not hide it – either from themselves or from others. They hoped in the world revolution; they hoped that the aid necessary to their existence would be fraternally offered them by the international Commune, rather than usuriously by a capitalist state; and they have not yet lost that hope. For the Russian comrades, until the world revolution, the question is one of surviving, gaining a breathing-space, and preserving the elementary conditions for communism – i.e. political power in the hands of the workers. It cannot be one of deep or permanent achievements.

The agreement with England does not have and cannot have any other significance. Having won power, the working class has succeeded in showing that it is the only social force capable of saving the Russian nation from foreign bondage, and the Russian economy from total ruin. But the strength of the Russian proletariat has been diminished economically by the agreement. Only in the world revolution, and in the solidarity of the workers' International become arbiter of the productive forces, can the Russian and other proletariats hope for a resolution of the conflicts and crises which are rending society today, and for their salvation from utter ruin.

Unsigned, *L'Ordine Nuovo*, 18 March 1921.

11. THE ITALIAN PARLIAMENT

It now seems certain that Hon. Giolitti intends to renew the Chamber of Deputies, and the poor representatives of the people's will are in great distress and great anguish. The deputies who represent the socialist will of the Italian people are the most disturbed and anguished. How will they succeed in convincing the electoral masses yet again that Parliament must be taken seriously, and that social progress and the emancipation of the oppressed can only be expressed through parliamentary action? Today, the Italian people has experimentally gained its own political education. Today, even the most agile mountebanks of parliamentary cretinism, such as Hon. Treves, if asked by a worker: What power and real influence does Parliament exercise over the State? what importance and what political function does the Italian Parliament have at the present moment? – would not know what to reply, since demagogic charlatanry can too easily be refuted by the data of direct experience.

But what is happening today is not a novelty. In Italy, even before the War, Parliament never exercised a constitutional function and power. In Italy, there has never existed a parliamentary régime, only a despotic régime, somewhat tempered before the War by periodic consultation of popular opinion. From the point of view of constitutional law, the Italian political régime is characterized by the absence of an independent judiciary power, with its personnel recruited strictly, to which the armed forces of the country are subordinated. In Italy, judiciary power does not exist, but merely a judiciary order; the armed forces depend directly on the government, which can use them at will against the people and against Parliament itself. Since no judiciary power exists, Parliament legislates for the archives. No guarantee exists that its laws will be applied and respected. The people has no means of control over the government, or of defence against the arbitrary acts of the government, other than armed insurrection.

The present situation of impunity for massacres and a magistrature in headlong flight is not a novelty. Even before the War, there existed no legal guarantee in Italy of the liberty and personal safety of the citizens. Even before the War, it was possible to hold citizens in custody for an unlimited period by a simple administrative decision. Even before the War, massacres of those in custody occurred. Even before the War, every agent of the police force, every armed functionary of the government, felt that he was invested not merely with the executive role of executioner, but also with the roles of legislator and judge: he could restore the death penalty, pronounce the verdict and carry out the sentence on the spot. Even before the War, the situation had got so bad in Italy that to prevent massacres, which had become an everyday occurrence, the Italian people in June 1914 rose against the government in an armed insurrection, seeing the impotence of parliamentary action.[17]

The cast of the Italian political régime can also be easily explained from the historical point of view. Parliamentarism, characterized by the separation of powers and the subordination of the police forces to the judiciary power, is a product of the struggle between the capitalist class and the landowning class, with the industrialists prevailing over the landowners. In Italy, this class struggle has not been decisive: Italian history is nothing but a compromise between the State and the landowners. The landowners have continued to hold the power of life and death over the poor peasants, and the magistrature is to a great extent recruited from the petty bourgeoisie of peasant origin, especially in southern Italy. In such conditions, it was impossible for a strong and independent judiciary power to arise and impose itself through parliamentary struggle, hence parliamentarism could not emerge. Thus Parliament in Italy has always been a mere consultative body, without any real influence on the governmental machine, without power of initiative or control. Even elections have never had any significance or value, other than that of allowing a despotic and paternalist government to sample opinion, and reassuring it that its arbitrary acts and its abuses would not provoke irreparable ruptures in the established order.

The new elections too, if Hon. Giolitti decides to call them, can have no other significance. Hon. Giolitti wants a Parliament that will appear as the popular expression of a reactionary will turned against the industrial workers and poor peasants. His desire will be abundantly satisfied. The petty bourgeoisie, which in November 1919 was convinced of the inevitability of a socialist government, has today aligned itself openly against the proletariat and against socialism. It is the petty bourgeoisie, especially in the country areas, which provides the forces for fascism. It is the petty bourgeoisie which has armed itself and organized itself militarily, before the proletariat and against the proletariat. The new Parliament will mark a violent recovery of the landowning classes over the industrial classes: the definitive subjugation of the cities – in the throes of economic crisis and incapable of supplying the national market with the products it desperately needs – to the countryside, which has a near monopoly of food-supplies and hence, in the present period, an unquestioned superiority. Military dictatorship and a new war of plunder will be the necessary consequences of this new equilibrium of the social classes, if the proletariat is not able to organize itself politically and win its battle.

It is certain that the Socialist Party, as it is composed today, will be smashed by the new popular consultation. To save itself politically, it would have to accept a programme of collaboration with the bourgeois government and repression against the working class. The right wing of the party, stimulated by the need for self-preservation, will end up by accepting this point of view, dragging the majority behind it. The Socialist Party will be smashed, because it is not capable of understanding Italian reality and the complicated play of the class struggle. It is unable to say a single concrete word to the industrial workers, the majority of whom have in fact abandoned it and gone over to the Communist Party. It is unable to orient the poor peasants who are hit hardest and most directly by fascism.

The present situation can be understood and politically exploited only by the anti-parliamentary and anti-democratic forces. By the bourgeois government, which knows what elections amount to, since it manipulates them and seeks to make use of them only in order to bring about a state of demoralization in the revolutionary proletariat, by putting it into a minority. And by the communists, who can make use of them as an agitational instrument to educate the working-class masses in a precise understanding of what proletarian dictatorship means, and to organize the sole popular institution capable of controlling and reducing to impotence the industrial and agrarian bourgeoisie: the people itself in arms, united in its system of Councils, which has incorporated in its revolutionary Councils the three powers of the State in order to use them as an axe to cut down its enemies.

Unsigned, *L'Ordine Nuovo*, 24 March 1921.

12. THE COMMUNISTS AND THE ELECTIONS

The Communist Party is the historically determined political party of the revolutionary working class.

The working class was born and organized itself on the terrain of bourgeois democracy, in the framework of the constitutional and parliamentary régime. Tied to the fate of large-scale modern industry, with its great factories and immense cities, teeming with diverse, chaotic multitudes, the working class has only become aware of its own unity and class destiny slowly and by way of the cruellest experiences and most bitter disappointments.

This is why, in the various phases of its development, the working class has supported the most widely differing political parties. It began by supporting the liberal parties: in other words, it united with the urban bourgeoisie and struggled to annihilate the remnants of economic feudalism in the countryside. The industrial bourgeoisie thus succeeded in breaking the monopoly of food-supplies, in introducing into the countryside too a little economic liberalism, and in bringing down the cost of living. But this whole enterprise turned out disastrously for the working class, which saw its average wages cut. In a second period the working class supported the petty-bourgeois democratic parties and struggled to enlarge the framework of the bourgeois State: to introduce new institutions and develop the existing institutions. It was tricked a second time. The whole of the new ruling personnel which had been formed in this struggle went over with their weapons and equipment to the camp of the bourgeoisie, renovating the old ruling class and furnishing new ministers and high functionaries for the bureaucratic parliamentary State. The State was not even transformed. It continued to exist within the limits fixed by the Albertine Statute; no real freedom was won by the people.[18] The Crown continued to remain the only real power in Italian society since, via the government, it continued to keep the magistrature, Parliament and the armed forces of the country subordinated to its every wish.

With the creation of the Communist Party, the working class has broken all its traditions and asserted its political maturity. The working class no longer wishes to collaborate with other classes in the development or transformation of the bureaucratic parliamentary State. It wishes to work positively for its own autonomous development as a class. It submits its candidature as a ruling class, and asserts that it can exercise this historical function only in an institutional context that is different from the existing one: in a new state system, and not within the framework of the bureaucratic parliamentary State.

With the creation of the Communist Party, the working class presents itself in the political struggle as an initiator, as a leader, and no longer as an inert mass of troops directed and led by the general staff of another social class. The working class wants to govern the country. It asserts that it is the only class capable, with its own means and with its national and international institutions, of solving the problems placed on the agenda by the general historical situation. What are the real forces of the working class? How many proletarians in Italy have gained a precise consciousness of the historical mission that belongs to their class? What following does the Communist Party have in Italian society? In the present confusion and chaos, do the main lines of the new historical configuration already exist? In this continuous process of disintegration and reintegration, decomposition and recomposition of the social forces, classes and strata of the Italian population, has there already been formed an initial nucleus, compact and solid, permanently loyal to the ideas and programmes of the Communist International and the world revolution, around which the new and definitive political, governmental, organization of the working class can take place?

These are the questions which will be answered by the elections. In order to obtain a positive, concrete answer which can be verified and documented historically, the Communist Party is contesting the elections. The Communist Party, in the process whereby social forces are drawn up into battle units by the electoral programmes, wants to identify its own units and to count its forces. This is a necessary phase of the historical process which must lead to the dictatorship of the proletariat and the foundation of the workers' State. The elections, for the communists, are one among the many forms of political organization characteristic of modern society. The party is the higher organizational form; the trade union and the factory council are intermediary organizational forms, in which the most conscious proletarians enrol for the daily struggle against capital, and in which the enrolment takes place on a trade-unionist platform. In elections, the masses declare themselves for the highest political goal, for the form of the State, for the assertion of the working class as a ruling class.

The Communist Party is essentially the party of the revolutionary proletariat, i.e. of the workers engaged in urban industry; but it cannot reach its goal without the support and consent of other layers, of the poor peasants and the intellectual proletariat. That is the statement of principle. What is the force of expansion today of the revolutionary proletariat? How many elements from the other toiling classes recognize in the proletariat the future ruling class and henceforward, notwithstanding the terrorism exercised by reaction, intend to support it in its labour of mobilization and organization? The Communist Party does not harbour any illusions about the results – especially since it has already shown that it is seeking to get away from the methods of fairground demagogy whereby the Socialist Party "drew a crowd" in the past. But the more the Italian population has plunged into chaos and disorientation, and the more the forces dissolving the past alignment of revolutionary forces have operated and continue to operate, the more evidently necessary it appears to bring about a new alignment of loyal and trusty soldiers of the world revolution and of communism. The murkier the situation, and the scantier the resources of the new party presenting itself in the field of general Italian politics, the greater will appear the dynamic and expansive value of this new alignment.

Unsigned, *L'Ordine Nuovo*, 12 April 1921.

13. THE ELECTIONS AND FREEDOM

The real, concrete terms of bourgeois equality are progressively being laid bare in all their naked reality, and they cannot fail to be understood even by the most benighted and backward layers of the proletariat.

The industrial and landowning bourgeoisie possesses thousands and thousands of newspapers and printing-presses: all the paper-mills are at its disposal. The proletarians can only print very few newspapers with their own resources. The acts of destruction which have occurred, and the threats which rain down on printing works which accept orders from the working-class parties, make the inferiority of the propertyless class even more grotesque. Not one of the thousands upon thousands of bourgeois papers has yet been destroyed by the proletarians. Out of the small number of working-class papers, however, the destruction has already taken place of *Il Lavoratore* from Trieste, of *Il Proletario* from Pula, of *La Difesa* from Florence, of *La Giustizia* from Reggio Emilia, and of *Avanti!* in both its Milanese and its Roman editions.

The industrial and landowning bourgeoisie possesses tens of thousands of meeting-halls, theatres and cinemas, where it can assemble its supporters peacefully and carry out all the propaganda it deems useful. But the premises of the working class, the Chambers of Labour and the Socialist and Communist sections, have been burned down in their tens and their hundreds. Even the streets are denied to the popular masses: the natural place where the proletariat can assemble without cost has become a field for surprise-attacks and ambushes. To keep its domination of the streets, the working class would have to remain mobilized day and night, neither going to the factory to work nor going home to rest. A hundred armed individuals – guaranteed impunity for any violent act they may commit and the unconditional assistance of the forces of public order in case of need; with no obligation to carry out productive work; and able to move about from one spot to another in the execution of an overall plan – is sufficient to hold the proletariat in check and deprive it of its freedom to come and go, its freedom to meet and to discuss.

What value could a Parliament elected in such conditions have? How could it be seen as representing the "free" will of the nation? What could it reveal about the real political position of the social classes? If simply posing these questions were enough to produce a widespread conviction, a universal state of awareness and an impulse towards the foundation of a new order of things, the political struggle would already long since have concluded in the victory of the working people over the bourgeois class. The insurrection of the oppressed and exploited classes against their dominators, with their false and hypocritical liberty and equality, would long since have taken place.

The truth is that words and propaganda are not enough to cause the broad masses to rise up, or to determine the necessary and sufficient conditions for the foundation of a new order of things. The historical process is accomplished through a real dialectic: not through education or verbal polemics, but through the violent counter-position of incontestable states of affairs, which are manifest to the great popular masses with the utmost clarity. It is certain that the forced resignations of the socialist municipal councillors did more than two years of demagogic propaganda from the Socialist Party to render the notion of proletarian dictatorship comprehensible. It is certain that fascism, in a few months, has contributed more to illustrating the theses of the Communist International empirically in the proletarian consciousness than two years of *Avanti!* and the entire output of its publishing house have done. It is certain that these elections will definitively extirpate Parliament and all the other bourgeois institutions from the popular consciousness; and that they will make the emergence of a new representative system, in which the will of the people and the new ideals of liberty and equality are asserted and ensured protection, historically necessary and irresistible.

That is why the Communist Party is not abstaining from the elections. Because it wants the experiment to be carried out with full effectiveness and educative force. Because the Communist Party is the party not just of the proletarian vanguard, but of the great popular masses – even those who are most backward and benighted. It wants to reach and defeat the democratic socialist illusion even in its deepest lair. Will the elections, staged as they are in the environment of freedom and equality which is specific to bourgeois democracy, give the working class even just one deputy? This single one will then represent the whole oppressed class. His voice will be heard by the whole class. A slogan proclaimed by this single deputy, under the mandate of the proletarian party, will be accepted and put into practice by the whole class.

Such a situation will inexorably provoke the explosion of new representative institutions, which will counterpose themselves to Parliament and replace it: no popular layer will regret it or fight for it. This real process has already taken place in Russia. It is quite understandable why the Soviet government, even a few months after the November Revolution, should have convened the Constituent Assembly.[19] If the Constituent Assembly had not been convened, many popular layers would have remained supporters of parliamentarism in Russia. Yet its dissolution provoked no discontent or rebellion. It had become obvious, even to the most backward peasant masses, that the Constituent Assembly, elected as it was on the basis of lists for parties which no longer occupied those specific positions, did not represent the people – did not represent the interests of the majority of the nation. The Bolsheviks wanted the experience to be gone through. They wanted the popular consciousness to be formed materialistically. They wanted no regret or vague illusion to persist among the broad masses.

Let us make the revolutionary hypothesis that a popular insurrection sweeps away the next Parliament and replaces it with a Congress of workers' and peasants' deputies. Certainly not even Filippo Turati will still dare to maintain then that bourgeois democracy is the "city" and the Soviets the "horde"....[20]

Unsigned, *L'Ordine Nuovo*, 21 April 1921.

14. ELEMENTAL FORCES

In an interview with the *Le Temps* correspondent, Hon. Giolitti has solemnly declared that he wants order to be re-established at all costs. The government has summoned the general who commands the *carabinieri*, the commander of the royal guards, the chief of the general staff, and all the army corps commanders: the matter has been discussed, the necessary measures will be taken. With what means? Within what limits? Is it possible for the government, even if it wanted, to take the necessary measures? The circulars and meetings of the government are accompanied by orders, appeals and excommunications from the fascist authorities, who are also seriously concerned by the turn which events are taking and by the inevitable counter-blows. But it does not seem that even these authorities, highly "respected and feared" though they be, are succeeding in winning much obedience from the rank and file of their followers. Just as there does not exist a political State, just as there no longer exist any cohesive bonds of morale or discipline in the organisms and between the individuals who make up the State machine, so there exist no cohesion or discipline in the fascist "organization" either — in the unofficial State which today can at will dispose of the lives and property of the Italian nation.

It has now become obvious that fascism can only be partially interpreted as a class phenomenon, as a movement of political forces conscious of a real aim. It has spread, it has broken every possible organizational framework, it is above the wishes and proposals of any central or regional Committee, it has become an unchaining of elemental forces which cannot be restrained under the bourgeois system of economic and political government. Fascism is the name of the far-reaching decomposition of Italian society, which could not but accompany the decomposition of the State, and which today can only be explained by reference to the low level of civilization which the Italian nation had been able to attain in these last sixty years of unitary administration.

Fascism has presented itself as the anti-party; has opened its gates to all applicants; has with its promise of impunity enabled a formless multitude to cover over the savage outpouring of passions, hatreds and desires with a varnish of vague and nebulous political ideals. Fascism has thus become a question of social mores: it has become identified with the barbaric and anti-social psychology of certain strata of the Italian people which have not yet been modified by a new tradition, by education, by living together in a well-ordered and well administered State. To understand the full force of these assertions, it is enough to recall: that Italy holds first place for murders and bloodshed; that Italy is the country where mothers educate their infant children by hitting them on the head with clogs – it is the country where the younger generations are least respected and protected; that in certain Italian regions it seemed natural until a few years ago to put muzzles on grape-pickers, so that they would not eat the grapes; and that in certain regions the landowners locked their labourers up in sheds when the workday was over, to prevent meetings or attendance at evening classes.

The class struggle has always assumed an extremely harsh character in Italy, as a result of this "human" immaturity of certain strata of the population. Cruelty and the lack of *simpatia* are two traits peculiar to the Italian people, which passes from childish sentimentality to the most brutal and bloody ferocity, from passionate anger to cold-blooded contemplation of other people's ills. The State, though still frail and uncertain in its most vital functions, was with difficulty gradually succeeding in breaking up this semi-barbaric terrain. Today, after the decomposition of the State, every kind of miasma pullulates upon it. There is much truth in the assertion of the fascist papers that not all those who call themselves fascists and operate in the name of the *fasci* belong to the organization. But what is to be said of an organization whose symbol can be used to cover actions of the nature of those which disgrace Italy daily? The assertion, moreover, endows these events with a very much more serious and decisive character than those who write in the bourgeois papers would like to accord them. Who will be able to check them, if the State is incapable and the private organizations are impotent?

Thus we can see that the communist thesis is justified. Fascism, as a general phenomenon, as a scourge which transcends the will and the disciplinary means of its exponents – with its violence, with its monstrous and arbitrary actions, with its destruction at once systematic and irrational – can be extirpated only by a new State power, by a "restored" State in the sense which the communists understand this term, in other words by a State whose power is in the hands of the proletariat, the only class capable of reorganizing production and therefore all the social relations which depend on the relations of production.

Unsigned, *L'Ordine Nuovo*, 26 April 1921

15. THE OLD ORDER IN TURIN

Avanti!'s correspondent, the archangel with the clyster, signor Mario Guarnieri, is right:[21] the old order has triumphed in Turin.[22] It is certain that even the 22,323 socialist votes cannot be considered as an affirmation of revolutionary will. The Turin socialists have moved so far to the right, they have shown such a frenzied desire to ruin the proletarian organization, that they have permanently secured the sympathies and the political support of the petty bourgeois — and the latter certainly do not want the proletariat to instal a new order. The 22,323 socialist votes can be added in with the 10,150 votes for the Popular Party, not with the 12,509 communist votes. And the significance of the Turin elections clearly emerges: a majority asserted by the middle parties (32,473 votes) against fascist capitalism (31,555 votes for the bloc), to protest against the uncivilized "excesses" of those who burned the Chamber of Labour and, by means of the civilized weapon of the ballot, to proclaim the possibility for the magnificent and progressive destiny of the working people to be realized within the framework of bourgeois legality and the old capitalist order.

The Popular Party, since the share-croppers' strike, has lost the support of the old landed nobility.[23] The socialists, since the split from the communists, have lost the support of the revolutionary proletariat. Together, they have given political expression to the feelings of share-croppers, sacristans, shop-keepers, foremen, clerks and a percentage (around 20 per cent of more skilled workers, who want to blackleg while still claiming to be socialists. It is noteworthy that the socialists achieved respectable votes in the wards of the city centre; and it is still more noteworthy that Hon. Casalini should have won 250 write-in votes on the Popular list. The links of the chain which now bind Turin socialism to the bourgeoisie have been revealed: Turin socialism — Casalini (250 write-in votes on the Popular list) — Popular Party (400 write-in votes for Hon. Facta and Hon. Rossi on the Popular list) — Giolittism.[24] *La Stampa* did not oppose the socialist list and only gave the bloc tepid support. All *La Stampa*'s propaganda during the municipal election campaign against the Communists; the fact that in the last few days *La Stampa* has been arguing that it was only due to the wisdom of the reformists that the occupation of the factories did not culminate in "Bolshevik madness"; the fact that *La Stampa* has always maintained (including in the last few days) that since the split the Socialist Party has become a party of right-thinking men and model citizens – these factors combined to produce the 22,323 votes for the socialists.

The communists were defeated. We do not hesitate to acknowledge it. Of the 48,000 votes won in the last administrative elections, 40,000 at least were cast by communist proletarians and could have been cast in these elections too. Why was there such a high degree of abstention in the proletarian camp? It is not hard to explain such abstention, even if it is not justified from the point of view of a high level of political education, such as might have been presumed and hoped for in an industrial centre like Turin. In Turin, we are passing through a terrible crisis of discouragement and demoralization. The communists are persecuted in the factories, two thirds of the members in the section have been subjected to "reprisals". The electoral struggle, because of the general interpretation given it by popular sentiment, had the significance of an affirmation of bourgeois legality against fascist barbarism and ferocity; the Turin proletariat believed that such an affirmation was of no interest to it. This apathy is not a sign of political capacity, it is a sign of dissolution and mental confusion. An electoral result has the same value as a big rally; it serves as a demonstration of numerical strength and a document of the popular consent to an idea and a programme. Just as occurs with big rallies and public meetings, so too the results of an election can have the virtue of raising the spirits and the enthusiasm of the popular masses – hence the results of an election can even become a revolutionary factor. Not to understand this little truth of political life means not to know the ABC of political struggle. That is why abstention cannot ever be viewed as proof of political capacity, but is only proof of dissolution and moral degradation.

The small enthusiasm of the masses is justified by the small enthusiasm and the lassitude of the organized communists. A huge job of reorganization must be carried out by the best and most conscious elements. However, the communists must not get tangled up in investigations to determine the formal responsibility. The best way of establishing who was responsible is to construct a more solid organization. The best way of eliminating the weary, the hesitant and the undisciplined is by mobilizing the energetic, the decisive, the disciplined, and those who are aware of the immense work of organization and propaganda which lies before the Communist Party, if it wishes to become the party of the broad masses and to be capable of leading the revolutionary proletariat to accomplish its historic mission.

Unsigned, *L'Ordine Nuovo*, 18 May 1921.

16 SOCIALISTS AND FASCISTS

The political position of fascism is determined by the following basic circumstances.

1. The fascists, in the six months of their militant activity, have burdened themselves with an extremely heavy baggage of criminal acts which will only remain unpunished as long as the fascist organization is strong and feared.

2. The fascists have been able to carry on their activities only because tens of thousands of functionaries of the State, especially in the public security forces (police, royal guards, *carabinieri*) and in the magistrature, have become their moral and material accomplices. These functionaries know that their impunity and their careers are closely linked to the fortunes of the fascist organization, and they therefore have every interest in supporting fascism in whatsoever attempt it may make to consolidate its political position.

3. The fascists possess, spread throughout the national territory, stocks of arms and ammunition in such quantities as to be at least sufficient to create an army of half a million men.

4. The fascists have organized a military-style hierarchical system which finds its natural and organic apex in the general staff.

It stands to reason that the fascists do not want to go to prison, and that instead they want to use their strength – all the strength which they have at their disposal – to remain unpunished and to achieve the ultimate aim of every movement: to hold political power.

What do the socialists and the leaders of the Confederation intend to do to prevent the Italian people from being subjected to the tyranny of the general staff, the great landowners and the bankers? Have they fixed upon a plan? Do they have a programme? It does not appear so. Might the socialists and the leaders of the Confederation have fixed upon a "clandestine" plan? This would be ineffective, because only an insurrection of the broad masses can break a reactionary *coup de force*; and insurrections of the broad masses, though they do need clandestine preparation, also need legal, open propaganda to give them direction, orient the spirit of the masses and prepare their consciousness.

The socialists have never seriously faced up to the possibility of a *coup d'état*, or asked themselves what provision they should make for defending themselves and going over to the offensive. The socialists, accustomed as they are to stupidly chewing over a few little pseudo-Marxist formulae, reject the idea of "voluntarist" revolutions, "hoping for miracles", etc. etc. But if the insurrection of the proletariat were *imposed* by the will of the reactionaries, who cannot have "Marxist" scruples, how should the Socialist Party conduct itself? Would it, without resistance, leave the victory to reaction? And if the resistance was victorious, if the proletariat rose in arms and defeated reaction, what slogan would the Socialist Party give: to hand over their arms, or to carry the struggle through to the end?

We believe that these questions, at this moment, are far from being academic or abstract. It may be, it is true, that the fascists, who are Italians, who have all the indecisiveness and weakness of character of the Italian petty bourgeoisie, will imitate the tactic followed by the socialists in the occupation of the factories: that they will draw back and abandon to the punitive justice of a government dedicated to the restoration of legality those of their own who have committed crimes and their accomplices. This may be the case. However, it is bad tactics to put one's trust in the errors of one's enemies, and to imagine one's enemies to be incapable and inept. Whoever has strength, uses it. Whoever feels that he is in danger of going to prison, will do the impossible to keep his freedom.[25] A *coup d'état* by the fascists, i.e. by the general staff, the landowners and the bankers, is the menacing spectre which has hung over this legislature from the start. The Communist Party has its line: to launch the slogan of insurrection and lead the people in arms to their freedom, guaranteed by the workers' State. What is the slogan of the Socialist Party? How can the masses still trust this party, which confines its political activity to groaning, and proposes only to ensure that its deputies make "magnificent" speeches in Parliament?

Unsigned, *L'Ordine Nuovo*, 11 June 1921.

17. REACTIONARY SUBVERSIVENESS

The largely irrelevant interplay of combinations between the various parliamentary groups, favourite subject-matter for the astrological predictions of the Rome correspondents, was followed in the Chamber yesterday by the debut of the man who likes to present himself and to be presented as the leader of Italian reaction: Mussolini.[26] And Mussolini in his debut thought good to recall, almost as a badge of merit, his subversive origins. Is this a pose or is it a desire thereby the better to win the favours of his new master? Both motives no doubt play their part, and it is indeed true that the past subversiveness of the newest reactionary is an element which contributes not a little to delineating his image. It is, however, necessary to discuss it impartially, and to strip a little of the foliage away from this Mussolinian myth, so dear to the leader of the former revolutionary wing of the Socialist Party.

Is it a merit of the greater maturity of consciousness which the concrete revolutionary experience of the past years has brought if, reconsidering the attitudes and events of that time, we cannot but see them reduced to proportions very different from those which appeared to us then? When speaking in the Chamber, Mussolini perhaps said just one true thing, when with reference to his way of conceiving political conflicts and acting he spoke of Blanquism.[27] This admission provides us with the best vantage-point from which to grasp and precisely define what we instinctively perceive today as illogical, clumsy, grotesque in the figure of Mussolini. Blanquism is the social theory of the *coup de main*; but, if one really thinks about it, Mussolinian subversiveness only took over its material aspect. It has also been said that the tactics of the IIIrd International have points of contact with Blanquism; but the theory of proletarian revolt that is disseminated from Moscow and that was realized by the Bolsheviks is simply the Marxist theory of the dictatorship of the proletariat. Mussolini took over only the superficial aspects of Blanquism. Or rather, he himself made it into something superficial, reducing it to the materiality of the dominant minority and the use of arms in a violent attack. The incorporation of the minority's actions within the mass movement, and the process which makes insurrection the means for transforming social relations – all this disappeared. The Red Week in Romagna, the typical Mussolinian movement, was thus most accurately defined by those who called it a revolution without a programme.

But this is not all: one may say that for the leader of the fascists things have not changed from that time to this. His position, at bottom, is still what it was formerly. Even today he is nothing but a theorist, if that is the word, and a stage-manager of *coups de main*. Blanquism, in its materiality, can be subversive today, reactionary tomorrow. However, it is always revolutionary and renovatory only in appearance, condemned to lack continuity and development, fated to be incapable of welding one *coup de main* to the next in a linear historical process. Today the bourgeois, half terrified and half stupefied, regard this man who has placed himself at their service as a kind of new monster, a revolutionizer of real situations and a creator of history. Nothing is further from the truth. The inability to weld together the links of a historical construction is as great in the Blanquism of this epileptic as it is in the Malthusian subversiveness of people like D'Aragona and Serrati. They are all members of the same family. They represent, the former and the latter alike, a common impotence.

If Italian reaction today appears to have consistency and continuity, this derives from other elements, from other factors, of a character which is not just national but common to all countries and of a very different nature from what this bombastic self-praiser would like people to believe. The struggle against working-class demands and resistance to working-class resurgence have a very much more concrete basis. But it is no doubt significant, for the seriousness of Italian political life, that at the apex of a construction that is held together by a massive system of real forces, there should be found this man who amuses himself with trials of strength and verbal masturbation.

The politicians of the bourgeoisie, who judge by their own impotence and their own fear, speak of Mussolini's reactionary subversiveness. But we – like all those who understand anything about the trial of strength constituted by politics – only see a coach-fly.[28]

Unsigned, *L'Ordine Nuovo*, 22 June 1921.

18. REFERENDUM

The working-class trade-union association can function in three ways: by a general assembly of the membership, by "referendum", or by an assembly of shop-floor delegates. Which of these three forms best expresses the conscious will of the mass of union members?

Questions concerning the structure and functioning of working-class trade-union associations aroused no interest and attracted no attention in the period before the imperialist war of 1914–18, because the unions then only organized a tiny part of the working masses. After the Armistice, there was a sudden gigantic growth of the workers' unions. In Turin, for instance, the FIOM section organized between 30 and 35,000 metalworkers, and the problem was at once posed: how could one enable a membership on this scale to participate in the union's internal life? How could one enable it to express its will and exercise its sovereign right of deliberation?

The problem was an extremely important one, vital for the communists. For what is communism in essence? It is the spontaneous, historically determined movement of the broad working masses, who want to free themselves from capitalist oppression and exploitation, and to found a society organized in such a way that it is able to guarantee the autonomous and unlimited development of men without property. The communists thus have every interest in ensuring that the broadest masses take a direct interest in general questions, in political discussion, in administrative and organizational problems. The indifference of the broad masses means the stagnation and death of communism; the interest and enthusiasm of the broad masses means the development and the victory of communism. But how does one go about enabling 30 or 35,000 workers to take part in the life of their union? Even if it were possible to get them all into one hall, would so gigantic an assembly have any deliberative value? It would be a rally, not a deliberative assembly. The speeches would have to be shouted through a megaphone. The proceedings would not even be understood by everybody. All educative utility would be annihilated by the impossibility of serious argument or discussion.

These problems did not interest the trade-union mandarins or the reformists in general – or rather, they interested them negatively. For the reformists, just like the bourgeois, do not want the intervention of the broad masses. Oh yes, they want the broad masses to join unions, to pay dues, to be orderly and obedient. But they fear enthusiasm and a revolutionary spirit like the plague, and always seek to avert any participation in discussion by the popular masses. The trade-union mandarins have the same mentality as the great war bankers: they see themselves as "bankers of men". The masses for them are a means, an instrument, not an end. They say: we, trade-union mandarins, stand politically for the hundreds of thousands, the millions of workers who are organized in the union federations and the Confederation. Just as a banker overturns a government by manipulating his millions, corrupting and depraving the political personnel of parliament and the bureaucracy, so we mandarins overturn a government by manipulating the masses organized in the trade unions. But if the workers participate directly in union life; if they want to see clearly in all things; if they want to control; if they want to have all the deliberative power and only leave the administrative, executive, bureaucratic function to the mandarins – how, under these conditions, is it possible to carry on manipulating? The mandarins would no longer be mandarins.

So thus it is that the mandarins seek by every means to prevent the broad masses from participating in discussion. The assemblies are rigged: when a critic speaks, the little groups of reformists resort to systematic heckling; but when a reformist takes the floor, bursts of applause punctuate his speech. The reformists deliver interminable orations, seek to divert attention from the main problems, provoke incidents, etc., etc. When the moment comes for discussion, the assembly has dwindled in size, because many have grown impatient and decamped. Those who have remained feel suffocated, bewildered, stupefied by all the manoeuvres; so the reformists win a majority.

The reformist cliques are so strong and well-organized in some centres, that the communists are denied any possibility of making propaganda. Let us give an example. Once last year, at the invitation of the young socialists, comrade Togliatti went to Milan to give a meeting on the Factory Councils. The young socialists advertised the meeting in *Avanti!* and notified the Internal Commissions. The reformists put about a rumour in the Internal Commissions that the meeting was postponed for three days. Still not sure of having done enough to sabotage the meeting, they managed to get the municipal council – which they controlled – to interrupt the tram service for two hours on all lines leading to the hall where it was taking place. This is how the Milan reformists took care to prevent the "Turin contagion" from infecting the Milanese proletariat. And what did Giuseppe Bianchi, secretary of the CGL, do at the PSI National Council meeting in Florence? He asked the party leadership to establish a *cordon sanitaire* around Piedmont, to prevent Factory Council propaganda from spreading – which would have endangered the economic and political positions of the mandarins. Had the general assembly then become physically impossible, because of the immense dimensions attained by the unions? What was to be done? Resort to the "referendum"? But the referendum cannot be a normal method of government, it can only be an exceptional method. If one had to have recourse to a referendum for every vote, the unions would cease to function. The communists are also on principle opposed to referendums, since they place the most advanced and active workers, who make the greatest sacrifices, on the same plane as the lazy, ignorant, idle workers. If one wants direct, individual consultation, then this must take place in assemblies, after an organized debate, and the vote must presuppose knowledge of what is at stake and a sense of responsibility. A referendum can only be called for in exceptional circumstances, if one wishes to avoid appearing as saboteurs and disrupters.

The communists worked out the system of workshop delegates, as a reasonable solution to the present organizational problems. The delegates' assembly is an assembly performing the function of a referendum. The delegate is elected by a work squad, imperatively mandated, and instantly recallable. The delegates' assembly thus represents the whole mass of workers, and can be assumed to be made up of the best elements from that mass. Since the mandate is imperative and revocable, it can also be assumed that the delegates' assembly represents the opinion of the mass of workers at all times.

The general membership assembly has the same relation to the delegates' assembly as the gathering of a Roman or Germanic tribe has to a bourgeois parliament. The representative principle was a great step forward in the practice of government, for every class. In Rome, the people or plebs took part in the running of public affairs by gathering together and appointing tribunes. In the Middle Ages, the Germanic tribes too gathered in great assemblies to discuss, beating their lances on the ground. Parliaments replaced these barbaric and irrational forms of popular government. The same thing has occurred in the working-class organizations. When general membership assemblies were called, they were deafened by words, swindled by reformist demagogy, and ruled by the clapping of hands and the raising of arms. The delegates' assembly, embryonic form of the soviet, is the natural form of representation of the working class. It is working-class "parliamentarism", which seeks to abolish monarchic absolutism in the trade unions, just as the national parliament abolished monarchic absolutism in the State. The communists wanted the whole mass of workers to interest themselves in union problems, and at the same time wanted to retain those elements contained in the general assembly that were beneficial from an educative point of view. They succeeded in solving the problem in a historically concrete manner with the system of delegates, which synthesizes the referendum and the general membership assembly.

The reformists, with the offensive they have launched in combination with that of the industrialists, are aiming to wreck the workers' organizations – which today can only live and develop in soviet-type forms. One of the reformists' weapons is the continual demand for referendums. The aim of these is to reduce the masses once more to the conditions of apathy and indifference which characterized the period preceding the imperialist war, and thus to restore the absolute power of the mandarins. The reformists frequently and readily accuse the communists of being ambitious and *arriviste*. The reply is simple: it may very well be that the communists are ambitious (ambition has always been one of the great forces in history); but at least the "ambitious" communists, as they rise, seek to raise the broad popular masses with them. But you, people who have already "arrived", in order to keep your positions you press the masses down and degrade them. The ambition of the communist, who knows he cannot rise without raising the mass of workers, is a noble thing. Yours, o mandarins, is not even ambition; it is an ignoble imitation of the bourgeois methods whereby one man oppresses another.

Unsigned, *L'Ordine Nuovo*, 29 June 1921.

19. LEADERS AND MASSES

The peace treaty which is about to be drawn up between socialist and fascist members of parliament will have considerable importance in Italian political life.[29] It will mark the failure of fascism as a political movement; and it will reduce socialist collaborationism to its objective and real terms, in other words will mark the beginning of the political failure of the Socialist Party.

The treaty will only have any meaning in parliament: it will be binding on the leaders, but will have no value for the masses. Hon. Mussolini, who aspires to the role of a highly shrewd and skilful deputy, will appear in his true colours: a coach-fly, a sorcerer's apprentice who has learnt the formula to call up the devil but does not know the one to send him back to hell again. The fascists will be preached at and disavowed as "false fascists" from the benches of parliament and the columns of *Il Popolo d'Italia*. The workers who put up a resistance to reactionary violence will be massacred as "communist criminals". And the treaty will be effective insofar as it allows Armando Bussi to be friendly to Benito Mussolini and Tito Zaniboni to shake hands with Farinacci or De Vecchi.

The peace between fascists and socialists is the result of a state of mind to which the two political failures contribute. Fascist tactics, insofar as they corresponded to a predetermined political plan, aimed to oblige the socialist leaders to return to constitutional legality and to persuade them to collaborate. Hon. Giolitti encouraged the fascist movement in order to direct it towards this precise goal. The masses were massacred with impunity, the Chambers of Labour, the *Case del popolo* and the cooperatives were burnt and sacked with impunity, in order to persuade the socialist leaders to reflect. A pedagogic method formerly employed in the English royal family was applied on a large scale: the young prince was always accompanied by a boy of humble rank who took his thrashings for him; pity for the sufferings and cries of this wretched creature was supposed to induce the prince, subject to freaks, whims and indolence, to mend his ways. Thus to induce the trade-union leaders and socialist deputies to drop their "intransigence" and collaborate with the government and the capitalists, Hon. Giolitti allowed fascism to martyrize whole regions, to terrorize millions upon millions of citizens, to organize 400,000 armed men for civil war. Hon. Giolitti's plan was a Machiavellian one. But reality is full of contradictions: only too often, the loutish jeers of Stenterello screech out beside the cynically pensive face of Machiavelli.[30] Fascist tactics and Giolittian political pedagogy have had the following result: Italian trade-union organization has fallen apart, and the masses no longer obey the leaders by whom they were basely abandoned at the moment of danger and carnage.

What purpose would socialist collaboration with the government still have? The socialists and union leaders are only of any use to capitalism when their slogans are accepted by the masses organized in the trade unions. The union leaders, as individuals, are considered worthless. Their ignorance is universally known; their administrative incapacity is proverbial. It is one thing to draw up industrial agreements, quite another to govern a country. The union leaders are only valued insofar as they are held to enjoy the confidence of the broad working masses; only insofar as they are able to prevent strikes and persuade the workers to accept with resignation the exploitation and oppression of capitalism "in order to save the nation from ruin". Today, the socialists and trade-union leaders have lost all control over the working class. Even if they wanted to, they could do nothing. This is what the result of fascist tactics and Hon. Giovanni Giolitti's political pedagogy has been. Replacing Labriola by Bruno Buozzi today would only mean replacing one coach-fly by another coach-fly.[31]

It is therefore natural that the fascists should become reconciled with the socialists: the intrinsic weakness of both will be less apparent. Both no longer have a function to fulfil in the country: they have therefore rightly become government parties, "practical" parties. Giovanni Giolitti is their representative figure: and we shall see, if the tutelary deities allow it because the masses have not yet found a revolutionary orientation and organization – we shall see Giovanni Giolitti head a government of Socialist, Fascist and Popular coach-flies.

Unsigned, *L'Ordine Nuovo*, 3 July 1921.

20. BONOMI

The new Prime Minister, Hon. Bonomi, is the true organizer of Italian fascism.[32] As War Minister, he did not merely allow officers to participate actively in political factions, he organized this participation minutely. When he demobilized the officers, he did not follow a technical plan but a reactionary political one, whereby the demobilized officers were systematically to become the cadres of a white guard. Stocks of arms and ammunition were put at the disposal of the fascists. The army and divisional staffs had orders to study the strategic position in case of civil war, and to draw up detailed plans of attack. Senior officers were sent off to tour the country, making reports and suggestions. Hon. Bonomi is the true representative of this bloody phase of bourgeois history. Like Noske, Millerand and Briand, he comes from the socialist ranks. The bourgeoisie places its trust in these men precisely because they have been militants and leaders in the working-class movement; they thus know its weaknesses and how to corrupt its members.

Bonomi's arrival in power, after the entry of the fascists into Parliament, has the following significance: Italian reaction to communism will become legal rather than illegal. To be a communist, to fight for the coming to power of the working class, will not be a crime merely in the judgement of a Lanfranconi or a Farinacci, it will be a crime "legally"; it will be systematically persecuted in the name of the law, and no longer merely in the name of the local Fascist squad. The same process will take place in Italy as has taken place in the other capitalist countries. The advance of the working class will be met by a coalition of all reactionary elements, from the fascists to the *popolari* and socialists: the socialists will indeed become the vanguard of anti-proletarian reaction, because they best know the weaknesses of the working class and because they have personal vendettas to pursue.

The communists have never had any illusions on this score. They know they must wage a struggle to the death, a struggle without quarter. Bonomi is the first link in the chain of crimes which social-democracy is girding itself to commit in Italy. This organizer of militarized fascism has the mission of concentrating in a single movement all the anti-proletarian and anti-communist currents which pullulate in our country, for a desperate attempt to check the ever more threatening insurrection of the masses against destructive capitalism. But massacres and attacks on freedom will not be able, in Italy either, to solve the economic crisis or to re-erect the social edifice ruined by the imperialist war.

Unsigned, *L'Ordine Nuovo*, 5 July 1921.

21. THE "ARDITI DEL POPOLO"

Hon. Mingrino's declarations to the press about his joining the *Arditi del Popolo*[33] serve magnificently to highlight the Communist Party's statement on the same subject. Mingrino's declarations correspond to the obsolete, worn-out psychology of the Socialist Party, which on other occasions we have baptized as neo-Malthusianism. If this conception were accepted, the *Arditi del Popolo* movement would inevitably lead to a repetition of the events of September 1920, when the metal-working proletariat was led on to the terrain of illegality, placed in a situation where it could not resist without arming itself and violating the most sacred privileges of capitalism, and then, suddenly, everything came to an end because the occupation of the factories only set itself . . . trade-union objectives.

Hon. Mingrino is joining the *Arditi del Popolo*. He is giving that institution his name, his rank as a socialist deputy, his personal prestige as someone liked by the revolutionary proletariat for his conduct during the fascist attack on comrade Misiano.[34] But what is the mission of the *Arditi del Popolo*, according to Hon. Mingrino? It should be limited to achieving a counter-weight to fascist violence; it should be one of pure resistance; in short, it should have purely . . . trade-union objectives.

Does Hon. Mingrino then believe that fascism is a superficial manifestation of post-war psychosis? Has he not yet been persuaded that fascism is organically linked to the present crisis of the capitalist order and will only disappear with the suppression of that order? Has he not yet been convinced that the patriotic, nationalistic, reconstructionist ideology of Mussolini and Co. is of purely marginal significance? That instead fascism must be seen in its objective reality, outside all predetermined schemas or abstract political models, as a spontaneous pullulation of reactionary energies which coalesce, dissolve and come together again, following the official leaders only when their directives correspond to the inner nature of the movement? For this is what it is, notwithstanding Mussolini's speeches, Pasella's official statements and the hurrahs of all this world's idealists.

To launch, or join, a movement of popular resistance, while setting in advance a limit to its expansion, is the most serious error of tactics that can be committed at this moment. It is essential not to sow illusions among the popular masses, who are suffering cruelly and are led by their sufferings to delude themselves, to believe that they can alleviate their pain simply by shifting their position. It is essential not to make them believe that a little effort will be enough to save them from the dangers which loom over the entire working people today. It is essential to make them understand, it is essential to compel them to understand, that today the proletariat is confronted not just by a private association, but by the whole State apparatus, with its police, its courts, its newspapers which manipulate public opinion as the government and the capitalists please. It is essential to make them understand what they were not made to understand in September 1920: when the working people leaves the terrain of legality but does not find the necessary spirit of sacrifice and political capacity to carry its actions through to the end, it is punished by mass shootings, by hunger, by cold, by inactivity which kills slowly, day by day.

Are the communists opposed to the *Arditi del Popolo* movement? On the contrary: they want the arming of the proletariat, the creation of an armed proletarian force which is capable of defeating the bourgeoisie and taking charge of the organization and development of the new productive forces generated by capitalism.

The communists are also of the opinion that when one wishes to launch a struggle, one should not wait for victory to be guaranteed by a notary's certificate. On many occasions in history, peoples have found themselves at a crossroads: either to languish day by day in starvation and exhaustion, strewing their paths with a few deaths each day – which, however, in the course of weeks, months and years become a host; or else to take a chance. This could mean to die fighting in an all-out effort; but it could also mean to win, to halt the process of dissolution at a single blow and initiate the enterprise of reorganization and development which will at least ensure a little more tranquillity and well-being for future generations. Those peoples who had faith in themselves and their own destinies, and who faced up to the struggle with audacity, were the ones who saved themselves.

But if the communists are of this opinion – as regards the objective elements of the situation; as regards the relation of forces with the enemy; as regards the ways in which the decadence and chaos created by the imperialist war can be overcome; as regards all those elements which cannot be inventoried, and concerning which it is not always possible to make an accurate calculation of probabilities – they nevertheless at least want the political objectives to be clear and concrete. They do not want what happened in September 1920 to be repeated today, at least so far as what can be foreseen is concerned – what can be assessed, and predetermined by political activity organized in a party.

The workers have the means to express their opinions. The socialist workers, who are revolutionaries and have drawn certain lessons from the experience of these last months, have the means to exert pressure on the Socialist Party, forcing it to abandon equivocation and ambiguity, and obliging it to take up a clear and precise position on this problem in which the actual physical safety of the worker and the peasant is at stake. Hon. Mingrino is a socialist deputy. If he is a sincere man, as we believe, let him take the initiative in bringing the masses which still follow his party out of their torpor and indecision. But let him not put limits on their expansion, if he does not wish to bear the responsibility of having brought the Italian people a new defeat and a new fascism, compounded by all the vengeance which reaction implacably wreaks upon the waverers and hesitaters, after it has massacred the assault troops in the vanguard.

Unsigned, *L'Ordine Nuovo*, 15 July 1921.

22. THE DEVELOPMENT OF FASCISM

The events of Grosseto, Viterbo and Treviso are the initial phase of a new and definitive development of fascism.[35] Punitive expeditions by small bands are giving way to actions by veritable army units, armed with machine-guns. In some areas fascist cavalry is making its appearance. In Siena, thousands upon thousands of fascists assembled, on the pretext of a provincial congress, to parade in military order with their own cavalry.

It would be foolish to believe that all this has only a choreographic significance. It is clear, in fact, that the local fascist formations are obeying a central directive and applying a minutely prearranged plan. Before long the Treviso episode, which so greatly stirred public opinion, will be surpassed by quite other sensational events. It seems that Turin is to be the scene of the next grandiose fascist exploit. It is said that between ten and fifteen thousand fascists will be demobilized, from all over the Po valley, to attack Turin and definitively crush its proletarian movement. Those in charge of public security allegedly know something about it: the Milan chief of police, Commander Gasti, who concerns himself so "lovingly" with *L'Ordine Nuovo*, allegedly knows something very definite about it.

There is every guarantee that these rumours are serious, and the working masses must be seriously concerned. The revolts against fascism which are now multiplying throughout the country contain the hope of a rebirth of popular energies; but they should also cause the weight of responsibility to be more keenly felt. The more it is shown that the people are not prepared to submit to white terror, the more it is necessary to foresee that fascism will extend, intensify and organize its activity. The very probability of socialist collaboration with the government increases the danger of a fascist *coup de main*. It is certain that the socialists will give their support to the government only if the government gives assurances that it will repress fascism. And it is also certain that fascism will not want to lose the position of predominance which it occupies in so many regions today. "Pacification"[36] is only a thin mask designed to allow them to continue with impunity the preparation and military organization of veritable armies to counterpose to the government and to the socialists.

After the episodes of Grosseto and Treviso, which have remained unpunished, a fascist attack on the great working-class cities is to be expected. We once again ask the General Confederation of Labour whether it has prepared a plan of defence, that will permit the local populations to be aided and assisted in any efforts they may make to resist the reactionary offensive – which undoubtedly also has "trade-union" consequences and implications. We ask the same question of the Railwaymen's Union.

The local populations, however, do not have much to hope for from these bodies, which have completely lost any sense of historical reality. It is up to the local forces to give thought to their own defence. Viterbo and Sarzana have given the example of what must be done.[37] We hope that in the big cities, another force too will come into play: the soldiers, who have everything to fear from a fascist government. A fascist *coup d'état* would mean a war, and not only in the East. The popular masses who want peace, freedom and bread must, in this period of dark onrush of events, always hold themselves ready to spring up as one man against every danger of new carnage and suffering threatened by the so heroic exploits of fascism.

Unsigned, *L'Ordine Nuovo*, 21 July 1921.

23. AGAINST TERROR

The invitation which the Communist Trade-union Committee has addressed to the Italian working-class organizations for concerted action against the employers' offensive also refers to the need to check the brigandry of the white guards.[38] It is necessary to stress this point particularly, in the propaganda which communists must carry out among the working masses, if we are to obtain the best possible outcome from the initiative of our trade-union committee. It has now become obvious that the tactic of compromises applied by the Socialist Party and the General Confederation of Labour *vis-à-vis* fascism, has only benefited the latter. The popular masses, tormented, continuously exposed to mortal danger from the punitive expeditions, without protection from the legal authorities, were rising violently against the white terror. Automatically, precisely because fascism had become a national scourge, an uprising of a national character was maturing, which would have had very great revolutionary significance. The Socialist Party and the General Confederation of Labour, with their pacifist attitude, succeeded in achieving: on the one hand, a collapse of the revolutionary energies which were developing progressively among the broad popular masses; on the other hand, an internal crisis of fascism, which is one not of decomposition but of reorganization and improved reactionary functioning.

By centring itself on Bologna in place of Milan,[39] fascism is in fact freeing itself from elements like Mussolini – always uncertain, always hesitating as a result of their taste for intellectualist adventures and their irrepressible need for general ideologies – and becoming a homogeneous organization supporting the agrarian bourgeoisie, without ideological weaknesses or uncertainties in action. Compromise tactics must be adopted by revolutionaries to procure moments of respite for the proletariat, and to permit reorganization and improved use of the working-class forces. Social-democratic pacifism, however, only benefited the fascist movement. Ir procured a respite for the fascist movement. It permitted the fascist movement to reorganize itself and eliminate from its own commanding body the uncertain, wavering elements who, at the moment of action, endanger victory by their oppositional attitude.

The situation has become objectively clear. The preaching of non-resistance to evil by the Socialist Party after the Livorno Congress had created many illusions among the working-class masses. The working-class masses, who conceive of the function of the political party concretely and positively and who continued to put their trust in the Socialist Party after the Livorno Congress, were convinced that the preaching of non-resistance to evil was a tactical camouflage, designed to allow meticulous and thorough preparation of a great strategic initiative against fascism. This explains the great enthusiasm with which the first appearances of the *Arditi del popolo* were greeted. *It was believed by many workers that the preaching of non-resistance to evil had precisely served to allow the Socialist Party and the Confederation to organize meticulously the forces of the* Arditi del popolo, *and thus give the popular insurrection a solid and compact form.* This illusion has now vanished. The great mass of the people must by now be convinced that behind the socialist sphinx there was nothing.

It is true that socialists too (even perhaps the most right-wing) took part in the creation of the first nuclei of the *Arditi del popolo*. It is nevertheless certain that the lightning speed with which the initiative spread was not the result of a general plan prepared by the Socialist Party, but was simply due to the generalized state of mind in the country – the desire to rise up in arms which was smouldering among the broad masses. This was resoundingly demonstrated by the pacification pact, which could not but cause the movement of proletarian resurgence to stagnate, and could not but bring about a reorganization of the reactionary elements and a new strategy on their part.

By now, the great mass of the Italian people must understand this. All the more so today, after the new events which have occurred in the fascist camp. The assembly of fascists opposed to the concordat at Bologna and the disavowal of Mussolini are clear indications of a renewal of the reactionary offensive on a large scale. Is it possible still to think of continuing with the tactic of non-resistance to evil? The broad proletarian masses must answer this question. What the Communist Party proposes to do is consult the will of the Italian workers and peasants.

There can be no doubt about the reply: battle or death; struggle or annihilation. This is how the problem is inescapably posed.

Unsigned, *L'Ordine Nuovo*, 19 August 1921.

24. THE TWO FASCISMS

The crisis of fascism, on whose origins and causes so much is being written these days, can easily be explained by a serious examination of the actual development of the fascist movement.

The *Fasci di combattimento* emerged, in the aftermath of the War, with the petty-bourgeois character of the various war-veterans' associations which appeared in that period.[40] Because of their character of determined opposition to the socialist movement – partly a heritage of the conflicts between the Socialist Party and the interventionist associations during the War period – the *Fasci* won the support of the capitalists and the authorities. The fact that their emergence coincided with the landowners' need to form a white guard against the growing power of the workers' organizations allowed the system of bands created and armed by the big landowners to adopt the same label of *Fasci*. With their subsequent development, these bands conferred upon that label their own characteristic feature as a white guard of capitalism against the class organs of the proletariat.

Fascism has always kept this initial flaw. Until today, the fervour of the armed offensive prevented any exacerbation of the rift between the urban petty-bourgeois nuclei, predominantly parliamentary and collaborationist, and the rural ones formed by big and medium landowners and by the farmers themselves: interested in a struggle against the poor peasants and their organizations; resolutely anti-trade-union and reactionary; putting more trust in direct armed action than in the authority of the State or the efficacy of parliamentarism.

In the agricultural regions (Emilia, Tuscany, Veneto, Umbria), fascism had its greatest development and, with the financial support of the capitalists and the protection of the civil and military authorities of the State, achieved unconditional power. If, on the one hand, the ruthless offensive against the class organisms of the proletariat benefited the capitalists, who in the course of a year saw the entire machinery of struggle of the socialist trade unions break up and lose all efficacy, it is nevertheless undeniable that the worsening violence ended up by creating a widespread attitude of hostility to fascism in the middle and popular strata.

The episodes at Sarzana, Treviso, Viterbo and Roccastrada deeply shook the urban fascist nuclei personified by Mussolini, and these began to see a danger in the exclusively negative tactics of the *Fasci* in the agricultural regions. On the other hand, these tactics had already borne excellent fruit, since they had dragged the Socialist Party on to the terrain of flexibility[41] and readiness to collaborate in the country and in Parliament.

From this moment, the latent rift begins to reveal itself in its full depth. The urban, collaborationist nuclei now see the objective which they set themselves accomplished: the abandonment of class intransigence by the Socialist Party. They are hastening to express their victory in words with the pacification pact. But the agrarian capitalists cannot renounce the only tactic which ensures them "free" exploitation of the peasant classes, without the nuisance of strikes and organizations. The whole polemic raging in the fascist camp between those in favour of and those opposed to pacification can be reduced to this rift, whose origins are to be sought only in the actual origins of the fascist movement.

The claims of the Italian socialists to have themselves brought about the split in the fascist movement, through their skilful policy of compromise, are nothing but a further proof of their demagogy. In reality, the fascist crisis is not new, it has always existed. Once the contingent reasons which held the anti-proletarian ranks firm ceased to operate, it was inevitable that the disagreements would reveal themselves more openly. The crisis is thus nothing other than the clarification of a pre-existing *de facto* situation.

Fascism will get out of the crisis by splitting. The parliamentary part headed by Mussolini, basing itself on the middle layers (white-collar workers, small shop-keepers and small manufacturers), will attempt to organize these politically and will necessarily orient itself towards collaboration with the socialists and the *popolari*. The intransigent part, which expresses the necessity for direct, armed defence of agrarian capitalist interests, will continue with its characteristic anti-proletarian activity. For this latter part – the most important for the working class – the "truce agreement" which the socialists are boasting of as a victory will have no validity. The "crisis" will only signal the exit from the *Fasci* movement of a faction of petty bourgeois who have vainly attempted to justify fascism with a general political "party" programme.

But fascism, the true variety, which the peasants and workers of Emilia, Veneto and Tuscany know through the painful experience of the past two years of white terror, will continue – though it may even change its name.

The internal disputes of the fascist bands have brought about a period of relative calm. The task of the revolutionary workers and peasants is to take advantage of this to infuse the oppressed and defenceless masses with a clear consciousness of the real situation in the class struggle, and of the means needed to defeat arrogant capitalist reaction.

Unsigned, *L'Ordine Nuovo*, 25 August 1921.

25. THE AGRARIAN STRUGGLE IN ITALY

As the policy being pursued by the landowners in Italy becomes more and more clearly defined, its significance for the workers grows accordingly. The landowners are not just arbiters of the situation in the countryside; indeed, this precisely serves them for other purposes, which are less well known, but far more important from the point of view of their class interests. It is a fact that the landowners today own the banks. To own the banks means, in a word, to hold in one's hands also the destiny of industry. This is how the working class is directly tied to the peasant class, and why the city proletariat must follow attentively all that happens among the workers on the land. The landowners, crushing the peasantry, aim also to obtain the subjugation of the city workers.

In this sense, when speaking of the rural fascism which is centred on the Bologna region, we have always maintained that the workers cannot be indifferent to the way in which the crisis of fascism is resolved. If the peasants continue to be terrorized in the countryside, the workers in their turn will feel the effects of this state of affairs. On the other hand, it is not just violence in the countryside which determines the crisis in the cities. Industry will only be able to take on a normal development, when it is freed from the influence of these adventurers from the land who have become captains of industry, without any specific merit of their own. Can this take place through an evolution of the State's internal policies, i.e. without causing violent clashes and conflicts? The attempt of the Popular Party to modify the relations between peasants and landowners, by seeking to associate labour with capital, can only be doomed to failure. The affair of the cancelled agricultural contracts too shows the impotence of the Popular Party – and of any other party which may follow in its tracks.[42]

In comparison with the *popolari*, the landowner deputies only represent a small minority. But the effective strength of the landowner deputies in the actual spheres of government surpasses that of the *popolari*. This is not the place to speak again of the weakness of parliamentary institutions. It is enough to demonstrate that what counts today is not the number of deputies one may have, but the organized strength which one possesses in the country. The landowners are, in this respect, far stronger than the *popolari*. Does the Treviso episode not tell us that the *popolari* are prisoners of the landowners or, if not prisoners, impotent in the face of their activity? In Treviso, a Popular newspaper was destroyed; the actual headquarters of the Popular organizations were stormed and sacked. But the *popolari*, although they have several ministers in what is supposed to be the cabinet, including to cap it all, the minister of justice, did not dare take even the usual measures that are adopted for the most ordinary crimes. Thus the *popolari* can only defend the interests of the peasants up to a certain point. They can do so only transitorily, i.e. until they come up against the interests of the landowners. This is precisely the case with the cancellations.

Minister Micheli has granted a postponement. This postponement is also supported by the socialists. The attitude of the landowners may drive the two parties – Popular and Socialist – to adopt a clearer position in the sphere of parliamentary collaboration. But this will not stop the landowners from having a preponderant weight in determining the direction of domestic policies. The landowners have direct means at their own disposal for organizing their defence against the working class. They have given proof of this with the organization of fascism in the countryside. They can thus still impose their will upon the peasantry when they want to, even when this means opposing government decisions. Socialists and *popolari* may, for electoral purposes, show that they are very concerned for the welfare of the peasants. But they do not realize they cannot point to any concrete way of preventing the landowners from carrying through their plans.

The problem of the land is now coming back on to the agenda of Italian politics. Everywhere, the peasant classes are in ferment. A revolutionary party alone (and in Italy that means only the Communist Party) can today understand this problem and fight for a solution to it.

The problem of the land is the problem of revolution, which in Italy is only possible if it coincides with the interests of the peasants and workers. This coincidence is present today. As in April 1920, today once more workers and peasants are united by a common interest in the struggle against exploitation by the employers. The problem of the Italian revolution, therefore, is one of worker and peasant unity. It is essential that this important aspect of the revolution in Italy should not escape the communists.

Unsigned, *L'Ordine Nuovo*, 31 August 1921.

26. THOSE MAINLY RESPONSIBLE

If in September 1920 the Turin communists had been anarchists instead of communists, the factory occupation movement would have had a very different outcome from the one it actually did have: this is the essence of an article from Turin in *Umanità Nova*, which reasserts our heavy responsibility for the failure to make a revolution.[43] What a pity! The Turin communists, in September 1920, were in fact communists and not anarchists. Even then, they believed that "proletarian revolution" means and can only mean creation of a revolutionary government. Even then, they believed that a revolutionary government can only be created if there exists a revolutionary party, nationally organized, which is capable of leading a mass action towards this historically concrete objective.

The Turin communists belonged to the Italian Socialist Party, and were members of its Turin section; the reformist leaders of the General Confederation of Labour also belonged to that party and that section. The movement had been launched by the reformists. The weekly *L'Ordine Nuovo* of 15 August 1920 clearly shows that the Turin communists were opposed to the action initiatied by FIOM – because of the way in which it had been initiated; because of the fact that it had not been preceded by any preparation; and because of the fact that it had no concrete aim.[44] Given these concrete conditions, the movement could only culminate in a revolution on condition that the reformists continued to lead it. If the reformists, once the action had begun and taken on the dimensions and the character which it did, had led it forward to its logical conclusion, certainly the great majority of the proletariat, and broad layers of the petty bourgeoisie and peasantry as well, would have followed their slogans.

If, on the other hand, the Turin communists had begun the insurrection on their own initiative, Turin would have been isolated, proletarian Turin would have been pitilessly crushed by the armed forces of the State. In September 1920, Turin would not even have had the solidarity of the Piedmont region, as it had had in the previous April. The evil campaign which the trade-union officials and Serratian opportunists had waged against the Turin communists after the April strike had had its effect, especially in Piedmont. The comrades from Turin could not even approach those from the region. Not a word of what they said was believed; they were always asked if they had an express mandate from the party leadership. The whole regional organization built up from Turin had completely fallen to pieces. The Turin correspondent of *Umanità Nova*, who perhaps knows the organizational efforts that were made in that period, certainly does not know many other things. The communists sought to put the Turin proletariat in the best conditions from the point of view of a probable insurrection. They knew, however, that elsewhere nothing was being done, nor any slogan being circulated. They knew that the union leaders responsible for the movement had no warlike intentions.

For a very brief period of time, three or four days, the union leaders were extremely favourable to an insurrection, they called wildly for an insurrection. Why? Apparently Giolitti, under pressure from the industrialists, who were openly threatening to overthrow the government by a military *pronunciamento*, wanted to go over from "homeopathy" to "surgery". He evidently made certain threats. The union leaders lost their heads. They wanted an "outrage", a local massacre which would justify their reaching an agreement at national level in accordance with reformist traditions. Were we right or wrong to refuse to take part in this infamous game, which was to be played with the blood of the Turin proletariat? By dint of repeating from April onwards that the Turin communists were irresponsible hotheads, "localists" and adventurers, the reformists had actually ended up by believing this – and by believing that we would lend ourselves to their game. They were not easy, those days of September 1920. In those days we acquired, perhaps belatedly, a precise and resolute conviction of the need for a split. How could men who mistrusted each other, who precisely at the moment of action saw that it was necessary to protect their backs from their own fellow-members, possibly remain together in the same party?

This was the situation, and we were not anarchists but communists, i.e. convinced of the need for a national party if the proletarian revolution was to have the least chance of a successful outcome. But even if we had been anarchists, would we have acted differently? There is a point of reference for answering this question: in September 1920 there did indeed exist anarchists in Italy, there existed a national anarchist movement. What did the anarchists do? Nothing. If we had been anarchists, we would not even have done what was done in Turin in September 1920 – i.e. carried out preparations that were certainly very considerable, seeing that they were accomplished by purely local effort, without assistance, without advice and without any national coordination.

If the anarchists reflect well upon the events of September 1920, they cannot fail to reach a single conclusion: the need for a strongly organized and centralized political party. Certainly the Socialist Party, with its incapacity and its subordination to the trade-union officials, was responsible for the failed revolution. But precisely for that reason, there must exist a party which puts its national organization at the service of the proletarian revolution, and which – through discussion and through an iron discipline – prepares capable men who can see ahead, and who do not know hesitation or wavering.

Unsigned, *L'Ordine Nuovo*, 20 September 1921.

27. PARTIES AND MASSES

The constitutional crisis in which the Italian Socialist Party is floundering interests the communists, insofar as it is a reflection of the deeper constitutional crisis in which the broad mass of the Italian people is floundering. From this point of view, the crisis of the Socialist Party cannot and should not be viewed in isolation: it is part of a more comprehensive picture which embraces the Popular Party and fascism.

Politically, the broad masses only exist insofar as they are organized within political parties. The changes of opinion which occur among the masses under pressure from the determinant economic forces are interpreted by the parties, which first split into tendencies and then into a multiplicity of new organic parties. Through this process of disarticulation, neo-association, and fusion of homogeneous entities, a more profound and intimate process of decomposition of democratic society is revealed. This leads to a definitive alignment of conflicting classes, for preservation or for conquest of power over the State and productive apparatus.

In the period which lasted from the armistice to the occupation of the factories, the Socialist Party represented a majority of the Italian working people, made up of three basic classes: the proletariat, the petty bourgeoisie and the poor peasants. Of these three classes, only the proletariat was essentially and therefore permanently revolutionary. The other two classes were "occasionally" revolutionary: they were "war socialists", who accepted the idea of revolution in general because of the sentiments of anti-governmental rebellion which germinated during the War. Since the Socialist Party was predominantly made up of petty-bourgeois and peasant elements, it could have made the revolution only in the first period after the armistice, when those sentiments of anti-governmental revolt were still alive and active. Furthermore, since the Socialist Party was predominantly made up of petty-bourgeois and peasant elements (whose mentality is not very different from that of urban petty bourgeois), it could not fail to waver and hesitate, without any clear or precise programme, without a line of march, and especially without an internationalist consciousness.

The occupation of the factories, basically proletarian, found the

Socialist Party – only partially proletarian and already, under the first blows of fascism, undergoing a crisis of consciousness in its other constitutive parts – unprepared. The end of the occupation of the factories threw the Socialist Party into total confusion. Its infantile and sentimental revolutionary beliefs were utterly confounded. The pains of war had been partly deadened (a revolution is not made because of memories of the past!). Bourgeois rule still appeared strong in the person of Giolitti and in the activity of the fascists. The reformist leaders asserted that to think of communist revolution at all was insane. Serrati asserted that it was insane to think of communist revolution in Italy, in that period. Only a minority of the party, made up of the most advanced and educated part of the industrial proletariat, did not change its communist and internationalist viewpoint; was not demoralized by what was occurring daily; and did not allow itself to be taken in by the bourgeois State's apparent strength and energy. Thus the Communist Party was born, first autonomous and independent organization of the industrial proletariat – the only class of the people that is essentially and permanently revolutionary.

The Communist Party did not at once become a party of the broadest masses. This proves only one thing: the conditions of great demoralization and dejection into which the masses had been plunged after the political failure of the occupation of the factories. In a great many leaders, faith was extinguished. What had previously been vaunted was now derided. The most intimate and sensitive feelings of the proletarian consciousness were vilely trampled on by these junior officers of the leadership, who had become sceptical, corrupted by repentance and remorse for their past of maximalist demagogy. The popular masses, who immediately after the armistice had aligned themselves around the Socialist Party, became dismembered, fluid, dispersed. The petty bourgeois who had sympathized with socialism now sympathized with fascism. The peasants, now without support in the Socialist Party, tended to give their sympathies to the Popular Party.

This confusion of the former forces of the Socialist Party with the fascists on the one hand and the *popolari* on the other was not without its consequences. The Popular Party drew closer to the Socialist Party. In the parliamentary elections, Popular "open" slates in every constituency were filled with hundreds and thousands of names of socialist candidates.[45] In the municipal elections which have taken place in some country districts since the political elections, the socialists have often not put forward a minority slate but advised their supporters to vote for the Popular one. In Bergamo, this phenomenon took a sensational form: the *popolare* left-wingers split away from the white organization and fused with the socialists, founding a Chamber of Labour and a weekly respectively led and written by socialists and *popolari* together.

Objectively, this process of Popular-Socialist *rapprochement* represents an advance. The peasant class is becoming united; acquiring consciousness and the idea of overall solidarity; breaking the religious carapace in the Popular camp; and breaking the carapace of petty-bourgeois anti-clerical culture in the Socialist camp. As a result of this tendency among its rural members, the Socialist Party is becoming further and further detached from the industrial proletariat, making it seem that the strong unitary bond which the Socialist Party appeared to have created between city and countryside is being broken. However, since this bond did not really exist, no real damage has derived from the new situation. On the contrary, a real advantage is becoming clear: the Popular Party is undergoing an extremely powerful swing to the left and becoming increasingly secular. The final result will be that its right wing, made up of big and medium landowners, will split off. In other words, it will decisively enter the field of the class struggle, with a consequent tremendous weakening of bourgeois rule.

The same phenomenon is beginning to appear in the fascist camp. The urban petty bourgeoisie, politically strengthened by all the defectors from the Socialist Party, had sought after the armistice to put to advantage the skill in military organization and action which it had acquired during the War. The Italian war was led, in the absence of an effective general staff, by the junior officers, i.e. by the petty bourgeoisie. The disappointments suffered during the War aroused extremely powerful sentiments of anti-governmental rebellion in this class which, having lost the military unity of its cadres after the armistice, became fragmented among the various mass parties and infused them with the ferment of rebellion – but also with uncertainty, wavering and demagogy.

When the strength of the Socialist Party declined after the occupation of the factories, this class, with lightning speed, under pressure from that same general staff which had exploited it during the War, reconstructed its cadres militarily and organized itself on a national scale. Extremely swift evolution; extremely swift appearance of a constitutional crisis. The urban petty bourgeoisie, a toy in the hands of the general staff and the most retrograde forces in the government, allied itself with the landowners and broke the peasant organizations on their behalf. The Rome pact between fascists and socialists marked the halting-point of this blind and politically disastrous policy of the urban petty bourgeoisie, which came to understand that it was selling its "birthright" for a mess of pottage.[46] If fascism had gone on with punitive expeditions of the Treviso, Sarzana or Roccastrada type, the population would have risen *en masse*. Moreover, even in the event of a popular defeat, it is certainly not the petty bourgeoisie who would have captured power, but rather the general staff and the big landowners. The fascists are once again drawing closer to the socialists; the petty bourgeoisie is seeking to break its links with large-scale landed property, and to have a political programme which ends up by strangely resembling that of Turati and D'Aragona.

This is the present situation of the Italian popular masses – great confusion, replacing the artificial unity created by the War and personified by the Socialist Party. A great confusion which has found its points of dialectical polarization in the Communist Party, independent organization of the industrial proletariat; in the Popular Party, organization of the peasantry; and in fascism, organization of the petty bourgeoisie. The Socialist Party, which from the armistice to the occupation of the factories represented the demagogic confusion of these three classes of the working people, is today the major exponent and the most notable victim of the process of disarticulation (towards a new, definitive order) which the popular masses of Italy are undergoing as a consequence of the decomposition of democracy.

Unsigned, *L'Ordine Nuovo*, 25 September 1921.

28. MASSES AND LEADERS

The struggle which the Communist Party has launched to form a trade-union united front against the capitalist offensive has had the merit of creating a united front of all the trade-union mandarins. Against the "dictatorship" of the Communist Party and the Moscow Executive, Armando Borghi finds himself in agreement with Ludovico D'Aragona, Errico Malatesta finds himself in agreement with Giacinto Menotti Serrati, Sbrana and Castrucci find themselves in agreement with Guarnieri and Colombino.[47] This does not surprise us communists at all. The worker comrades who followed the campaign waged for the Factory Council movement in the weekly *Ordine Nuovo* no doubt remember how we foresaw that this phenomenon would appear in Italy too. For it had already appeared in other countries and could therefore already be seen as universal – as one of the most characteristic features of the present historical period.

Trade-union organization, whether it had a reformist, anarchist or syndicalist label, had brought about the emergence of a whole hierarchy of lesser and greater leaders, whose best-known characteristics were vanity, a mania for wielding uncontrolled power, incompetence and unrestrained demagogy. The most ridiculous and absurd role in this whole comedy was that played by the anarchists. The more they shrieked at authoritarianism, the more authoritarian they were. The more they howled about wanting freedom, autonomy and spontaneous initiative, the more they sacrificed the real will of the broad masses and the spontaneous flowering of their libertarian tendencies. Especially in Italy, the union movement fell low and became a fairground hubbub: everyone wanted to create his own "movement", his own "organization", his own "real union" of workers. Borghi represented one registered trade-mark, De Ambris another registered trade-mark, D'Aragona a third, Sbrana and Castrucci a fourth and Captain Giulietti a fifth.[48] All these people, naturally, showed themselves hostile to the interference of political parties in the trade-union movement, asserting that the union is self-sufficient: that the union is the "true" nucleus of the future society; that in the union are to be found the structural elements of the new economic and political order of the proletariat.

In the weekly *Ordine Nuovo*, without *parti pris* and with a libertarian method, i.e. without letting ourselves be diverted by ideological preconceptions (hence with a Marxist method, given that Marx is the greatest libertarian to have appeared in the history of the human race), we examined what the real nature and structure of the trade union are. We began by showing that it is absurd and puerile to maintain that the trade union in itself possesses the capability to overthrow capitalism. *Objectively*, the trade union is nothing other than a commercial company, of a purely capitalistic type, which aims to secure, in the interests of the proletariat, the maximum price for the commodity labour, and to establish a monopoly over this commodity in the national and international fields. The trade union is distinguished from capitalist mercantilism only *subjectively*, insofar as, being formed necessarily of workers, it tends to create among the workers an awareness that it is impossible to achieve industrial autonomy of the producers within the bounds of trade-unionism; an awareness that for this it is necessary to take over the State (i.e. deprive the bourgeoisie of State power) and utilize its power to reorganize the entire apparatus of production and exchange.

We then showed that the trade union cannot be, or become, the basic cell of the future society of producers. The trade union, in fact, appears in two forms: the general assembly and the leading bureaucracy. The general assembly is *never* called upon to discuss and deliberate upon problems of production and exchange, or upon technical industrial problems. It is normally convened to discuss and decide upon the relations between entrepreneurs and labour-force, i.e. on problems which are specific to capitalist society and which will be transformed fundamentally by the proletarian revolution. Nor does the selection of trade-union officials take place upon the terrain of industrial technique. A metal-working trade union does not ask a would-be official if he is competent in the metal-working industry, or whether he is capable of administering the metal-working industry of a city, a region, or the entire country. It simply asks him if he is capable of arguing the workers' case in a dispute, if he is capable of drawing up a report and if he is capable of addressing a meeting.

The French syndicalists of *Vie Ouvrière* tried before the War to create industrial skills among trade-union officials. They promoted a whole series of research-studies and publications on the technical organization of production. (For example: how does it come about that hide from a Chinese ox becomes the shoe of a Paris *cocotte*? What route does this hide follow? How is the transport of this commodity organized? What are the costs of transport? How does the manufacture of international "taste" operate, so far as leather goods are concerned? etc.) But this attempt sank without trace. The trade-union movement, as it has expanded, has created a body of officials who are completely detached from the individual industries, and who obey purely commercial laws. A metal-workers' official can pass on indifferently to the bricklayers, the bootmakers or the joiners. He is not obliged to know the real technical conditions of the industry, just the private legislation which regulates the relations between entrepreneurs and labour force.

One may assert, without fear of being contradicted by any *experimental* demonstration, that the theory of syndicalism has now been revealed as an ingenious castle in the air constructed by politicians who only hated politics because, before the War, politics meant nothing except parliamentary activity and reformist compromise.

The trade-union movement is nothing but a *political movement*, the union leaders are nothing but political *leaders* who reach the posts they fill by appointment rather than by democratic election. In many respects a union leader represents a social type similar to the *banker*. An experienced banker, who has a good business head and is able to foresee with some accuracy the movement of stocks and bonds, wins credit for his institution and attracts depositors and investors. A trade-union leader who can foresee the possible outcome as conflicting social forces clash, attracts the masses into his organization and becomes a *banker of men*. From this point of view, D'Aragona, insofar as he was backed by the Socialist Party which called itself maximalist, was a better *banker* than Armando Borghi, distinguished confusionist, a man without character or political direction, a fairground pedlar more than a modern banker.

That the Confederation of Labour is essentially a political movement can be seen from the fact that its greatest expansion coincided with the greatest expansion of the Socialist Party. Its leaders, however, thought that they could ignore party policy, i.e. that they could follow *individual* policies without the nuisance of controls or disciplinary obligations. This is the reason for that noisy revolt of the union leaders against the "dictatorship" of the Communist Party and the notorious Moscow Executive. The masses instinctively understand that they are powerless to control the leaders or force them to respect the decisions of assemblies and congresses. Therefore, the masses want the trade-union movement to be controlled by a party. They want the union leaders to belong to a well-organized party which has a definite line, which is able to see that its discipline is respected and which will uphold freely contracted commitments.

The "dictatorship" of the Communist Party does not terrify the masses, because the masses understand that this "terrible dictatorship" is the best guarantee of their freedom, the best guarantee against betrayals and intrigues. The united front which the trade-union mandarins of every subversive variety form against the Communist Party shows just one thing: that our party has finally become the party of the broad masses, and that it truly represents the permanent interests of the working class and the peasantry. To the united front of all bourgeois strata against the revolutionary proletariat there corresponds the united front of all union mandarins against the communists. Giolitti, in order to defeat the workers, has made peace with Mussolini and given arms to the fascists. Armando Borghi, in order not to lose his position as the Grand Senusso of revolutionary syndicalism, will reach an agreement with D'Aragona, the High Bonze of parliamentary reformism.

What a lesson for the working class, which must follow not men, but organized parties that can subject individual men to discipline, seriousness and respect for voluntarily contracted commitments!

Unsigned, *L'Ordine Nuovo*, 30 October 1921.

29. ONE YEAR

The whole history of Italy since 1900 (i.e. since the assassination of Umberto I and the failure of the idiotic doctrinaire attempts to create a constitutional State with a rigid corpus of written laws),[49] and perhaps even the whole of our country's modern history since the achievement of national unity, would be an enigma if one neglected to take as the central focus of one's historical vision the ceaseless endeavours of certain governmental strata to incorporate into the ruling class the most eminent personalities from the working-class organizations. Italian democracy, as created after 1870, lacked a solid class structure because of the failure of either of the two propertied classes – the capitalists and the landowners – to become predominant. In other countries, the struggle between these two classes represented the terrain on which the modern liberal, parliamentary State was organized. In Italy, this struggle was almost entirely missing, or to be more accurate it took place in an equivocal manner as a bureaucratic and plutocratic subjugation of the central and southern regions of the country, inhabited by the rural classes, to the northern regions, where industrial and finance capital had developed.

The need to maintain a democratic régime, which was at once rule by bourgeois minorities and domination by a small part of the nation of the greater part of its territory, ceaselessly drove the representatives of northern industrialism and plutocracy to seek to broaden their own cadres as a ruling class, by integrating the working-class masses and eliminating the class struggle in their own area. Up to 1900, the northern capitalists in alliance with the big southern landowners sought to extinguish simultaneously the class struggle of the industrial proletariat and the violent eruptions of the poor peasant classes in the south. But it became clear that this alliance in the long run would have reversed the situation, giving State power to the big landowners and causing the North to lose the privileged position it had won with national unity.

The attempt by Umberto and Sonnino to give the State a rigid constitutional structure, removing from parliament the *de facto* prerogatives which it had succeeded in winning, was the decisive watershed in these struggles. With the assassination of Umberto, capitalism definitively got the upper hand. It sought to replace the alliance on a national scale of the propertied classes by a system of alliance with the urban proletariat, on the basis of which it could develop a true parliamentary democracy as in other capitalist countries. Giolitti is the typical representative of this tendency, and the whole history of the socialist movement from 1900 till today has simply been a result of the successive combinations thought up by Giolittism to secure the support of the working classes. In no country have the emergence and articulation of trade-union and cooperative organizations been encouraged as they have in Italy. Through the consolidation of these established interests, a whole stratification of petty-bourgeois officials was to emerge from within the working class, ready to lend a favourable ear to the seductive words of bourgeois statesmen. This twenty-year plan of the most intelligent part of the Italian bourgeoisie has today reached full maturity. In his extreme old age, Giolitti sees himself at last on the point of reaping the fruits of his long and patient labours. And this conclusion is being reached precisely in the days which mark the anniversary of the Livorno Congress.

One year ago, it was clear to the communists what the real line of development of Italian political life was. Despite the extreme difficulty of the moment, and despite the fact that their action might seem reckless and premature to a great part of the working class, the communists did not hesitate to adopt a clear position, separating off their own responsibility – and thus in the last analysis that of the entire Italian proletariat – from the political actions which were inevitably going to be carried out by the petty-bourgeois stratum which, for twenty years of history, had been forming and organizing powerfully within the working class.

The so-called unitary maximalists, with that ignorance of the social history of their country which has always distinguished them, believed instead that holding the class-collaborationist tendencies imprisoned in a verbally revolutionary party formation was sufficient to prevent the historical act from being accomplished. The maximalists maintained that the predetermined and daily preached collaboration was simply a question of will. They always refused, with the obstinacy of blinkered mules, to recognize that the whole of Italian history, because of its particular premisses and because of the way in which the unitary State was founded, necessarily had to lead to collaboration.

But Giolitti knew the history of the Italian socialist movement better than the maximalists. He knew (because to a great extent he was its creator) that the system of cooperatives and all the other organizations of resistance, insurance and production of the Italian working class were not born out of some original and revolutionary creative impulse, but depended on a whole series of compromises in which the strength of the government represented the dominant element. What the government had created, the government could destroy. What the government had created without officially compromising the authority of the State, could be destroyed by the government by the same method.

Thus fascism became the instrument for blackmailing the Socialist Party; for producing a split between the petty-bourgeois elements, encrusted like barnacles upon the established interests of the working class, and the rest of the Socialist Party – which limited itself to feeding on ideological formulae, since it had shown itself incapable of leading the revolutionary upsurge of the proletariat to a conclusion. Once again, economics prevailed over ideology. Today, the representatives of established interests – i.e. of the cooperatives, the employment agencies, the shared land-tenancies, the municipalities and the providential societies – although they are in a minority in the party, have the upper hand over the orators, the journalists, the teachers and the lawyers, who pursue unattainable and vacuous ideological projects.

In one year, intensifying to the point of absurdity the policy of compromise which is traditional for the Italian ruling classes, the bourgeoisie has succeeded in obtaining what it had patiently been preparing for twenty years. The great Socialist Party, which in 1919 seemed to have become the unifier of all the tendencies to revolt that were smouldering even among the lowest strata of the Italian population, has completely disintegrated. Two political forces have thereby resulted, neither of which is capable of dominating the situation: on the one hand, the reformist tendency, which will swiftly be incorporated within the bourgeoisie; and on the other, the Communist Party.

But these objective results of the Livorno Congress are not such as to discourage the communists. Indeed, the latter are strong precisely because they do not refuse to look the situation in the face and assess the real relationship of forces. For the proletariat to become an independent class, it was necessary for the edifice of false economic might that had been built up in twenty years of compromise to disintegrate. A collapse of such a kind could not fail to have very serious consequences that would weaken the proletariat itself. The communists had the courage to face up to the situation and bring it on. However, if this courage had been lacking, the collapse would have occurred just the same; but then not even the present strength preserved by the proletariat would have been saved from the catastrophe.

It is a necessary precondition for revolution that the complete dissolution of parliamentary democracy should occur in Italy too. The proletariat will become a dominant class and put itself at the head of all the revolutionary forces of the country only when experimentally, as a fresh proof of historical reality, the collaborationist tendencies show that they are incapable of resolving the economic and political crisis. At Livorno, the maximalists did not want to be convinced of this truth, which flows from the whole of Marxist doctrine. They believed that by the ideological coercion of an empty party discipline, they could prevent the historical process from being realized integrally in all its moments, and that a link in the chain could be leaped over. They were punished for their pride and belief in miracles. As a result of their lack of all political capability or understanding of the real history of the Italian people, they only achieved the wretched success of artificially postponing an experiment which, by now, would already have been liquidated by its own results. Thus to the pain and suffering imposed on the working class by capitalist oppression, they added new pains and new sufferings which could have been avoided.

Unsigned, *L'Ordine Nuovo*, 15 January 1922.

30. THE "ALLEANZA DEL LAVORO"

The leaders of the five most important trade-union organizations among which the Italian proletariat is divided have reached an agreement to set up a united national committee, with the task of realizing a programme of action drawn up on the basis of the minimum demands which form the most elementary connective substance of working-class organization.[50] The *Alleanza del Lavoro*, thus constituted, represents an undeniable advance over the original conception, which sought to make it into a coalition not just of the various trade-union organizations, but also of the various so-called subversive parties – and which thus sought to create in Italy a monstrous simulacrum of the English Labour Party. But despite this advance, for us communists the *Alleanza* only represents a first step towards realization of the united front programme.

The fact that the official leaders of the trade-union movement should reach agreement, and decide to give a permanent organizational form to their agreement by setting up a unitary national committee, is a historical fact whose importance for Italy we do not wish to belittle. But what would the agreement between the leaders be worth, if it were not based solidly on the agreement of the masses who fill the union ranks? In the case in question, we have seen that both the minority in the Confederation of Labour and the minority in the *Unione sindacale italiana* – i.e. in each, the supporters of their organization's adherence to the Red Trade-union International – were excluded from the constitutive meeting in Rome (and hence probably also from the committee that will be elected). The committee will have the following complexion: 5 reformists for the Confederation; 1 reformist and 1 anarchist for the Railwaymen's union; 2 anarchists for the *Unione Sindacale*; 2 syndicalists for the *Unione italiana del lavoro*; 1 reformist and 1 syndicalist for the Port-workers' Federation. In other words, the *Alleanza del Lavoro* will be made up of 7 reformists, 3 anarchists and 3 syndicalists. The communists, who certainly represent larger masses in the Italian workers' movement than do the anarchists or syndicalists, will have no representative in the *Alleanza del Lavoro*. The reformists, on the other hand, will have a majority from the first day. A rational distribution of mandates, in line with congress results, would give one 5 reformists, 2 communists, 2 anarchists and 4 syndicalists.

The fact that it produces situations of this kind is an additional reason why the agreement between the leaders can thus only be the beginning, the first step in an organizational activity that will culminate in the creation of the proletarian united front. Agreement among the leaders must be followed by agreement among the masses: what has happened at the leadership level must be reproduced at the bottom, in the heart of the proletariat, in all the centres where the working class and peasantry are struggling for their existence and their freedom. The national committee of the *Alleanza del Lavoro* must, if it wishes to live and develop, seek its organizational base in a system of local committees, directly elected by the masses organized in the various union federations. Only the formation of this new organizational system, in which all ideological tendencies which inhabit the working masses can find just representation, will signal the historical phase of the proletarian united front. This is the objective set for communist trade-union activity by the theses which the party's Central Committee will present to the next congress. To achieve it, the communists will work with all their energy as propagandists and organizers.

Unsigned, *L'Ordine Nuovo*, 21 February 1922.

31. A CRISIS WITHIN THE CRISIS

No solution was found yesterday either.[51] The crisis is certainly becoming daily more complex. Is any solution possible, given the existing Chamber? To pose the problem in this way means in a sense to shift it. Whatever government emerges from the present crisis, it can only be a transitional one. For a new element has entered the interplay of parliamentary combinations, and until this has been successfully inserted into its natural place, it cannot fail to unbalance things. This element is the socialist group – although the newspaper editorialists do not seem to be paying it much attention in their comments on the evolution of the crisis. The motion put to the vote yesterday in Rome,[52] protesting about the fact that this wretched country is still unable to give itself a government, shows that the parliamentary situation cannot be clarified if the socialist parliamentary group does not take the decision to abandon its habitual methods. The muddying of the parliamentary waters is due to the fact that the parties threshing about in them have not yet succeeded in finding their own equilibrium. Among these parties, the most uncomfortable, we repeat, is the Socialist Party.

Now that it has openly entered the orbit of legality and ceased to call itself a revolutionary party even by simple definition, it cannot fail to reach the ultimate consequences of its new attitude, which began with its abstention in Parliament. The Socialist Party, in other words, must collaborate not just in the corridors of Montecitorio, but in power.[53] This decision can only come to fruition through a series of crises. First of all, the Socialist Party must free itself from the last fetters of apparent intransigence, and must find its ally on the terrain of parliamentary combinations. But the socialist collaboration which was yesterday desired by all, today has greater obstacles to overcome, because of the shift of interests it would bring about. Not that Socialist collaboration is not still desired today; but the results which landowners and industrialists were hoping for from it have now been partially achieved. The treachery of the socialist union leaders, one might say, was a kind of indirect collaboration.

Thus today, the landowners and industrialists no longer even need the assistance of the social-reformists. So their participation in power is less straightforward today. But it is inevitable. The socialists must rise to power. They will do so even with the proletariat's worst enemy, but to power they will rise, because today this is their only wish. Now, until this process of Italian political life has been completed, the situation will remain obscure and complicated for all who seek a solution to it within the limits of Parliament. No government can achieve a stable existence without socialist collaboration. This is why the social-democratic government which is beginning to take shape on the horizon of Italian political life too, far from being the "best government" as the socialists are dishonestly saying, will be the worst that the proletariat could hope for.

Unsigned, *L'Ordine Nuovo*, 24 February 1922.

32. LESSONS

The conclusions to be drawn from the way in which this year's First of May demonstration went are comforting.

The demonstration succeeded as an intervention by the masses and an extension of working-class solidarity. It showed that the Italian proletariat is still *red*, despite reaction. And it also succeeded as a proof of the spirit of combativity reawakening among the ranks of the toilers.

The fascists were concerned to show by their attitude, and by their actual statements, that this was an anti-fascist demonstration. And such indeed was the meaning of the fact that large masses stayed away from work and turned out for the rallies, from one end of Italy to the other, without excepting the areas most hit by fascism. If there were no processions, this was due to the government ban. Had it been possible to hold them, today we would be counting a greater number of working-class dead, but also a greater number of fascist dead.

However, we must accompany this comforting recognition of the huge size and impressive character of the demonstration, and the high morale of the masses, with a recognition too of what its *organization* generally left to be desired.

This was not accidental: the united front tactic adopted on this First of May by all the proletarian organisms, as a test of the Italian *Alleanza del lavoro*, has had one good result and at the same time one disadvantage. Both must be carefully considered by the communists. We shall limit ourselves here to a brief allusion to the question, in connection with the statement put out by the *Alleanza del lavoro*'s Committee after the First of May.

By means of the united front tactic, it was possible to draw great masses of workers to the First of May rallies, even where it was perfectly clear to every individual attending that what was involved was not the habitual and tradition choreography, but a day of struggle. But this demonstration of the proletariat's aversion to reaction and to fascism, and of the class spirit which still animates the broad mass of toilers, is not enough in itself to overcome fascism and reaction. Fascism will not be stifled by platonic expressions of unanimity. Pistols and fists will not be rendered powerless by throwing a mattress over them. Fascism does not have the numbers, but it has organization, united and centralized, and in this lies its strength, integrated into the centralization of the official bourgeois power.

The *Alleanza del lavoro*, which has today made it possible to assemble vast masses, must become able to organize these and give them a unitary discipline. This is the task of the communists: to achieve this result, towards which only the first step has been taken. When it is possible for major rallies to count on a mass proletarian attendance, and at the same time on a rational preparation of our forces, then the proletariat will be able to dominate its enemies. On this First of May, it was evident that the meetings and demonstrations arranged by the allied organizations suffered from the absence of a little organizational preparation, even simply for the purpose of protecting them from enemy attacks. This circumstance was due to the fact that it was not really clear who had organized the meetings, or worked out the detailed plan for how they should proceed. The local committees of the Alliance have only recently been formed, and they do not have either a clear organizational structure or adequate powers.

Nevertheless, it is already a great advantage to have been able to hold united gatherings of the masses, because this raises proletarian morale and permits the communists to reach the whole proletariat with their plain speaking. If there is a whole further development of this interesting Italian experience of the united front tactic, it will have the effect of complementing this first undeniable advantage by a second: organizational unity of a real and intimate kind.

Some extremely important considerations arise in relation to this question. For the time being, we will only note that the trade-union terrain upon which the *Alleanza* has been set up allows the communists to press for it to become tighter and tighter organizationally, until it achieves the proletarian trade-union unity which we have always invoked and which the programme of the Communist Party alone can and must fill with revolutionary content.

For the present, it is necessary to react against the indolent and wavering character which the leadership of the *Alleanza del lavoro* has had up to now. The communists have already formulated, precisely and concretely, proposals for the development, revitalization and strengthening of the *Alleanza* – which could, if this campaign is not vigorously prosecuted in parallel with the eloquent experiences of proletarian action, degenerate into bureaucratic and cumbersome diplomacy on the part of hesitant, opportunistic leaders. The urgency of the communist proposals is shown by the *Alleanza*'s passive attitude in the face of the extremely serious provocations to which the working-class masses were subjected on the First of May. It is also shown, in spite of the invitations to action which reached it from all sides, by its insensitivity to the pressure coming today from the Italian proletariat, which is ready to proceed rapidly along the path of a counter-offensive. And it is shown by that extremely eloquent document, the statement put out by the national committee, which with its flat, banal phrases rejects what the masses panting for struggle suggest. We do not wish to make any further comment on the statement, confident that since the question is now irrevocably placed before the masses, the latter will not fail to make their own comment and judgement – and will draw from this fresh disappointment a new reason to proceed along the arduous but certain road to their resurgence.

Unsigned, *L'Ordine Nuovo*, 5 May 1922.

II

The Rome Congress

33. THESES ON THE TACTICS OF THE PCI ("ROME THESES")[54] – BORDIGA; TERRACINI

I

Organic Nature of the Communist Party

1. The Communist Party, political party of the proletarian class, presents itself in its action as a collectivity operating with a unitary approach. The initial motives which lead the elements and groups of this collectivity to incorporate themselves into an organism with a unitary action are the immediate interests of groups of the working class, arising out of their economic conditions. The essential characteristic of the Communist Party's function is utilization of the energies incorporated in this way for the attainment of objectives which are common to the entire working class and situated at the culmination of all its struggles; objectives which thus transcend – by integrating them – the interests of single groups, and such immediate and contingent aims as the working class may propose.

2. The integration of all elemental thrusts into a unitary action occurs by virtue of two main factors: one of critical consciousness, from which the party draws its programme; the other of will, expressed in the instrument with which the party acts, its disciplined and centralized organization. It would be wrong to see these two factors of consciousness and will as faculties which can be obtained from or should be demanded of individuals, since they are only realized through the integration of the activity of many individuals into a unitary collective organism.

3. The precise definition of the theoretical-critical consciousness of the communist movement, contained in the programmatic declarations of individual parties and of the Communist International, just like the organization of both of these, has been and is being arrived at through examination and study of the history of human society and its structure in the present capitalist epoch, carried out on the basis of data, on the basis of experience, and in the course of active participation in the real proletarian struggle.

4. The proclamation of these programmatic declarations, like the

designation of the men to whom the various levels of the party organizations are entrusted, take place formally with a democratic form of consultation of representative assemblies of the party. But in reality they must be understood as a product of the real process which accumulates elements of experience and carries out the preparation and selection of leaders, thus giving form to both the programmatic content and the hierarchical constitution of the party.

II

The Communist Party's Process of Development

5. The organization of the proletarian party takes form and develops insofar as there exists – because of the level of maturity to which the social situation has evolved – the possibility of a unitary collective consciousness and action in the direction of the general and ultimate interests of the working class. On the other hand, the proletariat appears and acts as a class in history precisely when the tendency to construct a programme and a common method of action, and hence to organize a party, takes form.

6. The process of formation and development of the proletarian party does not present a continuous and regular course, but is susceptible both nationally and internationally of highly complex phases and periods of general crisis. Many times there has occurred a process of degeneration whereby the action of the proletarian parties has lost, or has moved away from rather than towards, that indispensable character of a unitary activity inspired by the highest revolutionary aims. It has become fragmented in pursuit of the satisfaction of interests of limited groups of workers, or in achieving contingent results (reforms) at the cost of adopting methods which have compromised the work for revolutionary objectives and the preparation of the proletariat for such objectives. Thus the proletarian parties have often ended by extending the frontiers of their organization to the spheres of elements that could not yet place themselves upon the terrain of unitary and maximalist collective action. This process has always been accompanied by a deforming revision of doctrine and programme, and by such a slackening of internal discipline that instead of having a general staff of capable leaders resolute in the struggle, the proletarian movement has been placed in the hands of hidden agents of the bourgeoisie.

7. The path back from a situation of this kind towards the organization of a true class party, under the influence of new situations and new pressures to act exercised by events upon the working masses, takes place in the form of a separation of a part of the party which – through debates on the programme, a critique of unfavourable experiences in the struggle, and the formation within the party of a school and an organization with its own hierarchy (fraction) – reconstitutes that living continuity of a unitary organism, founded on the possession of a consciousness and a discipline, from which the new party arises. This is the process which, in general, led from the failure of the IInd International Parties to the birth of the communist IIIrd International.

8. The development of the Communist Party after the resolution of such a crisis, allowing for the possibility of subsequent critical phases produced by new situations, can to facilitate analysis be defined as "normal" development of the party. By displaying the maximum continuity in upholding a programme, and in the life of its leading hierarchy (apart from individual replacement of disloyal or worn out leaders), the party will also perform the maximum of effective and useful work in winning the proletariat to the cause of revolutionary struggle. This is not simply a question of exerting a didactic effect upon the masses; and even less is it a desire to exhibit an intrinsically pure and perfect party. It is rather a question of achieving the maximum yield in the real process whereby – as will be seen better below – through the systematic work of propaganda, proselytism and above all active participation in social struggles, the action of an ever increasing number of workers is caused to shift from the terrain of partial and immediate interests to the organic and unitary terrain of the struggle for the communist revolution. For only when a similar continuity exists is it possible, not merely to overcome the proletariat's mistrustful hesitations with respect to the party, but rapidly and effectively to channel and incorporate the new energies gained into a common thought and action, thus creating that unity of movement which is an indispensable revolutionary condition.

9. For all the same reasons, the aggregation to the party of other parties or parts detached from parties must be seen as entirely abnormal. A group which up to that moment was distinguished by a different programmatic position and independent organization does not bring with it an ensemble of elements that can be effectively assimilated *en bloc*; on the contrary, it impairs the solidity of the old party's political

position and internal structure, so that the increase in overall numbers is far from corresponding to an increase in the party's strength and potential – indeed could on occasion paralyse its work of organizing the masses rather than facilitate it.

It is desirable that as soon as possible it should be declared inadmissible within the world communist organization to depart from two fundamental principles of organization: in each country, there can only be a single communist party; and it is only possible to join the Communist International by individual admission to the communist party of the country in question.

III

Relations between the Communist Party and the Proletarian Class

10. The specification and definition of the characteristics of the class party, which is the basis for its constitutive structure as organ of the most advanced part of the proletarian class, does not mean that the party need not be bound by close relations with the remainder of the proletariat – indeed it demands that it should be.

11. The nature of these relations derives from the dialectical way of viewing the formation of class consciousness and a unitary organization of the class party, which transports a vanguard of the proletariat from the terrain of partial, spontaneous movements provoked by the interests of groups on to the terrain of general proletarian action; and which does not achieve this by rejecting those elemental movements, but accomplishes their integration and transcendence through living experiences, by pushing for their realization, taking active part in them, and following them attentively throughout their development.

12. The work of propagating its ideology and proselytizing for its ranks which the party continuously carries on is thus inseparable from the reality of the proletariat's activity and movement in all its myriad forms. It is a banal error to see as contradictory: participation in struggles for contingent and limited objectives, and the preparation of the final and general revolutionary struggle. The very existence of the party's unitary organism, with its indispensable conditions of clarity of programmatic vision and solidity of organizational discipline, gives a guarantee that partial demands will never be accorded the value of ends in themselves, and that oniy the struggle to fulfil them will be seen as a

means of experience and training for useful and effective revolutionary preparation.

13. Hence, the Communist Party participates in the organizational life of all forms of the proletariat's economic organization open to workers of all political faiths (unions, factory councils, cooperatives, etc.). If the party is to carry out its work effectively, it is a fundamental position to maintain that all organs of this nature must be unitary, in other words must include all those workers who are to be found in a specific economic situation. The party participates in the life of such organs by organizing those of its members who belong to them into groups or cells linked to the party organization. These groups, participating in the front line in the actions of the economic organs to which they belong, draw to themselves – and hence into the ranks of the political party – those elements who become ready for this as the action develops. They aim to win majority support and leading positions in their organizations, thus becoming the natural vehicle for transmitting the party's slogans. A whole activity is thus carried on, which is one of conquest and organization; this is not limited to propaganda or proselytism or internal electoral campaigns in the proletarian assemblies, but above all involves entering into the thick of struggle and action and helping the workers to derive the most useful experience from them.

14. The entire work and organization of the communist groups is designed to give the party definitive control over the leading bodies of the economic organisms, and first and foremost over national union executives, which seem the most secure mechanism for leading movements of the proletariat not integrated in the ranks of the party. The Communist Party – seeing it as its primary interest to avoid splits in the unions and other economic organs, so long as their leadership remains in the hands of other parties and political currents – will not enjoin its members to comport themselves, in the field of execution of movements led by such organisms, in contrast with the latter's directives as regards action, though they must express the most open criticism of the action itself and the work of the leaders.

15. Apart from taking part in this way in the life of those proletarian organisms that have arisen naturally through the pressure of real economic interests, and facilitating their extension and reinforcement, the party will strive to bring to the fore through its propaganda those problems of real interest to the workers which, in the evolution of social situations, can give life to new organisms of economic struggle. By all

these means, the party expands and strengthens the influence which via a thousand bonds stretches from its organized ranks to the proletariat as a whole, taking advantage of all its manifestations and potential manifestations in social activity.

16. Any conception of the party organism that was based on requiring a perfect critical consciousness and total spirit of sacrifice from each of its members considered individually, and that restricted the layer of the masses linked to the party to revolutionary unions of workers constituted in the economic field by a secessionist criterion and including only those proletarians who accepted given methods of action, would be totally erroneous. On the other hand, one cannot insist that by a given time, or on the eve of undertaking general actions, the party must have realized the condition of incorporating under its leadership – or actually in its own ranks – the majority of the proletariat. Such a postulate cannot be put forward aprioristically, abstracting from the real dialectical course of the party's process of development. And it is quite meaningless, even in the abstract, to compare the number of workers incorporated into the disciplined and unitary organization of the party, or following the latter, with the number of those who are unorganized and dispersed or attached to corporative organisms incapable of linking them together organically. The remainder of the present exposition will be an attempt to define the conditions to which relations between the party and the working class must correspond, in order to render given actions possible and effective, and how those conditions may be established.

IV

Relations between the Communist Party and other Proletarian Political Movements

17. One part of the proletariat is especially resistant to incorporation into the ranks of the Communist Party or into its periphery, because it is organized in other political parties or sympathizes with them. All the bourgeois parties have proletarian supporters, but here we are above all interested in the social-democratic parties and syndicalist and anarchist currents.

18. Faced with these movements, an incessant criticism of their programmes must be carried out, demonstrating their inadequacy for the purposes of proletarian emancipation. This theoretical polemic will

be all the more effective if the Communist Party can show that the criticism long made by it of such movements, in accordance with its own programmatic conceptions, are confirmed by proletarian experience. For this reason, in polemics of this kind it is essential not to hide the conflict between our respective methods – including that part which does not apply solely to problems of the moment, but reflects the subsequent developments of the proletariat's action.

19. Such polemics must, moreover, be reflected in the field of action. Communists taking part in struggles in proletarian economic organisms led by socialists, syndicalists or anarchists will not refuse to follow their actions unless the masses as a whole, in a spontaneous movement, should rebel against it. But they will demonstrate how this action, at a certain point in its development, was rendered impotent or utopian because of the incorrect method of the leaders, whereas with the communist method better results would have been achieved, serving the aims of the general revolutionary movement. In their polemics the communists will always distinguish between leaders and masses, leaving the former all responsibility for their errors and faults; moreover, they will not omit to denounce with equal vigour the activity of those leaders who, albeit with sincere revolutionary feelings, propose dangerous and incorrect tactics.

20. If it is an essential aim of the Communist Party to win ground among the proletariat by increasing its strength and influence at the expense of proletarian political parties and currents with which it disagrees, this aim must be achieved by taking part in the reality of the proletarian struggle upon a terrain which can be simultaneously one of common action and of mutual conflict – always on condition that the programmatic and organizational physiognomy of the party is never compromised.

21. In order to draw to itself those proletarians who support other political movements, the Communist Party cannot follow the method of constituting within them organized groups and fractions of communists or communist sympathizers. In the trade unions, this method is logically applied to carry out penetration work, without any aim of causing the communist groups organized in the unions to leave them; with political movements, a method of this kind would compromise the party's organic unity, for the reasons already mentioned with respect to the development of the party's organization.

22. In propaganda and polemics, it is opportune to bear in mind that many workers who are militants in the syndicalist and anarchist ranks

were ready to understand the unitary revolutionary struggle, but were set on the wrong path solely through a reaction to the past degeneration of the political parties led by social-democrats. The bitterness of polemics and struggle directed against the socialist parties will be an element of prime importance in bringing these workers back on to the revolutionary terrain.

23. The obvious incompatibility for a member of the Communist Party with simultaneously being a member of another party extends beyond political parties, to other organisms which, though they do not have the name or organization of a party, nevertheless have a political character, and to all associations which base their acceptance of members on political theses: the most important of these is freemasonry.

V

Elements of the Communist Party's Tactics derived from Study of the Situation

24. With the preceding elements, the general criteria which govern organizational relations between the Communist Party and other proletarian organisms have been established, in accordance with the former's essential nature. Before coming to the more properly tactical terms of the question, it is necessary to dwell on those elements for resolving any tactical problem that are provided by examination of the momentary situation through which one is passing. The Communist Party's programme contains a perspective of successive actions related to successive situations, in the process of evolution which is generally attributed to them. There is, therefore, a close connection between the programmatic directives and the tactical rules. Study of the situation thus appears as an integrating element for the solution of tactical problems, insofar as the party in its consciousness and critical experience had already foreseen a certain evolution of situations, and hence determined the tactical possibilities corresponding to the action to be followed in the various phases. Examination of the situation will be a check on the accuracy of the party's programmatic positions. The day that it necessitates any substantial revision of them, the problem will be far more serious than any that could be resolved by means of a simple tactical switch, and the inevitable rectification of programmatic outlook cannot but have serious consequences on the party's organization and

strength. The latter must, therefore, strive to foresee the development of situations, in order to exercise the maximum possible degree of influence in them; but waiting for situations, and then following the indications and suggestions they furnish in an eclectic and discontinuous manner, is a method characteristic of social-democratic opportunism. If communist parties were forced to adapt themselves to this, they would underwrite the ruin of the ideological and militant construction of communism.

25. The Communist Party succeeds in possessing its character of unity, and its tendency to realize a whole programmatic process, only insofar as it assembles in its ranks that part of the proletariat which, by becoming organized, has overcome the tendency to move only under the direct impulses of limited economic situations. The influence of the situation on general movements of the party ceases to be direct and deterministic, becoming a rational and voluntary dependence, insofar as critical consciousness and the initiative of will, which have only the most limited value for individuals, are realized in the organic collectivity of the party. This is all the more true in that the Communist Party presents itself as the forerunner of those forms of human association which will draw from their transcendence of the existing formless economic organization the faculty to direct rationally – instead of passively undergoing – the play of economic facts and their laws.

26. The party, however, cannot utilize its will and initiative in a capricious direction or to an arbitrary degree; the limits within which it must and can fix both of these are imposed upon it precisely by its programmatic directives, and by the possibilities and opportunities for movement which can be deduced from an examination of contingent situations.

27. From examination of the situation, a judgement must be drawn about the party's strength and the relation between it and the strength of enemy movements. Above all, it is necessary to take care to assess the breadth of that layer of the proletariat which would follow the party if the latter undertook an action or engaged in a struggle. This means forming a precise idea of the repercussions and spontaneous actions which the economic situation produces among the masses, and of the possibility of developing these actions, as a result of the initatives of the Communist Party and attitude of the other parties. The forms of influence of the economic situation on the class combativity of the proletariat are very complex, depending on whether we are passing through a period of growing prosperity of the bourgeois economy, or of

crisis with sharpening consequences. The effect of these phases on the activity and organizational life of the proletarian organisms is complex, and cannot be considered simply by embarking on an examination of the economic situation at one given moment, and deducing from it the proletariat's level of combativity. For it is necessary to take account of the influence of the whole course of previous situations, in all their oscillations and variations. For instance, a period of prosperity can produce a powerful trade-union movement, which in a subsequent crisis of immiseration can be rapidly drawn on to revolutionary positions, while preserving the breadth of its mass organization and thus favouring the success of the revolution. Or a period of progressive immiseration can disperse the trade-union movement, in such a way that in a subsequent period of prosperity it finds itself at a stage of construction that does not offer a sufficient framework for revolutionary organization. These examples, which could equally well be reversed, go to prove that "the curves of the economic situation and of class combativity are determined by complex laws, the latter by the former, but do not resemble each other in form".[55] To the rise (or fall) of the former, there may correspond in given cases indifferently a rise or a fall of the latter.

28. The integrative elements of this study are extremely varied. They consist in examining the effective tendencies involved in the constitution and development of the proletariat's organizations, and in the reactions – including psychological reactions – produced upon it on the one hand by economic conditions, and on the other by the specific attitudes and social and political initiatives of the ruling class and its parties. Examination of the situation is completed in the political field by examination of the positions and forces of the various classes and parties in relation to the power of the State. From this point of view, it is possible to classify into fundamental phases the situations in which the Communist Party may have to operate and which, in their normal succession, lead it to grow stronger by extending its membership and at the same time to define ever more precisely the limits of its tactical field. These phases can be specified as follows: Absolutist feudal power – democratic bourgeois power – social-democratic government – interregnum of social war in which the bases of the State become unstable – proletarian power in the dictatorship of the Councils. In a certain sense, the problem of tactics consists, not just in choosing the right course for an effective action, but also in preventing the party's activity from overspilling its appropriate limits and falling back upon

methods that correspond to situations now transcended – which would have the consequence of halting the party's process of development and causing revolutionary preparation to regress. The considerations which follow will refer above all to the party's action in the second and third of the above-mentioned political phases.

29. The Communist Party's possession of a critical method and a consciousness which lead to the formulation of its programme is a condition of its organic life. For that very reason, the party and the Communist International cannot limit themselves to establishing the greatest liberty and elasticity of tactics, by entrusting their execution to the relevant leading bodies, subject to examination of the situation, in their judgement. Since the party's programme does not have the character of a simple aim to be achieved by whatever means, but rather that of a historical perspective of mutually related routes and destinations, tactics in successive situations must be related to the programme; hence the general tactical norms for successive situations must be specified within certain limits, which though not rigid are ever more precise and less oscillating as the movement gains in strength and approaches its general victory. Only such a criterion makes it possible to draw ever closer to the maximum of effective centralization in the parties and the International with respect to leadership of the action, so that the execution of central directives is accepted without any reluctance not just within the communist parties, but also in the mass movement which these have succeeded in organizing. This is not to forget that at the base of such acceptance of the movement's organic discipline there lies a factor of initiative on the part of individuals and groups – depending on the influence and development of the situation – and a continuous logical progress of experience and rectifications of the course to be followed for most effective action against the conditions of life imposed on the proletariat by the existing system. Therefore, the party and the International must set out in a systematic manner the corpus of general tactical norms for whose application they may call the ranks of their members, and the layers of the proletariat which rally around them, to action and to sacrifice; and they must demonstrate how such norms and perspectives for action constitute the inevitable route leading to victory. It is, therefore, a practical and organizational necessity, and not the desire to theorize and schematize the complexity of the movements which the party may be called upon to undertake, which leads us to establish the terms and limits of the party's tactics. And it is for these entirely concrete reasons that the latter must take

decisions which appear to restrict its possibilities for action, but which alone give a guarantee of the organic unity of its activity in the proletarian struggle.

VI
"Indirect" Tactical Activity of the Communist Party

30. When the conditions are lacking for a tactical activity that can be defined as direct, having the character of an assault on bourgeois power with the forces at the Communist Party's disposal, and which will be discussed below, the party can and must – far from restricting itself to a pure and simple work of proselytism and propaganda – exert an influence on events through its relations with and pressures upon other parties and political and social movements, with the aim of determining developments of the situation in a direction favourable to its own objectives, and in such a way as to hasten the moment when resolutive revolutionary action will be possible. The initiatives and attitudes to adopt in such a case constitute a delicate problem, and for this reason the condition must be laid down that they must on no account be or appear in contradiction with the longer-term requirements of the party's specific struggle in accordance with the programme of which it is the sole proponent, and for which the proletariat must struggle at the decisive moment. Any attitude which causes or involves demotion to a secondary level of the integral affirmation of that propaganda, which does not merely have theoretical value, but is above all drawn from the daily positions taken up in the real proletarian struggle, and which must continuously highlight the necessity for the proletariat to embrace the communist programme and methods; any attitude which can be seen to make the conquest of given contingent strong points an end in itself rather than a means to proceed further; any such attitude would lead to a weakening of the party's structure and influence on the revolutionary preparation of the masses.

31. In the historico-political situation which corresponds to the democratic bourgeois power, there generally takes place a division in the political field into two currents or "blocs" – one of the left, the other of the right – which contest leadership of the State. The left bloc is normally supported more or less openly by the social-democratic parties, which favour coalitions on principle. The unfolding of this contest is not a matter of indifference to the Communist Party, both

because it revolves around points and demands which interest the proletarian masses and demand their attention, and because its resolution through a victory of the left really can smooth the path to the proletarian revolution. In examining the problem of the tactical advisability of coalitions with the left political elements – and wanting to avoid all falsely doctrinaire or stupidly sentimental and puritanical apriorism – one must above all bear in mind that the Communist Party enjoys freedom of movement insofar as it is capable of pursuing with continuity its process of organization and preparation, from which it draws that influence upon the masses which permits it to call them to action. It cannot propose a tactic with an occasional and transitory criterion, reckoning that it will be able subsequently, at the moment when such a tactic ceases to be applicable, to execute a sudden switch and change of front, transforming its allies of yesterday into enemies. If one does not wish to compromise one's links with the masses and their reinforcement at the very moment when it is most essential that these should come to the fore, it will be necessary to pursue in all public and official declarations and attitudes a continuity of method and intention that is strictly consistent with the uninterrupted propaganda and preparation for the final struggle.

32. The Communist Party's essential task in preparing the proletariat ideologically and practically for the revolutionary struggle for dictatorship is a ruthless criticism of the programme of the bourgeois left, and of any programme that seeks to derive the solution of social problems from the framework of bourgeois parliamentary democratic institutions. The content of the disagreements between the bourgeois right and left for the most part affects the proletariat only by virtue of demagogic falsifications, which naturally cannot be demolished through a pure process of theoretical criticism, but must be met and unmasked in practice, in the thick of struggle. In general, the political demands of the left – which do not at all include in their objectives that of taking a step forward and placing a foot upon some intermediary rung between the economic and political system of capitalism and that of the proletariat – correspond to conditions of greater freedom for and more effective defence of modern capitalism, both in their intrinsic value, and because they tend to give the masses the illusion that the existing institutions can be utilized for their process of emancipation. This is true of the demands for extension of the suffrage and for guarantees and improvements of liberalism, as it is of the anti-clerical struggle and the whole baggage of "masonic" politics. Legislative

reforms in the economic or social fields have a similar value: either they will not be carried through, or they will be carried through only insofar as they create an obstacle to the revolutionary dynamic of the masses — and with that intention.

33. The advent of a left bourgeois government, or even of a social-democratic government, may be seen as a preliminary to the definitive struggle for proletarian dictatorship; but not in the sense that their operation would create useful preconditions of an economic or political kind, and certainly not with the hope that they would accord the proletariat greater freedom for organization, preparation, and revolutionary action. The Communist Party knows and has the duty to proclaim, by force of critical reason and of bloody experience, that such governments would only respect the freedom of proletarian movements until such time as the proletariat recognized these and defended them as its own representatives, while before an assault by the masses against the machine of the democratic State they would respond with the most ferocious reaction. It is thus in a very different sense that the advent of such governments may be useful: in other words, insofar as their activity will allow the proletariat to deduce from the facts the real experience that only the installation of its dictatorship constitutes a real defeat of capitalism. It is evident that the utilization of such an experience will be effective only on condition that the Communist Party has denounced the government's failure in advance, and preserved a solid independent organization around which the proletariat can regroup when it is forced to abandon the groups and parties which it has partly supported in their experiment at government.

34. Thus not only would a coalition of the Communist Party with parties of the bourgeois left or of social-democracy damage revolutionary preparation and make it difficult to utilize a left government experiment, but also in practice it would normally postpone the victory of the left over the right bloc. These are rivals for the support of the bourgeois centre, which moves to the left because it is rightly convinced that the left is no less anti-revolutionary and conservative than the right, proposing concessions that are largely apparent and only minimally effective in order to brake the pressing revolutionary movement against the identical institutions accepted by right and left alike. Thus the presence of the Communist Party in a left coalition would lose the latter more support, above all on the terrain of electoral and parliamentary struggle, than it would bring it through its backing,

and the whole experiment would probably be delayed rather than accelerated by such a policy.

35. On the other hand, the Communist Party will not ignore the undeniable fact that the demands around which the left bloc centres its agitation draw the interest of the masses and, in their formulation, often correspond to their real demands. The Communist Party will not uphold the superficial position of refusing such concessions on the grounds that only the final and total revolutionary conquest merits the sacrifices of the proletariat. There would be no sense in proclaiming this, since the only result would be that the proletariat would certainly move behind the democrats and social-democrats, and remain enslaved to them. The Communist Party will thus call upon the workers to accept the left's concessions as an experiment; but it will emphasize in its propaganda its pessimistic forecast as to that experiment's outcome, and the necessity for the proletariat, if it is not to be ruined by this venture, not to stake its independence of organization and political influence upon it. The Communist Party will ask the masses to demand of the social-democratic parties – who guarantee the possibility that the promises of the bourgeois left can be realized – that they keep their commitments. And with its independent and uninterrupted criticism it will prepare to cull the fruits of the negative result of such experiments, by showing how the entire bourgeoisie is in fact arrayed in a united front against the revolutionary proletariat, and how those parties which call themselves workers' parties but support the coalition with a part of the bourgeoisie are merely its accomplices and agents.

36. The demands put forward by the left parties, and especially by the social-democrats, are often of such a kind that it is appropriate to call upon the proletariat to move directly to implement them. For if the struggle were engaged, the insufficiency of the means with which the social-democrats propose to arrive at a programme of benefits for the proletariat would at once become apparent. The Communist Party will then raise high those same demands, underlining them and making them more precise, as a banner of struggle for the entire proletariat, urging the latter forward to compel the parties which speak of them only through opportunism to engage themselves and commit themselves on the path to win them. Whether it is a question of economic demands, or whether they have a political character, the Communist Party will propose them as objectives for a coalition of trade-union organisms, avoiding the setting-up of committees to direct the struggle and agitation in which the Communist Party would be represented and

engaged alongside other political parties. The party's purpose in this is always to keep the attention of the masses on the specific communist programme, and to keep its own freedom of movement for the choice of moment in which to enlarge the platform of action, by-passing the other parties who have shown themselves impotent and been abandoned by the masses. The trade-union united front, understood in this way, offers the possibility of combined actions of the whole working class from which the communist method cannot fail to emerge victorious. For it alone is capable of giving content to the unitary movement of the proletariat, and free from any share in responsibility for the activity of the parties which express verbal support for the proletariat's cause through opportunism and with counter-revolutionary intentions.

37. The situation we are considering may take the form of an assault by the bourgeois right upon a democratic or social-democratic government. In such a case too, the attitude of the Communist Party cannot be one of proclaiming solidarity with governments of this kind. For one cannot present to the proletariat as a gain to be defended, a political order whose experiment one has greeted and followed with the intention of accelerating in the proletariat the conviction that it is not designed in its favour but for counter-revolutionary ends.

38. It may happen that the left government allows right-wing organizations, bourgeois white bands, to carry out their actions against the proletariat and its institutions; and that not only does it not ask for the proletariat's support, but claims that the latter does not have the right to respond by organizing armed resistance. In such a case, the communists will demonstrate that what is involved can only be an effective complicity, indeed a division of functions, between liberal government and reactionary irregular forces. The bourgeois is then no longer discussing whether the method of democratic and reformist lullabies or that of violent repression suits it best, but utilizes them both at the same time. In this situation, the true – and the worst – enemy of revolutionary preparation is the liberal element in government. It deludes the proletariat that it will take up its defence in the name of legality, in order to find it weaponless and disorganized and to be able to lay it low, in full accord with the whites, the day that the proletariat finds itself compelled by the force of events to struggle against the legal apparatus which presides over its exploitation.

39. Another hypothesis is that the government and the left-wing parties which compose it invite the proletariat to take part in armed struggle against the right-wing assault. This invitation cannot fail to

prelude a snare, and the Communist Party will greet it by proclaiming that the arms in the hands of the proletariat mean the advent of the proletarian power and State, and the disarmament of the traditional bureaucratic and military machinery of the State. For this will never carry out the orders of a left government which has reached power by legalitarian means if it calls the people to armed struggle; and only the proletarian dictatorship could give a victory over the white bands a stable character. As a consequence, no "loyalism" should be proclaimed or practiced towards such a government, and it will above all be necessary to indicate to the masses the danger that consolidation of its power, with the help of the proletariat, against the right-wing rising or attempted *coup d'état*, would mean consolidation of the very organism that will combat the revolutionary advance of the proletariat when this becomes inevitable as the only way out. This will be the danger if control over the armed organization of the State has remained in the hands of the democratic parties in government; in other words, if the proletariat has put down its arms without having used them to overturn the existing political and state forms, against all the forces of the bourgeois class.

VII

"Direct" Tactical Acitivity of the Communist Party

40. We have considered the case in which the attention of the masses is engaged by objectives which the parties of the bourgeois left and social-democracy have formulated as strong points to be conquered or defended, and in which the Communist Party proposes the same objectives in its turn, with greater clarity and energy, at the same time as it openly criticizes the insufficiency of the means proposed by others to realize them. In other cases, however, immediate and pressing demands of the working class, whether for conquest or for defence, find the left and social-democratic parties indifferent. Not having at its disposal sufficient forces to call the masses directly to those conquests, because of the influence upon them of the social-democrats, the Communist Party — avoiding offering any alliance to the social-democrats, indeed proclaiming that they betray even the contingent and immediate interests of the workers — in formulating these objectives of proletarian struggle will invoke a proletarian united front realized on the trade-union terrain for their attainment. The implementation of this front will

find at their posts the communist militants in the unions; but at the same time it will leave the party the possibility of intervening when the struggle takes a further development, against which the social-democrats will inevitably come out – and at times the syndicalists and anarchists too. On the other hand, the refusal of the other proletarian parties to implement a trade-union united front for these objectives will be utilized by the Communist Party to strike down their influence – not merely with criticism and propaganda which shows how what is involved is real complicity with the bourgeoisie, but above all by participating in the front line in those partial actions of the proletariat which the situation will not fail to provoke, by doing so on the basis of those precise strong points for which the party had proposed the trade-union united front of all local organizations and all categories, and by drawing from this a concrete demonstration that the social-democratic leaders by opposing the extension of activity are preparing its defeat. Naturally, the Communist Party will not limit itself to this task of pinning the responsibility for an incorrect tactic on the other parties; but with extreme caution and tight discipline it will study whether the moment has not arrived to overcome the resistance of the counter-revolutionaries, when in the course of the action a situation is produced among the masses such that they would follow a call to action of the Communist Party against any resistance. An initiative of this kind can only be a central one, and it is never admissible for it to be taken locally by organisms of the Communist Party or trade unions controlled by the communists.

41. The expression "direct" tactics is applied more specially to the activity of the party in a situation which suggests to it that it should take the independent initiative of an attack on bourgeois power, in order to bring it down or to strike it a blow which will gravely weaken it. The party, in order to be able to undertake an action of this kind, must have a solid internal organization at its disposal, which will give absolute certainty of strict discipline to the orders of the central leadership. It must, in addition, be able to count on the same discipline from the union forces which it leads, so as to be sure of the support of a broad segment of the masses. It also needs a military type of organization of a certain degree of efficiency, and all the equipment for illegal activity – above all for communications and forms of contact that cannot be checked by the bourgeois government – that will allow it to preserve its leadership of the movement securely in the predictable situation of being outlawed under emergency provisions. But above all, in taking a decision for

offensive action upon which may depend the fate of a whole, extremely long labour of preparation, the Communist Party must base itself on a study of the situation which does not just ensure it the discipline of the forces directly organized and led by it; which does not just encourage it to predict that the links which bind it to the best of the proletarian masses will not break in the struggle; but which gives it confidence that the party's support among the masses and the breadth of the proletariat's participation in the movement will grow progressively in the course of the action, since the order for this will serve to awaken and set in operation tendencies naturally diffused in the deepest layers of the masses.

42. It will not always be possible for a general movement initiated by the Communist Party for an attempt to overturn bourgeois power to be announced as having this open objective. The directive to engage the struggle may (other than in the case of an exceptional precipitation of revolutionary situations stirring the proletariat) refer to strong points which are something less than the conquest of proletarian power, but which are in part only to be realized through this supreme victory – even though the masses merely see them as immediate and vital demands: objectives which to a limited extent, insofar as they can be realized by a government which is not yet that of the proletarian dictatorship, leave open the possibility of halting the action at a certain point which leaves the level of organization and combativity of the masses intact, if it appears to be impossible to continue the struggle to the end without compromising, through the outcome, the conditions for resuming it effectively in subsequent situations.

43. It is not even to be excluded that the Communist Party may find it opportune to give the word for an action directly even though it knows that there is no question of arriving at the supreme revolutionary conquest, but only of waging a battle from which the enemy will emerge with his prestige and his organization damaged, and the proletariat materially and morally strengthened. In such a case, the party will call the masses to struggle by formulating a series of objectives which may either be the actual ones to be achieved, or appear more limited than those which the party proposes to achieve if the struggle is crowned with success. Such objectives, above all in the party's plan of action, must be arranged in progression, so that the attainment of each of them constitutes a position of possible reinforcement through a halt on the path towards successive struggles. It is necessary to avoid as far as possible the desperate tactic of launching oneself into struggle in

conditions such that only the supreme triumph of the revolution constitutes the favourable alternative, while in the opposite event there is a certainty of defeat and dispersal of the proletarian forces for a period impossible to foresee. Partial objectives are thus indispensable to maintain safe control over the action, and to formulate them does not conflict with criticism of their specific economic and social content, insofar as the masses might welcome them not as opportunities for struggle which are a means and a preliminary to the final victory, but as ends of intrinsic value with which to be satisfied once they have been won. Naturally, it is always a delicate and terrible problem to fix these goals and limits to action; it is through the exercise of its experience and the selection of its leaders that the party tempers itself for this supreme responsibility.

44. The party must avoid harbouring or spreading the illusion that, in a situation of stagnation of the proletariat's combativity, it is possible to bring about the awakening of the masses for struggle through the simple effect of the example given by a group of brave men launching themselves into combat, and attempting *coups de main* against bourgeois institutions. The reasons why the proletariat may lift itself out of a situation of depression are to be sought in the real unfolding of the economic situation; the party's tactics can and must contribute to this process, but with work that is far more profound and continuous than the dramatic deeds of a vanguard hurled into the attack.

45. The party, however, will use its strength and organization for actions that are properly controlled both in their conception and in their execution, on the part of armed groups, working-class organizations and street-crowds, which have a demonstrative and defensive value in giving the masses concrete proof that it is possible with organization and preparation to confront certain forms of resistance and offensive sallies by the ruling class, whether in the form of terrorist outrages by reactionary armed groups or in the form of police obstruction of given types of proletarian organization and activity. The aim will not be to provoke a general action, but to raise the depressed and demoralized masses up again to the highest level of combativity, with a series of actions designed to reawaken within them sentiments and a need of revolt.

46. The party will absolutely avoid, in such local actions, any infraction of the internal discipline of the trade-union organisms on the part of the local organs and the militants within them who are members of the Communist Party, since these must never be allowed to break

with the national executive bodies led by other parties. For as has already been stated, they must serve as indispensable footholds for winning those bodies to the party. The Communist Party and its members will, however, follow the masses actively and offer them all their help when they respond through a spontaneous impulse to bourgeois provocations, even if they go beyond the limits of discipline to the criteria of inaction and passivity of the reformist and opportunist union leaders.

47. In the situation which is characteristic of the moment in which the power of the State is shaken to its foundations, and is about to fall, the Communist Party, amid the full unfurling of its forces and of the agitation of the masses around its banner of maximum demands, will not miss the possibility of influencing moments of unstable equilibrium in the situation by taking advantage of all such forces as may momentarily be acting in harmony with its own independent activity. When it is quite certain that it will win control of the movement as soon as the traditional State organization has collapsed, it can have recourse to transitory and contingent agreements with other movements which have forces at their disposal in the field of struggle – but without raising such alliances to themes of propaganda or slogans addressed by the party to the masses. Success will in any case be the sole yardstick for assessing the correctness of having yielded to such contacts, and for judging what calculations are to be made in this respect. The entire tactics of the Communist Party is not dictated by theoretical preconceptions or by ethical and aesthetic preoccupations, but solely by the real appropriateness of the means to the end and to the reality of the historical process, in that dialectical synthesis of doctrine and action which is the patrimony of a movement destined to be the protagonist of the most immense social renewal, the commander of the greatest revolutionary war.

VIII

The Italian Communist Party and the Present Moment

48. The phase, and thus the problem, of the party's formation has now been completely surmounted in Italy. With the Socialist Congress of Milan – prior to which, the possibility was not definitively excluded of a substantive modification of the constitutive basis of the Italian Communist Party, through fusion with a left faction of the Socialist

Party, which would have assumed the significance of an essential and integrative element – with the Milan Congress and its decisions this possibility has vanished entirely. It now seems evident that only the far left faction which split away at Livorno could constitute the party's creative nucleus. And it is now equally clear that its normal progressive development will, in future, not proceed through a *rapprochement* with organized groups splitting off from other political formations; instead, it will proceed solely through individual recruitment of single persons who, as they enter its ranks designed precisely to receive them, will not introduce disorder or changes, but simply greater strength – in numbers, and hence in action.

49. The Party, therefore, freed from the cares inherent in every period of initiation, must devote itself completely to its work of ever more extensive penetration among the masses, establishing and multiplying the linking organs between them and itself. No field of proletarian activity must remain unknown to the communists: the trade unions, the cooperatives, the savings trusts, must be penetrated ever more deeply – with the establishment of communist groups and their linking together – and won to the Party's directives. While the various Aid Committees, for political victims, for Russia, etc., must see the communists represented and enjoy their collaboration. This, however, is simply because the party must not remain indifferent to any instrument which will put it in closer contact with the proletariat; and because it must take care to satisfy the latter's contingent necessities. It is never in order to establish lasting relations with other political parties, even subversive ones.

50. With respect to the latter, the polemics aimed at clarifying their attitude in the eyes of the workers, and at breaking the ambiguity of their programmatic declarations, must continue unflaggingly. Socialists and libertarians pursue the weakening of the proletarian class in two different ways in Italy today: the former with their tactics of submission and disarmament in the face of capitalism's attack; the latter with their struggle against the Republic of Soviets and against the principle of dictatorship of the proletariat, to which they counterpose the empty and theoretical apotheosis of an abstract freedom.

The present Italian situation, characterized by the ever vaster and more complete offensive of the bourgeoisie, daily offers a thousand unhappy documents for our polemics against the anarchists and social-democrats, who give manifest proof of their lack of understanding of the moment. For this, rather than representing anything exceptional and transitory, is in reality a natural and predictable stage of development of the capitalistic order: a specific manifestation of the function and purposes of the democratic State.

51. Today, in Italy, one can perceive a characteristic involution of the State with respect to its mode of functioning. The constitutive period of the bourgeois State, which marked a progressive centralization of all the functions of rule within the organization of a central authority, finds its counterpart and its negation in the present period, in which the stable unity of all powers – previously removed from the arbitrary decision of individuals – now crumbles and scatters. The powers of the State are once again exercised individually by each private person. And it would no longer even be necessary for the State to place its organs explicitly – though it does so – at the disposal of bourgeois conservation: from the army to the magistrature, from Parliament to the functionaries of the executive power. For each of these, in the person of its practitioners, uses its own powers to the same end, in an autonomous and uncontrollable manner.

In order then to prevent an unexpected halt in this crisis of dissolution from allowing the State to regain any control over the activity of individuals, the bourgeois class proceeds hastily to the establishment of supplementary organs. These, perfectly in agreement with the statutory organs when these function according to the explicit desires of conservation, instead counterpose themselves to those organs and replace them whenever they show signs of moving away from the most supine acquiescence (Civil Committees, Defence Committees, etc.).

To invoke, as the social-democrats do, a return to the authority of the State and to respect for the law shows that, even though they do assert that the democratic parliamentary State is a class State, they do not succeed in understanding that precisely for this reason it is today carrying out its essential task – by violating the written laws which were necessary to its progressive consolidation, but which would henceforward damage its conservation.

52. The present Italian situation contains synthetically within itself all the constitutive elements of the *coup d'état*, even though the external probative fact of the military deed has not occurred. The progressive occurrence of episodes of violence which successively annul the normal conditions of social life for a whole class of citizens; the superposition of the capricious will of groups and individuals over the dispositions of the written law; the immunity guaranteed to such groups and individuals; and the persecution ordained for their enemies – all this has produced

the same results as would have been produced by a more grandiose and more violent single act, which set more numerous forces in motion simultaneously.

The bourgeois class is perfectly aware of this state of affairs, but its interests require that the outward appearance of a formal democracy should not be destroyed; and that the general economy should not be deeply shaken by a violent change which ultimately would not offer any greater safeguard for its privilege than that which it enjoys today. It is thus probable that divided as it is on its evaluation of the necessity for it, and still being powerful enough to break it, the bourgeois class would oppose a disruptive military putsch motivated almost solely by personal ambitions. No new form of government could have more contempt than the present one for freedom; for rights already won and sanctioned; for the lives of the workers. Only in a further perfecting of the democratic State, rendering it more able to conceal the real substance of the bourgeoisie's dictatorial régime, can it find its goal. This will be achieved with the formation of a social-democratic government.

53. The present Italian situation engenders and brings to fruition precisely this further stage in the martyrdom of the proletariat. Work is proceeding towards this result from two sides: a strong current in the Socialist Party and the left parties of the bourgeoisie are alike testing the ground, in order to find the most favourable spot for a meeting and an alliance. Both, in fact, motivate their actions solely by the necessity of finding and constructing a defence against destructive fascist violence. And on this terrain they seek the assent of all the subversive parties, demanding an end to polemics and mutual attacks.

If a social-democratic government would have the strength to fight and defeat fascism – which we strongly doubt, both through our theoretical convictions and because of the examples of recent history – and it therefore becomes necessary to prepare a terrain favourable to its formation, this will be all the more easily and rapidly constituted insofar as the communists continue their present determined and unflagging polemic against the Socialist Party. The communist attack gives the Socialist Party credit in bourgeois eyes, as a target of revolutionary violence and as an impediment and obstacle to the unfurling of the class struggle, and thus makes more probable an agreement and an alliance between them. For it must not be forgotten that left groups of the bourgeoisie began to present socialist collaboration as attainable in Italy from the time that the Livorno split liberated the Socialist Party from any communist current. A quietening down of the struggle between communists and socialists would restore the latter to the ostensible, though false, position of being favourable to the doctrine and practice of the IIIrd International; it would thus impede the reinforcement of that trust which is the precondition for creation of the social-democratic bloc.

Hence, the most absolute intransigence towards the subversive parties should be practised in the field of political struggle, even allowing the perspective – which for us is fallacious – that a change of men in a formally unchanged State could conceivably occur in a sense that would favour the proletariat.

54. As for fascism, the PCI, though considering it as an inevitable consequence of the régime's development, does not draw the conclusion that an attitude of inert passivity should be taken up with respect to it. To combat fascism does not mean to believe that it is possible to annul one function of bourgeois society without destroying the latter's existence; nor to delude oneself that fascism can be defeated in itself, as an episode cut off and isolated from the overall offensive activity of capitalism. It aims instead at rendering less serious and painful the damage which enemy violence inflicts upon this combative and unyielding spirit.

55. The PCI does not exclude but indeed bears in mind the possibility that from the present unstable situation there may arise the opportunity for violent action by a part of the bourgeoisie. Preparing, therefore, a minimum of means necessary to confront and overcome this, it takes up with respect to the problem of direct action an attitude of preparation.

The world crisis of the capitalist economy has had a negative influence on the advance of the proletariat, which has seen its most solid organizations broken. For they had not foreseen the crisis, and hence had not prepared themselves to surmount it victoriously. The party believes that today it is necessary to reconstruct that former solidity, guided by the conviction that in a situation analogous to the one recently traversed, a proletariat solidly organized and led by a revolutionary party could justly go over to the attack. Thus to construct this party and enlarge its influence over the masses; to give its own members coherence, discipline and preparation; to draw behind it ever broader layers of the working class: these are the essential tasks of the Italian Communists, who will accomplish them taking as their norm the theses on the various questions (trade union, agricultural, etc.) which will be approved and discussed by the present Congress.

34. CONGRESS INTERVENTIONS

I

Gramsci argues that the creation of the *Alleanza del lavoro* has considerably modified the Italian trade-union situation. It is therefore necessary to include in the Theses some new programmatic points.[56] These will be contained in three theses to be inserted after the present number 10, and will be inspired by the following principles.

The creation of the *Alleanza del lavoro* is an attempt to resolve in a purely bureaucratic fashion the problem of the Italian trade-union movement's unity of action. For some time, as a result of the unfortunate outcome of the last strikes and the practical impossibility of embarking upon others with any hope of success, the organized masses had been asking that the problem of united trade-union action should be tackled and resolved. With the *Alleanza del lavoro*, the leaders of the mass organizations had proposed and implemented a purely bureaucratic form of unity, in order to discharge in the eyes of the masses the responsibility which weighed upon them. Tomorrow, these leaders will say to the masses: "You see, we have achieved unity, we have created the *Alleanza del lavoro*, and not even that has done any good."

At first, a tendency seemed to be taking shape to set up a kind of labour party, with the adherence of political and trade-union organizations to a single name and organism. It is no exaggeration to assert that this attempt failed as a result of the criticism and action of the communist minority – which every attempt was made to immunize. Unity has now been achieved in the trade-union domain, but in an exclusively bureaucratic form.

Having recalled the organic formation of the *Alleanza del lavoro*, comrade Gramsci said that the attitude of the Communist Party must now be motivated by a dual order of considerations. In the first place, the following problem arises: can we say that in the *Alleanza del lavoro* a basis exists for resolving the problem of the organizational unity of the Italian proletariat? This is not to be excluded, and there are some interesting indications in this respect. Two articles appeared in *Umanità*

Nova, one by Angelo Faggi and one by Luigi Fabbri, in which opinions are expressed which seem favourable to this thesis.[57] It is certain that at the present moment, small union organizations which till yesterday maintained themselves on the terrain of competition with the General Confederation of Labour, can see that their competition has less and less prospect of success. The possibility of an agreement cannot be excluded. Armando Borghi claims that he is nearer to D'Aragona than to the communists, and perhaps personal approaches have already taken place.[58] These are symptoms of a change of position which tomorrow might create a new situation, in which the organizational basis for the trade-union unity of the Italian proletariat might cease to be the General Confederation and become the *Alleanza del lavoro* itself.

In the second place, the communists must seek in what way the present bureaucratic unity might be the point of departure for a process of development that would be revolutionary in character. If the political situation grows worse and the Italian state returns once again to the conditions of disintegration of 1919, it might be that the tactic of unitary committees like the *Alleanza del lavoro*, but elected directly by the proletariat, could become more appropriate than that of Factory Councils, especially because of the impossibility in which we now find ourselves to carry on propaganda for the councils, and because of the disappointments which the tactic of councils has caused in more than one case. The Communist Party has already requested that local committees of the *Alleanza del lavoro* should have a wider formation, in closer contact with the masses. It is not excluded that the problem may arise of inducing the unorganized masses too to join these committees. It is true that today the number of organized workers is falling, but that occurs in part because the masses have lost faith in the form of organization by dues and by assemblies, while the interest of the masses would be reawoken by an organization of an elective kind. An instance of this is provided by the active participation of the masses in the nomination of leading committees for such elective organizations as already exist at present, like the Unemployment Funds, Cooperative Savings Trusts, etc.

If a situation arises in which propaganda for elective committees of the *Alleanza del lavoro* becomes appropriate, these will become formations of a quasi-Soviet type, and within this organization the tendencies at present existing in embryo form in the working class could be unified.

The theses on the *Alleanza del lavoro* will set out these fundamental orienting ideas. However, it is not thought necessary at once to change the content of the tenth thesis, in which it is stated that the basis of the Italian proletariat's organizational unity is considered by the communists to be the General Confederation of Labour, since for the moment it is only a question of tendencies that have not yet been clarified. Similarly, it is held that the position of our comrades within the union organizations should remain unaltered, even if at the forthcoming Paris Congress the USI decides to detach itself definitively from the Red Trade-union International.[59]

L'Ordine Nuovo, 25 March 1922.

II

Gramsci states that he is in agreement with the theses presented by comrades Bordiga and Terracini, and wishes to present the congress with a problem.

If the congress of the Communist Party accepts generic formulae in contradiction with the theses presented by the Party Executive and in which the possibility of a political united front is admitted, it will be believed that our thinking is in line with that which is widespread among the masses, according to which the political united front would be one that stretched as far as the Popular Party. It would be a good idea for there to be some discussion on this point. I am convinced that not just the Popular Party, but also a part of the Socialist Party must be excluded from the proletarian united front, in accordance with the conception of the theses approved by the Enlarged Executive Committee,[60] because to make an agreement with them would mean making an agreement with the bourgeoisie. The Popular Party is essentially based upon the peasant class. Now it is true that the peasants are prepared to engage in struggle against the State; but they are willing to struggle to defend their property, not to defend their pay or working hours. The struggle they wage is inspired by motives which belong to the sphere of the bourgeois civil code.

We too often confuse the workers with the peasants. They are two different classes. The Socialist Party based itself on both these classes, and that was why two spirits coexisted within it. The working class and the peasantry can reach agreements in an organic form, such as is proposed by the Communist Party in its theses on the agrarian question, but it must not be believed that the peasants can become communists. The Communist Party must maintain its physiognomy as a workers' party, with centres of action in the countryside.

Then it is necessary to bear in mind the Italian political situation. In Germany, the movement tending towards the establishment of a social-democratic government is based on the working-class masses; but the tactic of the united front has no value except for industrial countries, where the backward workers can hope to be able to carry on a defensive activity by conquering a parliamentary majority. Here, the situation is different. If we launched the slogan of a workers' government and tried to implement it, we would return to the socialist ambivalence, when that party was condemned to inactivity because it could not decide to be either solely a party of workers or solely a party of peasants. If we launched the slogan of a political united front, we would have against us the left faction of the Socialist Party, the *Maffisti*, based in the big cities where an industrial proletariat exists and in those regions where the category of rural workers prevails.[61] It is, therefore, necessary that the congress does not make generic assertions, which could give rise to extremely serious ambiguities, given the dark Italian situation and the scanty political culture in our country. The trade-union united front, by contrast, has an aim which is of primary importance for political struggle in Italy.

Certain speakers have asserted that the working class has become reformist. I think it is necessary to protest against this assertion. The workers today are dispersed, lack leaders, lack an organization which would permit them to utilize their strength. They are therefore opportunist through necessity; and the problem which faces the Communist Party is how to restore to the working class an organization in which its forces may be reconstituted. This organization is the product of a whole complex of factors and bonds which have been destroyed, and which the communists must create anew.

Concerning the bitterness of our polemics against the socialists, I think it is necessary for me to make some statement, since I am one of those responsible for it. I believed that carrying on so harsh a polemic against the social-democratic leaders was something necessary to the very interests of the working class. At the moment when reaction was descending on the workers, destroying all their hopes, it was necessary at least to manage to persuade the masses that blame for the defeat did not lie with them, so that they would not lose faith in themselves. And this had to be done above all in the big cities, where one can get a complete view of what the workers' needs are. Moreover, it is not true that the masses have abandoned the Communist Party. They are for the Communist Party and know that only the communists will be able to lead them. Our Party has won a solid position in their consciousness. The problem which faces us is rather, how to reconstitute an organization through which the masses can return to being a dominant force in the political situation.

L'Ordine Nuovo, 28 March 1922.

35. REPORT ON THE NATIONAL CONGRESS TO THE TURIN COMMUNIST SECTION

Comrade Gramsci reported on the question of tactics. He began by stressing the origin and character of the opposition that had arisen on this question, and the reasons upon which it was based.[62] He showed the inconsistency of the principal objections raised by the opposition, according to which the theses presented by the Central Committee should not have been discussed or voted upon, simply because there were points of divergence between them and those voted at the Enlarged Executive meeting in Moscow. He explained, therefore, in what this divergence consisted: it does not have a substantive value or one of principle, but only one of detail, concerning the modalities of practical implementation of the single principle of the united front accepted by everyone.

He stressed the special character of the Italian unions, which are infused with a far greater political spirit than is the case abroad, for example in Germany. This expresses itself unambiguously in the different effects which have been produced in different countries by the influence of events on these organisms. This is one of the main reasons why in Italy the united front has taken on a trade-union aspect, without thereby at all falling into the syndicalist error. He explained the reasons why the same practical application of the united front as was implemented in other countries, where it is extended to the political field, to the point of launching the slogan of a workers' government, is not possible in Italy. Here, launching the slogan of a workers' government would mean provoking confusion and chaos – without, moreover, having any possible practical significance. These, among others, are the reasons why the Communist Party has asserted the need to limit the united front to the trade-union sphere, through which in Italy it is possible to attain the aims the Communist International has proposed with the united front tactic.

The reporter then went on to explain another argument which makes the implementation of the political united front impossible in Italy, which is the relation of forces existing in Italy between workers and peasants. He explained the differing political value of the industrial and agricultural workers and the peasants, and the differing revolutionary character of the particular movements of these different categories of toilers, who although they do not both have a communist character can nevertheless join for a common purpose: the destruction of bourgeois power. When one speaks of a political united front, and hence of a workers' government, one must understand a "united front" between parties whose social base is furnished only by industrial and agricultural workers, and not by peasants (small-holders, share-croppers, husbandmen, etc.).

In Italy there do not exist, as in Germany, exclusively workers' parties between which a political united front too can be conceived. In Italy, the only party which has such a character is the Communist Party. Moreover, this was one of the principal reasons for its emergence – to give an independent character to the political organization of the working class. Even the Socialist Party is a party whose social base is not exclusively working-class (industrial or agricultural), but also peasant. Forming a united front with the Socialist Party would mean going as far as the Popular Party, which bases itself exclusively upon the peasants. This would be absurd. We must have relations with the peasants, and we must struggle together. But one thing is indispensable: to maintain the independence and primacy of the political organization of the working class (industrial and agricultural), which is the sole class whose revolutionary movement can be communist.

When we say that the peasants cannot have a communist movement, but only a revolutionary movement which is resolved in the sphere of property rights, we are speaking of the *peasant class* and not of individual peasants, who as individuals can be and become good communists – like all men who are sincere and in good faith, of whatever social class. Thus the principle remains firm that the working class must be the one to lead the revolutionary movement, but that the peasants too must take part in this movement, since only with the help of the workers will they be able to free themselves from the exploitation of the big landowners; while on the other hand, without the consent or at least neutrality of the peasants in the struggle against capitalism, the workers will not be able to accomplish the communist revolution.

The speaker then reviewed the points in the theses on tactics which had encountered a more or less opportunist opposition – relations with the Socialist Party; the *Arditi del popolo* – stressing the inconsistency of this opposition and the inadequacy of the motives on which it was based.

The speaker concluded by inviting the assembly to approve the attitude of the Central Committee, which at the congress had asked that the theses presented should be discussed and a vote taken upon them. The purpose of this was to demonstrate that the new Central Committee really represents the great majority of party members.

L'Ordine Nuovo, 6 April 1922.

III

Towards a New Leading Group

36. ORIGINS OF THE MUSSOLINI CABINET

Signor Giolitti's Policy – the Peasants – the Socialist Party – the Capitalist Offensive of March 1920

The elements of the Italian crisis, which was violently resolved when fascism came to power, can be briefly resumed in the following way.

The Italian bourgeoisie succeeded in organizing its State not so much through its own intrinsic strength, as through being favoured in its victory over the feudal and semi-feudal classes by a whole series of circumstances of an international character (Napoleon III's policy in 1852–60; the Austro-Prussian War of 1866; France's defeat at Sedan and the development of the German Empire after this event). The bourgeois State thus developed more slowly, and followed a process which has not been seen in many other countries. The Italian régime on the eve of the War did not go beyond the limits of a pure constitutional monarchy. No separation of powers had yet taken place; parliamentary prerogatives were very limited; there did not exist large-scale parliamentary political parties. At that time, the Italian bourgeoisie had to defend the unity and integrity of the State against repeated attacks by reactionary forces, represented above all by an alliance between the big landowners and the Vatican. The big industrial and commercial bourgeoisie, led by Giovanni Giolitti, sought to resolve the problem with an alliance between all the urban classes (the first proposal for governmental collaboration was made to Turati in the first years of the twentieth century) and the class of agricultural wage-labourers. What was involved, however, was not some parliamentary progress. It was rather a question of paternalist concessions of an immediate kind, which the régime made to the toiling masses organized in trade unions and agricultural cooperatives.

The world war swept away all these endeavours. Giolitti, with the agreement of the Crown, committed himself in 1912 to act alongside Germany in the 1914 War (the military treaty signed in Berlin in 1912 by General Pollio, the Italian Chief of Staff, came into force precisely on 2 August 1914; the General committed suicide during the period of Italian neutrality, as soon as the Crown showed itself favourable to a new pro-Entente political orientation). Giolitti was violently set aside by the new ruling groups, representing heavy industry, big landed property and the General Staff (which went so far as to inspire a plot to have him assassinated).

The new political forces which were to make their appearance after the Armistice consolidated their existence during the War. The peasants were grouped in three extremely powerful organizations: the Socialist Party, the (catholic) Popular Party, and the War-veterans' Association. The Socialist Party organized more than a million agricultural labourers and share-croppers in central and northern Italy; the Popular Party grouped as many small-holders and middle peasants in the same regions; the veterans' associations developed above all in southern Italy and in the backward regions without political traditions. The struggle against the big landowners quickly became very intense throughout Italian territory. The land was occupied, the owners had to emigrate to the provincial capitals of the agricultural areas – to Bologna, Florence, Bari and Naples. From 1919 on, they began to organize bourgeois squads to fight against the "peasant tyranny" in the countryside. But this immense uprising of the toiling classes in the countryside lacked any clear and precise slogan; any common, resolute, specific orientation; and any concrete political programme.

The Socialist Party should have dominated the situation; but it allowed it to slip from its grasp. Sixty per cent of the Party's members were peasants; of the 150 socialist deputies in Parliament, 110 had been elected in the countryside; of 2,500 local councils won by the Italian Socialist Party, 2,000 were exclusively peasant; four fifths of the cooperatives administered by the socialists were agricultural cooperatives. The Socialist Party, in its ideology and its programme, reflected the chaos which reigned in the countryside; its entire activity consisted in maximalist rhetoric, in noisy pronouncements in Parliament, in sticking up posters, and in songs and fanfares. All the attempts made from within the Socialist Party to bring working-class issues or proletarian ideology to the fore were combated ferociously, with the most unfair methods. For instance, in the session of the Socialist National Council held at Milan in April 1920, Serrati went so far as to say that the general strike which had broken out at that moment in Piedmont, and which was supported by all categories of workers, had been artificially provoked by irresponsible agents of the Moscow government.

In March 1920, the propertied classes began to organize their counter-offensive. On 7 March, the first National Conference of industrialists was convened, which created the General Confederation of Italian Industry. In the course of this conference, a detailed overall plan of united capitalist action was worked out. In it, everything was provided for, from the disciplined and methodical organization of the manufacturer and merchant class to the most minute study of all instruments of struggle against the working-class unions, and to the political rehabilitation of Giovanni Giolitti. In the first days of April, the new organization was already obtaining its first political success: the Socialist Party branded the great Piedmont strike, which had broken out in defence of the Factory Councils and to win workers' control of industry, as anarchic and irresponsible. The Party threatened to dissolve the Turin section, which had led the strike.

On 15 June, Giolitti formed a government of compromise with the landowners and the General Staff (represented by Bonomi, the War Minister). A feverish activity of counter-revolutionary organization then began, before the threat of the occupation of the factories – which was foreseen even by the reformist leaders assembled for the Conference of the Metalworkers' Federation (FIOM), held in Genoa in the same year. In July, the War Ministry under Bonomi's direction began the demobilization of some 60,000 officers in the following way: the demobilized officers kept four fifths of their pay, and for the most part were sent to the key political centres, under an obligation to join the *Fasci di combattimento*. The latter had previously remained merely a small organization of socialist, anarchist, syndicalist and republican elements who had been favourable to Italian participation in the War on the Entente side. The Giolitti government made immense efforts to bring the Confederation of Industry closer to the landowners' associations, especially those of central and northern Italy. It was in this period that the first armed fascist squads appeared, and that the first episodes of terrorism occurred. But the occupation of the factories by the metalworkers took place at a moment when all this activity was in gestation; the Giolitti government was compelled to take up a conciliatory attitude, and to resort to a homeopathic cure rather than a surgical operation.

Signed A. Gramsci, *La Correspondance Internationale*, 20 November 1922.

37. TOGLIATTI TO GRAMSCI
(Rome, 1 May 1923)

Dearest Antonio,

Comrades Terracini and Scoccimarro will explain to you the reasons why it has not been thought advisable to send me up there for the meeting of the Enlarged EC.[63] But I feel it is necessary to write and give you my views on the most important questions concerning us which will have to be decided up there.

The comrades will also explain to you how I have been absent from the party's life for almost a month. Now I have been brought up to date by them on many issues which have arisen and been resolved in that period, and on others which still remain to be resolved, and my general impression is that the internal conditions of the party are, if not serious, certainly very delicate, such as to require active assistance and great good will from everyone in order to overcome this phase without too much damage.

Little is being done here at present other than organizational work, but keeping the organization on a secure basis demands tenacity and sacrifice, and it is unnecessary to remind you of the great political importance that such work has today. However, it cannot be excluded that open political struggle too may shortly begin in Italy. The existence of an anti-fascist state of mind in certain layers of the non-proletarian population has been clearly demonstrated by the Popular congress, and this state of mind will provide a footing for the attempts by some political groups to prevent even the "formal" reforms of the Constitution which the fascists have in mind to put through. Moreover, the industrial classes are fairly mistrustful of the new régime, for fear of unforeseen developments of the class struggle via the fascist unions. There is also a widespread scepticism, which the fascists do not care if they justify more each day by their actions. Finally, I do not think it out of the question that – quite independently of new international developments – the Italian political situation may grow unstable again and the strength of the proletariat once more come to play a significant and positive role at the present time. If this happens, it is essential that the *party of the proletariat* should find itself at that moment not just strongly organized, but also politically oriented so as to be able to provide the workers with steady leadership, a leadership which enables them to obtain the maximum results from use of their strength.

I fear that this will not happen if we do not succeed in resolving correctly all the questions which confront us now, and which can really be reduced to one single question: our relations with the Communist International and with the PSI. The comrades will let you know about the invitation which Amadeo has addressed to us from prison. He wants the political group which has up to now exercised leadership in the PCI, which has had responsibility for its formation and for the action it has developed in these past three years, to address itself to the proletariat with a manifesto. This manifesto should declare that the action pursued by the Communist International towards the PSI has prevented this political group from carrying out successfully the historic task which it had set itself – i.e. the task of destroying the old pseudo-revolutionary tradition represented by the PSI, clearing this corpse out of the way and at the same time founding a new tradition and a new organization of struggle.

The merit of what Amadeo proposes is that it conforms to a rigorous logic (rigorous to excess) and I will not hide from you that for this reason his proposal is such as to exercise a great attraction on the most intelligent comrades, especially when one adds the weight of his personal ascendancy. In practice, given the present conditions, doing what Amadeo says will mean putting ourselves in open conflict with the Communist International; placing ourselves outside it; finding ourselves thus deprived of a powerful material and moral support; and being reduced to a tiny group, held together by links that are almost purely personal and condemned before long, if not to be scattered to the winds, certainly to lose all real and practical direct influence on the development of the political struggle in Italy. Is this immediate practical damage compensated for by the value of an absolute and intransigent statement of principles such as Amadeo would like to make? I confess to you that I am still somewhat perplexed as to what to reply.

I think that by initiating in 1919 and 1920 an action of revision and criticism in the interests of the Italian proletarian movement, which at the time was entirely represented by the PSI, we began a task that was historically necessary, an action that had to culminate in the foundation of a party which would stand for – and have the ability to give the proletariat – a radically different leadership than that which it had had before. On the other hand, it is also true that the link with the Communist International is what has allowed us to give our action an impact which it otherwise would not have had, and has indeed been one of its essential elements. To maintain this element, can we renounce, even partially, the other, which is the logical conclusion from our premisses?

This way of expressing myself will tell you that I think the maintenance of ambiguous relations with the PSI is making us lose the advantages of the creation of the Communist Party, and tending to take us back into analogous conditions to those from which we set out. The tactic of the International is tending, in other words, in my view, to bind us to the PSI in the same way as we were bound to it before Livorno, and even worse. There will no longer be a Right with its own clear programme (although lacking the ability to apply it), but there will always be the dead weight of the Centre, i.e. of all the traditional defects of the socialist movement, which will prevent us and the workers in general from doing or accomplishing anything worthwhile. Fusion would have allowed us to eliminate this dead weight – but a "bloc" with a party which will always refuse to merge with us will not allow it.

Have you seen how *Avanti!* has presented the question of the "freedom blocs"?[64] In a very dangerous way, which it is true contains the possibility of a struggle for a "workers' government", but which also contains the possibility of collaborationism of the kind the PSI engaged in after 1900, *vis-à-vis* reactionary, Giolittian democracy. This second possibility could only be excluded by the constitution, or rather the "tradition", of a communist party. But if you consider the fact that those people have refused to adopt such a tradition, and if you consider the fact that their leaders are Vella and Nenni, you can very well understand that the second hypothesis is the only real one, while the former is purely abstract.

There is the question of the masses. But I do not think that the SP has any greater following among the masses today than we do. The old traditions are falling to pieces, and why should it be us – ourselves and the Communist International – to hold them together, since whenever we have wanted to do something which *had to be done*, we have found them like shackles round our feet? The state of mind of the workers is that of a person who *physically* cannot express a political opinion; but this does not mean that they do not have any, or that they have different ones than we do. A while back, *Il Lavoratore* printed some articles on the life which the future leaders of the Russian CP were leading before the revolution. I cannot tell you how many workers spoke to me with emotion of those articles: workers with jobs, who no longer take any part in either party or union life, and who nevertheless feel that the destiny of their class today can only be safeguarded by a nucleus, however small, of militants who at the price of whatever sacrifices hold together the revolutionary party, and guarantee the integrity of its principles and tactics and the continuity of its existence. Another noteworthy example: ask for an explanation of how the publication by us of a trade-union bulletin calling for a strike on the First of May went. The thing conflicted with our tactics and we disapproved of it. And yet, innumerable workers have told me that this appeal was excellent, because "it was high time that the Communist Party distinguished itself from the socialists".

Generally, in my view, the movement and alternation of the masses' sympathies obey motives which are profoundly logical and rational, beyond whatever our attempts may be to draw them to us. I mean that, in order to lay down the basis of a future mass party, it may be more important to stick to the orientation which has made us known and given us a "personality", than to run after ... the supposedly high circulation of *Avanti!* Apropos this, the 1 May issue of *Avanti!* had a print run of around 50,000 copies, which means a normal run of around 26,000; not very many, when you compare it with the 16,000 of our *Lavoratore* published in Trieste.

Then it is not worth even speaking of organizational questions. The SP does not even have anything more than a fictitious organization now; and above all, its members do not have an "organizational mentality". They have remained in the epoch of rallies, meetings, etc. You can imagine to what advantage, given the conditions of today and those of tomorrow! In the whole of their party, there does not exist a group whose authority is accepted by everyone, and which has a stable political authority. And there are so many other things too, which are all summed up for me in the need for the renewal of the Italian proletarian movement to take place outside, and even if possible against, the tradition embodied by the PSI.

If, through discipline to the International, we have agreed in the past to abandon this point of view (manœuvring to win masses, at a time when this was not the problem of the hour), we can continue to do the same today – but not to the point where we can no longer develop the programme which was the very reason for the emergence of the Communist Party of Italy. It is this programme which allowed us to emerge as a living organism. Not to be able to realize it would deprive us of life.

I have thought long about these matters and think I am not far wide of the mark. Consider, too, that the fact I have not been on the central bodies except in this last period renders me immune to that sentiment of affection for the organization which those bodies have created — a sentiment which is perhaps prevalent in other comrades. I think, therefore, I can judge objectively.

Well, we do not really know what people think up there, but what we do know, and the way in which many questions are dealt with, and the proposals which have been made regarding our attitude to the socialists as a party, make us fear that the International sees things in a way that is too different from ours — so much so that one cannot go on in this way. Some comrades are more pessimistic than I am. Scocci is more optimistic. Amadeo is catastrophic and wants to break off at once. I have already told you that I think doing this would very soon disperse us. But the same thing, in my view, will happen if we do not reach an agreement with the International which allows our political group *to continue in substance* along the path it has followed up to now. In other words, what will happen is that little by little we will be dispersed just the same, either into an organization which will not be that which the moment requires, or outside it. The fruits of three years' work, criticism, organization and struggle will be lost. If we foresee having to "disappear" in this way, is it not perhaps better to agree to what Amadeo says, i.e. at least to assert to the last our own personality and the political will which has animated us from the first moment?

Apart from this general problem, there are many others of practical importance but no less serious. To mention them briefly.

— Amadeo's personal ascendancy and personal willpower are a strength for the party which must not be lost.

— It is also important that all misunderstanding should disappear between you and Umberto.[65] Do not forget it is largely to him that we owe the speed with which the party reorganized its ranks after the last blows. At moments like these, I do not know if we are so rich in steady wills as to be able to allow ourselves the luxury of neglecting those of which we are certain.

— I think that not just those comrades who hold the organizational threads of the party, but also some real "political leaders" must reside *in Italy* rather than outside. If there is an external political centre, it must be in closer contact with the centre based inside Italy than will be possible if outside they make use of comrades who have not previously become leaders of the party because they were not capable of being so.

In other words, I am afraid that repression and the International's control (correct and wished for, be it said) may make us carry out a kind of selection-process in reverse, absurd and damaging.

– You must come closer to Italy. You need very frequently to see comrades who have lived and still live in continuous contact with our reality. You need to be informed about everything better than is possible now. And we too need your guidance to make itself widely felt once again. I think you should live in Switzerland, very close to us, and that if there is an *external political bureau*, it should be headed by you, who together with Amadeo are one of the few who exercise an influence – including of a personal nature – on the mass of our party which is fully justified.

– Other questions of minor importance, but which are still not to be neglected, will be explained to you by the comrades.

Dear comrade Gramsci, you will excuse me if I write to you with such blunt and perhaps brutal frankness. I feel licensed to do so by the memory of our fraternal friendship, and by my awareness that the work we began then with such mutual enthusiasm is now threatened by a grave danger. It is necessary to do all that can be done to avoid any of what has been accomplished being lost.

Scocci will tell you how I think the Italian situation should be judged. But all forecasts aside, you must do whatever you can to ensure that the organizational and political activity of the party is not either truncated or seriously diminished. You can influence the International, and those comrades in the majority who are even more concerned and angry than I am. I am convinced that with a joint effort the crisis will be overcome. If it were not, the consequences would be too serious. I hope to see you again soon.

I embrace you affectionately,

Palmiro

38. GRAMSCI TO TOGLIATTI
(Moscow, 18 May 1923)

Dear Palmiro,

I will answer your letter at some length and set out my present opinion on the situation in the party, and on the perspectives which can be drawn up for its future development and for the attitudes of the groups which make it up. In general, I will tell you at once that you are too optimistic; the question is much more complex than would appear from your letter. During the Fourth World Congress, I had a few talks with Amadeo which make me think that an open and definitive discussion between us is necessary, on certain questions which today seem, or may seem, intellectual bickering, but which I think could, in the context of a revolutionary development of the Italian situation, become the cause of internal crisis or decomposition of the party. The basic issue today is the following (in other words, it is the one you posed yourself): it is necessary to create within the party a nucleus – which is not a faction – of comrades who have the highest degree of ideological homogeneity, and are therefore able to impress upon our practical activity the greatest possible unity of leadership. We, the old Turin group, have made many errors in this field. We avoided taking to their final consequences the ideal and practical differences which had arisen with Angelo, we did not clarify the situation, and today we find ourselves up against the following problem: the fact that a little band of comrades is exploiting for its own ends the tradition and forces which we created in Turin has become a document against us.[66]

In the general sphere, as a result of the revulsion we felt in 1919–20 against the idea of creating a faction, we remained isolated, mere individuals or little more than that; while in the other group, the abstentionist one, the tradition of work in common, as a faction, left deep traces which still have very considerable ideal and practical repercussions on the life of the party today. But I will write to you at length and in detail. I also want to write another, more general letter for the comrades of our old group, like Leonetti, Montagnana, etc., in which I will explain to them too my attitude at the Fourth World Congress – which, if they recall, exactly reproduced my 1920 position in Turin, when I did not want to enter the electionist communist faction, but argued for the necessity of a closer understanding precisely with the abstentionists.[67]

I think that today, up here, it is easier – given the general conditions of the movement in Europe – to resolve the questions that have arisen in a way that is favourable to us, at least so far as the substance is concerned. Formally, crude mistakes have been made on our part, which have done us enormous harm and made us appear infantile, light-minded, disruptive. But the situation is favourable to us all along the line. For Italy I am optimistic – provided of course, that we are able to work and remain united. The question of the PSI, in my opinion, should be viewed by us in a more realistic way, giving thought – indirectly – to the period after the seizure of power. Three years experience has taught us, not just in Italy, how deeply-rooted social-democratic traditions are, and how difficult it is to destroy the residues of the past simply through ideological polemics. An immense and at the same time painstaking political action is necessary, that can break down this tradition day by day, by breaking down the organism which embodies it. The tactics of the International are adequate for this purpose. In Russia, of 350,000 members of the CP only 50,000 are old Bolsheviks, the other 300,000 are Mensheviks and Social-Revolutionaries who have come over to us as a result of the political activity of the original nucleus. The latter has nevertheless not been submerged by this element, but continues to lead the party and indeed is continually being strengthened in terms of representation at congresses and in the general movement of the leading stratum.

In the German party, the same thing occurs: the 50,000 Spartacists have incorporated the 300,000 Independents completely; at the Fourth Congress, out of 20 German delegates only 3 were former Independents (and note that the representatives were mainly chosen by the local bodies).[68]

I think that there has been too much anxiety on our part, and if I examine its psychological roots I can only find one explanation: we are conscious of the fact that we are weak and could be submerged. Note that this has enormously important practical repercussions. In Italy, we have cultivated in a hot-house an opposition barren of any ideals or clear vision. What situation has been provoked? The mass of the party and its sympathizers forms its opinions on public documents which are on the line of the International and, indirectly, of the opposition. We are becoming separated from the masses. Between us and these masses a cloud of ambiguity, misunderstanding and obscure squabbles is being formed. At a certain point, we will appear like men who want to hold their positions at any price, i.e. the role that should properly belong to the opposition will be turned to our disadvantage. I believe that we, our group, must remain at the head of the party, because we are really in the line of historical development; because, despite all our errors, we have worked positively and created something. The others have done nothing, and today want to act so as to liquidate communism in Italy and take our young movement back into the traditional course. But if we continue to take up the formalistic positions which we have taken up hitherto (note that these are formalistic for me, for you, for Bruno, for Umberto, but not for Amadeo), we shall obtain the opposite result to the one we want. The opposition will *de facto* become the party's representative, and we will remain cut off. We will suffer a defeat in practice, one that is perhaps irremediable and that will undoubtedly mark the beginning of our disintegration as a group and of the defeat of our ideas and politics. Well, we should not be too concerned about our leadership function. We should move ahead, developing our political activity, without too much looking in the mirror. We are in the flow of the historical current and will succeed, provided we "row" well and keep a firm grasp on the rudder. If we can operate correctly, we shall absorb the Socialist Party and resolve the first and basic problem of revolution: to unify the proletarian vanguard and destroy the demagogic populist tradition.

The comment you make on the socialist congress did not satisfy me from this point of view. In it, you appear like a communist looking in the mirror. Instead of disintegrating the Socialist Party, your comment amounts to reinforcing it, placing the entire socialist movement in insuperable counter-position to us. As far as the leaders, Nenni, Vella, etc., are concerned, this cannot be doubted; but is it true of the mass of party members, and more importantly of the party's sphere of influence in the proletariat? Certainly not, and we are convinced that the proletarian vanguard will in its overwhelming majority be attracted and assimilated by us. So what must be done?

1. We must not continue to make *en bloc* counterpositions, but must distinguish between leaders and mass base.

2. We must find all the elements of disagreement between the leaders and the mass base and deepen these, enlarge them, generalize them politically.

3. We must develop a discussion of present politics and not a study of general historical phenomena.

4. We must make practical proposals and indicate to the masses practical paths of action and organization.

I will give an example so that you will understand better, and will enlarge the question to the Popular Party congress, which was not exploited politically by us although (together with the development of the situation in the Sardinian Action Party) it offered us the terrain for essential statements of position on the problem of relations between proletariat and rural classes.

The socialist problem was the following: to highlight the glaring contrast between the words and the deeds of the socialist leaders. When the International advised us to adopt the watchword of the right-wing socialists, for a bloc between the two parties, it did so because it was easy to foresee that, in the general situation, fusion had become impossible and it was necessary to imprison the Vellas and Nennis in their own paddocks, with the requisite confidence that their attitude was demagogic and their line different from ours. This was indeed shown by their response to our proposal. In our comments on the congress, we should have begun to note this: the prohibition barring the fusionists from organizing, their exclusion from the central leadership, the dissolution of the youth federation, were political elements of the first importance, to be exploited. The socialist masses should have been confronted by this precise fact. *Vis-à-vis* these masses, it was necessary for us to take the trouble to disentangle, from the welter of polemics and verbalism, the concrete master-lines, and set them out in a clear and comprehensive fashion.

The same for the Popular Party congress. I think that every movement of the Popular Party, in view of the links which connect this organization with the Vatican, has a special importance for us. The Popular Congress had the following significance, in my view. There exists a widespread discontent among the peasant masses with the party's policies, a discontent caused especially by the new tax on agricultural transporters. This state of mind is spreading from the countryside to the city, among wide layers of the petty bourgeoisie. The composition of the PP is the following: a reactionary and fascist right wing, based on the clerical aristocracy, a left wing based on the countryside and a centre made up of urban intellectual elements and priests. The campaign by *Il Corriere* and *La Stampa* is reinforcing the Popular Party's centre.[69] The elements who are detached from fascism by this wily campaign necessarily orient themselves towards the PP, the sole existing organization that offers a hope of being able, with its flexible, opportunist tactics, to counter-balance fascism and reintroduce governmental competition in the parliamentary sphere – i.e. liberty as liberals understand it.

Fascist tactics towards the Popular Party are very risky, and will necessarily result in making the party more leftist and in causing splits to the left. The same situation confronts the Popular Party as during the War, but immensely more difficult and risky. During the War, the catholics were neutralist in the parishes and villages, while the catholic press and the top circles of the Church vociferously supported the War. Then the government did not compel the centre to oppose the periphery or to homogenize it. But the fascists do not want to behave like that. They want to have open agreement and declarations of co-responsibility, especially before the masses in the basic cells of the mass parties. This is impossible to obtain from the PP, without implicitly demanding its death. It is obvious that we must heighten and enlarge the crisis of the Popular Party, by stimulating – including in our own press – statements by left-wing elements, as we once did in Turin with Giuseppe Speranzini.[70]

The letter has turned out to be longer and more complex than I had thought. Since I want to deal with some of these questions at greater length, I will stop for today.

Warm greetings to the comrades and yourself.

Antonio

39. REPORT BY THE MINORITY OF THE ITALIAN DELEGATION TO THE ENLARGED EXECUTIVE MEETING OF JUNE 1923[71]

1. When a battle is lost (and the Milan congress of the PSI certainly has been that for us), it is natural for a discussion about the responsibility to be unleashed.[72] But the battle lost at Milan cannot and must not bring about an end to the campaign, nor a cessation of the struggle to achieve the ends which the Fourth Congress fixed. The considerable vote obtained at Milan by the fusionists (3,908 votes, as against 5,361) indicates that the shift required was not very great; 43 per cent of the PSI aligned itself openly with the IIIrd International and for fusion with the PCI.

2. The majority of the Italian delegation to the Fourth Congress, once defeated on the question of fusion, turned all its efforts to imposing on the PSI the heaviest possible ransom for its entry into the IIIrd International; and the whole discussion, instead of pursuing the means to succeed, continued for almost two months on the terrain of "guarantees". This made us lose sight of the most important task, which was to "guarantee" fusion above all else. And while we were wasting our time drawing up protocols, our enemies – aided by the new wave of terrorism deliberately unleashed by Mussolini from February onwards – speedily took advantage of our mistakes and of the situation to seize control of *Avanti!* and the party. The Socialist Defence Committee did not go to war against us by counter-posing a rival plan for the future organization. It instead limited itself to general formulae, which allowed it to concentrate all its efforts in the present and to collect around itself the forces of inertia which the situation of terror has spawned within the party and at its edges. They defeated us because they understood better than we did what was most important: to get hold of the party apparatus. We became convinced of this too late. We found the real field of battle after a series of retreats which brought us there too late, and which weakened us.

3. I think I can assert that if the Italian delegation, after simply having fixed certain general lines for our future work, had returned in the second fortnight of December to Italy, the battle was won. But even at the end of January, even in the situation of total practical

immobilization in which we found ourselves, it was still possible to win – if the line of retreat that was to be fixed up in haste with Lazzari at the Milan Congress (when it only brought us a few hundred votes) had been fought for in the month preceding the congress. Comrade Rakosi, realizing the situation, had recognized at once upon his arrival in Italy the need for an immediate change of tactic. If the sections of the PSI had had to declare themselves on a resolution proclaiming "unconditional" adherence to the IIIrd International and an immediate bloc with the PCI as "preparation" for fusion, we would certainly have won and made it impossible for the Vella–Nenni grouping to do any harm. . . .

The proposal for a bloc was made too late, and the PSI sections and federations did not know about it before the congress. We followed the policy of "asking a lot" in order to "obtain somewhat less" (this was the tactical formula dear to the majority comrades on the PCI's Executive Committee, and supported by comrade Manuilsky). We thus lost sight of the masses, and played into the hands of the "Defence Committee". If, instead of concentrating our efforts on objectives which were changed and re-ordered under pressure from the situation, we had at once, from the first moment, adopted the slogans of "unconditional adherence" and "bloc" with the communists, we would have transformed the relationship of forces. But the change of tactics only occurred when the sections had already stated their positions: in other words, when there was no longer any advantage to be drawn from it, since the members of the "Defence Committee" – who alone knew about it – were naturally not moved by it and openly declared that "it did not fool them".

4. As for the PCI's responsibilities in these results, one may observe that if the Executive Committee of the Italian Communist Party had been convinced of the need for fusion and had worked in this direction, by mobilizing its forces immediately after the Rome Congress, the "public opinion" of the masses today grouped around the PSI would have been drawn behind it, at least to a degree sufficient to give us victory.

I have already indicated how the position taken up by our comrades in the majority of the Italian delegation to the Fourth Congress put the entire work of the commission appointed by the congress on the wrong track. In the period in which the "fusion commission" worked in Italy, the EC of the PCI maintained its attitude of reservation and some distrust towards the fusion activity. But when the commission entered Italy, the situation was already such that the attitude of the PCI could not and did not play any great role. It would be unjust to make it the scapegoat for a defeat whose roots lie in the tactics adopted – in Moscow and in Italy alike – by the fusion commission, and for which the commission as a whole bears responsibility: some for having imposed those tactics, the rest for not having opposed them as was necessary.

5. The attitude of the PCI since the Milan Congress must be denounced as clearly sabotaging fusion. The EC of the PCI is proposing to the PSI a bloc for joint action, since the Italian situation "imposes upon all those who claim to remain faithful to the principle of the class struggle to unite all their efforts for defence against the capitalist offensive and against the disintegrative manoeuvres of reformism" (*Il Lavoratore*, 2 May).

The PCI's letter was published in *Il Lavoratore* without commentary; no preparation was made, no wide distribution organized. The proposal for a bloc was an act of prime importance, which should have been given the widest publicity, to win the broadest consent among maximalist workers. On the contrary, it was made almost secretly; we published the letter, and then waited passively for whatever might ensue. What was, however, done was to publish an editorial which, after making a very detailed analysis of the faults of the Socialist Party, concluded: "No one can hold us responsible for the fact which, today as yesterday, makes us judge that they (the maximalist socialists) are bound to a corpse (the Socialist Party) which must be cleared out of the way" (*Il Lavoratore*, 8 May).

The only words which the PCI uttered to clarify its proposal for a "bloc" thus consisted in declaring that the PSI (this party with which the Fourth Congress had decided we should fuse) was a "corpse" to be cleared out of the way. One can well understand what advantage the anti-fusionists and anti-communists of the PSI were able to draw from that, by playing on the "patriotism" of workers who feel a certain attachment to their party and setting them against us and the International.

The PSI leadership replied that: "the two movements (maximalist and communist) are naturally indicated as those which should collaborate and form the first active nucleus of class unity, but the indispensable basis for collaboration is trust. Without that, there is only trickery, lies and polemical ruses. If we lack that, it is better for each to go his own way" (*Avanti!*, 10 May). In the same letter, the PSI leadership disavowed the attacks against the Socialist Party, and stated its intention of "extending" the united front to the parties which "really" want to realize it.

In other words, while the PCI was proposing a "bloc" of the two parties, the PSI replied by speaking of the "united front". It was necessary to stress that the question was one of a "bloc" and not a "united front", given the relations. Quite the contrary. In *Sindacato rosso*, the communist trade-union organ, the letter proposing the bloc was explained in these terms: "With this letter, the CP resolutely takes the initiative to form a united front between classist elements!" (28 April). And in the PCI answer to the PSI leadership's reply one may read: "We conceive the tactic of blocs and of the united front as a means to pursue the struggle against those who betray the proletariat on a new level.... That is why we have proposed it" (*Il Lavoratore*, 18 May).

No mention is made of the specific reasons which determine the tactics of the Communist International (which should also be the tactics of the PCI) towards the PSI. In the *Lavoratore* article on 8 May, an attempt was made to deny that the Rome Congress had any importance. But even if it were true that the Milan Congress had revised it (which even Vella and Nenni have had to deny), it is in our interests to use the Rome resolutions to strike at the enemies of the IIIrd International and the anti-fusionists.

What is more, an article in *Il Lavoratore* on 23 May contained the following: "We do not ask for testimonials of good conduct, and still less for promises, from Messrs Vella or Serrati or Nenni." Now Serrati at that very moment was in prison because he had rallied to the IIIrd International and favoured fusion. Language of this kind, if one did not know the comrade responsible for it, is what might be employed by an *agent provocateur* of the Vella–Nenni gang, and has certainly created some difficulties for the fusionists within the party.

The reality is that the comrades of the PCI Executive Committee have sought to create a *fait accompli* between the PSI and the International, which by playing the game of the anti-communists in the Socialist Party would deliver these comrades once and for all from the nightmare which the fusion of the two parties represents for them.

6. It is now necessary to consider two aspects of the situation in the Socialist Party: international relations; and the fusionist-maximalists.

So far as international relations are concerned, it will be useful to assemble here the most striking statements of the anti-fusionists in the PSI. The motion voted through at Milan, at the first meeting of the Defence Committee (14 January), rejects the "14 points" which were conditions for fusion and states that "in relations between the IIIrd International and the PSI, the latter has accepted the conditions which Moscow had hitherto posed for its admission and has proceeded at its Rome Congress to expel its centrist right wing" (*Avanti!*, 16 January). In other words, the expulsion of the reformists at the Rome Congress is presented as a "necessary and sufficient" condition for admission to the IIIrd International.

P. Nenni, in his speech to the Milan section, states that: "No one in the SP aims to withdraw from adherence to the IIIrd International" (*Avanti!*, 2 February); but the manifesto of the Defence Committee simply accepts "the spirit of the programmatic positions of the IIIrd International", while refusing to make the SP into "a headless section of the International, without a will of its own, and without power of decision, instead of an autonomous and free cell, which nevertheless respects the discipline of the federation of the world's workers (?)".

At the Milan Congress, P. Nenni declared: "the conclusions of the Rome Congress are not susceptible of any revision, and the Defence Committee absolutely does not intend to go back on the vote of adherence to the International" (*Avanti!*, 17 April). The motion on international questions approved at the congress sums up the attitude of the anti-fusionists in the following terms: "to act on the doctrinal and problematic terrain of the IIIrd International, supporting its actions against the capitalist offensive and against the social-democratic International, and committing itself as of now to support all attempts to unite the international proletarian and revolutionary forces. . . . The SP is confident that the IIIrd International will very soon recognize that in the proceedings of the Fourth Congress in Moscow it demanded a sacrifice which the PSI could not and cannot consent to" (*Avanti!*, 18 April).

It is necessary to underline this adherence to "all attempts to unite the international proletarian and revolutionary forces", which reminds us of certain dreams entertained by comrade Serrati in 1921 and on the occasion of the Berlin conference.[73] This attitude is also close to that of the French "dissidents".[74] It is interesting in this connection to note that the PSI leadership replied to a letter of invitation to the Saint-Ouen Congress as follows: "Comrade Vella has transmitted to us your circular of the 16 inst. with the relative documents. In the meantime, you will certainly have learnt of the results of our Milan Congress. As a result of the positions adopted, I have the duty to tell you frankly that the position of our party, with respect to the conditions established for its admission by the Fourth Congress of the Communist International, must in no way be interpreted as an expression of hostility towards the International itself, to which all our congresses since 1919 have confirmed our adherence. And even the motion approved in Milan asserts our loyal intention of following the actions of the Communist International" (*Egalité*, 3 May). In the same letter, the intention is repeated of backing all attempts to achieve working-class unity.

In any case, it is certain that the meeting of the two Internationals in Hamburg has completely demolished the plans which the Vella–Nenni–Sacerdote grouping had for international organization, and the articles published on the subject in *Avanti!* show the extent to which those people have been thrown off course.[75]

On 11 May, the leadership of the Italian Socialist Party decided to send the motion approved at the Milan Congress to Moscow, with an explanatory report.

7. From the documentation which we have thought it worthwhile assembling, it is clear that the leadership of the PSI, although formed by anti-fusionist and anti-communist elements, is obliged not to put itself openly against the IIIrd International and even to make official statements of "loyalty". Why is this? Have Vella and Nenni been converted? Obviously, they have had to do this not just because there are the 43 per cent of fusionists in the PSI, but because even among the others and among the working-class layers who follow the party and *Avanti!* the prestige of the IIIrd International has been unshakeable. The leadership of the Socialist Party will seek every means to escape a complete and unequivocal adherence. But if we operate correctly, it will break its head between our pressure and the wall of the unbreakable loyalty of the Italian workers to the IIIrd International. To achieve this end, we propose that:

1. the International takes note: (a) that at the Milan Congress 43 per cent of PSI members declared themselves for fusion and for adherence to the IIIrd International; (b) that the congress did not mean – even according to the statements of the Socialist Defence Committee – revision of the Rome Congress;

2. the International asserts, and demands recognition of the fact, that the coexistence of two member parties in the same country would not be possible for long, since such coexistence is absurd and inadmissible from a political and organizational point of view;

3. the only conditions which should be posed to the Socialist Party for its admission, even as a "sympathizer" – to use com. Zinoviev's formula – are the two following: (a) formation of an action bloc with the

Communist Party and between the two youth organizations; (b) freedom for the fusionists within the PSI to continue, within the bounds of discipline, their propaganda.

8. The comrades of the PCI Executive Committee are highly concerned by the "conditions" to be imposed on the PSI for its admission to the CI. They say that this is not with the aim of "sabotaging" fusion, to which they are resigned, but in order to safeguard the "quality" of the new party. We believe that there is only one way of achieving this safeguard in the present situation: by breaking the *cordon sanitaire* which the PSI leadership is trying to establish between its members and the PCI; and by bending all our efforts to making possible a certain period of joint work between maximalist and communist workers – after which no force, neither fascist terror nor the manoeuvres of the anti-communist socialists, will again be able to separate them. Whoever knows the Italian situation knows that if the maximalist and communist workers can really work in the same organs of struggle for a certain time, the anti-communists and the enemies of the IIIrd International will be rendered impotent.

Must we fear unfortunate consequences for the ideological clarity of the party which will emerge from this process? I think that the danger is not so great as is supposed: 1. because the Italian workers are quite capable of assimilating communist conceptions; 2. because in the new joint struggle organs the communists will certainly win a preponderant influence. The contact of our party apparatus with that of the PSI cannot fail to result in a marked superiority on our part. Our style of work, our methods of organization and even our ideological preparation will certainly give us the advantage. The "guarantees" which it would be vain to seek elsewhere can only be found in ourselves, in our determination to win over the maximalist masses. We will only have to mobilize all our efforts to that end, and the result cannot be in doubt.

This is why we believe that the most important condition to pose for the PSI's admission is precisely the formation of a "bloc" or "alliance", which must find their expression in the creation of networks of joint committees, both national and local (but above all local), through which we can make contact with broader proletarian layers and draw them decisively into the communist current. The pressure of the fusionists (who must be given the possibility of exercising it) within the PSI will accompany this activity and profit by it. The struggle will thus be able to develop with the greatest possible likelihood of success.

9. The comrades of the EC of the PCI have proposed (a) to break with the existing leadership of the Italian Socialist Party; (b) to consider the fusionist faction within the PSI as the latter's "official" representative in the International; i.e. to push the fusionist faction into a bitter struggle against the present leadership of the PSI, while supporting it from our side with an offensive in the same direction. What result would the application of this tactic have? The exodus or expulsion in the near future of a few hundred fusionists from the PSI, and their "individual" entry into the PCI. This is precisely what our comrades of the EC of the PCI want to arrive at; but it would be precisely the opposite solution to the one towards which the Fourth Congress considered we should proceed.

10. Does the Socialist Party have the possibility of living on for a long time in Italy as an "independent party"? From the point of view of the experience of all countries, which was strikingly confirmed at Hamburg, it is true that it is not possible for any party to remain for long in a centrist position between the communists and the reformists. Nevertheless, the situation is such that it could allow a situation of this kind for some time. As the possibilities for action are very limited, it will be possible for the maximalists of the PSI to continue to remain in that position of purely verbal "intransigence", demagogic and passive at the same time, which was characteristic of the party throughout the whole period from 1918 to 1922.

But even if the rapid dissolution of the Socialist Party was possible, only a part of the masses which follow it would come with us: perhaps a third, perhaps less. The others either would go with the reformists, or would become disgusted by all activity. We assert that given the Italian situation such a solution is in no way desirable, and that our interests lead us to try to draw along with us troops who are already assembled and ready to fight, rather than scattered elements of a routed army.

11. The Italian situation demands a close collaboration, a perfect articulation between the communists and the maximalists in the period which will precede fusion. The situation which *Il Lavoratore* is in allows us to think, even if the news of its legal suppression is not confirmed, that *Avanti!* even after the fusion could only be the ... legal organ of an illegal party. In this respect, it is necessary to examine a whole aspect of illegal activity which our party has not yet seriously considered.

In a situation of terror such as fascism has created in Italy, the problem of illegality is not just a problem of technical organization, but also and above all one of general political tactics. The slogans for action, the forms of propaganda, must be such as to allow us not to lose contact with the terrorized masses, making clear to them that the new tactic employed does not represent a weakening in our opposition to fascism.

To give a negative example, the formula "red against tricolour" (red flag against national flag), launched by the Communist Party at a moment in which all the inertial forces of the bourgeoisie and petty bourgeoisie were being galvanized and activated by nationalism, represented an absurdity. This is so true that our party had hardly launched it before it quickly dropped it and spoke of it no more. Well, the combat slogans which we adopt must be such as always to represent possibilities for development. They must not be mere rockets set off to "frighten the bourgeois" who, in this case, counterpose to our empty words solid arguments in wood and iron. For this, it is necessary that our slogans can be understood by the masses as concrete and practicable. If the opposite is the case, one becomes responsible for a greater demoralization of the masses themselves.

In a country in which all freedoms have been removed, in which the working class has been reduced to a state of slavery, in which even the marginal classes who had given a certain support to fascism (war veterans, petty bourgeoisie, small farmers) have had their interests seriously hurt, it will be easy to find agitational issues which can gain the agreement of very broad social layers.

12. The EC of the PCI has made a fairly detailed analysis of the Italian political situation in its report. So without repeating what has already been said, we stress that no serious improvement in this situation is probable with respect to our possibilities for action for a certain time to come. The internal conflicts within fascism do not for the moment express a development of "contradictions" inherent in the social composition of fascism. The conflicts between the "political" and the "military" elements do not as yet have great importance. There is no fascist "trade-unionism" developing a serious activity of resistance within the fascist party to the government's reactionary and anti-proletarian policies. Fascism will never decide to weaken its military apparatus, which constitutes its most certain bulwark, both against the "reds" and against the "attempts" of certain bourgeois groupings to get the direct administration of power in their hands. The liberal opposition and the tendencies towards a "return to legality" do not take up and will not take up a position of open struggle against fascism. Certain bourgeois layers are interested in eliminating fascism, which they

wanted to utilize as a machine whose controls they would keep entirely in their hands. But fascism (i.e. the politico-military organization of the fascist party) will not accept giving up the direct administration of power.

On the other hand fascism is abandoning and will increasingly abandon the baggage of demagogic formulae which has accompanied it in its bloody progress. Its policy does not depart from the routine framework of the programmes and solutions worked out by the bourgeois governments which preceded it. What constitutes the "novelty" of fascism is its combat apparatus organized into a political party and controlling the State. It is precisely this apparatus which will permit fascism to continue its domination for a long time to come, before the underground working of the economic contradictions which it has unleashed can sap its foundations.

The only opposition to fascism on which one can count in the months which separate us from the Fifth Congress is that of the proletariat. While not losing sight of the interplay of conflicting interests within and around fascism, all efforts must be directed to the constitution of a united front of the working class and peasantry on the elementary problems of their existence. The centre of this front must be represented by the communist-maximalist nucleus. But it must seek to extend itself to all parties which represent social layers directly interested in the struggle against fascism: Unitary Socialist Party (democratic petty bourgeoisie and peasants of the Po valley); Catholic Popular Party (artisans and small farmers). So far as the latter party is concerned, it is not practically possible to enter into relations to this end with the central organs; but one could well do so locally with the proletarian or semi-proletarian elements which it includes.

13. Our activity should thus be directed to two successive tasks: (a) formation of the communist-maximalist bloc; (b) united front with other political formations of the working class and peasantry. For this, it is necessary that our party be led by comrades who really want to achieve these ends. The unhappy experience of the years 1921–2 and the systematic sabotage applied by the leaders of our party to all practical and serious united front action; the experience of the same EC's attitude towards fusion—these give us the very firm conviction that the comrades in question are not capable, from the political point of view, of bringing our party to make the maximum effort towards the tasks of which we have spoken.

14. There is a further problem, which it is our duty to make clear to

the comrades of the International. The comrades who make up the Executive Committee of our party have remained entirely on the political line expressed in the Theses on Tactics approved by the Rome Congress and clearly rejected by the Fourth World Congress. They have not been converted; they still think today that it is the International which was and is mistaken. In this belief, they have thought it their duty to keep the leading bodies of the party strictly composed of those who agree with them. They have given themselves the role of vestal virgins charged with guarding the sacred fire, which the Fourth Congress merely covered over with a few cinders. They have therefore divided the party into two categories: the chosen and the rejected.

The conception which these comrades have of the party and its relations with the masses is perfectly designed to maintain the "sect" mentality which is one of the most serious defects of our organization. These comrades have systematically excluded from leading positions in the party those who were not in agreement with the Rome Theses. As a result of this same sect mentality, comrades who were wholly unworthy or incapable have been kept in positions of responsibility (Moscow, Berlin, trade-union movement);[76] comrades have ceased to be good comrades the moment they allowed themselves to make any criticisms; there has even been recourse to systematic defamation of those whose influence in the party they could fear. The comrades of the Executive Committee have abused the power entrusted to them by the whole party and by the International for factional and sectarian ends, and this not in a few occasional episodes, but in a systematic, constant and organized manner.

This sect mentality, in relation to the political attitude which it expresses, as in relation to the internal organization of the party, is one of the most serious obstacles which hinder the application of a truly communist tactics. We have thought it our duty, aside from all personal questions, to assert that it is absolutely necessary to break in a definitive fashion, both from the point of view of principle and from the point of view of organization, this anachronism of a communist party which continues to be led in the anti-Marxist spirit of the Rome Theses (March 1922) and which the leadership wants to organize with a view to preserving this spirit. We have spoken clearly, because it was our duty to do so, because we think that the possibilities for serious communist work in Italy depend on the radical liquidation of such a past.

40. WHAT THE RELATIONS SHOULD BE BETWEEN THE PCI AND THE COMINTERN

Up till now, we have adopted an attitude towards the Comintern that has appeared equivocal. While we have proclaimed the utmost formal discipline and used language more appropriate for inferiors speaking to their superiors than for use between equals, we have acted in such a way as to give the impression that we were ready to do anything effectively to evade the directives established by the International Congresses and by the Executive Committee. It is a principle of orientation that has now become fundamental that every local attitude must have an international reflection, and can lead to an international process of organization, or at least a movement, that will bring about the emergence of factions within the Comintern. It is certain that the Executive will combat sharply any manifestation of such a kind. One procedure which the Executive regards as being of the highest importance is that there should always be unanimity in votes. This is not simply a formal question. From the entire experience of the Russian revolution it is clear that the absence of unanimity in important public votes produces quite specific attitudes among the broad masses: political enemies are polarized towards the minority, enlarging and generalizing its positions; they clandestinely publish manifestoes and programmes, etc., perhaps even signed by the oppositionists or by a group of their friends; and they carry out a whole agitational activity which may become extremely dangerous at a certain juncture. A defensive approach to such manœuvres is unanimity in voting, which appears in the eyes of the public as an agreement reached and as proof of the most open unity. From this principle, which has become fundamental for the communist parties insofar as they must take up positions today with an eye to tomorrow, there flow corollaries which are relevant to our attitudes too: for example, the assertion that we will observe discipline even if we are not convinced, the threat of resignations, etc. Indeed, this attitude is more dangerous insofar as it gives rise to, or can give rise to rumours and whisperings, and can lead to pseudo-revelations from behind the scenes which can have very grave repercussions in the international arena. It is therefore better to raise questions in their full dimensions in private discussions, upholding one's own point of view proudly and showing that one is also ready to struggle. Naturally, such questions can arise only within the limits of the statutes and of the decisions already taken by the various Congresses and Conferences.

We are in a questionable position, in view of the international situation. The tactic of the united front, laid down with considerable precision by the Russian comrades, both technically and in the general approach to its practical application, has *in no country* found the party or the men capable of concretizing it. Germany, where it seemed until recently that exemplary things had been achieved, has been strongly criticized. The great majority of the German party has not understood this tactic, and the minority is the expression of this widespread state of mind.[77] The Frankfurt delegation sent to Amsterdam was only capable of pursuing a bureaucratic practice, and for that reason was recalled.[78] Obviously, all this cannot be accidental. There is something not functioning in the international field as a whole, there is a weakness and inadequacy of leadership. The Italian question must be seen in this framework, not as something which depends on the ill-will of individuals and which can be modified by the good will of the first rough fellow who decides to become a Marcellus.[79] We must argue that we want to pose the problem to the other parties in this way, and must utilize whatever elements are available to us if there is a refusal to recognize our good will and correct conduct.

The present majority of the CP intends to defend to the last its position and historical role in Italy, where the unified CP must be constituted with an ideological centre which is neither the traditional Socialist one nor a compromise with that. We are defending the future of the Italian revolution. The situation of the Socialist Party to a great extent depends upon a similar attitude in a group of Socialist leaders. They defend and will defend to the last and with every means their political profile and their future. We may have made mistakes and we are willing to amend them, but we are not willing to allow the centre of attraction and assimilation of new elements entering the Italian section of the Comintern to be shifted onto a new basis – represented by individuals who want to make a compromise with the Socialists on the fundamental issue.[30] The attitude of the Comintern and the activity of its representatives is bringing disintegration and corruption into the communist ranks. We are determined to struggle against the elements who would liquidate our Party and against the corrupt elements. The situation of illegality and exile makes this obligatory. We do not want what happened in Hungary and in Yugoslavia to be repeated in Italy.[81] If the Comintern too receives a few blows as we strike back, we should not be blamed for that: it is a mistake to ally oneself with untrustworthy elements.

> Handwritten notes, probably written in Moscow in June 1923.

41. FACTION MEETING
(12 July 1923)

(Fragment of the minutes)[82]

PRESENT: *Umberto [Terracini], Bruno [Fortichiari], Leonetti, Ravera, Palmiro [Togliatti]*

Umberto thinks we should first establish that we accept the decisions of the International, then begin factional activity designed to draw from these decisions the greatest possible advantage for our group. It will therefore be necessary to examine all the technical organizational questions, and take a series of decisions which will have the result of guaranteeing that the work of the new Executive Committee will be carried out in a way that conforms to our perspectives, and that we will keep positions such as to assure us control of the party and the political situation. We should make use of these positions to carry out an organic factional activity.

Palmiro wants us to treat it as a political question rather than a technical one of organization. He thinks that, if one does not clarify the position of the 'majority' political group with a series of open actions, acceptance is impossible – even if it is accompanied by a group agreement of the kind referred to by Umberto. Acceptance in these conditions would put us on the same level as the minority, i.e. would begin the transformation of our political group into a personal côterie, whose existence and whose positions would be unknown or misunderstood by the masses and which would sooner or later be condemned to fragment. Instead it is necessary, even if we accept, to do so in a way that guarantees that we continue to be what we have been up to now, i.e. a group that can be recognized by the masses for its theoretical physiognomy and its tactical conduct. We have made the mistake of not taking up earlier a position of open polemic *vis-à-vis* the International, before the whole party and the working-class masses. No organizational expedient can put us in a correct position, before the party and the masses, if we do not come to such an open polemic. He poses two conditions: 1. that the group should organize itself in such a way that all responsibilities are joint ones, and that members of mixed bodies are responsible to it; 2. that an open polemic is begun with the International and with the minority of the party, by way of a series of statements of principle and polemics, which must be not just communicated to the International but disseminated among the masses. If on this basis, or one that is not substantially different, an agreement or concrete conclusion is arrived at, he will accept, otherwise not.

(In code for Amadeo):

Basis of the agreement:
— polemical actions will be taken collectively, but you will have a key role above all in the drawing up of the basic statement. We think that it must be done leaving aside the contingent questions of the moment (fusion, mixed Executive, etc.), or at least only dealing with them in relation to and as a consequence of the theoretical and tactical positions which our group has taken and maintained since its origins.

42. THREE FRAGMENTS BY GRAMSCI[83]

I

To comrade Paolo Palmi [copy to Scoccimarro, Leonetti, Montagnana, Fortichiari, Platone, Terracini, Ravera, Peluso]

Dear comrade,
I am replying to your letter, setting out my point of view for you on the situation created for our party as a result of the decision of the Enlarged Executive, and suggesting to you a plan of general action whose realization, in my opinion, could offer a real, concrete solution to the situation itself. I am absolutely convinced that today any discussion on our part that is limited to the organizational and juridical aspects of the Italian question can have no useful result. It could only make things worse and make our task more difficult and dangerous. Instead, it is necessary to work concretely and show, through a general party activity and political work that is adequate to the Italian situation, that we are what we claim to be, instead of continuing any longer with the attitude of "misunderstood geniuses" which we have adopted hitherto.

1. You think that the discussion here in Moscow has revolved around fusionism and anti-fusionism. This is only apparently the case. Fusionism and anti-fusionism were the "polemical terminology" of the discussion, but not its substance. The discussion was the following: whether the PCI has understood the overall Italian situation, and whether it is capable of giving a lead to the proletariat; whether the PCI is capable of developing a vast political campaign, i.e. whether it is ideologically and organizationally equipped for a specific activity; whether the leading group of the PCI has assimilated the political doctrine of the Communist International, which is Marxism as it developed into Leninism, i.e. into an organic and systematic body of organizational principles and tactical viewpoints. . . .

II

The Italian socialist movement of the last thirty years has been an apparatus for selecting new leading elements for the bourgeois State.

The same goes for the *popolari*. Fascism is the last and most decisive of these movements, whch seeks to absorb the whole new social stratum that has been formed, by dissolving the bonds between leaders and masses.

The crisis of the SP was nothing other than an aspect of the proletariat's mighty effort to recover its unity and class homogeneity, and simultaneously to put itself at the head of the other classes of the population who cannot win freedom except by accepting the leadership of the revolutionary proletariat. What should the CP's attitude be to the present crisis of the SP? It must help the healthy elements to overcome it, and to overcome it in a way that is beneficial for the working class.... The (S.) party is today still struggling. It is disintegrating. This means disintegration of the masses. The masses organize around political parties. They shift and take up position in accordance with the "signals" of the party which they follow. If the p. instead of shifting disintegrates, then in the present period its mass following disintegrates too.

Political value of fusion. Reaction has set itself the aim of forcing the proletariat back into the conditions in which it found itself in the initial period of capitalism: dispersed; isolated; individuals, not a class which feels that it is a unity and aspires to power. The Livorno split (the separation of the majority of the Italian proletariat from the Communist International) was without a doubt the greatest triumph of reaction ...

III

Fascism aims to become an integral movement, of a new class, which has never been independent in the Italian State: the rural bourgeoisie, allied to the big landowners, against the peasants and against the workers.

The urban petty bourgeoisie, which had constituted the original fascist movement, is detaching itself today: the *fasci* of the towns are collapsing; D'Annunzio's attitude is highly symptomatic of this situation.[84]

43. GRAMSCI TO THE EXECUTIVE COMMITTEE OF THE PCI[85]

Vienna, 12 September 1923

Dear Comrades,

At its last session, the Presidium decided that a workers' daily should be published in Italy under the direction of the Executive Committee, as an organ with which the IIIrd-Internationalists expelled from the Socialist Party can collaborate politically. I want to give you my impressions and views on this matter.

Given the present situation in Italy, I think it is very important, indeed necessary, that the paper should be put together in such a way as to ensure its legal existence for as long as possible. So not only should it not carry any party identification, it should also be edited in such a way that its actual dependence upon our party does not appear too clearly. It should be a newspaper of the left: of the working-class left that has remained loyal to the programme and tactics of class struggle. It should publish the proceedings and discussions of our party, and possibly also those of the anarchists, republicans and syndicalists. It should give its judgements with a dispassionate tone, as if it had a position above the struggle and viewed things from a "scientific" point of view. I know that it is not very easy to lay down all of this in a written programme; but the important thing is not to lay down a written programme, but rather to ensure that the party itself — which historically holds a dominant position in the sphere of the working-class left — has a legal platform which will allow it continuously and systematically to reach the broadest masses.

The Communists and the followers of Serrati will contribute publicly to the paper. In other words, they will sign articles, as individuals who are known, and they will do so according to a political plan that takes account, month by month and I would say week by week, of the general situation in the country and the relations developing among the Italian social forces. It will be necessary to watch the Serratians, who will tend to transform the paper into a factional organ in their struggle against the PSI leadership. It will be necessary to be very strict about this, and to prevent any degeneration. A polemic will, of course, be carried out, but in a political rather than a sectarian spirit and within certain limits. It will be necessary to be on one's guard against attempts to create an "economic" situation for Serrati, who is unemployed and will in all probability be proposed by his comrades as a full-time member of the editorial staff. Serrati will contribute both signed and unsigned material; his signed articles, however, should be kept to a certain number, and the unsigned ones should be approved by our Executive Committee. It will be necessary to carry out principled polemics against the socialists, or rather against the socialist spirit of Serrati, Maffi, etc. These will help to reinforce the communist consciousness of the masses, and to prepare the unity and homogeneity of the Party that will be necessary ater the fusion, if we are to avoid a return to the chaotic situation of 1920.

I propose the name *L'Unità* pure and simple; this will mean something to the workers, and will also have a more general meaning. For since the decision of the Enlarged Executive on the workers' and peasants' government, I think we must pay special attention to the Southern question – in which the problem of relations between workers and peasants is posed not simply as a problem of class relations, but also and especially as a territorial problem, i.e. as one of the aspects of the national question. Personally, I think that the slogan "Workers' and Peasants' Government" should be adapted in Italy as follows: "Federal Republic of Workers and Peasants". I do not know if the present moment is suitable for this; but I think that the situation which fascism is creating, and the corporative and protectionist policy of the Confederation leaders, will bring our party to this slogan. *A propos* this, I am preparing a report for you to discuss and study. If it would be useful, after a few issues we might start a debate in the paper under pseudonyms and see what impact it has in the country – especially among the left layers of the Popolari and bourgeois democrats, who represent the real tendencies of the peasant class and have always had in their programmes the slogan of local autonomy and decentralization. If you accept the proposal to call it *L'Unità*, you will leave the field free for the solution of these problems; the name will be a guarantee against autonomistic degenerations, and against reactionary attempts to give tendentious, authoritarian interpretations of the campaigns we may wage. Moreover, I believe that the soviet régime, with its political centralization provided by the Communist Party and its administrative decentralization and coloration by local popular forces, will be ideologically prepared in excellent fashion by the slogan: Federal Republic of Workers and Peasants.

Communist greetings,

Gramsci

44. OUR TRADE-UNION STRATEGY

In the 15 September issue of *Sindacato rosso*, comrade Nicola Vecchi put forward once again an old thesis of his: "It is necessary to create a national class trade-union body, autonomous and independent from all parties and for the time being independent from all Internationals."[86]

What should be our attitude to this proposal? What should be the propaganda orientation of the communists, in order to block possible currents of opinion among the masses agreeing with the theses of comrade Vecchi? What is, concretely, in the present situation, our trade-union strategy. How, in other words, do we intend ourselves to keep in contact with the broad proletarian masses, to interpret their needs, to focus and concretize their will, to aid the process of the proletariat's development towards its emancipation – which continues, in spite of all the repression and violence of the disgraceful fascist tyranny?

We are, *as a matter of principle*, against the creation of new trade unions. In all capitalist countries, the trade-union movement developed in a particular way, resulting in the creation and progressive development of a specific great organization which embodied the history, the tradition, the customs and the ways of thinking of the great majority of the proletarian masses. Every attempt made to organize revolutionary union members separately has failed in itself, and has served only to reinforce the hegemonic positions of the reformists in the major organization. What advantage did the syndicalists in Italy draw from the creation of the *Unione sindacale*? They only succeeded in influencing partially and episodically the mass of industrial workers, i.e. of the most revolutionary class of the working population. During the period which lasted from the assassination of Umberto I to the Libyan war, they won the leadership of broad rural masses in the Po valley and in Apulia, with one sole result. These masses, who had only just entered the sphere of the class struggle (in that period there was precisely a transformation of agriculture which increased the mass of landless labourers by about 50 per cent), distanced themselves ideologically from the factory proletariat. Anarchist syndicalists up to the Libyan war, i.e. during the period in which the proletariat became radicalized, they subsequently became reformists. After the armistice and up till the occupation of the factories, they made up the passive cannon-fodder whom the reformist leaders at every decisive juncture threw beneath the feet of the revolutionary vanguard.

The American example is still more typical and significant than that of Italy. No organization has reached the level of abject, counter-revolutionary servility reached by Gompers's AFL. But does this mean that the American workers were abject slaves of the bourgeoisie? No, certainly not. And yet they remained attached to the traditional organization. The IWW (revolutionary syndicalists) failed in their attempt to win the masses controlled by Gompers from outside. Detaching themselves from those masses, they were massacred by the white guards. By contrast, the movement led by comrade Foster within the AFL, with slogans which interpreted the real situation of the movement and the deepest feelings of the American workers, is winning one union after another and showing clearly how weak and unstable the power of the Gompers bureaucracy is.

Hence, we are as a matter of principle against the creation of new unions. The revolutionary elements represent the class as a whole, they are the most highly developed form of its consciousness, on condition that they remain with the mass of the class and share its errors, illusions and disappointments. If a decree of the reformist dictators compelled the revolutionaries to leave the CGL and organize themselves separately (which, of course, cannot be excluded), the new organization would have to present itself as being – and really be – guided by the sole aim of achieving its reintegration; of achieving once again unity between the class and its most conscious vanguard.

The CGL as a whole still represents the Italian working class. But what is the present system of relations between the working class and the Confederation? Answering this question accurately, in my view, amounts to finding the concrete basis for our trade-union work and hence establishing our function and our relations with the broad masses. The CGL, as a trade-union organization, has been reduced to a bare minimum, to perhaps one tenth of its numerical strength in 1920. But the reformist faction which leads the Confederation has kept its organizational cadres almost intact, and has kept its most active, intelligent and capable militants in the workplace: militants who – let us speak the truth openly – know how to work better than our comrades, with greater tenacity and perseverance. By contrast, a great part, indeed almost all, of the revolutionary elements who in past years had acquired organizational and leadership capabilities and the habit of systematic work have been massacred or have emigrated or have been dispersed.

The working class is like a great army which has suddenly been deprived of all its junior officers. In such an army, it would be impossible to maintain discipline, cohesion, the will to fight, and unity of purpose, solely by virtue of the existence of a general staff. Every organization is an articulated whole, which only functions if there exists a proper numerical ratio between the mass base and the leaders. We do not have the cadres, we do not have the links, we do not have the services to spread our influence over the broad mass of union members, to strengthen it and to make it once again an effective instrument of revolutionary struggle. The reformists are in a far better condition that we are from this point of view, and they exploit their situation skilfully.

The factory continues to exist and naturally organizes the workers, groups them, puts them into contact with one another. The process of production has kept its 1919–20 level, characterized by a more and more obstructive role of capitalism and hence by a more and more decisive importance of the worker. The increase in cost prices, caused by the need to keep 500,000 fascist thugs permanently mobilized, is certainly not a brilliant proof that capitalism has won back its industrial youth. The worker is thus naturally strong inside the factory; he is concentrated and organized inside the factory. He is, however, isolated, dispersed, weak outside the factory.

In the period before the imperialist war, it was the opposite relationship which existed. The worker was isolated inside the factory and was socialized outside. He exerted pressure from outside to obtain better factory legislation, to win shorter working hours and conquer industrial freedom.

The working-class factory is today represented by the internal commission.[87] The question is at once asked: why do the capitalists and fascists, who sought to destroy the trade unions, not also destroy the internal commissions? Why, while the trade union has lost ground organizationally under the pressure of reaction, has the internal commission by contrast enlarged its organizational sphere? It is a fact that in almost all Italian factories the following has occurred: there is one single internal commission, and all the workers – not just the unionized ones – vote in elections for it. The entire working class is therefore organized today by the internal commissions, which have thus definitively lost their strictly corporate character. This, objectively, is a great achievement of the most far-reaching significance. It serves to indicate that, despite everything, in pain and beneath the oppression of the mailed heel of the fascist mercenaries, the working class – even if in a molecular fashion – is developing towards unity and a greater organizational homogeneity.

Why have the capitalists and fascists allowed, and why do they continue to allow, such a situation to arise and persist? For capitalism and fascism, it is necessary that the working class should be deprived of its historical function as leader of the other oppressed classes of the population (peasants, especially in the South and the Islands; urban and rural petty bourgeois). It is necessary, in other words, to destroy organizations that are external to the factory and territorially centralized (unions and parties), since they exercise a revolutionary influence on all the oppressed and remove from the government the democratic basis of its power. But the capitalists, for industrial reasons, cannot want all forms of organization to be destroyed. In the factory, discipline and the smooth flow of production is only possible if there exists at least a minimum degree of constitutionality, a minimum degree of consent on the part of the workers.

The most intelligent fascists, such as Mussolini, are the first to be convinced that their "supra-class" ideology is incapable of expanding beyond the sphere of that petty-bourgeois stratum which, having no function in production, has no consciousness of social antagonisms. Mussolini is convinced that the working class will never lose its revolutionary consciousness, and believes it is necessary to allow a minimal degree of organization. Holding the trade-union organizations within very narrow limits through terror, means giving power in the Confederation to the reformists. It is necessary that the Confederation should exist in embryonic form, and be grafted onto a scattered system of internal commissions, in such a way that the reformists control the whole working class, are the representatives of the whole working class.

This is the Italian situation, and this is the system of relations which exists today in our country between the proletarian class and its organizations. The implications for our tactics are clear:

1. To work in the factory to build revolutionary groups which control the internal commissions and push them continually to enlarge their sphere of activity;
2. To work to create links between factories, and to impress upon the present situation a movement which marks the natural course of

development of factory organization: from the internal commission to the factory council.

Only in this way will we remain on the terrain of reality, in close contact with the broad masses. Only in this way, through effective work in the hottest crucible of working-class life, will we succeed in recreating our organizing cadres; in drawing forth from the broad masses the capable, conscious elements, filled with revolutionary ardour because they are aware of their own value and importance – which cannot be eliminated – in the world of production.

Signed Antonio Gramsci, *Lo Stato operaio*, 18 October 1923.

45. WHAT IS TO BE DONE?

Dear Friends of the *Voce*,

I have read in *Voce*, no. 10 (15 September) the interesting discussion between comrade G.P. of Turin and comrade S.V.[88] Is the discussion closed? Might one ask that the discussion remain open for many more issues, and invite all young workers of good will to take part in it, expressing their opinions on the subject sincerely and with intellectual honesty?

How the Problem should be Posed

I shall start off, and I shall certainly say that, at least in my view, comrade S. V. has not posed the problem properly and has fallen into certain errors that are extremely serious from his own point of view.

Why was the Italian working class defeated? Because it was not united? Because fascism succeeded in defeating the Socialist Party, the traditional party of the toiling population, not only physically but also ideologically? Because the Communist Party did not develop rapidly in the years 1921–2, and did not succeed in grouping around itself the majority of the proletariat and the peasant masses?

Comrade S.V. does not pose these questions. He replies to all the anguished concern expressed in comrade G.P.'s letter with the assertion that the existence of a true revolutionary party would have been enough, and that its future organization will be enough in the future, when the working class has recovered the possibility of movement. But is all that true, or at least in what sense and within what limits is it true?

Comrade S.V. suggests to comrade G.P. that he should not go on thinking in fixed schemas, but should think in other schemas – which he does not specify. But it is in fact essential to specify. So here is what seems immediately necessary to do. Here is what the "beginning" of the working class's task must be. It is necessary to carry out a pitiless self-criticism of our weakness, and to begin by asking ourselves why we lost, who we were, what we wanted, where we wished to go. But there is also something else which must be done first (one always finds that the beginning always has another . . . beginning!): it is necessary to fix the criteria, the principles, the ideological basis for our very criticism.

Does the Working Class have its own Ideology?

Why have the Italian proletarian parties always been weak from a revolutionary point of view? Why have they failed, when they should have passed from words to action? They did not know the situation in which they had to operate, they did not know the terrain on which they should have given battle. Just think: in more than thirty years of life, the Socialist Party has not produced a single book which studies the socio-economic structure of Italy. There does not exist a single book which studies the Italian political parties, their class links, their significance. Why did reformism sink such deep roots in the Po valley? Why is the Catholic Popular Party more successful in northern and central than in southern Italy, where the population after all is more backward and should therefore more easily follow a confessional party? Why are the big landowners in Sicily separatists but not the peasants, whereas in Sardinia the peasants are separatists and not the big landowners? Why did the reformism of De Felice, Drago, Tasca di Cutò and their ilk develop in Sicily and not elsewhere?[89] Why was there an armed struggle between fascists and nationalists in southern Italy which did not occur elsewhere?

We do not know Italy. Worse still: we lack the proper instruments for knowing Italy as it really is. It is therefore almost impossible for us to make predictions, to orient ourselves, to establish lines of action which have some likelihood of being acurate. There exists no history of the Italian working class. There exists no history of the peasant class. What was the importance of the 1898 events in Milan?[90] What lesson did they furnish? What was the importance of the 1904 strike in Milan?[91] How many workers know that then, for the first time, the necessity of the proletarian dictatorship was explicitly asserted? What significance has syndicalism had in Italy? Why has it been successful among agricultural workers and not among the industrial workers? What is the importance of the Republican party?[92] Why are there republicans wherever there are anarchists? What is the importance and the meaning of the phenomenon of syndicalist elements going over to nationalism before the Libyan War, and the repetition of the phenomenon on a larger scale with fascism?

It is enough to pose these questions to perceive that we are completely ignorant, that we are without orientation. It seems that no one in Italy has ever thought, ever studied, ever done any research. It seems that the Italian working class has never had its own conception of the life, the history, the development of human society. And yet the working class does have its own conception: historical materialism. And yet the working class has had great teachers (Marx, Engels) who have shown how to examine facts and situations, and how to draw from one's examination guides to action.

This is our weakness, this is the main reason for the defeat of the Italian revolutionary parties: not to have had an ideology; not to have disseminated it among the masses; not to have strengthened the consciousness of their militants with certitudes of a moral and psychological character. What wonder that some workers have become fascists? What wonder if S.V. himself says at one point: "who knows, even we, if we were convinced, might become fascists"? (Such statements should not be made even as jokes, even as hypotheses for the sake of argument.) What wonder, if another article in the same issue of *Voce* says: "We are not anti-clerical"? Are we not anti-clerical? What does that mean? That we are not anti-clerical in a masonic sense, from the rationalist point of view of the bourgeois? It is necessary to say this, but it is also necessary to say that we, the working class, are indeed anti-clerical, inasmuch as we are materialists; that we have a conception of the world which transcends all religions and all philosophies born hitherto on the terrain of class-divided society. Unfortunately . . . we do not have that conception, and this is the reason for all these theoretical errors, which also have their reflection in practice and have so far led us to defeat and to fascist oppression.

The Beginning . . . of the Beginning!

What is to be done then? Where to begin? Well: in my view it is necessary to begin precisely from this. From a study of the doctrine which belongs to the working class, which is the philosophy of the working class, which is the sociology of the working class: from a study of historical materialism, from a study of Marxism. Here is an immediate task for the groups of friends of the *Voce*: to meet, buy books, organize lessons and discussions on this subject, form solid criteria for research and study, and criticize the past – in order to be stronger in the future and win.

The *Voce* should, in every possible way, help this attempt – by publishing courses of lessons and discussions, by giving rational bibliographical information, by replying to readers' questions, by stimulating their good will. The less that has been done up till now, the more it is necessary to do, and with the greatest possible rapidity. Destiny is pressing in upon us: the Italian petty bourgeoisie, which had placed its hopes and its faith in fascism, is daily seeing its house of cards collapse. Fascist ideology has lost its capacity to expand, and indeed is losing ground. The first dawn of the new proletarian day is appearing anew.

>Signed Giovanni Masci, *Voce della Gioventù*, 1 November 1923.

46. GRAMSCI TO SCOCCIMARRO
(Vienna, 5 January 1924)

Dear Negri,

I have received your letter of 25 December and Palmi's of the 29th.[93] I will reply to both together. Show this letter to Palmi, and if possible to Lanzi [Tresso] and Ferri [Leonetti] as well.

I will outline to you the reasons why I persist in regarding it as impossible that I should sign the manifesto, even after having read the second draft of it. For the manifesto, there exists neither the Enlarged Executive of February 1922, nor that of June 1922, nor the Fourth World Congress, nor the Executive of June 1923. For the manifesto, history finishes with the Third World Congress, and it is to the Third Congress that we must attach ourselves in order to proceed. All this may be plausible as the personal opinion of a single comrade and as the expression of a little group. It is simply crazy as the line of a majority faction which has administered the party since the Third Congress and still continues to administer it. It is crazy and absurd because at all the Enlarged Executives and at the Fourth Congress the representatives of the majority have always made the most extensive declarations in favour of centralism, of the single international party, etc. At the Rome Congress it was stated that the Theses on Tactics would be voted, on a consultative basis, but that after the discussion at the Fourth World Congress they would be annulled and not spoken of again. In the first half of March 1922, the Comintern Executive published a special statement in which the party's theses on tactics were refuted and rejected, and an article in the Statutes of the International says that every deliberation of the Executive must become law for the individual sections. That is what needs to be said on the formal and juridical aspect of the question. Which has its importance. Indeed, after the publication of the manifesto the majority could be totally disqualified and even expelled from the Comintern. If the Italian political situation did not prevent it, I think that expulsion would come. By the standards of the conception of the party which derives from the manifesto, expulsion should be obligatory. If one of our local federations did only half of what the majority of the party wants to do *vis-à-vis* the Comintern, its dissolution would be immediate. I do not want, by signing the manifesto, to appear a complete clown.

But I do not agree with the substance of the manifesto either. I have a different conception of the party, its function, and the relations which should be established between it and the masses outside any party, i.e. between it and the population in general. I absolutely do not believe that the tactics which have been developed by the Enlarged Executive meeting and the Fourth Congress are mistaken. Neither in their general approach, nor in significant details. I think the same is true for you and for Palmi, and therefore I cannot understand how you can so light-heartedly set sail in a vessel that is so unsafe. It seems to me that you are in the same state of mind that I was in during the period of the Rome Congress. Perhaps because in the meantime I have been far away from the party's internal work, this state of mind has disappeared. In reality, it has disappeared for other reasons as well. And one of the most important is this: one absolutely cannot make compromises with Amadeo. He is too forceful a personality, and has such a deep conviction of being in the right that to think of ensnaring him with a compromise is absurd. He will continue to struggle, and at every opportunity will always represent his theses unchanged.

I think that Palmi is wrong to believe that the moment is not propitious for us to begin an independent activity and create a new formation which only in a "territorial" sense would appear to be of the centre. It is undeniable that the conception of the party's function which has been the official one up till now has led to a crystallization in purely organizational debates, and hence to a real political passivity. Instead of centralism, we have managed to create an unhealthy minority movement; and if one speaks to comrades in exile, to persuade them to participate more actively in the party's external activity, one gets the impression that the party is really very little to them, and that they would be willing to give very little for it. The experience of the Petrograd School is very telling.[94] In reality, I am convinced that the main force which holds the party together is the prestige and ideals of the International, not the bonds which the specific action of the party has succeeded in creating. And we have created a minority precisely on this terrain, and allowed the minority to be the one to adorn itself with the title of true representative of the International in Italy.

It is precisely today, when it has been decided to take the discussion before the masses, that it is necessary to take up a definitive position and specific lineaments of our own. So long as the discussions took place within a tiny circle, and the problem was one of organizing five, six, ten individuals into a homogeneous body, it was still possible (although even then it was not entirely correct) to reach individual compromises and leave aside certain questions which were not immediately relevant. Today it is a question of going before the masses, discussing, bringing mass formations into being which will not just live for a few hours. Well, it is necessary that this should be done without ambiguity, without leaving anything unsaid; that these formations should be organic ones, that can develop and become the whole party. Therefore, I will not sign the manifesto.

I do not know yet exactly what to do. It is not the first time that I have found myself in this situation, and Palmi must remember how I split even with him and Umberto, in August 1920. Then it was I who wanted to maintain relations with the left rather than with the right, whereas Palmi and Umberto had rejoined Tasca, who had already split with us in January. Today it seems that the opposite is happening. But in reality the situation is very different. And just as then within the Socialist Party it was necessary to depend on the abstentionists if one wished to create the basic nucleus of the future party, so today it is necessary to struggle against the extremists if one wishes the party to develop and stop being nothing more than an external faction of the Socialist Party. In fact, the two extremisms, that of the right and that of the left, by imprisoning the party in a single and solitary discussion on relations with the Socialist Party, have reduced it to a secondary role. Probably I shall remain alone. I will write a report in which I will combat both of them, in my capacity as a member of the CC of the party and of the Comintern Executive. I will accuse both of them of the same fault, and take the doctrine and tactics of the Comintern as the basis for an action programme for our activity in the future. That is what I wanted to say. I assure you that no arguments from all of you will succeed in shifting me from this position. Naturally, I want to go on collaborating closely with you and I think that the experience of the past years has been of use to all of us – at least to teach us that within the ambit of the party one may have different opinions and nevertheless go on working together with the highest degree of mutual trust.

Urge those comrades who are within your reach to hurry up and send the articles I have requested.[95] Palmi should immediately do me a "Battle of Ideas" of at least three columns (the whole of the back page). I do not know what book or set of books or other publications to propose to him. He could make a critique of the viewpoint upheld by

Gobetti's *Rivoluzione liberale*,[96] showing how in reality fascism has posed a very crude, sharp dilemma in Italy: that of the permanent revolution, and of the impossibility not only of changing the form of the State, but even of changing the government, other than by armed force. And he could examine the new current that has emerged among the war-veterans and crystallized around *Italia libera*.[97] I think that the war-veterans' movement, in general, since it is really the formation of the first secular party of the peasantry especially in central and southern Italy, has had an immense importance. It has helped to overturn the old political structure of Italy and to bring about an extreme weakening of the bourgeoisie's parliamentary hegemony, and thus the triumph of the fascist petty bourgeoisie – reactionary and inconclusive, and yet full of utopian aspirations and dreams of palingensis. What precise significance does the birth of the *Italia libera* movement have in this general context? This is beyond me, and I would be really glad for Palmi to enlighten me too about it.

Naturally Palmi will have to be one of the pillars of the review and send general articles which make the rebirth of the old *Ordine Nuovo* possible in a substantive sense too. I have still omitted to make any proposals for Valle's [Tasca's] collaboration, because I think that he will want to have a free hand in this. Tell him, however, that I would like to have a synthetic article by him on the question of the Gentile school reform. Synthetic has, of course, a logical meaning, and does not refer to the length in metres. The article could even be one of five columns and become the central nucleus of an issue.

And what is Lanzi doing? He too should contribute. Especially on the trade-union question. Write to him and warn him that I want to know something about his activity and his opinions on what is going on.

Greetings

Gramsci

47. GRAMSCI TO TERRACINI
(Vienna, 12 January 1924)

Dear Urbani,

I am replying more specifically to your letter in which you pose the question of my position in terms which are very exaggerated and to a great extent incorrect.[98]

1. Your memory seems very fallible. In private conversation with you, I told you that I was "as a matter of principle" opposed to the publication of a manifesto polemicizing with the International. You assured me that the amendments made to the original which I had read were so numerous and of such a character as to completely change its nature, making it into a simple historical account of the events which have taken place in the last years, as a necessary and indispensable basis for any fruitful discussion.

2. I only saw the amended manifesto here. Not having the original to hand, I am not able to give a philological judgement on the extent of the amendments that have been made. Politically, the amendments have not altered the situation much. The absolute rejection of the development in the Comintern's tactics since the Third Congress remains. The position taken up by our party as a potential centre for all the lefts which may be formed in the international field remains, objectively, unaltered. There remains the spirit of fundamental opposition to the tactic of the united front, of the workers' and peasants' government and of a whole series of deliberations in the organizational field prior to the Third Congress or approved by the Third Congress itself.

3. From what I told you in the conversation we had immediately after your arrival in Moscow, it was clear that I would not be able to sign the second draft of the manifesto either. Your astonishment, therefore, seems to me very out of place. There is much more justification for my great astonishment at the extremely simple terms in which you and Negri, who were present at the June Plenum and made public statements, view the future. You must remember that in Moscow, in the conversation we three had with Tasca, we developed the following line of argument with him: the internal life of a communist party cannot be conceived as the arena for a parliamentary type of struggle, in which the

various factions fulfil a function which is determined, like that of the different parliamentary parties, by their different origins, which in turn depend on the different classes in society. In the party, one single class is represented and the different positions which from time to time become currents and factions are determined by divergent assessments of the events which are taking place; they therefore cannot become solidified into a permanent structure. The CC of the party may have had a given position in given conditions of time and context; but it can change this position if the time and the context are not what they were previously.

The minority presents the conflicts as something permanent, and seeks to reconstruct a general mentality characteristic of the majority which explains this permanent process. It has thus posed, poses and will continue to pose the majority as being in continuous conflict with the Comintern – i.e. with the majority of the revolutionary proletariat, and especially with the Russian proletariat which has made the revolution. In reality, it is raising the first elements of a question which should lead with certainty to the expulsion of the majority of the party from the Comintern. But we deny any basis for this abstractly dialectical procedure of the minority, and demonstrate by our actions that we are on the terrain of the Comintern; that we apply and accept its principles and its tactics; that we are not becoming crystallized in an attitude of permanent opposition, but know how to change our positions as the relation of forces changes and the problems to be solved are posed on another basis.

If, despite this, the minority continues to adopt the same attitude towards the majority as it has done hitherto, it will be we who will have to see whether there is not a basis there for showing that the minority is a result of the liquidatory tendencies which appear in every revolutionary movement after a defeat, and which are inherent in the waverings and panic characteristic of the petty bourgeoisie, i.e. of a class that is not that upon which our party is based. It will not be difficult to show how the minority's orthodoxy *vis-à-vis* the Comintern's tactics is only a mask in order to get the leadership of the party. An examination of the make-up of the groups which form the minority gives us an easy way of showing that it is basically opposed to the Comintern, and that it will not be long before it shows this true nature.

This is how we spoke to Tasca, and I remember that I said several times to you and Negri that I considered this line of argument not as a manoeuvre to intimidate Tasca momentarily and weaken him at the

Plenum, but as a new platform on which the majority of the party should resolutely place itself, in order to liquidate the past honourably and enable itself to solve its internal problems. And I remember that you and Negri were in agreement on this.

4. I think that you are still in agreement, and therefore I cannot find any explanation for your present position. The truth is that we are at a great historical turning-point of the Italian Communist movement. This is the moment in which it is necessary, with great determination and extreme precision, to lay the new basis for the party's development. The manifesto certainly does not represent this new basis. It provides every justification for viewing the minority as a faction which saw things correctly at the Fourth Congress and the Plenum, mistrusting the goodwill and sincerity of the majority and making the latter appear like a grouping of petty political adventurers who time and again save their positions by wretched tricks. Not even the most recent events in our party (the Bombacci affair authentically interpreted by the statements of Belloni and Remondino)[99] will succeed in saving us. In the present situation, which continues to be objectively revolutionary in Germany while it is extremely confused in Italy, the Comintern cannot peacefully allow there to be formed in the international sphere a majority of parties which are in opposition and which demand a re-discussion of all the decisions taken since the Third Congress. To allow this would mean strengthening enormously the extremist tendencies which have emerged in the German Communist Party, and would thus delay the latter's reorganization. You too often forget that our party has responsibilities of an international character, and that every position we take up has repercussions in the other countries, often in unhealthy and irrational forms.

5. I persist in my attitude, because I consider it the most appropriate and correct. Your letter only confirms me in this decision, especially because of what you say about the bridge which you three have represented in this last period. It is necessary for you, Negri and Palmi to decide in favour of clarity too; to decide on the position which is nearest to your innermost convictions and not to your role as 'bridges'. In that way, we shall be able to accomplish a great deal together and give our party all the development which the situation permits. It is useless to wish to preserve a formal factional unity which continually constrains us to equivocation and half measures. If Amadeo wants to persist in his attitude, as he certainly will, perhaps that will be a good thing, on condition that his stance is that of a single individual or a small

group. If, on the other hand, with your agreement it becomes the stance of the majority, this would compromise our party irretrievably.

I have received the two packets of material which you sent me. They were open. I would therefore ask you to provide better wrappings, so that there are no losses. Try to send me the rest as quickly as possible; if not all at once, at least in small successive doses. You have certainly seen the proposal I made to the Exec. for the publication of a quarterly journal in a large format (250–300 pages every three months) which could be called *Critica proletaria*.[100] I think that the proposal will be accepted, and that it could be carried out within a few months. I have worked out the contents of the first issue as follows:

1. Programmatic manifesto (which I could write)
2. Bordiga: problems of proletarian tactics
3. Graziadei: the accumulation of capital according to Rosa Luxemburg
4. Tasca: the problem of the schools and the Gentile reform
5. Scoccimarro: perspectives for a workers' and peasants' government in Italy
6. Longobardi or Pastore: the Italian industrial structure
7. Terracini: the programme of the Communist International
8. Togliatti: the problem of the Vatican
9. News reports: economic, financial, political, military, international, trade-union, on working-class life
10. Book reviews (The authors of the various articles should also send a critical/bibliographical survey of publications on the subjects with which they are dealing.)
11. Political diary
12. Index of reviews and newspapers.

You should immediately set to work to write your article, which must consist of at least twenty pages in the format of a review like *Nuova Antologia*. In it, you must make a study of the draft programmes that have been presented and the discussions which these provoked. I warn you that especially in Russia there has been a pretty extensive discussion. You could get the necessary references from Bukharin, and get the Russian material translated by the Press Office. It would be a good idea for the translations to be made in several copies and sent to parties which have set up commissions to discuss the programme, but which lack the basic elements for the discussion. One could pose the question to the secretariat. But your article will have to be ready within two months at most.

Warm greetings to yourself and to Alma

Masci

P.S. It would be a good thing to have your article on the situation in Germany at once, to be the main item in the first issue of *L'Ordine Nuovo*.

48. GRAMSCI TO TOGLIATTI
(Vienna, 27 January 1924)

Dear Palmi,

Since the letter you sent me just after leaving prison, I have received nothing more from you.[101] I think that you have been shown my two letters, one to Negri and the other to Urbani, in which I expressed at greater length my views on the present situation in the party and on the solutions which I consider appropriate to resolve its problems. I am still waiting for a letter from you that will refute me or say that I am right. Today I want to talk to you about a specific problem which I consider fundamental in the present situation, and which provides me with a touchstone for judging all the party's activity and the methods which have characterized the comrades who have led it up till now: the activity which (so that we may understand one another) I shall call that belonging to comrade Tito.[102]

Two key episodes justify me in asserting that in this field there has existed, and still does exist, a great confusion and lack of organization. Well, if it is theoretically correct to accuse the minority of being, at least partially, liquidatory, because it does not understand and enormously underestimates the importance of this work in the present situation, it is nevertheless necessary (for the sake of truth, and because only by knowing the truth precisely can one remedy the errors and deficiencies and restore the organization to health) to say that neither has the majority – in the person of those members of it who have had the responsibility – been able to do what was necessary, so that *de facto* even if not in theory it too has been liquidatory.

So far as the first episode is concerned, I think you know the disagreeable events of last March in Moscow, which had consequences for me personally which were far from brilliant. After the Executive had been arrested in the persons of Amadeo and Ruggero [Grieco], we waited in vain for about a month and a half for information that would establish precisely how things had gone, what limits the police action had had in destroying the organization, and what series of measures the Executive remaining at liberty had taken in order to renew organizational links and reconstitute the party apparatus. Instead, after a first letter written immediately after the arrests and in which it was said that all was destroyed and that the central leadership of the party had to be reconstituted *ab imis*,[103] we received no further concrete information, but merely polemical letters on the question of fusion, written in a style which seemed all the more arrogant and irresponsible in that the author had with his first letter created the impression that the party only continued to exist in his person.[104]

There was a stormy session of the commission for technical work, with the participation of a member of the Russian Central Committee who had been in Italy from a month before the fascists came to power to a fortnight afterwards.[105] The question was brutally posed of what the Italian party's central leadership was worth, and of the measures to be taken in view of its absence and its failure to make provision for reorganization. The letters which had been received were harshly criticized, and I was asked what I was going to propose. I will not hide from you that I too shared the disastrous impression caused by the letters, and since I did not have any other material at my disposal, I could not but recognize that the criticisms were justified and more than justified. I therefore went so far as to say that if it was thought that the situation was really such as it objectively appeared from the material available, it would be better to finish things once and for all and reorganize the party from outside, with new elements nominated by the International. I can tell you that in another similar situation I would again make the same proposal, and would have no fear of unleashing all the thunderbolts in the universe.

In reality, the Russian comrades are less centralist than it seems. Perhaps too they had, by other means, more information than I did, and were merely manoeuvring to produce a particular situation. Thus the upshot was that it was merely decided to send a letter to the party which, on the basis of the correspondence from Italy, indicated the measures to be taken and the course to be followed. This letter was answered by Tito with a long account from which it emerged: that the party's internal apparatus had remained completely intact; that the centre represented by Tito had not ceased functioning even for an instant; and that through its liaison, the entire organization had remained alive and vigorous. The scandal became still greater. Whom to believe? Tito, who represented a subordinate and only partially controlled activity, and who could therefore unless known personally be taken for just some confidence-trickster; or those who held the main political posts in the party, who presumably could not be ignorant of the situation and were therefore more believed when they said that all was destroyed? It is also necessary to consider that, in the history of revolutionary parties, the aspect represented by Tito's activity is always that which remains most obscure and lends itself most easily to blackmail, waste and swindles. When Tito came to Moscow, he was clearly furious about the letter he had received; but his fury abated when he was given the party's correspondence to read, and it was shown him, pencil in hand, that the phrases considered by him as offensive and without substance had been taken word for word from that correspondence. It then became clear – and Tito admitted – that the two centres operated independently of each other: without any liaison; without the one knowing at least the general lines of the other's activity; and thus with one defaming and discrediting the other. Since my statements had been placed in the minutes, and they had mortified Tito who thought that they were directed at him personally, it was not hard for me to show that although I had from time to time participated in commissions in which his activity was discussed, I had never had any information about it, did not have at my disposal any concrete element to criticize the information of the political centre, and therefore could not have taken any other attitude from the point of view of the narrower interests of the Italian movement.

Unfortunately, this situation has not changed much since. Recently, replying to a reprimand from the budget commission because the party had not handed over to the U.I. [Clandestine Bureau] the full amount which had been allocated to it, the Executive replied that it looked after a great part of the Bureau's activity itself and therefore spent its funds. All that is absurd, and against the most elementary norms of good organization. I have become convinced to my own cost that the so-highly praised and lauded centralism of the Italian party comes down in reality to a very ordinary lack of any division of labour, or precise allocation of responsibilities and spheres of authority. In the conversations I had with Tito, I got the definite impression that he too to a great extent shared this assessment, and is not a little demoralized by the scant regard with which his activity is treated and maltreated. Everyone takes initiatives without warning the centre responsible, which has often already initiated work along the same lines which it has to discontinue. All continuity of initiatives ends by disappearing. Too many people end up knowing the most highly confidential matters; every possibility of control or checking vanishes. People are introduced into the movement whose seriousness and responsibility have not been checked out in advance in any way. I had the impression that Tito was enormously tired and disheartened by this whole state of affairs, which is why he has tried so persistently to get himself put on leave. The question is a very serious one, and if it is not resolved according to good organizational criteria the situation could become catastrophic.

I am convinced that the situation of our party from the point of view of its legal existence will get worse and worse. The more the constitutional opposition to fascism, centred upon the Reformist party, endangers the real basis of Mussolini's government, the more the lives of our leaders and the security of our organization will be in danger. The fascists will seek to resolve every situation by a hunt for communists, and by raising the spectre of a revolutionary uprising. Constructing a good technical apparatus – with its cogs made up of picked elements, highly experienced, highly disciplined, tried and tested, sufficiently cool of nerve not to lose their heads in any emergency – is becoming a matter of life or death for us. To achieve this, it is really necessary to liquidate much of the party's past situation, with its habitual devil-may-care attitudes, failure to fix responsibilities precisely and clearly, failure to check and immediately punish acts of weakness and irresponsibility. The party must be centralized; but centralization means first and foremost organization and demarcation. It means that when a decision has been taken it cannot be modified by anybody, even one of those attached to centralism, and that no one can create *faits accomplis*.

I will not hide from you that in these two years I have spent out of Italy, I have become very pessimistic and very wary. I have myself often been in a very difficult situation because of the general state of the party: not so far as my personal position is concerned (about which I really do not give a damn, and which anyway I do not think has suffered very much: at most I have involuntarily won the reputation of being a fox of devilish cunning), but in my position as representative of the party, often called upon to resolve questions which would have an immediate effect upon the Italian movement. Having gone to Moscow without being briefed on even one tenth of the questions of the day, I had to pretend to know, and had to carry out unheard of acrobatic feats in order not to demonstrate how irresponsibly representatives were nominated, without any provisions for the journey other than Doctor Grillo's motto: "May God send you all the best".[106]

I tolerated many things because the situation in the party and the movement was such, that even the least appearance of a split in the ranks of the majority would have been disastrous and would have given oxygen to the disoriented, directionless minority. My conditions of health too, which did not allow me to work intensively or with intensive continuity, prevented me from taking up a position which would have required, apart from the burden of a general political responsibility, also the necessity for an intensive activity. The situation today has greatly changed. The questions have been brought out into the open, certainly not through my fault, but partly because people were not willing to follow in time certain suggestions I made and so resolve things automatically. Therefore, I thought it necessary to take the stand I have taken and which I will maintain to the end. I do not know what you are doing at the present time. Once you wrote to me that as soon as I arrived here you would try to make a trip so that we could exchange ideas. If, as I think, you are now provisionally replacing Tito, it would be a good idea if you could find the time to come. There are so many things we could talk about and it might perhaps not be useless.

I have not yet received any definite information concerning the publication of O.N., and although I have written to many comrades I have not yet had any articles as contributions. However, I will start sending the material this week. If necessary, I will put the first issues together entirely myself, while waiting for the contributors to stir themselves. The first issue will be largely devoted to comrade Lenin. I will write the main article, and try to bring out the main features of his personality as a revolutionary leader. I will translate a biography, and make a little anthology of his principal views on the Italian situation in 1920. In the last letter I sent to Negri, I wrote that I was counting not just on your general collaboration, but on a specific contribution from you that would consist in supplying material in each issue for the rubric "Battle of Ideas". I suggested Gobetti's journal and the *Italia libera* movement as the two first subjects to be dealt with. I now think that for the first issue it would be more appropriate for you to make a survey for the rubric of Lenin's books and pamphlets published in Italian, incorporating this survey within an assessment of the function which Lenin's work and prestige have had in Italy over the last years. In any case, I will inform Ruggero that you are permanently in charge of putting this rubric together, and that your material can be put to press without having to make the return journey between here and Italy. If I have any material for the rubric, I will send it you so that you can see it and arrange your work accordingly. I am waiting for a letter from you giving your opinions on the various questions I have discussed in this letter and the others which have been passed on to you.

Fraternal greetings
Gramsci

P.S. Naturally, I do not think that, in all I have outlined to you, only questions of organization are involved. The situation of the P., which is reflected in its organization, is the consequence of a general political conception. The problem is thus a political one, and involves not just the present activity but that in the future. Today, it is a problem of relations on the one hand between the party leaders and the mass of members, on the other between the party and the proletariat. Tomorrow, it will be a vaster problem, which will influence the organization and solidity of the workers' State. Not to pose the question to its full extent today would mean going back to the Socialist tradition, and waiting to differentiate oneself until the revolution is at the door, or even until it is already in course. We made a serious mistake in 1919 and 1920 in not attacking the Socialist leadership more resolutely, even if this meant running the risk of expulsion, by constituting a faction that could move out from Turin and be something more than the propaganda *L'Ordine Nuovo* could make. Today, it is not a question of going to such extremes; but, with the relationship reversed, the situation is almost identical and must be confronted with determination and courage.

49. GRAMSCI TO LEONETTI
(Vienna, 28 January 1924)

Dear Ferri,

Your letter pleased me very much, because it showed that I am not alone in having certain anxieties and in considering certain solutions to our problems necessary. I agree almost completely with the analysis which you have made. Unfortunately, however, the situation is much more serious and difficult than you could imagine, and therefore I think that a certain prudence is necessary. I am convinced that Amadeo is capable of going to the utmost extremes, if he sees that the situation in the party is becoming unfavourable to his cause. He is strongly and resolutely convinced of being in the right and of representing the most vital interests of the Italian proletarian movement, and he will not retreat even before the possibility of being expelled from the International. But something nevertheless must be done, and will have to be done, by us.

I do not share your view that we should revive our Turin group formed around O.N. In the last two years, I have seen how the campaign waged by *Avanti!* and the socialists against us has influenced and left deep traces even among the present members of our party. In Moscow, the exiles were divided into two camps on this point, and at times the arguments turned into actual brawls or scuffles. Moreover, Tasca belongs to the minority – having taken to its ultimate conclusions the position he assumed back in January 1920, and which culminated in the polemic between me and him.[107] Togliatti cannot make up his mind, as was always somewhat his way: the "forceful" personality of Amadeo has strongly affected him and keeps him in a half-way position, in a state of indecision which seeks justification in purely juridical quibbles. Umberto I believe to be fundamentally even more extremist that Amadeo, because he has absorbed his conceptions but does not possess his intellectual strength, practical sense or organizational ability. How then could our group come back to life? It would appear nothing but a clique assembled round me as an individual for bureaucratic reasons. The basic ideas themselves which characterized O.N.'s activity are today, or would be, anachronistic. Apparently, at least today, the question takes the form of problems of organization and especially of party organization. I say apparently, because in fact the problem is still the same: that of relations between the central leadership and the mass of the party, and between the party and the classes of the working population.

In 1919–20, we made extremely serious mistakes which ultimately we are paying for today. For fear of being called upstarts and careerists, we did not form a faction and organize this throughout Italy. We were not ready to give the Turin factory councils an autonomous directive centre, which could have exercised an immense influence throughout the country, for fear of a split in the unions and of being expelled prematurely from the Socialist Party. We should, or at least I will have to, say publicly that we made these mistakes, which have undoubtedly had grave repercussions. In reality, if after the April split we had taken up the position which I actually thought was necessary, perhaps we would have arrived at the occupation of the factories in different conditions, and would even have postponed this to a more propitious moment. Our merits are very much less than we have had to proclaim for propaganda and organizational reasons; we only succeeded – of course it is not a small thing – in bringing into being and organizing a strong mass movement, which gave our party the only real base which it has had in the past years. Today, the perspectives are different, and it is necessary scrupulously to avoid laying too much stress on the fact of the Turin tradition and the Turin group. One would end up in polemics of a personalized nature, aimed at securing an elder son's rights over an inheritance of words and memories.

From a practical point of view, I think I can influence the situation in the following way. If the manifesto of the so-called communist Left is published, and perhaps at this very moment it has already been published in the first issue of the revived *Stato Operaio*, I will write an article or a series of articles to explain why my signature does not appear on it, and to outline a short programme of practical tasks which the party must accomplish in the present situation. If a party conference is prepared and the discussion takes place internally, with only a minimal degree of publicity, I will draw up a kind of report for party functionaries and organizers, in which I will be more explicit and fuller. In any case, I consider it indispensable to avoid sharpening the polemic. I have seen how easy it is, with our temperament and with the sectarian and one-sided spirit proper to Italians, to arrive at the worst extremes and at a total rupture between the various comrades.

I would be grateful if you would write again to let me know about the main currents prevailing in the party and the attitude of the comrades whom I know, especially those from Turin.

50. GRAMSCI TO TOGLIATTI, TERRACINI AND OTHERS
(Vienna, 9 February 1924)

Dear Comrades,
I willingly accept the invitation addressed to me by com. Urbani to define, at least in broad outline, the reasons why I think it is necessary at this moment to bring about not merely a fundamental discussion before the mass of party members on our internal situation, but also a new alignment of the groups seeking leadership of the party. Reasons of expediency will, however, oblige me not to go too deeply into certain questions. I know the psychology that is widespread in our movement, and I know how the absence up till now of all internal polemics and of any vigorous attempt at self-criticism has left us too with an excessively obstinate and irascible cast of mind, which gets angry about every little thing.

The internal situation in the International. I am not at all convinced by the analysis made by Urbani concerning the new orientations supposedly emerging in the Comintern after the German events. Just as I did not believe a year ago that the International was moving to the right, as was the general view on our EC, so I do not believe today that it is moving to the left. The political nomenclature itself which com. Urbani uses seems to me absolutely mistaken and, to say the least, extremely superficial. So far as Russia is concerned, I have always known that in the topography of the factions and tendencies, Radek, Trotsky and Bukharin occupied a left position, Zinoviev, Kamenev and Stalin a right position, while Lenin was in the centre and acted as arbiter in the whole situation. This, of course, in current political language.

The so-called Leninist nucleus,[108] as is well known, maintains that these "topographic" positions are absolutely illusory and fallacious, and in its polemics it has continually demonstrated how the so-called lefts are nothing but Mensheviks, who cloak themselves in revolutionary language but are incapable of assessing the real relations of concrete forces. It is well known, in fact, that throughout the history of the Russian revolutionary movement Trotsky was politically to the left of the Bolsheviks, while on organizational questions he often made a bloc with or actually could not be distinguished from the Mensheviks. It is well known that in 1905, Trotsky already thought that a socialist and working-class revolution could take place in Russia, while the Bolsheviks only aimed to establish a political dictatorship of the proletariat allied to the peasantry that would serve as a framework for the development of capitalism, which was not to be touched in its economic structure. It is well known that in November 1917, while Lenin and the majority of the party had gone over to Trotsky's view and intended to take over not merely political power but also economic power, Zinoviev and Kamenev remained in the traditional party view and wanted a revolutionary coalition government with the Mensheviks and Social-Revolutionaries. They therefore left the CC of the party, published statements and articles in non-Bolshevik papers and came very close to a split. It is certain that if the *coup d'état* had failed in November 1917, as the German movement failed last October, Zinoviev and Kamenev would have detached themselves from the Bolshevik party and probably have gone over to the Mensheviks.

In the recent polemic which has broken out in Russia, it is clear that Trotsky and the opposition in general, in view of the prolonged absence of Lenin from the leadership of the party, have been greatly preoccupied about the danger of a return to the old mentality, which would be damaging to the revolution. Demanding a greater intervention of proletarian elements in the life of the party and a diminution of the powers of the bureaucracy, they want basically to ensure the socialist and proletarian character of the revolution, and to prevent a gradual transition to that democratic dictatorship – carapace for a developing capitalism – which was still the programme of Zinoviev and Co. in November 1917. Th's seems to me to be the situation in the Russian party, which is far more complicated and more substantive than is seen by Urbani; the only novelty is the passage of Bukharin to the Zinoviev, Kamenev, Stalin group.

So far as the German situation is concerned too, it seems to me that things happened rather differently from what Urbani has described. The two groups which are competing for the party leadership are both inadequate and incapable. The so-called minority group (Fischer–Maslov) undoubtedly represents the majority of the revolutionary proletariat; but it has neither the necessary organizational strength to lead a victorious revolution in Germany, nor a firm, stable line which can safeguard against still worse catastrophes than those of October. It is made up of elements who are new to party activity, who find themselves at the head of the opposition only because of the absence of leaders that is characteristic of Germany. The Brandler–Thalheimer group is stronger than the first ideologically and from the point of view of revolutionary experience, but it too has its weaknesses which are in certain respects much greater and more damaging than those of the other group. Brandler and Thalheimer have become revolutionary Talmudists. Wanting at all costs to find allies for the working class, they have ended up by forgetting the function of the working class itself. Wanting to win the labour aristocracy controlled by the social-democrats, they have thought they could do so not by developing a programme of an industrial nature, based on the Factory Councils and on workers' control, but by seeking to compete with the social-democrats on the terrain of democracy and thus leading the slogan of a workers' and peasants' government to degeneration.

Which of the two groups is on the right and which on the left? The question is rather Byzantine. It is natural that Zinoviev, who cannot attack Brandler and Thalheimer individually as incapable nonentities, should pose the question on a political level and seek in their errors the motives for accusing them of rightism. Moreover, the question becomes hellishly complicated. In certain respects, Brandler is a putschist more than a rightist – and one may even say that he is a putschist because he is a rightist. He had assured everybody that it was possible to carry out a *coup d'état* in Germany last October; had assured them that the party was technically ready for that. Zinoviev, however, was very pessimistic and did not think that the situation was politically ripe. In the discussions which took place on the Russian central leadership, Zinoviev was put in a minority and there appeared instead Trotsky's article: "Can the revolution be made on a predetermined day?".[109] In a discussion which took place at the Praesidium, this was said pretty clearly by Zinoviev.

Well, what is the nub of the question? Back in the month of July after the Hague Peace Conference, Radek came back to Moscow from a reconnaissance-trip and made a catastrophic report on the German situation. From this it appeared that the CC, led by Brandler, no longer enjoyed the confidence of the party; that the minority, although made up of incapable and in some cases shady elements, had the majority of the party with it and could have won a majority at the Leipzig Congress if centralism and Comintern support had not prevented this; and that the CC was only carrying out Moscow's decisions in a formal sense, since no systematic campaign had been waged for the united front or the workers' government, but merely newspaper articles of a theoretical and abstruse nature which were not read by the workers. It is obvious that after this report from Radek, the Brandler group started to move and in order to prevent the minority getting control prepared a new March 1921. If there were errors, they were committed by the Germans. The Russian comrades, i.e. Radek and Trotsky, made the mistake of believing the confidence tricks of Brandler and company; but in fact even in this case their position was not a right-wing but rather a left-wing one, laying them open to the accusation of putschism.

I have thought it worthwhile going into this subject at some length, because it is necessary to have a pretty clear orientation in this sphere. The Statutes of the International give the Russian party *de facto* hegemony over the world organization. It is, therefore, certain that one must know the different currents which appear in the Russian party in order to understand the orientations which at one time or another are imposed upon the International. It is, furthermore, necessary to take account of the more advanced situation of the Russian comrades, in that they have at their disposal not only the mass of information available to our organization, but also that which is available to the Russian State – which in certain areas is more abundant and more accurate. Their orientations are therefore grounded on a material basis which we will only be able to have after a revolution, and this gives their supremacy a permanent character which can hardly be eroded.

The manifesto of the communist Left. I now come to the questions which are more directly our own. Comrade Urbani writes that I have exaggerated a great deal in my judgments on the character of the manifesto. I still maintain that it is the beginning of an all-out fight against the International, and that it demands a revision of the entire tactical development since the Third Congress. Among the concluding points of the manifesto, the one under letter (b) says that it is necessary to bring about a discussion in the competent bodies of the International on the conditions of proletarian struggle in Italy during the last years, of wide scope and outside all contingent and ephemeral systematizations – which often stifle the examination and solution of the most important problems. What does this mean, except that one is asking for, and considers possible, a revision not only of the Comintern's tactics in Italy since the Third Congress, but also a discussion on the general principles upon which this tactic has been based?

It is not true that since the Third Congress, as is asserted in the last sentence of this section ('Communist Tactics in Italy'), the International has not said what it wanted to be done in Italy. In. No. 28 of the review *Internazionale comunista* there is published an open letter from the

International Executive to the CC of the PCI: a letter written towards the middle of March 1922, i.e. after the February Plenum.[110] In this letter, the entire conception of the theses on tactics presented to the Rome Congress is refuted and rejected and declared to be in complete disaccord with the resolutions of the Third Congress. In the letter, the following points in particular are dealt with: 1. the problem of winning the majority; 2. the situations in which battle becomes necessary and the possibilities for struggle; 3. the united front; 4. the slogan of a workers' government.

On the third of these points, the question of the united front in the trade-union field and in the political field is settled. In other words, it is said explicitly that the party must participate in mixed committees for struggle and agitation. On the fourth point, an attempt is made to trace an immediate tactical line for the Italian struggle, designed to lead to a workers' government. The letter ends with the following sentence: "It is preferable that the party should accept the theses worked out by the Third Congress and the February Plenum and renounce its own theses, rather than present the theses in question, which would compel the Executive to fight openly and in the most energetic fashion the conceptions of the Italian C.C." I do not know if after this letter from the Exec., which has a very precise significance and meaning, one can ask, as is done in the manifesto, for the whole discussion to be reopened at a more general level than that of contingent events. This would mean saying openly that the Italian party, since the Third Congress, has systematically and permanently found itself in disagreement with the line of the Comintern, and that it wants to begin a struggle on questions of principle.

The tradition of the party. I deny emphatically that the party's tradition is that which is reflected in the manifesto. What we see here is the tradition, the conceptions, of one of the groups which initially formed our party, and not a party tradition. In the same way, I deny that there exists a crisis of confidence between the International and the party as a whole. This crisis only exists between the International and a part of the party leadership. The party was formed at Livorno not on the basis of a conception which then continued to exist and develop, but on a concrete and immediate basis: separation from the reformists, and from those who took the part of the reformists against the International. The wider basis, that which brought the Imola provisional committee the sympathies of a section of the proletariat, was loyalty to the Communist International.[111] One may, therefore, assert precisely the opposite to what the manifesto maintains. Its signatories could, quite justifiably, be accused of not having known how to interpret and of having abandoned the tradition of the party.

But this question is purely verbal and Byzantine. We are dealing with a political fact: Amadeo, finding himself in the leadership of the party, wanted his views to prevail and become those of the party. Today, with the manifesto, he would still like that. That we should have allowed this attempt to succeed in the past is one thing; but to continue to want it today, and by signing the manifesto to sanction the whole situation and imprison the party in it, is quite another. In reality we never, in an absolute sense, allowed this situation to become consolidated. I, at least before the Rome Congress, in the speech I made to the Turin assembly, said clearly enough that I was accepting the theses on tactics only for a contingent motive of party organization, and declared myself in favour of the united front right through to its normal conclusion in a workers' government.[112] Moreover, the theses as a whole were never discussed thoroughly by the party, and at the Rome Congress the question was clear enough: if the Executive had not reached a compromise with the Comintern delegates, whereby the theses were only presented consultatively and would be changed after the Fourth Congress, it is not very likely that the majority of delegates would have sided with the Executive. The latter, moreover, faced with an ultimatum from the Comintern, would not have hesitated to follow its tradition of international loyalty. Certainly I would have acted thus and with me the Piedmontese delegations, with whom I had had a meeting after Kolarov's speech and with whom I found myself in agreement on the following points: to prevent the minority from winning the party by surprise, but not to give the vote a significance which went beyond the question of organization.

The conception of the manifesto. Aside from these more or less juridical questions, I consider that the moment has come to give the party a different orientation from the one it has had up till now. A new phase is beginning in the history not just of our party but of our country too. It is, therefore, necessary that we should enter a phase of greater clarity in relations within the party, and in relations between the party and the International. I do not want to run on too long, I will simply deal with a few points in the hope that they will suffice to illuminate also the questions left on one side.

One of the most serious errors which have characterized and continue to characterize our party's activity can be summed up in the same words as those used in the second of the theses on tactics: "It would be wrong to see these two factors of consciousness and will as faculties which can be obtained from or should be demanded of individuals, since they are only realized through the integration of the activity of many individuals into a unitary collective organism."[113] This concept, correct if it refers to the working class, is mistaken and extremely dangerous if referred to the party. Before Livorno, it was the conception of Serrati, who maintained that the party as a whole was revolutionary even if socialists of various shapes and colours cohabited within it. At the split congress of Russian social-democracy, this conception was upheld by the Mensheviks, who said it was the party as a whole that counted, not its individual members. So far as the latter were concerned, it was enough that they should declare themselves to be socialists. In our party, this conception has been partly responsible for the opportunist danger. For one cannot deny that the minority was born and won disciples as a result of the absence of discussion and polemic within the party, i.e. as a result of our failure to give importance to individual comrades or to seek to orient them a little more concretely than can be done through decrees and peremptory orders.

In our party, we have had another aspect of the danger to lament: the withering of all individual activity; the passivity of the mass of members; the stupid confidence that there is always somebody else who is thinking of everything and taking care of everything. This situation has had the most serious repercussions in the organizational field. The party has lacked the possibility of choosing, with rational criteria, the trustworthy elements to whom particular tasks could be assigned. The choice has been made empirically, according to the personal knowledge of individual leaders, and has most often fallen on elements who did not enjoy the confidence of the local organizations and therefore saw their work sabotaged. And it should be added that the work carried out has only been controlled to the most minimal extent, and that in the party there has therefore been produced a real separation between the membership and the leadership.

This situation still continues and seems to me to contain innumerable dangers. In my stay in Moscow, I did not find a single one of the political exiles, though they came from every different part of Italy and were among the most active elements, who understood the position of our party or did not criticize the CC harshly (while, of course, observing fully the norms of discipline and obedience). The error of the party has been to have accorded priority in an abstract fashion to the problem of party organization, which in practice has simply meant creating an apparatus of functionaries who could be depended on for their orthodoxy towards the official view. It was believed, and it is still believed, that the revolution depends only on the existence of such an apparatus; and it is sometimes even believed that its existence can bring about the revolution.

The party has lacked any organic activity of agitation and propaganda, although this should have had all our attention and involved the formation of genuine specialists in this field. No attempt has been made to stimulate the masses, at every opportunity, to express themselves in the same direction as the Communist Party. Every event, every anniversary of a local or national or world-wide nature should have served to agitate the masses by means of the communist cells: putting through resolutions; distributing leaflets. This has not been accidental. The Communist Party has even been against the formation of factory cells. Any participation of the masses in the activity and internal life of the party, other than on big occasions and following a formal decree from the centre, has been seen as a danger to unity and centralism. The party has not been seen as the result of a dialectical process, in which the spontaneous movement of the revolutionary masses and the organizing and directing will of the centre converge. It has been seen merely as something suspended in the air; something with its own autonomous and self-generated development; something which the masses will join when the situation is right and the crest of the revolutionary wave is at its highest point, or when the party centre decides to initiate an offensive and stoops to the level of the masses in order to arouse them and lead them into action. Naturally, since things do not work out in this way, areas of opportunistic infection have formed without the centre knowing anything about them. These have had their reflection in the parliamentary group, and subsequently, in a more organic form, in the minority.

This conception has had its influence on the fusion issue. The question that was always put to the Comintern was the following: "Do you think that our party is still at the nebular stage, or that its formation has been completed?" The truth is that historically a party is never definitive and never will be. For it will become definitive only when it has become the whole population, in other words when it has disappeared. Until it disappears because it has achieved the ultimate aims of communism, it will pass through a whole series of transitory phases, and will from time to time absorb new elements in the two forms which are historically possible: through individual recruitment, or through the recruitment of smaller or larger groups. The situation was made even more difficult for our party, as a result of its disagreements with the Comintern. If the International is a world party, even taking this with many pinches of salt, it is obvious that the development of the party and the forms it can take depend on two factors and not just on one. They depend, in other words, not just on the national Executive, but also and especially on the International Executive, which is the stronger. To repair the situation, to succeed in impressing the orientation which Amadeo wants on the development of our party, it is necessary to conquer the International Executive, in other words to become the hub of a general opposition. Politically this is the result one arrives at, and it is natural that the International Executive should seek to break the back of the Italian Executive.

Amadeo has a whole theory about this, and in his system everything is logically coherent and consistent. He thinks that the tactic of the International reflects the Russian situation, i.e. was born on the terrain of a backward and primitive capitalist civilization. For him, this tactic is extremely voluntaristic and theatrical, because only with an extreme effort of will was it possible to obtain from the Russian masses a revolutionary activity which was not determined by the historical situation. He thinks that for the more developed countries of central and western Europe, this tactic is inadequate or even useless. In these countries, the historical mechanism functions according to all the approved schemes of Marxism. There exists the historical determinism which was lacking in Russia, and therefore the over-riding task must be the organization of the party as an end in itself.

I think that the situation is quite different. Firstly, because the political conception of the Russian communists was formed on an international and not on a national terrain. Secondly, because in central and western Europe the development of capitalism has not only determined the formation of the broad proletarian strata, but also – and as a consequence – has created the higher stratum, the labour aristocracy, with its appendages in the trade-union bureaucracy and the social-democratic groups. The determination, which in Russia was direct and drove the masses onto the streets for a revolutionary uprising, in central and western Europe is complicated by all these political super-structures, created by the greater development of capitalism. This makes the action of the masses slower and more prudent, and therefore requires of the revolutionary party a strategy and tactics altogether more complex and long-term than those which were necessary for the Bolsheviks in the period between March and November 1917.

But the fact that Amadeo has this conception, and that he seeks to achieve its victory not merely on a national scale but also internationally, is one thing. He is a convinced man, and struggles with great skill and great elasticity to obtain his objective; to avoid compromising his theses; to postpone any Comintern sanctions which might prevent him from continuing until the historical period in which the revolution in western and central Europe deprives Russia of the hegemonic position it holds today. But that we, who are not convinced of the historical truth of this conception, should continue to ally ourselves with it politically and thereby give it the international status which it at present enjoys, is quite another thing. Amadeo approaches things from the viewpoint of an international minority, but we must approach things from the viewpoint of a national majority.

We cannot, therefore, wish the leadership of the party to be given to representatives of the minority on the grounds that they are in agreement with the International, even if after the discussion opened up by the manifesto the majority of the party remains with the present leaders. This in my view is the central point, which must determine our attitude politically. If we agreed with Amadeo's theses, of course, we ought to ask ourselves whether, having the majority of the party with us, it would be better to remain in the International, with a national leadership drawn from the minority, taking our time and waiting for a reversal of the situation to prove us correct theoretically; or whether it would be better to break away. But if we do not agree with the theses, to sign the manifesto means taking full responsibility for the following equivocal alternatives: either, if there is a majority for Amadeo's theses, to accept a Minority leadership – we who do not agree with the theses, and could therefore resolve the situation organically; or else to remain in a minority, when by virtue of our ideas we are in agreement with the majority which would align itself with the International. This would mean our political liquidation; and to split from Amadeo after such a state of affairs would appear extremely distasteful and odious.

Suggestions for our future work. I do not want to go very deeply into this subject, because it would require a great deal of space to deal with it adequately. I will content myself with a few suggestions. The future work of the party will have to be renewed both organizationally and politically.

In the organizational field, I think it is necessary to give a greater role to the CC and make it do more work, insofar as this is possible given the situation. I think it is necessary to establish more clearly the relations which should exist between the various party bodies, fixing more precisely and strictly the division of labour and the allocation of responsibilities. Two new bodies and activities must be created. A control commission, made up predominantly of old workers, should in the last instance adjudicate litigious questions which do not have immediate political repercussions, in other words which do not require an immediate intervention by the Executive. It should also keep the status of party members under continuous review, through periodic checks. And an agitation and propaganda committee should collect all such local and national material as is necessary and useful for the party's agitational and propaganda activity. It should study local situations, propose forms of agitation, and compose leaflets and programmes to orient the work of the local bodies. It should be based on a whole national organization, whose constitutive nucleus will be the ward in the big urban centres and the rural district in the countryside. It should begin its work by a census of party members who should be divided up for organizational purposes according to their seniority and the posts which they have held, the abilities they have shown, and of course their moral and political talents.

A precise division of labour must be established between the Executive and the Clandestine Bureau. Precise responsibilities and functions established, which cannot be violated without serious disciplinary sanctions. I think that this is one of the weakest sides of our party, demonstrating most clearly how the centralism installed has been more a bureaucratic formality and banal confusion of responsibilities and functions than a rigorous system of organization.

In the political field, it is necessary to draw up detailed theses on the Italian situation and the possible phases of its further development. In 1921–2, the party had the following official conception: that the advent of a fascist or military dictatorship was impossible.[114] With great difficulty, I managed to get this conception removed from the theses and prevent it from being written down, securing basic modifications in theses 51 and 52 on tactics.[115] Now, it seems to me that the party is falling into another error, closely linked to the previous one. Then, no importance was accorded to the silent, latent opposition to fascism of the industrial bourgeoisie, and a social-democratic government was not thought possible, but only one of these three solutions: dictatorship of the proletariat (least probable); dictatorship of the general staff on behalf of the industrial bourgeoisie and the court; dictatorship of fascism; this conception bound our political action and led us into many mistakes.

Now, once again, no account is being taken of the emerging opposition of the industrial bourgeoisie – especially that which is beginning to take shape in the South, with a more explicitly territorial character and thus presenting certain aspects of a national question. It is more or less believed that a proletarian revival can and must only benefit our party. I think, however, that if there is a revival our party will still be in a minority; that the majority of the working class will go with the reformists; and that the liberal-democratic bourgeois will still have a great deal to say. That the situation is actively revolutionary, I do not doubt; and that therefore within a given space of time our party will have the majority with it. But if this period will perhaps not be long chronologically, it will undoubtedly be packed with supplementary phases, which we will have to foresee with some accuracy in order to be able to manoeuvre and avoid making mistakes which would prolong the trials of the proletariat.

I believe, moreover, that the party should tackle in a practical sense certain problems which have never been confronted, and whose resolution has simply been left to such elements of the party as were directly affected by them. The problem of winning the Milanese proletariat is a national problem for our party, which should be solved with all means the party has at its disposal, rather than just with Milanese means. If we do not have with us, in a stable fashion, the overwhelming majority of the Milanese proletariat, we cannot carry out or keep going the revolution in Italy as a whole. It is, therefore, necessary to bring worker elements from other cities into Milan; to introduce them to work in the factories; to enrich the legal and clandestine organization in Milan with the best elements from all Italy. Thus, I think it is roughly speaking necessary to inject into the Milanese working class at least a hundred comrades willing to work themselves to death for the party.

Another problem of this kind is that of the seamen, closely linked to the problem of the military fleet. Italy lives from the sea; to fail to concern oneself with the problem of the seamen, as one of the most important questions and worthy of the party's maximum attention, would mean not to think concretely about revolution. When I think that for a long time the leader of our work among seamen was a boy like

Caroti's son, it makes me shudder.[116] Another problem is that of the railwaymen, which we have always looked at from a purely trade-union point of view, whereas it transcends that definition and is a national political problem of the first order.

Fourth and last of these problems is that of the South, which we have misunderstood just as the socialists did, considering that it could be solved within the normal framework of our general political activity. I have always been convinced that the South would become the grave of fascism, but I also think that it will be the greatest reservoir and the marshalling-ground for national and international reaction if, before the revolution, we do not adequately study its problems and are not prepared for everything.

I think I have given you a fairly clear idea of my position, and of the differences which exist between it and what comes out from the manifesto. Since I think that to a great extent you are more in agreement with my position, on which we found ourselves together for some considerable time, I hope that you still have the possibility of deciding otherwise than you were on the point of doing.

With the most fraternal greetings,

Masci

IV

The New Orientation

51. EDITORIAL: March 1924

L'Ordine Nuovo is resuming publication in the same format and with the same intentions as when it was first printed in Turin on 1 May 1919.[117] Its activity as a weekly in the years 1919–20 and as a daily in the years 1921–2 left extensive, deep traces in the history of the Italian working class. This was especially true with respect to the Turin proletariat, which helped it more directly through its sacrifices, followed its propaganda more closely and carried out its directives. The situation appears much changed from those years; but in reality, it has changed more on the surface than in substance. The problems to be solved have remained the same, though they have become more difficult and complicated.

Then, it was a question of forming an independent party of the revolutionary working class, at the same time as it was urgently necessary to organize the broad masses into a movement capable of overthrowing the rule of the bourgeoisie and setting up a new State: the dictatorship of the proletariat and of the toiling masses in the countryside. In the years 1919–20, *L'Ordine Nuovo* saw the two problems as closely inter-related. By directing the masses towards the revolution; by pushing for a break with the reformists and opportunists in the factory councils and the craft unions; by revitalizing the life of the Socialist Party with discussions of the most genuinely proletarian problems, in which ordinary workers thus had the advantage over the lawyers and demagogues of reformism and maximalism – *L'Ordine Nuovo* aimed also to create the new party of the revolution, as an imperative necessity of the existing situation.

But our forces were too tiny for so immense a task. It is also necessary to confess that sometimes we lacked the courage to carry things through to the end. Attacked from every side as *arrivistes* and careerists, we were not capable of rejecting with scorn the malicious accusations. We were too young, and still retained too much political naivety and too much formal pride. Thus we did not dare, in 1919, to create a faction with ramifications throughout the country. Thus we did not dare, in 1920, to organize an urban and regional centre of the factory councils, which could have addressed itself as an organization of the totality of Piedmontese workers to the Italian working class and peasantry – over the heads, and if necessary against the directives, of the General Confederation of Labour and the Socialist Party.

Today, the situation has changed. The independent party of the revolutionary proletariat exists, and has carried out an immense work since the Livorno Congress, drenching every city and every village with the blood of its most loyal and dedicated militants. Other struggles, in other forms from those of 1919–20, now confront the working class. And though it may appear scattered and disorganized, the latter nevertheless retains a strength which is perhaps still greater than that which it possessed in those years – if one takes into account its political education, its clarity of ideas, and its greater historical experience.

L'Ordine Nuovo is resuming its battle to deepen this education, to organize and revitalize this experience. As it resumes publication, it salutes the comrades who have fallen throughout Italy, and in particular salutes the memory of those who fell in Turin in December 1922, comrades Ferrero and Berruti, who were among its warmest friends and supporters in the first, hard moments.

Unsigned, *L'Ordine Nuovo*, March 1924.

52. "LEADER"

Every State is a dictatorship. Every State cannot avoid having a government, made up of a small number of men, who in their turn organize themselves around one who is endowed with greater ability and greater perspicacity. So long as a State is necessary, so long as it is historically necessary to govern men, whichever the ruling class may be, the problem will arise of having leaders, of having a "leader". The fact that socialists, even ones who call themselves Marxists and revolutionaries, say they want the dictatorship of the proletariat but not the dictatorship of leaders; say they do not want command to be individualized and personalized; in other words, say they want dictatorship, but not in the form in which it is historically possible – merely reveals a whole political stance, a whole "revolutionary" theoretical formation.

In the question of proletarian dictatorship, the key problem is not the physical personification of the function of command. The key problem consists in the nature of the relations which the leaders or leader have with the party of the working class, in the relations which exist between this party and the working class. Are these purely hierarchical, of a military type, or are they of a historical and organic nature? Are the leader and the party elements of the working class, are they a part of the working class, do they represent its deepest and most vital interests and aspirations, or are they an excrescence or simply a violent superimposition? How was this party formed, how did it develop, through what process did the selection of the men who lead it take place? Why did it become the party of the working class? Did this occur by chance?

The problem becomes that of the whole historical development of the working class, which is gradually formed in struggle against the bourgeoisie, winning a few victories and suffering many defeats: the historical development, moreover, not just of the working class of a single country, but of the entire working class of the world – with its superficial differentiations, which are nevertheless so important at any single moment in time, and with its basic unity and homogeneity. The problem also becomes that of the vitality of Marxism; of whether it is or is not the most certain and profound interpretation of nature and of history; of whether it can complement the politician's inspired intuition by an infallible method, an instrument of the greatest precision for exploring the future, foreseeing mass events, leading them and hence controlling them.

The international proletariat has had, and still has, the living example of a revolutionary party exercising working-class dictatorship. It has had, and unfortunately no longer has, the most typical and expressive living example of what a revolutionary leader is – comrade Lenin.[118]

Comrade Lenin was the initiator of a new process of development of history. But he was this, because he was also the exponent and the last, most individualized moment of a whole process of development of past history, not just of Russia but of the whole world. Did he become the leader of the Bolshevik Party by chance? Did the Bolshevik Party become the leading party of the Russian proletariat, and hence of the Russian nation, by chance? The selection process lasted thirty years; it was extremely arduous; it often assumed what appeared to be the strangest and most absurd forms. It took place, in the international field, in contact with the most advanced capitalist civilizations of central and western Europe, in the struggle of the parties and factions which made up the Second International before the War. It continued within the minority of international socialism which remained at least partially immune from the social-patriotic contagion. It was renewed in Russia in the struggle to win the majority of the proletariat; in the struggle to understand and interpret the needs and aspirations of a numberless peasant class, scattered over an immense territory. It still continues, every day, because every day it is necessary to understand, to foresee, to take measures.

This selection process was a struggle of factions and small groups; it was also an individual struggle; it meant splits and fusions, arrest, exile, prison, assassination attempts; it meant resistance to discouragement and to pride; it meant suffering hunger while having millions in gold available; it meant preserving the spirit of a simple worker on the throne of the Tsars; it meant not despairing even when all seemed lost, but starting again, patiently and tenaciously; it meant keeping a cool head and a smile when others lost their heads. The Russian Communist Party, with its leader Lenin, bound itself up so tightly with the entire development of its Russian proletariat, with the whole development therefore of the entire Russian nation, that it is not possible even to imagine one without the other: the proletariat as a ruling class without the Communist Party being the governing party; hence without the Central Committee of the party being the inspirer of government policy; and hence without Lenin being the leader of the State.

The very attitude of the great majority of Russian bourgeois, who used to say "our ideal too would be a republic headed by Lenin without the Communist Party", had great historical significance. It was the proof that the proletariat no longer merely exercised physical domination, but dominated spiritually as well. At bottom, in a confused way, the Russian bourgeoisie too understood that Lenin could not have become and could not have remained leader of the State without the domination of the proletariat, without the Communist Party being the government party. Its class consciousness prevented it as yet from acknowledging, beyond its physical, immediate defeat, also its ideological and historical defeat. But already the doubt was there, expressed in that typical sentiment.

Another question arises. Is it possible, today, in the period of the world revolution, for there to exist "leaders" outside the working class; for there to exist non-Marxist leaders, who are not linked closely to the class which embodies the progressive development of all mankind? In Italy we have the fascist régime, we have Benito Mussolini as fascism's leader, we have an official ideology in which the "leader" is deified, declared to be infallible, prophesied as the organizer and inspirer of a reborn Holy Roman Empire. We see printed in the newspapers, every day, scores and hundreds of telegrams of homage from the vast local tribes to the "leader". We see the photographs: the hardened mask of a face which we have already seen at socialist meetings. We know that face: we know that rolling of the eyes in their sockets, eyes which in the past sought with their ferocious movements to bring shudders to the bourgeoisie, and today seek to do the same to the proletariat. We know that fist always clenched in a threat. We know the whole mechanism, the whole paraphernalia, and we understand that it may impress and tug at the heart-strings of bourgeois school-children. It is really impressive, even when seen close to, and has an awesome effect. But "leader"?

We saw the Red Week of June 1914.[119] More than three million workers were on the streets, called out by Benito Mussolini, who for about a year since the Roccagorga massacre had been preparing them for the great day, with all the oratorical and journalistic means at the disposal of the then "leader" of the Socialist Party, of Benito Mussolini – from Scalarini's lampoon to his great trial at the Milan Assizes.[120]

Three million workers were on the streets: but the "leader", Benito Mussolini, was missing. He was missing as a "leader", not as an individual; for people say that as an individual he was courageous, and defied the cordons and the muskets of the *carabinieri* in Milan. He was missing as a "leader", because he was not one. Because, by his own admission, within the leadership of the Socialist Party he could not even manage to get the better of the wretched intrigues of Arturo Vella or Angelica Balabanoff.

He was then, as today, the quintessential model of the Italian petty bourgeois: a rabid, ferocious mixture of all the detritus left on the national soil by the centuries of domination by foreigners and priests. He could not be the leader of the proletariat; he became the dictator of the bourgeoisie, which loves ferocious faces when it becomes Bourbon again, and which hoped to see the same terror in the working class which it itself had felt before those rolling eyes and that clenched fist raised in menace.

The dictatorship of the proletariat is expansive, not repressive. A continuous movement takes place from the base upwards, a continuous replacement through all the capillaries of society, a continuous circulation of men. The leader whom we mourn today found a decomposing society, a human dust, without order or discipline. For in the course of five years of war, production – the source of all social life – had dried up. Everything was re-ordered and reconstructed, from the factory to the government, with the instruments and under the leadership and control of the proletariat, i.e. of a class new to government and to history.

Benito Mussolini has seized governmental power and is holding onto it by means of the most violent and arbitrary repression. He has not had to organize a class, but merely the personnel of an administration. He has dismantled a few of the State's mechanisms more to see how it is done and to learn the trade than from any primary necessity. His ideas are all contained in the physical mask, the eyes rolling in their sockets, the clenched fist ever raised in menace.

Rome has seen these dusty scenarios before. It saw Romulus, it saw Augustus Caesar, and at its twilight it saw Romulus Augustulus.[121]

> Unsigned, *L'Ordine Nuovo*, March 1924; republished with the title *Lenin, revolutionary leader*, signed Antonio Gramsci, *L'Unità*, 6 November 1924.

53. AGAINST PESSIMISM

There can be no better way of commemorating the fifth anniversary of the Communist International, of the great world association of which we Italian revolutionaries feel ourselves more than ever to be an active and integral part, than by carrying out a self-examination: an examination of the little we have achieved and of the immense amount that remains to be accomplished. In this way we will help to clarify our situation. In particular we will help to dissipate the dark cloudbanks of heavy pessimism which are today oppressing even the most experienced and responsible militants, and which represent a great danger – perhaps the gravest at the present moment – because of the political passivity, the intellectual torpor and the scepticism towards the future which they produce.

This pessimism is closely linked to the general situation in our country; the situation explains it, but of course does not justify it. What difference would there be between us and the Socialist Party, between our will and the tradition of that party, if we too were only capable of working and were only actively optimistic in the periods of the fat kine: when the situation is propitious, when the working masses move spontaneously through irresistible impulse, and when the proletarian parties can fall comfortably back into the brilliant role of the coach-fly?[122] What would be the difference between us and the Socialist Party if we too – even though for different reasons and with a different viewpoint; and even though we had a greater sense of responsibility, and showed that this was the case by our active concern to prepare adequate organizational and material forces to meet any eventuality – abandoned ourselves to fatalism? If we cherished the sweet illusion that events cannot fail to unfold according to a fixed line of development (the one foreseen by us), in which they will inevitably find the system of dykes and canals which we have prepared for them, be channelled by this system and take historical form and power in it? This is the central knot of the problem, which appears tangled in the most complicated way because passivity has the outward appearance of brisk activity; because there appears to be a line of development, a seam which workers are meritoriously sweating and toiling away to excavate.

The Communist International was founded on 5 March 1919, but its ideological and organic formation occurred only at the Second Congress, in July–August 1920, with approval of the Statutes and with the 21 Conditions. It was after the Second Congress that the campaign to restore the Socialist Party to health began in Italy – began on a national scale that is, since it had already been initiated in the previous March by the Turin section with the resolution drawn up for the party's imminent National Council meeting scheduled to be held precisely in Turin, but had produced no significant repercussions.[123] (The Florence Conference of the abstentionist faction, held in July 1920 before the Second World Congress, rejected the proposal made by a representative of *L'Ordine Nuovo* to enlarge the basis of the faction by making it a communist one, without the abstentionist precondition which in practice had lost much of its *raison d'être*.)[124]

The Livorno Congress, and the split which occurred there, were related to the Second World Congress and its 21 Conditions. They were presented as a necessary conclusion of the "formal" proceedings of the Second Congress. This was an error, and today we can appreciate its full extent by the consequences which it has had. In reality, the proceedings of the Second World Congress were a living interpretation of the Italian situation, as they were of the world situation in general. But we, for a whole series of reasons, did not determine our actions by what was happening in Italy: by the Italian events which proved the Second Congress correct; which were a part, and indeed one of the most important parts, of the political reality which animated the decisions and organizational measures taken by the Second Congress. Instead, we limited ourselves to putting the emphasis on the formal questions, those of pure logic and pure consistency. And we were defeated, because the majority of the politically organized proletariat disagreed with us and did not come with us – even though we had on our side the authority and prestige of the International, which were very great and on which we had relied.

We had not been capable of conducting a systematic campaign, of a kind that could have reached all the nuclei and constitutive elements of the Socialist Party and forced them to reflect. We had not been capable of translating into language that could be understood by every Italian worker and peasant, the significance of each of the Italian events of the years 1919 and 1920. We were not capable, after Livorno, of confronting the problem of why the congress had had the outcome it did. We were not capable of confronting the problem in practice, in such a way as to find the solution; in such a way as to continue our specific mission, which was to win the majority of the Italian people. We were – it must be said – overtaken by events. Without wanting to be, we were an aspect of the general dislocation of Italian society, which had become a burning crucible in which all traditions, all historical formations, all prevailing ideas were melted down, sometimes leaving no trace. We had a consolation – which we embraced with all our strength – in the thought that no one was escaping, but that we could claim to have foreseen mathematically the cataclysm, while the others were cherishing the most blissful and idiotic of illusions.

After the Livorno split, we entered a state of necessity. This is the only justification we can give to our attitudes and activity after Livorno: the necessity which was crudely posed, in the most intense way, in the dilemma of life or death. We had to organize ourselves into a party in the flames of civil war, cementing our sections with the blood of the most dedicated militants. We had to transform our groups, in the very act of their formation and recruitment, into detachments for guerrilla war – for the most atrocious and difficult guerrilla war that a working class has ever had to fight. Yet we succeeded: the party was created and created strongly. It is a phalanx of steel, too small certainly to go into battle against the forces of the enemy, but enough to become the framework for a broader formation: for an army which, to use Italian historical language, can ensure that the battle on the Piave will follow the rout of Caporetto.[125]

This is the problem which faces us today, inexorably: how to form a great army for the forthcoming battles, based on the forces which from Livorno to the present day have shown that they are capable of resisting, without wavering or retreating, the attack so violently unleashed by fascism. The development of the Communist International since the Second Congress has provided us with the appropriate terrain for this. It has interpreted once again – with the proceedings of the Third and Fourth Congresses, supplemented by those of the Enlarged Plenums of February and June 1922 and of June 1923 – the Italian situation and its needs. The truth is that we, as a party, have already taken several steps forward in this direction: it only remains for us to take note of them and to proceed boldly.

What is the real significance of the events which have taken place within the Socialist Party, first with the split from the reformists, secondly with the expulsion of the *Pagine Rosse* editorial group, and thirdly and finally with the attempt to expel the entire third-internationalist faction?[126] They have the following precise meaning. While our party as the Italian section was forced to limit its activity to the physical struggle of defence against fascism, and to the preservation of its primordial structure, as an international party it was operating – continuing to operate – to open new paths towards the future; to enlarge the sphere of its political influence; and to shift a part of the masses, who at first stood looking on indifferently or hesitantly, from their position of neutrality. The activity of the International was for a time the only activity which allowed our party to have an effective contact with the broad masses, and which preserved a ferment of discussion and the first stirrings of movement in significant strata of the working class – something which it was impossible for us to achieve otherwise in the given situation. It was undoubtedly a great success to have torn blocks away from the Socialist Party matrix; and at the very moment when the situation appeared worst to have managed to create nuclei, from the amorphous socialist jelly, who declared that despite everything they had faith in the world revolution: nuclei which, in action if not in words (which are it seems more painful than action), recognized that they had been wrong in 1920–21–22. This was a defeat of fascism and reaction: it was, if we want to be sincere, the only physical and ideological defeat of fascism and reaction in the last three years of Italian history.

It is necessary to react forcefully against the pessimism of certain groups within our party, including some of the most responsible and experienced comrades. This represents the most serious danger today, in the new situation which is emerging in our country and which will find its sanction and clarification in the first fascist legislature. Big struggles are imminent, perhaps yet more bloody and arduous than those of the last years. The maximum of energy is therefore necessary on the part of our leaders; the maximum degree of organization and centralization of the mass of party members; a great spirit of initiative and a very great swiftness of decision. Pessimism mainly adopts the following refrain: we are going back to a pre-Livorno situation; we shall have to carry out once again the same work which we carried out before Livorno, and which we thought was definitive. It is necessary to show every comrade how incorrect this position is, both politically and theoretically. Certainly, it will still be necessary to fight hard. Certainly, the task of the basic nucleus of our party formed at Livorno is not yet finished, and will not be for a while yet – it will still be a vital and present task even after the victory of the revolution. But we shall not find ourselves again in a pre-Livorno situation, because the world and Italian situation in 1924 is not what it was in 1920; because we ourselves are no longer what we were in 1920, and would not like ever again to become so. Because the Italian working class has changed greatly, and it will not again be the easiest thing in the world to get it to reoccupy the factories with stovepipes for cannons, after filling its ears and stirring its blood with the vile demagogy of maximalist fair-grounds. Because our party exists, which is something after all, which has proved that it is something, and in which we have limitless faith as the best, healthiest, most honourable part of the Italian proletariat.

Unsigned, *L'Ordine Nuovo*, 15 March 1924.

54. GRAMSCI TO TOGLIATTI, SCOCCIMARRO, LEONETTI, ETC. (Vienna, 21 March 1924)

Dearest Friends,

I have not yet received any reply from you to my last letter, indicating at least in general terms the practical steps you have decided to take. So in this letter too I shall have to concern myself solely with general questions, about which I do not know whether you have already discussed, or in what terms.

Among others, I have received two letters which have greatly moved me, and which seem to me to be the sign of a general situation about which we must think very seriously. Sraffa has written to me – you will read part of his letter, appropriately commented on, in the third issue of O.N. – and so has Zino Zini.[127] Both write that they are still with us, but both are extremely pessimistic. Sraffa is moving towards a position which seems to be precisely that of the maximalists. Zini remains in principle with the communists, but writes that he is old, tired, no longer has faith in anything or anybody, and has completely devoted himself – outside his academic work – to arranging his thoughts into a book which, to judge by the allusions contained in his letter, will be a pure reflection of this state of political passivity. Sraffa will collaborate with the Journal, and from things he has written I think his collaboration will be very interesting.[128] In his case, I do not think the problem is very difficult. He has remained isolated since the contacts he had with us in Turin, he has never worked among workers, but he is certainly still a Marxist. It will only be necessary to keep in contact once again in order to resuscitate him and make him an active element of our party, to which he will be able to render much useful service today and in the future.

In his letter, there is a passage which will not be published that is extremely interesting. *A propos* the trade-union question, he asks me how it is that our party has never thought of creating unions of the same type as the American IWW, which was precisely suited to the situation of lawlessness and violent repression on the part of the State and the private capitalist organizations. He has promised me an article on trade-union bureaucracy in which, I think, he will also develop this argument, which seems to me to merit our closest attention. It is certain that we have not yet in practice considered the question of whether it is possible to create a clandestine, centralized trade-union movement that could work to bring about a new situation in the working class. Our local groups and trade-union committee have retained a purely party character, as party fractions within the CGL – which must exist, but which do not resolve the question entirely. Nor could it be resolved by taking as a model the IWW, which was in effect the organization of the so-called "migratory" workers. But the IWW's organization may, nevertheless, give some indication and clarify the nature of the question.

After the June Executive meeting, I had proposed – and Negri and Urbani were in agreement (Tasca was totally against) – to try to organize clandestinely a little conference of representatives from the biggest Italian factories: twenty or thirty workers from Turin, Milan, Genoa, Pisa, Livorno, Bologna, Trieste, Brescia, Bari, Naples, Messina. The idea was that these, as representatives of their factories and not in the name of the party, would study the general situation, pass resolutions on various problems, and before they dispersed nominate a Central Committee of Italian factories. The conference would naturally have a purely agitational and propagandistic value. Our party, which organizes it, will prepare the necessary ideological material, and make certain that the decisions taken have the maximum impact on the masses. The CC elected will be a useful transmission-belt for industrial action, and if we can sustain it will become the embryo of a future organization of Factory Councils and Internal Commissions, which will become a rival to the CGL in a changed overall situation.

I think that on this basis an excellent work of reorganization and agitation can be carried out. The party must systematically avoid appearing the inspirer and leader of the movement, in the present situation. The organization must be clandestine, both in its national and its local centres. The national conference, once its decisions have been made known through posters and through our press, should be followed by local conferences, at city, provincial and regional level. In this way, the activity of our party groups will be revitalized. We shall have to study the question of whether it is not possible to get some small dues paid, for the national CC, for general propaganda, etc. Naturally, the problem will arise that we shall be accused of trying to create a rival organization. So it will be essential: 1. simultaneously to intensify the campaign for a return to the Confederation unions; 2. to stress the fact that what is involved is not new unions, but a factory movement like the Councils or Internal Commissions.

This, broadly speaking, was my plan, which was accepted by Negri and Urbani, but which has remained in the realm of good intentions so far. I do not think that it has now become out of date, quite the contrary. A letter from Losa (Turin), which will appear in the third issue of O.N., shows that since the take-over of the land workers' federation, the masses are even more resistant to joining unions, fearing that the union lists may become black lists.[129] The situation, already favourable for a clandestine trade-union movement, has thus become yet more favourable. The important thing is to be able to find an organizational solution which fits the circumstances and gives the masses the impression of an overall enterprise, a centralization. The question, in my view, is extremely important; I would therefore like you to discuss it in detail among yourselves and send me your opinions, your impressions, the perspectives which you consider to be probable or possible.

That is what Sraffa's letter made me think about. Zini's made me think about a different problem. Why, among the intellectuals who were actively with us in 1919–20, has this passive and pessimistic state of mind become widespread today? I think it is at least in part because our party does not have an immediate programme, based on perspectives of the likely solutions which the present situation may have. We are for the workers' and peasants' government, but what does that mean concretely in Italy? Today? No one would be able to say, because no one has bothered to say. The broad masses, whose spokesmen the intellectuals automatically become, do not have any precise orientation, they do not know how to get out of their present straits, so they accept the path of least resistance: the solution provided by the constitutional-reformist opposition. Sraffa's letter is clear on this point. Zini is more of an old militant, he certainly does not believe in the possibility of fascism being displaced by Amendola or Giolitti or Turati or Bonomi: he does not believe in anything. For Sraffa, we are in the same situation as in 1915–17; for Zini, we are barely in 1915, when the War had just broken out (this is literal), when everything was confusion and thick darkness. So I think a great deal of work needs to be done in this direction: involving political propaganda, and study of the economic basis of the situation. We must explore all the likely solutions which the present situation may have, and for each of these likely solutions we must work out a line.

For example, I have read Amendola's speech, which I consider very important; there is a remark in it which could have consequences.

Amendola says that the constitutional reforms ventilated by the fascists pose the problem of whether in Italy, too, it is not necessary to separate constituent activity from normal legislative activity. It is probable that this remark contains the germ of the opposition's political line in the next Parliament. Parliament, already discredited and deprived of any authority by the electoral mechanism which produced it, cannot discuss constitutional reforms, which could only be done by a Constituent Assembly. Is it likely that the demand for a Constituent Assembly will once again become relevant? If so, what will our position be on it? In short: the present situation must have a political resolution; what is the most likely form for this resolution to take? Is it possible to believe that we will pass directly from fascism to the dictatorship of the proletariat? What intermediate phases are possible and likely? We must carry out this task of political study, both for our own sake and for the mass of party members and for the masses in general. I think that in the crisis which the country will undergo, that party will gain the upper hand which has best understood this necessary transition process, and thus impressed its seriousness on the broad masses. From this point of view, we are very weak, undoubtedly weaker than the socialists – who, well or badly, do carry out some agitational work, and what is more have a whole popular tradition to sustain them.

It is in the light of this general problem that the question of fusion too is posed today. Do we think it possible to arrive at the eve of revolution with a situation like the present one? With three socialist parties? How do we think this situation can be eliminated? By the maximalists fusing with the reformists? It is possible that may happen, but I do not think it very probable. Maximalism will want to remain independent, in order to exploit the situation on its own account. Well then? Will we make an alliance with the maximalists for a Soviet government, as the Bolsheviks did with the Left Social-Revolutionaries? I think that if the situation arises, it will not be so favourable to us as it was to the Bolsheviks. It is necessary to bear in mind the tradition of the SP, the thirty-year links it has had with the masses. Those cannot be resolved either with machine-guns or with petty manoeuvres on the eve of the revolution. This is a great historical problem, which can only be resolved if we begin studying it today in its full dimensions, and initiating a solution to it.

I think that if we establish our group solidly, and if we accomplish a political and organizational work that succeeds in keeping the present majority of our party compact, neutralizing the unshakeable leftists and the liquidatory rightists, we can accept and automatically develop the

Comintern's tactics for winning the majority of the SP. This is an ultimate objective, an orientation, certainly not something which can be achieved in immediate practical terms. The question is to extend our influence over the majority of the masses influenced today by the SP. The question is to ensure that if there is a new revolutionary working-class upsurge, it will organize itself around the CP and not around the SP. How can we achieve this? It is necessary to press the SP until its majority either comes over to us or goes over to the reformists. This involves a whole process, which must be directed by us and must give us all the profitable results; it is not a mechanical thing. So I think your latest positions are very dangerous. We are falling back into the same situation as existed from the Fourth Congress up till June. The episode of the circular letter is very instructive.[130] Circular letters of such a kind should only be sent to a few extremely trustworthy comrades, not to organizations as such. In the present situation, to organizations one should only send "political", "diplomatic" circulars.

Did the Rome trial teach us nothing? And have you not considered the fact that in many centres the IIIrd-internationalists have become the true leaders of our movement?[131] And have you not considered the fact that Vella and Nenni may have tried to introduce some of their own agents among the IIIrd-internationalists who have left the SP? I am convinced of it, sure of it. Nenni used to be in the Republican Party, where they have some experience of intrigue, and in addition he has learnt the organizational methods of the Comintern for his own ends. In 1921–2, I visited many of our party organizations: in Como, for example, the centre of a fairly industrial region, we did not have a single organizing element; the federation had to be run from Sondrio. In Como, because of the position which Roncoroni had taken up at Livorno, the mass of communists had remained with the SP and they subsequently became IIIrd-internationalist. I would swear that in Como, just as an example, our party is in the hands of the IIIrd-internationalists, more or less directly, and that among those IIIrd-internationalists there are agents of Momigliano. That this is happening, I have proof. The section of Tortona has been reorganized. Who has been put in charge of the reorganization? A IIIrd-internationalist, believed to be a communist, who enjoys no sympathy among the rank and file members. At least, that is what a well-informed friend has written to me. In practice, the IIIrd-internationalist has had to turn to a communist for the reorganization, but the episode shows: 1. that the party has an organizational apparatus that is very defective; 2. that the entry into the party of socialist agents who may leak documents is possible.

I hope that the mail will bring me some communication from you, to which I will reply at once.

Affectionate greetings,

Masci

If you have the chance, send me a copy of this letter and another to Urbani. In the new apartment where I am now, I cannot use the typewriter very much, which causes a lot of complications.

55. THE PROGRAMME OF *L'ORDINE NUOVO*

Let us begin with a material observation: the first two issues already published of *L'Ordine Nuovo* have had a circulation (a *real* circulation) greater than the highest circulation achieved in the years 1919–20. Several conclusions could be drawn from this observation. We will refer just to two: 1. the fact that a journal of the *Ordine Nuovo* type represents a need that is strongly felt by the Italian revolutionary masses in the present situation; 2. the fact that it is possible to ensure for *L'Ordine Nuovo* conditions of existence that make it financially autonomous from the general budget of our party – for which it is necessary only to organize the consent that has been spontaneously given, in such a way that it can continue to express itself even if reaction (as is likely) seeks to intervene to stifle it; to prevent any link between *L'Ordine Nuovo* and its readers; or even, at a certain point, to prevent the journal from being printed in Italy any longer.

The circulation reached by the first two issues can only be due to the position which *L'Ordine Nuovo* occupied in the first years of its publication, which consisted essentially in the following. 1. In having been able to translate into the historical language of Italy the main postulates of the doctrine and tactics of the Communist International. In the years 1919–20, this meant putting forward the slogan of factory councils and workers' control of production: i.e. the organization of the mass of all producers for the expropriation of the expropriators, and for the replacement of the bourgeoisie by the proletariat in the government of industry – and hence, necessarily, of the State. 2. In having supported within the Socialist Party, which at that time meant the majority of the proletariat, the integral programme of the Communist International and not just some part of it. For this reason, at the Second World Congress, comrade Lenin said that the *Ordine Nuovo* group was the only tendency of the Socialist Party which faithfully represented the International in Italy. For this reason too, the theses compiled by the *Ordine Nuovo* editors and presented to the Milan national council meeting of April 1920 by the Turin section, were indicated explicitly at the Second Congress as the basis for revolutionary reorganization in Italy.[132]

Our present programme must reproduce, in the situation which exists in Italy today, the position taken up in the years 1919–20. It must reflect the objective situation of today, with the possibilities which are offered to the proletariat for autonomous action, as an independent class. It must continue, in present political terms, the tradition of faithful and integral interpreter of the programme of the Communist International. The urgent problem, the slogan that is necessary today is that of the workers' and peasants' government. It is a question of popularizing it; fitting it to concrete Italian conditions; showing how it springs from every episode in our national life, and how it resumes and contains in itself all the demands of the multiplicity of parties and tendencies into which fascism has disintegrated the political will of the working class, and above all of the peasant masses. This, of course, does not mean that we should neglect the more properly working-class and industrial issues, quite the contrary. Experience – including in Italy – has shown how important the factory organizations have become in the present period, from the party cell to the internal commission, i.e. to the representation of the whole mass of workers. We believe, for example, that today there does not exist even a reformist who would argue that in factory elections only unionized workers should have the right to vote. Anyone who remembers the struggles which it was necessary to wage on this question, has a yardstick to measure the progress that experience has compelled even the reformists to make. All the problems of factory organization will therefore be brought back into discussion by us, since only through a powerful organization of the proletariat, achieved with all the methods that are possible under a reactionary régime, can the campaign for a workers' and peasants' government avoid becoming transformed into a repetition of the ... occupation of the factories.

In the article "Against Pessimism" which was published in the last issue, we referred to the line which our party should follow in its relations with the Communist International. This article was not the expression of a single individual, but the result of a whole process of agreement and exchange of opinions among the former editors and friends of *L'Ordine Nuovo*. Thus before it became a beginning, it was the end-result of the thinking of a group of comrades who must certainly be acknowledged to know the needs of our movement through direct experience and long practice in active work. The article provoked some reactions which did not surprise us, because it is unavoidable that three years of terrorism, and hence of absence of major discussions, should have created a certain sectarian and factional spirit, even among excellent comrades. This observation could lead to a whole series of conclusions: the most important seems to us the fact that a great deal of work is necessary, in order to bring the mass of our party members up to the same political level as has been achieved by the major parties in the International. We are today, in relative terms, as a result of the conditions created by white terror, a little party. But we must consider our present organization, given the conditions in which it exists and develops, as the element that is destined to provide the framework for a great mass party. It is from this point of view that we must see all our problems and judge even individual comrades.

The fascist period is often compared to that of the War. Well: one of the weaknesses of the Socialist Party was the fact that during the War it did not attend to the nucleus of 20 or 25,000 socialists who remained faithful; that it did not consider them as the organizing element for the great masses who would flood in after the Armistice. It thus occurred that in 1919–20 this nucleus was submerged by the wave of new elements; and the organizational practice, the experience, which had been won by the working class in the blackest and hardest years were submerged with it. We would be criminals if we fell into the same error. Each of the present members of the party, because of the selection process which has taken place, and because of the strength of sacrifice which has been shown, must be personally dear to us. He must be helped by the central leadership to improve himself, and to draw from the experience undergone all the lessons and all the implications which it contains. In this sense *L'Ordine Nuovo* aims to carry out a special function in the general framework of the party's activity.

It is, therefore, necessary to organize the agreement which has already been demonstrated. This is the special task of the old friends of *L'Ordine Nuovo*. We have said that it will be necessary to collect 50,000 *lire* in the next six months, the sum necessary to guarantee the review's independent existence. To this end, it is necessary to form a movement of 500 comrades, each of whom will seriously aim to collect 100 *lire* over the next six months among his friends and acquaintances. We will keep a detailed list of all those elements who are willing to collaborate in our activity: they will be as it were our trustees. The collection of subscriptions can be made up as follows: 1. ordinary subscriptions, whether amounting to a few *soldi* or to many *lire*; 2. supporting subscriptions; 3. dues to meet the initial expenses of a correspondence course for party organizers and propagandists: these dues must not be less than 10 *lire*, and will give the right to have a number of lessons determined by the overall cost of printing and postage.

We think that through this system, we will be able to recreate an apparatus to replace that which existed in 1919–20 under the democratic régime, by means of which *L'Ordine Nuovo* kept itself in close contact with the masses in the factories and workers' clubs. The correspondence course must become the first phase of a movement to create small party schools, designed to create organizers and propagandists who are Bolsheviks and not maximalists: who in other words have brains as well as lungs and a throat. We will therefore maintain constant contact by letter with the best comrades – to inform them about the experiments which have been made in this field in Russia and other countries; to orient them; to advise them on books to read and methods to apply. We believe that in particular the comrades in exile should do a lot of work of this kind. Wherever there exists a group of ten comrades in a foreign country, a party school should be created. The older and more skilled elements should be the instructors in these schools. They should bring the younger comrades to share in their experience, and thus contribute to raising the political level of the mass of members.

Certainly, it is not with these pedagogic methods that the great historical problem of the spiritual emancipation of the working class can be resolved. But it is not some utopian resolution of this problem which we are aiming to achieve. Our task is limited to the party, made up as it is of elements who have already – simply by the fact of having joined the party – shown that they have reached a considerable level of spiritual emancipation. Our task is to improve our cadres; to make them capable of confronting the forthcoming struggles. In practice these struggles, moreover, will present themselves in the following terms. The working class, made prudent by bloody reaction, will for a certain time generally distrust the revolutionary elements. It will want to see them engaged in practical work, and will want to test their seriousness and competence. On this terrain too, we must render ourselves able to defeat the reformists, who are undoubtedly the party which today has the best and most numerous cadres. If we do not seek to achieve this, we will never take many steps forward.

The old friends of *L'Ordine Nuovo*, especially those who worked in Turin in the years 1919–20, understand very well the full importance of this problem. For they remember how, in Turin, we succeeded in eliminating the reformists from their organizational positions only *pari passu* as worker comrades, capable of practical work and not just of shouting "Long live the revolution", were formed from the factory council movement. They also recall how in 1921 it was not possible to seize certain important positions, such as Alessandria, Biella and Vercelli, from the opportunists, because we did not have organizing elements who were up to the job. Our majorities in those centres melted away, as a result of our organizational weakness. By contrast in certain centres, Venice for example, one capable comrade was enough to give us the majority, after a zealous work of propaganda and organization of factory and trade-union cells. Experience in all countries has shown the following truth: that the most favourable situations can be reversed as a result of the weakness of the cadres of the revolutionary party. Slogans only serve to impel the broad masses into movement and to give them a general orientation. But woe betide the party responsible if it has not thought about organizing them in practice; about creating a structure which will discipline them and make them permanently strong. The occupation of the factories taught us many things in this respect.

To help the party schools in their work, we propose to publish a whole series of pamphlets and a number of books. Among the pamphlets, let us mention: 1. elementary expositions of Marxism; 2. an explanation of the workers' and peasants' government slogan applied to Italy; 3. a propagandist's manual, containing the most essential data concerning Italian economic and political life, the Italian political parties, etc. – in other words, the indispensable materials for simple propaganda to be carried out through collective reading of the bourgeois press. We would like to publish an Italian edition of the *Communist Manifesto*, with comrade Ryazanov's notes: taken together, these notes are a complete exposition in popular form of our doctrines. We would also like to publish an anthology of historical materialism, in other words a collection of the most significant passages from Marx and Engels, to give a general picture of the works of these our two great teachers.

The results so far achieved authorize us to hope that it will be possible to continue confidently and successfully. To work then! Our best comrades must become convinced that what is involved is a political statement, a demonstration of the vitality and capacity for development of our movement, and hence an anti-fascist and revolutionary demonstration.

Antonio Gramsci on behalf of the editors, *L'Ordine Nuovo*, 1 and 15 April 1924.

56. PROBLEMS OF TODAY AND TOMORROW

From an old subscriber and friend of *L'Ordine Nuovo*, we have received the following letter:[133]

"It seems to me that our disagreement is especially of a chronological order. I accept a great deal of what you write to me, but as solutions to problems which will arise *after* the fall of fascism. It is very useful to study them and prepare oneself to confront them; but the problems of *today* are very different. Let us discuss this. I stand by my opinion that the working class is totally absent from political life. And I can only conclude that the Communist Party, *today*, can do nothing or almost nothing positive. The situation is strikingly similar to that of 1916–17; and so too is my state of mind, which you say is shared by other friends who write to you. My political opinions are unchanged – or worse still, I have become fixed in them; just as up till 1917, I was fixed in the pacifist socialism of 1914–15 – which I was shaken out of by the discovery, made after Caporetto and the Russian Revolution of November, that guns were precisely in the hands of the worker-soldiers. Unfortunately, the analogy does not extend so far. But just as at that time, although we knew rationally that the War would have to end one day, we all "felt" that it would never end and could not see *how* peace could come – so it is today with fascism. It is quite easy for me to accept your opinion that this state of affairs cannot last, and that major events are imminent: it is perfectly logical, but one cannot "feel" it or "see" it.

There will be no possibility of working-class political action, so long as the concrete problems which present themselves to each worker have to be resolved individually and privately, as is the case today. He has to preserve his job, his pay, his house and his family. The union and the party cannot help in any way, indeed the reverse is true. A little peace can only be won if one makes oneself as small as possible, if one scatters. One can only increase one's pay a bit by working a lot or looking for supplementary jobs, competing with the other workers, etc. The very negation of the party and the union. The economic crisis has now diminished, so that if there was even a minimum of trade-union freedom and public order, union organization, industrial action, etc., could start up again (as in England, for example). The urgent question, which conditions all others, is that of "freedom" and "order": the others will come later, but for now they cannot even interest the workers.

Now, I do not think that a relaxation of fascist pressure can be secured by the Communist Party; today is the hour of the democratic opposition, and I think it is necessary to let them proceed and even help them. What is necessary, first of all, is a "bourgeois revolution", which will then allow the development of a working-class politics. Basically, it seems to me that – just like during the War – there is nothing to be done except to wait for it to pass. I would like to know your opinion on this subject. I do not feel that my own is incompatible with being a Communist (though a non-active one). For the function which I attribute to the "lefts" will be accomplished very quickly, I believe. And it would certainly not be right for the Communist Party to compromise itself with them, since in any case it could not make any real contribution to a campaign of such a kind. But I also think that it is an error to set oneself openly against them, and to spend too much time (as *L'Unità* does, for example) deriding bourgeois "freedom". Fair or foul, it is what the workers feel most keenly the need for today, and it is the precondition for any further advance. Just as during the War neutralism was certainly not a socialist policy, but it was certainly the best policy for the Socialist Party out of those which were possible, because it meant most to the masses.

The Communist Party cannot – because of the contradiction it would involve – wage a campaign for freedom and against dictatorship in general. But it commits a grave error when it gives the impression it is sabotaging an alliance of the opposition forces – as it did with its sudden declaration that it would participate in the electoral struggle, when the other parties pretended to threaten abstention. Its function, for now, is that of a coach-fly, since *afterwards* it will be necessary for a mass party to have distinguished itself in the struggle against fascism: again, just as in the War.[134] Meanwhile, it would be a good thing to take advantage of this experience to prepare a concrete programme for afterwards: then, certainly, the Southern question and that of unity will be in the foreground. But not today. I do not think that the fascists' fight to have Orlando and Co. on their slate has the significance you attribute to it. It can be explained more simply as an obvious electoral expedient, necessary to avoid a fiasco. This explanation is also more worthy of the prefect of Naples and of Mussolini. You say that fascism is precisely destroying the unity of the State, hence the question is urgent and relevant today; but I do not think it is of the kind you say. It seems to me to be more of a police question than a social one. The fact is that fascism pays its supporters not so much with money as with crumbs of State authority; with permission to swagger and strut, for amusement and for private interest. The remedy will lie in an efficient police-force independent of the local chieftains, no matter whether it is centralized or local. In short, it comes back to a question of public order, not to a territorial one.

I was really moved at the sight of the first issue of *L'Ordine Nuovo*. I hope that, as in 1919, it will succeed in finding the slogan which is lacking today and which is needed. I hope too that it will be able to draw a balance-sheet of the past: not to determine the blame or merit of individuals or parties; not to repeat "I told you so"; above all, not to draw a balance-sheet of your enemies, but rather of yourselves and your own comrades — which is more useful, and alone can make experience useful. You certainly need great courage to carry out an autopsy on yourselves, but the old *Ordine Nuovo* will perhaps have that courage." S.

Liquidatory Elements

This letter contains all the necessary and sufficient elements to liquidate a revolutionary organization such as our party is and must be. And yet, this is not the intention of our friend S., who even though he is not a member, even though he is only on the fringes of our movement and our propaganda, has faith in our party and considers it the only one capable of permanently resolving the problems posed and the situation created by fascism. Is the position adopted in the letter purely personal? We do not think so. It cannot but be the position of a large circle of intellectuals who, in the years 1919–20, sympathized with the proletarian revolution, and who subsequently refused to prostitute themselves to triumphant fascism. It is also, unconsciously, the position of a part of the proletariat itself, even of members of our party, who have not succeeded in resisting the torturing daily drip of reactionary events, in the state of isolation and dispersal created for them by fascist terror. This is clear from a whole series of facts, and is openly confessed in private correspondence. Our friend S. does not adopt the viewpoint of an organized party. So he does not perceive the consequences of his views or the numerous contradictions into which he falls, but arrives at an absurd position and thus himself highlights the weakness and falsity of his argument.

S. believes that the future will belong to our party. But how could the Communist Party continue to exist, how could it develop, how in other words could it become capable of dominating and guiding events after the fall of fascism, if it annihilated itself today in the attitude of total passivity proposed by S. himself? Predestination does not exist for individuals, and even less does it do so for parties. All that exists is the concrete activity, the ceaseless work, the continuous contact with developing historical reality that give individuals and parties a position of preeminence, a role of guide and vanguard. Our party is an organized fraction of the proletariat and of the peasant masses, i.e. of the classes which are today oppressed and crushed by fascism. If our party did not find *for today* independent solutions of its own to the overall, Italian problems, the classes which are its natural base would turn *en masse* towards those political currents which give some solution to these problems that is not the fascist one.

If that occurred, the fact would have an immense historical significance. It would mean that the present is not a revolutionary socialist period, but we are still living in an epoch of bourgeois capitalist development. It would mean that not only the subjective conditions of organization and political preparation are lacking, but also the objective material conditions for the proletariat to attain power. Then, indeed, we too would face the problem of taking up not an independent revolutionary position, but that of a mere radical fraction of the constitutional opposition, called by history to realize the "bourgeois revolution" – in other words, an indispensable and inevitable stage in the process which will culminate in socialism. Does the Italian situation perhaps authorize one to believe this? S. himself does not believe it, because he writes that the task of the constitutional opposition will be chronologically very brief, without any direct development other than towards a proletarian revolution.

S. refers to the period of the War, and presents the stance of the Socialist Party during the War as exemplary. How absurd this reference is, and how much it proves its author wrong, is at once clear from even the briefest and most hasty analysis. Socialist neutralism was an essentially opportunist tactic, dictated by the tradititional need to balance the three tendencies making up the party (which we will indicate simply with the three names of Turati, Lazzari and Bordiga). It was not a political line established after an examination of the situation and of the relationship of forces which existed in Italy in 1914–15. Instead, it was a result of the conception of "party unity above all else, even above the revolution" which still characterizes maximalism. The fact that our friend S. only discovered that arms were in the hands of the worker-soldiers after the November revolution and the defeat at Caporetto, merely demonstrates the way in which this opportunist tactic had left the Socialist masses in the dark about the discussions which had already taken place on this subject at the international level. The Zimmerwald Left had made this "discovery" back in 1915, and it had determined the tactics of the Russian Bolshevik Party. For that reason, the defeat of the Russian armies, after the offensives imposed on the Kerensky government by the Entente, was followed by proletarian revolution and transformation of the imperialist war into a civil war. The defeat at Caporetto, however, was only followed by a resolution which confined itself to reasserting parliamentary opposition to the government and the rejection of war credits.

The attitude which the Socialist Party maintained during the War also illuminates subsequent events up to the Livorno Congress, the Socialists' Rome Congress and the formation of the Unitary Socialist Party. It is the same tactic, basically, taking on a new aspect for each new situation: the same tactic of passivity; "neutralism"; unity for unity's sake; the party for the party's sake; faith in the predestination of the Socialist Party to be the party of the Italian workers. The results which this attitude has today, when there exist the Unitary Socialist Party to the right and the Communist Party to the left, are clear even to our friend S.: permanent internal crises and split after split, none of which ever resolve the situation, because the communist tendency continually re-emerges and the right (favourable to fusion with the Unitary Socialists) is continually reinforced.

Residues of Old Ideologies

Our friend S. has not yet succeeded in destroying in himself all the ideological traces of his democratic-liberal intellectual formation, normative and Kantian rather than dialectical and Marxist. What meaning do his statements have that the working class is "absent"; that the situation is against unions and parties; that fascist violence is a problem of "order", i.e of "police", and not a "social" problem?

The Italian situation is certainly complicated and contradictory, but not so much so that one cannot grasp definite unitary lines of development in it. The proletariat, i.e. the revolutionary class *par excellence*, is a minority of the toiling population oppressed and exploited by capitalism, and is mainly concentrated in a single zone – that of the North. In the years 1919–20, the proletariat's political strength consisted in finding itself *automatically* at the head of all the working population; and in centralizing *objectively* – by its direct and immediate action against capitalism – all the revolts of the other popular strata, amorphous and directionless. Its weakness was revealed in its failure to organize these revolutionary relations; and in the fact that it did not even consider the problem of the need to organize these relations into a concrete political system and a government programme. Fascist repression, following the line of least resistance, began with these other social strata and came to the proletariat last.

Today, systematic and legal repression is kept up against the proletariat. But it has by contrast diminished at the periphery, against those strata who in 1920 were only objectively the proletariat's allies – and which are becoming reorganized; entering partially into struggle again; revealing the softer features of a constitutional opposition, i.e. their most markedly petty-bourgeois features. What then does it mean that the working class is 'absent'? The 'presence' of the working class, in the sense our friend S. understands this, would mean revolution; because it would mean that once more, as in 1919–20, not democratic petty bourgeois are standing at the head of the working population, but the most revolutionary class of the nation. But fascism is precisely the negation of such a state of affairs; fascism was born and developed precisely in order to destroy such a state of affairs, and to prevent it from reappearing.

How then is the problem posed today? It seems to us that it is posed in the following terms: the working class is, and will remain, "absent" to the extent that the Communist Party allows the constitutional opposition to monopolize the reawakening to struggle of the social strata which are historically the proletariat's allies. The emergence and consolidation of the constitutional opposition is infusing the proletariat with new strength, so that it is once again flocking into the party and the unions. If the Communist Party intervenes actively in the process whereby the opposition is formed, works to bring about a class differentiation in the social base of the opposition, and ensures that the peasant masses orient themselves towards the programme of a workers' and peasants' government, then the proletariat is no longer "absent" as before. Then there is a line of political work in which both the problems of today and those of tomorrow are resolved, and in which tomorrow is prepared and organized, not just awaited from the lap of fate.

This line of political work is thus opposed as much to the constitutional opposition as it is to fascism – even if the constitutional opposition upholds a programme of freedom and order which would be preferable to fascism's one of violence and arbitrary power. The truth is that the constitutional opposition will never realize its programme, which is a pure instrument of anti-fascist agitation. It will not realize it, because to do so would mean that so great a "catastrophe" would occur so soon; and because the entire development of the situation in Italy is controlled by the armed force of the national militia. Nevertheless, the development of the opposition and the features which it assumes are extremely important phenomena. They are the proof of fascism's powerlessness to resolve the vital problems of the nation. They are a daily reminder of the objective reality which no volley of insults can annihilate. For us, they represent the environment in which we must move and work, if we wish to remain in contact with historical reality, and not become a meditational sect; the environment in which we must seek the concreteness of our slogans and our immediate programmes for action and agitation.

Three Points to Summarize

We can sum up the main features of our conception of the present needs and tasks of the proletarian movement, in counter-position to that of our friend S., as follows: 1. to give our party a sharper awareness of the concrete problems which the situation created by fascism has posed for the working class, in such a way that organization becomes not an end in itself, but an instrument for spreading revolutionary slogans among the broadest masses; 2. to work for the political unity of the proletariat under the banner of the Communist International, hastening the process of decomposition and recomposition that was begun at the Livorno Congress; 3. to establish concretely the meaning in Italy of the workers' and peasants' government slogan, and to give this slogan a national political substance – which can only happen if we study the most crucial and pressing problems of the peasant masses, and therefore first and foremost those specific problems which are summed up in the general term "the Southern question".

Intellectuals like our friend S. who have not allowed themselves to be carried away by fascism, and who in one way or another have not been prepared to disavow their attitudes in the years 1919 and 1920, can once again find in *L'Ordine Nuovo* a centre of discussion and regroupment.

Unsigned, *L'Ordine Nuovo*, 1 and 15 April 1924.

57. GRAMSCI TO ZINO ZINI
(Vienna, 2 April 1924)

I too received your reply only after a long delay, and it gave me great pleasure to get news of you directly.[135] I had the most varied and contradictory reports about you, as about so many other friends, so that I could not get any idea of how you are thinking and how you see the future. I think our disagreement today depends a lot on the fact that in 1920 I was very pessimistic about how the events then taking place would be resolved. Fascism's rise to power, and the destruction which preceded and followed this, only surprised me moderately. Another thing which has certainly contributed to creating my present state of mind is the fact that I did not remain in Italy during this last period, so that I escaped the terrible spiritual pressure exerted on many comrades and friends by the torturing daily drip of violence and abasement. The daily spectacle which I, by contrast, had in Russia – of a people which is creating a new life, new customs, new relationships, new ways of thinking and confronting all problems – makes me today more optimistic about our country and its future. Something new exists in the world, and is working in a subterranean, one might say molecular fashion, but irresistibly. Why should our country be left out of this process of general renewal?

The attitude of many of the Italian workers who have emigrated to Russia shows that in 1920 we would not have held on to power, even if we had won it. They do not understand how the Russian workers, after six years of revolution, are able to suffer in good spirit the many travails to which they are still condemned. They, the Italians, want to avoid these, and try to ward them off by every means. Fascism, from this point of view, has transformed our people, and we have proof of this every day. It has given it a more robust temper, a healthier morality, a resistance to ill fortune which was previously unsuspected, a depth of feeling that had never existed before. Fascism has truly created a situation that is permanently revolutionary, as Tsarism once did in Russia. The pessimism which dominated me in 1920, especially during the occupation of the factories, has vanished today. Naturally, this does not mean that I see the Italian situation in rosy colours. Indeed, I think that much pain and struggle still awaits our proletariat, of a yet more bloody kind than those it has already experienced. But today there is a sure line of development, and this seems to me to be a highly significant thing to say of our country. Today, predictions can be made with some confidence, and it is possible to work with greater stamina than in 1919–20. There, you see, is my optimism, which I would like to communicate to all the friends and comrades with whom I am making contact again, and who appear to me to be crushed by the spiritual pressure of fascism.

I see that the masses are less pessimistic than the intellectuals. But they are looking for a point of reference, a centre. The most important question in our country today is to give the masses their point of reference. The intellectuals of the old generation, who have so much historical experience, who have seen the whole tormented development of our people over these last decades, would fail in their duty and mission if, precisely in this culminating phase, they stood aside and were unwilling to contribute to clarifying, organizing and centralizing the ideal forces which already exist – which, in other words, do not need to be brought into existence (that would be utopian), but merely to be centralized and given a direction. See what is happening with the periodical. It is printing double the number of copies today that it was in 1920. This is documentary evidence of what I am saying. In 1920, the situation appeared enormously propitious, but it was a quartan fever. Today, there is more depth, more solidity, even if the landscape is one of cataclysm.

I would be very happy to be able to recreate the community of work which was formed around the periodical in 1919–20. I think that your collaboration would be precious for that. Naturally, you would have to sign with a pseudonym, because we have already too often made the mistake of throwing our forces into the fray unarmed or virtually so against a well-equipped and implacable enemy. The idea too of your collaboration with Russian journals could be taken up again, and I could help to arrange it. In Russia, a whole number of great literary, artistic and philosophical journals are published, which would like to have regular contributions from Italy on all our cultural and intellectual movements. The articles or reports would also be very well paid, because the Russians value literary activity very highly (perhaps even too highly). This would in any case allow you to get hold of Russian books and periodicals, which are being produced in gigantic quantities in all fields, but especially in the natural sciences and the philosophy of Marxism.

I wanted to reply at once to your letter, so I have only touched on many of the things I should have liked to write about. I would be grateful if you would write to me again, at the same address as last time, and also tell me something about Prof. Cosmo, with whom I had an interesting conversation in Berlin in May 1922.[136]

Please accept my most cordial and affectionate greetings,

Gramsci

58. GRAMSCI TO TOGLIATTI, SCOCCIMARRO, ETC.
(Vienna, 5 April 1924)

Dearest Friends,

I have received comrade Silvia's letter, but I must confess it has greatly embarrassed me.[137] The situation is still totally confused, and I am unable to understand exactly what you all want me to do. What is the agenda for the CC meeting? To what specific issue, or item of discussion, should the resolution I am to write refer? I thought of writing an open letter to the CC to make a personal statement, but I abandoned the idea, fearing that I might in some way become separated from you and thus allow the resulting situation to be exploited. The article I wrote in the second number of ON can be taken as my statement to the meeting and as an indication of my position.[138] Please make a statement in my name to this effect, if it is necessary.

There is still too little coordination in our work. To tell the truth, I still do not know exactly what you concretely want. Do you accept all my proposals *en bloc*? But may there not still be disagreement on some detail, which could nevertheless be crucially important? How can I draw up a resolution under these circumstances? I think you know my point of view fairly fully, but I only know yours very imperfectly. If anybody can draw up a resolution, given that we want to produce something global and organic, then it is among you who can discuss and reach an understanding that this somebody exists. In general, if the meeting is going to discuss tactical questions and the orientation of the party, as you indicate is the case, I think it is necessary to take up a position, decisively and without hesitating: the one I have indicated, if you accept it *in toto*. In that case I think that a short resolution is enough, at the end of a speech by Palmi, for instance, outlining our attitude from the Rome Congress up till today.

At Rome, we accepted Amadeo's theses because they were presented as an opinion for the Fourth Congress and not as a line of action. We thought we would thus keep the party united around its basic nucleus, and considered that this concession could be made to Amadeo, given the very great role he had had in organizing the party. We do not regret this. Politically, it would have been impossible to lead the party without the active participation of Amadeo and his group in work at the centre.

Events which have occurred since have modified the situation. We face a new upsurge, which is reflected in Italy as well. At that time, we withdrew and had to do so in such a way that the retreat took place in good order, without new crises or new threats of splits within our movement, without ever adding new disintegrative ferments to those which defeat itself was producing in the revolutionary movement. Today, it is necessary to lay the foundations of a great mass party, and to clarify fully our own theoretical and practical positions. We have found ourselves in partial disagreement with the Comintern, not so much in our assessment of the general Italian situation, as in our evaluation of the repercussions which the measures proposed would have inside our party, whose weakness and constitutive fragility we knew. We have been somewhat sectarian, as occurs when the movement ebbs, partly as a reaction against the excessive optimism of the preceding period. On questions of principle, we have always been in agreement with the Comintern. But our attitude has had repercussions which have made us reflect. At the same time, we see that a clarification has occurred within the minority, and this has helped to orient us.[139] Two tendencies have now emerged within the minority, one of which has shown its true liquidatory charactor, foreseen by us and which had frightened us. With this wing, we could never have anything in common; we will fight against it. The other part, represented by comrade Tasca, has changed its nature and in practice accepted many of our positions. With it, or with the policy which it claims to represent, it is possible to work fruitfully. With the left, many discussions will still be needed to see exactly where the difference lies. But we must censure Amadeo's attitude, which has damaged the party.

We differ from the left on certain organizational principles, and it will be necessary to explore these to see how far they go. The attitude taken up by Amadeo implies denying the world party in practice, i.e. in the only way in which it could be concretized in the present situation.[140] In the national sphere, the party's development is hampered and it tends towards political passivity. But we continue to believe that Amadeo's collaboration in the work of the party is necessary. We believe that a man like him cannot become a simple militant, a rank-and-file member.[141] In practice, that would mean a perpetual state of unease among the party's membership; the perpetual existence of a non-organized faction. For at every moment, before every difficulty, each member of the party would wonder: "What does Amadeo think? If he was there, things would perhaps go better." The assertion that a leader can remain in the ranks like an ordinary member is false both theoretically and in practice. If Amadeo insists on this, we can do nothing to help him, but must envisage the need to struggle against him to prevent a wasting sickness in the party.

It will be necessary to be clear on these points and extremely open. Only in that way will it be possible to extricate the party from the toils in which it is caught and give it an orientation. If you agree, you can say that my article in ON roughly represents our orientation, and that our subsequent statements will develop points touched upon in the article: 1. our desire to put an end to the crisis and liquidate factionalism; 2. our intention of working in practical agreement with the International Executive Committee, whose deliberations we accept *en bloc* (i.e. not excluding that they could be improved in part); 3. our campaign to make the party capable of confronting the grave tasks which await it. If you are in agreement, you can yourselves draw up a short resolution based on these elements, putting my signature on it too and saying that it completely represents my point of view as well.

Warm greetings,

Sardi

I have received Negri's letter, which persuades me even more that there is insufficient coordination between you. His comments should, I think, be taken into consideration, at least so far as our group and its organization is concerned, because a lot of time has now been lost. With respect to the minority, I do not agree with him. I think it is absolutely indispensable, vital, to try to detach Tasca from the minority, at the price of any formal concessions whatsoever. You do not trust Tasca's words: yet another reason to detach him from the others.[142] Greetings.

59. THE COMO CONFERENCE: RESOLUTIONS[143]

I

The majority of the Central Committee of the Communist Party of Italy, at the moment in which the discussion on tactics and the internal situation in the party is being initiated, in order to clarify its position:

1. Declares that it feels itself to be and is continuing the activity of the groups which, by creating the Communist Party in Italy, laid the basis for resolving the historical problem posed for the class of workers and peasants in Italy by the defeat and disintegration of the movement which, for more than thirty years, had been led by the Italian Socialist Party.

2. Recognizes that after the split Congress at Livorno, all the party's activity had to take account of, and suffered the consequences of: the need to resolve before all else the problem of how to root in the consciousness of the masses the necessity for the Communist Party's existence; the need to give the Communist Party a definite personality and physiognomy; and the need to create a complete, solid organizational and political apparatus which would allow it to fulfil its tasks in a normal fashion.

3. As for the differences which have arisen between the party and the International, it asserts that these have not been the result of conflicting assessments of the general Italian situation, but have concerned the repercussions which the measures proposed by the International would have upon the party's internal constitution, upon its process of formation and evolution, and upon the position which it was slowly winning in the consciousness of the Italian working masses, as against the other proletarian or so-called proletarian parties.

4. Repeats that the theses of the Rome Congress were voted as an orientation for the discussion at the Fourth Congress, and not as an action programme; and that in voting for them the majority of the party had in mind the need to keep the entire party united around its fundamental nucleus, avoiding any differentiation which might have diminished and perhaps destroyed its capacity for development or for action. This was all the more the case because at the Rome Congress the

existence of liquidationist tendencies inside the party had already become clear, grouped in the form of an artificial, improvised minority.

5. Recognizes that from the time of the Fourth Congress and the June Plenum, the majority of the party has begun to revise and rework its positions, and that this has allowed the party as such to apply the Comintern's decisions loyally and in a disciplined way. It asserts that today, having overcome the period of greatest démoralization, in which every activity had to be designed to reduce the dispersal of our forces to the minimum, the party is in a position to arrive at a dispassionate and serene judgement of its past, acknowledging the errors and weaknesses there have been in its activity. However, it considers that it would be very damaging to deliver such a judgement on the party's work and positions without taking into account what the needs and vital requirements of our organism were in the past. Only in this way can examination of the past be a preparation for working out a political programme for the future. The deep political error of the comrades who at the Enlarged Executive meeting presented themselves at the head of the so-called minority group consists precisely, in our view, in having expressed judgements whereby they placed themselves and remained outside the essential continuity of our organism, and encouraged tendencies towards its liquidation.

6. Appeals to those comrades who have not accepted to collaborate in applying the Communist International's tactics in Italy, or its specific recommendations about relations between the Communist Party of Italy and the Italian Socialist Party, to draw back from their present attitude and to feel the duty of collaborating with the present majority of the Central Committee in leading the party; and asserts that collaboration with them must take place on the basis of a complete and loyal acceptance of the Communist International's programme, both as regards the united front tactic and as regards the action which the Comintern is carrying out to endow the sections of the International, conceived of as the world party of the revolutionary working class, with organizational solidity, theoretical awareness and a common line of action.

7. Hopes therefore that in pursuit of the struggle against tendencies and individuals who continue to question in practice the fundamental principles which the Communist Party must observe in its work, and who are recalcitrant to its discipline of thought and action, the formation of any faction within the Communist Party will be

eliminated; and that under the guidance of the International Executive Committee, the work of reinforcing and developing a great mass party will be carried forward, a party capable of leading the workers and peasants of Italy towards the struggles upon which their liberation depends.

> Signed: Egidio Gennari, Palmiro Togliatti, Mauro Scoccimarro, Ennio Gnudi, Vittorio Flecchia, Isidoro Azzario, Camilla Ravera, Alfonso Leonetti, Antonio Gramsci, Umberto Terracini

II

The minority of the Central Committee:

1. Indicates the great importance of the discussion which is about to open up inside the party, which for the first time since it was founded is being called upon to give its opinions on key problems of the international and Italian communist movement.

2. Considers that such a discussion must provide an organic and rational solution to the disarray and grave damage which have been inflicted on the party's activity and on the destiny of the proletarian movement in Italy by the disagreement between the former Executive Committee of the party – and the majority established at the Rome Congress in general – and the Communist International.

3. Points to the responsibility of the present majority of the Central Committee which, although not being in agreement with the Rome Theses, has guided the views of the party as a whole in their spirit, even when some of its members as they later claimed did not entirely agree with them; and which made those Theses the basis for its political position at the Fourth Congress, thus continuing and aggravating an artifical and arbitrary dispute between the Italian Communist Party and the Communist International, and reducing the effectiveness of the party's activity among the masses.

4. States that in such a discussion, the necessary examination of the Communist Party's political and organizational activity in Italy, and of the tactics followed by it in the years 1921–4, must be carried out – in conjunction with an examination of the situation in the various sections of the Communist International – in the spirit and with the aim of

deriving from it the lessons needed to determine the party's future tactics and future programme of work.

Signed: Angelo Tasca, Antonio Graziadei,
Giovanni Roveda, Giuseppe Vota

III

Following the passing of the well-known resolution from the majority of the party's Central Committee, since there does not exist within the party anything resembling a constituted faction, and in view of the short period within which the debate authorized by the leadership is to take place, I have thought it appropriate to simply draw up a resolution which reflects the thinking of those comrades who have followed the same course of action that I have with respect to the leadership of the party in recent years, without even having the time to consult them in advance. In the course of the debate, short though it will be, it will be possible to prepare theses which are a little less incomplete than this resolution, and in which the opinions of comrades who are prepared to support the resolution will be taken into acount.

Amadeo Bordiga

1. The group of comrades who led the party in the period following the Livorno Congress considers the need to render the theoretical and political consciousness of the part precise and complete, and its organization well-defined and solid, not to be just a preliminary and occasional task, but a permanent necessity for communist parties, which cannot be in contradiction with the development of the best tactical activity, just as the latter cannot come into in contradiction with the former. This is in accordance with the criteria formulated at length in the Theses on Tactics of the Rome Congress, which faithfully represent the opinions of the group in question.

2. The differences which have arisen between the Communist Party of Italy and the Communist International had their source in a different evaluation of the problems inherent in the tactics, in the internal organization, and in the leadership work of the International as a whole; only as a specific aspect of the overall difference were they reflected in the evaluation of the Italian situation and the task of the PCI.

3. The old Executive of the PCI was able to apply the line of action which corresponded to its views up till the strike of August 1922.[144]

That strike, with all the activity to which it led, amounted to an example of the application of the tactic of winning the masses through the united front, as set out in the Rome Theses. And the situation in which it culminated, with the defeat of the proletariat, for which the other parties and groups which took part in and led the strike were responsible, should have been further developed – despite the general retreat of the Italian working class – with a period of totally autonomous activity by the PCI, denouncing in the most explicit manner as incapable of class action all the other above-mentioned parties and groups, and making itself the centre of proletarian resistance and resurgence against the victorious capitalist offensive.

4. At such a culminating moment, it appeared to the Communist International that the path to win greater forces in Italy was, instead, through splitting the PSI and through fusion of the maximalists with our party. From that moment the International, as was its incontestable right, in practice abrogated to itself leadership of our activity in Italy and directed it towards the new objective. At once, the leaders of the PCI felt themselves and proclaimed themselves to be incompatible with conducting such a policy, with which they did not agree. At the Fourth Congress, after having once again upheld their point of view in the commission-meetings, they made clear their attitude by not speaking against the new policy in the Plenary Session of the Congress. They pledged the most total discipline of the whole party, and of themselves as militants of that party, but they explicitly declined the task of its political leadership.

5. The most important question which arose in this field after the Fourth Congress was not the PCI's sabotage of the Communist International's decisions. The old leaders loyally respected the line just indicated, which did not consist in taking responsibility for achieving fusion, which they believed to be in the first place harmful and – secondarily – impossible, but in demanding that they be immediately replaced. Fusion did not take place, as a result of the attitude of the maximalists, and in any case the International could, if it had so wished, have proceeded to the requested replacement of the party leaders before the Enlarged Executive of June 1923. No action against fusion can be cited on the part of the old leaders, as the documents bear witness.

6. The experience of the party's activity in that period, i.e. after August 1922 – although it cannot be denied that the change of course occurred at a moment which makes very problematical any judgement on the respective results of the old and of the new policy – while it does

not show a balance-sheet of speedy conquest of new forces and political positions, other than along the lines advocated by the old leaders, did not lead to any organic elaboration of a new political consciousness and practice. The oscillating attitudes towards the PSI and its left wing, the blurring of the boundary between the Communist forces and the others, the creation of dual political or press organisms, etc. — all these things show that to the method in question, there corresponded a weakening of the party's precise orientation and organizational discipline, leading to an undeniable state of disarray and discontent among the comrades. Nevertheless, possibilities for successful activity continued to present themselves to the party, which in the material which composes it and in its old structures continues to show its revolutionary capacities, in contrast with the continual criticisms with which some people have sought to teach it the best course — often factually mistaken, and sometimes fatuous and light-minded.

7. The problems of the PCI's activity can only be resolved on the basis of international discussions and decisions concerning the whole orientation of the Communist International. The Left of the PCI can formulate an action programme for the party for today and tomorrow, but only if it bases this on the premise that its own opinions on the tactics, organization and leadership of the Communist International will prevail in the international meetings, thus maintaining its classical programmatic postulates in full force, just as they are engraved in the founding documents provided by Lenin and inspired by the most powerful current of revolutionary Marxism.

8. Only if in such a discussion a totality of concordant views is achieved, and the PCI Left comes to find itself on the terrain of the Communist International majority in the deliberations in question, will the Left be able to participate in the new leadership of the party.

9. The minority of the PCI, i.e. its right wing, corresponds in part to the tendency which places itself on the present tactical terrain of the Communist International, but in part too it represents the survival of immature elements which retain a centrist mentality. Such a group could play the role of liquidating the tradition of the party, if it were to coincide with the activity of groups aiming to liquidate the glorious political tradition of the Communist International. Against this danger, the Left of the PCI will be the most energetic and resolute in the struggle.

10. It is undeniable that in the International, functioning as the world communist party, organic centralization and discipline exclude the

existence of factions or groups able to either take on the leadership of national parties or not, as now occurs in all countries. The PCI Left is for the most speedy attainment of this objective; but it considers that it cannot be achieved by mechanical decisions and fiats, but only by ensuring the correct historical development of the international communist party, which must involve a parallel clarification of political ideology, unambiguous definition of tactics and organizational consolidation.

The International without factions will be one in which there will prevail criteria of political coherence and continuity which make impossible: dual local organizations; fusions; the admission of members not according to the statutory provisions, but with a sudden allocation of important leading functions through negotiations and compromises; political blocs; agitation for unclear demands which may come into conflict with the content of our programme, like that for a workers' government, and so on. If the International were to threaten to evolve in the opposite direction, the emergence of an international left opposition would be an absolute revolutionary and communist necessity. The Left of the PCI is confident that this unhappy eventuality will, by clear decisions of the forthcoming Congress, be unequivocally excluded, for reasons of principle and as a consequence of the most recent experiences of international communist activity; and that the communists will continue, without the compromises and manœuvres of an illusory political diplomacy, a simultaneous pitiless struggle against bourgeois reaction, and against the opportunism of all kinds which comes to nestle among the workers, as a necessary and natural ally of the former.

> Signed: Amadeo Bordiga, Bruno Fortichiari, Ruggero Grieco, Luigi Repossi

> Resolutions published in *Lo Stato Operaio*, 16 May 1924.

60. GRAMSCI'S INTERVENTION AT THE COMO CONFERENCE

I have observed that the mood of comrades has above all been expressed against the so-called "Centre" of the party, and find it strange that a question of nomenclature should have such importance within the Communist Party. It is necessary to study the problems from a more serious and more concrete point of view.

Comrade Bordiga states that he has not even tried to constitute a real faction inside the party. But it is undeniable that when a comrade with a personality like that of Bordiga stands apart, and no longer takes any active part in the work of the party, this fact alone is enough to create a factional mentality among the comrades. It is necessary to take account of this fact in judging our attitude in the present debate. Moreover, we do not have to make any very great efforts to find what our origins were.

In 1919–20, there were three tendencies which later united to form the Communist Party: that represented by *L'Ordine Nuovo* of Turin, the abstentionists, and finally a third, which is only now tending to clarify its positions, and which included all those comrades who entered the party at the time of the Livorno split without having belonged to either of the two tendencies I have already mentioned. We of the *Ordine Nuovo* tendency have always believed it necessary – even before the party was established – to ally ourselves with the left rather than with the right. Any other course, in our view, would have led to promoting tendencies from which we feel very distant.

In this connection, I recall that in Turin, immediately before and after the general strike of April 1920, we were led to break with the group headed by comrade Tasca.[146] Seeing the opportunist danger of the Right, we preferred to ally ourselves with the abstentionists and, at a certain moment, even leave the whole leadership of the section in their hands.

According to many comrades, the occupation of the factories represented the highest point in the revolutionary development of the Italian proletariat. For us, that event initiated the period of decline of the working-class movement. Well, making an estimate at that time of which forces in the socialist movement were most capable of limiting the defeat, we were once again with the Left. And we thought that without the abstentionists, the Communist Party could not be established.

We still maintain that point of view today. But on the other hand, we cannot ignore the errors which the Left has made. In this respect, it is as well to remember that the vote on the Rome Theses had a purely generic and consultative character, and that those Theses should have been represented to the party – with certain modifications, perhaps – after the Fourth Congress of the Third International. Unfortunately, this could not be done because of the deterioration of the overall situation. But today the situation is no longer the same as that which existed in 1921 and 1922. There are the first signs of a recovery of the workers' movement. How will this develop? It is certain that it cannot fail to undergo the influence of the experience which all classes and political parties have acquired in the last few years. This experience has given every group its own physiognomy.

In 1919 and 1920, the whole working population – from the white-collar workers of the North and the capital to the peasants of the South – was following, albeit unconsciously, the general movement of the industrial proletariat. Today the situation has changed, and only through a long, slow process of political reorganization will the proletariat be able to return to being the dominant factor in the situation. We consider that this work cannot be carried out, if we continue to follow the orientation which comrade Bordiga would like the party to continue to follow. The recent electoral performance of our party certainly has great significance, but it is undeniable that our movement lacks the support of the majority of the proletariat.

Bordiga. We would have it, if we had not changed our tactics towards the Socialist Party! In any case, we are in no hurry.

Gramsci. Well *we* are in a hurry! There are situations in which "not being in a hurry" leads to defeat. In 1920, for instance, it was necessary to be in a hurry. I recall that in July of that year, I attended the Abstentionist conference in Florence to propose the creation and establishment of a national communist faction.[147] Comrade Bordiga then too "was in no hurry" and rejected our proposal, so that the occupation of the factories took place without there existing an organized communist faction in Italy, capable of giving the masses who followed the Socialist Party a national slogan. The 'time" factor is also important. Sometimes it is of capital importance.

I have the impression that the comrades who have so far expressed their opinions have forgotten what the fundamental problem which faces our party today is: its relations with the Communist International. Comrade Bordiga's attitude too can be useful, in a certain sense; but his error lies in not taking account of the party's need to resolve the problem of relations with the International. Bordiga's attitude besides can only result in the emergence of a group of heterogeneous elements who will be able to find a measure of unity and consistency in the fact of declaring themselves 'for the International'. This result, which we have already had to lament once, serves to prove how intrinsically incorrect Bordiga's attitude is. The origin of the 'minority' should be ascribed to it.

With respect to the comrades of the minority, the situation has been partly altered as a result of the statement they have produced; but not all the differences have disappeared. On the present political programme, the minority asserts that no disagreement exists. In reality, I recall that in Moscow, for example, comrade Tasca opposed the formula of replacing the unions within the factory. Today, this problem is one of the most important which confront our party. It is posed in the following terms: how must the Communist Party − effective centre of the revolutionary vanguard − lead the trade-union struggles of the working class? Create factory cells, very well: but what work must these carry out? We are convinced that now the Internal Commissions have disappeared, if not formally at least in a functioning sense, the workers will turn to the Communist cells not just for questions of a political character, but also for their trade-union defence; and that it is therefore necessary that comrades should be prepared to carry out this work too. It will be necessary for these problems to be fully studied and thought through, all the more because we are at a decisive turning-point in the history of the Italian workers' movement.

The comrades of the Left protest their disciplined attitude to the International. We say to them: "It is not enough to say that one is disciplined. It is necessary to situate oneself on the terrain of activity indicated by the International." If the International, for reasons known to all, has up to now made concessions, this cannot continue in the future, since this would lead to the fragmentation of the International itself. What has occurred recently inside the Russian party must serve as valuable experience for us.[148] Trotsky's attitude, initially, can be compared to comrade Bordiga's at present. Trotsky, although taking part "in a disciplined manner" in the work of the party, had through his attitude of passive opposition − similar to Bordiga's − created a state of unease throughout the party, which could not fail to get a whiff of this situation. The result was a crisis which lasted several months, and which only today can be said to have been overcome. This shows that opposition – even kept within the limits of a formal discipline – on the part of exceptional personalities in the workers' movement can not merely hamper the development of the revolutionary situation, but can put in danger the very conquests of the revolution.

A few words more on the workers' government. At the June 1923 Enlarged Executive meeting, comrade Trotsky predicted the creation of the *Cartel des Gauches* in France, and posed the problem of the attitude which the French communists should adopt in such a situation.[149] At the time, not much importance was given to this problem. Well, today we can see that the French workers have only given 850 thousand votes to the communists, while they have given millions to the *Cartel des Gauches*.[150] And if the communists at least won these 850 thousand votes, it was due to the fact that they presented the communist slate as the slate of a Workers' and Peasants' Bloc.

Bordiga. Yet a good third of the communist votes were won in Paris, where there are no peasants.

Gramsci. That is true, but one must not forget that all the revolutions of the Paris proletariat have been defeated because of the isolation in which it found itself, and that therefore the Paris workers understand perfectly the need to unite with the peasantry.

Bordiga. But why call it a "bloc" and not simply Communist Party? Does the Communist Party not have the alliance between workers and peasants in its programme?

Gramsci. Let us not quarrel about words. It is necessary to present things in the way one considers most effective to move even the most backward sections of the masses. Not all the workers can understand the whole development of the revolution. Today, for example, the Italian workers of the South are undoubtedly revolutionaries, yet they continue to swear by Di Cesarò and De Nicola.[151] We must take account of such states of mind, and seek means to overcome them. If the communists go among the peasants of the South and speak of their programme, they are not understood. If one of us went to my village to talk about "struggle against the capitalists", he would be told that "capitalists" do not exist in Sardinia. Yet even these masses must be won over. We have the possibility, given precisely the conditions created by fascism, to initiate a mass anti-reactionary movement in the South. But it is necessary to win over these masses, and this can be done only by participating in the struggles which they launch for partial victories and partial demands. The "workers' and peasants' government" slogan must serve to bring together and synthesize the content of these partial struggles, in a programme which can be understood even by the most backward masses.

These are our ideas on the problems of today. I repeat that the comrades must not make an issue of nomenclature: in 1919 Buozzi rebuked us for carrying out activity – through the Factory Councils – that was too reformist.[152] We laughed at the time, and the facts have shown who was reformist and who was revolutionary. Let comrades pose concrete questions, and let them remember that at the present time the most important question is that of our party's relations with the Communist International.

Lo Stato Operaio, 29 May 1924; *L'Unità*, 5 June 1924.

61. THE ITALIAN CRISIS

The radical crisis of the capitalist order, which in Italy as in the entire world began with the War, has not been cured by fascism. Fascism, with its repressive method of government, had made very difficult and indeed almost totally prevented the political manifestations of the general capitalist crisis. However, it has not succeeded in halting this crisis; and even less has it succeeded in renewing and developing the national economy. It is generally said, and even we communists are accustomed to assert, that the present Italian situation is characterized by the ruin of the middle classes. This is true, but it must be understood in all its significance. The ruin of the middle classes is damaging, because the capitalist system is not developing but instead is undergoing a contraction. It is not a phenomenon apart, which can be examined – and whose consequences can be provided against – independently from the general conditions of the capitalist economy. It is precisely the crisis of the capitalist order, which no longer succeeds and will not again succeed in satisfying the vital requirements of the Italian people; which does not succeed in guaranteeing bread and a roof over their heads to the great mass of Italians. The fact that the crisis of the middle classes is in the foreground today, is merely a contingent political fact. It is merely the form of the period, which precisely for that reason we call "fascist". Why? Because fascism arose and developed on the terrain of this crisis in its initial phase. Because fascism struggled against the proletariat and rose to power by exploiting and organizing the lack of consciousness and the lack of spirit of the petty bourgeoisie, drunk with hatred for the working class – which, through the strength of its organization, was succeeding in attenuating the repercussions upon it of the capitalist crisis.

For fascism is becoming exhausted and dying precisely because it has not kept any of its promises, has not satisfied any hopes, has not alleviated any misery. It has broken the revolutionary impetus of the proletariat, dispersed the class unions, lowered wages and increased hours; but this was not enough to guarantee even a limited vitality to the capitalist system. For that, a lowering of the living-standards of the middle classes was also necessary; the looting and pillaging of the petty-bourgeois economy; hence the stifling of all freedoms and not just of proletarian freedoms; and hence a struggle not just against the working-class parties, but also and especially at a given stage against all the non-fascist political parties, against all associations not directly controlled by official fascism.

Why has the crisis of the middle classes had more radical consequences in Italy than in other countries? Why has it created fascism and carried it to State power? Because in our country, given the scanty development of industry and the regional character of what industry there is, not only is the petty bourgeoisie very numerous, but it is also the only class that is "territorially" national. The capitalist crisis, in the years following the War, had also taken the acute form of a collapse of the unitary State and thus encouraged the rebirth of a confusedly patriotic ideology, so that there was no other solution than the fascist one – once the working class had in 1920 failed in its task of creating by its own means a State capable of also satisfying the unitary national needs of Italian society.

The fascist régime is dying because it has not merely failed to halt, but has actually helped to accelerate the crisis of the middle classes initiated after the War. The economic aspect of this crisis consists in the ruin of small and medium firms: the number of bankruptcies has multiplied rapidly in the last two years. The monopoly of credit, the fiscal régime and legislation on rents have crushed the small commercial and industrial enterprise. A real transfer of wealth has taken place from the small and medium to the big bourgeoisie, without any development of the productive apparatus. The small producer has not even become proletarian. He is simply permanently hungry; a desperate man without prospects for the future. Nor has the application of fascist violence to compel savers to invest their capital in a particular direction brought much advantage to the small industrialists. When it has been successful, it has only ricocheted the effects of the crisis from one stratum to another, increasing the already great discontent and distrust among savers caused by the existing monopoly in the sphere of banking, and further aggravated by the *coup de main* tactics which the big entrepreneurs have to resort to in the general distress in order to secure credit.

In the countryside, the development of the crisis is more closely linked with the fiscal policy of the fascist State. From 1920 to today, the average budget of a family of share-croppers or small-holders has undergone a deterioration of some 7,000 *lire*, through tax increases, worsened contractual conditions, etc. The crisis of the small farm in northern and central Italy is now typical. In the South new factors are intervening, the main one being the absence of emigration and the resulting increase in demographic pressure. This is accompanied by a diminution of the cultivated area and hence of the harvest. The grain harvest last year was 68 million quintals in the whole of Italy, i.e. it was above average taking the country as a whole, yet it was below average in the South. This year, the harvest was below average throughout Italy; it failed completely in the South. The consequences of this situation have not yet shown themselves in a violent fashion, because in the South there exist backward economic conditions which prevent the crisis from at once revealing itself fully as happens in advanced capitalist countries. Nevertheless, in Sardinia serious episodes of popular discontent brought about by economic hardship have already occurred.

The general crisis of the capitalist system has thus not been halted by the fascist régime. Under the fascist régime, the existential possibilities of the Italian people have diminished. A restriction of the productive apparatus has taken place, at the very time when demographic pressure was increasing due to the difficulties of overseas emigration. The limited industrial apparatus has only been able to save itself from complete collapse by lowering the living standards of the working class, squeezed by smaller wages, longer working hours and the high cost of living. The result has been an emigration of skilled workers, in other words an impoverishment of the human productive forces which were one of the greatest national riches. The middle classes, who placed all their hopes in the fascist régime, have been overwhelmed by the general crisis; indeed they themselves have become precisely the expression of the capitalist crisis in this period.

These elements, briefly alluded to, serve only to recall the full significance of the present situation, which contains within it no possibility of economic revival. The Italian economic crisis can only be resolved by the proletariat. Only by participating in a European and world revolution can the Italian people regain the ability to utilize fully its human productive forces, and to restore development to the national productive apparatus. Fascism has merely delayed the proletarian revolution, it has not made it impossible. Indeed, it has helped to enlarge and enrich the terrain of the proletarian revolution, which after the fasicst experiment will be a truly popular one.

The social and political disintegration of the fascist régime had its first mass demonstration in the elections of 6 April.[153] Fascism was put clearly into a minority in the Italian industrial zone, in other words where the economic and political power which dominates the nation and the State resides. The elections of 6 April, showing that the régime's stability was only apparent, gave heart again to the masses; stimulated a certain movement among them; and marked the beginning of that democratic wave which came to a head in the days immediately following the assassination of Matteotti, and which still characterizes the situation today.[154] After the elections, the opposition forces acquired an enormous political importance. The agitation they carried on in the press and in parliament, contesting and denying the legitimacy of the fascist government, acted powerfully to dissolve all the State organisms controlled and dominated by fascism. It had repercussions within the national Fascist Party itself, and it cracked the parliamentary majority. This was the reason for the unprecedented campaign of threats against the opposition, and for the assassination of the Unitary Socialist deputy. The storm of indignation provoked by the crime took the Fascist Party by surprise, and it shivered in panic and was lost. The three documents written at that painful moment by Finzi, Filipelli and Cesarino Rossi (and made known to the opposition) show how the very highest levels of the party had lost all confidence and were piling error upon error. From that moment, the fascist régime entered its death-agony. It is still sustained by its so-called fellow-travelling forces, but it is sustained in the way that the rope supports the hanged man.

The Matteotti murder gave the irrefutable proof that the fascist party will never succeed in becoming a normal government party, and that Mussolini possesses nothing of the statesman or dictator other than a few picturesque external poses. He is not an element of national life, he is a phenomenon of rustic folklore, destined to be remembered in stories like one of those mask-characters from the Italian provinces rather than like a Cromwell, a Bolivar or a Garibaldi.

The popular anti-fascist upsurge provoked by the Matteotti assassination found a political form in the secession of the opposition parties from the chamber of Parliament.[155] The opposition Assembly, in reality, became a national political centre around which the majority of the country was organized. The crisis which had exploded in the emotional and moral sphere thus acquired a distinct institutional character. A State was created within the State, an anti-fascist government against the fascist government. The Fascist Party was powerless to check the situation. The crisis had totally overwhelmed it, devastating the ranks of its organization. The first attempt to mobilize the national militia failed utterly, with only 20 per cent answering the call; in Rome, only 800 militiamen presented themselves at the barracks. The mobilization only produced substantial results in a few rural provinces, such as Grosseto and Perugia, which made it possible to bring down to Rome a few legions ready to face a bloody struggle.

The opposition forces still remain the fulcrum of the popular anti-fascist movement. Politically, they represent the upsurge of democracy which is characteristic of the present phase of the Italian social crisis. In the beginning, the opinion of the great majority of the proletariat was also oriented towards these opposition forces. It was the duty of us communists to seek to prevent such a state of affairs from becoming permanently consolidated. Therefore, our parliamentary group joined the Opposition Committee, accepting and emphasizing the main feature which the political crisis was assuming with the existence of two powers and two parliaments. If they had wanted to carry out their duty, which was indicated by the masses in movement, the opposition forces would have had to give a definite political form to the state of affairs that existed objectively – but they refused. It would have been necessary to launch an appeal to the proletariat, which is alone capable of giving substance to a democratic régime. It would have been necessary to intensify the spontaneous strike movement which was beginning to emerge. The opposition forces were afraid of being overwhelmed by a possible working-class insurrection. Hence, they did not want to leave the purely parliamentary terrain to enter upon political questions. They did not want to leave the terrain of a trial for Matteotti's assassins to enter upon a campaign to keep the agitation alive throughout the country. The communists, who could not accept the form of a bloc of parties which the opposition forces gave to the Committee, were ejected.

Our participation in the Committee in an initial stage, and our exit from it at a subsequent stage, have had the following consequences. 1. They have allowed us to survive the most acute phase of the crisis without losing contact with the broad working masses. If it had remained isolated, our party would have been overwhelmed by the democratic upsurge. 2. We have broken the monopoly of public opinion which the opposition forces threatened to establish. A greater and greater part of the working class is becoming convinced that the bloc of opposition forces represents a semi-fascism which wants to reform and soften the fascist dictatorship, without causing the capitalist system to lose any of the benefits which terror and illegality have secured for it in the last years, with the lowering of the Italian people's living standards.

The objective situation, after two months, has not changed. There still *de facto* exist two governments in the country, fighting each other in competition for the real forces of the bourgeois State organization. The outcome of the struggle will depend on the repercussions of the general crisis within the national Fascist Party, on the definitive attitude of the parties which make up the opposition bloc, and on the actions of the revolutionary proletariat led by our party.

In what does the crisis of fascism consist? To understand it, some say that it is first necessary to define the essence of fascism. But the truth is that there does not exist any essence of fascism as such. The essence of fascism in 1922–3 was provided by a particular system of relations of force that existed in Italian society. Today, this system has changed profoundly, and the "essence" has evaporated to some extent. The characteristic feature of fascism consists in the fact that it has succeeded in creating a mass organization of the petty bourgeoisie. It is the first time in history that this has happened. The originality of fascism consists in having found the right form of organization for a social class which has always been incapable of having any cohesion or unitary ideology: this form of organization is the army in the field. The militia is thus the fulcrum of the national Fascist Party: one cannot dissolve the militia without also dissolving the party as a whole. There does not exist a Fascist Party that can turn quantity into quality; that is an apparatus for political selection of a class or a stratum. There only exists a mechanical aggregate, undifferentiated and impossible to differentiate from the point of view of intellectual and political capabilities, which only lives because it has acquired in the civil war an extremely strong *esprit de corps*, crudely identified with the national ideology. Outside the sphere of military organization, fascism has not contributed and cannot contribute anything; and even in this sphere, what it can contribute is very relative.

The product of circumstances in this way, fascism is not capable of realizing any of its ideological premises. Fascism today says that it aims to conquer the State: at the same time, it says that it aims to become a prevalently rural phenomenon. How the two assertions can be reconciled is hard to understand. To conquer the State, it is necessary to be capable of replacing the dominant class in those functions which have an essential importance for the government of society. In Italy, as in all capitalist countries, to conquer the State means first and foremost to conquer the factory; it means to have the capability of taking over from the capitalists in governing the country's productive forces. This can be done by the working class, it cannot be done by the petty bourgeoisie, which has no essential function in the productive field; which in the factory, as an industrial category, exercises a function that is mainly of a police nature, not a productive one. The petty bourgeoisie can conquer the State only by allying itself with the working class, only by accepting the programme of the working class: soviet system instead of parliament in the State organization; communism and not capitalism in the organization of the national and international economy.

The formula "conquest of the State" is empty of meaning in the mouths of the fascists, or has only one meaning: to devise an electoral mechanism which gives a parliamentary majority to the fascists for ever, and at all costs. The truth is that all of fascist ideology is a toy for the state nurseries: a dilettantesque improvisation, which in the past under favourable circumstances was able to delude its followers, but which today is destined to become an object of ridicule even among the fascists themselves. The only active residue of fascism is the military *esprit de corps* cemented by the danger of an outburst of popular vengeance. The political crisis of the petty bourgeoisie, the passage of the overwhelming majority of this class beneath the banner of the opposition forces, the failure of the general measures announced by the fascist leaders can considerably reduce the military effectiveness of fascism, but they cannot annul it.

The system of democratic anti-fascist forces draws its main strength from the existence of the parliamentary Opposition Committee, which has succeeded in imposing a certain discipline on a whole spectrum of parties which goes from the maximalists to the *popolari*. The fact that maximalists and *popolari* obey the same discipline and work within the same programmatic plan – that is the most characteristic feature of the situation. This fact makes the process of development of events slow and painful, and determines the tactic of the opposition forces as a whole: a waiting tactic, of slow encircling manœuvres and patient pounding away at all the positions of the fascist government. The maximalists, with their membership of the Committee and their acceptance of its common discipline, guarantee the passivity of the proletariat. They assure the bourgeoisie, still hesitating between fascism and democracy, that autonomous action of the working class will no longer be possible – except much later, when the new government has already been set up and strengthened, and is already able to crush any uprising of the masses disillusioned both by fascism and by democratic anti-fascism. The presence of the *popolari* is a guarantee against an intermediate fascist-*popolare* solution like that of October 1922. Such a solution would become very likely, because imposed by the Vatican, in the event of a detachment of the maximalists from the bloc and an alliance on their part with us.

The main effort of the intermediate parties (reformists and constitutionalists), assisted by the left *popolari*, has so far been directed towards the following aim: to hold the two extremes together within the same bloc. The servile spirit of the maximalists has adapted itself to the role of the fool in the theatre: the maximalists have accepted to count for the same as the peasants' party or the *Rivoluzione Liberale* groups within the opposition bloc.[156]

The main forces have been contributed to the opposition by the *popolari* and the reformists, who have a considerable following in the cities and in the countryside. The influence of these two parties is complemented by Amendola's Constitutionalists, who bring to the bloc the adherence of broad strata of the army, the war-veterans and the Court. The agitational division of labour between the various parties is made according to their traditions and social roles. The Constitutionalists, since the tactics of the bloc aim to isolate fascism, have the political leadership of the movement. The *popolari* wage a moral campaign based on the trial and its interconnections with the fascist régime; with the corruption and criminality that have flourished around the régime. The reformists combine both these positions, and make themselves ever so tiny, so that everybody will forget their demagogic past; so that everybody will believe that they have redeemed themselves and become indistinguishable from Hon. Amendola or Senator Albertini.

The solid and united stance of the opposition forces has chalked up some considerable successes. It is undoubtedly a success to have provoked the crisis of "fellow-travelling"; in other words, to have compelled the liberals to differentiate themselves actively from fascism and pose conditions to it. This has had, and will have even more, repercussions within fascism itself; and it has created a duality of power between the Fascist Party and the central war-veterans' organization. But it has shifted the centre of gravity of the opposition bloc even further to the right; in other words, it has accentuated the conservative character of anti-fascism. The Maximalists have not noticed this; they are ready to provide the coloured troops not only for Amendola and Albertini, but also for Salandra and Cadorna.

How will this duality of power be resolved? Will there be a compromise between fascism and the opposition bloc? And if a compromise is impossible, will we have an armed struggle? A compromise cannot be totally ruled out; however, it is very unlikely. The crisis which the country is passing through is not a superficial phenomenon, curable with little measures and little expedients. It is the historic crisis of Italian capitalist society, whose economic system is shown to be insufficient for the needs of the population. All relations are exacerbated. Immense masses of people await something very different than a petty compromise. If such a thing occurred, it would mean the suicide of the major democratic parties. An armed insurrection with the most radical aims would at once be placed on the agenda of national life. Fascism, by the nature of its organization, does not tolerate collaborators with equal rights; it only wants chained slaves. There cannot exist a representative assembly under a fascist régime. Every assembly at once becomes a legionaries' encampment, or the antechamber of a brothel for drunken junior officers. Thus the chronicle of each day's events only records a succession of political episodes denoting the disintegration of the fascist system; the slow but inexorable detachment from the fascist system of all peripheral forces.

Will there be an armed clash then? Any struggle on a grand scale will be avoided equally by the opposition forces and by fascism. What will happen will be the opposite to the phenomenon of October 1922, when the March on Rome was the choreographic parade of a molecular process through which the real forces of the bourgeois State (army, magistrature, police, press, Vatican, free-masonry, court, etc.) had passed over to the side of fascism. If fascism were to attempt to resist, it would be destroyed in a long civil war in which the proletariat and the peasants could not fail to take part. The opposition bloc and fascism do not want an all-out struggle to break out, and will systematically avoid one. Fascism will instead seek to preserve the basis of an armed organization, which it can put back into the field as soon as a new revolutionary upsurge appears on the horizon – something which is very far from displeasing the Amendolas and Albertinis of this world, or even the Turatis and Treves.

The drama will unfold, in all likelihood, on a fixed date; it is arranged for the day when the Chamber of Deputies should reopen. The military choreography of October 1922 will be replaced by a more sonorous democratic choreography. If the opposition forces do not return to Parliament, and the fascists – as they are saying – convene the majority as a fascist Constituent Assembly, then we shall have a meeting of the opposition bloc and a show of struggle between the two assemblies.

However, it is possible that the solution will be found in the parliament chamber itself, where the opposition forces will return in the very likely event of a split in the majority putting the Mussolini government clearly into a minority. In that case, we shall have the formation of a provisional government of generals, senators and former Prime Ministers, the dissolution of Parliament and a state of emergency.

The terrain upon which the crisis evolves will continue to be the trial for Matteotti's murder. We shall see further highly dramatic phases of this, when the three documents of Finzi, Filipelli and Rossi are made public and the highest personalities of the régime are swept away by popular indignation. All the real forces of the State, and especially the armed forces, which are already beginning to be the subject of discussion, will have to align themselves clearly on one side or the other, imposing the solution that has already been mapped out and agreed upon.

What should be the political attitude and the tactics of our party in the present situation? The situation is "democratic", because the broad working masses are disorganized, dispersed and fragmented into the undifferentiated people. Hence, whatever the immediate evolution of the crisis may be, we can only foresee an improvement in the political position of the working class, not a victorious struggle for power. The crucial task of our party consists in winning the majority of the working class. The phase which we are passing through is not that of a direct struggle for power, but rather a preparatory phase, of transition to the struggle for power: in short, a phase of agitation, propaganda and organization. This, of course, does not rule out the possibility that savage conflicts may take place. And it does not mean that our party must not at once prepare itself and be ready to confront these. Quite the contrary. But these conflicts too must be seen in the context of the transitional phase, as elements of propaganda and agitation for winning the majority. If there exist within our party fanatical groups and tendencies which want to force the situation, it will be necessary to struggle against these in the name of the entire party, in the name of the vital and permanent interests of the Italian proletarian revolution.

The Matteotti crisis has offered us many lessons in this respect. It has taught us that the masses, after three years of terror and oppression, have become very prudent and want to cut their coat according to their cloth. This prudence is called reformism, it is called maximalism, it is called "opposition bloc". It is destined to disappear, certainly, and in the not too distant future. But for the moment it exists, and can only be overcome if at all times, on every occasion and at every moment, although moving forward, we maintain contact with the working class as a whole. Thus we must combat every rightist tendency which seeks a compromise with the opposition bloc, and which seeks to obstruct the revolutionary development of our tactics and our work of preparation for the next stage.

The first task of our Party consists in equipping itself to become fitted for its historic mission. In every factory and every village there must exist a communist cell, which represents the Party and the International; which knows how to work politically; which shows initiative. Hence, it is necessary to struggle against a certain passivity which still exists among our comrades, and against the tendency to keep the ranks of the Party narrow. On the contrary, we must become a great Party, we must seek to draw into our organizations the greatest possible number of revolutionary workers and peasants, in order to educate them for struggle, form them into mass organizers and leaders, and raise their political level. The workers' and peasants' State can only be built if the revolution has many politically qualified elements at its disposal. The struggle for the revolution can be waged victoriously only if the broad masses are, in all their local formations, organized and led by solid and capable comrades. Otherwise we are really going back, as the reactionaries clamour, to the years 1919–20: in other words, to the years of proletarian impotence; to the years of maximalist demagogy; to the years of working-class defeat. We communists do not want to go back to the years 1919–20 either.

The Party must carry out an enormous amount of work in the trade-union field. Without big trade-union organizations, there is no way out of parliamentary democracy. The reformists may want little trade unions, and may seek only to create guilds of skilled workers. We communists want the opposite from the reformists, and must struggle to re-unionize the broad masses. Certainly, it is necessary to pose the problem concretely and not just formally. The masses have abandoned the unions because the CGL although it has great political effectiveness (it is nothing other than the Unitary Socialist Party), is indifferent to the vital interests of the masses. We cannot propose to create a new body designed to make up for the Confederation's truancy. But we can and must set ourselves the problem of developing a real activity through the factory and village cells.

The Communist Party represents the totality of the interests and aspirations of the working class: we are not a mere parliamentary party. Our party therefore carries on a genuine trade-union activity. It puts itself at the head of the masses also in the little daily struggles for wages, for working hours, for industrial discipline, for accommodation, for bread. Our cells must push the internal commissions to incorporate all proletarian activities within their operations. It is, therefore, necessary to create a broad factory movement that can develop until it gives birth to an organization of city-wide proletarian committees, elected directly by the masses. These committees, in the social crisis that is looming, can become the strongholds of the general interests of the entire working people. This real activity in the factories and villages will revive the trade union and give it back some content and effectiveness, if in parallel all the vanguard elements go back into the organization, for the struggle against the present reformist and maximalist leaders. Whoever keeps his distance from the trade unions today is an ally of the reformists, not a revolutionary militant. He will be able to produce anarchoid phrases, but he will not shift by a hair's-breadth the iron conditions in which the real struggle is going on.

The extent to which the party as a whole, in other words the entire mass of members, succeeds in fulfilling its essential task of winning the majority of workers and transforming in a molecular fashion the bases of the democratic State, will also be the extent to which we shall advance along the path of revolution, and will permit us to pass on to a subsequent phase of development. The whole party, in all its bodies, but especially through its press, must work in a united way to secure the maximum benefit from each comrade's work. Today, we are forming up for the general struggle against the fascist régime. We reply to the stupid campaigns of the opposition press by showing our real determination to overthrow, not merely the fascism of Mussolini and Farinacci, but also the semi-fascism of Amendola, Sturzo and Turati. To achieve this, it is necessary to reorganize the broad masses and become a great party: the only party in which the working population sees the expression of its political will; the citadel of its immediate and permanent historical interests.

> Signed Antonio Gramsci, *L'Ordine Nuovo*, 1 September 1924. Previously published with the title "The crisis of the middle classes" in *L'Unità*, 26 August 1924.

62. DEMOCRACY AND FASCISM

In what sense should one say that fascism and democracy are two aspects of a single reality, two different forms of a single activity: the activity which the bourgeois class carries out to halt the proletarian class on its path? The assertion of this truth is contained in the theses of the Communist International, but only in Italy does the history of the last few years gives an unambiguous proof of it. In Italy, in the last few years, there has been a perfect division of labour between fascism and democracy.

It became clear after the War that it was impossible for the Italian bourgeoisie to go on ruling with a democratic system. Yet before the War, Italian democracy had already been a fairly singular system. It was a system which knew neither economic freedom nor substantial political freedoms; which strove through corruption and violence to prevent any free development of new forces, whether they committed themselves in advance to the existing framework of the State or not; and which restricted the ruling class to a minority incapable of maintaining its position without the active assistance of the policeman and the *carabiniere*. In the Italian democratic system, before the War, each year several dozen workers fell in the streets; and peasants were sent to pick grapes in some places with muzzles on, for fear they might taste the fruit. Democracy, for the peasants and workers, consisted only in the fact that at the base they had the possibility of creating a network of organizations and developing these, strand by strand, to the point where they included the majority of decisive elements of the working class. Even this very simple fact implied a death-sentence for the democratic system. The post-war crisis made it explicit.

The existence and development of a class organization of the workers create a state of affairs which cannot be remedied, either through the State violence which every democratic order permits itself, or with a systematic use of the method of political corruption of leaders. This could be seen in Italy after the first elections held under universal suffrage and with proportional representation.[157] After these, the democratic bourgeoisie felt impotent to solve the problem of how to prevent power slipping from its grasp. Despite the wishes of the leaders, and notwithstanding the absence of conscious guidance, the workers' movement could not fail to advance and achieve decisive developments. The handclasps for Filippo Turati, the winks at D'Aragona, and the favours done on the sly for the mandarins of the cooperative movement, were no longer sufficient to contain a movement which was impelled by the pressure of millions of men integrated, in however illogical and elementary a manner, in an organization: millions of men moved by the stimulus of elementary needs which had increased and been left unsatisfied. At this juncture, those democrats who wanted to remain consistent posed themselves the problem of how to "make the masses loyal to the State". An insoluble problem, so long as there did not exist a State for which the masses would be flesh and blood; a State which had emerged from the masses through an organic process of creation, and which was bound to them. In reality, at this juncture democracy understood that it must draw aside, leaving the field to a different force. Fascism's hour had come.

What service has fascism performed for the bourgeois class and for "democracy"? It set out to destroy even that minimum to which the democratic system was reduced in Italy – i.e. the concrete possibility to create an organizational link at the base between the workers, and to extend this link gradually until it embraced the great masses in movement. It set out too to annihilate the results already achieved in this field. Fascism has accomplished both these aims, by means of an activity perfectly designed for the purpose. Fascism has never manoeuvred, as the reactionary State might have done in 1919 and 1920, when faced with a massive movement in the streets. Rather, it waited to move until working-class organization had entered a period of passivity and then fell upon it, striking it as such, not for what it "did" but for what it "was" – in other words, as the source of links capable of giving the masses a form and physiognomy. The strength and capacity for struggle of the workers for the most part derive from the existence of these links, even if they are not in themselves apparent. What is involved is the possibility of meeting; of discussing; of giving these meetings and discussions some regularity; of choosing leaders through them; of laying the basis for an elementary organic formation, a league, a cooperative or a party section. What is involved is the possibility of giving these organic formations a continuous functionality; of making them into the basic framework for an organized movement. Fascism has systematically worked to destroy these possibilities.

Its most effective activity has, therefore, been that carried on in the localities; at the base of the organizational edifice of the working class; in the provinces, rural centres, workshops and factories. The sacking of subversive workers; the exiling or assassination of workers' and peasants' "leaders"; the ban on meetings; the prohibition on staying outdoors after working hours; the obstacle thus placed in the way of any "social" activity on the part of the workers; and then the destruction of the Chambers of Labour and all other centres of organic unity of the working class and peasantry, and the terror disseminated among the masses – all this had more value than a political struggle through which the working class was stripped of the "rights" which the Constitution guarantees on paper. After three years of this kind of action, the working class has lost all form and all organicity; it has been reduced to a disconnected, fragmented, scattered mass. With no substantial transformation of the Constitution, the political conditions of the country have been changed most profoundly, because the strength of the workers and peasants has been rendered quite ineffective.

When the working class is reduced to such conditions, the political situation is "democratic". In such conditions, in fact, so-called liberal bourgeois groups can, without fear of fatal repercussions on the internal cohesion of State and society: 1. separate their responsibilities from those of the fascism which they armed, encouraged and incited to struggle against the workers; 2, restore "the rule of law", i.e. a state of affairs in which the possibility for a workers' organization to exist is not denied. They can do the first of these two things because the workers, dispersed and disorganized, are not in any position to insert their strength into the bourgeois contradiction deeply enough to transform it into a general crisis of society, prelude to revolution. The second thing is possible for them because fascism has created the conditions for it, by destroying the results of thirty years' organizational work. The freedom to organize is only conceded to the workers by the bourgeois when they are certain that the workers have been reduced to a point where they can no longer make use of it, except to resume elementary organizing work – work which they hope will not have political consequences other than in the very long term.

In short, "democracy" organized fascism when it felt it could no longer resist the pressure of the working class in conditions even of only formal freedom. Fascism, by shattering the working class, has restored to "democracy" the possibility of existing. In the intentions of the bourgeoisie, the division of labour should operate perfectly: the alternation of fascism and democracy should serve to exclude for ever any possibility of working-class resurgence. But not only the bourgeois see things in this way. The same point of view is shared by the reformists, by the maximalists, by all those who say that present conditions for the workers of Italy are analogous to those of thirty years ago, those of 1890 and before, when the working-class movement was taking its first steps among us. By all those who believe that the resurgence should take place with the same slogans and in the same forms as at that time. By all those, therefore, who view the conflict between "democratic" bourgeoisie and fascism in the same way that they then viewed the conflicts between radical and conservative bourgeois. By all those who speak of "constitutional freedoms" or of "freedom of work" in the same way that one could speak of these at the outset of the workers' movement.

To adopt this point of view means to weld the working class inexorably within the vicious circle in which the bourgeoisie wishes to confine it. To hear the reformists, the workers and peasants of Italy today have nothing more to hope for than that the bourgeoisie should itself give them back the freedom to reconstruct their organization and make it live; the freedom to re-establish trade unions, peasant leagues, party sections, Chambers of Labour, and then federations, cooperatives, labour exchanges, worker-control offices, committees designed to limit the boss's freedom inside the factory, and so on and so forth – until the pressure of the masses reawoken by the organizations, and that of the organizations themselves, to transcend the boundaries of bourgeois society becomes so strong that "democracy" can neither resist it nor tolerate it, and will once again arm an army of blackshirts to destroy the menace.

How is the vicious circle to be broken? Solving this problem means solving, in practice, the problem of revolution. There is only one way: to succeed in reorganizing the great mass of workers during the very development of the bourgeois political crisis, and not by concession of the bourgeois, but through the initiative of a revolutionary minority and around the latter. The Communist Party, from the day in which the fascist régime went into crisis, has not set itself any other task than this. Is it a task of an "organizational" nature in the narrow sense of the word, or is it a "political" task? What we have said above serves to show that only insofar as the Communist Party succeeds in solving it, will it succeed in modifying the terms of the real situation. "Reorganizing" the working class, in this case, means in practice "creating" a new force and causing it to intervene on the political scene:

a force which today is not being taken into account, as if it no longer existed. Organization and politics are thus converted one into the other.

The work of the Communist Party is facilitated by two fundamental conditions. 1. By the fact that the shattering of the working class by fascism has left the Communist Party itself surviving, as the organized fraction of the class; as the organization of a revolutionary minority and of the cadres of a great mass party. The whole value of the line followed by the communists in the first years of the party consists in this, as does the value of the activity of purely technical organization carried on for a year after the *coup d'état*. 2. By the fact that the alternation from fascism to democracy and from democracy to fascism is not a process abstracted from other economic and political facts, but takes place simultaneously with the extension and intensification of the general crisis of the capitalist economy, and of the relations of force built upon it. There thus exists a powerful objective stimulus towards the return of the masses to the field, for the class struggle. Neither of these conditions exists for the other so-called workers' parties. They in fact all agree, not just in denying the value of conscious party organization, but in accepting the bourgeois thesis of the progressive stabilization of the capitalist economy after the wartime crisis.

But the political function of the Communist Party is revealed and develops with greater clarity and more effectively because of the fact that it alone is capable of calling for the creation of an organization which, transcending at one and the same time the limits of narrowly party organization and of trade-union organization, realizes the unity of the working class on a vaster terrain: that of preparation for a political struggle in which the class returns to the field arrayed for battle autonomously, both against the fascist bourgeois and against the democratic and liberal bourgeois. This organization is provided by the "workers' and peasants' committees" for the struggle against fascism.

To find in the history of the Italian movement an analogy with the "workers' and peasants' committees", it is necessary to go back to the factory councils of 1919 and 1920 and to the movement which emerged from them. In the factory council, the problem of the class's unity, and that of its revolutionary activity to overthrow the bourgeois order, were considered and resolved simultaneously. The factory council realized the organizational unity of all workers, and at the same time carried the class struggle to an intensity such as to make the supreme clash inevitable. Not only the fable of collaboration and the utopia of social peace, but also the foolish legend of an organization developing with bourgeois permission inside capitalist society until it transcends the latter's limits and empties it gradually of its content, found a total negation in the factory council. Working-class unity was achieved on the terrain of revolution, breaking the economic and political organization of capitalist society from below.

To what extent can the revolutionary function once fulfilled by the factory councils be carried out today by the workers' and peasants' committees? *L'Ordine Nuovo*, which in the first period of its existence devoted itself in particular to developing theses relating to the councils movement and to encouraging the spontaneous creation and the development of these organisms, is now basing its propaganda and agitational work on this other problem, to which the Communist Party is devoting itself today. The continuity between the two, whatever the points of similarity and difference between councils and committees may be, lies in the effort to induce the resurgent movement of the broad masses to express itself in an organic form, and to find in it the germs of the new order of things which we want to create. The odious alternation and the base division of labour between fascism and democracy will come to an end only insofar as this effort produces a result.

Unsigned, *L'Ordine Nuovo*, 1 November 1924.

63. THE FALL OF FASCISM

First: there is a contingent political problem, which is how to overthrow the government headed by Benito Mussolini. The bourgeois opposition forces, who have posed this problem in the most limited conceivable fashion, thinking that this would make their task easier to accomplish, have been trapped since June in a blind alley. For to think one can reduce the crisis of the Mussolini government to a normal governmental crisis is quite absurd. In the first place, there is the militia which obeys Mussolini alone, and puts him absolutely beyond the reach of a normal political manoeuvre. A struggle has been going on for several months to overcome the obstacle of the militia, but on an inadequate terrain. The Army has worked at it, the King has come into the open. But in the end they have found themselves just where they were at the beginning. Mussolini will not go.

In addition, even supposing it were possible to settle with the militia at no great cost, as soon as the question of Mussolini's elimination from the government is posed concretely, a problem arises that is not only more serious but also more decisive in character: who will hold the Matteotti trial? A Mussolini government cannot allow the Matteotti trial to be held. The reasons are well known. But neither can or will Mussolini go, until he is certain that the trial will not be held, either by him or by anybody else. Again, the reasons are known to everybody. Not to hold the trial, however – in other words to free, sooner or later and perhaps sooner rather than later, those at present under arrest – means to risk an open revolt of public opinion. It means placing the government at the mercy of any blackmailer or purveyor of confidential documents, and thus walking on a razor's edge. Not to hold the trial means to leave an ever-open wound, with the possibility of a "moral opposition" that can be far stronger and more effective, in certain circumstances, than any political opposition.

Now, there can be no doubting that every fraction of the bourgeoisie would be willing never to speak again either of the crime or of the trial, if that would restore the stability of the bourgeois order. It is said that this theme has indeed already been developed, at meetings of the opposition. But it is equally true that the campaign on the crime, and for a trial, cannot simply be bequeathed to anti-bourgeois groups – for instance, to a proletarian party. To consign things to silence would by no means mean that 39 million Italians would forget them. So nothing new can be achieved by normal means. The policies of fascism and the reactionary bourgeoisie – from the day when public opinion unanimously rose up against the Matteotti assassination, and Mussolini was overwhelmed by this revolt to the point of making certain moves which were bound to have, and will have, incalculable consequences – have been blocked by an unmovable obstacle. As a result of something similar, but much less serious, at the time of the Dreyfus Affair French society and the French State were brought to the brink of revolution. But, people say, what was involved there was something deeper than a moral question; what was involved was the rotation of classes and social categories in government. But the same is true in Italy, and moreover with the appropriate aggravating features.

So we come to the second aspect of the problem, to the problem of substance: not of the Mussolini government, or of the militia, or of the trial, and so on; but of the régime which the bourgeoisie has had to utilize, in order to break the strength of the proletarian movement. This second aspect, for us and for everybody, is the essential one; but it is indissolubly linked to the former. Indeed, all the dilemmas and uncertainties and difficulties which make it impossible to foresee any solution of a limited character, as the opposition and indeed the whole bourgeoisie has in mind, are a symptom of very deep and substantive contradictions. At the basis of everything, there is the problem of fascism itself: a movement which the bourgeoisie thought should be a simple "instrument" of reaction in its hands, but which once called up and unleashed is worse than the devil, no longer allowing itself to be dominated, but proceeding on its own account. The murder of Matteotti, from the point of view of defending the régime, was a very grave error. The "affair" of the trial, which nobody can manage to liquidate decently, is a wound in the régime's flank such as no revolutionary movement, in June 1924, was capable of opening. It was, in fact, simply the expression and the direct consequence of fascism's tendency not to present itself as a mere "instrument" of the bourgeoisie, but in its continual abuses, violence and crimes to follow an inner rationale of its own – which ends up by no longer taking any account of the interests of conservation of the existing order.

And it is this last point which we must examine and evaluate more carefully, to have a guide-line for resolving the problem we are discussing. The tendency of fascism which we have attempted to characterize breaks the normal alternation between periods of reaction and periods of "democracy", in such a way as may at first sight seem favourable to the maintenance of a reactionary line and to a more rigid defence of the capitalist order, but which in reality may resolve itself into the opposite. For there are, in fact, elements influencing the situation in a way that runs directly counter to any plan for preservation of the bourgeois régime and the capitalist order. There is the economic crisis; there is the hardship suffered by the broad masses; there is the anger provoked by fascist and police repression. There is a situation such that, while the political centres of the bourgeoisie are not succeeding in bringing off their salvage manoeuvres, there is a growing possibility of intervention in the field by the forces of the working class. Thus the dilemma fascism/democracy is tending to become converted into another: fascism/proletarian insurrection.

The thing can also be translated into very concrete terms. In June, immediately after the assassination of Matteotti, the blow suffered by the régime was so strong that immediate intervention by a revolutionary force would have put its fate in jeopardy. The intervention was not possible, because in majority the masses were either incapable of moving or oriented towards intermediate solutions, under the influence of the democrats and social-democrats. Six months of uncertainty and crisis, without any way out, have inexorably accelerated the process whereby the masses are becoming detached from the bourgeois groups and coming to support the revolutionary party and its positions. The complete liquidation of the opposition's position, which seems daily more certain, will give a definitive impetus to this process. Then, in the eyes of the masses too, the problem of the fall of fascism will present itself in its true terms.

Unsigned, *L'Ordine Nuovo*, 15 November 1924.

64. REPORT TO THE CENTRAL COMMITTEE: 6 February 1925[158]

Political Situation

At the last meeting of the Central Committee, it was said that the political and general situation was such as to permit the conclusion that the slogan of workers' and peasants' committees might be transformed from an agitational into an action slogan: in other words, it might enter the phase of concrete realization.[159] We stated that the activity of the party and all party bodies must be concentrated on realizing it; but so far we have not achieved any great results in this field.

How then has the political situation developed in this period of time? The opposition forces genuinely thought to bring about an anti-fascist movement, planned to culminate in Milan, which was to overthrow fascism and instal a military dictatorship. But when it became a question of facing up concretely to the execution of this plan, divergences and disagreements appeared within the Committee of Opposition, these were naturally hard to overcome, and in reality nothing serious was accomplished. Fascism, aware of this plan of the opposition forces, reacted with an activity whose culminating point was Mussolini's famous speech.[160] And the government, with new press measures which made it impossible to publish the sensational documents which the opposition had utilized for its campaign among the popular masses, stripped the Aventine of its only strength and beyond any question liquidated the opposition.[161]

The opposition forces had placed hopes in the king; but through their actions, they in fact drove the king to link himself more closely with Mussolini. For the king was afraid of the situation which the opposition was bringing about, so much so that some court elements even advised against the publication of the Rossi Memorandum, which marked the beginning of the fascist counter-offensive. With the hopes of the oppositions thus dashed, their activity was taken over by Giolitti, Salandra and Orlando, who took up a position against the electoral law and around whom there was formed a great democratic-Popular bloc, headed by Giolitti.

Today, the Aventine has finished its historical function. The bourgeois part of it is adopting a new position of its own, and creating a liberal-constitutional centre with its own physiognomy and political programme. Within the Aventine, there still remain elements who want a different outcome. These elements know that the constitutional forces of the Aventine only want to succeed Mussolini, and that they will make use of the Action Committee of the Opposition only as a committee of provocation (which, however, will do very, very little, since Giolitti wants to avoid any violent action). But they think they can remain with the constitutional opposition forces, in order to make use of their financial and material resources, and in order conspiratorially to enlarge and intensify their activity, so as to channel it towards different solutions from those which the constitutional forces are aiming at. Such elements have spoken with us in these terms, and even made us some proposals. We have no confidence in these elements. However, we think it necessary to follow their activity closely, to confront them with concrete problems, and to put to them clearly what our platform of action could be. The forces at the command of these groups are in any case very scanty, consisting of a few republicans, the supporters of *Italia libera*, the Migliolisti, and a few Unitary Socialists.[162]

The aim of fascism, or rather of Mussolini, is to gain by means of the new electoral law an electoral result similar to that of 6 April last, but in a peaceful manner and on a Mussolinian rather than a fascist platform. Mussolini is relying today, not so much on the extremist elements of his party, as on a reorganization of the General Confederation of Industry which will modify the situation. He really accepts the programme of the fellow-travellers, even if he has separated himself from them in the parliamentary sphere. Freeing himself from the extreme *squadrista* elements, Mussolini will form a conservative party and, with the new electoral law, will succeed without difficulty in forming a Mussolinian rather than a fascist majority, without physical violence and replacing such violence by fraud.

Among the anti-fascist forces, those of the Confederation are certainly the largest; but the entire tactic of the Confederation is aimed at eliminating the revolutionary forces, in order to give the impression they have disappeared. The tactic of the Confederation, moreover, is making it increasingly clear to the masses how necessary it is that the workers' and peasants' committees should become a reality, since the working-class masses as a class cannot but seek organs and forms in which they can find a political expression of their own. When in 1919 the unions abandoned the class terrain, the masses found their political expression in the Factory Councils; through these, they asserted a will that was different from that which the union leaders expressed through their trade-union bodies. Today, the leaders of the Confederation are once again compelling the workers to seek their own way and means of expression, and for this reason our slogan of workers' and peasants' committees is becoming more vital and real than ever.

The tactics of the Confederation is also creating a tendency not to be unionized, which helps to direct all our work, including in the trade-union field, towards the organization of workers' and peasants' committees.

The general economic situation, and above all the increase in the price of bread, give us the major themes for our propaganda and our campaign.

In the course of this last period, the party has not been given an opportunity to make proposals to the opposition. In general, the masses no longer believe in the opposition, yet at the same time they have felt that somebody among the opposition forces would be doing something. This is what has produced the state of uncertainty and disintegration which has characterized the recent period, and which has provided unfavourable terrain for any initiative.

An identical situation has also been produced in the parliamentary field. We returned to Parliament in the manner you all know, and then with Grieco's speech, which disproved many legends circulated about us by the opposition and had positive repercussions among the masses.[163] Nevertheless, our last intervention did not have the same success as our first intervention in the Chamber. Parliament has now lost all importance in the eyes of the country, and the very moment of our return had lost much of the dramaticity of the first moment when Parliament reopened. Moreover, the fascists – including even the least intelligent of them – have learnt during this period to become politicians; in other words, they have learnt how to swallow the bitterest of pills in order to achieve particular political ends. This increased the difficulties of our intervention, which from the parliamentary point of view, and as regards the way in which it occurred, did not have great success. We are not yet very skilled in parliamentary techniques.

In conclusion, we may say that this last period has had the value of leading to a greater clarification of the situation and of political positions. Today, we are faced with the formation of the conservative party which will allow Mussolini to remain on in power; with the formation of a liberal-constitutional centre, grouping all the constitutional opposition forces; and with a left represented by our party. All the other groups are gradually losing any importance: they are disappearing and they are destined to disappear. The Aventine has fragmented, though it continues to remain alive more than anything else as a collection of blocs. The *popolari* have fragmented the Aventine with their assertion that programmatic statements and statements of principle may be made by every individual party among the opposition forces. The Unitary Socialists have situated themselves entirely upon the terrain of constitutionality. As for the maximalists, they can sense that the opposition would like to drive them out, in order to form an electoral bloc which would naturally exclude those political groups which make anti-constitutional statements – even if only of a verbal nature. But the maximalists will do everything possible to find a compromise and remain inside the opposition.

We must maintain relations with those in the opposition who want an insurrection. First of all, because to do so is useful from an informational point of view; but also because it is as well to follow certain emerging currents, which come up with statements like the following: there is no longer any middle way between fascism and communism, and we choose communism. Statements of this kind, apart from having a real value, are also indications not to be ignored of the fragmention which is taking place – and intensifying – within the Aventine.

We are particularly interested in the positions of Miglioli and Lussu.[164] Miglioli is resuming publication of his newspaper, and by his request for funds from us is binding himself to us. He is accepting an editorial board partly composed of our elements. In this paper, which is for the moment remaining a far-left Popular organ, Miglioli will carry on a campaign in favour of joining the Red Peasants' International. In the organizational field, he will convene peasants' assemblies, in which representatives from us and from the Red Peasants' International will take part. Lussu's attitude too – he is asking to go to Moscow and making interesting statements – indicates a shifting of forces among the mass of peasants that is putting pressure on their leaders; and that is of significance for us.

In general, the disintegration of the Aventine has strengthened the revolutionary tendencies, and reveals a shifting of the masses at the base. In the past months, it has not been possible to obtain evidence of this shift in any organizational form; but it has occurred, and in our direction. It has been molecular in form, but it has occurred.

What practical work must the party carry out on the basis of this examination of the situation? We must intensify activity designed to illustrate to the masses the significance and value of our slogan of workers' and peasants' committees. We must develop political struggle in a form that is clearer to all workers. We must place on the agenda (as concrete preparation and not as an immediate solution) the problem of preparing for insurrection. The last political events mark the beginning of a phase in which insurrection is becoming a possibility. In which it is becoming the only means of expression for the political will of the masses, who have been stripped of every other form of expression. The party has the duty of equipping the masses with the appropriate means.

We must therefore enlarge the bases of our organization. We must organize street cells, which must also have the task of controlling the entire life of the population in the big cities, in such a way that at the right moment we shall be in a position to give those decisive blows which will ensure the success of the insurrection. We must confront the problem of arms, which should be considered from two points of view: the organization of men, and the necessary preparation for acquiring and storing arms (this second part of the problem can be resolved more easily if the party, as a whole, works properly in the street cells). We must indicate to the street cells the political work which they must carry out, including in relation to the slogan of workers' and peasants' committees – which cannot be created solely by the factory workers, but must become mass organisms, with the participation of all the population not grouped in the factories, and with the inclusion of women.

In all our political work, we must observe the fundamental principle: never advance slogans which are too distant from the forces at our disposal; ensure that to every slogan there corresponds real preparation and adequate material.

In addition, it is necessary to enlarge the party centre. It is necessary that the party should be able to have a political Executive Committee at its disposal (in the sense that it should devote itself mainly to the political work which it is necessary to carry out today), and also suitable bodies for organizational work. Our organizational forces are inadequate, and we must tackle the problem of increasing them. The Comintern would like the party to provide a full-timer for every federation. This will not be possible for us at present; but we must at least succeed in creating regional secretaries for all the regions in Italy, and especially for those where the movement is least developed and hence a greater effort and greater sustained activity is necessary.

The work of the cells is inadequate. It is necessary to ensure that every cell makes a report each week to its area; the area should report fortnightly to the federation; and the federations should send the Executive at least monthly detailed reports on the political work carried out and on the local situation. On the basis of these reports, the Executive Committee should continually dispatch to the federations instructions, information and suggestions aimed at making the work in each locality more extensive, complete and fruitful. This should be the main political work of the Executive within the party membership. Work of an organizational character should be entrusted to other bodies.

When an important slogan such as that of the workers' and peasants' committees is launched, one passes through a whole succession of interpretations. Between the phase of agitation and propaganda and the phase of realization of such a slogan, there lies what one might term a twilight period, which is precisely that which we have defined as one of "little success", but which does not at all mean that the slogan of workers' and peasants' committees has been, or should be, abandoned. After the last events, it has indeed become more radical, and remains our slogan, the centre of our activity, around which we must naturally carry on all the work of agitation to which comrade Valle [Tasca] has referred. I have already given instructions to our federations in this respect. All federations and sections must indeed be charged to study the local situation and the specific needs of the workers in the various localities. This preliminary examination constitutes the party's preparatory work. Next, our local organisms must organize factory assemblies, in which the problems of working-class life can be pointed out; these can then be summed up under the general organizational slogan calling for the creation of workers' and peasants' committees – mass organizations – charged with leadership of working-class struggles and demonstrations. All our work must be carried out in accordance with this orientation.

Certainly, we must stress the needs of the masses – but in order to organize them in a form which synthesizes them, which is that of the workers' and peasants' committees. We must be the motors of this formation; the process is slow, but it is taking place. Already, even now, our propaganda and agitation are coinciding with some first examples of realization, even though these are still uncertain.

As for our trade-union activity among the masses, I consider that it should also be carried out among the non-unionized masses. This faces us with the threat of a trade-union split, which formally we must avoid, but which should not immobilize us. Indeed, we will succeed in overcoming it to the extent that we succeed in ensuring that the movement is led by the workers' and peasants' committees, in the factories and urban [*word missing*].

As regards the Maximalist Party, comrade Serrati has done the pamphlet, which will be published and distributed.[165] It is certain that we must do something to illustrate the position of the Maximalist Party. In order to bring about great activity on the left of the party, and hasten the party's disintegration, I consider that we should attack the left itself. Serrati is exaggerating when he says that the situation has been totally reversed since the last Central Committee meeting. The opposition bloc did have mass influence; but we know, and have always said, that the bourgeoisie is attached to fascism. The bourgeois and fascism stand in the same relation to each other as do the workers and peasants to the Russian Communist Party.

Serrati. I said totally reversed in the sense of the hopes that were widespread among the masses.

Gramsci. Even this is not true.

Serrati. At least it is more true.

Gramsci. The masses were influenced by the bourgeoisie, but with a great deal of obscurity and confusion. Now, compared with one hundred measures of confusion, ten of clarity represent an advantage for us.

Serrati. You are right.

Gramsci. Today the classes have taken position on a national scale. Fascism has restored to the bourgeoisie class consciousness and organization. In this process of homogenization which has taken place, the working class too has made progress and achieved greater uniformity. The alliance between workers and peasants has taken a step forward; the attitudes of Miglioli and Lussu are an indication of this, and in this sense they have value and merit our attention. Insofar as a new disposition of the country's social forces has been created, we must recognize that there has been progress.

The party's activity has had weaknesses. But one cannot but recognize a notable improvement in the party generally, a greater degree of initiative in the local organizations. The party today is a better instrument of struggle than in the past, and will improve as the movement develops and activity is intensified.

Comrade Longo asks for precise information about the creation of workers' and peasants' committees and the function of cells. He who does not wish to work says: "Give me a precise model and I will start work." In reality, the cells were formed from the moment they began to work. Any definition would only lead to passivity and inaction.

The present situation is one which requires general agitation: the inadequacy of our organization, of course, prevents this. It is necessary to step up our work in all fields of organization and agitation.

As regards the Maximalist Party, I agree with Serrati: we will describe the situation in the Socialist Party to the masses, but for purposes of agitation, as agitation and nothing else.

Trade-union Question

The Trade-union Committee must become a mass organism, leading the working-class masses organized in the General Confederation of Labour and those outside it. Avoiding, of course, splits and clashes with the Confederation, but without renouncing any action for fear of such clashes. We must make use of our trade-union apparatus to generalize, sharpen and lead every moment, until workers' and peasants' committees have been created.

The present rules of the Confederation are designed to prevent any member of the Confederation from becoming a leader of a mass movement. We must thwart this design. The rules of the Confederation will never allow us to conquer this organism: as in Russia, we must create a centralized organization of factory councils which will replace the present trade-union organization for mass mobilization and action.

Our Trade-union Committee will be modified in the sense that comrade Azzario will be replaced by comrade Germanetto. We must say to comrade Azzario that his resolution violated party discipline, or rather party directives.[166] Certainly, the Confederation of Labour was only waiting for a pretext to expel us, and perhaps any resolution would have had the same result as that which was presented. But the first part of that resolution was certainly in contradiction to the directives given by the Trade-union Committee.

We must react against the tendency not to be unionized which the General Confederation of Labour's action has certainly helped to encourage among the workers.

Trotsky Question

The resolution should refer to the question of Bolshevizing all parties, a question put on the agenda for the Enlarged Executive meeting.[167] It should contain an exposition of Trotsky's thought: his predictions about American super-capitalism, which will apparently have a European arm in England and bring about a prolonged enslavement of the proletariat under the dominance of American capital.[168] We reject these predictions, which by postponing the revolution indefinitely would shift the whole tactics of the Communist International, which would have to go back to mere propaganda and agitation among the masses. They would also shift the tactics of the Russian State, since if one postpones the European revolution for an entire historical phase – if, in other words, the Russian working class will not for a long time be able to count on the support of the proletariat of other countries – it is evidence that the Russian revolution must be modified. This is why the democracy advocated by Trotsky meets with so much favour.

The resolution should also say that Trotsky's conceptions, and above all his attitude, represent a danger inasmuch as the lack of party unity, in a country in which there is only one party, splits the State. This produces a counter-revolutionary movement; it does not, however, mean that Trotsky is a counter-revolutionary, for in that case we would ask for his expulsion.

Finally, lessons should be drawn from the Trotsky question for our party. Before the last disciplinary measures, Trotsky was in the same position as Bordiga is at present in our party: he played a purely figurative role in the Central Committee. His position created a tendentially factional situation, just as Bordiga's attitude maintains an objectively factional situation in our party. Although Bordiga is formally correct, politically he is wrong. The Italian Communist Party needs to regain its homogeneity, and to abolish this potentially factional situation. Bordiga's attitude, like that of Trotsky, has disastrous repercussions. When a comrade with Bordiga's qualities withdraws, a distrust of the party is created among the workers, which leads to defeatism. Just as in Russia, when Trotsky took up this attitude, many workers thought that everything was in danger in Russia. Fortunately, it became clear that this was not true.

65. INTRODUCTION TO THE FIRST COURSE OF THE PARTY SCHOOL

Which specific need of the working class and its party, the Communist Party, has stimulated the initiative of a correspondence school, now finally beginning to be realized with the publication of the present batch of study notes?[169]

For almost five years, the Italian revolutionary workers' movement has been plunged into a situation of illegality or semi-legality. Freedom of the press, the rights of assembly, association and propaganda – all these have been virtually suppressed. The formation of leading cadres of the proletariat can, therefore, no longer take place in the ways and by the methods which were traditional in Italy up to 1921. The most active working-class elements are persecuted; all their movements and all their reading is controlled; the workers' libraries have been burnt or otherwise dispersed; the great mass organizations no longer exist, and great mass actions can no longer be carried out. Militants either do not take part at all, or only do so in the most limited way, in discussions and the clash of ideas. An isolated existence, or the occasional gathering of tiny restricted groups; the possibility of becoming habituated to a political life which in other times would have seemed exceptional: these engender feelings, states of mind and points of view which are often incorrect, and sometimes even unhealthy.

The new members whom the party gains in such a situation, clearly sincere men of vigorous revolutionary faith, cannot be educated in our methods by the broad activity, wide-ranging discussions and mutual checking which characterize a period of democracy and mass legality. Thus a very serious danger threatens. The mass of the party – growing accustomed in the illegal conditions to think only of the expedients necessary to escape the enemy's surprise attacks; growing accustomed to only seeing actions by little groups as possible and immediately organizable; seeing how the dominators have apparently won, and kept, power through the action of armed and militarily organized minorities – draws slowly away from the marxist conception of the proletariat's revolutionary activity. And while it seems to become radicalized, in that extremist statements and bloodthirsty phrases are often heard on its lips, in reality it becomes incapable of defeating the enemy.

The history of the working class, especially in the epoch through which we are passing, shows that this danger is not an imaginary one. The recovery of revolutionary parties, after a period of illegality, is often characterized by an irresistible impulse to action for action's sake; by the absence of any consideration of the real relation of social forces, the state of mind of the broad mass of workers and peasants, the degree to which they are armed, etc. It has thus too often occurred that the revolutionary party has let itself be massacred by a Reaction not yet destroyed, whose resources had not been correctly assessed, while the great masses – who after every reactionary period become extremely prudent, and are easily seized by panic whenever a return to the situation which they have only just left threatens – have remained indifferent and passive.

It is difficult, in general, to prevent such errors from being made. It is, therefore, incumbent on the party to be on its guard, and to carry out specific activity designed to improve the situation and its own organization, and to raise the intellectual level of the members in its ranks during the period of white terror. For these are destined to become the central nucleus, most able to sustain every trial and sacrifice, of the party which will lead the revolution and administer the proletarian State.

The problem thus appears bigger and more complex. The recovery of the revolutionary movement, and especially its victory, pour a great mass of new elements into the party. They cannot be rejected, especially if they are of proletarian origin, since precisely their recruitment is one of the most symptomatic signs of the revolution which is being accomplished. But the problem is posed of how to prevent the central nucleus of the party from being submerged and fragmented by the mighty new wave. We all recall what happened in Italy after the War, in the Socialist Party. The central nucleus, made up of comrades who had remained faithful to the cause during the cataclysm, was reduced to only about 16,000. Yet at the Livorno Congress 220,000 members were represented: in other words, the party contained 200,000 members who had joined since the War, without political preparation, lacking any or almost any notion of marxist doctrine, an easy prey to the rhetorical, petty-bourgeois blusterers who in the years 1919–20 constituted the phenomenon of maximalism. It is not without significance that the present leader of the Socialist party and editor of *Avanti!* should be precisely Pietro Nenni, who entered the Socialist Party after Livorno but who nevertheless sums up and synthesizes in himself all the ideological weaknesses and distinctive characteristics of post-war maximalism.

It would really be a crime if the same thing were to occur in the Communist Party with respect to the fascist period, as occurred in the Socialist Party with respect to the war period. But this would be inevitable, if our party were not to have an orientation in this field too: if it did not take care in good time to reinforce its present cadres and members ideologically and politically, in order to make them capable of absorbing and incorporating still greater masses, without the organization being too shaken and without the party's profile being thereby altered.

We have posed the problem in its most important practical terms. But it has a basis which goes beyond any immediate contingency. We know that the proletariat's struggle against capitalism is waged on three fronts: the economic, the political and the ideological. The economic struggle has three phases: resistance to capitalism, i.e. the elementary trade-union phase; the offensive against capitalism for workers' control of production; and the struggle to eliminate capitalism through socialization. The political struggle too has three principal phases: the struggle to check the bourgeoisie's power in the parliamentary State, in other words to maintain or create a democratic situation, of equilibrium between the classes, which allows the proletariat to organize; the struggle to win power and create the workers' State, in other words a complex political activity through which the proletariat mobilizes around it all the anti-capitalist social forces (first and foremost the peasant class) and leads them to victory; and the phase of dictatorship of the proletariat, organized as a ruling class to eliminate all the technical and social obstacles which prevent the realization of communism. The economic struggle cannot be separated from the political struggle, nor can either of them be separated from the ideological struggle.

In its first, trade-union phase, the economic struggle is spontaneous; in other words, it is born inevitably of the very situation in which the proletariat finds itself under the bourgeois order. But in itself, it is not revolutionary; in other words, it does not necessarily lead to the overthrow of capitalism, as the syndicalists have maintained – and as with less success they continue to maintain. So true is this, that the reformists and even the fascists allow elementary trade-union struggle; indeed, they assert that the proletariat as a class should not engage in any kind of struggle other than trade-union struggle. The reformists only differ from the fascists in that they say that, if not the proletariat as a class, at least proletarians as individuals and citizens should also struggle for "general democracy", i.e. for bourgeois democracy: in other words, should struggle only to preserve or create the political conditions for a pure struggle of trade-union resistance.

For the trade-union struggle to become a revolutionary factor, it is necessary for the proletariat to accompany it with political struggle: in other words, for the proletariat to be conscious of being the protagonist of a general struggle which touches all the most vital questions of social organization; i.e. for it to be conscious that it is struggling for socialism. The element of "spontaneity" is not sufficient for revolutionary struggle; it never leads the working class beyond the limits of the existing bourgeois democracy. The element of consciousness is needed, the "ideological" element: in other words, an understanding of the conditions of the struggle, the social relations in which the worker lives, the fundamental tendencies at work in the system of those relations, and the process of development which society undergoes as a result of the existence within it of insoluble antagonisms, etc.

The three fronts of proletarian struggle are reduced to a single one for the party of the working class, which is this precisely because it resumes and represents all the demands of the general struggle. One certainly cannot ask every worker from the masses to be completely aware of the whole complex function which his class is destined to perform in the process of development of humanity. But this must be asked of members of the party. One cannot aim, before the conquest of the State, to change completely the consciousness of the entire working class. To do so would be utopian, because class consciousness as such is only changed when the way of living of the class itself has been changed; in other words, when the proletariat has become a ruling class and has at its disposal the apparatus of production and exchange and the power of the State. But the party can and must, as a whole, represent this higher consciousness. Otherwise, it will not be at the head but at the tail of the masses; it will not lead them but be dragged along by them. Hence, the party must assimilate marxism, and assimilate it in its present form, as Leninism.

Theoretical activity, in other words struggle on the ideological front, has always been neglected in the Italian workers' movement. In Italy, Marxism (apart from Antonio Labriola) has been studied more by bourgeois intellectuals, in order to denature it and turn it to the purposes of bourgeois policy, than by revolutionaries. We have thus seen coexisting peacefully in the Italian Socialist Party the most disparate tendencies. We have seen the most contradictory ideas being official opinions of the party. The party leaders never imagined that in order to struggle against bourgeois ideology, i.e. in order to free the masses from the influence of capitalism, it was first necessary to disseminate Marxist doctrine in the party itself and defend it against all false substitutes. This tradition has not been, or at least has not yet been, broken with by our party; has not been broken with in a systematic manner and through a significant, prolonged activity.

People say, however, that Marxism has enjoyed good fortune in Italy, and in a certain sense this is true. But it is also true that this good fortune has not helped the proletariat; has not helped to create new means of struggle; has not been a revolutionary phenomenon. Marxism, or more precisely a few statements taken from Marx's writings, have helped the Italian bourgeoisie to show that it was an inevitable necessity of its development to do without democracy; that it was necessary to trample on the laws; that it was necessary to mock freedom and justice. In other words, what the philosophers of the Italian bourgeoisie called Marxism was the description which Marx gave of the methods the bourgeoisie (without any need for Marxist justifications) uses in its struggle against the workers.

The reformists, to correct this fraudulent interpretation, themselves became democrats, and made themselves into the incense-bearers for all the desecrated saints of capitalism. The theorists of the Italian bourgeoisie have had the astuteness to create the concept of the "proletarian nation"; in other words, to claim that Italy as a whole was "proletarian", and that Marx's conception should be applied not to the struggle of the Italian proletariat against Italian capitalism, but to Italy's struggle against other capitalist states. The "Marxists" of the Socialist Party let these aberrations go without a struggle; indeed, they were accepted by one person – Enrico Ferri – who passed for a great theoretician of socialism.[170] This was the good fortune of Marxism in Italy: that it served as parsley in all the indigestible sauces that most of the reckless adventurers of the pen have sought to put on sale. Marxists of this ilk have included Enrico Ferri, Guglielmo Ferrero, Achille Loria, Paolo Orano, Benito Mussolini. . . .[171] In order to combat the confusion which has been being created in this way, it is necessary for the party to intensify and systematize its activity in the ideological field; to make it a duty for the militant to know Marxist-Leninist doctrine, at least in the most general terms.

Our party is not a democratic party, at least in the vulgar sense commonly given to this word. It is a party centralized both nationally and internationally. In the international field, our party is simply a section of a larger party, a world party. What repercussions can this type of organization — which is an iron necessity for the revolution — have, and has it already had? Italy itself gives us an answer to this question. As a reaction against the usual custom in the Socialist Party — in which much was discussed and little resolved; where unity was shattered into an infinity of disconnected fragments by the continuous clash of factions, tendencies and often personal cliques — in our party we had ended up by no longer discussing anything. Centralization, unity of approach and conception, had turned into intellectual stagnation. The necessity of ceaseless struggle against fascism, which precisely at the moment of our party's foundation had passed over to its first active, offensive phase, contributed to this state of affairs. But it was also encouraged by the wrong conception of the party set out in the "Theses on Tactics" presented to the Rome Congress.[172] Centralization and unity were understood in too mechanical a fashion: the Central Committee, indeed the Executive Committee, was the entire party, instead of representing and leading it.

If this conception were to be applied permanently, the party would lost its distinctive political features and become, at best, an army (and a bourgeois type of army). In other words, it would lose its power of attraction and become separated from the masses. In order for the party to live and be in contact with the masses, it is necessary for every member of the party to be an active political element, a leader. Precisely because the party is strongly centralized, a vast amount of propaganda and agitation among its ranks is required. It is necessary for the party in an organized fashion to educate its members and raise their ideological level. Centralization means, in particular, that in any situation whatsoever — even when the most rigorous Emergency Laws are in operation, and even if the leading committees are unable to function for a given period or are put in a situation where they cannot maintain contact with the local organizations — all members of the party, and everyone in its ambit, have been rendered capable of orienting themselves and knowing how to derive from reality the elements with which to establish a line, so that the working class will not be cast down but will feel that it is being led and can still fight. Mass ideological preparation is thus a necessity of revolutionary struggle, and one of the indispensable conditions for victory.

This first course of lessons in the party school proposes, within the limits which the situation permits, to carry out a part of this general activity. It will contain three series of lessons: one on the theory of historical materialism; one on the fundamental elements of general politics; one on the Communist Party and its principles of organization. In the first part, which will follow − or simply give a translation of − comrade Bukharin's book on the theory of historical materialism, comrades will find a complete treatment of the subject.[173]

The second part, on general politics, will provide the most elementary notions of the following series of subjects: political economy; the development of capitalism up to the epoch of finance capital; the War and the crisis of capitalism; the development of economic forms; communist society and the transitional régime; communist doctrine of the State; the Ist and IInd Internationals; the IIIrd International; the history of the Russian Bolshevik Party; the history of the Italian Communist Party; soviet power and the structure of the republic of Soviets; the economic policies of Soviet power in the epoch of war communism; the origins and basis of the New Economic Policy; agrarian and peasant policy; trade and cooperation; financial policy; the trade unions, their functions and tasks; the national question.

The third part will systematically set out doctrine concerning the party and the principles of revolutionary organization, such as are developed through the Communist International's activity of leadership, and such as were fixed in a more complete fashion at the Organizational Conference held in Moscow in March of this year.[174]

This will be the school's basic course. It cannot be complete, and hence could not satisfy all comrades' needs. To obtain a greater completeness and organicity, it has been decided to publish each month, in the same format as the study-notes, separate dossiers on single subjects. One dossier will be devoted to the trade-union question, and will deal with the most elementary and practical problems of union life (how to organize a union; how to draw up rules; how to launch a wage struggle; how to frame a work-contract; etc.), thus representing a real organizer's manual. Another dossier will be designed to assemble every idea about the economic, social and political structure of Italy. In other dossiers, other specific subjects of working-class politics will be dealt with, in accordance with the doctrine of Marxism-Leninism. Furthermore, in every batch of study-notes, in addition to the three lessons, there will be published informative − and formative − notes designed to give direct backing to the lessons themselves; model discussions; didactic advice for study carried out without the help or direct guidance of a teacher, etc.

The study-notes must be seen by the pupils as material to be actually studied, not just read as one reads a newspaper or a pamphlet. The pupils must study as if they had to pass an examination at the end of the course. In other words, they must force themselves to remember and assimilate the subjects dealt with, so as to be capable of delivering reports or holding small meetings. The party will keep the list of pupils, and whenever it needs to will turn to them before anyone else.

So pupils must not be worried if at first many of them have difficulty in understanding certain ideas. The study-notes have been compiled bearing in mind the average formation of the party membership at large. It may happen that for some they will represent things already known, while for others they will be something new and somewhat difficult to digest. Indeed, it is inevitable that this will happen. In these circumstances, the pupils must help each other as far as possible. The establishment of groups and joint recital of the lessons received, may sometimes eliminate this problem. In any case, all pupils are entreated to write to the school administration, explaining their situation, asking for additional elucidation, and recommending other methods or forms of exposition.

Signed "Agitation and Propaganda Department of the Communist Party".

66. THE INTERNAL SITUATION IN OUR PARTY AND THE TASKS OF THE FORTHCOMING CONGRESS [175]

At its last meeting, the Enlarged Executive of the Communist International did not have to resolve any question of principle or of tactics that had arisen between the Italian party as a whole and the International.[176] This was the first time that such a thing had occurred, in the whole series of meetings of the International. For this reason, the most authoritative comrades of the Executive of the Communist International would have preferred there not even to have been any question of an Italian Commission: since there was no general crisis of the Italian party, there was no "Italian problem" either.

Indeed, it should be said at once that our party, although even before the World Congress and especially afterwards it had modified its tactical positions in order to draw close to the Leninist line of the Communist International, nevertheless suffered no crisis in the ranks of its members or in relation to the masses: quite the contrary. Having defined its new tactical positions with respect to the general situation created in the country after the 6 April elections, and especially after the assassination of Giacomo Matteotti, the party succeeded in growing as an organization and in extending its influence notably among the working-class and peasant masses. Our party is one of the few, if not the only, party in the International which can claim such a success in a situation as difficult as that which has been being created in all countries (especially in Europe) in relation to the relative stabilization of capitalism and the relative reinforcement of the bourgeois governments and of social-democracy – which has become an increasingly essential part of the bourgeois system. It is necessary to say, at least in parenthesis, that it is precisely because of the emergence of this situation, and in relation to the consequences it has had not only among the broad working masses but also within the communist parties, that the problem of Bolshevization must be confronted.

The Present Stage of Development of the Parties of the International

The crises which all the parties of the International have passed through since 1921, i.e. since the beginning of the period characterized by a slowing down of the rhythm of revolution, have shown that the overall composition of these parties was not ideologically very solid. The parties themselves oscillated, with often very violent shifts from right to far left; this produced the most serious repercussions on the entire organization, and general crises in relations between the parties and the masses. The phase which the parties of the International are passing through at present, on the other hand, is characterized by the fact that, in each of them, there has been being formed through the political experience of the last years – and there has been consolidated – a basic nucleus which is bringing about a Leninist stabilization of their ideological composition, thus ensuring that they will no longer be shaken by crises of too deep or oscillations of too wide a nature. By posing in this way the general problem of Bolshevization, both in the sphere of organization and in that of ideological formation, the Enlarged Executive has declared that our forces are on the point of resolving the crisis. In this sense, the Enlarged Executive meeting is a point of arrival. But at the same time its recognition of the very great progress achieved in consolidating the organizational and ideological bases of the parties is a point of departure, insofar as this progress must be coordinated and systematized, in other words must become the effective, generalized consciousness of the masses as a whole.

In some ways, the revolutionary parties of Western Europe find themselves today in the same conditions in which the Russian Bolsheviks found themselves from the moment of their party's foundation. In Russia before the War, there did not exist great workers' organizations such as those which by contrast characterized the entire period of the pre-War Second International in Europe. In Russia the party, not just as a general theoretical assertion but also as a practical necessity for organization and struggle, embodied within itself all the vital interests of the working class. Its factory and street cells guided the masses both in struggle around trade-union demands and in political struggle for the overthrow of Tsarism. In Western Europe, by contrast, an increasing division of labour grew up between the trade-union organization and the political organization of the working class. In the trade-union field, the reformist and pacifist tendency developed at an ever-increasing pace; in other words, the influence of the bourgeoisie over the proletariat grew steadily stronger. For the same reason, in the political parties, activity shifted increasingly towards the parliamentary sphere: in other words, towards forms which were in no way distinguished from those of bourgeois democracy. During the War, and in the period which followed it and which immediately preceded the creation of the Communist International and the splits in the socialist camp that led to the formation of our parties, the syndicalist-reformist tendency became increasingly consolidated as the organizational leadership of the trade unions. Thus a general situation came to be created, which precisely places the Communist Parties of Western Europe in the same conditions as those in which the Bolshevik Party found itself in Russia before the War.

Let us look at what happened in Italy. Through the repressive activity of fascism, the trade unions in our country came to lose all effectiveness, in terms alike of numbers and combativity. Taking advantage of this situation, the reformists gained complete mastery of their central machinery, and devised every conceivable measure and arrangement to prevent any minority from forming, organizing, developing or becoming a majority capable of taking over the central leadership. But the broad masses – rightly – want unity, and reflect this unitary sentiment in the traditional Italian trade-union organization: the General Confederation of Labour. The masses want to struggle and become organized, but they want to struggle with the General Confederation of Labour and to become organized in the General Confederation of Labour. The reformists oppose the organization of the masses. Recall D'Aragona's speech at the recent Confederation congress, in which he asserted that there should not be more than a million organized workers in the Confederation. If one bears in mind that the Confederation itself claims to be the unitary organism of all Italian toilers, i.e. not only of the industrial and agricultural workers but also of the peasants, and that there are at least fifteen million non-organized toilers in Italy, then it seems that the Confederation wishes, as a programme, to unionize one fifteenth, i.e. 7·5 per cent of Italian toilers, while we would like 100 per cent to be organized into unions and peasants' organizations.

But if the Confederation, for reasons of its own internal politics, i.e. in order to keep the leadership of the Confederation in the hands of the reformists, wants only 7·5 per cent of Italian toilers to be unionized, it also wants – for reasons of general politics, i.e. so that the reformist party can collaborate effectively in a bourgeois-democratic government – the Confederation as a whole to have an influence over the disorganized mass of industrial and agricultural workers; it wants, by preventing the unionization of the peasantry, to ensure that the democratic parties with which it intends to collaborate preserve their social base. It therefore manoeuvres especially in the field of the internal commissions, which are elected by the entire mass of unionized and non-unionized workers.

In other words, the Confederation would like to prevent the organized workers, apart from those in the reformist tendency, from presenting lists of candidates for the internal commissions. They would like the communists, even where they are in a majority in the local trade-union organization and among the unionized workers in individual factories, to vote for the lists of the reformist minorities as a matter of discipline. If this organizational programme were to be accepted by us, we would arrive *de facto* at the absorption of our party by the reformist party, and our sole activity would remain that in parliament.

The Task of the "Cells"

Moreover, how can we struggle against the application and organization of such a programme, without bringing about a split which we absolutely do not want to bring about? The only way to do so is through the organization of cells, and their development in the same way that they developed in Russia before the War. As a trade-union fraction, the reformists, holding the pistol of discipline at our throats, prevent us from centralizing the revolutionary masses either through trade-union or through political struggle.

It is, hence, obvious that our cells must work directly in the factories to centralize the masses around the party: pushing them to reinforce the internal commissions where these exist, and to create agitation committees in the factories where no internal commissions exist or where they do not carry out their tasks; pushing them to seek centralization of the factory institutions, as mass organisms not simply of a trade-union kind, but for general struggle against capitalism and its political régime. It is certain that the situation in which we find ourselves is much more difficult than that in which the Bolsheviks found themselves, since we have to struggle not just against reaction as represented by the fascist State, but also against reaction as represented by the reformists in the unions. Precisely because the situation is more difficult, our cells must be organizationally and ideologically stronger. In any case, Bolshevization as it is reflected in the organizational sphere is an imperative necessity. No one will dare to claim that the Leninist criteria for party organization are peculiar to the Russian situation, and that their application to Western Europe is purely mechanical. To oppose the organization of the party by cells means to still be tied to old social-democratic conceptions. It means to be situated objectively on right-wing terrain, i.e. on terrain where there is no desire to fight against social-democracy.

Bordiga's Failure to Intervene in Moscow

On all these issues, there is no disagreement today between our party as a whole and the International. They were therefore able to have no repercussions on the work of the Italian Commission, which concerned itself solely with the problem of Bolshevization from the ideological and political point of view, with particular respect to the situation created within our party. Comrade Bordiga was insistently invited to participate in the work of the Enlarged Executive. To have done so would have been his strict duty, insofar as he had accepted at the Fifth World Congress to become a member of the Executive of the International. It was all the more incumbent upon comrade Bordiga to participate in the proceedings in that in an article (whose publication he had himself, however, made subject to the approval of the International Executive), he had taken up a position on the Trotsky question that was radically opposed not only to that of the International Executive, but also to that adopted in practice by comrade Trotsky himself.[177] It is absurd and deplorable from every point of view that comrade Bordiga should not have been willing to take part personally in the discussion of the Trotsky question. That he should not have been willing to take sight directly of all the relevant material. That he should not have been willing to submit his opinions and information to the test of an international debate.

It is certainly not with such attitudes that one can show one has the necessary qualities and talents to embark upon a struggle which should have as its practical result a change, not only of policies, but also of personnel, in the leadership of the Communist International.

Lenin's Five Points for a Good Bolshevik Party

The Commission, which should have discussed specially with comrade Bordiga, in his absence fixed the line which the party should follow in order to resolve the question of tendencies, and of the possible factions which may emerge from these: in other words, to ensure that the Bolshevik conception prevails in our party. Let us examine the general situation of our party by the yardstick of the five basic qualities which comrade Lenin posed as necessary conditions for the effectiveness of the revolutionary party of the proletariat in the period of revolutionary preparation, that is to say: 1. every communist must be a Marxist (today we would say: every communist must be a Marxist-Leninist); 2. every communist must be in the first line in the struggles of the proletariat; 3. every communist must abhor revolutionary poses and superficially scarlet phrases, in other words must be not only a revolutionary, but also a realistic politician; 4. every communist must feel that he is always subject to the will of his party, and must judge everything from the point of view of his party, i.e. must be sectarian in the best sense which that word can have; 5. every communist must be an internationalist.

If we examine the general situation in our party by the yardstick of these five points, we can see that, although one may say of our party that the second quality constitutes one of its characteristic features, one cannot say the same so far as the other four are concerned. Our party lacks any deep knowledge of the doctrine of Marxism, and hence also of Leninism. We know that this is related to the traditions of the Italian socialist movement, which have not contained any theoretical discussion that has deeply interested the masses and contributed to their ideological formation. It is also true, however, that our party up till now has not helped to destroy this state of affairs. Indeed comrade Bordiga – confusing on the one hand, the reformist tendency to substitute a generic cultural activity for the revolutionary political action of the masses with, on the other, inner-party activity designed to raise the level of all party members to a total awareness of the immediate and long-term aims of the revolutionary movement – has helped to preserve it.

The Phenomenon of Extremism

Our party has sufficiently developed the sense of discipline. In other words, every member acknowledges his subordination to the party as a whole. But one cannot say the same so far as relations with the Communist International are concerned; i.e. so far as the consciousness of belonging to a world party is concerned. In this sense, it is only necessary to say that the internationalist spirit is not very much practised, certainly not in the general sense of international solidarity. This was a situation which existed in the Socialist Party, and which was reflected to our disadvantage at the Livorno Congress. It continued to subsist partially, in other forms, due to the tendency which comrade Bordiga encouraged of considering it a particular badge of honour to call oneself the adherents of a so-called "Italian Left". In this sphere, comrade Bordiga has re-created a situation resembling that created by comrade Serrati after the Second World Congress, which led to the exclusion of the Maximalists from the Communist International. In other words, he has created a kind of party patriotism which shrinks from becoming integrated into a world organization.[178]

But the greatest weakness of our party is that characterized by Lenin under point three. The love for revolutionary poses and for superficial scarlet phrases is the most striking feature not of Bordiga himself, but of the elements who claim to follow him. Naturally, the phenomenon of Bordigan extremism is not suspended in mid air. It has a double justification. On the one hand, it is related to the general situation of the class struggle in our country; in other words, to the fact that the working class is the minority of the working population and is concentrated mainly in one area of the country. In such a situation, the party of the working class can be corrupted by infiltration from the petty-bourgeois classes which, although they have interests which as a whole run counter to the interests of capital, nevertheless are not willing to take the struggle to its ultimate consequences.

On the other hand, what also helped to consolidate Bordiga's ideology was the situation in which the Socialist Party found itself prior to Livorno, which Lenin characterized as follows in his book *"Left-wing" Communism – An Infantile Disorder*: "In a party where there is a Turati, and a Serrati who does not fight against Turati, it is natural that there should be a Bordiga."[179] However, it is not natural that comrade Bordiga should have become ideologically crystallized even when Turati was no longer in the party, when even Serrati was not there, and when Bordiga was in personal charge of the struggle against both of them. Obviously, the element of the national situation was preponderant in the political formation of comrade Bordiga, and had crystallized in him a permanent state of pessimism on the possibility for the proletariat and its party to remain immune from infiltrations of petty-bourgeois ideologies, without the application of extremely sectarian political tactics which made impossible the application and realization of the two political principles which characterize Bolshevism: the alliance between workers and peasants, and the hegemony of the proletariat in the anti-capitalist revolutionary movement. The line to be adopted in order to combat these weaknesses of our party is that of the struggle for Bolshevization. The campaign to be waged must be a mainly ideological one. However, it must become a political one so far as the far left is concerned, i.e. the tendency represented by comrade Bordiga, which from latent factionalism will necessarily pass over to open factionalism, and at the congress will seek to change the political line of the International.

The Question of Tendencies

Do there exist other tendencies in our party? What is their character and what danger can they represent? If we examine the internal situation of our party from this point of view, we must recognize that it not only has not achieved the level of revolutionary political maturity which we sum up in the term 'Bolshevization' but has not even achieved a total unification of the various parts which came together at the moment of its formation. This has been helped by the absence of any broad debate which has unfortunately characterized the party since its foundation. If we take account of the elements which came out for the Communist International at the Livorno Congress, we can say that of the three currents which constituted the Communist Party – i.e.1. the abstentionists of the Bordiga faction; 2. the elements grouped around *L'Ordine Nuovo* and the Turin *Avanti!*; 3. the mass elements who followed what we can call the Gennari-Marabini group, i.e. the followers of the most typical figures of the leading stratum of the Socialist Party who had come with us – only two, i.e. the abstentionist current and that of *L'Ordine Nuovo*/Turin *Avanti!*, had prior to the Livorno Congress carried on a certain autonomous political work, discussed among themselves the key problems of the Communist International, and thus acquired a certain communist political ability and experience. But these currents, although they succeeded in getting the upper hand in the leadership of the new Communist Party, did not constitute the majority of its base. Furthermore, of these two currents only one, the abstentionists, had since 1919 – i.e. for two years before Livorno – had a national organization and formed among its adherents a certain organizational party experience. But in the preparatory period it had exclusively concerned itself with internal party questions and the specific factional struggle, without having as a whole passed through political experiences of a mass nature, other than on the purely parliamentary question.

The current which had formed around *L'Ordine Nuovo* and the Piedmont edition of *Avanti!* had created neither a national faction, nor even a real faction within the confines of the Piedmont region where it had arisen and developed. Its activity was prevalently of a mass nature. Internal party problems were systematically related by it to the needs and aspirations of the general class struggle: general to the working population of Piedmont, and especially to the Turin proletariat. This fact, though it gave the members of the current a better political preparation and, as individuals, even at the base, a greater ability to lead real movements, nevertheless placed it in a condition of inferiority in the general organization of the party. If one excepts Piedmont, the great majority of our party was made up of the elements who came out for the Communist International at Livorno. For a whole series of comrades of the old leading stratum of the Socialist Party remained with the Communist International: comrades like Gennari, Marabini, Bombacci, Misiano, Salvadori, Graziadei, etc. The local abstentionist groups were grafted onto this mass – which in its conceptions in no way differed from the maximalists – and gave it the form of organization of the new Communist Party.

If one were not to take account of this real formation of our party, one would understand neither the crises through which it has passed nor the present situation. The origins of our party coincided with the most ferocious unleashing of fascist reaction, so that one can say that each part of the organization was baptized with the blood of our best comrades. As a result of exigencies of a struggle without quarter which were thus imposed on our party from its very beginnings, the experience of the Communist International – i.e. not just of the Russian party, but also of the other fraternal parties – did not reach us, and was not assimilated by the mass of the party, other than in an irregular and episodic fashion. In reality, our party came to be detached from the international whole. It came to develop its own incoherent, chaotic ideology on the sole basis of our immediate national experience. In other words, there came to be created in Italy a new form of maximalism.

This general situation was aggravated last year by the entry into our ranks of the IIIrd-internationalist faction.[180] The weaknesses which were characteristic of us existed in a still more serious and dangerous form in this faction, which for two and a half years had existed in an autonomous form within the Maximalist Party, thus creating internal bonds among its adherents which were to persist even after the fusion.

Moreover, the IIIrd-internationalist faction too, for two and a half years, was completely absorbed by the internal struggle against the leadership of the Maximalist Party: a struggle which was mainly of a personal and sectarian nature, and only occasionally dealt with fundamental questions, whether political or organizational.

Bolshevization

It is thus obvious that the Bolshevization of the party in the ideological field cannot solely take account of the situation which we can sum up in the existence of a far left current and in the personal attitude of comrade Bordiga. It must tackle the general situation of the party; in other words, it must confront the problem of raising the theoretical and political level of all our comrades. It is certain, for example, that there is also a Graziadei question, in the sense that we must utilize his most recent publications to improve the Marxist education of our comrades, by combating the so-called scientific deviations defended in them.[181] No one, however, can think that comrade Graziadei represents a political danger; i.e. that on the basis of his revisionist conceptions of Marxism there can emerge a vast current and hence a faction which endangers the organizational unity of the party. On the other hand, it should not be forgotten either that Graziadei's revisionism leads to support for the right-wing currents which exist in our party, even if only in a latent state.

The entry into the party of the IIIrd-internationalist faction, i.e. of a political element which has not lost many of its maximalist features and which, as has already been said, automatically tends to prolong – beyond its existence as a faction within the Maximalist party – the bonds created in the previous period, can undoubtedly give this potential right-wing current a certain organizational base, thus posing problems which must absolutely not be neglected. At all events, no violent differences can arise on the following series of opinions. The above-mentioned difficulties created by the original composition of our party face us mainly with ideological problems closely related to the following two necessities: 1. that the old guard of the party should absorb the mass of new members who have come into the party since the Matteotti affair, and who have tripled its numbers;[182] 2. that we create party organizational cadres who are able to resolve not just the daily problems of party life, both as an organization in itself and in its relations with the unions and other mass organizations, but also the more complex problems related to our preparation for winning power and exercising that power once won.

The Right-wing Danger

One may say that a right-wing danger potentially exists in our party. It is linked to the general situation in the country. The constitutional opposition forces, however much they may have failed in their historical function since they rejected our proposal to create an anti-parliament, nevertheless continue to subsist politically side by side with a consolidated fascism. The losses suffered by the opposition, though they have reinforced our party, have done so to the same extent to which fascism, which holds the entire State apparatus in its hands, has been consolidated. It is therefore evident that within our party a right-wing tendency could emerge, if it does not already exist, in counterposition to a far-left tendency which believes at every moment that the time has come to go over to a frontal attack on the régime, which cannot be disintegrated by the manoeuvres of the opposition. The elements of this right-wing tendency, demoralized by the apparently overwhelming power of the dominant party and despairing of the possibility that the proletariat may be able speedily to overthrow the régime as a whole, will begin to think that the best tactic is that which leads, if not straight to a bourgeois-proletarian bloc for the constitutional elimination of fascism, at least to a tactic of real passivity, with no active intervention by our party, thus allowing the bourgeoisie to use the proletariat as electoral cannon-fodder against fascism.

The party must take account of all these possibilities and probabilities, so that its correct revolutionary line is not affected by deviations. It should consider the right-wing danger as a possibility, to be combated by means of ideological propaganda and normal disciplinary means whenever this proves necessary. But it should consider the far-left danger as an immediate reality: as an obstacle not merely to the ideological but to the political development of the party; as a danger which must be combated not just by means of propaganda, but also by means of political action – since it leads directly to the disintegration even of the formal unity of our organization, and since it tends to create a party within the party, a discipline against the discipline of the party.

Does this mean that we want to break with comrade Bordiga and those who say they are his friends? Does it mean that we want to modify the fundamental basis of the party, such as it was constituted at the Livorno Congress and preserved at the Rome Congress? Certainly and absolutely not. But the fundamental basis of the party was not a purely mechanical fact: it was founded on unconditional acceptance of the principles and discipline of the Communist International. It is not we who have brought these principles and this discipline into question. It is not in us, therefore, that a desire to modify the fundamental basis of the party should be sought. Moreover, it is necessary to say that 90 per cent or more of the party members are ignorant of the questions which have arisen between our organization and the Communist International. If, especially after the Rome Congress, the party as a whole had been enabled to know the situation of our international relations, it would probably not now be in the conditions of confusion in which it finds itself. In any case, we wish to assert most forcefully, in order to thwart the wretched schemes of certain irresponsible elements who seem to find their political satisfaction through exacerbating the wounds of our organization, that we believe it is possible to reach an agreement with comrade Bordiga, and we think that this is also the opinion of comrade Bordiga himself.

The Framework of the Discussion

We consider that the framework for our congress discussion should be defined in accordance with this general approach. In the period which we have passed through since the last parliamentary elections, the party has carried out a real political activity which has been agreed to by the great majority of our comrades. On the basis of this activity, the party has tripled its membership and notably developed its influence in the proletariat – to such an extent that one may say that our party is the strongest of those with a base in the General Confederation of Labour.

We have succeeded in this last period in posing concretely the fundamental problem of our revolution: that of the alliance between workers and peasants. Our party, in a word, has become an essential factor of the Italian situation. On this terrain of real political activity, a certain homogeneity has been created among our comrades. This element must continue to be developed in the congress discussion, and must be one of the essential determinants of Bolshevization. This means that the congress must not be conceived of solely as a moment of our general politics: of the process through which we bind ourselves to the masses and arouse new forces for the revolution. The main nucleus of the congress activity must, therefore, be seen in the discussions which will take place to establish through which phase of Italian and international life we are passing: in other words, what the present relation of social forces is in Italy; which are the motor forces of the situation; what the present phase of the class struggle represents.

From this examination, two fundamental problems arise. 1. How we can develop our party so that it becomes a unity capable of leading the proletariat into struggle; capable of winning and winning permanently. This is the problem of Bolshevization. 2. What real political activity our party should continue to carry out, in order to bring about a coalition of all the anti-capitalist forces led by the (revolutionary) proletariat in the given situation: so as to overthrow the capitalist order in the first stage, and constitute the basis of the revolutionary workers' State in a second stage. In other words, we must examine what the essential problems of Italian life are; and which solution to them will encourage and bring about the revolutionary alliance of the proletariat with the peasants, and accomplish the hegemony of the proletariat. The congress must, therefore, at least prepare the general outline of our government programme.

This is an essential phase of our party life. To perfect the instrument necessary for the proletarian revolution in Italy – that is the major task of our congress. That is the work to which we invite all comrades of good will, who put the unitary interests of their class before petty and sterile factional struggles.

L'Unita, 3 July 1925.

67. ELEMENTS OF THE SITUATION[183]

The importance of the present political moment derives from the fact that it allows us to draw certain general conclusions from the experience of the period of conflicts opened up by the 1924 elections, which reached their greatest degree of acuteness as a result of the Matteotti assassination. It is clear today that the political perspectives outlined by the Communist Party during the course of this period have been fully confirmed, and this confirmation is the best justification for the party's slogans.

The "Matteotti" period – understood in a broad sense as the period of political crisis initiated by fascism after the March on Rome – is characterized by a conflict between the various groups of the bourgeoisie, and by the attempt of a part of the petty bourgeoisie itself to lead the struggle to overthrow the fascist régime, drawing behind itself the other classes mobilized for this struggle, in particular the proletariat and the peasantry. The Aventine policy was the expression of this attempt. Its failure – which today no one can deny – gives fresh proof of the impossibility, in the period of imperialism, of the petty bourgeoisie leading a struggle against reaction, the form and instrument of the dominion of capital and the landowners. The collapse of the Aventine has allowed fascism to achieve a vigorous impetus for its policy, which should be seen from *two basic points of view*.

On the one hand, fascism continues with ever greater determination to carry through its plan of *organic unification of all the forces of the bourgeoisie under the control of a single centre* (leadership of the Fascist Party, Grand Council and government), and has achieved results in this sense which cannot be doubted. The activity aimed at 'fellow-travelling' groups, to eliminate them as autonomous groups and incorporate their remnants into fascism, has now been successful. After the passage of the national-liberals to fascism, there no longer exists outside fascism a centre of forces openly calling themselves reactionary. At the same time, the struggle against the old leading groups continues with increasing bitterness. Its most notable aspect is the struggle against freemasonry, which in Italy was the organization of all the forces which supported and gave cohesion to the State. Fascism has understood the need to arrogate this function integrally to itself.[184] The opposition press, which guaranteed to the remnants of the old leading groups a prestige and influence upon public opinion, no longer carries out that function. Fascism is systematically storming all centres of organized resistance – even partial and Platonic – to its activity. In the economic field, the plan of unification and centralization is being accomplished through a series of measures which aim to guarantee the unchallengeable supremacy of an industrial and land-owning oligarchy, ensuring its control over the whole economy of the country (restoration of the duty on grain; unification of banking; changes in mercantile law; agreements for payment of debts to America, etc.).

The second aspect of fascist policy concerns the repression that is exercised upon the workers, in order to prevent any kind of organization of their forces and to exclude them systematically and permanently from any participation in political life. Particularly worthy of attention at present are the following: 1. fascism's new trade-union policy (the 'Fascist Trade-union Law'); 2. the law on associations, also approved by the Senate; 3. the reform of administrative structures (the institution of the *podestà* for rural municipalities, and the decision whereby municipal consultative bodies are nominated by the corporations; the exclusion of subversives from the municipal councils in the cities).

It seems at first sight that fascism is chalking up only successes in the realization of its policy. But in fact, its actions are intensifying all the social conflicts more deeply day by day, and are bringing about new shifts and regroupments in which lie the preconditions for an inevitable proletarian renewal. The end of the Aventine will certainly not close the series of attempts by the old ruling classes to impede – even without merging into fascism – the rise of the proletariat to the position of dominant class. Indeed, we can see occurring today a vast phenomenon of adjustment and recomposition. The various groups and parties which made up the Aventine, or remained outside both it and fascism, are seeking the positions from which it will be easiest for them to continue to fulfil their counter-revolutionary function. For the proletariat and the Communist Party, the positions of the parties which chained the mass working-class movements to the Aventine are particularly significant.

The Maximalist Party, which was the first to take cognizance of the failure of the Aventine, is orienting itself ever more decisively for counter-revolution. Witness the propaganda which its leaders are carrying out against the Russian proletarian state, adopting as their own the theses of the reactionary democrats of Western Europe; and witness the adhesion given by *Avanti!* to the social-democratic point of view concerning the advantages of an 'intervention of American capital' in Italy. A complete examination of the attitude of the Maximalist leaders in all the other fields allows a full definition of their position. It corresponds in part, no doubt, to the tendency of certain layers of the working population to consider it sufficient to resist reaction passively, without making any systematic effort to reorganize their own forces, reconstitute a class front or prepare for revolution. The leaders of the Maximalist Party mask their inertia and passivity with empty revolutionary verbalism and extremist poses. The propaganda which they carry out for the constitution of a new political grouping that will assemble some of the débris of the Aventine is the latest form of this verbalism. It is accompanied by a negative activity in those fields in which the activity of a working-class party ought to be carried on today.

An activity analogous to that of the Maximalists is carried on by the Unitary Socialists and Republicans among other strata of the working class and anti-fascist petty bourgeoisie; by the *popolari* among the rural population; by the Sardists among the agricultural masses of Sardinia; by the National Union and social democracy among those of the South and Sicily. In this way, the formation of a new 'centre' group is being prepared, which will have a function analogous to that which the Aventine had during the Matteotti crisis. For the revolutionary preparation of the proletariat, and the success of the struggle against reaction, it is indispensable that this new formation should be decisively unmasked, forced to reveal its true nature before the masses, and rendered incapable of exercising any influence over them.

The fundamental problem which the Communist Party must set out to resolve in the present situation is that of leading the proletariat back to an autonomous position as a revolutionary class; free from all influence of counter-revolutionary classes, groups and parties; capable of collecting around itself and leading all the forces which can be mobilized for the struggle against capitalism. The Communist Party must, therefore, intervene actively in all fields open to its activity, and must take advantage of all movements, all conflicts, all struggles, even of a partial and limited character, in order to mobilize the proletarian masses and transport the resistance and opposition to fascism of the Italian working population onto a class terrain.

The Communist Party must systematically combat and unmask those groups and political parties which are vehicles for the influence on the proletariat of other classes, and of non-revolutionary social categories. It must strive to remove from their influence even the most backward strata of the working class, so that a united front of class forces may arise from below. This united front must have an organized form, and this is provided by the workers' and peasants' committees. All attempts to create representative mass organisms must be encouraged and developed with tenacity and constancy, as a first step towards practical realization of the united front of workers' and peasants' committees.

Unsigned, *L'Unità*, 24 November 1925.

V

The Lyons Congress

68. MINUTES OF THE POLITICAL COMMISSION NOMINATED BY THE CENTRAL COMMITTEE TO FINALIZE THE LYONS CONGRESS DOCUMENTS[185]

(*Present:* Gramsci, Bordiga, Ercoli [Togliatti], Rienzi [Tasca], Morelli [Scoccimarro], Massimo, Naples F. – not a delegate to the Congress, Calabria, Turin 1, Turin 2, Milan, Emilia, Rome, Sicily, Naples, Veneto.)
Chair: Milan; *Minutes:* Ercoli.

After a brief exchange of views on the agenda, it was decided to preface an analytic examination of the draft theses presented by the Central Committee with a general discussion concerning the principles upon which these theses were based.

Gramsci. Recapitulates the general principles on which the draft theses presented by the Central Committee of the party to the Congress are based. Advances a historical justification of the value of the process of "Bolshevization" of the proletarian parties that was begun after the Fifth World Congress and the Enlarged Executive meeting of April 1925. There is a fundamental analogy between the process of 'Bolshevization' being carried out today, and the activity of Karl Marx within the workers' movement. Today as then, it is a question of combating every deviation in the doctrine and practice of the revolutionary class struggle. This battle is fought in the ideological field, in the field of organization, and in that which concerns the tactics and strategy of the proletarian party. In our party, however, the fullest discussion has taken place on the terrain of organization. This is to be explained by the fact that, today, it is upon this terrain that the consequences of the different ideological and tactical positions appear immediately evident to all comrades – even to those least prepared for a purely theoretical debate.

All the points of disagreement between the central leadership of the party and the far left can be grouped around three fundamental problems: 1. the problem of relations between the central leadership of the party and the mass of comrades enrolled in its ranks; 2. the problem of relations between the central leadership and the working class; 3. the problem of relations between the working class and the other anti-capitalist classes.

All these relations must be established accurately, if one wishes to attain the historical destination of the dictatorship of the proletariat. In order to reach this destination, in fact, it is necessary for the working class to become the class that leads the anti-capitalist struggle; for the Communist Party to lead the working class in this struggle; and for the party to be structured internally in such a way that it can fulfil this its basic function. Each of the three problems alluded to is thus linked to the fundamental problem of the accomplishment of the Communist Party's revolutionary task.

To the two first problems is linked the question of the nature of the party and the bodies which lead it. We consider that in defining the party, it is necessary today to underline the fact that it is a 'part' of the working class, while the far left ignores and undervalues this side of the definition of the party, giving fundamental importance instead to the idea that the party is an 'organ' of the working class. Our position derives from the fact that we consider one must put maximum emphasis on the fact that the party is united to the working class not merely by ideological bonds, but also by bonds of a 'physical' character. And this is closely related to the tasks which must be set for the party *vis-à-vis* the working class.

According to the far left, the process of the party's formation is a 'synthetic' process, whereas for us it is a process of historical and political character, closely linked to the whole development of capitalist society. The difference of conception leads to different ways of determining the function and tasks of the party. All the work which the party must accomplish to raise the political level of the masses, to convince them and lead them onto the terrain of the revolutionary class struggle, is downgraded and impeded as a result of the far left's incorrect conception, because of the initial rift that has been created between the party and the working class.

The incorrect conception which the far left has on the nature of the party undeniably has a class character. Not that, as occurred within the Socialist Party, there is any tendency to cause the influence of other classes to prevail within the political organization of the proletariat; but in the sense that an incorrect evaluation is made of the weight which the various elements which make up the party should have in it. The conception of the far left, which places the workers and the elements who come from other social classes on the same plane, and is not concerned to safeguard the proletarian character of the party, corresponds to a situation in which the intellectuals were the most politically and socially advanced elements, and were therefore destined to be the organisers of the working class. Today, in our view, the organizers of the working class must be the workers themselves. It is therefore necessary, in defining the party, to stress particularly that part of the definition which highlights the intimacy of the relations which exist between it and the class from which it arises.

This problem of a technical nature has given rise to the discussion about organization by 'cells', in other words on the basis of production. Indeed, this is the point which has been taken up most, and by the largest number of comrades, in the pre-conference discussion. All the arguments of a practical character which make it useful and indispensable to transform the party organization on the basis of cells have, therefore, been fully expounded and the comrades know them. The far left puts forward objections, of which the most important consist in an exaggeration of the problem of overcoming competition between different categories of workers; in other words, of the problem of class unification of the proletariat. It is certain that this problem exists, but it is an error to make it into a fundamental one, which determines the form the party gives to its organization. This problem, moreover, has been resolved for some time in Italy in the trade-union field, and experience has shown that organization on a factory basis makes it possible to fight with the greatest effectiveness against every residue of corporatism and sectionalism. In reality, if the problem which the far left seems to present as fundamental, and which determines its anxieties, were really the essential problem of the present historical period in Italy, then indeed the intellectuals would be organizationally the vanguard of the revolutionary movement. However, this is not the case.

A second fundamental question is that of the relations which should be established between the working class and the other anti-capitalist classes. This is a problem which can be resolved only by the party of the working class, through the medium of its policies. In no country is the proletariat capable of winning power and keeping it with its own forces alone. It must therefore obtain allies: in other words, it must follow a policy that will enable it to place itself at the head of the other classes who have anti-capitalist interests, and guide them in the struggle to overthrow bourgeois society. The question is of particular importance for Italy, where the proletariat is a minority of the working population and geographically distributed in such a manner, that it cannot presume to lead a victorious struggle for power unless it has previously resolved very precisely the problem of its relations with the peasant class. Our party must devote itself especially to tackling and solving this problem in the immediate future. Furthermore, there exists a reciprocity between the problem of the alliance between workers and peasants and the problem of the organization of the working class and its party. The latter will be more easily solved if the former has been brought near to a solution.

The problem of the alliance between workers and peasants has already been confronted by the party leadership; but one cannot claim that all comrades have properly understood its terms, or have the capacity to work to resolve it – and this is especially the case in those regions where it would be necessary to work most and best, i.e. in the South. Thus the far left criticizes the entire activity of the leadership with respect to Miglioli, the representative of the peasant left in the Popular Party.[186] These criticisms show that the far left does not grasp the terms and the importance of the problem of relations between the proletariat and the other anti-capitalist classes. The party's activity with respect to Miglioli was carried out precisely with the aim of opening the path to an alliance between the workers and the peasants, in the struggle against capitalism and the bourgeois State. The question of the Vatican as a counter-revolutionary political force is posed on the same plane. The Vatican's social base is precisely provided by the peasants, whom the clerical forces have always considered as a reserve army of reaction and whom they have always striven to keep under their control. The accomplishment of an alliance between workers and peasants in the struggle against capitalism presupposes the destruction of the Vatican's influence over the peasants of central and northern Italy in particular. The tactics pursued by the party towards Miglioli were aimed precisely at achieving this.

The problem of the relations between the proletariat and the other anti-capitalist classes is only one of the problems concerning the party's tactics and strategy. On other points too, there exists a profound disagreement between the leadership and the far left. The leadership considers that the party's tactics should be determined by the situation, and by the aim of winning a decisive influence over the majority of the working class, in order actually to lead it towards the revolution. The far left considers that tactics should be determined by considerations of a formal character, and that the party should not at every moment pose the problem of winning a majority, but for long periods of time should limit itself to simple propaganda activity for its general political principles.

The best example of the nature and extent of the disagreement is provided by the tactics followed by the party after the Matteotti assassination, and by the criticisms which the far left makes of these. It is certain that at first, i.e. immediately after Matteotti's murder, the constitutional opposition was the predominant factor in the situation, and that its forces were essentially provided by the working class and the peasantry. It was, therefore, in effect the working class which found itself on incorrect positions, and operated without being conscious of its own function, or of the political position which was appropriate for it in the context of the conflicting forces. It was necessary to see to it that the working class acquired consciousness of this function and position.

What attitude should our party have adopted to this end? Would it have been enough to emit propaganda slogans and conduct a campaign of ideological and political criticism directed both at fascism and at the constitutional opposition (Aventine)? No, this would not have been sufficient. The propaganda and political criticism which are carried in the party organs enjoy a very restricted circle of influence; they do not reach very far outside the membership at large. It was necessary to carry out a political activity, and this had to be different in the case of fascism and in the case of the Opposition. In fact, the far left too says that there were three factors in the situation at that time: fascism, the Opposition and the proletariat. This means that we had to make a distinction between the two former, and pose ourselves the problem – not merely theoretically, but in practice – of how to disintegrate the Opposition, socially and thus politically, in order to deprive it of the base it had among the masses. The party's political activity with respect to the Opposition was directed to this end.

It is certain that a fundamental problem existed at that time, for us and for the proletariat: that of overthrowing fascism. Precisely because they wanted fascism to be overthrown, by whatever means, the masses to a very great extent followed the Opposition. And, in reality, it must not be denied that if the Mussolini government had fallen, whatever the means which had caused it to fall, an extremely deep political crisis would have opened up in Italy, whose development no one could have foreseen or halted. But the Opposition forces too knew this, and they therefore excluded right from the beginning 'one' way of bringing fascism down, which was the only possible one, i.e. the mobilization and struggle of the masses. By excluding this sole possible way to bring down fascism, the Opposition in reality kept fascism upright, and were the most effective prop of the régime in dissolution. Well we, with the political activity we carried out in relation to the Opposition (exit from Parliament; participation in the oppositional assembly; exit from that), succeeded in making this fact obvious to the masses: something which we would certainly not have been able to do by mere propaganda or critical activity, etc. We consider that the party's tactics must always have the character that our tactics had then. The party must take problems to the masses in a real and political way, if it wants to obtain results.

The problem of winning a decisive influence over the majority of the working class, and that of the alliance between the workers and the peasants, are both tightly bound up with the military problem of the revolution. This is posed for us today in a quite particular manner, given the disposition of the armed forces which the Italian bourgeoisie has at its command. First of all, there is a national army; however, this is extremely reduced in size, and contains a high percentage of officers controlling the mass of soldiers. It is, therefore, far from easy to exert any influence on the army, so as to have it as one's ally at a time of revolution. In the best eventuality – and to the extent that it is possible to foresee this today – the army could remain neutral. But apart from the army, there are very numerous armed corps (police, *carabinieri*, national militia), who can only be influenced by the proletariat with the greatest difficulty. In short, out of 600,000 armed men whom the bourgeoisie has in its service, 400,000 at least cannot be won to the policies of the working class. The relation of forces which exists between the proletariat and the bourgeoisie can, therefore, only be modified as the result of a political struggle which the party of the working class has conducted, and which has enabled it to gain sway over and lead the majority of the working population. The tactical conception of the left is an obstacle to the accomplishment of this task.

All the problems which have arisen in the discussion between the party leadership and the far left are linked to the international situation, and to the problems of the proletariat's international organization, the Communist International. The far left adopts a strange attitude in this domain, analogous in part to that of the Maximalists, insofar as it considers the Communist International as a *de facto* organization to which it counterposes the 'true' International which still remains to be created. This way of presenting the issue contains within it, potentially, the problem of a split. The stance adopted by the far left in Italy before and during the pre-congress discussion (factionalism) has, moreover, given proof of this.

It is necessary to examine what our party's situation as an international organism is. In 1921, our party was founded on the terrain indicated by the theses and resolutions of the first two congresses of the Communist International. Who departed from these theses, to take up a position in conflict with those of the International? Not the party leadership – which is still basically the same one that was elected by the Livorno and Rome Congresses – but a group of party leaders, those who make up the far left tendency. The position of this group is incorrect, and the party, in opposing and condemning it, is merely continuing its own political tradition.

The broad scope of the discussion which has taken place and which will have to take place at the Congress with the comrades of the far left is a consequence of the fact that these comrades, in order to distinguish themselves in the party as a faction, have felt the need to differentiate themselves on all problems which could be brought under discussion, and at the same time have carried on an activity which could have led to the disintegration of the party's base. This activity must be condemned by the Congress, and the possibility of its being repeated in the future must be excluded.

The discussion which will take place at this Congress has enormous importance, inasmuch as it touches on all the problems of the Italian revolution and hence profoundly interests the development of our party. The decisions which will be taken at it will characterize the party's activity for a whole historical period. It is, therefore, necessary for every comrade to be aware of the proletarian and revolutionary responsibility which rests upon him.

Bordiga. Gramsci's exposition of the basic points of disagreement between the party's central leadership and the far left has convinced me of the need for a complete differentiation. The far left will, therefore, present its own draft theses, completely opposed to those of the leadership, and which will serve to complete the part which has already been published in the party daily.[187]

Basically, there exists just one fundamental disagreement between us and the leadership and the International, and all the points of conflict can be reduced to this. While reserving the right to develop a full exposition in the plenary session, I shall limit myself here to indicating the basic points.

First of all, as regards ideology, we consider that we are on the line of revolutionary Marxism, while it is the comrades of the leadership who have departed from it, aligning themselves with idealistic philosophical conceptions which the International itself condemns.

With respect to the nature of the party, we maintain that it is an 'organ' of the working class. To maintain that the party is a 'part' and not an 'organ' of the working class indicates a concern to identify the party and the class in a statistical manner, and is symptomatic of an opportunist deviation. The statistical identification of party and class has always been one of the characteristics of opportunistic labourism.

We deny that organization by cells tends to give the party a proletarian spirit. Indeed, we assert that it tends to deprive it of that spirit, by causing a corporate spirit to prevail. It is incorrect to state that the problem of combating corporatism no longer exists in Italy. This problem does exist and only the party, as unitary organ of the working class, can resolve it. In debating this problem, we have seen a remarkable example of the method which consists in presenting the positions of the left as right-wing positions. It has been said that we do not have faith in the proletariat. Well, we recall that this very argument was put forward against the revolutionaries by the reformists. Today, as in those times of the struggle against reformism, we are against demagogic workerist optimism and consider it a dangerous deviation.

So far as tactics are concerned, in other words the party's activity in relation to specific situations, we consider that the formulations presented by the party leadership are very dangerous. For example, it is now said that the party must remain 'in all situations' in contact with the masses, in order to exert a predominant influence upon them. This is no longer even Lenin's thesis. Lenin formulated the thesis of conquering the majority in a period that was considered as preceding a struggle for the conquest of power. Lenin counterposed this thesis to the thesis of the 'offensive', in other words to the thesis according to which it would be possible for the communist party to struggle for the conquest of power even without having a decisive part of the masses under its control. We accept Lenin's thesis as he formulated it, i.e. for the period which precedes the conquest of power. But we reject the extension of it which is now being proposed, and indeed consider this extension as a step towards opportunism. It is, moreover, in contradiction with the history of Bolshevism. This history has shown that there are periods in which it is better to be few than many. This difference is viewed by us with alarm.

With respect to international questions, which we deliberately put to the fore, we assert that there exists a crisis in the Communist

International. This crisis has its source in the fact that the correct path has not always been followed in building the communist parties. It has been forgotten that sometimes one must be concerned not so much with immediate success, as with winning stable positions which will not ever be lost in the future. In a first period, the sole concern was to assemble forces, without caring if these were truly communist forces. Subsequently, it became necessary to initiate a series of purges, and all the parties had to pass through deep crises. This state of affairs has repercussions upon the present situation in the International too.

Questions of tactics were resolved with the same system: i.e. not in accordance with a clear, precise and immutable line, but with a deplorable 'eclecticism', which is justified by the aim of taking account of changes in the objective situation. The most obvious example concerns relations between the political movement and the trade-union movement. In a first period, organizations of a trade-union character were accepted into the ranks of the Communist International, in this way flouting fundamental principles of organization (IWW, Spanish syndicalists, etc.). Then the Red Trade-union International was founded, and a whole plan of action was drawn up to get the trade-union movements of individual countries to join it; naturally, it was claimed that this was the only correct method. But at the Fifth Congress, and – which is more serious – without any adequate preparation or discussion, a third course was adopted: that of struggling for the organic unity of the international trade-union movement. It is this method of eclectic and 'politicking' analysis, dominated by the sole preoccupation of immediate success, which has led us to failure. We counted on taking everything, but nothing went right and today we are weaker than before.

This wrong approach to political problems and to general tactics goes together with a fundamental defect in the internal method of work of the International. The system followed in creating leaderships for the individual parties is incorrect, as is the system whereby discussions for the World Congresses are imposed and directed. In this field, we accept the criticisms formulated by Trotsky of the International's method of work.

The idea now is to repair the crisis which exists in the International through so-called Bolshevization. We reject this slogan, inasmuch as it signifies an artificial and mechanical transposition to the Western parties of methods which were specific to the Russian party. With Bolshevization, an attempt is being made to resolve questions which are political with formulae of an organizational character. This is occurring, for example, with respect to factionalism. On this point, is there a direct counter-position between our position and that of the central leadership of our party? The leadership has waged a campaign against factionalism that was an out and out campaign of disintegration. The workers have been repelled by this campaign towards pure unitarism, which is an incorrect position. The question of factionalism cannot be resolved on the organizational and disciplinary plane, but only on the political and historical plane. If the International is not led well, factionalism will perforce arise, because its origin lies precisely in the inadequacy of the international organization for resolving the historical problems of the proletariat at the present moment. A campaign against factionalism waged with the methods used by the central leadership of our party would have led to extremely grave consequences, if we had not been determined to avoid all danger to the integrity of the party.

Another of the fundamental aspects of the Bolshevization campaign is that which concerns the organizational transformation by cells. We are against making organization by cells a question of principle. Moreover, we consider that so far as the non-Russian parties are concerned the basis of organization must be territorial, and the cells must be organs created by the party for work to be carried out in the factories.

So far as tactics are concerned, we maintain our long-standing criticisms of the united front and workers' government slogans. To these, we add new criticisms of the new tactical positions, of which we have seen the first examples in the tactics followed by the Italian leadership with respect to the Aventine; in the tactics recommended to the German party for the presidential elections; and in the tactics followed by the French party in the municipal elections (Clichy).[188] These new tactical attitudes are related to the evaluation of the objective situation. It is as well it be known that we are fundamentally in agreement with this evaluation (temporary stabilization of capitalism), but that the tactical and political deductions which it is proposed should be drawn from it alarm us. We consider that even in this period, there is a revolutionary policy to be followed. By contrast, on the part of the current which is dominant in the International and in our party, the policy of the party in this period is determined in accordance with an artificial and non-Marxist counter-position of two fractions of the bourgeoisie. The dualism between the bourgeois right and left is over-estimated. The spectre is invoked of a part of the bourgeoisie which wishes to destroy the advances that have been made in the last decades; and the conclusion is drawn that the working class should manoeuvre to preserve these advances. We consider that an error made in this direction is more serious than an error made in the opposite direction, i.e. in the direction of under-estimating the contradictions between the various fractions of the bourgeoisie.

Gramsci. It was partly because of an error of this last kind made by our party that fascism was able to come to power so easily.

Bordiga. Your error is precisely to overestimate the danger of the victory of a right-wing bourgeois group. The victory of fascism was made possible by the policy of concessions to the workers' movement that was followed by the left bourgeoisie during the democratic period. Those concessions served to prevent the formation of working-class unity. The proletariat's freedom of movement in the democratic period was thus a counter-revolutionary condition, and we must prevent any return to the same situation by fighting from this moment against the illusion that there exists a left bourgeoisie. You have not contributed to destroying that illusion, and have allowed the proletariat to fall under the influence of other classes.

It is perfectly true that the party cannot limit itself to merely proselytizing, just as it cannot limit itself to leading partial actions. It must, however, pose today the problem of tomorrow, fortifying itself against the counter-revolutionary influences of the two policies of the bourgeoisie. Hence, your tactics against the Aventine were fundamentally mistaken. In the proposal for an Anti-parliament, you posed the problem of freedom, etc., as a prejudicial problem; in other words, you accepted the terrain of the opposition. This meant prejudicing our situation also with respect to a possible revolutionary development. We consider, in fact, that even if the opposition had launched a struggle against fascism, we would only have been able usefully to intervene in that struggle and turn it to our own ends, if the masses had never seen any point of contact between us and the opposition. Any contact, or appearance of contact, between us and the opposition in fact contributed to keeping the workers under the latter's control.

So far as the tradition of the party is concerned, the left considers that it represents the tradition and continuity of the struggle against opportunist deviations and against centrism.

We do not believe that one can make proposals for action, or solve the problems of the Italian party, if first the problems are not resolved at the international level. The fundamental problem for us is that of the Communist International. To resolve this problem, the method of theorizing the experience of the Russian Communist Party is absolutely inadequate. Our opinion, on the contrary, is that the questions of the Russian Communist Party themselves cannot be resolved today, other than on the basis of elements drawn from the experience of the class struggle as it unfolds in other countries.

A confirmation of the accuracy of this opinion is provided by the recent discussion which has taken place in the Russian party.[189] We only have minimal information on this discussion, but it is certain that it touches on problems which are related to the entire international situation. These problems must be discussed in all Sections of the International, and for this reason we were extremely astonished to read a letter from the Russian Communist Party expressing the wish that the problems recently discussed at the Russian Congress should not be the subject of discussion in other parties. Apart from this, the way in which the recent discussion took place shows that the platform which is presented to us as permitting a resolution of all the problems which confront the various parties in the present historical period (Leninism) is a very unstable platform, inasmuch as even while holding to it one can perform oscillations as violent as those which appeared during the Russian discussion.

In conclusion, we consider that the only way to resolve our crisis and that of the International is by initiating a serious and exhaustive discussion on the problems of the International itself.

Rienzi [Tasca]. Agrees that it is necessary to have a full and serious discussion.

With respect to the philosophical question alluded to by Bordiga, asserts that the conception which the far left has of the party as an organ of the working class is far from being fully in accordance with the doctrine of historical materialism. Moreover, there is an obvious rift between the conception which the far left has of the nature of the party and its conception of the relations that the party must have with the masses.

There is no doubt that if the party proposed to 'remain' at every moment and in all situations a mass party, then 'situationism' would represent a danger. But the problem of winning a majority cannot be achieved in this way. It must be conceived in the sense that in every situation there must exist conditions of possibility for the party to win the majority of the working class, and that there do not exist situations in which this conquest is impossible. We win the masses when they have lost the capacity to delude themselves; but even at these moments, we only obtain results if at no moment have we ever abandoned the masses. There is an identity of destiny between the masses and the party. In Italy, for example, if the opposition forces had overthrown fascism, would they have succeeded in lulling the masses with the democratic illusion? On the contrary, precisely the opposite would have occurred.

Assessment of the situation and the consequent determination of the party's tactics can never be separated from considerations of time. One may never abstract from time. The best example is provided by the tactics followed by the Communist International to resolve the problem of relations between parties and unions. It is certain that in '19 and '20, it was right to make every effort to assemble the broadest possible masses under the International's control. It was for this reason that even trade-union organizations were welcomed into the International; but this attitude was modified when the situation was seen to have changed. The policy followed by the International in this field cannot be understood if it is separated from the general situation.

Bordiga is right when he asks that we discuss international problems; but only in the sense that it is necessary to accelerate the rhythm of the political experience of the various parties, by utilizing the experience which the individual Sections of the International have passed through in their recent past. In order to make a contribution to this process of formulating an international experience, the speaker passes in rapid review the problems which have faced the various parties in the last period.

So far as France is concerned, our party has made errors in the way it has posed, and conducted, the campaign against the war in Morocco. The party has limited itself to agitational propaganda based on clearly communist slogans against the war and for defeatism; it has not bothered to seek intermediate slogans which, without conflicting with the communist slogans, would make it possible to regroup the masses around us. This was an ultra-left error, and was responsible for the fact that the French party, in a very favourable situation, did not increase its influence among the masses very greatly or obtain the successes it could have.

Another error made by the French party is that of insisting mechanically on identifying fascism with the bourgeoisie and the bourgeoisie with social-democracy. These errors generate wrong tactical positions. The question – comrade Rienzi states – is one of general significance, and it is necessary to modify certain expressions which have become currently used in our parties. I do not accept the point of the political theses in which it is denied that social-democracy is the right wing of the working-class movement, and it is made instead into the left wing of the bourgeoisie. If this were the case, the tactic of the united front would be absurd, because it would be a tactic of coalition with an enemy class. By an assertion of this kind, one in effect justifies the criticisms made of the united front tactic by the far left. It is true that social-democratic ideology is a reflection of the bourgeoisie's influence on the working-class movement. It is true that this influence, which acts very powerfully upon the leaders, also affects broad layers of the masses. But this does not take away the class character or social structure of the workers' movement, even when it follows social-democracy. This is especially true when social-democracy constitutes an historical phase as the next step for the whole working class, as with the English "Labour Party"; if that were not the case, the affiliation of the communists to the LP would be an absurdity. I therefore ask that this point in the theses should be reworked, so as to avoid the base of the party being able to interpret a united front tactic of the CP with the mass of social-democratic workers as a united front tactic with the left wing of the bourgeoisie.

Going on to speak of the German situation and the workers' and peasants' government, comrade Rienzi observes that criticism of the Saxon episode has not been directed at participation of the communists in a government with the social-democratic left (a participation authorized by the Communist International), but at the fact that this was not accompanied by any proper political or military preparation at the base, or by any serious mobilization for revolutionary struggle. He considers that participation in an externally parliamentary form of government is a possible episode – a transitory and very brief episode, but a possible one – of the civil war in the context of which the tactic and development of the workers' and peasants' government are located. In this connection, he observes that if the workers' and peasants' government had been realized in Bulgaria to prevent Zankov coming to power, it would have had to be realized on the parliamentary terrain.[190]

In general, the speaker considers that the reasons for the failure of the German revolution of 1923 cannot be ascribed solely to an error made in the application of the united front and workers' government tactic. The reasons were far deeper and more complex, and it cannot be denied that a part of the responsibility lies also with the central leadership of the Communist International. These reasons were not analysed at the Fifth World Congress, for motives which I do not share. It is claimed that it was not possible to make this analysis fully at the Fifth Congress, because the prime necessity was to avoid demoralization spreading among the masses. These concerns no doubt have some value, but in addition to them one must also have a concern to clarify for the masses themselves what the tactic of the proletariat's party is. This latter concern should not be pushed into the background by problems of an internal nature.

As for Russia and the discussions which have taken place within the Russian party, the speaker justifies the expression used in the RCP's letter to the western parties with the anxiety to avoid the same thing happening with this last discussion as occurred with the first and second Trotsky discussions, i.e. a mechanical transposition of the conflict into the western parties. The problems of socialist construction in Russia are problems which must interest the whole proletariat. This, moreover, was clearly stated by Stalin in his speech to the Russian party Congress. The problems of Russia must be felt by all workers as their own problems.

The speaker considers that the expression 'State capitalism' applied to the present situation in Russia is ambiguous. The socialist character of the present Russian economic system consists in the fact that it allows the Russian revolution to ensure that conditions are produced, in which it will be possible for it to expand on a European and world scale. It is certain that the possibility exists to give the proletarian dictatorship in Russia organic foundations, such as will enable it to resist until the revolution breaks out in other countries. The workers must know that the concessions which Russia is having to make in the present historical period serve to link the Russian revolution to the revolution of the other countries. Resources are needed for this waiting-period, and these are created through a form of primitive accumulation made possible by the State's monopoly of foreign trade.

With respect to the situation of the International in general, the speaker states that the presentation of this problem which has been made by Bordiga is absolutely superficial and banal. It is necessary to see things from a far wider point of view, bearing in mind the characteristics of the present historical period, of partial recovery of the capitalist order. It is further necessary to examine the situation of the revolution from a world viewpoint, and to recognize that – if one takes account of the progress it has made (movement of the Eastern peoples) and of the positions it has held onto (Soviet Russia) through the work of the International – then the balance-sheet of the International itself must be presented as positive. There is no doubt that the work of constructing parties presents great difficulties and is influenced by the conditions in which the working masses find themselves. The essential problem is that of creating a leading centre, and of rendering the parties capable at the periphery too of fulfilling well all the tasks which belong to the political organization of the proletarian vanguard. It cannot be denied that this problem has been somewhat neglected by the International in certain parties.

In our party, a political evolution has commenced. This must become thorough-going and complete. Here the problem of the faction is posed. The existence of the faction may mean that at the gravest moments a part of the party, petrified on the positions of the far left, will not be able to move. If this occurs, the danger for us will be very great.

Naples F. (not a formal delegate to the Congress). He states that the discussion to prepare the party Congress was a discussion of dirty names and insults and not an ideological discussion. The far left wishes to win the masses precisely through its tactical inflexibility. During the Matteotti period, the party Centre did not know what to do, and it was pressure from the periphery which imposed on it the little good that it achieved. He protests because in the discussion published in *L'Unità*, the thinking of the left was distorted by editorial comments prefacing or appended to its articles.[191]

Morelli [Scoccimarro]. The essential problems under debate between the far left and the party leadership are, no doubt, those which concern the nature of the party and the tactics to be followed *vis-à-vis* the masses, in order to acquire a decisive influence over them. Comrade Bordiga, however, in his intervention did not reply to those things which the leadership maintains, but criticized assertions and points of view which no one has ever dreamed of maintaining. Perhaps in this way he thought he would make his own task easier.

None of us thinks that there exists a statistical coincidence between the party and the working class, and that every worker because he is a worker should be a member of the party. The criticisms made against this point of view are therefore not made against us, and Bordiga could have spared us them. We, having defined the party as a 'part' of the working class, clearly define which is the part in question, i.e. the vanguard, and say what the qualities are that this part must have.

Comrade Bordiga, on the other hand, limits himself to defining the party as the 'association of those' who accept that specific programme. This is a non-Marxist definition, because it entirely under-estimates the mass character of the party. Bordiga's definition, in that form, could be applied to any party.

Nor is it true that we say that the party must 'in all situations' be a mass party. However, we do say that in all situations it must 'aim' to be one. The two things are very different, and it is against the latter opinion that Bordiga ought to polemicize, not against the former which for polemical convenience he attributes to us.

Another point of disagreement concerns the way in which the internal struggles and conflicts between different groups of the bourgeoisie should be evaluated and exploited by the party of the proletariat. This tactic does not exist and has never been applied in our party. What is certain is that we do not accept Bordiga's formulation, according to which it is a matter of indifference whether Mussolini or Amendola is in power.

Similarly, with respect to the united front and the 'new tactics' of the Communist International, nobody has ever maintained that the communist parties should carry out a tactic of alliance with the left bourgeois parties, as Bordiga claims. We distinguish between the different groups of the bourgeoisie, and regulate and modify our tactics in accordance with these differences, in order to draw the maximum possible advantage from situations for the interests of the proletariat and the class struggle. In this respect, what Lenin wrote and the tactics he persuaded the party to follow at the epoch of the Kornilov coup are of decisive importance. It is always necessary to take account of the repercussions which the party's slogans and political positions have among the masses. For example, when we made the proposal for an Anti-parliament, we immediately felt that the workers understood that this was a revolutionary slogan. In fact, that slogan served to get the masses to take a step forward, detaching them from the Aventine in which they had had faith.

From all the points which are under discussion between the party leadership and the far left, it is clear that there exists a fundamental disagreement. Two ideologies are involved, which are tending to diverge. It is impossible to unify the party and give it internal cohesion, so long as two ideologies coexist within it. The party must be unified on the basis of a single ideology, that of Leninism. Must we then proceed to expel those comrades who do not share this ideology? We do not think so, because we still hope that they will be convinced and come over onto our terrain.

The things which comrade Rienzi has said about the character of social-democracy and the workers' and peasants' government represent his personal opinion, but are not at all the opinion of the majority of the party's Central Committee. Comrade Rienzi has basically repeated what was advanced by Graziadei at the Fourth World Congress with respect to the workers' government and the possibility of realizing it on the parliamentary terrain. I consider that the position of Rienzi is mistaken. It has, moreover, been condemned by the congresses of the International themselves. The workers' and peasants' government in Bulgaria, if it had been established, would have been a government created to direct the civil war and not a government of parliamentary coalition.

Milan. This Third Congress must create a new situation in the party. On the one hand, it must put an end to factionalism and signal the death of factions; and on the other, it must constitute a step forward towards the acquisition of a greater political capacity by the party. The far left, by its activities and by the positions it takes, tends to create obstacles to the attainment of these two objectives. But there must exist a discipline for the far left as well.

With respect to the tactics which the party followed from the Matteotti assassination onwards, the fact that they were correct is shown by the actual results which were obtained among the masses. Our influence grew and is still growing. We can work well among the masses to extend it. This means that the tactics were correct.

With respect to the party's ideology and its nature, the theses of the Central Committee pose these questions in their precise terms, whereas the assertions of the far left are such that if the tactics of the party were to be fixed in accordance with them, our organization would certainly be damaged and see the development of its influence among the masses checked.

Calabria. States that once it is said that the comrades of the far left have a mistaken ideology, and uphold theses whose application would damage the party, one should no longer demand that they enter the Central Committee, indeed one should want them to remain outside it.

During the Matteotti crisis, the peasants of the South were with us and the party Centre, not understanding the situation, was unable to take any advantage of this orientation on their part.

Gramsci. The discussion being carried on between the Central

Committee and the far left of the party is not a purely academic discussion. The far left, for example, gives a definition of the party which leads it to make errors of tactics. This occurred when it was leading the party. The same can be said with respect to its analysis of the movements and parties of the bourgeoisie. Of fascism, for instance. When fascism emerged and developed in Italy, how was it to be seen? Was it only a combat organ of the bourgeoisie, or was it also a social movement? The far left which then led the party only considered the former aspect; and the consequence of this error was that we did not succeed in stemming the advance of fascism, as might perhaps have been possible. No political action was carried out to prevent fascism from coming to power. The leadership of that time committed the error of thinking that the situation of '21–'22 might continue and become consolidated, and that the coming to power of a military dictatorship was neither necessary nor possible. This error of evaluation was the consequence of an incorrect system of political analysis, i.e. of the system which Bordiga is counterposing today to that upheld by the Central Committee, which is the Leninist system.

The Italian situation is characterized by the fact that the bourgeoisie is organically weaker than in other countries and maintains itself in power only insofar as it succeeds in controlling and dominating the peasantry. The proletariat must struggle to tear the peasants from the bourgeoisie's influence, and place them under its own political guidance. This is the central point of the political problems which the party must resolve in the immediate future.

It is certain that it is also necessary to examine attentively the different stratifications of the bourgeois class. Indeed, it is necessary to examine the stratifications of fascism itself; for given the totalitarian system which fascism tends to instal, it will be within fascism itself that the conflicts which cannot express themselves in other ways will tend to re-emerge. The party's tactics in the Matteotti period always strove to take account of the stratifications of the bourgeoisie, and our proposal for an Anti-parliament was made with the aim of managing to make contact with backward masses which had, until then, remained under the control of layers of the big or petty bourgeoisie. It is certain that there are masses of peasants in the South who only when we made the proposal for an Anti-parliament came to know of the existence of a Communist Party.

With respect to the problem of cells, comrade Bordiga confuses the corporate competition between different categories of worker with the political division of the working class. Today, it is essential to combat the political division of the working class, and it is political division which the fascists are seeking to keep open within the proletariat; whereas the struggle against corporate competition, even if it has to be waged, is not an essential problem.

It is certainly not true, as Bordiga asserts, that the problem of party organization is posed in essentially different terms for us than for the Russian party, which was organized on the basis of production. Bordiga asserts that Tsarism was a reactionary form, and not a capitalist force. This is not true. It is enough to know the history of the 1905 revolution, and of the way in which capitalism developed in Russia before and during the War, to be in a position to disprove Bordiga's statement.

The problem posed for us today, and which is basically the same that was posed for the Russian party under the reaction, is that of the political levelling and unification of the working class. To resolve this problem, the party must be organized on the basis of factory cells. The solution advocated by the far left of making the cells mere working bodies of the party is absolutely inadequate. Today, there exist in the party two working bodies – the trade-union committee and the parliamentary group – and they are precisely the party's two weakest points. There can be no working body which is not at the same time a political body. If we applied the solution advocated by the far left to the problem of the cells, the only result would be that either the cells would no longer work politically, as they must however do, or they would become the vehicle for a party deviation.

Then it is untrue that the question of the cells, as Bordiga says, is not a question of principle. In the organizational field, it is a question of principle. Our party is a class party, the political organization of the vanguard of the proletariat. The task of the vanguard of the proletariat is to lead the whole working class to the construction of socialism. But in order to implement this task, it is precisely necessary for the vanguard of the proletariat to be organized on the basis of production.

As regards tactics, comrade Bordiga, when he is compelled to give his criticisms a concrete form, limits himself to saying that there exist 'dangers' in the application of Leninist tactics. But there equally exist very serious dangers as a result of the application of the tactic which he proposes. It is true that one must look at the consequences which the party's tactics have on the working-class masses, and it is also true that tactics which induce the masses to passivity are to be condemned. But precisely this occurred in 1921–2, as a result of the party leadership's attitude on the question of the *Arditi del Popolo*.[192] That tactic, even if on the one hand it corresponded to a need to prevent the party members from being controlled by a leadership that was not the party's leadership, on the other hand served to disqualify a mass movement which had started from below and which could instead have been exploited by us politically.

It is absurd to assert that there is no difference between a democratic situation and a reactionary situation, and indeed that in a democratic situation the task of winning the masses is more arduous. The truth is that today, in a reactionary situation, we are struggling to organize the party, while in a democratic situation we would be struggling to organize an insurrection.

Bordiga. But it is necessary for the masses to be ready to place themselves on that terrain.

Gramsci. For that, it is necessary to destroy the intermediate formations, which cannot be achieved with the tactics you advocate.

Bordiga has said that he is favourable to winning over the masses in the period which immediately precedes the revolution. But how does one know when one is in this period? It depends precisely on the work we are able to carry out among the masses whether this period begins or not. Only if we work and achieve successes in winning over the masses will a pre-revolutionary situation be reached.

Comrade Naples has protested against the way in which the campaign against the far left's factionalism has been conducted. I maintain that this campaign was fully justified. It was I who wrote that to create a faction in the Communist Party, in our present situation, was to act as *agents provocateurs*, and I still stand by that assertion today. If factionalism is tolerated for some, it must be tolerated for all. And one of the methods the police may use to destroy revolutionary parties is precisely that of causing artificial opposition movements to appear within them.

Comrade Naples has also stated that if the leadership has done anything good, this was because of pressure from the localities. It is very strange that if there was such a strong 'left' pressure in the localities, all this left strength should subsequently have melted away, as the result of a few comments attached to the articles in the discussion. The reality is that a vast left movement at the base did not exist, and that the establishment of the faction was something entirely artificial. As for the political orientation of the party at the base in the Matteotti period, this was far from being to the left. The party leadership had to make an effort to drag the party onto positions of opposition to both fascism and the Aventine. This, by the way, was a result of the situation in which the party found itself in 1923, in which it had not carried out any political activity. Therefore, while it became isolated from the masses, at the same time the party was subjected to the influence of the masses themselves, who in their turn were under the influence of other parties.

On the present situation of the party, we cannot be pessimistic. Our party is in a phase of development that is more advanced than with other parties of the International. It contains a basic stable proletarian nucleus, and is establishing a homogeneous and solid central leadership. But precisely for this reason, it is necessary to ask more of our party than is asked of other parties in the International, and the struggle against factionalism can and must be waged within it with the greatest determination.

* * * * *

After Gramsci's summing up, the draft political theses presented by the Central Committee were put to the vote. The Commission decided to adopt this draft as a basis for the detailed discussion, with three votes against (one of which was that of comrade Naples F. who is not a Congress delegate), and to reject the draft presented by the far left.

The Commission then proceeded to an analytic examination of the individual sections of the draft theses presented by the Central Committee.

Section I

Introduction, Theses 1–3

Bordiga. States that these sections do not accord adequate value to the far-left tendency which had appeared in the Socialist Party even prior to the War, and which was a genuine 'Marxist Left'.

Gramsci. What is said in the theses is true, in the sense that a 'Marxist Left' tendency did not exist in the Socialist Party in a permanent fashion.

Section II

Analysis of the Italian structure – Theses 4–9

Bordiga. In this part, the importance of the industrial class is under-estimated and the weakness of Italian industrialism over-estimated. Moreover, in the North too agriculture has had great economic and social importance.

Veneto. Also considers that the strength of Italian industrialism is under-estimated.

Rienzi. Considers that greater stress should be laid on the importance which the movement of the rural proletariat had in the Po Valley. The rural proletariat is a force which must be inserted in the process of construction of the workers' State, and is a force which has dominated entire periods of social struggle in Italy.

Gramsci. The weakness of industrialism is relative both to the strength which it has in other countries, and to the importance in Italy of other economic and social factors.

Bordiga. In thesis 9, it would be better to make a reference to the phenomenon of emigration. Many peasants emigrate to become workers. When they return, they constitute a link between the peasantry and the proletariat.

Section III

Policy of the Italian bourgeoisie – Theses 10–14

Bordiga. Perhaps the crisis of the general staffs of the bourgeois parties is over-estimated in this part. This crisis was not always matched by an internal disintegration of the political groupings of the bourgeoisie.

Ercoli. What matters is to stress the disintegration of the State apparatus, provoked by the internal conflicts of the bourgeoisie and by a balance of forces between different groups in conflict, each pursuing its own interests. This concept was already expressed in the Rome Theses.

Bordiga. That point of the Rome Theses was not written by me, but by Gramsci.

Rienzi. It is necessary to make clear that it was not fascism which, by coming to power, defeated the revolution, but on the contrary the defeat of the revolution which gave the victory to fascism. With respect to the disintegration of the State, brought about by the balance between the different groups in conflict, it is necessary to define more closely the concept of State. Apart from an instrument of class domination, the State is also an apparatus which serves to ensure the satisfaction of elementary and universal needs. Now, the Italian experience of 1919–20 shows that the bourgeoisie in its activity makes use of the fact that, with the State, it monopolizes also the satisfaction – however this is done – of certain elementary needs, which might be called physiological, of social life. In a period of revolutionary crisis, it is necessary to take account of the fact that the assault on the bourgeois State also disorganizes certain forms of social life. Thus the revolutionary struggle cannot be reduced to repeated stoppages in social life itself, unless one is aware that such activity may, if not directed to the seizure of power, change broad layers of the population from possible allies or neutrals into elements of revolutionary decline.

Gramsci. The concept of State in an absolute sense as it has been expounded by Rienzi cannot be accepted. As for the crisis which the Italian State passed through in the 1920 period, this had the character of a real split between the leading elements of the State apparatus. Fascism carries out policies designed to prevent this situation being repeated in the future. In characterizing the situation after the fascist seizure of power, it is necessary to take account of the fact that for two years the proletariat continued to struggle against fascism arms in hand, even though it retreated from the positions it had held in the preceding years.

Section IV

Fascism and its policies – Theses 15–18

Bordiga. In setting out the results which the repressive action of fascism tends to produce, the impression must not be given that the situation might have some immediate resolution because of this.

Milan. The party's thinking has never been that the situation could have an immediate resolution. However, it is necessary to insist on setting out the real consequences of the fascist policy of repression of the masses, because this is an element which serves to counteract discouragement.

Bordiga. It seems to me that in these paragraphs the error is made of putting the proletariat, as a revolutionary force, on the same level and the same plane as the intermediate social layers.

Ercoli. On this point, there is no under-estimation of the proletariat's function in bringing about a modification of the present political situation.

Gramsci. The preeminent function of the proletariat derives from the very fact that fascism, while it seeks to exert the same pressure on the proletariat and on the peasants, in fact has more difficulty in repressing the workers. Hence, it is certain that the peasants, if they fought alone against fascism, would be beaten. Their victory is only possible if they fight under the leadership of the workers.

Section V

Motor forces and perspectives of the revolution – Theses 19–22

Bordiga. It is necessary to stress the importance of the rural proletariat, from a political and organizational point of view. The organization of the rural proletariat should be dealt with by the party's Trade-union Section, not by the Agrarian Section.

Gramsci. It is certain that from the political viewpoint there exists something like a series of interlocking links, whereby the rural proletariat is the vehicle for the proletariat's influence over the peasantry.

Ercoli, Morelli and Massimo explain that both in the theses under discussion, and in the party's past practice, account has always been taken of the rural proletariat in the correct manner. It has always been the Trade-union Committee which has dealt with the organization and demands of the agricultural wage-labourers.

Section VI

Fundamental tasks of the Communist Party – Thesis 23

Ercoli. Asks Bordiga if he accepts this formulation of the party's tasks.

Bordiga. I accept it.

Section VII

The construction of the Communist Party as a 'Bolshevik' party – Thesis 24

Section VIII

The party's ideology – Theses 25–28

Rienzi. Asks, in line with what he said in the general discussion, that the passage where it is asserted that social-democracy is the left wing of the bourgeoisie should be changed.

Gramsci. States that the modification asked for by Rienzi cannot be accepted. If what he maintains were true, we would not be able, on occasion, to fight social-democracy even with arms.

Christophe [Humbert-Droz, delegate from the International Executive]. It is true that social-democracy sometimes has a social base in the proletariat, but it is a left wing of the bourgeoisie because of the political function which it fulfils.

Bordiga. Rienzi is right. If one says that social-democracy is a left wing of the bourgeoisie, one has to concede that the united front tactic is a tactic of coalition with a bourgeois party. However, there is a contradiction between what Rienzi says about social-democracy's social base and what he says about the nature of the party. If it is true that one judges the nature of a party from its social basis, then social-democracy is in fact a proletarian and revolutionary party.

*   *   *   *   *

After a brief discussion on the concept of the party, Rienzi's proposal is rejected.

Sections IX, X, XI – Theses 29–35

Veneto. Asks comrade Bordiga to define the far left's thinking on centralism in the party.

Bordiga. For us, centralism is not a point of departure, but a point of arrival: in other words, the result of the whole policy which the party carries out. The speaker acknowledges that the majority system cannot be accepted as a norm. In given situations, the party leadership can lead the party even against the will of the majority. Hence, it would be better to substitute the formula of 'organic centralism' for that of 'democratic centralism'.[193] The essential condition for centralism to be applied is that there should be homogeneity of organizational criteria for the whole party. This has not been the case in our party, in the last period of its life.

Morelli. It is clear what Bordiga's words mean. For him, centralism only exists when the party follows the political line which he approves of. The speaker explains what the limits of centralism and democracy in the party are.

Section XII

Strategy and tactics of the party – Theses 36–44

Veneto. Asks that the slogan and tactic of the workers' and peasants' government should be explained better.

69. THE ITALIAN SITUATION AND THE TASKS OF THE PCI ("LYONS THESES")[194] – *GRAMSCI; TOGLIATTI*

1. The transformation of the communist parties, in which the vanguard of the working class is assembled, into Bolshevik parties can be considered at the present moment as the fundamental task of the Communist International. This task must be related to the historical development of the international workers' movement, and in particular to the struggle which has taken place within it between Marxism and the currents which represented a deviation from the principles and practice of the revolutionary class struggle.

In Italy, the task of creating a Bolshevik party takes on its full dimensions only if one bears in mind the vicissitudes of the workers' movement since its origins, and the fundamental deficiencies which have revealed themselves therein.

2. The birth of the working-class movement took place in different forms in every country. What was common everywhere was the spontaneous revolt of the proletariat against capitalism. This revolt, however, took a specific form in each nation, which was a reflection and consequence of the particular national characteristics of the elements which, originating from the petty bourgeoisie and peasantry, contributed to forming the great bulk of the industrial proletariat.

Marxism represented the conscious, scientific element, superior to the particularism of the various tendencies of a national character and origin; and it waged a struggle against these, both in the theoretical field and in the field of organization. The whole formative process of the Ist International was hinged upon this struggle, which concluded with the expulsion of Bakuninism from the International. When the Ist International ceased to exist, Marxism had already triumphed in the working-class movement. The IInd International was, in fact, formed of parties which all called themselves Marxist and took Marxism as the basis of their tactics on all essential questions.

After the victory of Marxism, the tendencies of a national character over which it had triumphed sought to manifest themselves in other ways, re-emerging within Marxism itself as forms of revisionism. This process was encouraged by the development of the imperialist phase of capitalism. The following three facts are closely connected with this phenomenon: the disappearance in the ranks of the working-class movement of criticism of the State, an essential element of Marxist doctrine, and its replacement by democratic utopias; the formation of a labour aristocracy; and a new mass transfer of petty bourgeois and peasants into the working class, hence a new dissemination within the proletariat of ideological currents of a national character, conflicting with Marxism. The process of degeneration of the IInd International thus took the form of a struggle against Marxism which unfolded within Marxism itself. It culminated in the collapse provoked by the War.

The one party which escaped degeneration was the Bolshevik Party, which succeeded in maintaining itself at the head of the workers' movement in its own country, expelled the anti-Marxist tendencies from its own ranks, and through the experience of three revolutions evolved Leninism, which is the Marxism of the epoch of monopoly capitalism, imperialist wars and proletarian revolution. Thus, the position of the Bolshevik Party in the foundation and at the head of the IIIrd International was historically determined, and the terms of the problem of forming Bolshevik parties in every country were laid down: it is the problem of recalling the proletarian vanguard to the doctrine and practice of revolutionary Marxism, overcoming and completely liquidating every anti-Marxist current.

3. In Italy, the origins and vicissitudes of the workers' movement were such, that before the War there was never constituted a Marxist left current with any permanent or continuous character. The original character of the Italian working-class movement was very confused. Various tendencies converged within it, from Mazzinian idealism to the generic humanitarianism of the cooperators and proponents of mutual help; and to Bakuninism, which maintained that the conditions existed in Italy – even before a development of capitalism – to pass immediately to socialism. The late origin and weakness of industrialism meant that the clarifying element provided by the existence of a strong proletariat was missing. One consequence was that even the split of the anarchists from the socialists took place after a delay of twenty years (1892, Genoa Congress).

In the Italian Socialist Party as it emerged from the Genoa Congress, there were two dominant currents. On the one hand, there was a group of intellectuals who represented nothing more than a tendency towards democratic reform of the State: their Marxism did not go beyond the aim of arousing and organizing the forces of the proletariat in order to make them serve to establish democracy (Turati, Bissolati, etc.). On the other hand, there was a group more directly tied to the proletarian movement, representing a working-class tendency, but lacking any adequate theoretical consciousness (Lazzari). Up till 1900, the Party set itself no aims other than ones of a democratic character. After 1900, once the freedom to organize had been won and a democratic phase began, the incapacity of all the groups which made it up to give it the physiognomy of a Marxist party of the proletariat was manifest.

The intellectual elements indeed detached themselves more and more from the working class. Nothing, moreover, came of the attempt by another layer of intellectuals and petty bourgeois to create a Marxist left in the shape of syndicalism. As a reaction to this latter attempt, the Party was conquered by the integralist faction. This was the expression, with its empty conciliationist verbalism, of a fundamental characteristic of the Italian working-class movement – also to be explained by the weakness of industrialism and the deficient critical consciousness of the proletariat. The revolutionism of the years preceding the War kept this characteristic intact, never managing to transcend the limits of a generic populism or to construct a party of the working class and apply the method of the class struggle.

Within this revolutionary current, even before the War, a "far left" group began to separate itself off; this upheld the theses of revolutionary Marxism, but in a spasmodic manner and without managing to exercise a real influence on the development of the workers' movement.

This is what explains the negative and ambiguous character which the Socialist Party's opposition to the War assumed; it also explains how the Socialist Party after the War found itself confronted by an immediately revolutionary situation, without having either resolved or so much as posed any of the fundamental problems which the political organization of the proletariat must resolve in order to fulfil its tasks: first of all, the problem of "choice of class" and the organizational form appropriate to it; then the problems of the party's programme and ideology; and lastly problems of strategy and tactics, whose solution could have grouped around the proletariat those forces which are its natural allies in the struggle against the State, and could thus have led it to the conquest of power.

The systematic accumulation of an experience which could contribute in a positive way to the resolution of these problems began in Italy only after the War. Only with the Livorno Congress were laid down the constitutive bases of the proletariat's class party, which, if it is to become a Bolshevik party and carry out its function to the full, must liquidate all the anti-Marxist tendencies that traditionally characterize the working-class movement.

Analysis of the Italian Social Structure

4. Capitalism is the predominant element in Italian society, and the force which is decisive in determining its development. This fundamental fact means that there is no possibility of a revolution in Italy that is not the socialist revolution. In the capitalist countries, the only class which can accomplish a real, deep social transformation is the working class. Only the working class is capable of translating into action the changes of an economic and political character which are necessary, if the energies of our country are to have complete freedom and possibility to develop. The way in which it will accomplish this revolutionary function is related to the degree of development of capitalism in Italy, and to the social structure which corresponds to it.

5. Industrialism, which is the essential part of capitalism, is very weak in Italy. Its possibilities for development are limited, both because of the geographical situation and because of the lack of raw materials. It therefore does not succeed in absorbing the majority of the Italian population (4 million industrial workers exist side by side with $3\frac{1}{2}$ million agricultural workers and 4 million peasants). To industrialism, there is counterposed an agriculture which naturally presents itself as the basis of the country's economy. The extremely varied conditions of the terrain, and the resulting differences in cultivation and in systems of tenancy, however, cause a high degree of differentiation among the rural strata, with a prevalence of poor strata, nearer to the conditions of the proletariat and more liable to be influenced by it and accept its leadership. Between the industrial and agrarian classes, there lies a fairly extensive urban petty bourgeoisie, which is of very great significance. It consists mainly of artisans, professional men and State employees.

6. The intrinsic weakness of capitalism compels the industrial class to adopt expedients to guarantee its control over the country's economy. These expedients are basically nothing more than a system of economic compromises between a part of the industrialists and a part of the agricultural classes, specifically the big landowners. One does not, therefore, find here the traditional economic struggle between industrialists and landowners, nor the rotation of ruling groups which this produces in other countries. The industrialists, in any case, do not

need to defend against the landowners an economic policy ensuring a continuous flow of labour from the countryside into the factories, since this flow is guaranteed by the abundant poor rural population which is characteristic of Italy. The industrial–agrarian agreement is based on a solidarity of interests between certain privileged groups, at the expense of the general interests of production and of the majority of those who work. It produces an accumulation of wealth in the hands of the big industrialists, which is the result of a systematic plundering of whole categories of the population and whole regions of the country. The results of this economic policy have in fact been: to create a deficit in the economic budget; to halt economic development in entire regions (South, Islands); to block the emergence and development of an economy better fitted to the structure and resources of the country; growing poverty of the working population; and the existence of a continuous stream of emigration, with the resulting demographic impoverishment.

7. Just as it does not naturally control the entire economy, so too the industrial class does not succeed in organizing single-handed the whole of society and the State. The construction of a national State is only made possible for it by the exploitation of factors of international politics (so-called Risorgimento). Its reinforcement and defence necessitate a compromise with the classes upon which industry exercises a limited hegemony: in particular, the landowners and petty bourgeoisie. Thence derives a heterogeneity and weakness of the entire social structure, and of the State which is its expression.

7 *bis*. There was a typical reflection of the weakness of the social structure, before the War, in the Army. A restricted circle of officers, lacking the prestige of leaders (old agrarian ruling classes, new industrial classes), had beneath it a bureaucratized caste of junior officers (petty bourgeoisie), which was incapable of serving as a link with the mass of soldiers, undisciplined and abandoned to themselves. During the War, the Army was forced to reorganize itself from the bottom up, after an elimination of the upper ranks and a transformation of organizational structure which corresponded to the appearance of a new category of junior officers. This phenomenon foreshadowed the analogous upheaval which fascism was to accomplish with respect to the State on a vaster scale.

8. The relations between industry and agriculture, which are essential for the economic life of a country and for the determination of its political superstructures, have a territorial basis in Italy. In the North,

agricultural production and the rural population are concentrated in a few big centres. As a result of this, all the conflicts inherent in the country's social structure contain within them an element which affects the unity of the State and puts it in danger. The solution of the problem is sought by the bourgeois and agrarian ruling groups through a compromise. None of these groups naturally possesses a unitary character or a unitary function. The compromise whereby unity is preserved is, moreover, such as to make the situation more serious. It gives the toiling masses of the South a position analogous to that of a colonial population. The big industry of the North fulfils the function *vis-à-vis* them of the capitalist metropoles. The big landowners and even the middle bourgeoisie of the South, for their part, take on the role of those categories in the colonies which ally themselves to the metropoles in order to keep the mass of working people subjugated. Economic exploitation and political oppression thus unite to make of the working people of the South a force continuously mobilized against the State.

9. The proletariat has greater importance in Italy than in other European countries, even of a more advanced capitalist nature: it is comparable only to that which existed in Russia before the Revolution. This is above all related to the fact that industry, because of the shortage of raw materials, bases itself by preference on the labour force (specialized skilled layers). It is also related to the heterogeneity and conflicts of interest which weaken the ruling classes. In the face of this heterogeneity, the proletariat appears as the only element which by its nature has a unificatory function, capable of coordinating the whole of society. Its class programme is the only "unitary" programme: in other words, the only one whose implementation does not lead to deepening the conflicts between the various elements of the economy and of society, or to breaking the unity of the State. Alongside the industrial proletariat, there also exists a great mass of rural proletarians, centred above all in the Po valley; these are easily influenced by the workers in industry, and hence easily mobilized for the struggle against capitalism and the State.

In Italy, there is a confirmation of the thesis that the most favourable conditions for the proletarian revolution do not necessarily always occur in those countries where capitalism and industrialism have reached the highest level of development, but may instead arise where the fabric of the capitalist system offers least resistance, because of its structural weakness, to an attack by the revolutionary class and its allies.

The Policy of the Italian Bourgeoisie

10. The aim which the Italian ruling classes set themselves from the origin of the unitary State onwards, was to keep the great mass of the working people subjugated and prevent them from becoming – by organizing around the industrial and rural proletariat – a revolutionary force capable of carrying out a complete social and political transformation, and giving birth to a proletarian State. The intrinsic weakness of capitalism, however, compelled it to base the economic disposition of the bourgeois State upon a unity obtained by compromises between non-homogeneous groups. In a vast historical perspective, this system is clearly not adequate to its purpose. Every form of compromise between the different groups ruling Italian society in fact becomes an obstacle placed in the way of the development of one or other part of the country's economy. Thus new conflicts are produced and new reactions from the majority of the population; it becomes necessary to intensify the pressure on the masses; and the result is a more and more decisive tendency for them to mobilize in revolt against the State.

11. The first period in the life of the Italian State (1870–90) was that of its greatest weakness. The two elements which composed the ruling class, the bourgeois intellectuals on the one hand and the capitalists on the other, were united in their aim of maintaining unity, but divided on the form to be given to the unitary State. There was no positive homogeneity between them. The problems which the State tackled were limited: they concerned rather the form than the substance of the bourgeoisie's political rule. Everything was dominated by the problem of balancing the budget, which is a problem of pure conservation. Awareness of the need to enlarge the basis of the classes which ruled the State appeared only with the beginnings of "transformism".[196]

The greatest weakness of the State in this period consisted in the fact that outside it, the Vatican grouped around itself a reactionary and anti-State bloc made up of the landowners and the great mass of backward peasants, controlled and led by the rich landlords and priests. The Vatican's programme had two elements: it sought to struggle against the unitary, "liberal" bourgeois State; and at the same time, it aimed to form the peasants into a reserve army against the advance of the socialist proletariat, stimulated by the development of industry. The State reacted to the sabotage carried out by the Vatican at its expense, with a whole quantity of legislation that was anti-clerical in content and aim.

12. In the period from 1890 to 1900, the bourgeoisie boldly tackled the problem of organizing its own dictatorship, and resolved it through a series of political and economic measures which determined the subsequent history of Italy.

First of all, the conflict between the intellectual bourgeoisie and the industrialists was resolved: Crispi's rise to power was the sign of this.[197] The bourgeoisie, thus strengthened, solved the question of its foreign relations (Triple Alliance), and so won the necessary security to try and enter the field of international competition for colonial markets.[198] At home, the bourgeois dictatorship established itself politically by restricting the right to vote, so reducing the electorate to little more than one million voters out of a population of 30 million. In the economic field, the introduction of industrial–agrarian protectionism corresponded to capitalism's aim to obtain control of all the national wealth. Through it, an alliance was forged between the industrialists and the landowners. This alliance stripped the Vatican of a part of the forces it had grouped around itself, especially among the landowners in the South, and brought these into the framework of the bourgeois State. The Vatican itself, moreover, saw the need to put more stress on the part of its reactionary programme which related to resisting the working-class movement, and took position against socialism in the encyclical *Rerum Novarum*.[199] The ruling classes, however, reacted to the danger which the Vatican continued to represent for the State by giving themselves a unitary organization with an anti-clerical programme, in the form of freemasonry.

The first real progress of the working-class movement in fact took place in this period. The establishment of the industrial-agrarian dictatorship posed the problem of revolution in its real terms, determining its historical conditions. In the North, an industrial and rural proletariat emerged, while in the South the rural population, subjected to a "colonial" system of exploitation, had to be held down with a stronger and stronger political repression. The terms of the "Southern question" were laid down clearly in this period. And spontaneously – without the intervention of any conscious factor, and without the Socialist Party even drawing any indication from this fact for its strategy as the party of the working class – for the first time in this period there occurred a convergence of insurrectionary attempts by the

Northern proletariat with a revolt of Southern peasants (Sicilian Fasci).[200]

13. Once it had broken the first attempts by the proletariat and the peasantry to rise up against the State, the strengthened Italian bourgeoisie was able to adopt the external methods of democracy to impede the progress of the working-class movement. The bourgeoisie also used the political corruption of the most advanced part of the working population (labour aristocracy), in order to make the latter an accomplice to the reactionary dictatorship which it continued to exercise, and to prevent it from becoming the centre of popular insurrection against the State (Giolittism). However, between 1900 and 1910 there was a phase of industrial and agrarian concentration. The rural proletariat grew by 50 per cent at the expense of the categories of tied labourers, share-croppers and tenant farmers.

The result was a wave of agricultural agitation, and a new orientation of the peasantry which forced the Vatican itself to react, with the foundation of Catholic Action and with a "social" movement which in its most advanced forms actually took on the appearance of a religious reform (Modernism).[201] This reaction on the part of the Vatican, aimed at maintaining its grip on the masses, was matched by an agreement between Catholics and the ruling classes to give the State a more secure basis (abolition of the *non expedit*, Gentiloni pact).[202] Again towards the end of this third period (1914), the various partial movements of the proletariat and the peasantry culminated in a new unconscious attempt to weld the different mass anti-State forces into an insurrection against the reactionary State. This attempt already posed with great clarity the problem which was to appear in its full dimensions after the War: i.e. the problem of the proletariat's need to organize within itself a class party which would give it the ability to place itself at the head of the insurrection and give it leadership.

14. The greatest economic concentration in the industrial field occurred in the post-war period. The proletariat reached its highest level of organization; and this corresponded to the maximum disintegration of the ruling classes and the State. All the contradictions inherent in the Italian social organism came to the surface with extreme violence, as a result of the reawakening to political life of even the most backward masses that was brought about by the War and its immediate consequences. As always, the advance of the industrial and agricultural workers was accompanied by a massive agitation of the peasant masses, both in the South and in the other regions. The great strikes and

the occupation of the factories took place simultaneously with occupations of the land.

The resistance of the reactionary forces once again operated along traditional lines. The Vatican allowed a real party to be formed, alongside Catholic Action, which aimed to integrate the peasant masses into the framework of the bourgeois State by apparently satisfying their aspirations for economic redemption and political democracy.[203] The ruling classes in their turn implemented in the grand style their plan to corrupt the working-class movement and destroy it from within, by dangling before the eyes of the opportunist leaders the possibility that a labour aristocracy might collaborate in government, in an attempted "reformist" solution of the problem of the State (left government). But in a poor and disunited country like Italy, the appearance of a "reformist" solution to the problem of the State inevitably provokes a disintegration of the cohesion of State and society; for this cannot resist the shock of the numerous groups into which the ruling classes themselves and the intermediate classes fragment. Each group has its own need for economic protection and political autonomy; and in the absence of a homogeneous class nucleus capable of imposing – through its dictatorship – a discipline of work and production on the whole country, routing and eliminating the capitalist and landowning exploiters, government is made impossible and the crisis of power is continuously open.

The defeat of the revolutionary proletariat in this decisive period was due to political, organizational, tactical and strategic deficiencies of the workers' party. As a consequence of these deficiencies, the proletariat did not succeed in placing itself at the head of the insurrection of the great majority of the population, and channelling it towards the creation of a workers' State. Instead, it was itself influenced by other social classes, which paralysed its activity. The victory of fascism in 1922 must be seen, therefore, not as a victory won over the revolution, but as a consequence of the defeat suffered by the revolutionary forces through their own intrinsic weakness.

Fascism and its Policy

15. Fascism, as a movement of armed reaction which set itself the task of fragmenting and disorganizing the working class in order to immobilize it, fitted into the framework of traditional Italian ruling-class policies, and into capitalism's struggle against the working class. It was,

therefore, favoured in its origins, in its organization and in its development by all the old ruling groups without exception – but especially by the landowners, who felt most threatened by the pressure of the rural populace. Socially, however, fascism found its base in the urban petty bourgeoisie, and in a new rural bourgeoisie thrown up by a transformation of rural property in certain regions (phenomena of agrarian capitalism in Emilia; origin of a category of middlemen in the countryside; "land grants"; new divisions of holdings).

This circumstance – together with the fact that it found an ideological and organizational unity in the military formations in which wartime tradition lives again (*arditismo*), and which serve for guerrilla actions against the workers – allowed fascism to conceive and carry out a plan of conquest of the State, against the old ruling strata. It would be absurd to call this a revolution. The new categories which are regrouped around fascism, however, derive from their origin a homogeneity and a common mentality of "nascent capitalism". This explains how it has been possible for them to fight against the politicians of the past, and how they have been able to justify this by an ideological construction which conflicts with traditional theories of the State and its relations with citizens. In substance, fascism merely modifies the programme of conservation and reaction which has always dominated Italian politics, through a different way of conceiving the process of unification of the reactionary forces. It replaces the tactic of agreements and compromises by the project of achieving an organic unity of all the bourgeoisie's forces in a single political organism under the control of a single centre, which would simultaneously direct the party, the government and the State. This project corresponds to the determination to resist to the last against any revolutionary attack; it thus allows fascism to win the support of the most decisively reactionary part of the industrial bourgeoisie and of the landowners.

16. The fascist method of defending order, property and the State tends, even more than the traditional system of compromises and left policies, to shatter social cohesion and the political superstructures which go with it. The reactions which it provokes must be examined in relation to its application in both the economic and in the political field.

In the political field, first of all, the organic unity of the bourgeoisie in fascism was not achieved immediately after the winning of power. Centres of a bourgeois opposition to the régime remain outside fascism. On the one hand, the group which remains faithful to the Giolittian solution of the problem of the State has not been absorbed. This group is linked to a section of the industrial bourgeoisie and, with a programme of "labourist" reformism, exerts an influence on layers of workers and petty bourgeois. On the other hand, the programme of basing the State upon a rural democracy in the South and upon the "healthy" part of Northern industry (*Corriere della sera*, free-traders, Nitti) is tending to become the programme of a political organization of opposition to fascism with a mass base in the South (National Union).[204]

Fascism is compelled to struggle very fiercely against these surviving groups, and to struggle even more fiercely against freemasonry, which it rightly considers as the organizing centre of all the traditional forces supporting the State. This struggle, which is the sign of a break in the bloc of conservative and anti-proletarian forces, whatever the intentions, may in certain circumstances favour the development and self-assertion of the proletariat as a third and decisive factor of the political situation.

In the economic field, fascism acts as the instrument of an industrial and agrarian oligarchy, to concentrate control over all the wealth of the country in the hands of capitalism. This cannot fail to provoke discontent in the petty bourgeoisie, which believed that with the arrival of fascism the hour of its rule had struck.

A whole series of measures are being adopted by fascism to encourage a new industrial concentration (abolition of death duties; financial and fiscal policy; heightening of protectionism), and to these there correspond other measures favouring the landowners and directed against small and medium farmers (taxes; duty on grain; "the grain battle"). The accumulation which these measures achieve is not an increase in the national wealth, but the plundering of one class in favour of another: in other words, that of the working and middle classes in favour of the plutocracy. The intention of favouring the plutocracy is shamelessly revealed in the plan to legalize the preference share system in the new commercial code; a little handful of financiers will in this way be enabled, without restriction, to dispose of vast masses of savings originating from the middle and petty bourgeoisie, and these categories will be stripped of the right to dispose of their wealth.

On the same level, but with bigger political consequences, must be placed the plan to unite the issuing banks, i.e. in practice to eliminate the two big Southern banks. These two banks today fulfil the function of absorbing the savings of the South and the remittances of the emigrants (600 million): in other words, the function which in the past was fulfilled by the State through issuing treasury bonds, and by the *Banca di*

Sconto in the interests of a part of Northern heavy industry. The Southern banks have been controlled until now by the ruling classes of the South themselves, which have found in this control a real basis for their political domination. The elimination of the Southern banks as issuing banks will transfer this function to the Northern big industry which controls, via the *Banca Commerciale*, the Bank of Italy. We shall thus see the "colonial" economic exploitation and impoverishment of the South increased, and the slow process of detachment of the Southern petty bourgeoisie from the State accelerated.

The economic policy of fascism is completed by the measures aimed at raising the value of the *lira*, stabilizing the trade balance, paying war debts and encouraging the intervention of Anglo-American capital in Italy. In all these fields, fascism is carrying out the programme of the plutocracy (Nitti) and of an industrial landowning minority, at the expense of the great majority of the population, whose conditions of life are being made progressively worse.

All the ideological propaganda and the political and economic activity of fascism is crowned by its tendency to "imperialism". This tendency expresses the need felt by the industrial/landowning ruling classes of Italy to find outside the national domain the elements to resolve the crisis of Italian society. It contains the germs of a war which in appearance will be fought for Italian expansion, but in which fascist Italy will in reality be an instrument in the hands of one of the imperialist groups which are striving for world domination.

17. As a consequence of fascism's policies, deep reactions are provoked among the masses. The most serious phenomenon is the sharper and sharper detachment of the rural populations of the South and the Islands from the system of forces which rule the State. The old local ruling class (Orlando, Di Cesarò, De Nicola, etc.) no longer exercises in a systematic fashion its function as a connecting link with the State. The petty bourgeoisie thus tends to draw closer to the peasantry. The system of exploitation and oppression of the Southern masses is being carried to extremes by fascism; this facilitates the radicalization of the intermediate categories too, and poses the Southern question in its true terms, as a question which will only be resolved by the insurrection of the peasants allied to the proletariat, in a struggle against both capitalists and landowners.

The middle and poor peasants of the other parts of Italy too are taking on a revolutionary function, although in a slower fashion. The Vatican – whose reactionary function has been taken over by fascism –

no longer controls the rural populations completely through the priests, Catholic Action and the Popular Party. There is a part of the peasantry which has been reawoken to struggle in defence of its own interests, precisely by the organizations authorized and directed by the ecclesiastical authorities. Now, under the economic and political pressure of fascism, this element is intensifying its own class orientation and beginning to feel that its destiny cannot be separated from that of the working class. A sign of this tendency is the Miglioli phenomenon. A very interesting symptom of it is also the fact that the White organizations – which since they are a part of Catholic Action are directly controlled by the Vatican – have had to enter inter-union committees with the Red peasant leagues: an expression of that proletarian period which the catholics indicated from 1870 onwards was imminent for Italian society.

As for the proletariat, activity to shatter its forces is finding a limit in the active resistance of the revolutionary vanguard, and in a passive resistance of the broad masses, who remain fundamentally class-conscious and give signs that they will begin to move again, as soon as the physical pressure of fascism is relaxed and the stimuli of class interest make themselves more strongly felt. The attempt via the fascist unions to split their ranks can be considered to have failed. The fascist unions, changing their programme, are now becoming direct instruments of reactionary repression in the service of the State.

18. Fascism reacts to the dangerous shifts and new recruitment of forces provoked by its policies, by subjecting the whole of society to the weight of a military force and repressive system which hold the population riveted to the mechanical fact of production – without any possibility of having a life of its own, expressing a will of its own, or organizing to defend its own interests.

So-called fascist legislation has no purpose other than to consolidate this system and make it permanent. The new political electoral law, the modifications to the administrative structure with the introduction of the *podestà* in rural communes, etc., are designed to mark the end of any participation by the masses in the country's political and administrative life. The control over associations prevents any permanent "legal" form of organization of the masses. The new trade-union policy strips the Confederation of Labour and the class unions of any possibility of negotiating agreements, in order to exclude them from contact with the masses who had been organized around them. The proletarian press is suppressed. The class party of the proletariat is reduced to a purely illegal existence. Physical violence and police persecution are utilized systematically, above all in the countryside, to strike terror and preserve a situation of emergency.

The result of this complex activity of reaction and repression is an imbalance between the real relationship of social forces and the relationship of organized forces, so that an apparent return to normality and stability in fact corresponds to an intensification of contradictions ready to break out at any instant in new ways.

18 *bis*. The crisis which followed the Matteotti assassination furnished an example of the possibility that the apparent stability of the fascist régime might be shaken from below, by the sudden outbreak of economic and political conflicts which have grown sharper without being noticed. At the same time, it furnished proof of the incapacity of the petty bourgeoisie in the present historical period to lead the struggle against industrial/landowning reaction to any outcome.

Motor Forces and Perspectives of the Revolution

19. The motor forces of the Italian revolution, as is now clear from our analysis, are in order of their importance the following:

(a) the working class and the rural proletariat;
(b) the peasantry of the South and the Islands, and the peasantry in the other parts of Italy.

The development and speed of the revolutionary process cannot be predicted without an evaluation of subjective elements: i.e. of the extent to which the working class succeeds in acquiring its own political profile, a precise class consciousness and an independence from all the other classes; and of the extent to which it succeeds in organizing its own forces, i.e. in *de facto* exercising leadership over the other elements and above all in concretizing politically its alliance with the peasantry.

One may in general assert, basing oneself moreover upon Italian experience, that one will pass from the period of revolutionary preparation to an "immediately" revolutionary period when the industrial and rural proletariat of the North has succeeded in regaining – thanks to the development of the objective situation, and through a series of specific and immediate struggles – a high level of organization and combativity.

As for the peasantry, that of the South and Islands must be included in the front line among the forces upon which the insurrection against the industrial/landowning dictatorship must rely, although one should not attribute to them decisive importance unless they are allied to the proletariat. The alliance between them and the workers is the result of a natural and deep historical process, encouraged by all the past experience of the Italian State. For the peasants of the other parts of Italy, the process of orientation towards an alliance with the proletariat is slower and will have to be encouraged by careful political activity on the part of the proletarian party. The successes already obtained in Italy in this field indicate, moreover, that the problem of breaking the alliance of the peasantry with the reactionary forces must be posed, to a great extent, in other western European countries too, as the problem of destroying the influence of Catholic organizations on the rural masses.

20. The obstacles to the development of the revolution do not derive only from fascist pressure, but are also related to the variety of groups into which the bourgeoisie is divided. Each of these groups strives to exert an influence on a section of the working population, to prevent the influence of the proletariat being extended; or on the proletariat itself, to cause it to lose its profile and autonomy as a revolutionary class. In this way a chain of reactionary forces is created, which starts from fascism and includes: anti-fascist groups which do not have a large mass base (liberals); those which have a base among the peasants and petty bourgeoisie (democrats, war-veterans, Popular Party, republicans) and in part also among the workers (Reformist Party); and those which have a proletarian base, and tend to maintain the working-class masses in a condition of passivity and to induce them to follow the policies of other classes (Maximalist Party). The group which leads the Confederation of Labour should also be considered from this point of view, i.e. as the vehicle of a disintegrative influence of other classes upon the workers. Each of the groups we have mentioned holds a part of the Italian working population in its grip. Modification of this state of affairs can only be conceived of as the result of a systematic and uninterrupted political activity of the proletarian vanguard organized in the Communist Party.

Particular attention must be accorded to the groups and parties which have a mass base – or seek to create one as either democratic or regional parties – among the agricultural population of the South and Islands (National Union; Sardinian Action Party; Action Parties of Molise, Irpinia, etc.). These parties do not exercise any direct influence upon the proletariat; but they are an obstacle to realizing the alliance between workers and peasants. Orienting the agricultural classes of the South towards a rural democracy and towards regional democratic solutions, they break the unity of the liberation process of the Italian working people; prevent the peasants from bringing their struggle against the economic and political exploitation of the bourgeoisie and the landowners to an outcome; and prepare their transformation into white guards of reaction. The political success of the working class in this field too is dependent upon the political activity of the proletariat's party.

21. The possibility that action by so-called democratic anti-fascist groups might bring down the fascist régime would only exist if these groups succeeded in neutralizing the activity of the proletariat, and in controlling a mass movement that would enable it to brake the latter's development. The function of the democratic bourgeois opposition is rather to collaborate with fascism, in preventing the reorganization of the working class and the realization of its class programme. In this sense, a compromise between fascism and bourgeois opposition is in train, and will inspire the policies of every "centre" formation which emerges from the ruins of the Aventine. The opposition will only be able to become once again the protagonist of the capitalist régime's defence activity, when fascist repression itself no longer succeeds in preventing the unleashing of class conflict, and the danger of a proletarian insurrection, welded to a peasant war, appears grave and imminent. The possibility that the bourgeoisie and fascism itself may resort to the system of reaction concealed by the appearance of a "left government" must, therefore, be permanently present in our perspectives (division of functions between fascism and democracy, *Theses of the Fifth World Congress*).

22. From this analysis of the factors of revolution and its perspectives, the tasks of the Communist Party can be deduced. The criteria for the Party's organizational and political activity must be related to the analysis, from which the basic coordinates of its programme derive.

Fundamental Tasks of the Communist Party

23. Having victoriously resisted the reactionary wave which sought to engulf it (1923); having contributed with its own actions to marking a first halt in the process of dispersal of the working-class forces (1924 elections); having taken advantage of the Matteotti crisis to reorganize

a proletarian vanguard which, with notable success, opposed the attempt to instal a petty-bourgeois predominance in political life (Aventine); and having laid the basis of a real peasant policy of the Italian proletariat – the party today finds itself in the phase of political preparation of the revolution.

Its fundamental task can be indicated by these three points:

(a) to organize and unify the industrial and rural proletariat for the revolution;
(b) to organize and mobilize around the proletariat all the forces necessary for the victory of the revolution and the foundation of the workers' State;
(c) to place before the proletariat and its allies the problem of insurrection against the bourgeois State and of the struggle for proletarian dictatorship, and to guide them politically and materially towards their solution, through a series of partial struggles.

The Construction of the Communist Party as a "Bolshevik" Party

24. The organization of the proletarian vanguard in a Communist Party is the essential feature of our organizational activity. The Italian workers have learnt from their experience (1919–20) that where the leadership of a Communist Party, built as the party of the working class and as the party of revolution, is missing, no victorious outcome of the struggle to overthrow the capitalist order is possible. The construction of a Communist Party which really is the party of the working class and the party of revolution – in other words, that is a "Bolshevik" party – is directly related to the following basic points:

(a) the party's ideology;
(b) its form of organization and degree of cohesion;
(c) its capacity to operate in contact with the masses;
(d) its strategic and tactical capacity.

Each of these points is closely linked with the others, and cannot logically be separated from them. Each of them, in fact, points to and contains a series of problems whose solutions are mutually interconnected and overlapping. Examining them separately will only be useful if it is borne in mind that none of them can be resolved, without all being tackled simultaneously and brought to a solution.

The Party's Ideology

25. The Communist Party needs complete ideological unity in order to be able at all moments to fulfil its function as leader of the working class. Ideological unity is an element of the Party's strength and political capacity; it is indispensable, to make it into a Bolshevik Party. The basis of ideological unity is the doctrine of Marxism and Leninism, this last being understood as Marxist doctrine adapted to the problems of the period of imperialism and the start of the proletarian revolution (*Theses on Bolshevization* of the April 1925 Enlarged Executive meeting, numbers 4 and 6).

The Communist Party of Italy formed its ideology in the struggle against social-democracy (reformists) and against the political centrism represented by the Maximalist Party. However, it did not find in the history of the Italian workers' movement any vigorous or continuous current of Marxist thought that it could invoke. Moreover, there is no deep or widespread knowledge in its ranks of the theories of Marxism and Leninism. Hence, deviations are possible. Raising the Party's ideological level must be achieved by a systematic internal activity designed to ensure that all members have a thorough awareness of the immediate aims of the revolutionary movement, a certain capacity of Marxist analysis of the situation, and a corresponding capacity for political orientation (party school). Any conception must be repudiated which asserts that factors of revolutionary consciousness and awareness, which constitute ideology, can be realized in the Party without being realized in a vast number of the individuals who make it up.

26. In spite of the beginnings of a struggle against rightist and centrist degenerations of the workers' movement, the danger of rightist deviations is present within the Communist Party of Italy. In the theoretical field, this danger is represented by the attempts to revise Marxism made by comrade Graziadei, in the guise of a "scientific" refinement of some of the basic concepts of Marx's doctrine.[205] Graziadei's attempts certainly cannot lead to the creation of a current, and hence a faction, which endangers the ideological unity and the cohesion of the party. However, they imply a support for rightist currents and political deviations. In any case, they point to the need for the party to carry out a deep study of Marxism and to acquire a higher and more solid theoretical consciousness.

The danger that a right-wing tendency might be created is linked to the general situation in the country. The very repression exercised by fascism tends to nourish the view that, since the proletariat cannot soon overturn the régime, the best tactic is one whose aim is, if not an actual bourgeois-proletarian bloc for the constitutional elimination of fascism, at least a passivity of the revolutionary vanguard and non-intervention of the Communist Party in the immediate political struggle, thus allowing the bourgeoisie to use the proletariat as electoral troops against fascism. This programme is expressed through the formula that the Communist Party must be the "left wing" of an opposition of all the forces conspiring to bring down the fascist régime. It is the expression of a profound pessimism concerning the revolutionary capacities of the working class.

The same pessimism and the same deviations lead to an incorrect interpretation of the nature and historical function of the social-democratic parties at the present time. They lead to forgetting that social-democracy, although it still to a great extent conserves its social base in the proletariat, must so far as its ideology and the political function it fulfils are concerned be considered, not as a right wing of the working-class movement, but as a left wing of the bourgeoisie, and as such must be unmasked in the eyes of the masses.

The right-wing danger must be fought through ideological propaganda, by counterposing the revolutionary programme of the working class and its party to the right-wing programme, and by ordinary disciplinary means whenever the necessity arises.

27. There is a similar connection between the origins of the Party and the general situation in the country on the one hand, and the danger of a leftist deviation from Marxist and Leninist ideology on the other. This is represented by the ultra-left tendency led by comrade Bordiga. This tendency was formed in the specific situation of disintegration and programmatic, organizational, strategic and tactical incapacity in which the Italian Socialist Party found itself from the end of the War up to the Livorno Congress. Its origin and fortunes are, moreover, related to the fact that, since the working class is a minority in the Italian working population, there is a constant danger that its party will be corrupted by infiltrations from other classes, and in particular from the petty bourgeoisie. The far left tendency reacted to this condition of the working class and to the situation in the Italian Socialist Party with a particular ideology, i.e. a conception of the nature of the Party and its function and tactics which conflicts with that of Marxism and Leninism.

(a) The far left, ignoring or under-estimating the Party's social content, defines it as an "organ" of the working class, constituted through the synthesis of heterogeneous elements. In reality, when defining the party it is necessary above all to stress that it is a "part" of the working class. The error in defining the party leads to an incorrect approach to organizational problems and problems of tactics.

(b) For the far left, the function of the Party is not to lead the class at all moments, striving to remain in contact with it through all changes in the objective situation, but to form and prepare cadres, who can lead the masses when the evolution of the situation has brought them to the party and made them accept the programmatic and principled positions it has fixed.

(c) As regards tactics, the far left maintains that these must not be determined on the basis of the objective situation and the position of the masses, in such a way as always to be in line with reality and provide a constant contact with the broadest layers of the working population; instead, they must be determined on the basis of formalist concerns. Ultra-leftism is characterized by the idea that deviations from the principles of communist politics are not to be avoided by the construction of "Bolshevik" parties capable of carrying out, without deviating, any political action required to mobilize the masses and for the victory of revolution; but that they can be avoided only by imposing rigid formal limits of an external kind upon the party's tactics. (In the organizational field: "individual recruitment", i.e. rejection of "fusions" – which can in fact, always given the right conditions, be a very effective means of extending the party's influence. In the political field: misrepresentation of the terms of the problem of winning a majority; trade-union united front, but no political united front; no difference in the way of combating democracy, according to the degree of mass support for counter-revolutionary democratic formations, or to the imminence and gravity of a reactionary danger; rejection of the slogan of workers' and peasants' government.) As a consequence, the situation of mass movements is only examined in order to check the line which has been deduced on the basis of formalistic and sectarian concerns. Thus, in determining the party's policy, the specific element is always missing; the unity and completeness of vision which characterizes our method of political enquiry (dialectic) is broken; the activity and the slogans of the party lose their effectiveness and value, remaining simply propaganda activity and propaganda slogans.

As a consequence of these positions, political passivity of the party is inevitable. "Abstentionism" was an aspect of this in the past. This allows us to relate ultra-leftism to maximalism and to rightist deviations. It is, moreover, like the right-wing tendencies, the expression of a scepticism concerning the possibility for the working-class masses to organize, from within themselves, a class party capable of leading the broad masses and at the same time striving to keep them bound to it at all times. The ideological struggle against ultra-leftism must be waged by counterposing to it the Marxist and Leninist conception of the proletarian party as a mass party. And by demonstrating the need for the latter to adapt its tactics to situations in order to be able to modify them; in order not to lose contact with the masses; and in order to acquire continually new zones of influence.

Ultra-leftism was the official ideology of the Italian party in the first period of its existence. It is advocated by comrades who were among the founders of the party and made a very great contribution to its construction after Livorno. There are, therefore, factors which explain how this conception was for a long time deeply rooted in the majority of comrades. It was not so much critically evaluated by them in any thorough-going manner, as it was the consequence of a widespread state of mind. It is thus evident that the leftist danger must be seen as an immediate reality; as an obstacle not only to ideological unification and refinement, but to the party's political development and the effectiveness of its activity. It must be combated as such, not just through propaganda, but through political action and, if necessary, through organizational measures.

28. One element of the party's ideology is the degree of internationalist spirit which has penetrated its ranks. This is very strong among us as a spirit of international solidarity, but as the awareness of belonging to a world party it is not so strong. One thing which contributes to this weakness is the tendency to present the far left's conception as a national conception ("originality" and "historical" value of the positions of the "Italian Left"), which is counterposed to the Marxist and Leninist conception of the Communist International and seeks to replace it. Hence, the origins of a kind of "party patriotism", which shrinks from becoming integrated into a world organization, in accordance with the principles which are proper to that organization (refusal of responsibilities, international faction struggle, etc.). This weakness of internationalist spirit provides the terrain for an echo within the party of the campaign which the bourgeoisie wages against the Communist International, describing it as an organ of the Russian State. Certain of the far left's theses on this question coincide with

habitual theses of the counter-revolutionary parties. They must be combated with extreme vigour, and with propaganda designed to show how the Russian party historically plays a predominant and directive function in the construction of a Communist International, and to show what the position of the Russian workers' State – first and sole real conquest of the working class in the struggle for power – is, with respect to the international workers movement (*Theses on the International Situation*).

The Basis of Party Organization

29. All problems of organization are political problems. Their solution must enable the party to carry out its fundamental task of ensuring that the proletariat acquires complete political independence; giving it a physiognomy, a personality and a precise revolutionary consciousness; and preventing any infiltration or disintegrative influence from classes and elements which, even if they have interests contrary to capitalism, are not willing to take the struggle against the latter to its ultimate consequences.

First and foremost, there is a political problem: that of the basis for organization. The party organization must be constructed on the basis of production and hence of the work-place (cells). This principle is essential for the creation of a "Bolshevik" party. It depends on the fact that the party must be equipped to lead the mass movement of the working class, which is naturally unified by the development of capitalism in accordance with the process of production. By locating the organizational basis in the place of production, the party performs an act of choice of the class on which it bases itself. It proclaims that it is a class party and the party of a single class, the working class.

All objections to the principle that bases party organization on production derive from conceptions which are related to classes alien to the proletariat, even if they are presented by comrades and groups who call themselves "far left". They are based on a pessimistic view of the revolutionary capacities of the worker and of the communist worker, and are an expression of the anti-proletarian spirit of the petty-bourgeois intellectuals, who believe they are the salt of the earth and see the workers as the material instrument of social transformation rather than as the conscious and intelligent protagonist of revolution.

There are being reproduced in the Italian party, with respect to cells, the discussion and conflict which led in Russia to the split between

Bolsheviks and Mensheviks, with respect to the same problem of choice of class: of the party's class character, and the way in which non-proletarian elements can join the party. This fact, moreover, has a very great importance in relation to the Italian situation. For it is the social structure itself, and the conditions and traditions of political struggle, which in Italy make the danger of building the party on the basis of a "synthesis" of heterogeneous elements – i.e. the danger of opening the way through these for a paralysing influence of other classes – far more serious than elsewhere. This danger, moreover, will be made all the more serious precisely by the policies of fascism, which will drive whole strata of the petty bourgeoisie on to the terrain of revolution.

It is certain that the Communist Party can be solely a party of workers. The working class and its party cannot do without intellectuals, nor can they ignore the problem of grouping around themselves and giving a lead to all those elements who, in one way or another, are driven to rebel against capitalism. Thus the Communist Party cannot close its doors to peasants; indeed it must contain peasants and use them to tighten the political bond between the proletariat and the rural classes. But it is necessary to reject vigorously, as counter-revolutionary, any conception which makes the party into a "synthesis" of heterogeneous elements – instead of maintaining, without any concessions of this kind, that it is a part of the proletariat; that the proletariat must mark it with the imprint of its own organization; and that the proletariat must be guaranteed a leading function within the party itself.

30. There is no consistency in the practical objections to organization on the basis of production (cells), according to which this organizational structure would not allow us to transcend the competition between different categories of worker and would leave the party at the mercy of functionarism. The practice of the factory movement (1919–20) has shown that only an organization adapted to the place and system of production makes it possible to establish a contact between the upper and lower strata of the working masses (skilled workers, unskilled workers and labourers), and to create bonds of solidarity which eliminate the basis for any phenomenon of 'labour aristocracy'.

Organization by cells leads to the formation within the party of a very large layer of leading cadres (cell secretaries, members of cell committees, etc.), who are part of the masses and remain within them even though they exercise leading functions – unlike the secretaries of territorial branches, who were necessarily elements detached from the working masses. The party must pay particular care to the education of these comrades, who form the connecting fabric of the organization and are the instrument for binding it to the masses. From whatever point of view it is considered, the transformation of its structure on the basis of production remains the party's fundamental task in the present period, and the means to solve the most important of its problems. We must insist upon it, and intensify all ideological and practical work relative to it.

Solidity of the Party Organization. Factionalism

31. The organization of a Bolshevik Party must at all moments in the life of the party be a centralized organization, led by the Central Committee not just in words but also in deed. An iron proletarian discipline must reign in its ranks. This does not mean that the party must be ruled from on high with autocratic methods. Both the Central Committee and the subordinate leading bodies are formed on the basis of election, and on the basis of a selection of capable elements carried out through the test of work and through the experience of the movement. This second element guarantees that the criteria for the formation of the local leading groups and of the central leading group are not mechanical, external and "parliamentary", but correspond to a real process of formation of a homogeneous proletarian vanguard linked to the masses.

The principle of election of the leading bodies – internal democracy – is not an absolute one, but relative to the conditions of political struggle. Even when it is restricted, the central and local organs must always consider their power not as being super-imposed, but as springing from the party's will, and must strive to accentuate their proletarian character and to multiply their links with the mass of comrades and with the working class. This last necessity is felt particularly keenly in Italy, where reaction has imposed and continues to impose a strict limitation of internal democracy.

Internal democracy is also relative to the degree of political capacity possessed by the local bodies, and by the individual comrades working in the localities. The activity which the centre carries on to increase this capacity makes possible an extension of "democratic" methods, and a growing reduction of the system of "cooptation" and of interventions from above to sort out local organizational questions.

32. The centralization and cohesion of the party require that there should not exist organized groups within it which take on the character of factions. A Bolshevik Party is sharply differentiated in this respect from social-democratic parties, which contain a great variety of groups, and in which factional struggle is the normal method of working out a political orientation and selecting a leading group. The Communist Parties and International emerged after a factional struggle waged inside the IInd International. Establishing themselves as the parties and the world organization of the proletariat, they chose as the norm of their internal life and development, in place of factional struggle, the organic collaboration of all tendencies through participation in the leading bodies.

The existence of, and struggle between, factions are in fact incompatible with the essence of the proletarian party, since they break its unity and open a path for the influence of other classes. This does not mean that tendencies may not arise in the party, and that these tendencies may not on occasion seek to organize themselves as factions; but it does mean that a vigorous struggle must be conducted to prevent this latter eventuality, by reducing tendency conflicts, theoretical discussions and the selection of leaders to the form appropriate to communist parties, i.e. to a process of real and unitary (dialectical) evolution and not to "parliamentary" modes of debate or struggle.

33. The working-class movement failed as a result of the impotence of the PSI, brought about by the faction struggle and by the fact that each faction, independently of the party, carried on its own policy, thus paralysing the activity of the other factions and that of the party as a whole. This experience provides a good terrain for creating and maintaining the cohesion and centralization which must characterize a Bolshevik party.

Among the different groups from which the Communist Party of Italy drew its origin, there subsists some differentiation, which must disappear as the common Marxist and Leninist ideology strikes deeper roots. Only among the followers of the anti-Marxist ideology of the far left have a homogeneity and solidarity of a factional kind been long maintained. Indeed, an attempt was made to pass from concealed factionalism to an open factional struggle, with the setting up of the so-called *Comitato d'Intesa*.[206] The intensity of the party's reaction to this crazy attempt to split its forces gives a sure guarantee that any attempt in this field to take us back to the habits of social-democracy will meet with no response.

The danger of factionalism to some extent also exists as a result of fusion with the IIIrd-Internationalists from the Socialist Party. The IIIrd-Internationalists do not possess a common ideology, but there exist links between them of an essentially corporate nature, created during the two years in which they were a faction inside the PSI. These links have been steadily weakening, and it will not be difficult to eliminate them totally.

The struggle against factionalism must above all involve propaganda for correct organizational principles. But it will not succeed until the Italian party is once again able to consider the discussion of its own current problems and those of the International as something normal, and to orient its tendencies in relation to these problems.

The Functioning of the Party Organization

34. A Bolshevik Party must be organized in such a way that it can function in contact with the masses, whatever the conditions may be. This principle takes on the greatest importance among us, because of the repression exercised by fascism with the aim of preventing the real relation of forces from being translated into a relation of organized forces. Only with the greatest concentration and intensity of party activity can one succeed in neutralizing at least in part this negative factor, and in preventing it from hampering greatly the revolutionary process. It is, therefore, necessary to take into account the following.

(a) The number of members and their political capacity; they must be enough to allow a continous extension of our influence. It is necessary to combat the tendency artificially to restrict membership; this leads to passivity and to atrophy. Every member, however, must be a politically active element, capable of disseminating the party's influence and translating its directives into action on a daily basis, and leading a part of the working masses.

(b) The utilization of all comrades in some practical work.

(c) The unitary coordination of the various kinds of activity, by means of committees in which the whole party is articulated as a working body among the masses.

(d) The collegiate functioning of the party's central organs, seen as a condition for the establishment of a homogeneous and cohesive, 'Bolshevik' leading group.

(e) The capacity of comrades to work among the masses, to be continuously present among them, to be in the first line in every struggle, to be able on all occasions to take and keep the position which is appropriate for the vanguard of the proletariat. This point is stressed because the need to work clandestinely, and the incorrect ideology of the "far left", have resulted in a limitation of our capacity to work among the masses and with the masses.

(f) The capacity of the local organisms and of individual comrades, to confront unforeseen circumstances and take up correct positions even before directives arrive from the leading bodies. It is necessary to combat the form of passivity – once again a residue of the false organizational conceptions of ultra-leftism – which consists in only being able to "wait for orders from above". The party must be characterized by "initiative" at the base; in other words, the base organs must be able to react immediately to every unforeseen and unexpected situation.

(g) The ability to carry out "underground" (illegal) activity and defend the party from reaction of every kind, without losing contact with the masses – indeed making that very contact with the broadest layers of the working class serve as a defence. In the present situation, defence of the party and its apparatus that is achieved by confining oneself to carrying on simply an activity of 'internal organization' must be considered as an abandonment of the revolutionary cause.

Each of these points must be considered with attention, because it indicates both a weakness of the party and a progress which it must achieve. They are all the more important insofar as it is to be foreseen that the blows of reaction will further weaken the apparatus linking the centre and the local organizations, however great the efforts made to keep it intact.

Strategy and Tactics of the Party

35. The strategic and tactical capacity of the party is the capacity to organize and unify around the proletarian vanguard and the working class all the forces necessary for revolutionary victory; and to lead these in fact towards the revolution, taking advantage of objective circumstances and of the shifts in the balance of forces which they bring about, both among the working population and among the enemies of the working class. With its strategy and tactics, the party "leads the working class" in major historical movements and day-to-day struggles alike. One form of leadership is linked to the other and conditioned by it.

36. The principle that the party leads the working class must not be interpreted in a mechanical manner. It is not necessary to believe that

the party can lead the working class through an external imposition of authority. This is not true, either with respect to the period which precedes the winning of power, or with respect to the period which follows it. The error of a mechanical interpretation of this principle must be combated in the Italian party, as a possible consequence of the ideological deviations of the far left. For these deviations lead to an arbitrary, formal over-estimation of the party, so far as its function as leader of the class is concerned. We assert that the capacity to lead the class is related, not to the fact that the party "proclaims" itself its revolutionary organ, but to the fact that it "really" succeeds, as a part of the working class, in linking itself with all the sections of that class and impressing upon the masses a movement in the direction desired and favoured by objective conditions. Only as a result of its activity among the masses, will the party get the latter to recognize it as "their" party (winning a majority); and only when this condition has been realized, can it presume that it is able to draw the working class behind it. The need for this activity among the masses outweighs any party "patriotism".

37. The party leads the class by penetrating into all the organizations in which the working masses are assembled; and by carrying out, in and through these, a systematic mobilization of energies in line with the programme of the class struggle, and an activity aimed at winning the majority to communist directives.

The organizations in which the party works, and which tend by their nature to incorporate the whole mass of workers, can never substitute for the Communist Party, which is the political organization of revolutionaries, in other words of the vanguard of the proletariat. This excludes any relationship of subordination, or of "equality" between the mass organizations and the party (Stuttgart trade-union pact; pact of alliance between the Italian Socialist Party and the General Confederation of Labour).[207] The relationship between trade unions and party is a special one of leadership, which is realized through the activity which the communists carry out inside the unions. The communists organize themselves into fractions in the unions, and in all the mass formations, and participate in the front rank in the life of these formations and the struggles which they wage, upholding their party's programme and slogans there. Every tendency to separate oneself off from the life of those organizations, whatever they may be, in which it is possible to make contact with the working masses, is to be combated as a dangerous deviation, indicating pessimism and generating passivity.

38. In the capitalist countries, trade unions are the specific organs grouping the working masses. Activity in the unions must be considered essential for the accomplishment of the party's aims. The party which renounces the struggle to exercise its influence in the unions and to win leadership of them, *de facto* renounces winning the mass of workers and renounces the revolutionary struggle for power.

In Italy, activity in the unions takes on particular importance; for such activity makes it possible to work with greater intensity, and with better results, at that reorganization of the industrial and rural proletariat which must restore it to a predominant position *vis-à-vis* the other social classes. However, fascist repression, and especially fascism's new trade-union policy, are creating a quite particular state of affairs. The Confederation of Labour and the class unions are finding themselves stripped of any possibility of carrying on an activity of organization and economic defence in the traditional forms. They are tending to become reduced to mere propaganda offices. At the same time, however, the working class is being driven by the pressure of the objective situation to reorder its own forces on the basis of new forms of organization. Thus the party must manage to carry out activity to defend the class union and demand freedom for it; and at the same time it must encourage and stimulate the tendency to create representative mass organisms adapted to the system of production. With the class union's activity paralysed, defence of the workers' immediate interests tends to be carried out through a fragmentation of resistance and struggle – by factory, by category, by workplace, etc. The Communist Party must be able to follow all these struggles and exercise a real leadership over them: ensuring that the unitary and revolutionary character of class conflicts is not lost in them, and indeed taking advantage of them to aid the mobilization of the whole proletariat and its organization along a fighting front (*Trade-union Theses*).

39. The party leads and unifies the working class by taking part in all struggles of a partial nature, and by formulating and agitating around a programme of demands of immediate interest to the working class. Partial and limited actions are considered by it as necessary steps to achieving the progressive mobilization and unification of all the forces of the working class.

The party combats the conception according to which one should abstain from supporting or taking part in partial actions, because the problems which interest the working class can be solved only by the overthrow of the capitalist order and by a general action on the part of all the anti-capitalist forces. It is aware of the impossibility for the workers' conditions to be improved in a serious or lasting way, in the period of imperialism and before the capitalist order has been overthrown. However, agitation around a programme of immediate demands and support for partial struggles is the only way of reaching the broad masses and mobilizing them against capital. Moreover, any agitation carried out or victory won by categories of workers in the field of immediate demands makes the crisis of capitalism more acute, and accelerates its fall subjectively too, insofar as it shifts the unstable economic equilibrium upon which it bases its power today.

The Communist Party links every immediate demand to a revolutionary objective; makes use of every partial struggle to teach the masses the need for general action and for insurrection against the reactionary rule of capital; and seeks to ensure that every struggle of a limited character is prepared and led in such a way as to be able to lead to the mobilization and unification of the proletarian forces, and not to their dispersal. It upholds these conceptions inside the mass organizations leading partial movements, or against the political parties which initiate them. Or else it gives force to them by itself taking the initiative in proposing partial actions, either within the mass organizations or to other parties (united front tactics). In every case, the party utilizes the experience of the movement in question, and of the outcome of its own proposals, to increase its influence – demonstrating through facts that its action programme is the only one which corresponds to the interests of the masses and to the objective situation – and to transport a backward section of the working class onto a more advanced position.

Direct initiatives by the Communist Party for partial actions may occur when it controls a notable part of the working class through mass organisms; or when it is certain that one of its direct slogans is followed likewise by a notable part of the working class. The party will not, however, take this initiative unless – depending on the objective situation – it leads to a shift in its favour of the balance of forces, and represents a step forward in the unification and mobilization of the class upon revolutionary terrain.

It is excluded that a violent action by individuals or groups can serve to shake the working-class masses out of their passivity, if the party is not closely linked with them. In particular, the activity of armed groups, even as a reaction to the physical violence of the fascists, only has value insofar as it is linked to a reaction of the masses or succeeds in provoking or preparing one. Then it can acquire the same value in the field of mobilization of material forces that strikes and specific economic struggles have for the general mobilization of the workers' energies in defence of their class interests.

39 *bis*. It is an error to believe that immediate demands and partial actions can have a purely economic character. With the deepening of the crisis of capitalism, the capitalist and landowning ruling classes are compelled, in order to preserve their power, to limit and suppress the proletariat's organizational and political freedoms. Consequently, the demand for these freedoms furnishes an excellent terrain for agitation and partial struggles which may lead to the mobilization of vast layers of the working population. All the legislation with which the fascists in Italy suppress even the most elementary freedoms of the working class, must therefore provide the Communist Party with themes for agitating among the masses and mobilizing them. It will be the Communist Party's task to link each of the slogans it launches in this field with the general directives of its activity: in particular, with the practical demonstration of the impossibility for the régime installed by fascism to undergo radical limitations and transformations in a "liberal" and "democratic" direction, without a mass struggle being unleashed against fascism that will inevitably culminate in a civil war. This conviction must be disseminated among the masses insofar as we succeed, linking the partial demands of a political character with those of an economic character, in transforming "revolutionary democratic" movements into working-class, socialist revolutionary movements.

This must be achieved in particular with respect to agitation against the monarchy. The monarchy is one of the props of the fascist régime; it is Italian fascism's State form. The anti-monarchic mobilization of the mass of the Italian population is one of the aims which the Communist Party must set itself. It will serve effectively to unmask certain of the so-called anti-fascist groups who have coalesced in the Aventine. It must, however, always be accompanied by agitation and struggle directed against the other basic pillars of the fascist régime, the industrial plutocracy and the landowners. In anti-monarchic agitation, the problem of the form of the State will, moreover, always be posed by the Communist Party in close connection with the problem of the class content which the communists intend to give the State. In the recent past (June 1925), the connection between these problems was achieved by the party through basing its political activity on the slogan: "Republican Assembly on the basis of Workers' and Peasants'

Committees; Workers' Control of Industry; Land to the Peasants."

40. The task of uniting the forces of the proletariat and all the working class on a terrain of struggle is the "positive" part of the united front tactic; in Italy, in the present circumstances, this is the party's fundamental task. Communists must see the unity of the working class as a concrete, real result to be achieved, in order to prevent capitalism from implementing its plan of permanently fragmenting the proletariat and making all revolutionary struggle impossible. They must be capable of working in every way to achieve this end. Above all, they must become capable of drawing close to the workers of other parties and those without a party, overcoming unwarranted hostility and incomprehension, and in all cases presenting themselves as the advocates of unity of the class in the struggle for its defence and liberation.

The "united front" of anti-fascist and anti-capitalist struggle which the communists are striving to create must aim at being an organized united front, i.e. at being based on bodies around which the masses as a whole can regroup and find a form. Such are the representative bodies which the masses themselves are tending to create today, from the factories and on the occasion of every struggle, since the possibilities for the trade unions to function normally began to be limited. The communists must take account of this tendency among the masses and be capable of stimulating it, developing the positive elements which it contains and combating the particularist deviations to which it may give rise. The matter must be considered without fetishization of any particular form of organization, bearing in mind that our fundamental purpose is to achieve an ever-increasing mobilization and organic unity of forces. To accomplish this purpose, it is necessary to be able to adapt ourselves to every terrain offered us by reality; to make use of every agitational theme; and to stress one form of organization or another, depending on what is needed and depending on each one's possibilities for development (*Trade-union Theses*: chapters dealing with internal commissions, agitational committees and factory conferences).

41. The slogan of workers' and peasants' committees must be considered as a synthetic formula for all the party's activity, insofar as it proposes to create an organized united front of the working class. The workers' and peasants' committees are organs of unity of the working class, whether mobilized for a struggle of an immediate nature or for political actions of broader scope. The slogan calling for the creation of workers' and peasants' committees is thus a slogan to be implemented

immediately, in all cases where the party succeeds through its activity in mobilizing a fairly extensive section of the working class (more than a single factory, or a single category in a locality). But at the same time it is a political solution and an agitational slogan appropriate for a whole period of the party's existence and activity. It makes evident and concrete the need for the workers to organize their forces, and counterpose them in practice to those of all groups of bourgeois origin and nature, in order to become the determining and preponderant element in the political situation.

42. The tactic of the united front as political activity (manoeuvre) designed to unmask so-called proletarian and revolutionary parties and groups which have a mass base, is closely linked with the problem of how the Communist Party is to lead the masses and how it is to win a majority. In the form in which it has been defined by the World Congresses, it is applicable in all cases in which, because of the mass support of the groups against which we are fighting, frontal struggle against them is not sufficient to give us rapid and far-reaching results.[208] The success of this tactic is related to the degree to which it is preceded or accompanied by an effective unification and mobilization of the masses, achieved by the party through action from below.

In Italy, the united front tactic must continue to be utilized by the party, insofar as it is still far from having won a decisive influence over the majority of the working class and the working population. The specific Italian conditions ensure the vitality of intermediate political formations, based on ambiguity and favoured by the passivity of a great part of the masses (Maximalists, Republicans, Unitary Socialists). The centre group which will very probably emerge from the collapse of the Aventine will be a formation of this kind. It is not possible to struggle fully against the danger which these formations represent other than through the united front tactic. But one should not rely on achieving success except on the basis of the work carried out simultaneously to wrench the masses from their passivity.

42. *bis*. The problem of the Maximalist party must be considered in the context of the problem of all the other intermediate formations which the Communist Party combats as obstacles to the revolutionary preparation of the proletariat, and towards which it adopts (depending on the circumstances) the united front tactic. There is no doubt that in certain regions the problem of winning a majority is specifically linked for us to the problem of destroying the influence of the PSI and its newspaper. The leaders of the Socialist Party, moreover, are situating

themselves more and more clearly among the counter-revolutionary forces acting to preserve the capitalist order (campaign for the intervention of American capital; *de facto* solidarity with the reformist union leaders). Nothing allows us to rule out entirely the possibility of their aligning themselves with the Reformists, and subsequently fusing with them. The Communist Party must bear this possibility in mind and must already set itself the aim of ensuring that – in the event of it occurring – the masses still controlled by the Maximalists but nevertheless conserving a class outlook detach themselves decisively from them, and link themselves as closely as possible to the masses grouped around the communist vanguard. The good results achieved by the fusion with the IIIrd-Internationalist faction that was decided upon by the Fifth Congress have taught the Italian party how, in given conditions, with a shrewd policy, results can be achieved which could not be obtained through the normal activity of propaganda and organization.

43. While it advances its programme of immediate class demands, and concentrates its activity upon achieving the mobilization and unification of the working-class forces, the party – in order to facilitate the development of its own activity – may present immediate solutions to general political problems, and put forward these solutions among the masses still supporting counter-revolutionary parties and formations. This presentation of, and agitation around, intermediate solutions – far removed both from the party's own slogans, and from the programme of inertia and passivity of the groups we wish to combat – allows us to assemble broader forces behind the party; to counterpose the words of the leaders of the counter-revolutionary mass parties to their real intentions; to push the masses towards revolutionary solutions; and to extend our influence (example: the "Anti-parliament"). These intermediate solutions cannot all be foreseen, because they must in all cases be adapted to reality. But they must be such as to be able to constitute a bridge towards the party's slogans; and it must always be evident to the masses that if they were to be realized, this would lead to an acceleration of the revolutionary process and a beginning of wider struggles.

The presentation of, and struggle for, such intermediate solutions is the specific form of struggle which must be used against the so-called democratic parties – which are in reality one of the strongest props of the tottering capitalist order, and as such alternate in power with the reactionary groups – when these so-called democratic parties are linked to sizeable and decisive layers of the working population (as in Italy, in the first months of the Matteotti crisis), and when a serious reactionary danger is imminent (tactic adopted by the Bolsheviks towards Kerensky during the Kornilov coup). In such cases, the Communist Party will obtain the best results by advancing the actual solutions which would be those of the so-called democratic parties, if they were in fact capable of waging a consistent struggle for democracy with all the means required by the situation. These parties, thus subjected to the test of deeds, will unmask themselves before the masses and lose their influence over them.

44. All the particular struggles led by the party, and its activities on every front to mobilize and unite the forces of the working class, must come together and be synthesized in a political formula which can be easily understood by the masses, and which has the greatest possible agitational value for them. This formula is the "workers' and peasants' government". It indicates even to the most backward masses the need to win power in order to solve the vital problems which interest them; and it provides the means to transport them onto the terrain of the more advanced proletarian vanguard (struggle for the dictatorship of the proletariat). In this sense, it is an agitational slogan, but only corresponds to a real phase of historical development in the same sense as the intermediate solutions dealt with in the preceding paragraph. The party cannot conceive of a realization of this slogan except as the beginning of a direct revolutionary struggle: i.e. of a civil war waged by the proletariat, in alliance with the peasantry, with the aim of winning power. The party could be led into serious deviations from its task as leader of the revolution if it were to interpret the workers' and peasants' government as corresponding to a real phase of development of the struggle for power: in other words, if it considered that this slogan indicated the possibility for the problem of the State to be resolved in the interests of the working class in any other form than the dictatorship of the proletariat.

Lyons, January 1926.

VI

Rearguard Action

70. THE PARTY'S FIRST FIVE YEARS

Given the difficulty of publishing at once a journalistic account of the proceedings of our party's Third Congress, we nevertheless think it proper to provide comrades and the readership as a whole with a general report and general information on the results of the Congress itself.[209] But we hasten to announce that the proceedings of the Congress will be published in our paper in the very near future, and that the discussion and theses in their definitive form will subsequently be assembled in a volume.

The numerical results of the voting at the congress were as follows:

Absent and not voting   18·9 per cent.
Of those attending the Congress:
votes for the Central Committee   90·8 per cent.
votes for the far left 9·2 per cent.

Our party was born in January 1921, i.e. at the most critical moment of the general crisis of the Italian bourgeoisie and of the crisis of the workers' movement. The split, even though it was historically necessary and inevitable, nevertheless found the broad masses unprepared and reluctant. In such a situation, the material organization of our party encountered the most difficult conditions. The result was, therefore, that purely organizational work, given the difficulty of the conditions in which it had to be carried out, absorbed the creative energies of the party almost completely. The political problems which confronted us, on the one hand due to the decomposition of the old bourgeois leading groups, on the other hand due to an analogous process in the workers' movement, could not be adequately analysed. The whole political line of the party in the years immediately following the split was primarily conditioned by this necessity: to keep the ranks of the party closed, as it was assaulted from one side physically by the fascist offensive, and from the other by the corpse-like stench of the Socialist decomposition. It was natural that, in such conditions, there should have developed within our party attitudes and outlooks of a corporate and sectarian character. The general political problem inherent in the presence and development of our party was not seen in terms of an activity through which the party should have aimed to win over the broadest masses and organize the social forces necessary to defeat the bourgeois and win power. Instead, it was seen in terms of the party's existence itself.

The Livorno Split

The fact of the split was seen in terms of its immediate and mechanical value, and we were guilty, even if in another direction, of the same error as Serrati. Comrade Lenin had given the lapidary formula for the significance of the split in Italy, when he had told comrade Serrati: "Separate yourselves from Turati, and then make an alliance with him." This formula should have been adapted by us to the split, which occurred in a different form from that foreseen by Lenin. In other words, we should – as our indispensable and historically necessary task – have separated ourselves not just from reformism, but also from the maximalism which in reality represented and still represents the typical Italian opportunism in the workers' movement. But after that, and though continuing the ideological and organizational struggle against them, we should have sought to make an alliance against reaction. But for leading elements in our party, every action of the International designed to obtain a reorientation along these lines appeared as if it were an implicit disavowal of the Livorno split – a sign of repentance. They said that if such an approach to the political struggle were accepted, this would mean admitting that our party was nothing but a vague nebula; whereas it was correct and necessary to assert that our party, by its birth, had definitively resolved the problem of the historical formation of the party of the Italian proletariat. This view was reinforced by the not-so-distant experiences of the Soviet revolution in Hungary, where the fusion between communists and social-democrats had certainly been one of the elements which contributed to the defeat.

The Significance of the Hungarian Experience

In reality, the way in which this problem was viewed by our party was false, and increasingly appeared as such to the mass of party members. Precisely the Hungarian experience should have convinced us that the line followed by the International in the formation of the communist parties was not that which we attributed to it. It is in fact well known that comrade Lenin sought strenuously to prevent the fusion between communists and social-democrats in Hungary, in spite of the fact that the latter declared themselves in favour of the dictatorship of the proletariat. Can one, therefore, say that comrade Lenin was generally opposed to fusions? Certainly not. The problem was seen by comrade Lenin and by the International as a dialectical process, through which the communist element, i.e. the most advanced and conscious part of the proletariat, both in the organization of the party of the working class and in the task of leading the broad masses, puts itself at the head of everything healthy and active that has been created and that exists in the class.

In Hungary, it was an error to destroy the independent communist organization at the moment of the seizure of power; it was an error to dissolve and dilute the regroupment that had been achieved, into the vaster and more amorphous social-democratic organization which could not fail to regain predominance. In the case of Hungary too, comrade Lenin had formulated the line of our former party as an alliance with social-democracy, not as a fusion. Fusion would have been achieved at a later stage, when the process of predominance of the communist regroupment had developed on the broadest scale in the fields of party organization, trade-union organization and the State apparatus — in other words, with the organic and political separation of the revolutionary workers from the opportunist leaders.

For Italy, the problem was posed in even simpler terms than in Hungary, because not only the proletariat had not won power, but also, precisely at the moment of the party's formation, a great movement of retreat began. To pose in Italy the question of the party's formation in the way which comrade Lenin indicated, in the formula he gave to Serrati, meant — in the conditions of proletarian retreat which were then emerging — giving our party the possibility of regrouping around itself those elements of the proletariat which wanted to resist, but which under Maximalist leadership were caught up in the general rout and falling progressively into passivity. This meant that the tactic proposed by Lenin and by the International was the only one capable of reinforcing and developing the results of the Livorno split, and of making our party genuinely, from that moment on, not just abstractly and as a historical affirmation, but in an effective form, into the leading party of the working class. As a result of this false approach to the problem, we maintained our advanced positions, alone and with the fraction of the masses immediately closest to the party. But we did not do what was necessary to hold the proletariat as a whole on our positions, though the latter was still imbued with a strong will to fight, as is shown by the numerous heroic episodes of the resistance that was opposed to the enemy advance.

The Party in the Years 1921–2

Another of the elements of weakness of our organization consisted in the fact that such problems – given the difficulty of the situation and given that the forces of the party were absorbed by the immediate struggle for its own physical defence – did not become the object of discussion at the base, and hence an element in developing the ideological and political capacity of the party.

As a result, the First Congress of the party, the one held in the San Marco theatre at Livorno immediately after the split, merely carried out tasks of a directly organizational nature: formation of the central organs and overall structuring of the party. The Second Congress could, and perhaps should, have examined and confronted the problems outlined above; but the following factors prevented this.

1. The fact that not only the rank and file, but also a great part of the most responsible elements in the party and those nearest to the leadership, literally did not know that there were deep and fundamental differences between the line being followed by our party and that advocated by the International.

2. The fact that the party was absorbed in the direct physical struggle led to an underestimation of ideological and political questions, as opposed to purely organizational ones. It was thus natural for there to appear within the party a state of mind that was *a priori* opposed to going deeply into any question that might hold the danger of serious conflicts within the leading group constituted at Livorno.

3. The fact that the opposition which emerged at the Rome Congress, and which claimed to be the sole representative of the International's directives, was – in the given situation – an expression of the state of mind of weariness and passivity that existed in certain areas of the party.

The crisis which both the ruling class and the proletariat passed through in the period before fascism came to power once again placed our party face to face with problems which the Rome Congress had not had the possibility of resolving. In what did this crisis consist? The left groups of the bourgeoisie, favourable in words to a democratic government that would aim to stem the fascist movement with real energy, had left it to the free choice of the Socialist Party whether or not to accept this solution, in order to liquidate the party politically under the weight of responsibility for the failure to reach an anti-fascist agreement. In this very way in which the democrats posed the question, there was implicit their previous capitulation before the fascist movement – a phenomenon which was then reproduced during the Matteotti crisis.

However, such an approach, although it could at first have brought about a clarification within the Socialist Party, since the split between Maximalists and Reformists had already taken place at the base, nevertheless made the situation of the proletariat worse.[210] In fact, the split made the tactic proposed by the democrats fruitless, insofar as the left government proposed by them was supposed to include the united Socialist Party, in other words was supposed to signify the capture of the majority of the organized proletarian class within the machinery of the bourgeois State, anticipating fascist legislation and making the directly fascist experiment politically unnecessary. Moreover, the split (as appeared more clearly subsequently) had only led in a mechanical sense to a leftward leap on the part of the Maximalists. For the latter, although they claimed they wanted to join the Communist International and thus to recognize the mistake they had made at Livorno, nevertheless proceeded with so many unspoken mental reservations as to neutralize the revolutionary reawakening which the split had stimulated among the masses, and thus led those masses to fresh disappointments and a new relapse into passivity, which fascism exploited to carry out the March on Rome.

The Party's New Course

This new situation was reflected at the Fourth Congress of the Communist International, where the formation of a fusion committee was achieved after uncertainties and resistance that were related to the conviction, rooted in the majority of our party's delegates, that the change of position on the part of the Maximalists merely represented a transitory oscillation leading nowhere. In any case, it was from that moment that there began within our party a process of differentiation within the Livorno leading group: a process which steadily continued, and which left the phase of a group phenomenon to become a feature of the party as a whole when the elements of the crisis of fascism which began with the Turin Congress of the Popular Party first started to appear and develop.[211]

It seemed increasingly clear that it was necessary to move the party away from the position that had been maintained in 1921–2, if the communist movement was to develop *pari passu* with the crisis through which the ruling class was passing. The premise which had been so important in the past, according to which the first essential was to maintain the organizational unity of the party, ceased to operate now. For in the situation of conflict between our party and the International, a state of latent faction was being created in our ranks, which found its expression in groups that were clearly right-wing and often liquidationist in character. To delay any longer in posing to their fullest extent the fundamental tactical questions, on which hitherto we had hesitated to open up a discussion, would have meant bringing about a general crisis of the party, with no way out.

New regroupments thus occurred and developed further and further, up to the eve of our Third Congress, when it was possible to ascertain that not only the great majority of the party base (which had never openly been appealed to), but also the majority of the old leading group had detached itself clearly from the political conceptions and positions of the far left, and had moved over completely on to the terrain of the International and Leninism.

The Importance of the Third Congress

What has been said hitherto makes it clear how great the importance and the tasks of our Third Congress were. It had to close a whole epoch in the life of our party, putting an end to the internal crisis and achieving a stable combination of forces capable of allowing a normal development of the party's capacity to provide political leadership for the masses, and hence of its capacity for action.

Has the Congress really fulfilled these tasks? Undoubtedly, all the proceedings of the Congress have shown how, notwithstanding the difficulties of the situation, our party has succeeded in resolving its crisis of development, achieving a remarkable level of homogeneity, cohesion and stabilization – and one that is certainly higher than that in many other sections of the International. The intervention of delegates from the base in the Congress debates, delegates who in some cases had come from those regions where party activity encounters most difficulty, showed the way in which the fundamental elements of the debate between the International and the Central Committee on the one hand, and the opposition on the other, had not simply been absorbed mechanically by the party, but had brought about a conscious and widespread conviction, so that they contributed to raising the tone of the intellectual life of the mass of comrades and their capacity for political leadership and initiative to a degree that was not foreseen even by the most optimistic comrades.

This seems to me to have been the key significance of the Congress. The result is that our party can call itself a mass party, not simply because of the influence it exercises on broad strata of the working class and the peasant masses, but because it has acquired in the single elements of which it is composed a capacity for analysing situations, for political initiative and for strong leadership which in the past it lacked, and which is the basis for its capacity for collective leadership.

Moreover, the whole way in which the work was carried on at the base to organize the congress, both ideologically and practically, in those regions and provinces where police repression keeps the most intensive watch over every movement on the part of our comrades, and the fact that we succeeded for seven days in keeping more than sixty comrades assembled for the party congress, and almost as many again for the youth congress, are in themselves a proof of the development referred to above. It is clear to everyone that all this activity of comrades and units of the organization is not just a purely organizational fact, but constitutes in itself a very striking demonstration of political ability.

A few figures in this respect. In the first phase of the Congress preparations, between two and three thousand meetings were held at the base; these culminated in more than one hundred provincial congresses where, after thorough discussion, the Congress delegates were chosen.

Political Significance and Results Achieved

Every worker is able to appreciate the full significance of these few figures which can be published, at five years distance from the epoch of the occupation of the factories, and after three years of fascist government which has intensified its general control over every mass activity and accomplished an organization of the police which is far superior to the police organizations which existed previously.

The greatest weakness of the traditional working-class organization lay essentially in the permanent imbalance – which became catastrophic at the climactic moments of mass activity – between the capacity of the organizing cadres of the party and the spontaneous upsurge from the base. It is thus clear that our party has succeeded, in spite of the extremely unfavourable conditions of the present period, in overcoming this weakness to a notable degree, and in predisposing coordinated and centralized organizational forces which can insure the working class against the errors and inadequacies which appeared in the past. This is another of the most important ways in which our congress was significant. The working class is capable of action, and shows that it is historically capable of accomplishing its mission of leadership in the anti-capitalist struggle, to the extent that it succeeds in producing from within itself all the technical elements which in modern society have proved to be indispensable for the concrete organization of the institutions in which the proletarian programme will be realized.

It is from this point of view that the entire activity of the fascist movement from 1921 up to the most recent ultra-fascist laws must be analysed: it has been systematically directed towards destroying the cadres which the proletarian and revolutionary movement has painstakingly formed over almost fifty years of history. In this way, fascism has succeeded in an immediate, practical sense in depriving the working class of its political autonomy and independence, and in reducing it either to a state of passivity, i.e. to an inert subordination to the State apparatus, or else, at moments of political crisis like the Matteotti period, to seeking cadres for its struggle in other classes that have been less exposed to the repression. Our party has remained the sole mechanism which the working class has at its disposal for selecting new leading cadres for the class: in other words, for winning back its political independence and autonomy. The Congress has shown that our party has succeeded brilliantly in fulfilling this essential task.

There were two fundamental objectives which the congress had to achieve.

1. After the debates and the new alignment of forces which took place in the way we have already described, it was necessary to unite the party, both on the terrain of organizational principles and practice and on the more narrowly political terrain.

2. The congress had the task of establishing the political line of the party for the immediate future, and of working out a programme of practical work in all fields of mass activity.

The problems which faced us if various concrete objectives were to be achieved were, of course, not mutually independent one from another, but coordinated in the framework of the overall conception of

Leninism. The Congress discussion, therefore, even when it revolved around the technical aspects of each particular practical question, posed the general question of the acceptance or non-acceptance of Leninism. Thus the Congress served to show to what degree our party had become a Bolshevik party.

The Fundamental Objectives

Starting off from a historical and directly political assessment of the function of the working class in our country, the congress gave a solution to a whole series of problems which can be grouped as follows.

1. Relations between the Central Committee of the party and the membership.

(a) This group of problems includes the general discussion on the nature of the party; on the need for it to be a class party, not just abstractly, i.e. insofar as the programme accepted by its members expresses the aspirations of the proletariat, but so to speak physiologically, i.e. insofar as the great majority of its members is made up of proletarians and it reflects and focuses only the needs and ideology of a single class: the proletariat.

(b) The complete subordination of all the party's energies, socially unified in this way, to the leadership of the Central Committee. The loyalty of all the elements of the party towards the Central Committee must become not just a purely organizational and disciplinary fact, but a real principle of revolutionary ethics. It is necessary to infuse in the membership as a whole so rooted a conviction of this necessity that factional initiatives and, in general, any attempt to disrupt the cohesion of the party will meet with a spontaneous and immediate reaction at the base that will stifle them at birth. The authority of the Central Committee, between one congress and the next, must never be put in question, and the party must become a homogeneous bloc. Only on these conditions will the party be capable of conquering its class enemies. How could the masses who are outside any party have confidence that the instrument of revolutionary struggle, the party, will succeed in waging an implacable struggle to win and keep power, without hesitation or wavering, if the party's Central Committee does not have the capacity and energy necessary to eliminate all the weaknesses which can crack its solidarity?

The two preceding points would be impossible to realize if, within the party, the social homogeneity and monolithic solidity of the organization were not accompanied by the widespread consciousness of an ideological and political homogeneity.

Concretely, the line which the party must follow can be expressed in the following formula: the nucleus of the party organization consists in a strong Central Committee, closely linked to the proletarian base of the party itself, on the terrain of the ideology and tactics of Marxism-Leninism.

On this series of problems, the overwhelming majority of the congress clearly declared itself in favour of the Central Committee's positions, and rejected — not only without the least concession, but indeed insisting on the need for theoretical intransigence and inflexibility in practice — the conceptions of the opposition, which could maintain the party in a state of deliquescence and of political and social amorphism.

2. Relations between the party and the proletarian class (i.e. the class of which the party is the direct representative; the class which has the task of leading the anti-capitalist struggle and organizing the new society). This group of problems includes the assessment of the proletariat's function in Italian society: in other words of the degree to which that society is ripe for a transformation from capitalism to socialism, and hence of the possibility for the proletariat to become an independent and dominant class. The Congress, therefore, discussed: (a) the trade-union question, which for us is essentially a question of the organization of the broadest masses, as a class apart, on the basis of immediate economic interests and as a terrain for revolutionary political education; (b) the question of the united front, i.e. of the relations of political leadership between the most advanced part of the proletariat and the less advanced fractions of it.

3. Relations between the proletarian class as a whole and the other social forces which are objectively on the anti-capitalist terrain, though led by parties and political groups linked to the bourgeoisie: hence, in the first place, the relations between the proletariat and the peasants. On this whole series of problems too, the overwhelming majority of the congress rejected the incorrect conceptions of the opposition and pronounced itself in favour of the solutions given by the Central Committee.

The Alignment of Forces at the Congress

We referred earlier to the attitude which the overwhelming majority at the Congress took up with respect to the solutions to be given to the key problems of the present period. It is, therefore, worth analysing in greater detail the attitude taken up by the opposition; and referring, however briefly, to other positions which were presented to the Congress as individual ones, but which could in the future coincide with specific transitory moments in the development of the Italian situation, and which therefore must be denounced and combated at once. We have already referred in the first paragraphs of this report to the modes and forms which characterized the crisis of development of our party in the years from 1921 to 1924. Let us briefly recall how at the Fifth World Congress the crisis itself met with a provisional organizational solution, with the constitution of a Central Committee which as a whole placed itself totally on the terrain of Leninism and the tactics of the Communist International, but which was composed of three parts. One of these, which had a majority plus one on the committee, represented the elements of the left which had detached themselves from the old Livorno leading group after the Fourth World Congress. A second represented the opposition which had formed at our Second Congress against the Rome Theses. The third represented the "IIIrd Internationalists", who had entered the party after the fusion. Despite its intrinsic weaknesses, since the leading role within it was clearly played by the so-called "centre" group, i.e. by the left elements who had detached themselves from the Livorno leading group, the Central Committee succeeded in confronting and forcefully resolving the problem of Bolshevizing the party and securing its complete agreeement with the directives of the Communist International.

Positions of the Far Left

Certainly there was some resistance, and the culminating episode in this, which all comrades will recall, was the creation of the *Comitato d'Intesa*; i.e. the attempt to create an organized faction which would counterpose itself to the Central Committee in the leadership of the party. In reality, the creation of the *Comitato d'Intesa* was the most striking symptom of the disintegration of the far left, which, since it felt itself progressively losing ground in the ranks of the party, sought by a dramatic act of rebellion to galvanize the few forces remaining to it. It is noteworthy that, after the ideological and political defeat suffered by the far left in the pre-congress period, its hard nucleus began to adopt positions that were increasingly sectarian and hostile to the party, from which each day it felt more distant and detached. These comrades not only continued to remain on the terrain of the most determined opposition to certain concrete points of the ideology and politics of the party and the International; they systematically sought motives for opposition on every point, in such a way as to present themselves *en bloc* almost like a party within the party. It is easy to imagine how, starting off from such a position, they should have arrived during the course of the congress at theoretical and practical positions in which the drama which was a reflection of the general situation in which the party has to operate could only with difficulty be distinguished from a certain histrionicism, which appeared affected to anybody who had really struggled and and sacrificed themselves for the proletarian class.

In this category should be included, for example, the procedural motion presented by the opposition, right at the start of the congress, contesting its deliberative validity and in this way seeking to create in advance an alibi for a possible renewal of factional activity and for a possible refusal to recognize the authority of the new party leadership.[212] To the mass of congress delegates, who knew what sacrifices and what organizational efforts the preparation of the congress had cost, this procedural motion appeared as an out and out provocation; and it is not without significance that the only applause (the congress regulations for understandable reasons prohibited any noisy demonstration of agreement or condemnation) was that bestowed on the speaker who stigmatized the attitude adopted by the opposition, and argued for the need to demonstratively reinforce the new committee which was to be elected, by giving it a specific mandate for implacable sternness against any initiative that in practice cast doubt on the authority of the congress and the validity of its deliberations.

In this same category, and in a way that was aggravated by its mannered and theatrical form, must be included also the attitude taken up by the opposition, before the congress ended, when we were about to draw the political-organizational conclusions of the proceedings of the congress itself. But the elements of the opposition themselves could see clear proof of the general state of mind in the ranks of the party. The party does not intend to allow any more playing at factionalism and indiscipline. The party wishes to achieve the maximum degree of collective leadership, and will not allow any individual – whatever his personal merits – to counterpose himself to the party.

First Signs of Right Deviations

In the plenary sessions of the congress, the far left opposition was the only official and declared opposition. The position of opposition on the trade-union question that was taken up by two members of the old Central Committee, because of its improvised and impulsive character, should be considered more as an individual phenomenon of political hysteria than as one of opposition in a systematic sense.[213] During the work of the political commission, however, there was a demonstration which, if for now it can be regarded as being of a purely individual character, must — given the ideological elements which formed the basis for it — be seen as an out and out right-wing platform, which could be presented to the party in a given situation and, therefore, must be (as it was) rejected without hesitation, especially in view of the fact that a member of the old Central Committee made himself the spokesman for it.[214]

The ideological elements involved are: 1. the assertion that the workers' and peasants' government can be constituted on the basis of the bourgeois parliament; 2. the assertion that social-democracy should not be seen as the left wing of the bourgeoisie, but as the right wing of the proletariat; 3. the assertion that, in assessing the bourgeois State, it is necessary to distinguish the function of oppression by one class or another from the function of production of certain satisfactions for certain general requirements of society. The first and second of these elements are contrary to the decisions of the Third Congress; the third is outside the Marxist conception of the State. All three together reveal an orientation towards conceiving of the solution to the crisis of bourgeois society outside revolution.

The Political Line Defined by the Party

Since the forces represented at the Congress aligned themselves in this way, i.e. as a most inflexible opposition on the part of the relics of "ultra-leftism" to the theoretical and practical positions of the majority of the party, we will refer rapidly only to a few points concerning the line established by the congress.

Ideological Question. On this question, the congress declared that it was necessary for the party to develop a whole process of education which would reinforce knowledge of our Marxist doctrine in the ranks of the party, and develop the capacity of the broadest leading stratum. The oppposition sought to create a skilful diversion here: it exhumed some old articles and extracts from articles by comrades of the majority in the party, in order to show that they have only relatively recently accepted integrally the conception of historical materialism as derived from the works of Marx and Engels, and that they were previously supporting the interpretation of historical materialism given by Benedetto Croce. Since it is well known that the Rome Theses too have been judged to be essentially inspired by Crocean philosophy, this line of argument by the opposition appeared animated by the purest congress demagogy. In any case, since the question is not one of single individuals but of the mass of members, the line fixed by the congress, concerning the need for specific educational work to raise the level of general Marxist culture in the party, reduces the opposition's polemic to an erudite exercise in research on more or less interesting biographical details in the intellectual development of individual comrades.

Party Tactics. The congress approved and forcefully defended against the opposition's attacks the tactic followed by the party in the last period of Italian history, characterized by the Matteotti crisis. It should be said that the opposition did not attempt to counterpose to the analysis of the Italian situation made by the Central Committee for the congress, either another analysis which would lead to the establishment of a different tactical line, or partial corrections sufficient to justify a position of principle. Indeed, the fact that its observations and criticisms were based neither on a deep study, nor even on a superficial one, of the relation of forces and general conditions existing in Italian society was characteristic of the far left's false position. It was thus clear to all that the method of the far left, which the latter declares to be dialectical, is not the method of Marx's materialist dialectics, but the old method of conceptual dialectics which characterized pre-Marxist and even pre-Hegelian philosophy.

In place of an objective analysis of the forces in conflict and the direction which these take – in contradictory fashion – in relation to the development of the material forces of society, the opposition substituted a claim that they possessed a special and mysterious 'nose' according to which the party should be led. A strange aberration, which authorized the congress to judge as extremely dangerous and damaging for the party such a method, which would lead only to a policy of improvisation and adventures.

The fact that the opposition never possessed a real method capable of developing the forces of the party and the revolutionary energies of the proletariat, which could be counterposed to the Marxist and Leninist method, was shown by the activity carried out by the party in 1921 and 1922, when it was led politically by some of the present irreducible oppositionists. In this connection, two moments of the Italian situation were analysed by the Congress: the first was the attitude assumed by the party leadership in February 1921, when fascism launched its frontal offensive in Tuscany and Apulia; and the other was the attitude of the same leadership towards the *arditi del popolo* movement.[215] From an analysis of these two moments, it clearly emerged that the method advocated by the opposition only leads to passivity and inaction; it consists in the last resort simply in drawing lessons of a purely pedagogic and propagandistic kind from events that have already taken place without the intervention of the party as a whole.

The Trade-union Question In the trade-union field, the difficult task of the party consists in finding a harmonious balance between the following two lines of practical activity.

1. Defending the class unions, by seeking to maintain the maximum degree of trade-union cohesion and organization among the masses who have traditionally participated in the union organization itself. This is a task of exceptional importance, since the revolutionary party must always, even in the worst objective situations, aim to preserve all the accumulated experience and technical and political skill which have been formed through the developments of past history in the proletarian masses. For our party, the C.G.L. constitutes in Italy the organization which historically expresses, in the most organic manner, this accumulated experience and skill, and hence represents the terrain upon which this defence must be conducted.

2. Taking account of the fact that the present dispersal of the great working masses is essentially due to motives which are not internal to the working class, and that therefore there exist immediate organizational possibilities of a not strictly trade-union character, the party must aim to encourage and promote these possibilities in an active way. This task can be carried out only if the mass organizational work is transferred from the corporate terrain onto the industrial terrain of the factory, and if the links of mass organization become elective and representative as well as by individual membership through the union card.

It is clear, moreover, that this tactic of the party corresponds to the normal development of proletarian mass organization, as was shown during and after the War, i.e. in the period when the proletariat began to confront the problem of an all-out struggle against the bourgeoisie for the conquest of power. In this period, the traditional organizational form of the craft union was completed by a whole system of elective representation in the factory; in other words, by the internal commissions. It is also well known that, especially during the War, when the trade-union federations joined the committees of industrial mobilization[216] and thus brought about a situation of "industrial peace" in some aspects analogous to the present one, the working-class masses in all countries (Italy, France, Russia, England and even the United States) rediscovered the paths of resistance and struggle under the guidance of the elected representatives of the workers in the factories.

The trade-union tactic of the party consists essentially in developing all the organizational experience of the broad masses, but stressing those possibilities that can most immediately be realized – given the objective difficulties which are created for the trade-union movement by the bourgeois régime on the one hand, and by the reformism of the national union leaders on the other.

This line was approved *in toto* by the overwhelming majority of the congress. However, the most passionate debates took place around it, and the opposition was represented not only by the far left but also by two members of the Central Committee, as we have already mentioned. One speaker argued that the trade union is historically superseded, since the only mass action of the party should be that which is carried on in the factories. This thesis, linked to the most absurd positions of infantile leftism, was clearly and forcefully rejected by the congress.

For another speaker, on the other hand, the sole activity of the party in this field should be organizational activity of a traditional trade-union type. This thesis is closely related to a right-wing conception, i.e. to the desire not to clash too sharply with the reformist trade-union bureaucracy, which strenuously opposes all mass organization.

The far left opposition developed two basic lines of argument. The first, designed essentially for debating purposes at the congress, aimed to show that the tactic of factory organizations supported by the Central Committee and the majority of delegates was linked to the views of the weekly *Ordine Nuovo*, which according to the far left used to be Proudhonian and not Marxist. The second was related to the question of principle whereby the far left clearly counterposes itself to

Leninism: Leninism says that the party leads the class through mass organizations, and hence says that one of the key tasks of the party is to develop mass organization; for the far left, by contrast, this problem does not exist, and the party is given functions which can lead either to the worst disasters or to the most dangerous forms of adventurism.

The congress rejected all these distortions of communist trade-union tactics, while considering it necessary to stress with particular force the need for a greater and more active participation by communists in work in the traditional union organization.

The Agrarian Question. The party has sought, so far as its activity among the peasants is concerned, to leave the sphere of simple ideological propaganda aimed at disseminating in a purely abstract sense the general terms of the Leninist solution to the problem itself, and to enter the practical terrain of real political organization and action. It is obvious that this was easier to achieve in Italy than in other countries, because in our country the process of differentiation of the broad masses of the population is in certain aspects more advanced than elsewhere, as a result of the present political situation. Moreover, in view of the fact that the industrial proletariat in Italy is only a minority of the working population, this question is posed more sharply than elsewhere. The problems on the one hand of what the motor forces of the revolution are, and on the other of the leading role of the proletariat, present themselves in Italy in forms such as to require particular attention from our party, and a search for concrete solutions to the general problems which can be summed up in the expression: agrarian question.

The overwhelming majority of the congress approved the approach of the party to these problems, and asserted the need for an intensification of the work according to the general line that is already partially being applied. In what does this activity consist in practice? The party must aim to create, in every region, regional unions of the Peasants' Defence Association.[217] However, within this broader organizational framework, it is necessary to distinguish four basic groupings of the peasant masses, for each of which it is necessary to find a precise and complete political position and solution.

One of these groupings consists in the mass of Slav peasants in Istria and Friuli, the organization of whom is closely linked to the national question. A second consists in the particular peasant movement which can be classified under the heading of the Peasant Party, and which has its base especially in Piedmont; for this grouping, of a non-confessional and more strictly economic character, it is enough to apply the general terms of the agrarian tactics of Leninism – especially since it exists in the region where there is to be found one of the most effective proletarian centres in Italy. The two other groupings are far more important, and require most attention from the party: 1. the mass of catholic peasants, grouped in central and northern Italy, who are directly organized by Catholic Action and the Church apparatus in general, in other words by the Vatican; 2. the mass of peasants in southern Italy and the Islands.

So far as the catholic peasants are concerned, the congress decided that the party must continue and develop the line which consists in encouraging the left-wing groupings which emerge in this field, which are closely linked to the general agrarian crisis that began even before the War in central and northern Italy. The congress declared that the position taken up by the party towards the catholic peasants, although it contains within it some of the essential elements for a solution to the politico-religious problem in Italy, must in no way lead us to encourage any ideological movements of a strictly religious nature that may emerge. The party's task consists in explaining the conflicts that arise on the terrain of religion as deriving from class conflicts; and in aiming to bring out with increasing clarity the class features of these conflicts. It does not, by contrast, consist in encouraging religious solutions to class conflicts, even if such solutions appear left-wing insofar as they call into question the authority of the official religious organization.

The question of the southern peasants was examined by the congress with particular attention. The congress recognized as correct the assertion contained in the theses of the Central Committee, according to which the function of the southern peasant masses in the evolution of the anti-capitalist struggle in Italy must be examined independently, and must lead to the conclusion that the southern peasants are – after the industrial and agricultural proletariat of northern Italy – the most revolutionary social element of Italian society.

What is the material and political basis for this function of the peasant masses in the South? The relations which link Italian capitalism and the southern peasants do not consist solely in the normal historical relations between city and countryside, as they were created by the development of capitalism in all countries in the world. In the context of this national society, these relations are aggravated and radicalized by the fact that, economically and politically, the whole zone of the South and the Islands functions as an immense countryside in relation to northern Italy, which functions as an immense city. This situation leads to the formation and development in southern Italy of specific aspects of a national question, even though in the immediate these do not assume an explicit form of such a question as a whole, but only that of an extremely powerful struggle of a regionalistic kind, and of deep currents in favour of decentralization and local autonomy.

What makes the situation of the southern peasants a specific one is the fact that, unlike the three groupings described previously, they do not – taken as a whole – have any autonomous organizational experience. They are incorporated within the traditional structures of bourgeois society, so that the landowners, an integral part of the agrarian/capitalist bloc, control the peasant masses and direct them in accordance with their own aims.

As a result of the War and the working-class upheavals of the post-war period, which profoundly weakened the State apparatus and almost destroyed the social prestige of the above-mentioned upper classes, the peasant masses of the South awoke to a life of their own and painfully sought their own structures. Thus we saw movements of war-veterans, and the various so-called parties of "renewal", which attempted to exploit this reawakening of the peasant masses: at times supporting it, as in the period of the land occupations; more often seeking to sidetrack it, and thus stabilize it on a position of struggle for so-called democracy – as has been the case most recently with the establishment of the National Union.

The most recent events of Italian life, which have caused the southern petty bourgeoisie to go over *en masse* to fascism, have made the necessity to give the southern peasantry an orientation of its own, for removing itself definitively from the influence of the rural bourgoisie, still more urgent. The only possible organizer of the mass of peasants in the South is the industrial worker, represented by our party. But for this work of organization to be possible and effective, it is necessary for our party to draw close to the southern peasant: for it to destroy in the industrial worker the prejudice instilled by bourgeois propaganda, that the South is a ball and chain which hinders the greatest developments of the national economy; and for it to destroy in the southern peasant the yet more dangerous prejudice, whereby he sees in the North of Italy a single bloc of class enemies.

To obtain these results, it is necessary for our party to carry out an intensive propaganda activity, including within its own organization, to give all comrades a precise awareness of the terms of this question — which, if it is not resolved in a far-sighted, revolutionary and wise manner by us, will make it possible for the bourgeoisie, defeated in its own area, to concentrate its forces in the South and make this part of Italy into the marshalling-ground of counter-revolution.

On this whole series of problems, the far left opposition had nothing to contribute except jokes and clichés. Its basic position consisted in denying *a priori* that these concrete problems exist as such, without any analysis or evidence even of a potential nature. Indeed, one can say that it was precisely with respect to the agrarian question that the true essence of the far left's conception was revealed. This conception consists in a kind of corporatism, which mechanically awaits the realization of revolutionary aims from the mere development of the general objective conditions. Such a conception was, as we have said, clearly rejected by the overwhelming majority of the congress.

Other Problems Dealt With

So far as the question of the concrete organization of the party in the present period is concerned, the congress ratified without discussion the deliberations of the recent organizational conference, already published in *L'Unità*.[218]

The Congress was not able — in view of the conditions under which it was held and the aims it set itself, which concerned in particular the internal organization of the party and the healing of the crisis — to deal amply with certain questions which are nonetheless crucial ones for a revolutionary proletarian party. Thus only in the Congress Theses was the international situation examined, in relation to the political line of the Communist International. In the discussion at the Congress, this question was only touched upon; and the only aspect of international problems that was dealt with was that related to the organizational forms and relations of the Comintern, since this was an element of the party's internal crisis. The Congress did, however, have a very full and exhaustive report on the proceedings of the recent congress of the Russian party, and on the significance of the discussions which took place at it.[219]

Similarly, the Congress did not deal with the problem of organization in the women's field, nor with the organization of the press — key questions for our movement which should have merited a separate discussion. The question of drawing up the party's programme, which had been placed on the agenda, was also not dealt with by the congress. We think it is necessary to remedy these defects by party conferences, specially convened for the purpose.

Conclusion

In spite of these partial deficiencies, one may say, in conclusion, that the quantity of work which the congress accomplished was really impressive. The congress drew up a series of resolutions, and a programme of concrete work, which will enable the proletarian class to develop its energies and its capacity for political leadership in the present situation.

One condition is especially necessary, if the congress resolutions are not just to be applied, but are to bear all their possible fruits. It is necessary for the party to remain closely united; for no germ of disintegration, of pessimism, of passivity to be allowed to develop within it. All comrades in the party are called upon to realize this condition. No one can doubt that the achievement of this will be greeted with the most intense disappointment by all the enemies of the working class.

Unsigned, *L'Unità*, 24 February 1926.

71. A STUDY OF THE ITALIAN SITUATION[220]

I

It is necessary to study three basic elements of the Italian political situation.

1. The positive revolutionary element, i.e. the progress achieved by the united front tactic. The present situation in the organization of the Committees of Proletarian Unity, and the tasks of the communist factions in these committees.[221]

2. The political element represented by the disintegration of the fascist landowner/bourgeois bloc. Internal situation in the ruling party, and significance of the crisis it is passing through.

3. The political element represented by the tendency to constitute a left democratic bloc, with its pivot in the Republican Party, in that a republican stance is supposed to provide the basis for this democratic coalition.

United Front Tactics

The study of the first point must have the aim of testing the correctness of the political line fixed by the Third Congress. The Third Congress of our party was characterized by the fact that it has not merely posed, in a generic sense, the problem of the need to realize the leadership of the Communist Party within the working class, and of the working class within the working population of Italy; but it has also sought to concretize, in a practical way, the political elements through which this leadership might be accomplished. In other words, it has sought to identify those parties and associations through which bourgeois or petty-bourgeois influence over the working classes is disseminated, and which are open to the possibility of an overturning, a reversal of class values. Thus it is necessary to test, by results, the correctness of the organizational terrain fixed by the party as that most appropriate for immediate regroupment of the forces set in motion by the united front tactic: i.e. the agitation committees.

On the positive side, one may say that our party has succeeded in winning a clear position of political initiative among the working masses. In this last period, all the journalistic organs of the parties which control the mass of the Italian people have been filled with polemics against the successful actions of our party. All these parties are on the defensive against our actions; in fact, they are indirectly led by us, since at least 60 per cent of their activity is devoted to repelling our offensives, or is devised to give their mass base some satisfaction that will free it from our influence.

It is clear that in the conditions of oppression and control represented by fascist politics, the results of our tactics cannot be statistically measurable at the level of the broad masses. However, it is undeniable that when specific elements of democratic and social-democratic parties shift over, even in a molecular fashion, towards the tactical terrain argued for by the communists, this shift cannot be ascribed to chance or have a purely individual significance. In practical terms, the question can be posed as follows: in every party, and especially in the democratic and social-democratic parties in which the organizational apparatus is very loose, there exist three strata.[222] The very tiny top stratum, which is usually made up of parliamentary deputies and intellectuals often closely linked to the ruling class. The bottom stratum, made up of workers, peasants and urban petty-bourgeois, which provides the mass of party members or the mass of those influenced by the party. An intermediate stratum, which in the present situation has an even greater importance than it had in normal periods, insofar as it often represents the only active and politically alive stratum in these parties. It is this intermediate stratum which maintains the link between the leading group at the top, and the mass of members and those influenced by the party. It is on the solidity of this middle stratum that the leading groups are counting, for a future renewal of these various parties and their reconstruction on a broad basis.

Now, it is precisely on a significant part of these middle strata of the various popular parties that the influence of the movement in favour of a united front is making itself felt. It is in this middle stratum that there is occurring this molecular phenomenon of disintegration of the old ideologies and old political programmes, and that the beginnings of a new political formation on the terrain of the united front can be seen. Old reformist or maximalist workers who exercise a wide influence in certain factories or certain urban neighbourhoods. Peasant elements who in the villages or little provincial towns represent the most advanced individuals in the rural world, to whom the peasants of those villages or little towns regularly turn for advice and practical directives. Petty intellectuals in the cities, who as exponents of the left catholic movement radiate an influence in the surrounding areas which cannot and must not be measured by their modest stature, but must instead be measured by the fact that outside the city they appear as a tendency of the party which the peasants were accustomed to follow. These then are the elements on which our party exercises a constantly growing power of attraction, and whose political exponents are a sure index of movements at the base that are often even more radical than appears from these individual shifts.

Particular attention must be paid to the function fulfilled by our youth in the activity for the united front. It is, therefore, necessary to keep in mind the fact that a greater flexibility must be allowed in the actions of the youth organization than is allowed to the party. It is obvious that the party cannot go in for fusion with other political groups, or for recruitment of new members on the basis of the united front, whose purpose is to create unity of action of the working class and the alliance between workers and peasants, and which cannot be the basis for party formations. For the young communists, on the other hand, the question is posed differently. By their very nature, the young communists represent the party's elementary, formative stage. In order to join the "youth organization", candidates cannot be required already to be communists in the complete sense of the word, but simply to have the desire to struggle and to become a communist. Hence this factor must serve as a general point of reference, in order to define more clearly the tactics appropriate for the communist youth.

One element which must always be taken into account, because its historical significance is not negligible, is the following. The fact that a maximalist, a reformist, a republican, a member of the Popular party or the Sardinian movement, or a democrat from the South should support the programme of the proletarian united front and workers' and peasants' alliance is certainly important. But the fact that a member of Catholic Action as such should support such a programme is of far greater importance. In fact, the opposition parties, albeit in inadequate and inchoate ways, tend to create and maintain a separation between the popular masses and fascism. Catholic Action, on the other hand, today represents an integral part of fascism. It tends through religious ideology to give fascism the agreement of broad masses of the people. And it is destined in a certain sense, in the minds of a very strong tendency within the Fascist Party (Federzoni, Rocco, etc.), to replace the Fascist Party itself in its function as a mass party and organism for political control of the population. Every success on our part, however limited, in the Catholic Action field therefore means that we are succeeding in preventing the accomplishment of fascist policy in a field which seemed shut off from any kind of proletarian initiative.

To conclude on this point, we may assert that the political line of the Third Congress has been verified as correct, and the balance-sheet of our actions for the united front is extremely positive.

It is necessary to include a special point on trade-union activity — both in the sense of the position which we occupy today in the class unions, and also in the sense of a real trade-union activity to be carried out and in that of our position with respect to the corporations.

The Two Tendencies of Fascism

On point 2, it is necessary to define with precision the internal situation of the fascist bourgeois/agrarian bloc, and of the fascist organization properly speaking. On the one hand, the Federzoni, Rocco, Volpi, etc., tendency wants to draw the conclusions from this whole period since the March on Rome. It wants to liquidate the Fascist Party as a political organism, and incorporate into the State apparatus the bourgeois position of strength created by fascism in its struggles against all the other parties. This tendency is working together with the Crown and the general staff. It wants to incorporate into the central forces of the State, on the one hand, Catholic Action, i.e. the Vatican, putting an end *de facto* and possibly even formally to the quarrel between the House of Savoy and the Vatican; and on the other hand, the more moderate elements of the former Aventine opposition. It is certain that while fascism in its nationalist wing, given the past and the traditions of old Italian nationalism, is working towards Catholic Action, on the other hand the House of Savoy is once again trying to exploit its traditions in order to draw into government spheres the members of the Di Cesarò and Amendola groups.

The other tendency is officially represented by Farinacci. It objectively represents two contradictions of fascism. 1. The contradiction between landowners and capitalists, whose interests clash in particular over tariffs. It is certain that the fascism of today typically represents the clear predominance of finance capital over the State: capital which seeks to enslave all the country's productive forces. 2. The second contradiction, which is far more important, is that between the petty bourgeoisie and capitalism. The fascist petty bourgeoisie sees in the party the instrument for its defence, its Parliament, its democracy. Through the party, it seeks to put pressure on the government to prevent it from being crushed by capitalism.

One element which must be kept in mind is the fact of the total enslavement to America to which Italy has been subjected by the fascist government. In the liquidation of its war debt to both America and England, the fascist government did not take the trouble to obtain any guarantee of the negotiability of Italian obligations. The Italian stock-market and exchequer are at all times exposed to the political blackmail of the American and English governments, who can at any moment release enormous quantities of Italian currency onto the world market. Moreover, the Morgan debt was incurred under even worse conditions.[223] Of the hundred million dollars of this loan, the Italian government has only 33 million at its disposal. The other 67 million, the Italian government can only make use of with the generous personal consent of Morgan, which means that Morgan is the real head of the Italian government. These elements may cause the petty bourgeoisie, in defending its interests through the Fascist Party as such, to take on a nationalist intonation – against the old nationalism and the present leadership of the party, which has sacrificed the country's national sovereignty and political independence to the interests of a small group of plutocrats. In connection with this, one of our party's tasks must be that of putting especial stress on the slogan of the United Soviet States of Europe, as an instrument of political initiative among the fascist rank-and-file.

In general, it can be said that the Farinacci tendency in the Fascist Party lacks unity, organization, general principles. It is more a diffuse state of mind than a tendency properly speaking. It will not be very hard for the government to disintegrate its constitutent nuclei. What is important, from our point of view, is that this crisis, insofar as it represents the detachment of the petty bourgeoisie from the fascist bourgeois/landowner coalition, cannot fail to be an element of military weakness for fascism.

The general economic crisis is the fundamental element of the political crisis. It is necessary to study the elements of this crisis, because certain of them are inherent in the general Italian situation and will operate negatively in the period of proletarian dictatorship as well. These main elements can be defined as follows: of the three elements which traditionally make up the assets in the Italian balance of trade, two – remittances from emigrants and the tourist industry – have collapsed. The third element, exports, are going through a crisis. If to the two negative factors (emigrants' remittances and tourist industry) and to the third, partially negative factor (exports), one adds the need for heavy imports of grain due to the failure of the harvest, it is clear that the perspectives for the coming months look catastrophic.

It is necessary to keep these four elements in mind, in order to understand the impotence of the government and the ruling class. Certainly, if the government can do nothing, or next to nothing, to increase remittances from emigrants (take account of the initiative proposed by signor Giuseppe Zuccoli, expected successor to Volpi at the Ministry of Finance) or to make the tourist industry prosper, it can nevertheless do something to increase exports. At all events, a grand strategy is possible here, which even if it did not heal the wound would at least tend to cicatrize it. Some people are thinking in terms of the possibility of a labour policy based on inflationism. Naturally this possibility cannot be absolutely excluded, but: 1. even if it came to pass, its results in the economic field would be relatively minimal; 2. its results in the political field, on the other hand, would be catastrophic.

In reality, it is necessary to keep the following elements in mind. 1. Exports represent only a part of the credit side of the Italian balance of trade, at most two-thirds. 2. To wipe out the deficit, it would be necessary not only to obtain the maximum yield from the existing productive base, but to enlarge the productive base itself by buying new machinery abroad, which would increase the trade deficit even further. 3. The raw materials for Italian industry are imported from abroad, and must be paid for in a hard currency. An increase of production on a large scale would lead to the necessity for an enormous mass of circulating capital for the acquisition of raw materials. 4. It must be borne in mind that fascism as a general phenomenon has, in Italy, reduced the wages and salaries of the working class to a minimum. Inflation makes some sense in a country with high wages, as an alternative to fascism, in order to lower the standard of living of the working classes and thus restore freedom of manoeuvre to the bourgeoisie. It makes no sense in Italy, where the working class's standard of living is already at subsistence level.

Among the elements of the economic crisis: the new organization of joint-stock companies with preferential voting, which is one of the elements of rupture between petty bourgeoisie and capitalism; and the imbalance which has recently appeared between the gross capital of the joint-stock companies, which is becoming concentrated in fewer and fewer hands, and the gross national savings. This imbalance shows that the sources of savings are drying up, since current incomes are no longer sufficient for needs.

The Democratic Coalition

On the third political element. It is clear that a certain regroupment is taking place in the democratic field, of a more radical character than in the past. Republican ideology is becoming stronger, in the same sense as for the united front, i.e. among the middle strata of the democratic parties, and in this case also to a considerable degree among the higher strata.

Old former Aventine leaders have refused the invitation to resume contact with the monarchy. It is said that even Amendola himself had become totally republican in the last period of his life, and carried out personal propaganda along these lines. The *popolari* have apparently become disposed to republicanism too, etc. It is certain that great efforts are being made to bring about a neo-democratic regroupment on the terrain of republicanism: a regroupment designed to take power when fascism collapses, and to instal a dictatorship aimed both against the reactionary right and against the communist left. The most recent European events, like the Pilsudski adventure in Poland and the dying convulsions of the French cartel, have contributed to this democratic republican reawakening.[224] Our party must confront the general problem of the country's political perspectives.

The elements can be established as follows. Though it is true that, politically, fascism may be succeeded by a dictatorship of the proletariat – since no intermediate party or coalition is capable of giving even the most minimal satisfaction to the economic requirements of the working classes, who will burst violently onto the political scene the moment existing relations are broken – it is nevertheless not certain, and not even probable, that the passage from fascism to the dictatorship of the proletariat will be a direct one. It is necessary to take account of the fact that the existing armed forces, given their composition, cannot at once be won over, and that they will be the determining element in the situation.

Hypotheses may be made with a continually increasing degree of verisimilitude. It is possible that the present government will give way to a coalition government, in which men like Giolitti, Orlando, Di Cesarò,

De Gasperi will provide a greater immediate flexibility. The most recent parliamentary events in France show what flexibility bourgeois policy is capable of, in order to postpone the revolutionary crisis, dislodge adversaries, tire them out and disintegrate them. A sudden, unexpected economic crisis, not improbable in a situation like the Italian one, could bring the republican democratic coalition to power, since it would present itself to the officers of the army, to a part of the fascist militia itself, and to the state functionaries in general (an element which has to be taken great account of in situations such as the Italian one), as capable of checking the revolution.

These hypotheses only serve us as a general perspective. They serve to fix the following points. 1. We must, from today, reduce to a minimum the influence and organization of the parties which may constitute the left coalition, in order to make more and more probable a revolutionary collapse of fascism, insofar as the energetic and active elements of the population are on our ground at the moment of the crisis. 2. In any case, we must strive to make the democratic interlude as brief as possible, by beginning from today to arrange the greatest number of favourable conditions to our advantage.

It is from these elements that we must derive the guidelines for our immediate, practical activity.

Intensification of the general activity of the united front and the organization of more and more new agitation committees, in order to centralize them at least on a regional and provincial level. In the committees, our fractions must seek first of all to obtain the maximum representation of the various left political currents, systematically avoiding all party sectarianism. The questions must be posed objectively by our fractions as an expression of the interests of the working class and the peasants.

Tactic towards the Maximalist party.

Need to pose the Southern problem more energetically. If our party does not begin to work seriously in the South, the South will be the strongest base for the left coalition.

Tactic towards the Sardinian Action Party, in view of its forthcoming congress.

For Southern Italy and the Islands, creation of regional work groups in the rest of Italy.

II

So far as the international situation is concerned, it seems to me to be dominated especially by the question of the English general strike, and the conclusions to be drawn from it.[225] The English strike has posed two fundamental problems for our movement.

The first of these is the problem of general perspectives; i.e. the problem of a precise assessment of the phase through which the capitalist order is currently passing. Is the period of so-called stabilization over? What point have we reached, with respect to the capacity of the bourgeois order for resistance? It is clear that not only from a theoretical and scientific point of view, but also from a practical and immediate point of view, it is interesting and necessary to verify precisely the exact point which the capitalist crisis has reached. But it is also clear that any new political orientation based on a different assessment of the precise level of the capitalist crisis would be stupid, if this different assessment is not immediately reflected in genuinely different political and organizational directives.

The problem to be posed, it seems to me, is the following. In the international field – and this, in practice, means two things: 1. in the field of the group of capitalist states which form the keystone of the bourgeois system; 2. in the field of those states which represent, as it were, the periphery of the capitalist world – are we about to pass from the phase of political organization of the proletarian forces, to the phase of technical organization of the revolution? Or, on the other hand, are we about to pass from the former of the phases mentioned to an intermediate phase, in which a particular form of technical organization can accelerate the political organization of the masses, and hence accelerate the passage to the concluding phase of the conquest of power? These problems in my view should be discussed. But it is obvious that it is not possible to solve them at a purely theoretical level. They can only be solved on the basis of concrete data, with respect to the real effectiveness both of the revolutionary and of the bourgeois forces.

A certain number of observations and criteria must form the basis for this study. The first of these concerns the fact that in the advanced capitalist countries, the ruling class possesses political and organizational reserves which it did not possess, for instance, in Russia. This means that even the most serious economic crises do not have immediate repercussions in the political sphere. Politics always lags behind economics, far behind. The state apparatus is far more resistant than is often possible to believe; and it succeeds, at moments of crisis, in organizing greater forces loyal to the régime than the depth of the crisis might lead one to suppose. This is especially true of the more important capitalist states.

In the typical peripheral states, like Italy, Poland, Spain or Portugal, the state forces are less efficient. But in these countries, one finds a phenomenon of which the greatest account must be taken. This phenomenon, in my view, consists in the following. In these countries, a broad stratum of intermediate classes stretches between the proletariat and capitalism: classes which seek to carry on, and to a certain sense succeed in carrying on, policies of their own, with ideologies which often influence broad strata of the proletariat, but which particularly affect the peasant masses. France too, although it occupies a prominent position in the first group of capitalist States, belongs by virtue of certain of its characteristics to the situation of the peripheral states.

What seems to me to be characteristic of the present phase of the capitalist crisis is the fact that, unlike in 1920–2, today the political and military formations of the middle classes have a left radical character, or at least they present themselves to the masses as left radicals. The development of the Italian situation, given its particular features, seems to me to be able, in a certain sense, to serve as a model for the various phases traversed by other countries. In 1919 and 1920, the military and political formations of the middle classes were represented in our country by primitive fascism and by D'Annunzio. It is well known that in those years, the fascist movement and D'Annunzio's movement alike were willing to ally themselves even with the revolutionary proletarian forces in order to overthrow the Nitti government, which appeared as American capital's go-between for the enslavement of Italy (Nitti was the precursor of Dawes in Europe).[226]

The second phase of fascism – 1921 and 1922 – was clearly reactionary. From 1923 on, a molecular process began through which the most active elements of the middle classes moved over from the reactionary fascist camp to the camp of the Aventine opposition. This process crystallized in a manner which might have proved fatal to fascism in the period of the Matteotti crisis. Because of the weakness of our movement, a weakness which moreover was itself significant, the phenomenon was interrupted by fascism and the middle classes were thrown back into a new state of political pulverization. Today, the molecular phenomenon has begun again, on a scale far greater than that which was started in 1923, and is accompanied by a parallel phenomenon of regroupment of the revolutionary forces around our party, which ensures that a new crisis of the Matteotti type could hardly culminate in a new 3 January.[227]

These phases traversed by Italy, in a form which I would call classical and exemplary, we find in all those countries which we have called peripheral capitalist countries. The present phase in Italy, i.e. a regroupment of the middle classes on the left, we can find in Spain, Portugal, Poland and in the Balkans. Only in two countries, Czechoslovakia and France, do we find a continuity in the permanency of the left bloc – a fact which in my view should be particularly closely studied.

The conclusion to be drawn from these observations, which of course will have to be improved and set out in a systematic manner, it seems to me might be the following. In reality, we are entering a new phase in the development of the capitalist crisis. This phase takes different forms, on the one hand in the countries of the capitalist periphery, and on the other in the advanced capitalist countries. Between these two series of states, Czechoslovakia and France represent the two connecting links. In the peripheral countries, the problem arises of the phase which I have called intermediate between the political and the technical preparation of the revolution. In the other countries, including France and Czechoslovakia, it seems to me that the problem is still one of political preparation. For all the capitalist countries, a fundamental problem is posed – the problem of the transition from the united front tactic, understood in a general sense, to a specific tactic which confronts the concrete problems of national life and operates on the basis of the popular forces as they are historically determined.

From a technical point of view, the problem concerns the appropriate slogans and forms of organization. If I did not have a certain fear of hearing cries of *Ordine Nuovo*-ism, I would say that today one of the most important problems we face, especially in the major capitalist countries, is the problem of factory councils and workers' control – as the basis for a new regroupment of the proletarian class, which will permit a more effective struggle against the trade-union bureaucracy and will permit us to organize the immense masses of non-unionized workers, not just in France, but also in Germany and in England.

In the case of England, it seems to me that in any case the problem of regrouping the proletarian masses can even be posed on the trade-union terrain itself. Our British party must have a programme for the democratic reorganization of the Trade Unions. Only insofar as local trade-union branches in England begin to coordinate their activities like our Chambers of Labour, and give these Chambers of Labour adequate powers, will it be possible: 1. to free the English workers from the influence of the trade-union bureaucracy; 2. to reduce the influence exercised within the Labour Party by MacDonald's party (I.L.P.), which today functions precisely as a local centralizing force in a context of trade-union fragmentation; 3. to create a terrain upon which it is possible for the organized forces of our party to exercise a direct influence on the mass of English workers. I think that this kind of reorganization of the trade unions, stimulated by our party, would have the significance and importance of a veritable soviet germination-process. Moreover, it would be in the line of the historical traditions of the English working class, from Chartism to the Action Committees of 1919.

The second fundamental problem posed by the English general strike is that of the Anglo-Russian Committee.[228] I think that despite the indecision, weakness and if you like betrayal of the English left during the general strike, the Anglo-Russian Committee should be maintained, because it is the best terrain to revolutionize not only the English trade-union world, but also the Amsterdam unions. In only one event should there be a break between the communists and the English left: if England was on the eve of the proletarian revolution, and our party was strong enough to lead the insurrection on its own.

Postscript. These notes have been written solely to prepare the work of the leading Committee. They are far from being definitive, but simply represent the draft for a first discussion.

72. THE PEASANTS AND THE DICTATORSHIP OF THE PROLETARIAT
(Notes for *Il Mondo*)

So we have a new article in *Il Mondo*, entitled – in accordance with the technique beloved of the old Barzinism and the new Calzinism – "Looking for Communism".[229] Naturally, it is in workers' and peasants' Russia that *Il Mondo* looks for communism. If we wanted to imitate the dialectical technique beloved of *Il Mondo*, we might write a whole series of articles entitled 'Looking for democracy', and demonstrate that democracy has never existed. And indeed, if democracy meant, as it cannot but mean, rule of the popular masses, expressed through a Parliament elected by universal suffrage, then in which country has the government ever existed which meets such criteria? In England itself, homeland and cradle of the parliamentary régime and of democracy, Parliament is flanked in government by the House of Lords and the Monarchy. The powers of democracy are in reality null. It does not exist. Before the War, in other words when the social-democrats and all the "friends of the people" could not yet accuse Bolshevism of having "provoked" the bourgeoisie and induced it (poor thing!) to abandon legality and resort to dictatorial means, Lord Carson was already able to arm and raise an army against the parliamentary bill on Irish freedom.[230]

And does democracy perhaps exist in France? Alongside Parliament there exists in France the Senate, which is elected not by universal suffrage, but by two levels of electors who in their turn are only partially an expression of universal suffrage; and there also exists the institution of the President of the Republic. The different terms of power fixed for the three basic institutions of the French Republic are intended to serve, according to official statements, to temper the possible excesses of the Parliament elected by universal suffrage. In reality, they are the mechanism through which the ruling class prepares to organize civil war in the best conditions for agitation and propaganda.

In Germany, there does not exist any institution of an aristocratic or oligarchic nature alongside Parliament. Yet we have recently been able to see the formidable braking power exerted on the so-called national will by the fact that the President of the Republic has an electoral base that is temporally different from the one which forms the national assembly. The votes obtained in the referendum for expropriating the former princes without indemnity were more numerous than those won by Marshal Hindenburg for his nomination as President of the Republic.[231] Nevertheless, Hindenburg did not resign. Having issued the blackmailing threat of a grave political crisis during the referendum campaign, after the referendum he continued to exert pressure to render the will of the popular masses null and void.

Certainly, we do not propose to convince the writers of *Il Mondo*. We know them, as we know their various bosses, from the Perrone brothers to Max Bondi, Count Matarazzo, Commander Pecoraino and the Banca Commerciale[232] – in whose service they write the most contradictory articles, but always designed to deceive the toiling masses. It is only for the masses' sake that we are writing to inquire: "Is it fair to ask of the new working-class régime that emerged in Russia in 1917, during the World War, after the greatest social and economic disaster that history has known, a one hundred per cent application of the maximum programme of the party which is in power in Russia, if one oneself represents and supports a régime which – in some centuries of existence – has not succeeded in realizing any of its programmatic promises, but has failed shamefully, capitulating before the most reactionary currents only to merge with them forthwith?"

Our paper must publish a whole series of documents which reply exhaustively to the questions raised by the writers of *Il Mondo*, questions which are essential for the international workers' movement, even if *Il Mondo* raises them in the most contorted and unintelligent way one could imagine. One confession which is implicit in a whole series of articles and in *Il Mondo's* prose must be taken up at once: for what exactly does *Il Mondo* mean by seeking to demonstrate that in Russia there does not exist the least element of social life, and by systematically keeping silent about the working-class character of the Russian State institutions, including cooperatives, banks and factory managements? *Il Mondo* means only to maintain the illusion among the broad mass of the people, that it is at least possible to obtain what exists today in Russia without a revolution, and without the total conquest of State power by the working class and peasants.

All *Il Mondo*'s arguments – from the one about the historical judgment to be made on Italian fascism, to this genuinely wretched critique on principle of the Russian economic and social structure – aim at this single goal. For us communists, the fascist régime is the expression of the most advanced stage of development of capitalist society. It precisely serves to demonstrate how all the conquests and all the institutions which the toiling classes succeed in realizing in the relatively peaceful period of development of the capitalist order are destined for annihilation, if at a given moment the working class does not seize State power with revolutionary means. So one can understand how the writers of *Il Mondo* have an interest in maintaining that fascism is a pre-democratic régime; that fascism is related to an incipient and still backward phase of capitalism.

So one can understand how the writers of *Il Mondo* – by presenting the readership of their paper (a readership unfortunately made up in large measure of workers and peasants) with a model of Russian society in which the bourgeois and petty-bourgeois elements are permeating the structure of the workers' State, over which they are destined inevitably to triumph through a restoration of the old régime – are seeking to re-present, in an updated form, the old utopian schema of democracy and reformism. According to this, the socialist elements – such as trade unions, cooperatives, socialist local councils, etc., etc. – which exist under the capitalist order could permeate the structure of the latter to the point where they would modify it completely, so leading to the bloodless victory of socialism. But, precisely, fascism has implacably destroyed such schemas, by destroying all the socialist (insofar as linked to the working class) elements which had been being formed in the period of development of the capitalist class.

There exist today in Russia socialist elements which are preponderant, and elements of petty-bourgeois economy which theoretically can develop, just as theoretically the socialist elements which existed in Italy before fascism could develop. But in Italy the proletariat has not conquered State power. The old capitalist organization, at a certain moment, put an end to the concessions it had made to the cooperatives, the unions, the socialist local councils: i.e. to the working class. In Russia, the working class in power – the working class which regulates and manages the essential parts of the national economy, the control-levers of the whole economic structure of Russian society – has made and does make concessions: not to the old society of the capitalists and big landowners, which was overthrown arms in hand and has been stripped of all property and all political rights, but to the peasant masses from whom theoretically the new capitalism could emerge.

There is, however, a little question which the gentlemen of *Il Mondo* seem to want to ignore, which is the following. Capitalism, as it emerges and develops, creates proletarians in numbers which far exceed that of the capitalists themselves. So the question – which the writers of *Il Mondo* think can be ignored – of establishing which class holds State power in its hands becomes a key question. In Russia today, the working class which has the State in its hands has an interest, if it wants to create an internal market capable of absorbing industrial production, in promoting and encouraging the development of agriculture. Since agriculture in Russia is still backward and can only be organized on an individual basis, the economic development of the Russian agricultural classes necessarily leads to a certain enrichment of an upper layer in the countryside. Every worker understands that if one carries out a policy to ensure that one hundred peasants will move from a yearly income of one thousand *lire* to one of two thousand *lire*, so that they will become able to buy more objects from socialized industry than they were able to with their original thousand *lire*, it is impossible to prevent certain of those one hundred peasants from moving not just from one to two thousand *lire*, but as a result of specific highly favourable circumstances reaching five or six thousand. While, at the other extreme, five or six peasants not only do not succeed in moving from an income of one to an income of two thousand *lire*, but as a result of extremely unfavourable circumstances (death of stock, hurricanes, etc.) will see their income of a thousand *lire* reduced to zero.

What is essential for the policies of the working class in Russia is that the central mass of peasants, through legislative provision, should achieve the results which the workers' State proposes: i.e. should become the basis for the formation of national savings which will serve to sustain the general apparatus of production in the hands of the working class, allowing this apparatus not just to maintain itself, but to develop. There does, however, exist this 4 or 5 per cent which develops beyond the limits foreseen by the legislation of the workers' State. And in a country like Russia, where the peasant masses represent a population of 100 million inhabitants, this 4 or 5 per cent becomes a social force – which can appear quite massive – of 4 or 5 million inhabitants. But if the working class, which in Russia today numbers at least 20 million inhabitants, retains its links to the great mass of peasants, which numbers scores of millions, the figure represented by the enemies of socialism is reduced to its just proportions in the overall picture, and the relatively peaceful victory of the socialist forces over the capitalist forces is ensured. We say relatively peaceful, because in fact in Russia the prisons are in the hands of the workers, the courts are in the hands of the workers, the police is in the hands of the workers, the army is in the hands of the workers. In other words, in Russia there exists a dictatorship of the proletariat, a socialist element which we are so foolish as to judge just a tiny bit more important than it is judged to be by the friends of the Perrone brothers, of Max Bondi, of Count Matarazzo and of Commander Pecoraino!

Unsigned, *L'Unità*, 17 September 1926.

73. ONCE AGAIN ON THE ORGANIC CAPACITIES OF THE WORKING CLASS [233]

Six years have passed since September 1920. In the intervening period, many things have changed among the working-class masses who in September 1920 occupied the factories in the metal-working industry. A notable part of the most active and combative workers, who in those years of heroic struggle represented the vanguard of the working class, are outside Italy. Marked with a triple cross on the black lists; after months and months of unemployment; after having tried every way (by changing trade, isolating themselves in small plants, etc., etc.) of remaining in their homeland to continue the revolutionary struggle, and to reconstruct each day the links which each day reaction was destroying; after unheard of sacrifices and sufferings – they were forced to emigrate. Six years are a long time. A new generation has already entered the factories: of workers who in 1920 were still adolescents or children, and who at most took part in political life by acting out in the streets the war between the Red Army and the Polish Army, and by refusing to be the Polish one even in a game. Yet the occupation of the factories has not been forgotten by the masses, and this is true not just of the working-class masses but also of the peasant masses. It was the general test of the Italian revolutionary class, which as a class showed that it was mature; that it was capable of initiative; that it possessed an incalculable wealth of creative and organizational energies. If the movement failed, the responsibility cannot be laid at the door of the working class as such, but at that of the Socialist Party, which failed in its duty; which was incapable and inept; which was at the tail of the working class not at its head.

The occupation of the factories is still on the agenda in the conversations and discussions which take place at the base, between vanguard elements and those who are more backward and passive, or between the former and class enemies. Recently, in a meeting of peasants and artisans in a village of Southern Italy (all sympathizers of our party), after a brief report on the present situation two kinds of questions were raised by those present.

1. What is happening in Russia? How are the local authorities organized in Russia? How do they succeed in getting the workers and

peasants to agree, given that the former want to buy foodstuffs cheap and the latter want to sell them at a decent price? Are the officers of the Red Army and the functionaries of the Soviet State like officers and functionaries in our country? Are they a different class, or are they workers and peasants?

2. Explain to us why we workers (an artisan was speaking, a blacksmith) abandoned the factories which we had occupied in September 1920. The gentry still say to us: "Did you occupy the factories, yes or no? Why then did you abandon them? Certainly because without 'capital' one cannot do anything. You sent away the capitalists and so the 'capital' was not there, and you went bankrupt." Explain the whole question to us, so that we will be able to reply. We know that the gentry are wrong, but we do not know how to put our arguments and often have to shut our mouths.

The revolutionary impact of the occupation of the factories was enormous, both in Italy and abroad. Why? Because the working masses saw in it a confirmation of the Russian revolution, in a Western country more industrially advanced than Russia, with a working class that was better organized, technically more skilled, and industrially more homogeneous and cohesive than was the Russian proletariat in October 1917. Are we capable of running production for ourselves, in accordance with our interests and a plan of our own? – wondered the workers. Are we capable of reorganizing production in such a way as to transfer society as a whole onto new tracks leading to the abolition of classes and economic equality? The test was positive, within the limits in which it took place and developed; within the limits in which the experiment could be carried through; in the sphere of the problems that were posed and resolved.

The experiment was limited, in general, to relations within the factory. Contacts between one factory and another were minimal from the industrial point of view; they occurred only for purposes of military defence, and even in this sense they were rather empirical and rudimentary.

The positive aspects of the occupation of the factories can be briefly resumed under the following headings.

1. Capacity for self-government of the mass of workers. In normal mass activity, the working class generally appears as a passive element awaiting orders. During struggles, strikes, etc., the masses are required to show the following qualities: solidarity, obedience to the mass organization, faith in their leaders, a spirit of resistance and sacrifice.

But the masses are static, like an immense body with a tiny head.

The occupation of the factories required an unprecedented multiplicity of active, leading elements. Each factory had to put together its own government, which was invested at once with political and with industrial authority. Only a part of the technicians and white-collar employees remained at their posts; the majority deserted the plants. The workers had to choose from their own ranks technicians, clerks, managers, foremen, accountants, etc. etc. This task was performed brilliantly. The old management, when it took up its functions again, had no administrative difficulties to overcome. The normal functions of an enterprise had been kept up to date, in spite of the fact that the technical and administrative personnel was extremely limited and made up of "crude, ignorant" workers.

2. Capacity of the mass of workers to maintain or exceed the capitalist order's level of production. The following occurred. The work force was reduced – because a tiny proportion did desert their work; because a certain proportion was assigned to military defence; because a certain proportion was working to produce objects that were not precisely for current use, although they were very useful for the proletariat;[234] and because workers had had to replace the majority of technicians and white-collar workers who had deserted – and in spite of all this, production kept up to the earlier level and often exceeded it. More cars were produced at FIAT than before the occupation, and the "workers'" cars displayed to the public daily by proletarian FIAT were not among the least of the reasons for the undeniable sympathy which the occupation enjoyed among the general population of the city of Turin, including among intellectuals and even tradesmen (who accepted the workers' goods as excellent currency).

3. Limitless capacity for initiative and creation of the working masses. An entire volume would be needed to cover this point fully. Initiative developed in every direction. In the industrial field, because of the need to resolve technical questions of industrial organization and production. In the military field, in order to turn every slight possibility into an instrument of defence. In the artistic field, through the capacity shown on Sundays to find ways of entertaining the masses by theatrical and other performances, in which *mise-en-scène*, production, everything was devised by the workers. It was really necessary to see with one's own eyes old workers, who seemed broken down by decades upon decades of oppression and exploitation, stand upright even in a physical sense during the period of the occupation – see them develop

fantastic activities; suggesting, helping, always active day and night. It was necessary to see these and other sights, in order to be convinced how limitless the latent powers of the masses are, and how they are revealed and develop swiftly as soon as the conviction takes root among the masses that they are arbiters and masters of their own destinies.

As a class, the Italian workers who occupied the factories revealed themselves to be up to their tasks and functions. All the problems which the needs of the movement posed for them to resolve were resolved brilliantly. They could not resolve the problems of re-stocking or communications, because the railways and merchant fleet were not occupied. They could not resolve the financial problems, because the institutes of credit and commercial firms were not occupied. They could not resolve the big national and international problems, because they did not conquer State power. These problems should have been confronted by the Socialist Party and by the unions, which instead capitulated shamefully, giving the immaturity of the masses as a pretext. In reality, it was the leaders who were immature and incapable, not the class. This was the reason why the Livorno split took place and a new party was created, the Communist Party.

First Note. The *Tribuna* finds that our method of reading is "subjective". On questions of method, *Tribuna*'s author gives a helping hand to the *Mondo* correspondent, who despite the intellectual vicinity of Adriano Tilgher has managed to call in question Einstein and relativism.[235] With the "objective" method of *Tribuna*, men would still be clinging to the idea that the earth stands still while the sun moves round it. We think *Tribuna*'s correspondent is confusing "subjectivism" with common "intelligence".

Second note. A correspondent from *Regime Fascista* has intervened in the discussion about the organic capacity of the working class, demonstrating merely that he does not know even the political nomenclature in Soviet Russia. We are told that the *Regime Fascista* writer is a certain Father Pantaleo, who has thrown off the habit. It is remarkable how many talented unfrocked priests and monks are fuelling the anti-working-class and anti-Bolshevik campaign in our country, under the banner of religion and Catholicism – they who are at least excommunicated: Romolo Murri, political columnist of *Il Resto del Carlino*; Don Preziosi of *Vita Italiana* and *Il Mezzogiorno*; Aurelio

Palmieri, the former Jesuit who serves as parsley in every anti-Soviet sauce; and this Father Pantaleo of *Regime Fascista*.

Unsigned, *L'Unità*, 1 October 1926

74. WE AND THE REPUBLICAN CONCENTRATION

In the article which we reported on at length yesterday, *Voce Repubblicana* seeks to convince us to replace our analysis of the Italian situation and our perspectives by its own fossilized models.[236] The *Voce*'s model is as follows: the 'Republican Concentration' should be seen by the communists as a favourable element for its own game [*sic*], because it is potentially capable of breaking the present equilibrium and endowing political struggle with a rapid tempo, pregnant with possibilities. In short, we ought to reason as follows. Before the October Revolution, there was the February Revolution. Before Lenin, there was Kerensky. Come on then! Conscious Communists, let us set about looking for the Italian Kerensky. Who will it be? Who will it not be? Found him. It will be Arturo Labriola, the theorizer of the "Republican Concentration".

Well, this whole way of reasoning proposed by *Voce* seems enormously puerile to us. We communists do not have any "game", we are not "playing" with history. We seriously want to do a great deal, and do not have any pre-arranged model to apply, not even the Russian model. We have principles; a doctrine; concrete ends to achieve. It is only in relation to our principles, our doctrine and the ends to be achieved that we establish our real political line. Our 'Machiavelli' is the works of Marx and Lenin, not the editors of *Voce Repubblicana* and Hon. Arturo Labriola – who, in any case, only resemble Master Nicolò Machiavelli in the sense of the well-known lines:

> Behind the tomb of Machiavello
> Lie the bones of Stenterello[237]

For us, the form which our relations with the Republican Concentration should take is clear. In Italian society, which has attained the highest degree of capitalist development which it historically could attain, given the conditions of time and place, only one class is revolutionary in a complete and permanent sense: the industrial proletariat. But as a result of its specific development, the specific national conditions of capitalist development, Italian society has conserved many relics of the past: a whole series of institutions and political relations which weigh on the situation and cloud its fundamental lines. In other countries too, where capitalist forces are far more developed than in Italy, ancient institutions and political relations survive. In England, there is the monarchy, despite the fact that 85 per cent of the population is industrial. In England, the Church is a very powerful institution, even if it is not formally centralized like the Vatican. In England, the Upper Chamber carries out a function of prime importance, especially when the Conservative Party does not have a majority in the House of Commons. Shall we, therefore, say that England is a backward, pre-capitalist, semi-feudal country? And again: in England there is no republican party, although the monarchy exists. This means that the republican party does not necessarily exist and develop because there is a monarchy; but because there exist a class and considerable social groups which find the republican terrain most suitable for defending their own position and their own class or group interests.

However, we recognize that in the Italian situation the specific weight of the "relics" mentioned earlier is greater than in other countries. Precisely for this reason, within the general world situation there exists a specific Italian situation: in other words, a situation in which there exist certain peculiar features; in which the fascist government exists and not that of Baldwin or that of Poincaré – to express ourselves like the Seigneur de La Palice.[238] So the question is the following: what assessment should we make of the specific weight of the "relics" peculiar to Italy? They exist, they must be overcome. We are in agreement about that. But do they represent the content of the historical work of a whole epoch, a whole generation or more than a generation? Are they the main item on the agenda which history implacably compels us to complete? Or are they not rather only details, secondary aspects of our hard historical work? This is the problem that is posed. For us, the content of the historical work imposed upon the present generations is the realization of socialism. On the arduous and difficult road leading to this realization, we find corpses to be buried, relics to be brushed aside. We must do this, and we will do it because it is necessary. But there is one particular corpse which we have the specific task of burying: that of capitalism. And one road which we have to open up: that which leads to socialism. This is our specific duty, and nothing else. As we proceed along this road, we shall attend to the secondary tasks and questions of detail.

The Republican Concentration expresses these secondary questions of detail in the Italian situation. We recognize the existence and relative weight of the issues which it raises. Therefore, we pay attention to the Concentration, we discuss with its representatives, we have sought and will in all probability continue to seek a relationship of alliance with it. But if we take into consideration the historically positive sides of this political current, we cannot and must not hide from ourselves or from the proletariat its negative sides. Two classes face each other today: proletariat and bourgeoisie. The present situation is determined by the fundamental struggle between these two classes. But neither of these two classes is isolated; each has real and potential allies. The bourgeoisie has the upper hand because it is helped by its allies, because it has at its disposal a system of forces which it controls and leads. The proletariat struggles partly in order to take these allies away from the bourgeoisie and make them into its own auxiliary forces.

The Republican Concentration is the political expression of this oscillation of the intermediate forces; of this latent disequilibrium of the forces which will decide the outcome of the historic duel between the two fundamental classes. If these forces shift *en masse*, if there is a social landslide of the intermediate layers towards the Republican Concentration, the bourgeoisie as a "class" will at once shift onto the same terrain and will become republican in twenty-four hours. For it will not want to remain isolated, and will understand that only by moving in this way could it preserve its essential positions. The *Voce* is touchingly naive when it invokes the attitude of the left groups of the anti-fascist bourgeoisie (*Popolari* and Constitutional Democrats). Today in Germany, the President of the Republic is called Hindenburg and the Prime Minister is called Dr. Marx, of the Catholic Centre: it is very probable that as recently as October 1918, neither one of them thought to become the Head of State or Prime Minister of a German Republic.

For (and this is the point) when could the social landslide of the intermediate layers occur? It could only occur in the event of a menacing renewal of the proletariat's revolutionary energies; only if capitalism showed itself incapable of satisfying any longer the essential needs of national life. But we believe that precisely at that moment it is necessary for the proletariat to be politically and ideologically united as a class, so that it will be able to resolve its essential problems – coordinating them naturally with the solution of the other national questions linked to classes and social groups which will fight at its side.

There: we are working for the proletariat to be the ruling class in a renewed Italian society. The Republican Concentration is working to subordinate the proletariat to other social forms – which in practice can only be capitalism, because only one of these two classes can govern the country. On this terrain, no Machiavellism – whether an old or a new brand – will succeed in disturbing the limpidity of the relationships which fascism has so brutally created. Only one republican concentration has a 'permanent' and historically stable perspective of success in Italy today: that which has the proletariat as its fundamental axis. Our party has seen the problem in its full dimensions since June 1923, and it is no accident that the present 'concentrationists' have only marked time.

Unsigned, *L'Unità*, 13 October 1926.

75. ON THE SITUATION IN THE BOLSHEVIK PARTY

I

Gramsci to Togliatti

Dearest Friend,

I enclose the document mentioned to you in another letter.[239] You will have it recopied and translated, adding if you wish our names, which in any case should not be published. You can go over the text and make any changes of detail or form, in view of the haste with which it was composed. The essential terms of it, however, must be kept intact. Since we want to help the majority of the Central Committee, you can come to an agreement with the more responsible of them about these changes. Send immediately a copy of the definitive text. Our impression is fairly pessimistic; that is why we felt the letter was necessary.

I am waiting for the corrected and collated text of Antonio Labriola's letters, with Ryazanov's preface. It is needed for the first issue of *L'Ordine Nuovo*.[240] The utmost speed is necessary.

I will send the articles for I.C. shortly, I hope. Greetings to all.

Antonio

II

To the Central Committee of the Soviet Communist Party

Dear comrades,

The Italian communists and all the conscious workers of our country have always followed your discussions with the greatest attention. On the eve of every congress and every conference of the Russian Communist Party we were confident that, despite the sharpness of the polemics, the unity of the Russian party was not in danger. We were indeed confident that, having achieved a greater ideological and organizational homogeneity through such discussions, the party would be better prepared and equipped to overcome the multiple difficulties which attend the exercise of power in a workers' state. Today, on the eve of your XV Conference, we no longer have the confidence we had in the past. We cannot free ourselves from a sense of anguish. It seems to us that the present attitude of the opposition bloc and the sharpness of the polemics within the Communist Party of the USSR necessitate intervention by the fraternal parties. It is precisely by this conviction that we are motivated, in addressing this letter to you. It may be that the isolation in which our party is forced to exist has led us to exaggerate the dangers in connection with the internal situation in the Communist Party of the USSR. In any case, our judgement of the international repercussions of this situation is certainly not exaggerated, and as internationalists we wish to carry out our duty.

The present situation in our brother party in the USSR seems to us different and far more serious than in previous discussions, because today we see occurring, and deepening, a split in the Leninist central group which has always been the leading nucleus of the party and the International. A split of this kind, independently of the numerical results of the congress votes, can have the most serious repercussions, not only if the oppositional minority does not accept with the greatest loyalty the fundamental principles of revolutionary party discipline, but also if, in carrying on its polemics and its struggle, it goes beyond certain limits which are above all formal democracy.

One of Lenin's most precious lessons was that we should pay great attention to the opinions of our class enemies. Well, dear comrades, it is certain that the strongest press organs and statesmen of the international bourgeoisie are counting on this organic character of the conflict that exists within the fundamental nucleus of the Communist Party of the USSR: are counting on a split in our brother party, and are convinced that this must lead to the disintegration and slow death-agony of the proletarian dictatorship; that it will bring about the ruin of the revolution, which the invasions and the white-guard revolts did not succeed in bringing about. The very coolness and circumspection with which the bourgeois press today seeks to analyse Russian events, and the fact that it seeks to avoid so far as it can the violent demagogy which was more characteristic of it in the past, are symptoms which should cause the Russian comrades to reflect and make them more conscious of their responsibility.

For another reason too, the international bourgeoisie is counting on a possible split or on a worsening of the internal crisis in the Communist Party of the USSR. The workers' state has now existed in Russia for nine years. It is certain that only a little minority, not merely of the working classes but even of the communist parties themselves, in the other countries is capable of reconstructing in its entirety the whole development of the revolution, and of finding even in the details of which everyday life is made up in the Soviet state the continuity of the red thread which leads to the general perspective of the construction of socialism. This is true, not only in those countries where freedom of association no longer exists and freedom of the press has been totally suppressed or subjected to unprecedented limitations, as in Italy (where the courts have confiscated and forbidden the printing of the books of Trotsky, Lenin, Stalin, Zinoviev and most recently of the *Communist Manifesto* as well), but also in those countries where our parties still have the possibility of supplying their members and the masses in general with an adequate documentation.

In these countries, the great masses cannot understand the discussions which are taking place in the Communist Party of the USSR, especially if they are as violent as the present one and concern not some question of detail, but the political line of the party in its entirety. Not just the working masses in general, but even the mass of members within our parties see, and wish to see, in the Republic of the Soviets and in the party which is in power there, a single combat unit that is working in the general perspective of socialism. Only insofar as the West European masses see Russia and the Russian party from this point of view, do they accept freely and as a historically necessary fact that the CPSU should be the leading party in the International; only for that reason, are the Republic of the Soviets and the CPSU today a formidable element of revolutionary organization and propulsion.

The bourgeois and social-democratic parties, for the same reason, exploit the internal polemics and the conflicts which exist within the CPSU. They want to combat this influence of the Russian revolution; to combat the revolutionary unity which is being forged around the CPSU throughout the world. Dear comrades, it is extremely significant that in a country like Italy – where the fascist State and party organization succeeds in stifling every noteworthy manifestation of autonomous life on the part of the great mass of workers and peasants – it is significant that the fascist papers, especially those in the provinces, are full of articles, technically well constructed for propaganda purposes, with the minimum of demagogy or insulting comment, in which an attempt is made to demonstrate with a manifest effort to achieve objectivity that now, as is proved by the best-known leaders of the Joint Opposition in the CPSU themselves, the State of the Soviets is inexorably becoming a purely capitalist State, and that hence in the world duel between fascism and Bolshevism, fascism will come out on top. This campaign, if it shows that the Republic of the Soviets still enjoys limitless sympathy among the great mass of the Italian people, who in some regions have only received a trickle of illegal party literature for six years now, also shows that fascism, which knows very well the real internal situation in Italy and has learnt to deal with the masses, is seeking to utilize the political stance of the Joint Opposition to break definitively the firm aversion of the workers to Mussolini's government, and to bring about a state of mind in which fascism can appear at least as an ineluctable historical necessity, notwithstanding the brutalities and other ills which accompany it.

We believe that, in the entire International, our party is the one which feels most keenly the repercussions of the serious situation which exists in the CPSU. This is the case, not just for the reasons set out above, which are so to speak *external* ones, which relate to the general conditions of revolutionary development in our country. You know that all the parties of the International have inherited, both from the old social-democracy and from the differing national traditions that exist in the various countries (anarchism, syndicalism, etc., etc.), a mass of prejudices and ideological features which represent the breeding-ground for all deviations, of both the right and the left. In the last years, but especially after the Fifth World Congress, our parties were beginning to achieve, through painful experience and through wearisome, exhausting crises, a secure Leninist stabilization; they were beginning to become true Bolshevik parties. New proletarian cadres were being created from below, from the factories. The intellectual elements were subjected to a rigorous selection-process, and to a pitilessly strict test on the basis of their practical work, on the terrain of action. This reworking took place under the guidance of the CPSU as a united ensemble and of all the great leaders of the CPSU.

Well, the sharpness of the present crisis, and the threat of an open or latent split that it contains, is halting this process of development and elaboration; crystallizing right and left deviations; putting off once again the achievement of an organic unity of the world party of workers. It is upon this aspect, in particular, that we believe it is our duty as internationalists to call the attention of the most responsible comrades of the CPSU. Comrades, in these past nine years of world history you have been the organizing and propulsive element of the revolutionary forces in all countries. The function which you have fulfilled has no precedent to equal it in breadth and depth, in the entire history of humanity. But today you are destroying your work. You are degrading, and run the risk of annihilating, the leading function which the CPSU won through Lenin's contribution. It seems to us that the violent passion of Russian affairs is causing you to lose sight of the international aspects of Russian affairs themselves; is causing you to forget that your duties as Russian militants can and must be carried out only within the framework of the interests of the international proletariat.

The Political Bureau of the Italian Communist Party has studied with the greatest care and attention of which it was capable all the problems which are today under discussion in the CPSU. The questions which are posed for you today, may be posed for our party tomorrow. In our country too, the rural masses make up the majority of the working population. Moreover, all the problems inherent in the proletariat's hegemony will certainly present themselves in our country in a more complex and sharp form even than in Russia – because the density of the rural population in Italy is enormously greater; because our peasants have an extremely rich tradition of organization, and have always succeeded in making their specific mass weight felt very keenly in national political life; because the organizational apparatus of the Church has two thousand years of tradition behind it in our country, and has specialized in propaganda and in the organization of the peasants in a way which has no equal in other countries. If it is true that industry is more developed in our country, and the proletariat has a considerable material basis, it is also true that this industry does not have raw materials within the country and is therefore more exposed to crises. Hence, the proletariat will only be able to carry out its leading function if it is very rich in the spirit of sacrifice, and has freed itself completely from every residue of reformist or syndicalist corporativism.

From this realistic and we believe Leninist point of view, the Political Bureau of the Italian Communist Party has studied your discussions. Hitherto, we have expressed a party view only on the strictly disciplinary question of factions, since we wished to respect the request you made after your XIV congress not to take the Russian discussion into the other sections of the International. Now we declare that we consider basically correct the political line of the majority of the Central Committee of the CPSU, and that the majority of the Italian Party will certainly take the same position, if it becomes necessary to pose the whole question. We do not wish, and we think it useless, to carry out agitation or propaganda *vis-à-vis* you, or *vis-à-vis* the comrades of the Joint Opposition. We will not, therefore, make a list of all the specific questions with our opinion in the margin. We repeat that we are struck by the fact that the attitude of the opposition concerns the entire political line of the Central Committee, and touches the very heart of the Leninist doctrine and the political action of our Soviet party. It is the principle and practice of the proletariat's hegemony that are brought into question; the fundamental relations of alliance between workers and peasants that are disturbed and placed in danger: i.e. the pillars of the workers' State and the revolution.

Comrades, history has never seen a dominant class, in its entirety, experiencing conditions of living inferior to those of certain elements and strata of the dominated and subjected class. This unprecedented contradiction has been reserved by history as the destiny of the proletariat. In this contradiction lie the greatest dangers for the dictatorship of the proletariat, especially in those countries where capitalism has not had any great development or succeeded in unifying the productive forces. It is from this contradiction, which moreover already appears in certain forms in those capitalist countries where the proletariat has objectively reached a high social function, that reformism and syndicalism, the corporate spirit and the stratifications of the labour aristocracy are born.

Yet the proletariat cannot become the dominant class if it does not overcome this contradiction through the sacrifice of its corporate interests. It cannot maintain its hegemony and its dictatorship if, even when it has become dominant, it does not sacrifice these immediate interests for the general and permanent interests of the class. Certainly, it is easy to be demagogic in this sphere. It is easy to insist on the negative sides of the contradiction: "Are you the ruler, o badly dressed and badly fed workers? Or is the Nepman in his furs, with all the goods of the earth at his disposal, the real ruler?" Similarly the reformists, after a revolutionary strike which has increased the cohesion and discipline of the masses, but which as a result of its long duration has yet further impoverished the individual workers involved, say: "What was the point of struggling? You are ruined and impoverished!" It is easy to be demagogic in this sphere, and it is hard not to be when the question has been posed in terms of corporate spirit and not in those of Leninism, the doctrine of the hegemony of the proletariat, which historically finds itself in one particular position and not in another.

For us, this is the essential element in your discussions; it is in this element that the root of the errors of the Joint Opposition, and the origin of the latent dangers contained in its activities, lie. In the ideology and practice of the Joint Opposition are born again, to the full, the whole tradition of social-democracy and syndicalism which has hitherto prevented the Western proletariat from organizing itself as a leading class.

Only a firm unity and a firm discipline in the party which governs the workers' State can ensure proletarian hegemony under the régime of the New Economic Policy – i.e. amid the full development of the contradiction to which we have referred. But the unity and discipline in this case cannot be mechanical and enforced. They must be loyal and due to conviction, and not those of an enemy unit imprisoned or besieged, whose only thought is of escape or an unexpected sortie.

This, dearest comrades, is what we wished to say to you, brothers and friends, even if younger brothers. Comrades Zinoviev, Trotsky, Kamenev have contributed powerfully to educating us for the revolution; they have at times corrected us with great force and severity; they have been among our masters. To them especially we address ourselves, as those principally responsible for the present situation, because we like to feel certain that the majority of the Central Committee of the USSR does not intend to win a crushing victory in the struggle, and is disposed to avoid excessive measures. The unity of our brother party in Russia is necessary for the development and triumph of the world revolutionary forces. To this necessity, every communist and internationalist must be prepared to make the greatest sacrifices. The damage caused by the error of a united party is easily mended; that caused by a split, or a prolonged condition of latent split, may easily be irreparable and fatal.

With communist greetings.

The Political Bureau of the PCI

III

Togliatti to Gramsci[241]

18 October 1926

Dearest Antonio,

This is to give you, very briefly, my opinion concerning the letter of the Political Bureau of the Italian Communist Party to the Central Committee of the Communist Party of the USSR. I do not agree with that letter, for several reasons, which I will mention in a very schematic fashion.

1. The basic defect of the letter lies in its point of departure. The fact of the split that has taken place in the leading group of the Union's Communist Party is put in the foreground, and the problem of the correctness or otherwise of the line being followed by the majority of the Central Committee is only confronted at a secondary level. This procedure is characteristic of the way in which many comrades in the Western parties consider and judge the problems of the Communist Party in the Union; but it does not correspond to an adequate approach to these problems. There is no doubt that the unity of the leading group of the Russian Communist Party has a value which cannot be compared with the value of unity in the leading groups of other parties. This value derives from the historical task which has fallen to this group in the constitution of the International. Yet however great this may be, it should not lead us to judge the problems of the Russian Communist Party on the basis of a line other than the line of political principles and positions.

The danger inherent in the position that is taken in your letter is a great one, because probably, from now on, the unity of the Leninist old guard will no longer be – or will be only with difficulty – realized in a continuous manner. In the past, the main factor in this unity was provided by the enormous prestige and the personal authority of Lenin. This element cannot be replaced. The line of the party will be fixed through discussion and debate. We must become accustomed to remain cool, and to see to it that the comrades at the base remain cool. And we must initiate ourselves and the party militants into a knowledge of Russian problems, in such a way as to be able to judge them according to the line of political principles and positions. It is in this study of Russian problems, and not in appeals to the unity of the leading group, that the help which the other parties of the International should give to the Russian Communist Party consists. What you say about the need for an intervention of these parties in the clash between the Central Committee and the opposition is therefore correct; but this intervention can only take place in the form of a contribution – on the basis of our revolutionary experience – towards fixing and confirming the correct Leninist line in the solution of the Russian problems. If our intervention has any other point of departure, there is a danger that it will not be useful, but damaging.

2. The consequence of this incorrect point of departure is the fact

that in the first half of your letter, that precisely in which are set out the consequences which a split in the Russian party (and in its leading nucleus) can have in the Western movement, you speak indifferently of all the leading Russian comrades: i.e. you make no distinction between the comrades who are leading the Central Committee and the leaders of the opposition. On page two of Antonio's handwritten text, the Russian comrades are invited "to reflect and be more conscious of their responsibility". There is not the slightest hint of a distinction between them. On page six the text says: "It is upon this aspect, in particular, that we believe it is our duty as internationalists to call the attention of the most responsible comrades of the CPSU. Comrades, in these past nine years of world history you have been the organizing and propulsive element of the revolutionary forces in all countries. The function which you have fulfilled has no precedent to equal it in breadth and depth, in the entire history of humanity. But today you are destroying your work. You are degrading, and run the risk of annihilating, the leading function which the CPSU won through Lenin's contribution. It seems to us that the violent passion of Russian affairs is causing you to lose sight of the international aspects of Russian affairs themselves; is causing you to forget that your duties as Russian militants can and must be carried out only within the framework of the interests of the international proletariat." Here again, even the faintest distinction is lacking. The only possible conclusion to be drawn is that the Political Bureau of the Italian Communist Party considers that all are responsible, all must be called to order.

It is true that in the last part of the letter, this attitude is corrected. Zinoviev, Kamenev and Trotsky are said to be those "mainly" responsible, and the letter goes on: "we like to feel certain that the majority of the Central Committee of the USSR does not intend to win a crushing victory in the struggle, and is disposed to avoid excessive measures." The expression "we like to feel certain" implies certain reservations, i.e. it means that *one is not certain.*

Now, aside from any considerations about whether it is expedient, when intervening in the present Russian debate, to say that the Central Committee is partly to blame too; aside from the fact that such a position can only end up by benefiting *solely* the opposition; aside from these considerations of expediency – can one say that the Central Committee is partly to blame? I do not think so. The proof lies in the attempts made before the Fourteenth Congress to reach an agreement; and, more importantly, it lies in the policy followed after the Fourteenth

Congress, which was prudent and can in no way be accused of being a policy followed blindly in one direction. As for the internal life of the party, the Russian central leadership is no more responsible for the discussion, for the factionalism of the opposition, for the sharpness of the crisis, etc., than were we, the Italian central leadership, responsible for Bordiga's factionalism, for the establishment and the activity of the *Comitato d'Intesa*, etc. There is no doubt a certain rigour in the internal life of the Communist Party of the Union. But there must be. If the Western parties sought to intervene with the leading group to secure the disappearance of that rigour, they would be committing a very serious error. If they did that, the dictatorship of the proletariat could really be compromised.

Thus I think that the first half of your letter, and the observations which are appended in its conclusion, are politically a mistake. This mistake spoils what is good in the letter (including in its first part).

Another observation on this point. It is true that the foreign parties view with anxiety a sharpening of the crisis in the Russian Communist Party, and it is true that they seek as far as they can to render it less sharp. However, it is certain that, when one agrees with the line of the Central Committee, the best way of contributing to overcoming the crisis is to express one's own support for that line without putting any limits to it. If the Russian opposition had not counted on the support of certain opposition groups, or of entire parties in the International, it would not have taken the attitude that it has taken since the Fourteenth Congress. Experience shows that the opposition also utilizes the least waverings that are manifested in the positions of groups and parties known to agree with the Central Committee.

3. In the passage which I have already quoted, where the Russian comrades are reminded of their responsibilities, it is stated that they are losing sight of the international aspects of Russian questions. This statement loses sight of the fact that after the Fourteenth Congress, the Russian discussion shifted from mainly Russian problems to international ones.[242] The failure to remember this explains the fact that the letter makes no reference to these international problems, and this is a third serious defect.

4. Your letter is too optimistic when it speaks of the Bolshevization that has been carried out since the Fifth Congress, and it seems that you attribute the halt in the process of consolidation of the communist parties solely to the Russian discussion. Here, too, there is a limited judgement, and an incorrect assessment. It must be recognized,

on the one hand, that the Bolshevik solidity of certain of the leading groups placed at the head of our parties by the Fifth Congress was purely external (France, Germany, Poland), so that the subsequent crises were inevitable.[243] In the second place, it is also necessary to recognize that these crises are related to the change in the objective situation, and its repercussions within the vanguard of the working class, far more than they are to the Russian discussion. The Russian crisis too is related to this change, in the same way incidentally as all the previous crises and discussions, and in particular, for example, as that which was closed by the Tenth Congress and which has the greatest analogy with the present one.[244]

5. The letter is too pessimistic, by contrast, not merely with respect to the consequences of the Russian discussion, but in general with respect to the ability of the proletarian vanguard to understand what the line of the Russian Communist Party is, and to get it understood by the mass of workers. For this reason, you overestimate the damaging consequences of the Russian discussion within the Western proletariat, and your pessimism gives the impression that you consider the line of the party to be not entirely correct. If this line is correct and corresponds to the objective conditions, we must be able to ensure that the masses understand its validity, and we must also be able to keep the masses closely assembled around Russia and the Bolshevik Party, in spite of the discussions. Through discussions and splits, the Bolshevik Party succeeded in winning the leadership of the Russian proletariat. It seems to me that today you see the historic function of the Russian party and the Russian revolution in an external manner. It is not so much the unity of the leading group (which anyway has never been something absolute) that has made the Russian party the organizer and propulsive force of the world revolutionary movement since the War. It is rather the fact that the Russian party has enabled the working class to win power and maintain itself in power. Does the party's present line condemn it to fall short in this historic task, yes or no? This is the way in which the question of the Russian party's position in the international workers' movement should be posed, if one does not wish to fall straight into the opposition's arguments.

These are just a few observations made in haste. But they are, I believe, the fundamental ones. Let me know what you think.

Fraternally,

Palmiro Togliatti

IV

Gramsci to Togliatti

26 October 1926

Dearest Ercoli,

I have received your letter of the 18th. I am replying personally, although I am sure that I also express the view of the other comrades.

Your letter seems to me too abstract and too schematic in its manner of reasoning. We started off from the point of view, which seems to me correct, that in our countries there do not exist just parties, in the sense of technical organizations, but also the great working masses, which are politically stratified in a contradictory fashion, but which as a whole tend towards unity. One of the most forceful elements in this unitary process is the existence of the USSR, linked to the real activity of the CPSU and to the widespread conviction that the USSR is moving along the road to socialism. Insofar as our parties represent the entire active complex of the USSR, they have a specific influence on all political layers of the broad masses; they represent the unitary tendency; they operate on a historical terrain which is basically favourable, despite the contradictory superstructures.

But it should not be thought that this factor, which makes the CPSU the most powerful mass organizer that has ever appeared throughout history, has now been acquired in a stable and decisive form: quite the contrary. It is always unstable. Thus it should not be forgotten that the Russian revolution already has nine years of existence behind it, and that its present activity is an ensemble of partial actions and acts of government which only a very highly developed theoretical and political consciousness can grasp as an ensemble, and in its overall movement towards socialism. Not only for the great working masses, but also for a considerable part of the membership of the Western parties, who are distinguished from the masses only by that radical but initial step towards a developed consciousness which entry into the party represents, the overall movement of the Russian revolution is concretely represented by the fact that the Russian party moves in a united fashion: that the representative figures, whom our masses know and are used to knowing, work and move together. The question of unity, not only of the Russian party but also of the Leninist nucleus, is therefore a question of the greatest importance in the international field. It is, *from the mass point of view*, the most important question in this historical period of intensified contradictory process towards unity.

It is possible, and probable, that unity cannot be preserved – at least in the form which it had in the past. It is also certain that in any case the world will not come to an end, and that it is necessary to prepare the comrades and the masses for the new situation. That does not alter the fact that it is our absolute duty to recall to the political consciousness of the Russian comrades, and recall forcefully, the dangers and weaknesses which their attitudes are going to cause. We would be pretty miserable, irresponsible revolutionaries if we passively allowed *faits accomplis* to come into being, simply justifying their inevitability *a priori*.

The fact that our fulfilment of this duty may, as a side effect, *also* help the opposition, should worry us to some extent. In fact, our aim is to contribute to the maintenance and creation of a unitary plan, in which the various tendencies and personalities can draw closer and merge, even ideologically. But I do not think that in our letter, which naturally should be read as a whole and not in isolated passages torn out of context, there is any danger whatever of weakening the position of the Central Committee majority. In any case, precisely in view of this and the possibility of any such appearance, in a covering letter I had authorized you to modify the form. You could perfectly well have reversed the two parts, and put our statement about the opposition's "responsibility" right at the beginning. For this reason, the way in which you argue has made a very painful impression on me.

I would also like to inform you that there is not the least shadow of alarmism in our attitude, only careful, cool reflection. We are certain that the world will not come to an end in any case; but it would be stupid only to act if the world were about to come to an end, it seems to me. Thus no stock phrases are going to shift us from our conviction that we have the right line, the Leninist line, in our way of looking at the Russian questions. The Leninist line consists in struggling for the unity of the party, and not just for external unity, but for the rather more intimate variety which consists in there not being within the party two political lines which are completely different on all questions. Not just in our countries with respect to the ideological and political leadership of the International, but also in Russia with respect to the hegemony of the proletariat and thus the social content of the State, the unity of the party is a condition of existence.

You confuse the international aspects of the Russian question, which are a reflection of the historical fact of the link between the working masses and the first socialist state, and the problems of international organization in the trade-union and political spheres. The two orders of facts are closely inter-related, but nevertheless distinct. The difficulties which are met, and which have been arising, in the narrower organizational field are dependent on the fluctuations which take place in the wider field of diffuse mass ideology: i.e. on the shrinking of the Russian party's influence and prestige in certain popular areas. As a question of method, we wished to speak only of the more general aspects. We wished to avoid falling into the "first school essay" style which unfortunately appears in the documents of certain other parties, and robs their intervention of all seriousness.

Thus it is not true, as you say, that we are too optimistic about the real Bolshevization of the Western parties. Quite the contrary. The process of Bolshevization is so slow and difficult that even the tiniest obstacle halts it and slows its progress. The Russian discussion and the ideology of the opposition contribute all the more to this halting and slowing down, in that the opposition represents in Russia all the old prejudices of class corporatism and syndicalism which weigh upon the tradition of the Western proletariat, and delay its ideological and political development. Our observation was entirely directed against the opposition. It is true that the crises of the various parties, including that of the Russian party, are linked to the objective situation, but what does that mean? Does it perhaps mean that we should therefore cease struggling? That we should cease striving to modify the subjective elements in a favourable direction? Bolshevism consists precisely also in keeping a cool head, and in being ideologically and politically firm even in difficult situations. Your comment is therefore inert and has no validity.

So is the one contained in point 5, since we were speaking of the broad masses and not of the proletarian vanguard. However, in a secondary sense, the difficulty also arises for the latter, which is not suspended in mid air but united to the masses. And it arises all the more in that reformism, with its tendencies to class corporatism – i.e. to not understanding the leading role of the vanguard: a role to be preserved even at the price of sacrifices – has far deeper roots in the West than it had in Russia. Then you forget too easily the technical conditions in which the work is carried on in many parties, which do not permit the dissemination of more complex theoretical problems, except among small groups of workers. Your whole argument is tainted by "bureaucratism". Today, at nine years distance from October 1917, it is no longer *the fact of the seizure of power* by the Bolsheviks which can revolutionize the Western masses, because this has already been allowed for and has produced its effects. What is active today, ideologically and politically, is the conviction (if it exists) that the proletariat, once power has been taken, *can construct socialism*. The authority of the party is bound up with this conviction, which cannot be instilled in the broad masses by the methods of school pedagogy, but only by those of revolutionary pedagogy, i.e. only by the *political fact* that the Russian Party as a whole is convinced of it, and is fighting in a united fashion.

I am sincerely sorry that our letter was not understood by you, first of all, and that you did not in any case, in view of my personal note, try to understand better. Our letter was a *whole* indictment of the opposition, not made in demagogic terms, but precisely for that reason more effective and more serious. Please transmit this letter formally, together with the Italian text of the letter and my personal note.

Warm greetings,

Antonio

76. SOME ASPECTS OF THE SOUTHERN QUESTION

These notes were initially stimulated by the publication of an article on the Southern question by "Ulenspiegel" in the 18 September issue of the journal *Quarto Stato*, and by the somewhat comical editorial presentation which preceded it.[245] "Ulenspiegel" informed his readers of Guido Dorso's recent book *La Rivoluzione meridionale* (pub. Piero Gobetti, Turin, 1925), and alluded to the author's assessment of our party's position on the southern question.[246] In their presentation, the editors of *Quarto Stato* – who proclaim themselves to be "young people who know the Southern problem *thoroughly in its general lines*" [*sic*] – protest collectively at the idea that the Communist Party can be accorded any "merits". Nothing wrong so far: young people of the *Quarto Stato* type have always and everywhere expressed extreme opinions and violent protests on paper, without the paper rebelling. But then these "young people" add the following words: "We have not forgotten that the magical formula of the Turin Communists used to be: divide the big estates among the rural proletariat. This formula is at the antipodes from any sound, realistic vision of the Southern problem." And here it becomes necessary to set the record straight, since the only thing that is "magical" is the impudence and superficial dilettantism of the "young" writers of *Quarto Stato*.

The "magical formula" is a complete invention. And the "young people" of *Quarto Stato* must have a low opinion indeed of their extremely intellectual readers if they dare to distort the truth in this way, with such garrulous presumption. Here, in fact, is a passage from *L'Ordine Nuovo*, no. 3, January 1920, which sums up the viewpoint of the Turin Communists:

The Northern bourgeoisie has subjugated the South of Italy and the Islands, and reduced them to exploitable colonies; by emancipating itself from capitalist slavery, the Northern proletariat will emancipate the Southern peasant masses enslaved to the banks and the parasitic industry of the North. The economic and political regeneration of the peasants should not be sought in a division of uncultivated or poorly cultivated lands, but in the solidarity of the industrial proletariat. This in turn needs the solidarity of the peasantry and has an "interest" in ensuring that capitalism is not reborn economically from landed property; that Southern Italy and the Islands do not become a military base for capitalist counter-revolution. By introducing workers' control over industry, the proletariat will orient industry to the production of agricultural machinery for the peasants, clothing and footwear for the peasants, electrical lighting for the peasants, and will prevent industry and the banks from exploiting the peasants and subjecting them as slaves to the strongrooms. By smashing the factory autocracy, by smashing the oppressive apparatus of the capitalist State and setting up a workers' State that will subject the capitalists to the law of useful labour, the workers will smash all the chains that bind the peasant to his poverty and desperation. By setting up a workers' dictatorship and taking over the industries and banks, the proletariat will swing the enormous weight of the State bureaucracy behind the peasants in their struggle against the landowners, against the elements and against poverty. The proletariat will provide the peasants with credit, set up cooperatives, guarantee security of person and property against looters and carry out public works of reclamation and irrigation. It will do all this because an increase in agricultural production is in its interests; because to win and keep the solidarity of the peasants is in its interests; because it is in its interests to orient industrial production to work which will promote peace and brotherhood between town and countryside, between North and South.[247]

That was written in January 1920. Seven years have gone by and we are seven years older politically too. Today, certain concepts might be expressed better. The period immediately following the conquest of State power, characterized by simple workers' control of industry, could and should be more clearly distinguished from the subsequent periods. But the important thing to note here is that the fundamental concept of the Turin communists was not the "magical formula" of dividing the big estates, but rather the political alliance between Northern workers and Southern peasants, to oust the bourgeoisie from State power. Furthermore, precisely the Turin communists (though they supported division of the land, subordinated to the solidary action of the two classes) themselves warned against 'miraculist' illusions in a mechanical sharing out of the big estates. In the same article of 3 January, we find: "What can a poor peasant achieve by occupying uncultivated or poorly cultivated lands? Without machinery, without accommodation on the place of work, without credit to tide him over till harvest-time, without cooperative institutions to acquire the harvest (if – long before harvest time — the peasant has not hung himself from the strongest bush or the least unhealthy-looking wild fig in the undergrowth of his uncultivated land!) and preserve him from the clutches of the usurers – without all these things, what can a poor peasant achieve by occupying?"

We were still for the very realistic and in no way "magical" formula of land to the peasants. But we wanted it to be incorporated in a general revolutionary action of the two allied classes, under the leadership of the industrial proletariat. The writers of *Quarto Stato* have invented entirely the "magical formula" they attribute to the Turin Communists; they have thus revealed their journalistic unseriousness and a lack of scruple proper to village pharmacy intellectuals (and these too are significant political factors, which bring their own consequences).

In the proletarian camp, the Turin communists had one undeniable "merit": that of bringing the Southern question forcibly to the attention of the workers' vanguard, and identifying it as one of the essential problems of national policy for the revolutionary proletariat. In this sense, they contributed in practice to bringing the Southern question out of its indistinct, intellectualistic, so-called "concretist" phase and impelling it into a new phase.[248] The revolutionary worker of Turin and Milan became the protagonist of the Southern question, in place of the Giustino Fortunatos, the Gaetano Salveminis, the Eugenio Azimontis and the Arturo Labriolas[249] – to mention only the names of the patron saints beloved of the "young people" of *Quarto Stato*.

The Turin communists posed concretely the question of the "hegemony of the proletariat": i.e. of the social basis of the proletarian dictatorship and of the workers' State. The proletariat can become the leading [*dirigente*] and the dominant class to the extent that it succeeds in creating a system of class alliances which allows it to mobilize the majority of the working population against capitalism and the bourgeois State.[250] In Italy, in the real class relations which exist there, this means to the extent that it succeeds in gaining the consent of the broad peasant masses. But the peasant question is historically determined in Italy; it is not the "peasant and agrarian question in general". In Italy the peasant question, through the specific Italian tradition, and the specific development of Italian history, has taken two typical and particular forms – the Southern question and that of the Vatican. Winning the majority of the peasant masses thus means, for the Italian proletariat, making these two questions its own from the social point of view; understanding the class demands which they represent; incorporating these demands into its revolutionary transitional programme; placing these demands among the objectives for which it struggles.

The first problem to resolve, for the Turin communists, was how to modify the political stance and general ideology of the proletariat itself, as a national element which exists within the ensemble of State life and is unconsciously subjected to the influence of bourgeois education, the bourgeois press and bourgeois traditions. It is well known what kind of ideology has been disseminated in myriad ways among the masses in the North, by the propagandists of the bourgeoisie: the South is the ball and chain which prevents the social development of Italy from progressing more rapidly; the Southerners are biologically inferior beings, semi-barbarians or total barbarians, by natural destiny; if the South is backward, the fault does not lie with the capitalist system or with any other historical cause, but with Nature, which has made the Southerners lazy, incapable, criminal and barbaric – only tempering this harsh fate with the purely individual explosion of a few great geniuses, like isolated palm-trees in an arid and barren desert. The Socialist Party was to a great extent the vehicle for this bourgeois ideology within the Northern proletariat. The Socialist Party gave its blessing to all the "Southernist" literature of the clique of writers who made up the so-called positive school: the Ferri's, Sergi's, Niceforo's, Orano's and their lesser followers, who in articles, tales, short stories, novels, impressions and memoirs, in a variety of forms, reiterated one single refrain.[251] Once again, "science" was used to crush the wretched and exploited; but this time it was dressed in socialist colours, and claimed to be the science of the proletariat.

The Turin communists reacted energetically against this ideology, precisely in Turin itself, where war-veterans' reminiscences and descriptions of "banditry" in the South and the Islands had most powerfully influenced the popular traditions and outlook. They reacted energetically, in practical forms, and succeeded in achieving concrete results of the greatest historical significance. They succeeded in achieving, precisely in Turin, embryonic forms of what will be the solution to the Southern problem.

Moreover, even before the War, an episode occurred in Turin which potentially contained all the action and propaganda carried out by the communists in the post-war period. When in 1914 the death of Pilade Gay left the city's fourth ward vacant and posed the question of a new candidate, a group in the Socialist Party section which included the future editors of *L'Ordine Nuovo* floated the idea of putting up Gaetano Salvemini.[252] Salvemini was at the time the most radical spokesman for the peasant masses in the South. He was outside the Socialist Party, indeed was waging a vigorous campaign against the Socialist Party, and one that was extremely dangerous, since his assertions and accusations aroused in the working masses of the South hatred not simply for such individuals as Turati, Treves and D'Aragona, but for the industrial proletariat as a whole. (Many of the bullets discharged by the royal guards in 1919, 1920, 1921 and 1922 against the workers were cast from the same lead which served to print Salvemini's articles.) Nevertheless, the Turin group wanted to take a stand on Salvemini's name, in the sense which was explained to Salvemini himself by comrade Ottavio Pastore, who had gone to Florence to obtain the former's agreement to the candidature.

"The Turin workers want to elect a deputy for the peasants of Apulia. The Turin workers know that in the general elections of 1913, the peasants of Molfetta and Bitonto were overwhelmingly in favour of Salvemini. But the administrative pressure of the Giolitti government, and the violence of hired thugs and police, prevented the Apulian peasants from expressing their wishes. The Turin workers do not ask Salvemini for guarantees of any kind: neither to the party, nor to a programme, nor to the discipline of the Socialist parliamentary group. Once elected, Salvemini will be answerable to the Apulian peasants, not to the workers of Turin, who will carry out electoral propaganda according to their own principles and will in no way be committed by Salvemini's political activity."

Salvemini did not agree to stand, although he was shaken and even moved by the proposal (in those days, no one yet spoke of communist "perfidy", and manners were honourable and unconstrained). He proposed that Mussolini should be the candidate, and promised to come to Turin to support the Socialist Party in the electoral campaign. In fact he held two huge meetings, at the Chamber of Labour and in Piazza Statuto, where he spoke to mass audiences who saw and applauded in him the representative of the Southern peasants, oppressed and exploited in yet more odious and bestial ways than the Northern proletariat. The approach that was potentially contained in this episode, and which was not developed further purely because of Salvemini's decision, was taken up again and applied by the communists in the post-war period. Let us recall the most significant and symptomatic facts.

In 1919 the *Giovane Sardegna* association was formed, first prelude of what was later to become the Sardinian Action Party.[253] *Giovane Sardegna* aimed to unite all Sardinians – both on the island itself and on the mainland – into a regional bloc capable of exerting effective pressure on the government, to ensure that the promises made during the War to the soldiers were kept. The organizer of *Giovane Sardegna* on the mainland was a certain professor Pietro Nurra, a *Socialist*, who is very probably today a member of the group of "young people" who discover each week in *Quarto Stato* some new horizon to explore. The association was joined – with the enthusiasm which every new chance to get hold of badges, titles and little medals arouses – by lawyers, teachers and civil servants. The constituent assembly held in Turin, for Sardinians living in Piedmont, saw an impressive roster of interventions. The majority was made up of humble folk: men of the people with no discernible qualifications; unskilled labourers; retired people living on pensions; former *carabinieri*, former prison warders and former frontier guards now engaged in a wide variety of petty commercial enterprise. All of these were fired with enthusiasm by the idea of finding themselves among fellow-countrymen and hearing speeches about their native land, to which they remained bound by innumerable bonds of kinship, friendship, memory, suffering and hope: the hope of returning to their country, but to a country more prosperous and wealthy, which would offer conditions for living, albeit modestly.

The Sardinian communists, who numbered precisely eight, attended the meeting, presented a resolution of their own to the Chair, and asked to be allowed to make a counter-report. After the fiery rhetoric of the official report, embellished with all the Venuses and Cupids of provincial oratory; after those who intervened in the debate had wept at the memories of past griefs and of the blood spilled in battle by the Sardinian regiments, and had been fired with enthusiasm to the point of delirium at the idea of a united bloc of all the generous sons of Sardinia – after all this, it was very difficult to "pitch" the counter-report right. The most optimistic forecasts were for – if not a lynching – at least a trip to police headquarters, after being rescued from the "righteous indignation of the crowd". However, the counter-report, though it provoked great astonishment, was in fact listened to attentively. And once the spell had been broken, the revolutionary conclusion was reached swiftly and methodically. The dilemma – Are you poor devils from Sardinia for a bloc with the gentry of the island, who have ruined you and who are the local overseers of capitalist exploitation? Or are you for a bloc with the revolutionary workers of the mainland, who want to destroy all forms of exploitation and free all the oppressed? – this dilemma was rammed into the heads of all those present. The vote, by division of the assembly, was a tremendous success: on one side, there was a handful of smartly dressed gentry, top-hatted officials, professional people, livid with rage and fear, with a circle of forty-odd policemen to garnish the consensus; on the other side, there was the whole mass of poor folk, with the women dressed up in their party best, clustered around the tiny communist cell. An hour later, at the Chamber of Labour, the Sardinian Socialist Education Circle was set up, with 256 members. The founding of *Giovane Sardegna* was put off *sine die*, and never in fact took place.

This was the political basis for the activity carried out among the soldiers of the Sassari Brigade, a brigade with an almost totally regional composition. The Sassari Brigade had taken part in the repression of the insurrectional movement of August 1917 in Turin. It was confidently believed that it would never fraternize with the workers, because of the legacy of hatred which every repressive action leaves behind it – both in the masses, as a hatred which is also turned against the material instruments of the repression, and in the ranks, because of the memory of the soldiers who have fallen beneath the blows of the insurgents. The Brigade was welcomed by a throng of ladies and gentlemen, who offered the soldiers flowers, cigars and fruit. The state of mind of the soldiers is well captured by the following account, given by a tannery worker from Sassari involved in the first propagandistic soundings: "I approached a bivouac on X Square (in the first days, the Sardinian soldiers bivouacked in the squares as if in a conquered city) and I spoke with a young peasant, who had welcomed me warmly because I was from Sassari like him. 'What have you come to do in Turin?' 'We have come to shoot the gentry who are on strike.' 'But it is not the gentry who are on strike, it is the workers and they are poor.' 'They're all gentry here: they have collars and ties; they earn 30 *lire* a day. I know poor people and I know how they are dressed, yes indeed, in Sassari there are lots of poor people; all of us "diggers" are poor and we earn $1\frac{1}{2}$ lire a day.' 'But I am a worker too and I am poor.' 'You're poor because you're a Sardinian.' 'But if I go on strike with the others, will you shoot me?' The soldier reflected a bit, then put a hand on my shoulder: 'Listen, when you go on strike with the others, stay at home!'."

Such was the attitude of the overwhelming majority of the Brigade, which contained only a small number of mine-workers from the Iglesias field. And yet, within a few months, on the eve of the general strike of 20–21 July, the Brigade was moved away from Turin, the older soldiers were discharged and the unit was split into three: one third was sent to Aosta, one third to Trieste and one third to Rome. The Brigade was moved out at night, without advance warning. No elegant throng applauded them at the station. Their songs, though still songs of war, no longer had the same content as those they sang on their arrival.

Did these events have no consequences? On the contrary, they have had results which still subsist to this day and continue to work in the depths of the popular masses. They illuminated, for an instant, brains which had never thought in that way, and which remained marked by them, radically modified. Our archives have been scattered, and we have destroyed many papers ourselves for fear they might lead to arrests and harassment. But we can recall dozens and indeed hundreds of letters sent from Sardinia to the *Avanti!* editorial offices in Turin; letters which were frequently collective, signed by all the Sassari Brigade veterans in a particular village. By uncontrolled and uncontrollable paths, the political attitude which we supported was disseminated. The formation of the Sardinian Action Party was strongly influenced by it at the base, and it would be possible to recall in this respect episodes that are rich in content and significance. The last verifiable repercussion of this activity occurred in 1922, when, with the same aim as in the case of the Sassari Brigade, 300 *carabinieri* from the Cagliari Legion were sent to Turin. At the editorial offices of *L'Ordine Nuovo* we received a statement of principle, signed by a large proportion of these *carabinieri*. It echoed in every way our positions on the Southern problem, and was decisive proof of the correctness of our approach.

The proletariat had itself to adopt this approach for it to become politically effective: that goes without saying. No mass action is possible, if the masses in question are not convinced of the ends they wish to attain and the methods to be applied. The proletariat, in order to become capable as a class of governing, must strip itself of every residue of corporatism, every syndicalist prejudice and incrustation. What does this mean? That, in addition to the need to overcome the distinctions which exist between one trade and another, it is necessary – in order to win the trust and consent of the peasants and of some semi-proletarian urban categories – to overcome certain prejudices and conquer certain forms of egoism which can and do subsist within the working class as such, even when craft particularism has disappeared. The metal-worker, the joiner, the building-worker, etc., must not only think as proletarians, and no longer as metal-worker, joiner, building-worker, etc.; they must also take a further step. They must think as workers who are members of a class which aims to lead the peasants and intellectuals. Of a class which can win and build socialism only if it is aided and followed by the great majority of these social strata. If this is not achieved, the proletariat does not become the leading class; and these strata (which in Italy represent the majority of the population), remaining under bourgeois leadership, enable the State to resist the proletarian assault and wear it down.

Well, what has occurred on the terrain of the Southern question shows that the proletariat has understood these duties. Two events should be recalled: one took place in Turin; the other occurred at Reggio Emilia, i.e. in the very citadel of reformism, class corporatism and working-class protectionism which is cited as a prime example by the "Southernists" in their propaganda among the peasants of the South.

After the occupation of the factories, the Fiat board proposed to the workers that they should run the firm as a cooperative. Naturally, the reformists were in favour. An industrial crisis was looming; the spectre of unemployment tormented the workers' families. If Fiat became a cooperative, a certain job security might be obtained by the skilled workers, and especially by the politically most active workers, who were convinced that they were marked out for dismissal. The Socialist Party section, led by the communists, intervened energetically on the question. The workers were told the following:

"A great firm like Fiat can be taken over as a cooperative by the workers, only if the latter have resolved to enter the system of bourgeois political forces which governs Italy today. The proposal of the Fiat board forms a part of Giolitti's political plan. In what does this plan consist? The bourgeoisie, even before the War, could not govern peacefully any longer. The rising of the Sicilian peasants in 1894 and the Milan insurrection of 1898 were the *experimentum crucis* of the Italian bourgeoisie.[254] After the bloody decade 1890–1900, the bourgeoisie was forced to renounce a dictatorship that was too exclusive, too violent, too direct. For there had risen against it *simultaneously*, even if not in a coordinated fashion, the Southern peasants and the Northern workers.

"In the new century, the ruling class inaugurated a new policy of class alliances, class political blocs: i.e. bourgeois democracy. It had to choose: either a rural democracy, i.e. an alliance with the Southern peasants, a policy of free trade, universal suffrage, administrative decentralization and low prices for industrial products; or a capitalist/worker industrial bloc, without universal suffrage, with tariff barriers, with the maintenance of a highly centralized State (the expression of bourgeois dominion over the peasants, especially in the South and the Islands), and with a reformist policy on wages and trade-union freedoms. It chose, not by chance, the latter solution. Giolitti personified bourgeois rule; the Socialist Party became the instrument of Giolitti's policies.

"If you look closely, it was in the decade 1900–1910 that the most radical crises occurred in the socialist and working-class movement. The masses reacted spontaneously against the policy of the reformist leaders. Syndicalism was born: the instinctive, elemental, primitive but healthy expression of working-class reaction against the bloc with the bourgeoisie and in favour of a bloc with the peasants – and *first and foremost with the Southern peasants*. Precisely that. Indeed, in a certain sense, syndicalism is a weak attempt on the part of the Southern peasants, represented by their most advanced intellectuals, to lead the proletariat. Who forms the leading nucleus of Italian syndicalism, and what is its ideological essence? The leading nucleus of syndicalism is made up almost exclusively of southerners: Labriola, Leone, Longobardi, Orano. The ideological essence of syndicalism is a new liberalism, more energetic, more aggressive, more pugnacious than the traditional variety. If you look closely there are two fundamental themes around which the successive crises of syndicalism and the gradual passage of the syndicalist leaders into the bourgeois camp took place: emigration and free trade, two themes closely bound up with Southernism. The phenomenon of emigration gave birth to the idea of Enrico Corradini's 'proletarian nation'; the Libyan war appeared to a whole layer of intellectuals as the beginning of the 'great proletariat's' offensive against the capitalist and plutocratic world.[255] A whole group of syndicalists went over to nationalism; indeed the Nationalist Party was orginally made up of ex-syndicalist intellectuals (Monicelli, Forges-Davanzati, Maraviglia). Labriola's book *History of Ten Years* (the ten years from 1900 to 1910) is the most typical and characteristic expression of this anti-Giolittian and Southernist neo-liberalism.

"In the ten years in question, capitalism was strengthened and developed, and directed a part of its activity towards the agriculture of the Po Valley. The most characteristic feature of those ten years was the mass strikes of the agricultural workers of the Po Valley. A profound upheaval took place among the Northern peasants: there occurred a deep class differentiation (the number of *braccianti* [landless labourers] increased by 50 per cent, according to the 1911 census figures), and to this there corresponded a recasting of political currents and spiritual attitudes. Christian democracy and Mussolinism were the two most outstanding products of the period. Romagna was the regional crucible of these two new activities; the *bracciante* seemed to have become the social protagonist of the political struggle. The left organs of social democracy (like *Azione* in Cesena) and Mussolinism too soon fell under the control of the 'Southernists'. *Azione* in Cesena was a regional edition of Gaetano Salvemini's *Unità. Avanti!*, under Mussolini's editorship, slowly but surely became transformed into a tribune for syndicalist and Southernist writers. People like Fancello, Lanzillo, Panunzio and Ciccotti became frequent contributors. Salvemini himself did not hide his sympathies for Mussolini, who also became the darling of Prezzolini's *Voce*. Everyone remembers that, in fact, when Mussolini left *Avanti!* and the Socialist Party, he was surrounded by this cohort of syndicalists and Southernists.[256]

"The most notable repercussion of this period in the revolutionary camp was the Red Week of June 1914: Romagna and the Marches were the epicentre of Red Week.[257] In the field of bourgeois politics, the most notable repercussion was the Gentiloni pact.[258] Since the Socialist Party, as a consequence of the rural movements in the Po Valley, had returned after 1910 to an intransigent tactic, the industrial bloc supported and represented by Giolitti lost its effectiveness. Giolitti shifted his rifle to the other shoulder. He replaced the alliance between bourgeoisie and workers by an alliance between bourgeoisie and the catholics, who represented the peasant masses of Northern and Central Italy. As a result of this alliance, Sonnino's Conservative Party was totally destroyed, preserving only a tiny cell in Southern Italy, around Antonio Salandra.[259]

"The War and post-war period saw a series of molecular processes of the highest importance take place within the bourgeois class. Salandra and Nitti were the first two Southern heads of government (leaving aside Sicilians, of course, such as Crispi, who was the most energetic representative of the bourgeois dictatorship in the nineteenth century).[260] They sought to realize the industrial bourgeois/Southern landowner plan – Salandra on a conservative basis, Nitti on a democratic one. (Both these heads of government were solidly assisted by *Il Corriere della Sera*, i.e. by the Lombard textile industry.) Salandra was already trying during the War to shift the technical forces of the State organization in favour of the South: i.e. to replace the Giolittian State personnel with a new personnel which embodied the bourgeoisie's new political course. You remember the campaign waged by *La*

Stampa, especially in 1917–18, for close collaboration between Giolittians and Socialists to prevent the 'Apulianization' of the State. This campaign in *La Stampa* was led by Francesco Ciccotti, i.e. it was *de facto* an expression of the agreement which existed between Giolitti and the reformists.[261] The question was not a small one, and the Giolittians, in their defensive obstinacy, went so far that they passed the limits allowed to a party by the big bourgeoisie; they went as far as those demonstrations of anti-patriotism and defeatism which are fresh in every memory.

"Today, Giolitti is once more in power, and once more the big bourgeoisie is putting its trust in him, as a result of the panic which has filled it before the impetuous movement of the popular masses. Giolitti wants to tame the Turin workers. He has beaten them twice: in the strike of last April, and in the occupation of the factories – with the help of the CGL, i.e. of corporative reformism. He now thinks that he can tie them into the bourgeois State system. What in fact will happen if the skilled workforce of Fiat accepts the board's proposals? The present industrial shares will become debentures: in other words, the cooperative will have to pay to debenture-holders a fixed dividend, whatever the turnover may be. The Fiat company will be cut off in every way from the institutions of credit, which remain in the hands of the bourgeoisie, whose interest it is to get the workers at its mercy. The skilled workforce will perforce have to bind itself to the State, which will 'come to the assistance of the workers' through the activity of the working-class deputies: through the subordination of the working-class political party to government policies. That is Giolitti's plan as applied in full. The Turin proletariat will no longer exist as an independent class, but merely as an appendage of the bourgeois State. Class corporatism will have triumphed, but the proletariat will have lost its position and role as leader and guide. It will appear to the mass of poorer workers as privileged. It will appear to the peasants as an exploiter just like the bourgeoisie, because the bourgeoisie – as it has always done – will present the privileged nuclei of the working class to the peasant masses as the sole cause of their ills and their misery."

The skilled workers of Fiat accepted almost unanimously our point of view, and the board's proposals were rejected. But this experiment could not be sufficient. The Turin proletariat, in a whole series of actions, had shown that it had reached an extremely high level of political maturity and capability. The technicians and white-collar workers in the factories were able to improve their conditions in 1919 only because they were supported by the workers. To break the militancy of the technicians, the employers proposed to the workers that they should themselves nominate, through elections, new squad and shop foremen. The workers rejected the proposal, although they had many points of difference with the technicians, who had always been an instrument of repression and persecution for the bosses. Then the press waged a rabid campaign to isolate the technicians, highlighting their very high salaries, which reached as much as 7,000 *lire* a month. The skilled workers also gave support to the agitation of the hodmen, and it was only thus that the latter succeeded in winning their demands. Within the factories, all privileges and forms of exploitation of the less skilled by the more skilled categories were swept away. Through these actions, the proletarian vanguard won its position as a social vanguard. This was the basis upon which the Communist Party developed in Turin. But outside Turin? Well, we wanted expressly to take the problem outside Turin, and precisely to Reggio Emilia, where there existed the greatest concentration of reformism and class corporatism.[262]

Reggio Emilia had always been the target of the "Southernists". A phrase of Camillo Prampolini: "Italy is made up of Northerners and filthy Southerners" could be taken as the most characteristic expression of the violent hatred disseminated among Southerners against the workers of the North.[263] At Reggio Emilia, a problem arose similar to the one at Fiat: a big factory was to pass into the hands of the workers as a cooperative enterprise. The Reggio reformists were full of enthusiasm for the project and trumpeted its praises in their press and at meetings.[264] A Turin communist[265] went to Reggio, took the floor at a factory meeting, outlined the problem between North and South in its entirety, and the "miracle" was achieved: the workers, by an overwhelming majority, rejected the reformist, corporate position. It was shown that the reformists did not represent the spirit of the Reggio workers; they represented merely their passivity, and other negative aspects. They had succeeded in establishing a political monopoly – thanks to the notable concentration in their ranks of organizers and propagandists with certain professional talents – and hence in preventing the development and organization of a revolutionary current. But the presence of a capable revolutionary was enough to thwart them and show that the Reggio workers are valiant fighters and not swine raised on government fodder.

In April 1921, 5,000 revolutionary workers were laid off by Fiat, the

Workers' Councils were abolished, real wages were cut.[266] At Reggio Emilia, something similar probably happened. In other words, the workers were defeated. But the sacrifice that they had made, had it been useless? We do not believe so: indeed, we are certain that it was not useless — though it would certainly be difficult to adduce a whole series of great mass events which prove the immediate, lightning effectiveness of these actions. In any case, so far as the peasants are concerned, such proof is always difficult, indeed almost impossible: and it is yet more difficult in the case of the peasant masses in the South.

The South can be defined as a great social disintegration. The peasants, who make up the great majority of its population, have no cohesion among themselves (of course, some exceptions must be made: Apulia, Sardinia, Sicily, where there exist special characteristics within the great canvas of the South's structure). Southern society is a great agrarian bloc, made up of three social layers: the great amorphous, disintegrated mass of the peasantry; the intellectuals of the petty and medium rural bourgeoisie; and the big landowners and great intellectuals. The Southern peasants are in perpetual ferment, but as a mass they are incapable of giving a centralized expression to their aspirations and needs. The middle layer of intellectuals receives the impulses for its political and ideological activity from the peasant base. The big landowners in the political field and the great intellectuals in the ideological field centralize and dominate, in the last analysis, this whole complex of phenomena. Naturally, it is in the ideological sphere that the centralization is most effective and precise. Giustino Fortunato and Benedetto Croce thus represent the keystones of the Southern system and, in a certain sense, are the two major figures of Italian reaction.

The Southern intellectuals are one of the most interesting and important social strata in Italian national life. One only has to think of the fact that more than three fifths of the State bureaucracy is made up of Southerners to convince oneself of this. Now, to understand the particular psychology of the Southern intellectuals, it is necessary to keep in mind certain factual data.

1. In every country, the layer of intellectuals has been radically modified by the development of capitalism. The old type of intellectual was the organizing element in a society with a mainly peasant and artisanal basis. To organize the State, to organize commerce, the dominant class bred a particular type of intellectual. Industry has introduced a new type of intellectual: the technical organizer, the specialist in applied science. In the societies where the economic forces

have developed in a capitalist direction, to the point where they have absorbed the greater part of national activity, it is this second type of intellectual which has prevailed, with all his characteristics of order and intellectual discipline. In the countries, on the other hand, where agriculture still plays a considerable or even preponderant role, the old type has remained predominant. It provides the bulk of the State personnel; and locally too, in the villages and little country towns, it has the function of intermediary between the peasant and the administration in general. In Southern Italy this type predominates, with all its characteristic features. Democratic in its peasant face; reactionary in the face turned towards the big landowner and the government: politicking, corrupt and faithless. One could not understand the traditional cast of the Southern political parties, if one did not take the characteristics of this social stratum into account.

2. The Southern intellectual mainly comes from a layer which is still important in the South: the rural bourgeois. In other words, the petty and medium landowner who is not a peasant, who does not work the land, who would be ashamed to be a farmer, but who wants to extract from the little land he has – leased out either for rent or on a simple share-cropping basis – the wherewithal to live fittingly; the wherewithal to send his sons to a university or seminary; and the wherewithal to provide dowries for his daughters, who must marry officers or civil functionaries of the State. From this social layer, the intellectuals derive a fierce antipathy to the working peasant – who is regarded as a machine for work to be bled dry, and one which can be replaced, given the excess working population. They also acquire an atavistic, instinctive feeling of crazy fear of the peasants with their destructive violence; hence, they practise a refined hypocrisy and a highly refined art of deceiving and taming the peasant masses.

3. Since the clergy belong to the social group of intellectuals, it is ncessary to note the features which distinguish the Southern clergy as a whole from the Northern clergy. The Northern priest is generally the son of an artisan or a peasant, has democratic sympathies, is more tied to the mass of peasants. Morally, he is more correct than the Southern priest, who often lives more or less openly with a woman. He therefore exercises a spiritual function that is more complete, from a social point of view, in that he guides a family's entire activities. In the North, the separation of Church from State and the expropriation of ecclesiastical goods was more radical than in the South, where the parishes and convents either have preserved or have reconstituted considerable

assets, both fixed and movable. In the South, the priest appears to the peasant: 1. as a land administrator, with whom the peasant enters into conflict on the question of rents; 2. as a usurer, who asks for extremely high rates of interest and manipulates the religious element in order to make certain of collecting his rent or interest; 3. as a man subject to all the ordinary passions (women and money), and who therefore, from a spiritual point of view, inspires no confidence in his discretion and impartiality. Hence confession exercises only the most minimal role of guidance, and the Southern peasant, if often superstitious in a pagan sense, is not clerical. All this, taken together, explains why in the South the Popular Party (except in some parts of Sicily) does not have any great position or possess any network of institutions and mass organizations. The attitude of the peasant towards the clergy is summed up in the popular saying: "The priest is a priest at the altar; outside, he is a man like anyone else."

The Southern peasant is bound to the big landowner through the mediation of the intellectual. The peasant movements, insofar as they do not take the form of autonomous, independent mass organizations, even in a formal sense (i.e. capable of selecting out peasant cadres, themselves of peasant origin, and of registering and accumulating the differentiation and progress achieved within the movement), always end up by finding themselves a place in the ordinary articulations of the State apparatus – communes, provinces, Chamber of Deputies. This process takes place through the composition and decomposition of local parties, whose personnel is made up of intellectuals, but which are controlled by the big landowners and their agents – like Salandra, Orlando, Di Cesarò.

The War appeared to introduce a new element into this type of organization, with the war-veterans' movement. In this, the peasant-soldiers and the intellectual-officers formed a mutual bloc that was more closely united, and that was to some extent antagonistic to the big landowners. It did not last long, and its last residue is the National Union conceived of by Amendola, which has some phantom existence thanks to its anti-fascism. However, given the lack of any tradition of *explicit* organization of *democratic* intellectuals in the South, even this grouping must be stressed and taken into account, since it might be transformed from a tiny trickle of water into a swollen, muddy torrent, in changed general political conditions.

The only region where the war-veterans' movement took on a more precise profile, and succeeded in creating a more solid social structure, was Sardinia. And this is understandable. Precisely because in Sardinia the big landowner class is very exiguous, carries out no function, and does not have the ancient cultural and governmental traditions of the mainland South. The pressure exerted from below, by the mass of peasants and herdsmen, finds no suffocating counterweight in the higher social stratum of the big landowners. The leading intellectuals feel the full weight of this pressure, and take steps forward which are more remarkable than the National Union.

The Sicilian situation has very specific features, which distinguish it both from Sardinia and from the South. The big landowners are far more compact and resolute there than in the mainland South. Moreover, there exists there a certain developed industry and commerce (Sicily is the richest region of the entire South and one of the richest in Italy). The upper classes feel very keenly their importance in national life and make its weight felt. Sicily and Piedmont are the two regions which have played a pre-eminent role since 1870. The popular masses of Sicily are more advanced than in the South, but their progress has taken on a typically Sicilian form. There exists a mass Sicilian socialism, which has a whole tradition and development that is peculiar to it. In the 1922 Chamber, it had around 20 of the 52 deputies who had been elected from the island.

We have said that the Southern peasant is tied to the big landowner through the mediation of the intellectual. This type of organization is most widespread, throughout the mainland South and Sicily. It creates a monstrous agrarian bloc which, as a whole, functions as the intermediary and the overseer of Northern capitalism and the big banks. Its single aim is to preserve the *status quo*. Within it, there exists no intellectual light, no programme, no drive towards improvements or progress. If any ideas or programmes have been put forward, they have had their origins outside the South, in the conservative agrarian politicians (especially in Tuscany) who were associated in Parliament with the conservatives of the Southern agrarian bloc. Sonnino and Franchetti were among the few intelligent bourgeois who posed the Southern problem as a national problem, and outlined a government plan to solve it.[267]

What was the point of view of Sonnino and Franchetti? They stressed the need to create in Southern Italy an economically independent middle stratum which would fulfil the role (as was said at that time) of "public opinion" – and would, on the one hand, limit the cruel and arbitrary actions of the landowners, on the other, moderate the insurrectionism of the poor peasants. Sonnino and Franchetti had been terrified by the popularity which the Bakuninist ideas of the First International had enjoyed in the South. This terror made them make blunders which were often grotesque. In one of their publications, for instance, reference is made to the fact that a popular tavern or *trattoria* in a village in Calabria (I am quoting from memory) is named "The Strikers" [*Scioperanti*], to demonstrate how widespread and deep-rooted internationalist ideas are. The fact, if true (and it must be true, given the intellectual probity of the authors), can be more simply explained if one recalls that there are numerous Albanian colonies in the South, and that the word *skipetari* [Albanians] has undergone the most strange and bizarre distortions in the various dialects (thus certain documents of the Venetian Republic speak of military formations of "*S'ciopetà*").[268] The fact is that it is not so much that Bakunin's theories were widespread in the South, as that the situation there was such as to have probably suggested to Bakunin his theories. Certainly, the poor Southern peasants were thinking about a "great revolt" long before Bakunin's brain had thought out the theory of "general destruction".

The government plan of Sonnino and Franchetti never even began to be put into practice. And it could not be. The nexus of relations between North and South in the organization of the national economy and the State is such, that the birth of a broad middle class of an economic nature (which means the birth of a broad capitalist bourgeoisie) is made almost impossible. Any accumulation of capital on the spot, any accumulation of savings, is made impossible by the fiscal and customs system; and by the fact that the capitalists who own shares do not transform their profits into new capital on the spot, because they are not from that spot. When emigration took on the gigantic dimensions it did in the twentieth century, and the first remittances began to flood in from America, the liberal economists cried triumphantly: Sonnino's dream will come true! A silent revolution is under way in the South which, slowly but surely, will change the entire economic and social structure of the country. But the State intervened, and the silent revolution was stifled at birth. The government offered treasury bonds carrying guaranteed interest, and the emigrants and their families were transformed from agents of the silent revolution into agents for giving the State the financial means to subsidize the parasitic industries of the North. Francesco Nitti, on the democratic level and formally outside the Southern agrarian bloc, might seem an effective realizer of Sonnino's programme; but he was, in fact, Northern capitalism's best agent for raking in the last resources of

Southern savings. The thousands of millions swallowed up by the *Banca di sconto* were almost all owed to the South: the 400,000 creditors of the *Banca Italiana di Sconto* were overwhelmingly Southern savers.[269]

Over and above the agrarian bloc, there functions in the South an intellectual bloc which in practice has so far served to prevent the cracks in the agrarian bloc becoming too dangerous and causing a landslide. Giustino Fortunato and Benedetto Croce are the exponents of this intellectual bloc, and they can thus be considered as the most active reactionaries of the whole peninsula.

We have already said that Southern Italy represents a great social disintegration. This formula can be applied not only to the peasants, but also to the intellectuals. It is a remarkable fact that in the South, side by side with huge property, there have existed and continue to exist great accumulations of culture and intelligence in single individuals, or small groups of great intellectuals, while there does not exist any organization of middle culture. There exist in the South the Laterza publishing house, and the review *La Critica*.[270] There exist academies and cultural bodies of the greatest erudition. But there do not exist small or medium reviews, nor publishing houses around which medium groupings of Southern intellectuals might form. The Southerners who have sought to leave the agrarian bloc and pose the Southern question in a radical form have found hospitality in, and grouped themselves around, reviews printed outside the South. Indeed, one might say that all the cultural initiatives by medium intellectuals which have taken place in this century in Central and Northern Italy have been characterized by Southernism, because they have been strongly influenced by Southern intellectuals: all the journals of the group of Florentine intellectuals, like *Voce* and *Unità*; the journals of the Christian democrats, like *Azione* in Cesena; the journals of the young Emilian and Milanese liberals published by G. Borelli, such as *Patria* in Bologna or *Azione* in Milan; and lastly, Gobetti's *Rivoluzione liberale*.

Well, the supreme political and intellectual rulers of all these initiatives have been Giustino Fortunato and Benedetto Croce. In a broader sphere than the stifling agrarian bloc, they have seen to it that the problems of the South would be posed in a way which did not go beyond certain limits; did not become revolutionary. Men of the highest culture and intelligence, who arose on the traditional terrain of the South but were linked to European and hence to world culture, they had all the necessary gifts to satisfy the intellectual needs of the most sincere representatives of the cultured youth in the South; to comfort their restless impulses to revolt against existing conditions; to steer them along a middle way of classical serenity in thought and action. The so-called neo-protestants or Calvinists have failed to understand that in Italy, since modern conditions of civilization rendered impossible any mass religious reform, the only historically possible reformation has taken place with Benedetto Croce's philosophy. The direction and method of thought have been changed and a new conception of the world has been constructed, transcending catholicism and every other mythological religion. In this sense, Benedetto Croce has fulfilled an extremely important "national" function. He has detached the radical intellectuals of the South from the peasant masses, forcing them to take part in national and European culture; and through this culture, he has secured their absorption by the national bourgeoisie and hence by the agrarian bloc.

L'Ordine Nuovo and the Turin communists – if in a certain sense they can be related to the intellectual formations to which we have alluded; and if, therefore, they too have felt the intellectual influence of Giustino Fortunato or of Benedetto Croce – nevertheless represent at the same time a complete break with that tradition and the beginning of a new development, which has already borne fruit and which will continue to do so. As has already been said, they posed the urban proletariat as the modern protagonist of Italian history, and hence also of the Southern question. Having served as intermediaries between the proletariat and certain strata of left intellectuals, they succeeded in modifying – if not completely at least to a notable extent – their mental outlook.

This is the main factor in the figure of Piero Gobetti, if one reflects carefully.[271] Gobetti was not a communist and would probably never have become one. But he had understood the social and historical position of the proletariat, and could no longer think in abstraction from this element. Gobetti, in our work together on the paper, had been brought by us into contact with a living world which he had previously only known through formulae in books. His most striking characteristic was intellectual loyalty, and the total absence of every kind of petty vanity or meanness. Therefore, he could not fail to become convinced of the way in which a whole series of traditional ways of viewing and thinking about the proletariat were false and unjust.

What consequence did these contacts with the proletarian world have for Gobetti? They were the source and stimulus for a conception which we have no wish to discuss or develop: a conception which is to a great extent related to syndicalism and the way of thinking of the intellectual syndicalists. In it, the principles of liberalism are projected from the level of individual phenomena to that of mass phenomena. The qualities of excellence and prestige in the lives of individuals are carried over into classes, conceived of almost as collective individualities. This conception usually leads, in the intellectuals who share it, to mere contemplation and the noting down of merits and demerits; to an odious and foolish position, as referees of contests or bestowers of prizes and punishments. In practice, Gobetti escaped this destiny. He revealed himself to be an organizer of culture of extraordinary talents, and during this last period had a function which must be neither neglected nor under-estimated by the workers. He dug a trench beyond which those groups of honourable, sincere intellectuals who in 1919–1920–1921 felt that the proletariat would be superior as a ruling class to the bourgeoisie did not retreat.

Some people in good faith and honestly, others in extremely bad faith and dishonestly, went around saying that Gobetti was nothing but a communist in disguise: an agent, if not of the Communist Party, at least of the *Ordine Nuovo* communist group. It is unnecessary even to deny such fatuous rumours. The figure of Gobetti and the movement which he represented were spontaneous products of the new Italian historical climate. In this lies their significance and their importance. Comrades in the party sometimes reproved us for not having fought against the *Rivoluzione liberale* current of ideas. Indeed, this absence of conflict seemed to prove the organic relationship, of a Machiavellian kind (as people used to say), between us and Gobetti. We could not fight against Gobetti, because he developed and represented a movement which should not be fought against, at least so far as its main principles are concerned.

Not to understand that, means not to understand the question of intellectuals and the function which they fulfil in the class struggle. Gobetti, in practice, served us as a link: 1. with those intellectuals born on the terrain of capitalist techniques who in 1919–20 had taken up a left position, favourable to the dictatorship of the proletariat; 2. with a series of Southern intellectuals who through more complex relationships, posed the Southern question on a terrain different from the traditional one, by introducing into it the proletariat of the North (of these intellectuals, Guido Dorso is the most substantial and interesting figure). Why should we have fought against the *Rivoluzione liberale* movement? Perhaps because it was not made up of pure communists who had accepted our programme and our ideas from A to Z? This could not be asked of them, because it would have been both politically and historically a paradox.

Intellectuals develop slowly, far more slowly than any other social group, by their very nature and historical function. They represent the entire cultural tradition of a people, seeking to resume and synthesize all of its history. This can be said especially of the old type of intellectual: the intellectual born on the peasant terrain. To think it possible that such intellectuals, *en masse*, can break with the entire past and situate themselves totally upon the terrain of a new ideology, is absurd. It is absurd for the mass of intellectuals, and perhaps it is also absurd for very many intellectuals taken individually as well – notwithstanding all the honourable efforts which they make and want to make.

Now, we are interested in the mass of intellectuals, and not just in individuals. It is certainly important and useful for the proletariat that one or more intellectuals, individually, should adopt its programme and ideas; should merge into the proletariat, becoming and feeling themselves to be an integral part of it. The proletariat, as a class, is poor in organizing elements. It does not have its own stratum of intellectuals, and can only create one very slowly, very painfully, after the winning of State power. But it is also important and useful for a break to occur in the mass of intellectuals: a break of an organic kind, historically characterized. For there to be formed, as a mass formation, a left tendency, in the modern sense of the word: i.e. one oriented towards the revolutionary proletariat.

The alliance between proletariat and peasant masses requires this formation. It is all the more required by the alliance between proletariat and peasant masses in the South. The proletariat will destroy the Southern agrarian bloc insofar as it succeeds, through its party, in organizing increasingly significant masses of poor peasants into autonomous and independent formations. But its greater or lesser success in this necessary task will also depend upon its ability to break up the intellectual bloc that is the flexible, but extremely resistant, armour of the agrarian bloc. The proletariat was helped towards the accomplishment of this task by Piero Gobetti, and we think that the dead man's friends will continue, even without his leadership, the work he undertook. This is gigantic and difficult, but precisely worthy of every sacrifice (even that of life, as in Gobetti's case) on the part of those intellectuals (and there are many of them, more than is believed) – from North and South – who have understood that only two social forces are essentially national and bearers of the future: the proletariat and the peasants.

NOTES

I

1 The Communist Party was born during the first period of widespread fascist violence. This had begun, in the autumn of 1920, to take the form of raids on behalf of the landowners of Northern and Central Italy both against the Socialist and Catholic peasant associations, and against Socialist-controlled municipalities such as that of Bologna or Socialist papers such as the Trieste daily *Il Lavoratore*. This article was Gramsci's first comment on the Livorno Congress, which had ended a week earlier, on 21 January 1921. The communist delegates had arrived at the PSI congress with 58,783 votes, as against 98,028 for the "Maximalist" Centre under Serrati and 14,695 for the reformist wing led by Turati. After six days of fruitless attempts to induce Serrati to expel the reformists and apply the Comintern's 21 Points, the communists left to found the new Communist Party in a neighbouring hall. The military analogy used here by Gramsci to characterize the situation derives from the vicissitudes of Italian participation in the First World War: at Caporetto, in October 1917, Italian forces were massively defeated by Austro–Hungarian troops. Luigi Cadorna, the Italian commander-in-chief, was held responsible: he is often taken by Gramsci as the symbol of an authoritarian leader who makes no attempt to win the "consent" of those he leads. The battles on the Piave and at Vittorio Veneto, by contrast, were Italian victories in 1918, in the final stages of the War.
2 The Congress of Bologna was held from 5–8 October 1919. It saw the defeat of the reformists and the adoption, by an overwhelming majority, of a motion from Serrati which among other things called for the PSI's adherence to the IIIrd International. A small minority voted for Bordiga's abstentionist position.
3 This episode from the Thirty Years' War is the subject of a famous passage in the Prison Notebooks; see *QC* III, pp. 1788–9.
4 *Panciafichismo* ("belly full of figs"-ism), a play on words with *pacifismo* (pacifism), was a term of abuse for the business lobby campaigning to draw Italy out of the War.
5 A reference to Giovanni Giolitti, prime minister of Italy 1892–3, 1906–9, 1911–14 and 1920–1, who was unpopular with the nationalist and fascist Right for his advocacy of Italian neutrality in 1914, and who had been brought back to power in 1920 in time to confront the occupation of

the factories – negotiating an end to the episode with an offer of "workers' control". *La Stampa* of Turin was the principal Giolittian newspaper.

6 See *SPN*, p. 198 for another reference to the syndicalist movement of 1915–21 in Catalonia, and "Italy and Spain" on pp. 23–4 below for a discussion of the Spanish reaction which had begun in 1918.

7 This bill on workers' participation in the management of industry was the one that Giolitti had promised in order to bring the occupation of the factories to an end. It should be remembered that *controllo*, although it is here translated as "control", in fact has a different meaning in Italian. As Giolitti himself once wrote: "In America and England, 'control' virtually means command and statutory authority, whereas in Italy it means 'check'."

8 In view of the subsequent importance of the *dominante/dirigente* couplet for Gramsci (see *SPN*, pp. 55 ff.), I have given the original in parenthesis here, and have preferred the somewhat clumsy "leading class" to a rendering which, though better English, would not bring out the distinction.

9 The first post-war congress of the CGL took place from 26 February to 3 March 1921. At that time, the Confederation had two million members; its leadership was firmly in the hands of reformists like its secretary Ludovico D'Aragona. The communist fraction intervened at the congress with a resolution proposing a radical overhaul of the structure and functioning of the unions; separation from the Amsterdam trade-union International; an end to the "pact of alliance" with the PSI; and adherence to the Moscow trade-union International.

10 In fact, the body in question was the All-Russian Central Executive Committee of the Soviets of Workers' and Soldiers' Deputies, elected from the All-Russian Congress of Soviets of Workers' and Soldiers' Deputies held on 26 October (8 November) 1917.

11 This motto of Romain Rolland's appeared on the front page of every issue of the weekly *Ordine Nuovo*, until its conversion on 1 January 1921 into a "communist daily".

12 A reference to the "Trade-union Debate" which raged in the latter part of 1920 and the first months of 1921, culminating in an overwhelming majority for Lenin's position at the Tenth Congress of the Bolshevik Party in March 1921. The All-Russian Extraordinary Commission to Combat Counter-revolution and Sabotage (Cheka) was set up on 7 December 1917.

13 The real figures were some 10 million dead and 20 million wounded.

14 In Emilia, fascist squads had launched a massive offensive against the rural proletariat, aimed at destroying Socialist Party sections, peasant leagues, cooperatives, etc. Similar actions were carried out in Apulia on behalf of the landowners, directed against the powerfully organized strength of the agricultural labourers there: on 25 February, workers in

Bari went on strike in protest at the attacks which had taken place five days earlier on Socialist leaders. There was also a wave of repressive violence in Tuscany – at Florence, Empoli, Grosseto, Siena – after the murder of Spartaco Lavagnini (a communist railwaymens' leader) had provoked angry demonstrations. At Casale Monferrato, workers fought off an attack on the Chamber of Labour by fascists brought from all over Piedmont; but there were many dead and wounded, and the Socialist Party premises were destroyed.

15 In a speech on 10 March in Parliament, Giacomo Matteotti reaffirmed the PSI's position with respect to the fascist offensive: "We must not let ourselves be provoked, for even cowardice is a duty, an act of heroism.'"

16 The Anglo-Soviet trade agreement was signed on 16 March 1921. Following as it did the Soviet defeat in Poland, and the final victory over Wrangel at home, it initiated a stabilization of the Soviet Union's relations with the capitalist powers.

17 A reference to the "Red Week", see note 119 below.

18 Carlo Alberto, King of Sardina (Piedmont), granted a constitution to Piedmont on 4 March 1848. This "Albertine Statute" provided for a parliament, with ministers responsible to it rather than to the King. It was subsequently extended to the other regions which were annexed to form the Kingdom of Italy.

19 The Constituent Assembly was convened in early December 1917, and dissolved by decree of the All-Russian Central Executive Committee on 6 January 1918.

20 In January 1921, *Critica Sociale* had published an open letter from Arturo Labriola, comparing the Soviet Republic to the Paris Commune "slandered by all", and declaring that it was the duty of all socialists to support the new socialist state. Turati had appended a comment to the letter, in which he wrote: "We never suspected that conquest of power by the proletariat meant usurpation of power and systematic terror by a sect; suppression of the *zemstva* and the Constitution; replacement of Parliament by the Soviet (which is like replacement of the city by the horde)...."

21 Gramsci carried on a long polemical feud with Mario Guarnieri in 1921–2, as numerous articles in *Socialismo e Fascismo: L'Ordine Nuovo 1921–1922* (Turin, 1966) and in *Per la Verità* (Rome, 1974) testify. Guarnieri, like Nenni, had joined the PSI after the Livorno Congress, and had specialized in polemics against the Communist Party, especially in Turin. In Gramsci's first attack on Guarnieri (see *Per la Verità*, op. cit., pp. 146–7), provoked by the latter's threat of serious "revelations" concerning the Turin communists, he had written: "It seems that signor Guarnieri has a whole arsenal of communist outrages: cockroach powders, asphyxiating gases, all kinds of plagues and poisons, corrosive sublimates, chemicals, various stenches, clysters for horses, dirty shirts,

etc., etc. So let us patiently wait for the archangel Guarnieri to sound his clyster, and open this amazing performance of an extraordinary Last Judgement upon the Turin communists."

22 This article comments on the results in Turin of the general election of 15 May 1921, when the working-class parties won 137 seats in parliament (122 for the PSI, 15 for the PCI), as compared with 156 in the 1919 election. The Popular Party won 107 seats; the fascists 35 out of the 275 won by a "nationalist bloc" which also included Liberals, Conservatives, Giolittians and Nationalists.

23 Giuseppe Speranzini from Verona, former editor of *Azione*, the newspaper of the white (i.e. Popular) unions and of the League of Catholic Municipalities – and who subsequently became editor of *Conquiste Sindacali*, founded in May 1921 – was expelled from the Popular Party at the end of 1920 because the share-croppers union of Verona, which he led, came out with a demand for transformation of the share-croppers' contract into a tenant farmers' contract. Gramsci took this episode as the occasion for his article "Crisi dei Popolari?" (*Socialismo e Fascismo: L'Ordine Nuovo 1921–1922*, Turin, 1966, pp. 18–20).

24 Armando Casalini was a fascist deputy, subsequently to be assassinated in 1924. Luigi Facta was a conservative politician who in 1922 headed the weak last government before the March on Rome. Cesare Rossi was a leading fascist, until his resignation as Mussolini's press officer in the wake of the Matteotti assassination.

25 Literally "will climb mirrors".

26 Mussolini made his first speech in Parliament on 21 June 1921, with a nationalist peroration on the questions of the Alto Adige region, Fiume and Montenegro. On domestic issues, he made overtures to the Popular Party and to the Vatican, and attacked the Socialists and Communists – though proposing reconciliation to the General Confederation of Labour, provided it detached itself from the Socialist Party.

27 In his speech, Mussolini boasted of having "been the first to infect those people [the communists] when [he had] put into circulation in Italian socialism a little Bergson mixed with a lot of Blanqui".

28 *Mosca cocchiera*, one of Gramsci's favourite terms of abuse: an allusion to La Fontaine's fable *Le Coche et la Mouche*, about a fly who thinks it is thanks to his efforts that a coach succeeds in ascending a steep hill.

29 On 3 August 1921, the PSI parliamentary group signed a "*patto di pacificazione*" (conciliation pact) with the fascist deputies, in the hope of securing an end to fascist violence; but the raids in fact barely abated, and the pact was abortive. It was precisely at this moment that the *Arditi del popolo* movement was developing, with the participation of many individual socialists.

30 Stenterello is a traditional Florentine mask-character in Italian theatre:

tall, thin, clumsy, at once fatuous and crafty. See also note 237 below.
31 Arturo Labriola, one of the main syndicalist leaders before the War, became Giolitti's Minister of Labour at the time of the occupation of the factories in 1920. Bruno Buozzi, the secretary of the metal-workers' union FIOM, played a key "centrist" role in the occupation of the factories; he was a consistent, but courageous reformist.
32 Bonomi was a former socialist (expelled in 1912), who became War Minister in Giolitti's government in the summer of 1920, and himself Prime Minister on 27 June 1921. Involved in the negotiations preceding the "conciliation pact", he was reported in the press as having said of the communists to a fascist delegation: "We will try to isolate them, and then we can all come down on them together" (*Il Popolo d'Italia*, 18 August 1921).
33 During the War, the *arditi* were volunteer commando squads in the Italian army, and the term was subsequently adopted by D'Annunzio for his nationalist volunteer "legions". The *arditi del popolo* movement emerged in the spring and summer of 1921 to combat the fascist squads. Although it was formed outside the left parties, the mass of its local leaders and members were communists or socialists. The PSI, when they signed the "conciliation pact" with the fascists, condemned the organization, advocating a policy of non-resistance. The PCI also condemned the organization, for sectarian reasons, shortly after the appearance of this article; party policy was to form its own, purely communist defence squads.
34 On 13 June 1921, some thirty fascist deputies attacked the communist deputy Francesco Misiano inside Parliament, beat him and threw him into the street. They accused him of desertion, because as a conscientious objector he had emigrated to Switzerland during the War (where he edited *L'Avvenire dei Lavoratori*). In 1919 he took part in the Spartacist uprising in Berlin. Mingrino, who tried to defend Misiano from his assailants, was himself to be the object of a fascist attack on 18 July, three days after the publication of this article.
35 Grosseto, run by a socialist council, was terrorized by fascist bands from all over the region, between 27 June and 1 July 1921. There were numerous dead and wounded, and a whole series of buildings was destroyed, including the Chamber of Labour and a socialist print shop. Viterbo, another working-class stronghold, was attacked on 9 July by fascist squads drawn from Perugia, Orvieto and Rome; but the popular forces resisted and prevented the fascists from entering the city. At Treviso, on 13 July, fascist columns from Padua and Bologna destroyed the premises of the local Catholic newspaper and attacked the strong local Republican and Catholic organizations.
36 A reference to the "conciliation pact": see note 29 above.

37 At Sarzana, for the first time, a force of eleven *carabinieri* opposed fascist violence, when an armed expedition of 600 men arrived to free ten fascists imprisoned for violent crimes. At the first shots, the fascist force fled, leaving three dead and a number of wounded. The scattered remnants of the force were subsequently given a hard time by the town's inhabitants and the peasants of the surrounding countryside.

38 On 15 August 1921, the Communist Trade-Union Committee launched an appeal to the General Confederation of Labour, the *Unione Sindacale Italiana* and the Railwaymens' Union, calling for "a class action of the whole organized proletariat with the aim of confronting the present critical situation".

39 On 7 August 1921, Dino Grandi organized in Bologna a meeting of the fascists of Emilia and Romagna, in opposition to Mussolini. The latter was accused of betrayal because of his support for the "conciliation pact"; behind this lay a revolt of "agrarian fascism" against parliamentary compromise and the abandonment of violence. Mussolini resigned from the Executive Committee of the *Fasci*, together with the vice-secretary-general Cesare Rossi, but these resignations were rejected.

40 See on this, "Origins of the Mussolini Cabinet", p. 130 below.

41 Literally "transigence", by contrast with "intransigence".

42 See note 23 above.

43 *Umanità Nova* was the newspaper of the *Unione Anarchica Italiana*, whose leading spirit was Errico Malatesta.

44 See "Partito e Sindacati", in *L'Ordine Nuovo 1919–1920*, Turin, 1955, pp. 404–8. This article, in fact dated 21 August rather than 15 August, must be the one referred to by Gramsci. It is in fact mainly directed against the Socialist Party leadership's failure to prepare the proletariat politically. It expresses no opposition to the action as such, though it implicitly criticizes FIOM: "the metalworkers' executive (not bothering with the Party? not bothering to inform the Party or reach agreement with it? It would be useful to have some information about this, in order to assess the spirit of discipline and the political intuition of certain comrades) has by its initiative determined the opening of a new phase of agitation and strikes on a national scale, without the Party's central organization having yet thought it useful to express its opinion, to propose any slogan for the metalworker comrades, or to discipline them to achieve the Party's own ends."

45 See note 24 above.

46 See note 29 above.

47 Borghi was the anarcho-syndicalist secretary of the USI, D'Aragona the reformist secretary of the CGL, Malatesta the anarchist "leader", Serrati the main leader of the PSI, Leone Sbrana and Augusto Castrucci were prominent in USI, Mario Guarnieri (see note 21 above) and Emilio Colombino were socialists.

48 Giuseppe Giulietti was a reformist leader of the seamens' union and a deputy, prominent in encouraging the CGL towards conciliation *vis-à-vis* fascism. Alceste De Ambris was secretary of USI until 1914, when he came out for intervention in the War.

49 Umberto I was king from 1878 until his assassination by an anarchist in 1900. In 1897, Sidney Sonnino, a conservative politician subsequently twice prime minister (1906 and 1909–10) and wartime foreign minister (1914–19), wrote an article entittled "Return to the Constitution" in which he called for an end to any attempt to create an English-style parliamentary democracy in Italy and for a considerable strengthening of the executive powers of the monarchy, to which alone ministers should henceforth be responsible as was ordained by the constitution. In fact, the King himself apparently shared the widespread hostile reaction to Sonnino's article. A weak and indecisive character, in general he tended to play little independent political role; the only exception was a half-hearted move to exceed his constitutional powers following the Milan rising of 1898 – and this was speedily abandoned. Thus Gramsci oversimplifies somewhat here when he presents Umberto as Sonnino's partner in the latter's attempt to curtail the powers of parliament.

50 The *Alleanza del lavoro* was established on 20 February 1922, between the leaders of the CGL, the USI, the UIL, the Railwaymens' Union and the National Federation of Portworkers. The Communist Trade-Union Committee was not invited to take part in the meeting, and the party's position was summed up in *L'Ordine Nuovo* on 23 February: "United front for Communists means 'action' of all the proletarian forces united for struggle. If this is also the purpose of the *Alleanza del lavoro*, it must seek to base itself directly on the masses. Without the weight of the latter, its National Committee can only become a factory for Platonic resolutions." On the *Alleanza*, see *SPN*, Introduction, pp. l–li.

51 After an attempt by Giolitti to form a new cabinet to replace that of Bonomi – which resigned on 2 February 1922, as a result of the withdrawal of support by Amendola's liberal democrats – had failed because of the Popular Party's opposition, a second attempt by De Nicola and Orlando to form a new administration also came to nothing, due to the refusal of Facta (see note 24 above) to take part.

52 For the essential passages of the PSI motion, see *Socialismo e Fascismo, L'Ordine Nuovo 1921–1922*, Turin, 1966, p. 461 n.

53 Montecitorio is the building in Rome which houses the Italian Chamber of Deputies.

II

54 This was the main document presented by the Party leadership to the Second Congress of the PCI, held at Rome from 20 to 25 March 1922. (This was the first true party congress, since the founding congress of

January 1921 immediately after the split from the PSI was simply a demonstration, accompanied by a provisional settlement of organizational questions.) The document was published in *L'Ordine Nuovo* on 3 January 1922, and was complemented by "Theses on the Agrarian Question" drafted by Sanna and Graziadei, and "Theses on Trade-union Tactics" drafted by Gramsci and Tasca. There was little disagreement with the "Rome Theses" prior to the Congress. But at Rome the Comintern delegates, notably Kolarov, expressed strong criticism of the party leadership's refusal to extend the united front beyond the trade-union sphere. Kolarov stressed that in the view of the Comintern Executive, the status of the Rome Theses should only be to provide the basis for a future discussion throughout the International. Kolarov's intervention was coldly received; a series of speakers, including Gramsci as well as Bordiga, argued against his views on the united front and workers' government (see pp. 120–4 below). A resolution moved by Bordiga was passed unanimously, to the effect that the Rome Theses should be seen as "a formulation which can in no way prejudice international discipline". This ambiguous compromise was to set the tone for relations with the Comintern over the next two years. At the Congress itself, two "rightist" oppositions emerged. The more extreme of these, however, led by Bombacci and Presutti and aligned with the views expressed by Kolarov, subsequently withdrew its own resolution in favour of a more nuanced one put forward by Graziadei (in agreement with Tasca) – with the direct encouragement of the Comintern delegates. In the final voting, the majority resolution approving the Romes Theses received 31,089 votes, the Graziadei resolution 4,151. At the Congress Gramsci, whatever his reservations about the Rome Theses, was *primarily* concerned about: 1. the danger of "liquidation" into social democracy if the political united front were to be accepted; 2. the danger that the right wing in the Party, led by Tasca and Graziadei, might come to power with Comintern backing if a compromise with the International was not reached. He was not to express any criticism of the Rome Theses before 1924, and then in private letters (see e.g. p. 196 below); for a later judgement, see e.g. *SPN*, pp. 200–1.

55 It has not been possible to identify the source of this quotation, probably a Comintern document, but cf. the "Theses on the World Situation and the Tasks of the Communist International" passed at the IIIrd Congress of the Communist International: 'Even though it is undeniable that in the present epoch the curve of capitalist development is a generally descending one, despite fleeting movements of revival, the curve of revolution is a rising one, though it shows a few dips."

56 The "Theses on Trade-union Tactics" drafted by Gramsci and Tasca (mainly by the latter) for the Rome Congress had been published in nine instalments between 31 January and 9 February 1922; they numbered

thirty. The *Alleanza del lavoro* was formally constituted on 20 February 1922. The article by Gramsci on pp. 83–4 above had represented an initial, individual reaction, but this intervention at the Congress should certainly be seen as reflecting the collective view of the PCd'I leadership. The "Theses on Trade-union Tactics" are included as an appendix to *Socialismo e Fascismo: L'Ordine Nuovo 1921–1922* (Turin, 1966), but the three additional theses mentioned here by Gramsci were probably never drafted.

57 See note 43 above. Among the anarchists, Malatesta was particularly enthusiastic about the new organization.

58 "ad' *Aragno*" in the original clearly is a misprint for "*a D'Aragona*" (see note 47 above).

59 There was a debate in progress within USI on the question of whether or not formally to join the Red Trade-union International. At the organization's March 1922 congress, the current led by Borghi in fact won a majority against joining, on the grounds that the International was subordinate to the Communist Parties.

60 In December 1921, the Executive Committee of the Comintern drew up a 24-point document formulating the united front policy *vis-à-vis* the social-democratic parties and the "yellow" unions. An appeal to the international proletariat in January 1922 motivated the new policy. At the end of February 1922, the first "Enlarged Executive" meeting took place – these were to become almost as important as the World Congresses in the next few years. At this meeting, the Italian delegates (together with the French and Spanish) clashed with the Comintern leadership. Though attacked by all the Bolshevik leaders present – Lunacharsky, Radek, Trotsky, Zinoviev – they voted against the majority on the united front question. Nevertheless, they at the same time promised to maintain a disciplined stance towards the policy of the International. Gramsci's position here was typical of the PCI's attitude in this period: to pay verbal homage to the line of the International, while in fact rejecting the whole spirit of the united front policy.

61 The "Maffisti" were the "third-internationalist" current within the PSI, led by Fabrizio Maffi and Costantino Lazzari. The current was constituted before the party's Milan Congress in October 1921, to fight for adhesion to the IIIrd International in the face of Serrati's view that this was no longer on the agenda.

62 See note 54 above for the emergence of the minority at the Rome Congress.

III

63 Gramsci had left Italy for Moscow in May 1922, soon after the Rome Congress, as the PCd'I's representative on the Comintern Executive. His first six months in the Soviet Union were mainly spent in a sanatorium,

but in September he was well enough to send a letter to Trotsky on Italian futurism (at the latter's request). In November he wrote "The Origins of the Mussolini Cabinet", and participated (with Zinoviev, Trotsky, Radek, Rakosi, Zetkin, etc.) in the "Italian Commission" at the Fourth World Congress of the IIIrd International, where he had a long discussion with Bordiga, and another with Rakosi.

Camilla Ravera, another of the Italian delegates to the Congress, has given an account of the former: "With Bordiga, Gramsci wanted to have detailed discussion on Italian and international problems: conversations – he said – an exchange of views, to clarify their ideas mutually; with the aim, by means precisely of this formal approach, of excluding any idea of counter-position or open disagreement and rupture. The relations that existed between Gramsci and Bordiga were affectionate. Bordiga felt and displayed a very keen concern for Gramsci's health; and a deep admiration for his intelligence and wisdom. Gramsci admired Bordiga's vigorous personality and general abilities and capacity for work, and appreciated the positive aspect of what he had achieved, in very difficult circumstances, in the initial construction and organization of the party" (see too Gramsci's own comment, p. 138 below).

On the discussion with Rakosi, Gramsci wrote in another letter: "At the IVth Congress, I had only been out of the sanatorium for a few days (a few numerically, and not just in a metaphorical sense), after a stay of around six months which had not helped much – which had merely prevented an aggravation of my illness and a paralysis of the legs which could have kept me confined to my bed for years. From a general point of view, my exhaustion and inability to work as a result of losses of memory and insomnia continued. The Penguin [Rakosi], with the diplomatic delicacy which distinguishes him, assailed me with the aim of once more offering me to become the leader of the party, eliminating Amadeo, who was literally to be excluded from the Comintern if he continued on his line. I said that I would do my best to help the International Executive to resolve the Italian question, but I did not believe that one could in any way (and certainly not with my person) replace Amadeo, without a preliminary activity designed to reorient the party. To replace Amadeo in the Italian situation, furthermore, meant having more than one element, since Amadeo, in effect, in terms of general and working capacity, is worth at least three – even allowing that it is possible to replace a man of his worth. I was walking upon burning coals, and this was not the most suitable activity for my condition of chronic weakness. . . . What would have happened if I had not 'wriggled', as unfortunately I had to do? The majority of the delegates would have been with me, apart from a few elements like Azzario, and we would have had a crisis of the Party at long distance, without any agreement with all of you. Urbani, Bruno, Luigino, Ruggero and Amadeo [Terracini, Fortichiari, Repossi, Grieco and

Bordiga, the members of the party's Executive Committee] would have resigned, and the minority – even less prepared than it was subsequently – would have taken over a handful of flies...."

At the Fourth World Congress, the discussion on Italy was mainly concerned with the question of fusion with the PSI, who a month previously had expelled their reformist wing (who formed the Unitarian Socialist Party (PSU), led by Turati and Momigliano) and renewed their application to join the Comintern. The PCI Executive Committee was opposed to any fusion with the socialists. At the other extreme, Tasca, Vota and Graziadei were in favour of fusion of the two parties as advocated by the Comintern leaders. Gramsci and Scoccimarro, and the majority of the Italian delegates to the Congress, initially were only prepared to accept fusion with the so-called IIIrd-Internationalist current inside the PSI (formed at the previous congress, see note 61 above). However, under Comintern pressure, and frightened by the identity of views between the International leadership and the Italian minority, they finally accepted the principle of fusion. At the end of the World Congress, a mixed commission was created of Gramsci, Scoccimarro and Tasca for the PCI, Serrati, Tonetti and Maffi for the PSI. However, the work of this commission, in Moscow and subsequently in Italy, was soon rendered fruitless by the emergence of a new anti-fusion majority in the PSI under Nenni (see note 72 below).

After the Congress, Gramsci remained in Moscow. The Congress had taken no decision about the composition of the PCI leadership, pending the outcome of the fusion talks, but shortly after his return to Italy Bordiga was arrested (February 1923), and the same fate befell Grieco and many other leading cadres soon after. Terracini assumed responsibility for rebuilding the party organization, but soon afterwards was shifted to Moscow and replaced by Togliatti, who was coopted on to the Executive for this purpose. In this situation, an Enlarged Executive meeting of the Comintern was scheduled in Moscow from 18 to 23 June 1923, to discuss all aspects of the "Italian Question". It was attended, in the event, by Gramsci, Terracini, Tasca, Vota and Scoccimarro. Togliatti was originally supposed to be present too; in fact, he stayed in Italy, but wrote this letter to Gramsci to explain the situation in the party.

64 After its Turin Congress in April 1923, the Popular Party – which despite its participation in the government, was in its majority opposed to unconditional collaboration with its coalition partners, notably the fascists – had launched the idea of "freedom blocs" to defend the constitution against fascist illegality. These were taken up by the reformist socialists, but in fact were rejected by the PSI and *Avanti!*, in keeping with their maximalist traditions. However, Togliatti was not wrong to point to a deep-going ambiguity in the PSI's positions, which tended to immobilize it in practice.

65 When the Nenni group's ascendancy in the PSI made fusion effectively unattainable in early 1923 (see note 72 below), Zinoviev proposed that the Italian communists should seek to form a political bloc between the two parties. Terracini, then leading the party in Italy after the arrest of Bordiga and Grieco (and most of the party's Central Committee and regional organizers), had sent an angry letter to the International's Presidium attacking Zinoviev's proposal as a capitulation to the anti-fusionist majority in the PSI, before even the question of fusion had been fought out at the party's April congress. Gramsci had considered Terracini's letter ill-judged, and had proposed that the latter be transferred to Moscow while he himself moved to Vienna. Terracini did indeed move to Moscow, though Gramsci's transfer to Vienna was in fact delayed until November 1923.

66 In other words, the activity of Tasca and the minority tended, Gramsci feared, to discredit the entire former *Ordine Nuovo* group – or risked doing so if the latter were to detach themselves from the Bordiga leadership.

67 For the Fourth World Congress and Gramsci's role, see note 63 above. For Gramsci's position in the summer of 1920, see introduction to *SPN*, pp. xli–ii.

68 The USPD (Independent Social-Democratic Party of Germany) was formed in the spring of 1917, mainly on the basis of opposition to the voting of war credits, in defiance of party discipline in the SPD. It applied for admission to the IIIrd International, but split after its Halle Congress in October 1920 on the question of full application of the Comintern's 21 Points. Although the communists won a comfortable majority at the congress, they failed to carry the key trade-union leaders. They emerged, in practice, with not more than 300,000 of the USPD's 800,000 members; these then merged with the 50,000 members of the Spartakusbund to form the Communist Party of Germany. The rump of the USPD merged with the SPD in 1922.

69 *La Stampa, Il Corriere della Sera* and *Il Mondo*, the main organs of the "liberal" bourgeoisie, waged a press campaign against fascism during 1923 that was interpreted by the PCI as reflecting the anti-protectionist interests of the engineering and textile employers (in contrast to the pro-fascist steel employers).

70 See note 23 above.

71 At the Enlarged Executive meeting in Moscow on 18–23 June 1923 (see note 63 above), there was a confrontation all along the line between, on the one hand, Zinoviev and the Comintern leadership (participants included Trotsky, Lunacharsky, Bukharin, Zetkin, Kolarov, Rakosi and Manuilsky), together with Tasca and the representatives of the fusionist wing of the PSI; on the other hand, the representatives of the majority leadership in the PCI – Gramsci, Scoccimarro, Terracini, Fortichiari,

Gennari – who closed ranks in defence of the record and organizational unity of the Communist Party as constituted at Livorno. (For all this, see introduction to *SPN*, pp. lvi–lvii.) This report by the minority of the PCI delegation, delivered by Tasca, provided the basis for the Comintern's critique of the Italian majority leadership.

72 At the PSI's Rome Congress in September–October 1922, the party had split more or less in half (32,106 votes for the maximalist resolution, 29,119 for the reformist one), and the reformist wing had formed the Unitary Socialist Party. The majority had renewed its intention of joining the IIIrd International, and decided to send an official delegation to Moscow to discuss the modalities. (For the discussions, at the Fourth World Congress and thereafter, see note 63 above.) However, on 14 January 1923, a group of socialist leaders headed by Nenni and Vella formed the National Committee of Socialist Defence, to fight against any liquidation of the PSI through fusion with the Communist Party. At the Milan Congress of the PSI, in April 1923, the anti-fusionists won a majority by 5,361 votes to 3,908 over the "III-internationalist" wing of the party (i.e. the Maffisti – see note 61 above – together with Serrati and the old leadership, who now genuinely favoured fusion).

73 At the conference of the three internationals in April 1922, the social democrats led by Vandervelde, when asked for IInd International support for the Soviet Union at the impending conference with the Western Powers at Genoa, made this conditional upon Russian acceptance of three political demands: self-determination for Georgia, freedom of press and propaganda for non-Bolshevik socialist parties, and freeing of the "social-revolutionary" leaders about to be tried for high treason in Moscow. Radek and Bukharin, who led the Soviet delegation, made some concessions on these demands to achieve agreement, but were criticized by Lenin and the party leadership subsequently (see Lenin's "We Have Paid Too Much", *Collected Works*, Vol. 33, London, 1966, pp. 330–4), as having allowed united front tactics to be utilized to the disadvantage rather than the advantage of the Communists. In any case, the limited agreements achieved at Berlin soon proved to be still-born. For Serrati's illusions about what the Berlin Conference had achieved, see four articles by Gramsci entitled "Words and Deeds", published in *L'Ordine Nuovo* on 12, 13, 15 and 18 April 1922 (*Socialismo e Fascismo*: *L'Ordine Nuovo 1921–1922*, Turin, 1966, pp. 482–8; *Per la Verità*, pp. 255–6), and the corresponding articles by Serrati in *Avanti!*, on 11, 12, 14 and 16 April 1922.

74 The French "dissidents" or *résistants* were the heterogeneous bloc of Communist Party members who rejected the recommendation of the Fourth World Congress that the French party should purge its ranks of freemasons (like its general secretary Frossard, who resigned in protest), supporters of the *Ligue des Droits de l'Homme*, etc. The St-Ouen

Congress referred to was the 1923 congress of the French Socialist Party.
75 Following the merger of the German SPD with the rump of the USPD in the summer of 1922 (see note 68 above), the basis no longer existed for the so-called Two-and-a-Half International, which merged with the IInd International at a Conference in Hamburg in the spring of 1923.
76 The comrades in question were Ersilio Ambrogi (delegate of the PCI first in Moscow, then in Berlin), and Luigi Repossi, responsible for trade-union work.
77 After the failure of the "March Action" in Germany in 1921, Brandler and the majority leadership of the German Communist Party drew conclusions which adumbrated the International's united front policy, though they went much further to the right in the way in which they interpreted it. A left minority emerged in the German party, initially still wedded to the "theory of the offensive" which had proved so disastrous in March. By the time of the IVth World Congress in late 1922, both majority and minority accepted the principle of the united front, though the differences in interpretation between them remained very wide. Lenin's interventions at the Congress, and the final resolution adopted there on the German question, sought to strike a balance between the two factions, making criticisms of both.
78 In March 1923, the Comintern convened an international conference at Frankfurt on the danger of fascism in Europe, and invited the social-democratic political and trade-union organizations. The conference itself decided to pursue this initiative *vis-à-vis* the social democrats by appointing a German delegation to the "yellow" trade-union headquarters in Amsterdam, but this was to bear little fruit.
79 Cf. "Il disco dell'immaturita", in *Socialismo e Fascismo: L'Ordine Nuovo 1921–22*, Turin, 1966, p. 139: "Every rough fellow who joins up with his bludgeon and his knife, can become a political leader, a chief, a Marcellus, someone capable of resolving the existential problems of society in its death-throes." Marcellus, during the Punic Wars between Rome and Carthage, was the first Roman general to show that Hannibal was not invincible, and was often portrayed as the symbol of military virtues and saviour of the Republic. Gramsci, in the article quoted here, was arguing that the collapse of the liberal bourgeois political order in Italy had created a situation in which only adventurers – the fascists and their collaborators on the one hand, the maximalists on the other – could prosper. In his notes on relations with the Comintern, he is saying that the role of communist leadership must be qualitatively different.
80 A clear reference to Tasca and the minority. This passage gives an unambiguous record of the decisive difference of attitude between Gramsci at this moment – determined to prevent a minority leadership – and Bordiga, who saw a minority leadership as the correct and inevitable consequence of the line of the International.

NOTES 477

81 In Hungary, the Communist Party was effectively eliminated from the country after the Soviet government was crushed by Rumanian troops in August 1919. In Yugoslavia, too, the Communist Party virtually disappeared as a force within the country (after briefly having been the second largest political party) when it was banned by government decree in 1919. In both cases, the parties proved unable to organize mass resistance, and the leaderships went into exile.

82 The decision to turn the old majority leadership into a faction was a response to the attack on that leadership's record made by Tasca and the minority at the Enlarged Executive meeting a month earlier (see preceding text), and represented a closing of the ranks in respect of the divisions which had opened up in the majority at the IVth World Congress (see note 63 above). Only the two interventions published here have survived, probably because they were copied for transmission to Bordiga in prison (he was considered to be the natural leader for the faction).

83 The first of these fragments is an unfinished reply to a 16 July letter from Togliatti expressing his doubts as to whether he should agree to continue on the party's Executive Committee. The second is probably a draft for part of the "plan of general action" spoken of in the first fragment; in other words, it might have been incorporated in the letter to Togliatti if this had been completed. There is no way of ascertaining whether the third fragment was also intended to find its place in the same "plan of general action", or whether it dates from an earlier period. The fragments were found among Gramsci's papers after his arrest, and copied by Tasca. One can only speculate as to why the fragments were not completed: perhaps either because Gramsci was expecting to move imminently to Vienna (though his departure was in fact to be postponed until November); perhaps because he did not feel confident that he would find a receptive response, in view of the closing of ranks in the majority leadership of the PCI after the Enlarged Executive meeting of June.

84 In April 1921, Gramsci made an abortive attempt to meet D'Annunzio and drive a wedge between his "legionaries" – disillusioned by their fiasco at Fiume (see note 226 below) and by Mussolini's collaboration with Giolitti in the 1921 parliamentary elections – and the fascists. Again in the spring of 1922, the CGL leaders had meetings with D'Annunzio, in an attempt to persuade him to lead an anti-fascist front and perhaps even a kind of Italian "labour" party. In the autumn of 1922, it was the turn of the traditional bourgeois and monarchist forces to look to D'Annunzio to save them from fascism. However, real though the tensions between Mussolini and D'Annunzio were, the latter was never again after Fiume to prove capable of organizing any serious independent initiative.

85 This letter, written by Gramsci shortly before he left Moscow for Vienna, arose from a decision of the Comintern Executive at the beginning of September that a new communist daily newspaper must be launched in

Italy, "to counter-balance the influence of *Avanti!* over the masses". This decision was taken when the new majority leadership that had emerged at the PSI's Milan Congress (see note 72 above) expelled a number of key "IIIrd-internationalist" leaders (the editors of the review *Pagine Rosse*) from the party: these included Serrati and Maffi. The name *L'Unità* proposed by Gramsci was inspired by the pre-war journal of that name edited by the "southernist" Salvemini (see note 252 below). The meeting of the Comintern Enlarged Executive referred to is that of June 1923 (see notes 63 and 71 above).

86 *Sindacato Rosso* was the organ of the communist tendency within the General Confederation of Labour. Nicola Vecchi was the leader of the anarcho-syndicalist tendency in USI, the other main trade-union federation; he was favourable to rapprochement with the communists and the IIIrd International.

87 Internal commissions – elected factory grievance committees – multiplied throughout Italian industry during the First World War, often serving to organize rank-and-file militancy independently of the trade unions. For their key importance in the development of the factory council movement, see *SPWI*, pp. 66–7, 94–7, 114–24, and *passim*.

88 This letter was sent from Moscow in October to the Milan periodical *Voce della Gioventù*, which had replaced the official organ of the Communist Youth Federation after its suppression by the police.

89 Giuffrida Giuseppe De Felice, Aurelio Drago and Alessandro Tasca di Cutò were Sicilian reformist politicians, before the War oriented towards Giolitti's policy of alliance with the organized labour movement, during the War allies of Salandra in his pro-War policies. De Felice had been a leader of the Fasci movement of 1893–4 (see note 199 below); he became a syndicalist, and rallied to a nationalist perspective during the Libyan War.

90 In 1898 the Milan workers demonstrated against rising prices and food shortages, and were bloodily repressed by General Bava Beccaris.

91 The national general strike of September 1904, sparked off by massacres of mine-workers in Sardinia and peasants in Sicily, was launched by the revolutionary syndicalist leaders of the Milan Chamber of Labour and lasted four days. This was the high point of revolutionary syndicalist influence in the PSI and the unions; but the collapse of the strike – Giolitti, the prime minister, simply waited it out, then called parliamentary elections – weakened the entire trade-union movement, and presaged a revival of reformism and decline of syndicalism. Many of the latter's leaders were to be absorbed by the ruling class in the process described by Gramsci as transformism (see *SPN*, p. 58 notes; also note 195 and p. 450 below).

92 After the Risorgimento, the republican tradition stemming from Mazzini was of diminishing importance, caught as it was between the emerging

socialist movement and the parliamentary "radicals" who had come to terms with the monarchy. However, in 1905 a Republican Party was organized with some success, and in Romagna even won a mass base, coming to dominate the share-croppers unions and an important section of the agricultural labourers. The opposition of the majority of the party to the Libyan War led to a split, but by contrast it was among the first forces to come out for Italian intervention in World War One. After the War, the Republican Party supported the *Alleanza del Lavoro* and later participated in the Aventine opposition to fascism. Never a large party, at the extreme left of the bourgeois spectrum, it won 29 seats in the 1900 elections, 24 in 1904 and again in 1909, 17 in 1913, and together with "democratic" allies 43 seats in 1919, 22 in 1921 and 9 in 1924.

93 For Bordiga's proposal that the majority leadership of the PCI should draft a manifesto to the party membership and the Italian working class, see Togliatti's letter, p. 133 above. From another letter from Togliatti to Gramsci, written on 29 December 1923, we know that Gramsci had refused to sign the manifesto – though it is not clear whether he had read the original or the second draft – whereas Togliatti, Terracini and Scoccimarro had accepted to sign the revised version, despite their differences with Bordiga. These differences concerned tactics *vis-à-vis* the International (they were effectively running the party in Italy, while Bordiga was for a policy of refusing leadership responsibilities), and the purpose of the manifesto (they wanted it to provide a basis for opening a political discussion on perspectives throughout the party, while Bordiga was mainly concerned with the reaffirmation of past positions).

94 The Petrograd School was set up in 1922 to train Communist cadres from many countries, both politically and militarily. The Italian communists in fact took their courses at the Tolmachev Political and Military Institute.

95 *L'Ordine Nuovo* was to be re-launched as a fortnightly review on 1 March 460–62 below.

96 Piero Gobetti (1901–26) was a young liberal intellectual, who despite his non-socialism had been powerfully influenced by the October Revolution and the Turin factory council movement. He shared the view of *L'Ordine Nuovo* in the post-war period that the key strategic problem was to forge a worker–peasant alliance – though he saw this, unlike the communists, as replacing fascism with a "democratic" stage. He collaborated as theatre critic with the daily *Ordine Nuovo* in 1921. In January 1922, Gobetti founded *La Rivoluzione Liberale*, with a wide range of anti-fascist contributors. For Gobetti, see the long footnote 42 in *SPN*, p. 73, and pp. 460–62 below.

97 *Italia libera* was founded as an anti-fascist war-veterans' movement in 1923, and achieved wide support in 1924 after the murder of the socialist deputy Matteotti (see note 154 below), even beginning to form its own militias.

98 The reference is to Terracini's letter of 2 January 1924, criticizing Gramsci's refusal to sign the manifesto drafted by Bordiga. Terracini argued that at the Enlarged Executive meeting in June 1923, Gramsci had accepted the need for the old majority leadership to consolidate their unity in the face of pressure from the International leadership and the threat from Tasca and the minority. His refusal to sign was jeopardizing precisely that unity, and undermining the fragile understanding that had been reached with Bordiga in the course of drafting the manifesto (the latter had modified his initial position that "there is nothing to be done with the Maximalists", under pressure from Scoccimarro).

99 In December 1923 Nicola Bombacci (former vice-secretary of the PSI and delegate to the Second Comintern Congress in June 1920; perhaps the most prestigious and typical representative of Italian "maximalism" won to the new Communist Party; founder-member of the communist faction within the PSI in October 1920, and member of the fifteen-strong Central Committee elected after the Livorno split) was at the centre of a minor political scandal. He had moved to the right during the first years of the party's existence, and though a parliamentary deputy was isolated within the party itself. Now, on the occasion of a new trade agreement between Italy and the Soviet Union, Bombacci made a speech in parliament referring to an "affinity" between the two revolutions (i.e. fascist and communist). Bombacci was forced by the party executive to resign from parliament. He was subsequently to be expelled from the party (1927) and to rally to fascism, becoming an adviser to Mussolini in his last days under the Salò Republic; he was shot with Mussolini in 1945. Belloni and Remondino were both communist deputies in 1923.

100 This project, conceived as a Marxist counterpart to Croce's journal *La Critica* (see note 270 below), was never in fact realized.

101 This refers to Togliatti's letter of 29 December 1923, see note 93 above.

102 "Tito" was Bruno Fortichiari, who had been in charge of the party's so-called "illegal" activity. Gramsci was under the impression that this area of work had been taken over by Togliatti after Fortichiari's refusal – together with Bordiga – to join the new Executive Committee. In fact, it was Scoccimarro who had replaced Fortichiari.

103 "From the very bottom".

104 The reference is to Terracini, who had been leading the party organization inside Italy after the arrest of Bordiga and Grieco.

105 The identity of this Russian CC member has not been established.

106 Dr Grillo was a sixteenth-century charlatan, a self-proclaimed doctor of peasant origin, who became the subject of numerous popular rhymes and stories after his death.

107 See *SPW I*, pp. 239–98.

108 In other words, the Zinoviev, Kamenev, Stalin triumvirate.

109 See Trotsky's *First Five Years of the Communist International*, Volume

2, New York, 1953, pp. 346–53, where its title is rendered as "Is it possible to fix a Definite Schedule for a Counter-revolution or a Revolution?"

110 For the February 1922 Enlarged Executive meeting, at which the Italian delegation headed by Terracini clashed with the International leadership, see introduction to *SPN*, p. *l*. Immediately following this, the Comintern's Executive Committee met to discuss the Rome Theses, and Trotsky and Radek criticized them in detail and proposed their rejection. It was finally decided that the Theses should be presented to the Italian Party Congress with a simply consultative status, as a contribution to the preparation of the Fourth World Congress. The Comintern Presidium thereupon drafted its own detailed criticisms and transmitted these in the form of an official letter to the Central Committee of the PCI. This letter was not published by the Italians until April 1924, but the International leadership made it public on the eve of the Fourth Congress by printing it in its official organ, with an editorial note explaining that it had been sent to the Italian comrades in mid-March 1922. See "Une contribution au projet de programme du PCd'I" (Observations by the ECCI Presidium), in *L'Internationale Communiste*, Year III, No. 23, October–November 1922.

111 The reference is to the Imola convention of the communist faction inside the PSI, in November 1920.

112 In a report entitled "The Tactics of the Communist Party discussed in the Turin Section", which appeared in *Il Comunista* on 19 February 1922, we find the following: "After a substantive report by comrade Gramsci, the assembly unanimously approved the theses which have been prepared on tactics, for presentation to the party congress ... the assembly unanimously acknowledged that there are circumstances of time and place in which the Communist Party can and must make compromises with other parties which enjoy the trust of the more backward layers of the working class and peasantry, and must insistently urge these parties to break all links with the bourgeoisie and establish a political coalition on the exclusive terrain of the working classes ... for these reasons the assembly judged that the only possible and useful tactic today is that of the trade-union united front". Since Gramsci's speech has not survived, it is hard to judge to what extent he really made his position as clear as he claims in this letter; the report certainly gives no such indication.

113 See p. 93 above.

114 In his "And Now?" (in *Whither France*), Trotsky wrote in 1931: "The (Italian) Communist Party did not appreciate the dimensions of the fascist danger, it entertained revolutionary illusions ... Fascism was only pictured as 'capitalist reaction'. The *specific* characteristics of fascism, determined by the mobilization of the petty bourgeoisie against the proletariat, were not discerned by the Communist Party. According to the information given by our Italian friends, with the exception of Gramsci

the Communist Party did not even admit the possibility of a seizure of power by the fascists. Since the proletarian revolution had suffered a defeat; since capitalism had managed to survive and the counter-revolution had thus won, what counter-revolutionary *coup d'état* could still take place? It was impossible after all that the bourgeoisie should rise up against itself! This was, in essence, the political orientation of the Italian Communist Party. Nevertheless, one should not forget that Italian fascism was at that time a new phenomenon, in the process of formation: it would have been difficult even for an experienced party to define its specific features." This passage from Trotsky, based presumably on what he knew from Leonetti and Tresso who had recently been expelled from the PCI for their opposition to the Third Period and their contacts with Trotsky, fully confirms Gramsci's own account here. Nevertheless, the passage which immediately follows seems hard to explain, since there Gramsci says that the party ignored the possibility of a social-democratic government and *did* consider a fascist dictatorship possible! In fact, the social-democratic "solution" was that generally seen as most probable by the PCI leadership in 1921–2, and Gramsci himself wrote of it as imminent, e.g. on 13 February 1922 ("Il processo della crisi", now in *Socialismo e Fascismo*: *l'Ordine Nuovo 1921–1922*, Turin, 1966). What is certainly true is that Gramsci, whatever the uncertainty of his political perspectives in 1921–2, did differ from the rest of the Bordiga leadership in that he accorded real importance to the *particular form* of bourgeois régime.

115 See pp. 115–16 above. No first draft of the theses in question has survived, so that it is not possible to identify corrections introduced by Gramsci.
116 Arturo Caroti was an important maximalist leader from Pisa, a parliamentary deputy, who joined the Communist Party when it was founded. His son Leopoldo, referred to here, had launched a journal called *Spartacus* at Livorno in 1919, while still a student.

IV

117 *L'Ordine Nuovo*, Third Series, was launched as a fortnightly at the beginning of March 1924, just two weeks after the appearance of the first issue of the new party daily *L'Unità*. It had a print run of 6,000 copies, and six issues appeared in 1924: two in March, a double issue in April, one in September and two in November.
118 Lenin had died on 21 January 1924.
119 On 7 June 1914, an anti-militarist demonstration at Ancona, organized by Malatesta and Nenni (then a republican), was fired on by the police, resulting in three deaths. The PSI called a general strike, and there were insurrectionary outbreaks throughout the country. Ancona was held by the insurgents for ten days, and it took 10,000 troops to subdue it.
120 Mussolini became editor of *Avanti!* in December 1912, and gained

immediate wide publicity with his fiery editorials on the occasion of a police massacre of agricultural labourers at Roccagorga in January 1913. (In the *Prison Notebooks*, Gramsci was to cite Roccagorga as the real origin of the train of events culminating in the Red Week, see *QC* II, pp. 1010–11). As a result of the *Avanti!* campaign, Mussolini and a number of other journalists and contributors to the paper were put on trial in Milan between 26 March and 1 April 1914; some of the *braccianti* who had escaped the massacre testified as defence witnesses. One of Mussolini's co-defenders was Giuseppe Scalarini, who was to continue as one of the principal contributors to *Avanti!* until its suppression in the mid-twenties.

121 Romulus Augustulus, last of the Western Emperors of Rome, was overthrown in A.D. 476 by the Heruli under Odoacer.

122 See note 28 above.

123 See "Towards a Renewal of the Socialist Party", in *SPW I*, pp. 190–6. This was written for the National Council meeting of the PSI, originally scheduled to take place in Turin, but moved to Milan when the Turin general strike broke out – the meeting lasted from 18 to 22 April 1920.

124 The proposal was in fact made by Gramsci himself, who intervened in the abstentionist convention of 8–9 May (not July) 1920 as an "observer" (see p. 251 below).

125 See note 1 above.

126 See note 85 above. The fortnightly *Pagine Rosse*, organ of the "IIIrd-internationalists" in the PSI, was founded on 29 June 1923 and suppressed in August 1924 after the current fused with the Communist Party.

127 See pp. 229–31 and 237–9 below. Piero Sraffa had been a young communist student influenced by *L'Ordine Nuovo* in 1920. He did not subsequently, as Gramsci hoped, contribute to the PCI press; but he maintained a friendship which was to be of prime importance in sustaining Gramsci during his imprisonment. Sraffa was mainly responsible for supplying Gramsci with books; he visited him and reported on his situation to the party leadership in exile; and he helped to organize the international campaign of protest against the conditions of his imprisonment. Zino Zini was a philosopher and long-standing socialist from Turin, who had written regularly for *L'Ordine Nuovo* in 1919–20.

128 See note 100 above.

129 In 1921–2, the fascist squads systematically destroyed socialist union organization among the peasants and agricultural labourers, forcing them instead into fascist unions. In 1921, membership of the socialist National Federation of Land Workers dropped from 890,000 to 294,000. (In 1922, the fascists turned their attention to the catholic unions on the land, smashing them in the same way.)

130 This "circular letter No. 11" to all local organizations of the Party said in no uncertain terms that the entire activity of the Party and the Comintern *vis-à-vis* the PSI, and in particular the electoral bloc for the April 1924 elections between communists and "IIIrd-internationalists", had the sole aim of destroying the Socialist Party. The letter went on to warn all Party sections to combat the danger that the pact with the "IIIrd-internationalists" might create the basis for some new centrist party. The circular letter fell into the hands of the PSI and was published in *Avanti!* on 5 March 1924, provoking the extreme indignation of the Comintern delegate in Italy, Jules Humbert-Droz. Togliatti describes the episode in a letter to Terracini on 15 March 1924, stressing the fact that even Tasca had agreed to the drawing up of the circular letter, and that this had led to something of a rift between him and the "IIIrd-internationalists".

131 For the "IIIrd-internationalists", see notes 61, 72, 85, 126 above.

132 See note 123 above.

133 The reference is to Piero Sraffa, see p. 218 and note 127 above.

134 See note 28 above.

135 See p. 218 and note 127 above.

136 For Umberto Cosmo, see introduction to *SPN*, p. xxi.

137 "Silvia" (Camilla Ravera) had written to Gramsci asking him to draft a resolution to be voted on at the Central Committee meeting scheduled to take place on 18 April, which was to prepare for the party's forthcoming consultative conference at Como.

138 The reference is to "Against Pessimism", see pp. 213–17 above.

139 On 30 March, Scoccimarro had written to Gramsci describing the disarray of the minority (Bombacci expelled; a growing divergence between Tasca and Vota on the one hand, Graziadei and the deputies Remondino and Belloni – see note 99 above – on the other), but without making any political discrimination between them of a qualitative kind.

140 Bordiga was increasingly moving on from an intransigent defence of the PCI's past positions in the face of Comintern criticism and pressure, to a critique of the Comintern itself, and in particular Russian dominance within it. This passage is extremely important in showing Gramsci's contrasting attitude to the Comintern and its discipline, which was to be maintained throughout his subsequent leadership of the Party.

141 Since the time of the June 1923 Enlarged Executive meeting in Moscow (see note 71 above) – when the Comintern had decided to instal a temporary "mixed" leadership composed of Fortichiari, Scoccimarro and Togliatti from the old majority, and Tasca and Vota from the minority – Bordiga had advocated non-cooperation. When released from prison, he refused to come onto the leadership, and he also persuaded Fortichiari to withdraw. Bordiga's position was quite simply that the party must accept the Comintern's wrong line in a disciplined fashion, but that it must have a leadership made up of those who support that line, whereas the majority

formed at Livorno and Rome should fight for their line not only within the party but also and above all throughout the International.
142 See note 139 above. Scoccimarro had referred to Tasca's proclaimed desire to withdraw for personal and family reasons from the Executive Committee, and his view that now that the question of fusion with the PSI had been buried, the motivation which had led the Comintern Executive to nominate him to the PCI leadership no longer operated. Scoccimarro had expressed scepticism concerning Tasca's motives.
143 For the PCI's consultative conference at Como, see introduction to *SPN*, p. lxiv. These resolutions were in fact presented and put to the vote at the Central Committee meeting of 18 April 1924 (see note 137 above) – though in fact no representative of the Left attended the meeting in question. Each of the three tendencies then drafted substantial sets of political theses for the Conference itself (see *Annali* of the Istituto Feltrinelli, 1966, pp. 186–240). Togliatti was subsequently to draw attention to the contrast between the resolution put forward by the new "centre" majority here and the indications contained in Gramsci's letter of 5 April (see pp. 240–2 above). At the 18 April CC meeting, the main clash was an organizational one, since Tasca launched a violent attack on the new CC majority, accusing them of political insincerity, complicity with Bordiga, duplicity in their acceptance of the united front, factionalism, etc. – in short, presenting them as simply making an unprincipled bid for power in the party. At the conference itself, which took place in mid-May just a few days after Gramsci's return to Italy, the centre and left were still closer on domestic issues, while the centre and right were closer on international questions (relations with the Comintern). The vote at the conference demonstrated Bordiga's strength in the party: 35 federation secretaries out of 45 voted for the Left, 4 out of 5 inter-regional secretaries, the representative of the youth federation and one member of the Central Committee. The Centre was supported by 4 federation secretaries and 4 members of the Central Committee; the Right by 5 federation secretaries, one inter-regional secretary and 4 members of the Central Committee. Thus the Centre was very much a minority in the party as a whole; it did, however, hold a real majority on the Central Committee, since the three members of that body who did not attend the conference were all Centre supporters. (The Left, of course, had withdrawn from all national leadership positions.) The three resolutions published here were all printed in *Lo Stato Operaio*, 16 May 1924.
144 On 19 July 1922 the fall of the Facta government opened a political crisis, and the *Alleanza del Lavoro* (see note 50 above) cautiously raised the possibility of a general strike to express popular opposition to a right-wing resolution of the crisis. On 26 July, Bordiga expressed the PCI attitude succintly in *L'Ordine Nuovo*: "Do the fascists want to demolish

the parliamentary side-show? Well we would be only too delighted. Do the collaborationists want a general strike – which they have always opposed and sabotaged when it was for the direct and effective defence of the workers – if it is necessary to help their manoeuvres in the crisis? Excellent. The greatest danger is still that they will all get together and agree not to rock the boat, in the interests of a legal and parliamentary solution." The *Alleanza del Lavoro* finally called the so-called "legalitarian" general strike on 31 July, to begin on 1 August. Taking place as it did after a whole series of fascist attacks on socialist and working-class institutions, and in the absence of any real national coordination of resistance to the armed attacks now unleashed, the strike met with only a weak response; by 3 August, the *Alleanza del Lavoro* had called it off. The strike had been a demonstration, on the one hand, of working-class demoralization (with only a few, isolated struggles, where a local armed organization existed and the local leaders were capable of using it); on the other hand, of fascist military organization on a national scale, with more or less open connivance of the government and state authorities. When the strike formally ended, the fascist assault intensified, turning the failure into a rout – though in the face of the savage reprisals, there was a desperate resistance in a whole number of working-class strongholds (Ancona, Brescia, Milan, Bari, Genoa, Livorno and above all Parma). In sum, the strike represented the last real manifestation of popular resistance to fascism; a telling demonstration of the inadequacy of the *Alleanza del Lavoro*, whose leaders capitulated under government pressure almost as soon as the strike began; and a decisive watershed in the fascist advance to power.

145 See note 143 above. When the conference began Togliatti, in his report on behalf of the new "centre" majority on the Central Committee, spoke of the key importance of active participation in the leadership by the Left; but this was rejected by Bordiga, who was more than ever determined to maintain an intransigent stance *vis-à-vis* the International. The delegates, who had previously known nothing of the differences that had emerged on the leadership, for the most part expressed dismay at the outbreak of factional divisions, and rallied to Bordiga. Most speeches expressed hostility to the Right and deep suspicion of the Centre. It was in this climate that Gramsci made his intervention in the discussion.

146 See the debate with Tasca, in *SPW I*, pp. 239–99.

147 See p. 214 and note 124 above. Again, Gramsci gets the month wrong.

148 At the Twelfth Congress of the Bolshevik Party, in April 1923, Trotsky – despite major disagreements with the majority on the Central Committee, above all in the economic domain – did not openly move into opposition. He had not taken up Lenin's proposal in December 1922 (prior to his stroke) that they should form a bloc at the Congress to defend the monopoly of foreign trade. Although Lenin and he had joined forces on

the question of the right to self-determination of the non-Russian peoples of the Soviet Union (notably the Georgians), and though Lenin's attacks on the bureaucratic excesses of Rabkrin in January 1923 had certainly coincided with his own views, Trotsky perhaps hesitated to appear as an open contender for the role of Lenin's successor, when the latter was incapacitated in March. At the Congress, Trotsky contented himself with warning – in his Theses on Industry – of the dangers of the "scissors" effect (growing industrial prices and falling agricultural prices), and with calling for a central economic plan to be administered by Gosplan: his Theses were accepted by the Congress, but his recommendations were not in fact acted upon.

Opposition both to the prevailing economic policies and to the growth of bureaucracy surfaced in October 1923, with the publication of the Platform of the Forty-Six, which called for an open discussion throughout the party. At more or less the same time, Trotsky, who did not identify himself with the Forty-Six although these included many of his principal co-thinkers, was moved by the defeat in Germany himself to write two letters to the Central Committee expressing parallel criticisms and indicating his intention to take these to the party membership as a whole if they were not met. The majority on the leadership responded by drafting the so-called "New Course" Resolution, which was unanimously adopted by the Politburo (i.e. with Trotsky's signature too). This recognized the growth of bureaucracy as a danger, and provided for a discussion throughout the party up till the Thirteenth Conference in January 1924. During December 1923, Trotsky published a series of articles in *Pravda* (they were assembled in book form as *The New Course* in January 1924). On the other side, on 15 December 1923 Stalin wrote an article attacking the Forty-Six, and bringing up against Trotsky all his pre-1917 disagreements with Lenin: this article initiated a widespread press campaign against the Opposition.

Elections for delegates to the Thirteenth Conference took place under a system which sharply reduced oppositional representation from district to province level, and again from province to national level. At the Conference itself, the Opposition thus had little presence, and was overwhelmingly defeated: Stalin threatened to suppress it under the Tenth Congress resolution banning factions. Trotsky was ill and unable to attend. In the next months, following Lenin's death at the end of January, some quarter of a million new members were taken into the Party in the so-called Lenin Enrolment. Trotsky returned to Moscow for the Thirteenth Congress of the Bolshevik Party in May, and made a speech defending his actions over the past year. The Congress declared that the discussion which had been opened by the New Course Resolution had been resolved. Since the Thirteenth Congress more or less exactly coincided with the Como conference, Gramsci must be referring here to the outcome of the Thirteenth Conference four months earlier, when he says that the crisis has "today . . . been overcome".

149 The June 1923 Enlarged Executive meeting was that made famous by Radek's "Schlageter speech". It was also of key importance for the PCI (see Introduction to *SPN*, pp. lvi–lix and above pp. 143–53 and note 71). However, although Trotsky was nominated to the Presidium of this meeting and to several of its Commissions, there is no indication from the proceedings in *Inprecorr* that he in fact attended – he certainly did not intervene. Thus it seems virtually certain that Gramsci is really referring to the June 1922 Enlarged Executive meeting, at which a Resolution on the French Question was adopted on the basis of Trotsky's report. This resolution contains a precise passage devoted to the danger of a "Left Bloc" and the tactics which the Party should follow in counterposition to it (see Trotsky, *The First Five Years of the Communist International*, Vol. 2, New York, 1953, pp. 147–8). In fact, throughout 1923 the PCF was vainly to seek a united front with the socialists against the Poincaré government, which had occupied the Ruhr in January of that year, and in solidarity with the German workers. In December, the socialists refused this option definitively, in favour of a *Cartel des Gauches* or bloc with left bourgeois parties, above all the radicals.

150 In the May 1924 elections, the *Bloc National* headed by Poincaré was swept from office after an overwhelming defeat by the *Cartel des Gauches*, under Herriot's leadership.

151 Giovanni Antonio Colonna di Cesarò, the aristocratic leader of a Sicilian party called the Democratic Social Party (which mobilized a section of the peasantry behind the big landlords), was a minister in the coalition headed by Mussolini until the murder of Matteotti in June 1924, when he went into opposition to the fascists. Enrico De Nicola, president of the Chamber of Deputies in 1921, was a traditional bourgeois politician from Naples. During the 1924 election campaign, Bordiga challenged him to a public debate, but he refused and in fact shortly afterwards withdrew his candidature.

152 For Buozzi, see note 31 above.

153 The April 1924 elections represented a significant stage in the consolidation of fascism's hold on Italy. A new electoral law gave the party which won a plurality – provided it managed to get over 25 per cent of the popular vote – two thirds of the seats in parliament. The Mussolini government had gained increasing bourgeois support by its economic policies and its repression of working-class militancy (hours lost in strikes had been reduced from 18,800,000 in 1919 and 16,400,000 in 1920 to 295,929 in 1923). The PCI proposed an electoral bloc in this situation to the other working-class parties (January 1924), and Togliatti explained how the party understood this tactic in a letter to the Comintern secretariat: "If, in general, the communists base their propaganda on a

critique of bourgeois democracy and a demonstration of the incapacity of bourgeois democracy to bring about and initiate a process of liberation of the proletariat in Italy, then since the victory of fascism and the creation of a dictatorship which aims merely to preserve the mask of democratic legality, the theses of the communists have become so self-evident that they cannot be denied. Fascism has opened a period of *permanent revolution* for the proletariat, and the proletarian party which forgets this point and helps to sustain the illusion among the workers that it is possible to change the present situation while remaining on the terrain of liberal and constitutional opposition will, in the last analysis, give support to the enemies of the Italian working class and peasantry." Thus the offer of a pact to the reformists – who precisely based their strategy on the attempt to create a coalition of liberal bourgeois and petty-bourgeois anti-fascist forces – was intended to meet with a refusal (as it in fact did from Giacomo Matteotti, secretary of the PSU – see note 72 above – on 24 January). A refusal was also expected from the PSI, and this was intended to provide a terrain upon which the "IIIrd-internationalist" current could agitate. Although the PSI at first kept the door open, at least if the PSU could be pulled into the pact as well, the negotiations soon broke down and the "IIIrd-internationalists" alone formed common slates with the communists (see note 130 above). In the event, the fascists won 66·9 per cent of the popular vote – 4,305,936 votes – with the *Popolari* getting 637,649, the Unitary Socialists 415,148, the maximalists 341,528 and the communists 268,191.

154 The new parliament opened on 24 May 1924, and on 30 May Giacomo Matteotti (see preceding note) made a long and courageous speech denouncing the violence, fraud and intimidation which had dominated the election and calling for it to be annulled. Mussolini responded with an article which said that Matteotti's provocation deserved something more concrete than a merely verbal reply. On 10 June it became known that Matteotti had disappeared, and it transpired that he had been kidnapped and stabbed to death by a fascist squad belonging to the so-called "Cheka", which was directly under the control of Cesare Rossi, head of Mussolini's Press Office. The car used had been borrowed from Filippo Filipelli, editor of a fascist paper. There was a huge wave of reaction to the murder throughout the country, and the fascist party was at first shaken and demoralized. Mussolini made conciliatory speeches, and police investigation of the crime led quickly to the heart of the fascist apparatus. Mussolini ordered the resignations of Rossi, De Bono the Chief of Police, and Aldo Finzi, under-secretary at the Ministry of the Interor; Rossi, Filipelli and others were arrested shortly after. On 13 June, all sections of the opposition in parliament – the liberal-democrats led by Amendola and Di Cesarò, the *popolari*, the Republicans, the two socialist parties and the communists – decided to take no further part in the proceedings of

parliament until the whole affair had been cleared up and the degree of government complicity established. This led to the so-called Aventine Secession, during which the opposition deputies met separately in another part of Rome.

Meanwhile, three of the prominent fascists involved in the crime, Finzi, Rossi and Filipelli, angry or frightened at being cast as scapegoats, drew up memoranda claiming that Mussolini had always had ultimate responsibility for the Cheka's actions. These memoranda were transmitted to the opposition, and thence to the King, who, however, refused to become involved in any way. Throughout the summer and autumn of 1924, as the crisis dragged on, the Aventine opposition concentrated its hopes on the possibility that the King would ultimately decide to move against Mussolini. But since nothing was done to mobilize the masses against the regime, the popular indignation of June soon gave way once again to apathy. However, the crisis continued throughout the year, and was rekindled in November and December by new evidence of the complicity of leading fascists in violent assaults on political opponents. Finally, when Amendola's liberal *Il Mondo* published the Rossi memorandum in full on 29 December, Mussolini was forced to act. On 3 January 1925 he made a speech denying all complicity in the crime, but at the same time assuming full responsibility for all that had happened: "If fascism has been a criminal association, I am the head of that association", etc.

155 For the beginning of the Aventine Secession, see preceding note. The communists returned to parliament on 12 November 1924, judging the Aventine impotent (see pp. 276–9 and note 163 below). They were followed by the PSI and some of the bourgeois democrats in the course of 1925, though the Aventine in fact lasted until 1926, when the *popolari* finally decided to return to parliament.

156 For *Rivoluzione Liberale*, see note 96 above.

157 The 1913 General Election.

158 This Central Committee meeting took place on the eve of Gramsci's departure for Moscow, where he was to participate in the Enlarged Executive meeting of the Comintern.

159 In the autumn of 1924, the Communist Party leadership launched the slogan of Workers' and Peasants' Committees. These were explicitly linked to the 1919–20 factory councils, and were seen as the organizational form which could realize the united front among the masses: "Before fascism is driven from power, the Italian political crisis will no doubt take on much deeper forms than it has done hitherto. The question of power will be placed before the workers and peasants in a direct and immediate way. And they will be in a much better position to resolve it if they have already given birth to organisms in which class unity is realized" (PCI internal bulletin, October 1924). Gramsci referred to

these committees in a speech to the communists of Lazio (24 November) as "a basis for the creation of soviets".
160 I.e. the speech of 3 January 1925, see note 154 above.
161 For the documents in question – the Rossi and other memoranda – see note 154 above. The press laws in question were adopted in July 1924, but not used to the full until the beginning of 1925, when Mussolini's speech on 3 January was followed by a new wave of repression aimed at the Aventine opposition forces.
162 For republicans, see note 92 above. Guido Miglioli was leader of the catholic unions among the dairy farms of southern Lombardy. A left catholic deputy, he was attacked and badly hurt by fascists during the May 1921 election campaign, after sharing a platform with a communist speaker. In June 1922, during the fascist campaign to smash the catholic unions (see note 129 above), he was once again the object of an attack and his house in Cremona was burned down, leading to the fall of the Facta government and the "legalitarian strike" (see note 144 above). Leader of the left wing of the Popular Party, Miglioli was expelled in June 1925. For *Italia Libera*, see note 97 above.
163 On 12 November 1924 (see note 155 above), the communists formally returned to parliament. Just one deputy, Repossi, entered the chamber, read out a statement of principles which publicly accused the government of complicity in the Matteotti Affair, then left at once. Grieco spoke on 14 January 1925, in a parliamentary debate on fascist proposals for a new electoral law. This marked the real – as opposed to purely formal – return of the communist deputies to parliament.
164 For Miglioli, see note 162 above. Emilio Lussu led the anti-fascist wing of the Sardinian Action Party which split in 1922 when the fascists came to power. His followers were a small component of the Aventine opposition. Exiled in 1926, Lussu returned to revive the party during the Resistance (1943–5).
165 Serrati and 2,000 "IIIrd-internationalists" fused with the Communist Party (which in this period grew in a few months from 12,000 to 20,000) in August 1924. The pamphlet referred to here was entitled "The situation of the Socialist Party (Open letter to a socialist worker of good faith)".
166 In December 1924, the CGL held its Congress in Milan. Of 269,754 members (at least on paper), 153,596 votes went to the reformists (PSU), 54,792 to the maximalists (PSI), 33,596 only to the communists, who challenged the validity of the vote. On 29 and 30 January 1925, the Confederation organized a conference to discuss the way forward. After a PCI motion attacking the Aventine and reformism, the communist delegates were ejected. On 5 February the CGL formally expelled all communists from membership. As the comrade in charge of trade-union work, Azzario was responsible for the content of the motion.

167 The Vth Congress of the Communist International had decided on the "Bolshevization" of all communist parties in order to strengthen discipline and centralization and combat "factionalism". The Comintern was thus to become a "true world party, homogeneous, communist, Bolshevik, Leninist". The model was to be the Russian party, after the defeat of the 1923 Opposition had been consecrated at the Thirteenth Congress (see note 148 above). The parties were to be reorganized on the basis of factory cells (as the Comintern Presidium had proposed as early as February 1924). The Enlarged Executive meeting in Moscow in March–April 1925 was to review the progress made in the Bolshevization campaign during the preceding year, and in particular to coordinate the struggle against "Trotskyism". (The struggle in the Russian party had exploded into the open again following the publication of Trotsky's *The Lessons of October* in October 1924; prevented from expressing his political positions outside the Politburo after the Thirteenth Congress, Trotsky had taken the opportunity offered him by the publication of a volume of his 1917 writings to include an introduction which contained, *inter alia*, embarrassing references to Zinoviev's and Kamenev's opposition to the insurrection of October 1917, and which defended his own record – which had been under attack in the press campaign against him before the Thirteenth Congress.)

168 The reference is to Trotsky's speech of 28 July 1924, published in *Izvestia* on 5 August under the title "The Premisses for the Proletarian Revolution". Trotsky argued that hegemony among the capitalist powers was passing into the hands of the United States, which would therefore be the arbiter of all attempts by the European governments, above all that of Germany, to stabilize their currencies and redress their economic situations. He depicted European social-democracy as American capitalism's ally in establishing its world domination, and suggested that the former's prospects were dependent above all upon the latter's success. But "the more American capitalism expands internationally, the more commands the American bankers issue to the governments of Europe, all the greater, all the more centralized, all the more resolute will be the resistance of the broadest masses of Europe". America "needs to secure her profits at the expense of the European toiling masses ... without the American labour aristocracy, American capitalism cannot maintain itself ... it is possible to keep the American labour aristocracy in its privileged position only by placing the 'plebeians', the proletarian 'rabble' of Europe on rations of cold and hunger.... The further this development unfolds along this road ... all the more urgent, all the more practical and warlike will the slogan of the all-European revolution and its state form – the Soviet United States of Europe – become for the European workers.... As against the little English isle, which rests on colonies all over the world, America is mighty. But we say: As against the

united proletarian-peasant Europe, bound together with us into a single soviet federation, America will prove impotent." And Trotsky concluded: "If we Americanize our still frail socialist industry, then we can say with tenfold confidence that the future is completely and decisively working in our favour. Americanized Bolshevism will crush and conquer imperialist Americanism." Gramsci's comments make it virtually certain that he had not read this text of Trotsky, but was relying on polemical accounts of it given during the later discussion sparked off by *The Lessons of October* (see preceding note). At all events, his presentation of the issues at stake in the Russian inner-party discussion here effectively reversed the real positions of the participants, since it was precisely Trotsky's adversaries of the majority who argued that "the Russian working class will not for a long time be able to count on the support of the proletariat of other countries".

169 Only two such batches of study notes were in fact ever sent out, both compiled entirely by Gramsci, and the text translated here constituted the introduction to the first of these, printed and distributed in April–May 1925.

170 Enrico Ferri (1856–1929) penologist and politician, began his political career as a socialist (editor of *Avanti!* 1900–1905), but rallied to fascism in 1922. (See p. 246 and note.)

171 Achille Loria (1857–1943) was an academic economist who put himself forward as an original thinker and enjoyed a certain vogue, not only in Italy, in the 1880s and 1890s. His vulgarization and plagiarism of Marx were attacked by Engels in the Preface to *Capital*, Vol. II. Gramsci took Loria as the archetype of "certain degenerate and bizarre aspects of the mentality of a group of Italian intellectuals and therefore of the national culture . . ." to which he gave the name *lorianismo* (see *SPN*, p. 458, n. 108, etc.). Gugliemo Ferrero and Paolo Orano were frequently cited by Gramsci in the Prison Notebooks as examples of the same phenomenon. Ferrero (1871–1942) was a sociologist and popular historian; Orano (1875–1945) a writer and journalist, for a time on the staff of *Avanti!* and subsequently (1924–5) editor of the Roman edition of *Il Popolo d'Italia*.

172 See pp. 93–117 above.

173 The reference is to Bukharin's *Historical Materialism; a System of Sociology* (New York, 1925). For Gramsci's own critique of this work, see *SPN*, pp. 419–72.

174 The Enlarged Executive meeting of March–April 1925 (see note 167 above) was preceded by an Organizational Conference.

175 This was a report to the Central Committee on 11–12 May 1925, and was published in *L'Unità* on 3 July with the following prefatory note: "Comrade Gramsci's report which we publish today had been unanimously approved by the Central Committee of our party at its session last May, in other words before the Executive had any knowledge

of the factional initiative of the *Comitato d'Intesa*. It expresses the thinking of the Central Committee itself on the internal situation in the party and on the tasks of the forthcoming congress" (for the *Comitato d'Intesa*, see note 191 below).

176 See note 167 above.
177 Bordiga's article "The Trotsky Question" was written on 8 February 1925 and sent to *L'Unità* for publication. The Executive Committee of the Party blocked its publication and sent it to the Comintern secretariat, proposing that the matter should be placed on the agenda of the Enlarged Executive meeting in March. Bordiga was pressed to attend the meeting both by the Italian leadership and by the Comintern secretariat, but he refused on the grounds that his wife was not well. At the Enlarged Executive, the campaign against "Trotskyism" in the Russian party and the struggle against Bordiga were repeatedly linked by both Russian and Italian participants, most notably by Scoccimarro (Gramsci did not intervene in the formal sessions). The 11–12 May Central Committee meeting to which Gramsci gave this report opened a pre-congress discussion in the Italian party, and Bordiga's article was finally published in this context, on 4 July 1925.
178 On party patriotism or "conceit" (*boria*), see *SPN*, p. 151, note 41.
179 What Lenin in fact wrote (see *Selected Works* in three volumes, Vol. III, Moscow, 1961, pp. 375–6) was: "Comrade Bordiga and his faction . . . are certainly wrong in advocating non-participation in parliament. But on one point, it seems to me, Comrade Bordiga is right . . . Comrade Bordiga and his group are right in attacking Turati and his partisans, who remain in a party which has recognized Soviet power and the dictatorship of the proletariat, and yet continue their former pernicious and opportunist policy as members of parliament. Of course, in tolerating this, Comrade Serrati and the entire Italian Socialist Party are making a mistake . . . Such a mistaken, inconsistent, or spineless attitude towards the opportunist parliamentarians gives rise to "Left-wing" communism, on the one hand, and *to a certain extent* justifies its existence, on the other."
180 See notes 61, 72, 85 and 126 above.
181 Count Antonio Graziadei (1873–1953) joined the PCI at Livorno, wrote the theses on the agrarian question for the 1922 Rome Congress, and became one of the main leaders of the Right after the congress. At the Fourth World Congress, he was the principal spokesman for the minority in the Italian party, arguing for a full acceptance of the united front policy. Coopted into the CC after the wave of arrests of communist leaders in early 1923, he was violently attacked by Zinoviev at the Fifth World Congress for his revision of Marxism – in his *Prezzo e sopraprezzo nell'economia capitalistica* ("Price and surplus price in capitalist economy"), subtitled "A Critique of Marx's Theory of Value", Milan, 1923. Graziadei was expelled from the party in 1928.
182 The party in fact had 25–27,000 members in early 1925, as compared

with perhaps little more than 5,000 in April 1923 after the first anti-communist drive, 8,619 in November 1923, 12,000 (including candidate members) in the spring of 1924, 20,000 by the autumn of that year.

183 The Prefect of Milan had suspended publication of *L'Unità, Avanti!* and the PSU paper *La Giustizia* from 9 to 23 November 1925, following an attempt on Mussolini's life by Tito Zaniboni, a former PSU deputy and CGL leader. The discovery of his plot was made the pretext for dissolving the reformist party, for a massive attack on freemasonry throughout Italy, and for a new battery of repressive measures.

184 Freemasonry was strong in Italy from the time of the Risorgimento, and flourished after the country's unification – being assisted by the half-century rift between the new State and the Vatican. Many leading politicians, such as Depretis and Crispi, were freemasons. So too were a number of the reformist leaders in the early Socialist Party, up to the Ancona conference of April 1914; then, however, the dominant Mussolini secured their expulsion. Ironically, a year later they and Mussolini were to find themselves allies in advocacy of Italian intervention in the War. After the War the freemasons were prominent in their support for D'Annunzio's Fiume expedition, and many of them helped to fund the March on Rome. Many leading fascists were initially freemasons – Ciano, Balbo, De Bono, Farinacci, Rossi, etc. – but in February 1923, as Mussolini pursued a policy of reconciliation with the Vatican, membership of the Fascist Party was declared incompatible with freemasonry. In May 1925, a parliamentary bill was introduced by Mussolini and Rocco to ban "secret associations". Ostensibly directed against freemasonry, it could clearly serve also against opposition parties.

The debate on this bill in parliament was the occasion for Gramsci's only intervention there. He argued that freemasonry had been "the only real and effective party which the bourgeois class possessed for a long time . . . the real ideology and organization of the capitalist bourgeois class"; that the Vatican had represented the "rural classes" in the past, but that it had subsequently been replaced in that role by fascism; that fascism's vaunted spiritual reunification of the nation thus represented a subordination of the capitalist bourgeoisie – which had shown itself incapable of controlling the working class – to the backward, rural ruling classes. He went on to speak of the weakness of Italian capitalism and its political order, and to outline the two strategies of the bourgeois for reinforcing it: 1. Giolitti's pursuit of an alliance between Northern industrialists and labour aristocracy, to subjugate the mass of peasants; 2. *Il Corriere della Sera*'s support for a bloc between Northern industrialists and Southern bourgeois-democratic politicians (Salandra, Orlando, Nitti, Amendola), on the terrain of free trade. What did fascism offer? No alternative strategy, but "the replacement of one administrative personnel by another". This was the significance of the attack on freemasonry. Gramsci's speech is in *La Costruzione del Partito*

Comunista 1923–1926, Turin, 1971, pp. 75–85. It was much interrupted, but the line of argument originally planned is also developed in "La Conquista Fascista dello Stato", *Per la Verità*, Rome, 1974, pp. 303–6.

V

185 The "Political Commission" met in the first stages of the PCI's Third Congress at Lyons (21–26 January 1926).
186 See note 162 above.
187 *L'Unità* had published the first part – "General Questions" – of the "Draft Theses of the Left" on 12, 14, 23 and 26 January 1926. (The majority's Theses had been published in the course of October and November, and the Left was repeatedly to complain of the late publication of oppositional contributions.) The Draft Theses as a whole – i.e. including "International Questions" and "Italian Questions" – were published in pamphlet form.
188 For the Aventine, see notes 154 and 155 above. In the German presidential elections called after Ebert's death in early 1925, in the first ballot Thälmann the communist candidate won 1,800,000 votes, compared with 8,000,000 for the social-democratic candidate Braun and 4,000,000 for the right-wing centre politician Wilhelm Marx. In the second ballot, the German party decided against withdrawing Thälmann, although the social-democrats voted for Marx as the lesser evil. The election was won by Hindenburg, with 14,600,000 votes against 13,700,000 for Marx; Thälmann's 1,900,000 votes thus could have tipped the balance. The recommendations spoken of by Bordiga were expressed, *post facto*, at the March/April 1925 Enlarged Executive meeting, where Zinoviev and others criticized the intransigent "leftism" of the new Fischer/Maslov leadership in the German party.

At the fourth congress of the French Communist Party, held at Clichy on 17 January 1925, Cachin presented theses on the application of united front tactics to the forthcoming municipal elections in May 1925: in the first ballot, the party-sponsored Worker and Peasant Bloc was to put forward its own candidates; in the second ballot a week later, it should be prepared to negotiate a common list with any other party on the basis of immediate demands where failure to do so might mean a victory of the Right. In the event, following these prescriptions, the PCF withdrew all its candidates in the second ballot in favour of the Socialist/Radical Bloc of the Left. In all these three episodes, Bordiga identified the common factor as "non-Marxist counterposition of two fractions of the bourgeoisie".
189 The inner-party conflict had exploded again in Russia following the publication of Trotsky's *The Lessons of October* in October 1924 (see note 167 above). In sharp contrast to the "New Course" discussion of the previous year, the Russian press now only published one side in the

dispute. A campaign continued for several months, in which Trotsky's views since 1904 were said to constitute a consistent trend hostile to Leninism and Bolshevism. In particular, in December 1924 Stalin opened an attack on Trotsky's 1906 "theory of permanent revolution" – which had hitherto only been conceived of as applying to the future course of the Russian revolution (it was not to be extended by Trotsky to colonial and semi-colonial countries in general before 1927). Throughout 1925, Trotsky remained silent on major political issues, but from the summer of that year a new rift began to appear between Zinoviev and Kamenev on the one hand and Stalin and Bukharin on the other, centring on the issues of industrialization, town-country relations, "socialism in one country", etc. This struggle came into the open at the Fourteenth Party Congress in December 1925 – the first congress not preceded by a full and open discussion. Trotsky still remained silent at this time, though shortly afterwards he was to form the Joint Opposition with Zinoviev and Kamenev. The new split in the Russian leadership took most foreign Communist Parties by surprise, and there was no substantive discussion of it at the Lyons Congress, nor of the issues – above all "socialism in one country" – which were at stake.

190 In June 1923, Stambulisky's Peasant Party government was overthrown by a Macedonian-based military coup led by Zankov. The Communist Party, which had flourished under Stambulisky, remained passive, regarding the form of bourgeois rule as a matter of indifference. It did nothing to mobilize the masses, despite their high level of combativity. Subsequently, however, in September of the same year, under pressure from the Comintern directed against their abstract "leftism" and under the impact of anti-working-class repression by the Zankov military government, they organized a suicidal uprising without any mass support; the inevitable defeat was followed by a terrible wave of repression and the shattering of one of the strongest IIIrd International parties.

191 The pre-congress discussion had been opened as early as the May 1925 Central Committee meeting (see notes 175 and 177 above), since the Lyons Congress was originally scheduled to take place in early autumn of that year. On 7 June 1925, *L'Unità* reported the formation, by four communist deputies (including Fortichiari and Repossi from the original Livorno Executive) and a number of other prominent party members from the Left, of the *Comitato d'Intesa tra gli elementi della Sinistra* (Committee of Accord between components of the Left). The letter which announced this posed a series of demands concerning the organization of the pre-congress discussion. Although Bordiga was not initially associated with the *Comitato d'Intesa* (at least formally), he solidarized with it in an Open Letter to the Executive a few days later, after its leaders had been relieved of all their party functions. The subsequent pre-

congress discussion was to a great degree dominated by mutual accusations of "factionalism" and "anti-democratic procedures". The *Comitato d'Intesa* was dissolved by urgent request of the Comintern; both the latter's letter (signed by Humbert-Droz) and the acceptance (though formally protesting) by Bordiga, Fortichiari and their co-thinkers, were published in *L'Unità* on 18 July 1925.

192 See note 33 above.
193 For a discussion of these concepts, see *SPN*, pp. 186–90, etc.
194 Five series of Theses were drafted by the majority of the PCI leadership and published in *L'Unità* during October and November 1925: 1. on the international situation; 2. on the national and colonial question; 3. on the agrarian question; 4. on the Italian situation and the Bolshevization of the PCI; 5. on the trade unions. By far the most important was the fourth, translated here. It was republished in pamphlet form with the new title given here after it had been approved by the Lyons Congress – by a majority of 90·8 per cent to 9·2 per cent for the Left.
195 See pp. 362–3 below.
196 For transformism – a term initially used from the 1880s onwards to describe the process whereby the so-called "historic" Left and Right parties which emerged from the Risorgimento tended to converge in terms of programme, while the personnel of the Left were absorbed progressively into the dominant political conservative élite – see *SPN*, p. 58, note 8, etc.
197 Francesco Crispi (1818–1901) broke with the parliamentary Left and Mazzini in 1865, rallying to the monarchy. He became Minister of the Interior and Prime Minister on various occasions between 1876 and 1896, and was the most consistent advocate of Italian colonial expansion (see *SPN*, pp. 66–70).
198 The Triple Alliance between Italy, Germany and Austro-Hungary was concluded in 1882; it was directed principally against France.
199 The encyclical *Rerum Novarum* on "The Condition of the Working Classes" appeared in March 1891. It was, in fact, to some extent a modification of earlier anti-socialist encyclicals, and advocated confessional trade unions and mixed corporations of employers and employees. It condemned laissez-faire capitalism and called for class collaboration at all times. It laid the basis for what was to become modern Christian democracy.
200 *Fasci dei lavoratori* ("workers' leagues"), led by socialists, spread through Sicily in 1892–3. They were basically peasant organizations, and their main aim was the break-up of the big estates and distribution of the land. They had considerable success in securing improved contracts between peasants and landowners in 1893. In 1893–4, under the impact of the economic crisis of that year, the peasantry rose throughout the island and was repressed with great brutality by Crispi.

201 The modernist movement developed among catholic intellectuals in the late nineteenth and early twentieth centuries. Its proclaimed aims were to bring the Church into harmony with the culture and society of the contemporary world – especially with new developments in scientific and sociological thinking. It was thus in sharp contrast with the "anti-progress" stance of the Papacy's 1864 "Syllabus of Errors", which had dominated catholic thinking in the late nineteenth century. Modernism was condemned by the Papal decree *Lamentabili* and the encyclical *Pascendi* in 1907. However, via the work notably of Romolo Murri, it was an important ideological ancestor of contemporary Christian democracy.

202 In 1871 the Vatican declared that it was "not expedient" (*non expedit*) for Catholics to vote in parliamentary elections (the ban was strengthened to a *non licet* – "it is not lawful" – in 1877). The *non expedit* was relaxed in 1904 and further in 1909, and finally abolished in 1919. The Gentiloni Pact was concluded in 1913 between Giolitti and Count Gentiloni, the president of the Catholic Electoral Union. It provided for Catholic voters to support government candidates in the elections of that year, in order to check the advance of the Socialists.

203 The Popular Party was founded by Luigi Sturzo and others in January 1919, and was initially encouraged by the papacy (as a political movement directed outwards, rather than towards reform of the Church itself like Modernism). It grew swiftly, especially in the agricultural areas of North and Central Italy, where it set up "white" unions whose strength among the small peasants often outstripped that of their "red" rivals. In the 1919 general election, the *Popolari* won 100 seats, and in 1921 108. After vacillating in its attitude towards fascism between 1921 and 1925 (Sturzo resisted Papal pressure for an accommodation), the Popular Party was suppressed at the same time as other opposition parties in October 1926 (though Sturzo had in fact been in exile since 1924).

204 The anti-fascist National Union of Liberal and Democratic Forces was launched by the Liberal leader Amendola in November 1924, with the aim of winning back the middle classes from fascism to bourgeois democracy, with the goodwill of the working class. It held its only congress in June 1925, but by that time Amendola himself saw little hope for it in view of the stabilization of the fascist régime after Mussolini's 3 January 1925 speech, which put an end to the Matteotti crisis of the year before.

205 See note 181 above.

206 See note 191 above.

207 At the 1907 Congress of the IInd International at Stuttgart, a compromise resolution was passed on the question of what the proper relations should be between socialist parties and trade unions. The resolution stressed the need to permeate unions with the spirit of

socialism, without going so far as to jeopardize their unity; it pronounced in favour of trade-union autonomy in the economic field, and for close relations between party and unions, without taking any position on the question of organic links between them. The "pact of alliance" between PSI and CGL was signed in September 1918, and involved mutual recognition of the authority of each in its respective "sphere".

208 See the passages on war of position and war of manoeuvre in *SPN*, pp. 229–39, etc.

VI

209 This report on the proceedings of the Lyons Congress was dictated by Gramsci to Riccardo Ravagnan, on the editorial staff of *L'Unità*, then read over and approved by him for publication. It appeared in the newspaper on 26 February 1926.

210 See note 72 above.

211 At the Popular Party's Turin Congress on 12–13 April 1923, a "centrist" resolution was passed, after a right-wing proposal to give unconditional support to the fascist government had been defeated.

212 As soon as the Lyons Congress opened, the Left challenged its validity on the grounds that the pre-congress discussion had not been conducted democratically, and formally appealed to the International to intervene. The Comintern Presidium passed a resolution, on the basis of a decision by the International Control Commission, which rejected Bordiga's appeal and confirmed "the entire validity of the Congress and the authority of its decisions, as of the Central Committee elected from it".

213 Unfortunately, the minutes of the "Trade-union Commission" at the Lyons Congress have not survived in legible form. According to a report in February 1926 by "Aquila" (the Hungarian Sachs), who was briefly charged by the Comintern's Latin Secretariat with the task of reporting on the Italian situation, the two comrades in question were Bordiga and Tasca, who despite differences between them both wished to centre the party's trade-union activity around the slogan of "Defend the Trade Unions", and who were both sceptical about the practical viability of the Workers' and Peasants' Committees (see note 159 above). But see p. 394 below, where the account given fits Tasca but hardly Bordiga.

214 The reference is to Tasca's intervention, see pp. 324–8 above.

215 For these episodes, see "Socialists and Communists", "The Arditi del Popolo" and "Against Terror", pp. 25–6, 56–8 and 61–2 above; see too notes 14 and 33 above. The attitude of the whole PCI leadership at the time tended to be that the destruction of the liberal bourgeois state was hardly a matter of concern for communists; that the advance of fascism would lead to the exposure of the reformists and maximalists of the PSI; and that these would be eliminated as direct rivals to the Communist

Party, though they might find themselves in government as a last line of defence for the bourgeois order.
216 In August 1915, the government issued a decree setting up seven "Regional Committees of Industrial Mobilization", with the principal function of settling labour disputes. The question of whether or not to cooperate with them became a subject of controversy between reformists and intransigents within the PSI.
217 This Association was launched by the Communist Party in late 1924, in connection with the slogan of "Workers' and Peasants' Committees" (see note 159 above). It had some initial success, notably in the South, and Grieco gave a figure of 75,000 members in November of that year. The main responsibility for building up the Association fell to Giuseppe di Vittorio, who joined the PCI with the "IIIrd-Internationalists". The Association developed a series of demands aimed at defending the interests of share-croppers, tenant-farmers and small-holders – none of them adequately represented in the past by the PSI. This led to friction with the socialists on this terrain, and the Federterra (the national peasants' trade-union federation) was strongly opposed to the new association.
218 See notes 167 and 174 above.
219 See note 189 above. Although there was no discussion of the new inner-party struggle in Russia, there was a report on the Fourteenth Congress of the Russian Party by Humbert-Droz.
220 Report to the 2–3 August 1926 meeting of the Party's Executive Committee. The first part was published in March 1928 in *Stato operaio*, the second not until 14 April 1967 (*Rinascita*).
221 Since the launching of the slogan of Workers' and Peasants' Committees (see note 159 above), the main effort of the PCI in the trade-union field had been directed towards the creation of so-called Agitational Committees of Proletarian Unity, within which other forces could be grouped around communist nuclei. In March 1926, as a result of the dispute on the trade-union question at the Lyons Congress (see note 213 above) and Sachs's report which was critical of party policy, the Enlarged Executive of the Comintern discussed the PCI's trade-union tactics. Lozovsky and other delegates were predisposed to accept Tasca's and Sachs's view that the party had not rid itself of lingering "*Ordine Nuovo*" ideas, or of residues of ultra-leftism in the form of acceptance of the united front only "from below". They saw the concentration on the "Committees" as a manifestation of this, and argued that priority should instead be given to defence of the trade unions. However, in reality, the hostility of the PSI to any collaboration with the Communist Party that might jeopardize their relations with the reformist leaders of the CGL made the idea of united action in defence of the trade unions illusory. At

the least, the "Committees" grouped a limited layer of workers still prepared to resist actively.
222 See *SPN*, pp. 152–3 for a development of this analysis.
223 J. P. Morgan lent over a hundred million dollars to Italy in early 1926, on the assumption that fascism had created the conditions for profitable investment.
224 In May 1926, Marshall Josef Pilsudski headed a military rising which overthrew the conservative bourgeois government. As a former socialist and anti-Tsarist terrorist, Pilsudski was violently opposed by the right-wing parties in Poland; similarly, the Polish communists interpreted the "united front" policy – in the form in which it was advocated under Zinoviev's leadership in 1925 – to mean that they should take advantage of this contradiction in the ranks of the bourgeoisie and fight alongside Pilsudski. They expected Pilsudski's coup to initiate a process leading to revolution. In fact, however, Pilsudski installed a régime which had much in common with fascism, and threw the communists who had fought for him into gaol.

French diplomatic policy following the First World War had as a principal aim the establishment of a system of alliances with the smaller Central and Eastern European countries, against both Germany and Russia. In 1925, the Locarno Pact was accompanied by French–Polish and French–Czechoslovak military alliances, and France was also to conclude treaties with Rumania in 1927 and Yugoslavia in 1928. In fact, the Pilsudski coup did not decisively worsen relations with France; moreover, it was the aristocratic pre-coup government, rather than the semi-fascist Pilsudski régime which followed it, which pursued a policy of rapprochement with liberal-bourgeois Czechoslovakia. In the event, it was the rise of German Nazism which was finally to destroy the French system of alliances, in the thirties.
225 The General Strike took place from 4–13 May 1926.
226 Nitti was prime minister from June 1919 until June 1920. It was only at the end of 1920, after the failure of the occupation of the factories, that fascism began to get real financial backing (at first from landlords in Central and Northern Italy) and to become a mass, anti-working-class phenomenon. Before that, fascism had been a marginal and "subversive" movement, directing its main (verbal) fire against "plutocracy" and the government. D'Annunzio and his "legionaries" seized Fiume in September 1919 to press Italian claims on the Eastern shores of the Adriatic; they held the town until – after Italy and Yugoslavia had signed the Treaty of Rapallo – they were forced to evacuate it in December 1920. D'Annunzio was certainly violently opposed to both Nitti's government and that of Giolitti which followed it. For his relations with the Communists in 1921–2, see note 84 above. In the earlier period referred to here, Gramsci had described him at the time (October 1919) as a "cast-

off lackey of Anglo–French freemasonry", and said that he "stands in relation to Nitti as Kornilov did to Kerensky".
227 For Mussolini's 3 January speech which brought the Matteotti crisis to a close, see note 154 above.
228 The Anglo–Russian Trade-union Unity Committee was officially founded on 14 May 1925, with the proclaimed object of promoting international trade-union unity and struggling against capitalist reaction and the danger of new wars. After the capitulation of the General Council and the failure of the General Strike, the question of continued participation in the Committee became a central point of conflict between the majority on the Russian leadership led by Stalin and Bukharin and the Joint Opposition led by Trotsky, Zinoviev and Kamenev. The Committee was in fact maintained in existence until the British union leaders withdrew from it in September 1927, on the grounds that the Russians were interfering in their "domestic affairs".
229 The reference is to reports of visits to Russia published in *Il Corriere della Sera* in the preceding years by Luigi Barzini and Raffaele Calzini. The article commented on here was published in *Il Mondo* on 17 September 1926.
230 Sir Edward Carson organized a Protestant, Unionist army called the Ulster Volunteers in 1913, to prevent the north-eastern part of Ulster becoming part of an Irish (home rule) state.
231 For Hindenburg's election, see note 188 above. The German Left lost the referendum over the indemnification of the former princes in March 1926, but obtained $14\frac{1}{2}$ million votes.
232 Mario and Pio Perrone were the owners of Ansaldo, the Ligurian shipbuilding firm, which between 1914 and 1918 increased its capital from 30 to 500 million *lire* and its employees from 4,000 to 56,000, acquiring iron mines, and building steelworks and hydro-electric plants. Ansaldo, through the personal share-holdings of the Perrone brothers, also controlled the Banca Italiana di Sconto, one of the "big four" Italian banks. Max Bondi was the dominant figure among the directors of the giant steel trust Ilva, which during the War had branched out into arms manufacture, shipbuilding, shipping, etc. Count Francesco Matarazzo (1854–1937) built up a vast industrial empire in Brazil; during World War I, he was in charge of all supplies for the Province of Naples, and became an early and heavy contributor to the coffers of fascism. It has not been possible to identify "Commander Pecoraino".
233 This article formed part of a series of polemical pieces collectively entitled "The Mondo-Tribuna United Front" which appeared on 24, 25, 26 September, 1 and 14 October 1926.
234 Obviously a reference to arms.
235 Tilgher (1887–1941) was an essayist and literary critic, author of books on "The World Crisis" and on Pirandello, among many others. He was a

frequent contributor to *Il Mondo* and for a time one of its editors. One of the most eminent Italian intellectuals of the twenties, he is frequently referred to by Gramsci in the Prison Notebooks, often with considerable contempt. In 1921, he published a book entitled "Contemporary Relativists", which was perhaps in Gramsci's mind here.

236 The formation of a Republican–Socialist bloc (the "Republican Concentration") had been proposed by Pietro Nenni and Carlo Rosselli in *Quarto Stato*, and by Arturo Labriola in *La Voce Repubblicana*. In response, on 9 October 1926, in *L'Unità*, the PCI had reproposed the slogan of a "Republican assembly on the basis of workers' and peasants' committees". *La Voce Repubblicana* responded at length on 11 October, and *L'Unità* reported on this article on 12 October, giving its own comments.

237 For Stenterello, see note 30 above. The lines "Dietro l'avello/ Di Machiavello/ Dorme lo scheletro/ Di Stenterello" are by Giuseppe Giusti (*Il Mementomo*, stanza 2). Some commentators have suggested a physical proximity of Machiavelli's tomb to that of Stenterello's creator, Luigi Del Buono, but in fact they were in different Florentine churches.

238 The Seigneur de La Palice was a French military captain, killed at the battle of Pavia in 1525. His soldiers composed a song in his honour with the lines: "Un quart d'heure avant sa mort, Il était encore en vie . . ." (A quarter of an hour before he died, he was still alive . . .). A "La Palicean truth" became a common expression for a self-evident truth, so obvious that it does not require pointing out.

239 This note to Togliatti accompanied the following letter written by Gramsci in October 1926, on behalf of the Political Bureau of the PCI and addressed to the Central Committee of the CPSU, during the course of the inner-party struggle between the Stalin–Bukharin majority and the Trotsky–Zinoviev–Kamenev opposition. The Joint Opposition had been formed in April–June 1926, and was officially announced at a Central Committee meeting in July by Trotsky. Disciplinary measures followed, with Zinoviev being removed from the Political Bureau. *L'Unità* carried a report at the end of July which gave unconditional support to the majority, but purely on the grounds of preserving party unity; there was no comment on the issues at stake in the debate. In September, Gramsci wrote a series of articles on the Soviet Union (of which "The Peasants and the Dictatorship of the Proletariat" on pp. 412–16 above was one). On 4 October 1926, the Opposition proposed a truce in the inner-party struggle, declaring that they would cease to organize as a faction.

240 Gramsci planned to relaunch *L'Ordine Nuovo* as a theoretical review, but his arrest intervened before the project could be realized. His essay on the Southern Question (see pp. 441–62 below) was written for this journal.

241 Togliatti, in Moscow, did not transmit the letter from the PCI Political

Bureau to the Russian Central Committee, but instead sent this reply to Gramsci.

242 See note 189 above. During the course of 1926, the divisions in the Soviet leadership had been sharpest over the Anglo–Russion Trade-union Committee (see note 228 above) and over the course of events in China.

243 The French, German and Polish "Left" leaderships had all been replaced since the Fifth World Congress. When Comintern policy moved to the right in early 1925, Zinoviev organized the removal of the Fischer/Maslov group leading the German party. Souvarine, Monatte and Rosmer all came out in support of the Russian opposition and were expelled; Treint, who had also been guilty of "leftism" in the eyes of the 1925 Comintern leadership, and was even more suspect by 1926 as a protégé of Zinoviev's, only managed to survive in the leadership by extraordinary suppleness in complying with international pressure. Warski, Kostrzewa and Walecki were replaced by a "Left" group headed by Lenski and Domski at the Fifth World Congress; but in the summer of 1925, Domski's leftism was no longer in favour, and by the end of the year his association with Zinoviev was a further point against him: he was replaced by the reinstated Warski in December, while Lenski rallied to the new majority. In these and other parties, Zinoviev during 1925 helped to remove precisely those leading communists who might have been allies for him in the inner-party struggle in Russia; thus he was never in fact able to use the International as a political power base, despite his long dominant role within it.

244 The reference is to the Trade-Union Debate, which divided the Bolshevik leadership in the autumn and winter of 1920, and which was brought to a close by the Tenth Congress in March 1921 and by the adoption of NEP in May 1921.

245 This essay was planned (see note 240 above) to be included in a new theoretical journal. Written in the period immediately prior to Gramsci's arrest, it was not completed or corrected. It was subsequently found among his papers by Camilla Ravera, and published in 1930 in Paris by *Stato Operaio*. As Gramsci writes, the piece was originally stimulated by an article in *Quarto Stato*, a socialist review edited by Carlo Rosselli in Milan between March and October 1926. The author, "Ulenspiegel", was Tommaso Fiore, a contributor to Gobetti's *La Rivoluzione Liberale*.

246 The "Southernist" Guido Dorso together with Piero Gobetti represented the most progressive wing of Italian liberalism in the post-war period.

247 See *SPW I*, pp. 148–9.

248 Salvemini (see note 252 below), when he left the Socialist Party, defined his political views as "concretism".

249 Fortunato was a liberal conservative, author of *Il Mezzogiorno e lo Stato Italiano* (1911). Eugenio Azimonti was an agrarian, who contributed to Salvemini's *L'Unità* and to Gobetti's *La Rivoluzione Liberale*; he

published a book called *Il Mezzogiorno agrario qual è* in 1919. For Labriola, see note 31 above.
250 See note 8 above.
251 Alfredo Niceforo, a prominent sociologist and criminologist, argued in his book *Italiani del Nord e Italiani del Sud* that Southern Italians were biologically inferior. Similar arguments were put forward by Giuseppe Sergi, Enrico Ferri (see note 170 above) and Paolo Orano.
252 Gaetano Salvemini was a considerable influence on the young Gramsci, see *SPN*, Introduction pp. xx, xxvi, xxix. Leaving the PSI in 1910, he founded a journal called *L'Unità* (implying that the real unity of Italy — i.e. that between South and North — remained to be accomplished); this was published 1911–15 and 1918–20.
253 See note 164 above. The party was founded by Lussu in 1919.
254 See notes 199 and 90 above.
255 Enrico Corradini (1865–1931) was, together with D'Annunzio, the dominant figure in the pre-war nationalist movement in Italy. He founded the first nationalist review *Il Regno* in 1903. He made a particular study of Italian emigration, visiting the United States, Latin America and North Africa, and advocated colonial expansion into Africa so that Italians should go abroad as conquerors rather than as cheap labour. He developed the concept of Italy as a "proletarian nation" among the plutocracies — above all Britain and France.
256 For Mussolini's role in the PSI in 1914–15, see *SPN*, Introduction pp. xxvi–xxvii and xxx; *SPW I*, pp. 6–10 and Introduction p. xii. In the present volume, see pp. 211–12 and note 120 above.
257 See note 119 above.
258 See note 201 above.
259 For Sonnino, see note 49 above. For Salandra (1853–1931), see note 261 below.
260 See note 196 above.
261 Francesco Ciccotti was editor of the Rome edition of *Avanti!* in 1917. *La Stampa*, of course, was Giolitti's mouthpiece. Antonio Salandra, the conservative prime minister in 1914–15 and 1915–16, was a native of Foggia in Apulia. His government had been brought down in 1916 after disagreements with the Army high command; it was opposed both by Giolitti's neutralists and by those bourgeois forces who considered Salandra's conduct of the War too cautious. After the defeat of the Italian army at Caporetto, in October 1917, the Minister of the Interior Orlando took over the premiership. Although not a Giolittian or neutralist, he was unpopular with the pro-War forces for his "appeasement" of Giolitti and of the socialists. Giolitti's aim was to keep Orlando out of the embrace of the extreme pro-War lobby, and to prevent at the same time his being

replaced by a more right-wing prime minister – perhaps Salandra or some other Southern conservative politician.
262 Reggio Emilia had for long been the symbol of reformist socialism: see e.g. *SPW I*, p. 360.
263 Camillo Prampolini (1859–1930), the man who built up the foremost base of Italian social-democracy at Reggio Emilia, was one of the leaders of the reformist socialist party (PSU) and editor of its paper *La Giustizia* until its suppression in 1925. The pun in the original Italian "*nordici e sudici*" is impossible to translate: "*nordici*" means northerners, but although "*sud*" is indeed "south", "*sudici*" does not mean "southerners" but "filthy" (plural).
264 See "Un asino bardato" ("An ass in harness") in *Socialismo e Fascismo: L'Ordine Nuovo 1921–1922*, Turin, 1966, pp. 64–7, for this episode.
265 Umberto Terracini.
266 See "L'avvento della democrazia industriale" and "Uomini di carne e ossa" ("The advent of industrial democracy" and "Men of flesh and blood") in *Socialismo e Fascismo: L'Ordine Nuovo 1921–1922*, Turin, 1966, pp. 120–30 and 154–6.
267 Sonnino (see note 49 above) and Leopoldo Franchetti were both wealthy Tuscan conservatives; in 1873–5, they conducted an extensive private investigation into the social and administrative conditions of the Neapolitan region and Sicily. Franchetti published *Condizioni economiche ed ammistrative delle province Napoletane* in 1875; they jointly published *La Sicilia nel 1876* in 1877.
268 Gramsci himself had a Greek–Albanian great-grandfather, who had come from Epirus after 1821: "I myself have no race: my father is of recent Albanian origin" (*Lettere dal Carcere*, Turin, 1965, p. 506). The very name Gramsci was originally Albanian; there is a village called Gramshi in south-eastern Albania today.
269 The Banca Italiana di Sconto (see note 232 above) collapsed in December 1921, with lasting political consequences.
270 *La Critica* was a review founded by Benedetto Croce in 1903, and edited by him until 1944; in 1945 he re-launched it as *Quaderni della Critica*.
271 See note 96 above.

INDEX

Albania, 458, 507 n. 268
Albertini, Luigi, 262–3
Alessandria, 228
Alleanza del Lavoro, 83–4, 87–9, 118–19, 469 n. 50, 471 n. 56, 485 n. 144, 486 n. 144
Alma: *see* Lex
Amadeo: *see* Bordiga
Amendola, Giovanni, 200–1, 262–3, 266, 329, 403, 406, 456, 469 n. 51, 489 n. 154, 490 n. 154, 495 n. 184, 499 n. 204
America: *see* United States
American Federation of Labour (AFL), 165
Amsterdam, 155, 411
Angelo: *see* Tasca
Anglo-Russian Trade-union Committee, 411, 503 n. 228, 505 n. 242
Aosta, 447
Apulia, 26, 164, 393, 445, 452, 454
Arditi del Popolo, 56–8, 62, 124, 333, 393, 466 n. 29, 467 n. 33
Assyria, 12
Augustus Caesar, 212
Austria, 24
Avanti!, 35–6, 41, 49, 134–5, 143, 145, 147–8, 150, 188, 286, 300–1, 308, 448, 451
Aventine Secession; Assembly, 258, 276–7, 279, 306–8, 317, 322–3, 329, 334, 356–7, 371, 373, 403, 406, 409, 489 n. 154, 490 n. 154, n. 155
Azimonti, Eugenio, 443, 505 n. 249
Azione, L' (Cesena), 451, 459
Azione, L' (Milan), 459
Azzario, Isidoro, 283, 491 n. 166

Babylonia, 12
Bakunin, Mikhail, 340–1, 458
Balabanoff, Angelica, 212
Baldwin, Stanley, 423

Balkans, 410
Banca Commerciale Italiana, 352, 413
Banca Italiana di Sconto, 351–2, 459, 503 n. 232
Bank of Italy, 352
Barcelona, 7, 24
Bari, 130, 219
Barzini, Luigi, 412
Bavaria, 4, 15
Belloni, Ambrogio, 179
Bergamo, 73
Berlin, 129, 147, 153, 239, 475 n. 73
Berruti, Carlo, 208
Bianchi, Giuseppe, 50
Biella, 228
Bissolati, Leonida, 341
Bitonto, 445
Blanqui, Louis-Auguste, 46–7
Bolívar, Simón, 258
Bologna, 5, 61, 130, 219, 458
Bologna Congress of PSI (1919), 4, 463 n. 2
Bolshevik Party; CPSU, etc., 13, 21, 46, 134, 139, 183, 191–2, 194, 200, 210–11, 221, 233, 252, 282, 291, 294, 295–7, 301, 320, 324, 327, 332, 341, 362–3, 375, 398, 426–40, 464 n. 12, 486 n. 148, 487, n. 148, 492 n. 167, 497 n. 189, 503 n. 228, 504 n. 239, 505 n. 241, n. 242, n. 244
Bombacci, Nicola, 179, 301, 470 n. 54, 480 n. 99
Bondi, Max, 413, 416, 503 n. 232
Bonomi, Ivanoe, 54, 131, 220, 467 n. 32, 469 n. 51
Borelli, Giovanni, 459
Bordiga, Amadeo, 120, 133, 136–7, 138, 140, 158, 174, 179–80, 182, 188, 196, 199–200, 232, 240–2, 250–2, 284, 297–300, 302–4, 324–5, 327–9, 331–3, 337–9, 359, 435, 463 n. 2, 470 n. 54, 472 n. 63, 473 n. 63, 476 n. 80,

INDEX 509

Bordiga, Amadeo—*cont.*
  479 n. 93, 480 n. 98, 484 n. 140, n. 141,
  485 n. 143, n. 144, 486 n. 144, n. 145,
  494 n. 177, n. 179, 496 n. 188, 497 n.
  191, 500 n. 212, n. 213
Borghi, Armando, 75–8, 119, 468 n. 47,
  471 n. 59
Brandler, Heinrich, 192–4, 476 n. 77
Brescia, 219
Briand, Aristide, 54
British Communist Party, 410
Bruno: *see* Fortichiari
Bukharin, Nikolai, 180, 191–2, 291, 493
  n. 173, 497 n. 189
Bulgaria, 326, 330, 497 n. 190
Buozzi, Bruno, 53, 254, 467 n. 31
Bussi, Armando, 52

Cadorna, Luigi, 3, 7, 263, 463 n. 1
Cagliari Legion, 448
Calabria, 458
Calvin, John, 460
Calzini, Raffaele, 412
Camilla: *see* Ravera
Caporetto (battle), 3–4, 7, 215, 229, 233,
  463 n. 1, 506 n. 261
Caroti, Arturo, 203
Carson, Sir Edward, 412, 503 n. 230
Cartel des Gauches, 253, 488 n. 149, n.
  150, 496 n. 188
Casalese (Piedmont), 26
Casalini, Guido, 41
Castrucci, Augusto, 75
Catholic Action, 348–9, 353, 396, 402–3
CHEKA, 20, 464 n. 12
"Cheka" (in fascist Italy), 489 n. 154, 490
  n. 154
China, 12, 76, 505 n. 242
Ciccotti-Scozzese, Francesco, 451–2,
  506 n. 261
Clichy Congress of PCF (1925), 322, 496
  n, 188
Colombino, Emilio, 75
Colonna di Cesarò, Giovanni Antonio,
  253, 352, 403, 406, 456, 488 n. 151,
  489 n. 154
Comitato d'Intesa, 365, 389, 435, 493 n.
  175, 497 n. 191, 498 n. 191

Como, 222
Como Conference of PCI (1924),
  243–54, 484 n. 137, 485 n. 143
Conservative Party, 451
Constitutional democrats: *see* Liberal-
  democrats
Constitutionalists: *see* Liberal-democrats
Corradini, Enrico, 450, 506 n. 255
Corriere della Sera, Il, 141, 351, 451,
  474 n. 69, 495 n. 184
Cosmo, Umberto, 239
Crispi, Francesco, 347, 451, 498 n. 197,
  n. 200
Critica, La, 459, 507 n. 270
Critica Proletaria, 180
Croce, Benedetto, 392, 454, 459–60, 507
  n. 270
Cromwell, Oliver, 258
Czechoslovakia, 410

D'Annunzio, Gabriele, 6, 160, 409, 467
  n. 33, 477 n. 84, 502 n. 226
D'Aragona, Ludovico, 47, 74, 75–8, 119,
  268, 295, 445, 464 n. 9
Dawes, Charles, 409
De Ambris, Alceste, 75
De Felice, Giuffrida Giuseppe, 170, 478
  n. 89
De Gasperi, Alcide, 407
De Nicola, Enrico, 253, 352, 488 n. 151
De Vecchi, Cesare, 52
Di Cesarò: *see* Colonna di Cesarò
Difesa, La, 35
Dorso, Guido, 441, 461, 505 n. 246
Drago, Aurelio, 170
Dreyfus, Alfred, 274

Égalité, 148
Einstein, Albert, 420
Emilia, 26, 63–4, 350, 458
Engels, Friedrich, 170, 228, 392
England, 21, 27, 229, 284, 326, 352, 394,
  404, 408, 410–11, 412, 423
Entente (England, France, Italy, Russia,
  etc.), 23, 233
"Ercoli": *see* Togliatti
Europe; West Europe, 23–4, 139, 199,
  200, 210, 257, 284, 293–6, 308, 327,

Europe; West Europe—*cont.*
345, 355, 404, 409, 428, 459–60, 492
n. 168

Fabbri, Luigi, 119
Facta, Luigi, 41
Faggi, Angelo, 119
Fancello, Francesco, 451
Farinacci, Roberto, 52, 54, 266, 403–4
Fascist Party; fascists, etc., 4, 5–9, 23–4,
26, 30–1, 36, 38–40, 41–3, 44–5,
46–7, 52–3, 54–5, 56, 58, 59–60,
61–2, 63–5, 66–7, 71–4, 81, 87–8,
116–17, 129, 132, 141–2, 150–2, 160,
166–7, 169, 170–1, 183–4, 201–3,
211, 215–16, 221, 226, 229–38, 253,
255–72, 274–5, 276–8, 282, 287–8,
290, 295–6, 301, 303, 306–8, 317–18,
323, 325, 331–7, 344, 349–56, 359,
366, 369–71, 379, 382–3, 385–6, 397,
400–7, 409, 413–14, 423, 425, 428–9,
464 n. 14, 466 n. 22, 467 n. 35, 468 n.
37, n. 39, 476 n. 78, 481 n. 114, 482 n.
114, 483 n. 129, 486 n. 144, 488 n.
153, 489 n. 153, n. 154, 490 n. 154,
491 n. 161, 495 n. 184, 499 n. 203, 502
n. 226
Ferderzoni, Luigi, 402–3
Ferrero, Guglielmo, 289, 493 n. 171
Ferrero, Pietro, 208
"Ferri": *see* Leonetti
Ferri, Enrico, 289, 444
FIAT, 419, 449–52
Filipelli, Filippo, 258, 264, 489 n. 154,
490 n. 154
Finzi, Aldo, 258, 264, 489 n. 154, 490 n.
154
FIOM (Metalworkers' Federation), 48,
68, 131, 468 n. 44
Fischer, Ruth, 192, 496 n. 188
Flanders, 4
Florence, 35, 50, 130, 214, 251, 445, 458
Forges-Davanzati, Roberto, 450
Fortichiari, Bruno, 140, 182–4, 186, 480
n. 102, 484 n. 141, 497 n. 191
Fortunato, Giustino, 443, 454, 459–60,
505 n. 249
Foster, William Z., 165

France, 76, 129, 253, 274, 325, 394,
406–7, 409–10, 412, 436, 488 n. 149,
502 n. 224
France, Communist Party (PCF), 147,
253, 322, 325, 475 n. 74, 488 n. 149,
496 n. 188, 505 n. 243
Franchetti, Leopoldo, 457–8, 507 n. 267
Frankfurt, 155, 476 n. 78
Friuli, 395

Garibaldi, Giuseppe, 258
Gasti, Giovanni, 59
Gay, Pilade, 444
General Confederation of Italian
Industry *(Confindustria)*, 131, 277
General Confederation of Labour (CGL),
5, 12–14, 17–19, 20, 44–5, 49–50, 60,
61, 68, 77, 83, 119–20, 162, 165, 167,
208, 219, 265, 277–8, 283, 295–6,
304, 353, 355, 368–9, 393, 452, 464 n.
9, 491 n. 166, 500 n. 207
Gennari, Egidio, 300–1
Genoa, 131, 219
Genoa Congress of PSI (1892), 341
Gentile, Giovanni, 176, 180
Gentiloni, Vincenzo, 348, 451, 499 n. 202
Germanetto, Giovanni, 283
Germany, 4, 24, 121, 123–4, 129, 155,
179, 181, 191–2, 326, 410, 412–13,
424, 436, 496 n. 188, 503 n. 231
Germany, Communist Party (KPD), 139,
155, 179, 194, 322, 476 n. 77, 496 n.
188, 505 n. 243
Giolitti, Giovanni, 10–11, 29–30, 38, 41,
52–3, 69, 72, 78, 80–1, 129–31, 134,
220, 276–7, 348, 350, 406, 445,
449–52, 463 n. 5, 464 n. 5, 464 n. 7,
469 n. 51, 478 n. 91, 495 n. 184, 499 n.
202, 506 n. 261
Giovane Sardegna, 445–7
Giuletti, Giuseppe, 75
Giustizia, La, 35
Gobetti, Piero, 176, 186, 441, 458–62,
479 n. 96, 505 n. 246
Gompers, Samuel, 165
Gramsci, Antonio, 319, 334–5, 434
Graziadei, Antonio, 180, 301–2, 330,
358, 470 n. 54, 484 n. 139, 494 n. 181

INDEX

Grieco, Ruggero, 182, 186, 278, 491 n. 163
Grillo, Doctor, 185, 480 n. 106
Grosseto, 59–60, 259
Guarnieri, Mario, 41, 75, 465 n. 21

Hague, The, 193
Hamburg, 148, 150, 476 n. 75
Hegel, Georg W.F., 392
Hindenburg, Paul Ludwig, 413, 424, 496 n. 188
Holy Roman Empire, 211
Hungary, 4, 8, 15, 24, 156, 380–1, 477 n. 81

Iglesias, 447
Imola, 195
Independent Labour Party, 411
Independents (German USPD), 139, 474 n. 68
International, Ist, 291, 340, 458
International, IInd, 210, 291, 294, 340–1, 365, 476 n. 75
International, IIIrd, Executive Committee (ECCI), etc., 3, 26, 36, 46, 75, 77, 93, 96, 103, 117, 133–7, 139, 141, 154–6, 157, 159–60, 161–2, 173–4, 177–80, 183, 188, 191, 193–5, 198–200, 213–15, 224–5, 235, 241–2, 243–9, 252, 254, 265, 267, 280, 284, 290–1, 293–5, 297–301, 304, 318–29, 334, 338, 340–1, 361–2, 365–6, 380–4, 389–90, 398, 427–30, 433, 438, 463 n. 2, 470 n. 54, 471 n. 60, 473 n. 63, 474 n. 65, 481 n. 110, 484 n. 140, n. 141, 492 n. 167
Ist World Congress, 214
IInd World Congress, 20, 214, 224, 299
IIIrd World Congress, 173, 177, 179, 194–5, 214, 391, 470 n. 55
IVth World Congress, 173–4, 179, 214, 222, 243–5, 247, 251, 383, 472 n. 63, 476 n. 77, 477 n. 82, 481 n. 110
Vth World Congress, 297, 313, 321, 327, 374, 389, 429, 435–6, 492 n. 167

1st Enlarged Executive, 120, 123, 173, 195, 214, 471 n. 60, 481 n. 110
2nd Enlarged Executive, 173, 214, 253, 488 n. 149
3rd Enlarged Executive, 132, 143–53, 159, 173–4, 177, 179, 214, 219, 244, 247, 473 n. 63, 474 n. 71, 477 n. 82, 484 n. 141, 488 n. 149
5th Enlarged Executive, 284, 291, 293, 297, 313, 358, 492 n. 167, 494 n. 177
International Workers of the World (IWW), 165, 218–19, 321
Internazionale Comunista, L', 194, 426
Ireland, 15
Irpinia, 355
Istria, 395
Italia Libera, 176, 186, 277, 479 n. 97

Joint Opposition, 426–40, 497 n. 189, 504 n. 239

Kamenev, Lev, 191–2, 432, 434, 492 n. 167, 497 n. 189
Kerensky, Alexander, 233, 375, 422
Kolarov, Vasil, 196, 470 n. 54
Kornilov, Lavr, 329, 375
Kronstadt, 27

Labour Party (England), 83, 326, 411
Labriola, Antonio, 288, 426
Labriola, Arturo, 53, 422, 443, 450, 465 n. 20, 467 n. 31, 504 n. 236
Landworkers' Federation, 220, 483 n. 129
Lanfranconi, Luigi, 54
"Lanzi": *see* Tresso
Lanzillo, Agostino, 451
La Palice, Seigneur de, 423
Laterza (publishing house), 459
Lavoratore, Il, 35, 134–5, 145–6, 150
Lazzari, Constantino, 144, 232, 342, 471 n. 61
Leipzig Congress of KPD (1923), 193
Lenin, Vladimir Ilich, 186, 191–2, 210–11, 224, 248, 297–9, 320, 329, 380–1, 422, 427–8, 430, 433–4, 482 n. 118, 486 n. 148, 487 n. 148, 494 n. 179

Leone, Enrico, 450
Leonetti, Alfonso, 138, 173
Lex, Alma, 181
Liberal-democrats (*see also* National Union), 262, 424, 469 n. 51, 489 n. 154
Libya, 164, 170, 450
Livorno Congress of CGL (1921), 12–14, 17–19, 20–1
Livorno Congress of (PSI) PCI (1921), 3, 13, 25, 61–2, 80–2, 114, 116, 134, 160, 195, 197, 208, 214–16, 219, 222, 233, 235, 243, 246, 250, 286, 299, 300–1, 304, 319, 342, 359, 361, 380–3, 389, 420, 463 n. 1, 470 n. 54
Lloyd George, David, 27
Lombardy, 451
Longo, Luigi, 283
Longobardi, Ernesto Cesare, 180, 450
Loria, Achille, 289, 493 n. 171
Losa, 220
Luigino: *see* Repossi
Lussu, Emilio, 279, 282, 491 n. 164
Luxemburg, Rosa, 180
Lyons Congress of PCI (1926), 311–75, 379–99, 400, 403, 496 n. 185, 497 n. 191, 498 n. 194, 500 n. 209, n. 212, n. 213, 501 n. 221

MacDonald, James Ramsay, 411
Machiavelli, Nicolò, 53, 422
Maffi, Fabrizio, 162, 47¹ n. 61, 478 n. 85
Maffisti: *see* Third-internationalist Faction
Malatesta, Errico, 75, 468 n. 43, 482 n. 119
Malthus, Thomas, 56
Manuilsky, Dimitri, 144
Marabini, Anselmo, 300–1
Maraviglia, Maurizio, 450
Marcellus, 155, 476 n. 79
Marches, 451
Marx, Karl, 170, 228, 289, 313, 392, 422
Marx, Wilhelm, 424, 496 n. 188
"Masci": *see* Gramsci
Maslov, Arkadij, 192, 496 n. 188
Matarazzo, Francesco, 413, 416, 503 n. 232
Matteotti, Giacomo, 258–9, 264, 273–5, 293, 302, 306, 308, 317, 328, 330–1, 333, 354, 356, 375, 383, 386, 392, 409–10, 465 n. 15, 489 n. 153, n. 154
Mauro: *see* Scoccimarro
Mazzini, Giuseppe, 341
Mensheviks, 21, 139, 191–2, 197, 363
Messina, 219
Mezzogiorno, Il, 420
Micheli, Giuseppe, 67
Miglioli, Guido; *Migliolisti*, 277, 279, 316, 353, 491 n. 162
Milan, 35, 49–50, 59, 61, 130, 146, 170, 202, 211–12, 219, 224, 276, 443, 449, 458, 478 n. 90, n. 91
Milan Congress of PSI (1921), 113–14
Milan Congress of PSI (1923), 143–8, 475 n. 72
Millerand, Alexandre, 54
Mingrino, Giuseppe, 56, 58, 467 n. 34
Misiano, Francesco, 56, 301, 467 n. 34
Molfetta, 445
Molise, 355
Momigliano, Riccardo, 222, 473 n. 63
Mondo, Il, 412–16, 420, 474 n. 69
Mongolia, 12
Monicelli, Tommaso, 450
Montagnana, Mario, 138
"Morelli": *see* Scoccimarro
Morgan, John Pierpont, 404, 502 n. 223
Morocco, 325
Moscow, 21, 27, 46, 75, 77, 123, 130, 145, 147–8, 153, 159, 177, 182, 184–5, 188, 193, 197, 252, 279, 291, 471 n. 63
Murri, Romolo, 420, 499 n. 200
Mussolini, Benito, 46–7, 52, 56, 61–2, 64, 78, 129, 143, 185, 211–12, 230, 258, 264, 266, 273–4, 276–8, 289, 317, 329, 429, 445, 451, 466 n. 26, 468 n. 39, 482 n. 120, 483 n. 120, 488 n. 153, 489 n. 154, 490 n. 154, 491 n. 161, 495 n. 183, n. 184

Naples, 130, 219, 230
"Naples, F.", 333–4
Napoleon III, 129
Nationalist Party, 450
National Liberals, 306, 499 n. 204

INDEX 513

National Union of Liberals and Democrats, 308, 351, 355, 397, 456–7, 499 n. 204
"Negri": *see* Scoccimarro
Nenni, Pietro, 134, 140–1, 144, 146–8, 222, 286, 465 n. 21, 473 n. 63, 474 n. 65, 475 n. 72, 482 n. 119, 504 n. 236
New Economic Policy (NEP), 432, 505 n. 244
Niceforo, Alfredo, 444, 506 n. 251
Nitti, Francesco, 351–2, 409, 451, 458, 495 n. 184, 502 n. 226
Noske, Gustav, 54
Nuova Antologia, 180

Opposition Committee, 259, 261, 276–7
Orano, Paolo, 289, 444, 450, 493 n. 171
Ordine Nuovo, L', 5, 18, 59, 68, 75–6, 176, 181, 186–7, 188, 207, 214, 218, 220, 224–7, 229, 231, 236, 240, 242, 250, 272, 300–1, 394, 410, 426, 441, 444, 448, 460–1, 464 n. 11, 479 n. 95, n. 96, 482 n. 117, 504 n. 240
Orlando, Vittorio Emanuele, 230, 276, 352, 406, 456, 495 n. 184, 506 n. 261

Pagine Rosse, 215, 478 n. 85, 483 n. 126
"Palmi, Paolo": *see* Togliatti
Palmieri, Aurelio, 420–1
Pantaleo, Paolo, 420–1
Panunzio, Sergio, 451
Paris, 76, 253
Paris Congress of USI (1922), 120
Pasella, Umberto, 56
Pastore, Ottavio, 180, 445
Patria, La, 459
Peasant Party, 262, 395
Peasants' Defence Association, 395, 501 n. 217
Pecoraino, Commander, 413, 416, 503 n. 232
Perrone, Mario and Pio, 413, 416, 503 n. 232
Perugia, 259
Petrograd School, 174, 479 n. 94
Piave (battle), 3–4, 215, 463 n. 1
Piedmont, 50, 68–9, 130–1, 196, 208, 301, 396, 446, 457, 465 n. 18

Pilsudski, Józef, 406, 502 n. 224
Pisa, 219
Po valley, 58, 152, 170, 335, 345, 450–1
Poincaré, Raymond, 423
Poland, 406, 409–10, 417, 436, 502 n. 224, 505 n. 243
Pollio, Alberto, 129
Popolo d'Italia, Il, 52
Popular Party; *popolari*, 41, 53, 54, 64, 66–7, 71–4, 120, 124, 130, 132, 141–2, 152, 160, 162, 170, 261–2, 276, 279, 308, 316, 353, 355, 383, 402, 406, 424, 456, 466 n. 22, n. 23, 469 n. 51, 473 n. 64, 489 n. 154, 490 n. 155, 491 n. 162, 499 n. 203, 500 n. 211
Portugal, 409–10
Port-workers' Federation, 83
Prampolini, Camillo, 453, 507 n. 263
Preziosi, Giovanni, 420
Prezzolini, Giuseppe, 451
Proletario, Il, 35
Proudhon, Pierre-Joseph, 394
Pula, 35

Quarto Stato, Il, 441, 443, 446, 505 n. 245

Radek, Karl, 191, 193–4, 481 n. 110, 488 n. 149
Railwaymen's Federation, 60, 83
Rakosi, Matyas, 144, 472 n. 63
Ravera, Camilla, 240, 472 n. 63, 484 n. 137, 505 n. 245
Red Army, 20, 417–18
Red Peasants' International, 279
Red Trade-union International, 120, 321, 464 n. 9, 471 n. 59
Reggio Emilia, 35, 449, 453–4, 507 n. 262
Regime Fascista, Il, 420–1
Remondino, Duilio, 179
Repossi, Luigi, 476 n. 76, 491 n. 163, 497 n. 191
Republican Concentration, 422–5, 504 n. 236
Republican Party, 170, 222, 277, 308, 355, 373, 400, 479 n. 92, 489 n. 154

Rerum Novarum (Encyclical), 347, 499 n. 199
Resto del Carlino, Il, 420
"Rienzi": *see* Tasca
Risorgimento, 344
Rivoluzione Liberale, La, 176, 262, 458, 461, 479 n. 96
Roccagorga, 211, 483 n. 120
Roccastrada, 64, 74
Rocco, Alfredo, 402–3
Romagna, 47, 451, 479 n. 92
Rome, 35, 46, 50, 74, 212, 222, 259, 263, 306, 383, 403, 447
Rome Congress of PCI (1922), 91–125, 153, 173–4, 195–6, 240, 243, 245–7, 251, 290, 304, 319, 335, 382, 389, 392, 469 n. 54, 470 n. 56, 475 n. 72, 481 n. 110
Rome Congress of PSI (1922), 144, 146–8, 233
Romulus, 212
Romulus Augustulus, 212, 483 n. 121
Roncoroni, 222
Rossi, Cesare, 41, 258, 264, 276, 466 n. 24, 489 n. 154, 490 n. 154
Ruggero: *see* Grieco
Russia, 21, 27–8, 37, 114, 139, 178, 180, 191–2, 194, 199–200, 210–1, 227, 237–8, 283–4, 294–6, 307, 327–8, 332, 345, 361–2, 394, 408, 412–16, 417–18, 420, 422, 426–40, 471 n. 63, 503 n. 229, 504 n. 239
Russian Revolution (1905), 332
Russian Revolution (February 1917), 422
Russian Revolution (October 1917), 4, 13, 21, 37, 154, 229, 233, 284, 345, 418, 422, 440
Russian Social-Democratic Party, 197
Ryazanov, David, 228, 426

Sacerdote, Gustavo, 148
Saint-Ouen Congress of French Socialist Party, 147, 475 n. 73
Salandra, Antonio, 263, 276, 451, 456, 495 n. 184, 506 n. 259, n. 261
Salvadori, Riccardo, 301
Salvemini, Gaetano, 443–5, 505 n. 248, 506 n. 252
"Sardi": *see* Gramsci
Sardinia, 170, 253, 257, 308, 344, 352, 354–5, 396–7, 407, 441–2, 444, 446–8, 450, 454, 457
Sardinian Action Party, 141, 308, 355, 402, 407, 445, 448, 491 n. 164
Sarzana, 60, 64, 74
Sassari; Sassari Brigade, 447–8
Savoy Monarchy, 403
Saxony, 326
Sbrana, Leone, 75
Scalarini, Giuseppe, 211
"Scocci": *see* Scoccimarro
Scoccimarro, Mauro, 132, 136–7, 177–80, 182, 186, 219–20, 242, 473 n. 63, 479 n. 93, 480 n. 98, n. 102, 494 n. 177
Sedan, 129, 132
Sergi, Giuseppe, 444
"Serra": *see* Tasca
Serrati, Giacinto, 47, 68, 75, 130, 146–7, 161–2, 197, 282–3, 299, 380–1, 463 n. 1, n. 2, 471 n. 61, 473 n. 63, 475 n. 72, n. 73, 478 n. 85, 491 n. 165, 494 n. 179
Sicilian Fasci, 348, 449, 498 n. 200
Sicily, 170, 308, 344, 352, 354–5, 396–7, 407, 441–2, 444, 450–1, 454, 456–7
Siena, 59
"Silvia": *see* Ravera
Sindacato Rosso, 146, 164, 478 n. 86
Socialist Defence Committee, 143–4, 146, 148
Socialist Party (PSI); Maximalists, 3–4, 12–13, 24, 25–6, 31, 34, 36, 41, 44–5, 46, 50, 52–3, 54, 56, 58, 61–2, 63–4, 67, 68, 70, 71–4, 77, 80–2, 85, 113–14, 116, 120–1, 124, 129–31, 133–5, 139–41, 143–50, 155, 159–60, 161, 169–70, 175, 187, 188–9, 203, 207–8, 211–12, 213–16, 218, 221–2, 224, 226, 230, 232–3, 243–4, 247–8, 251, 261–2, 265–6, 270, 282–3, 286–7, 289–90, 298–302, 307–8, 314, 318, 334, 341–2, 347, 349, 355, 359, 365–6, 368, 373–4, 379, 382–3, 407, 417, 420, 444–5, 449–52, 463 n. 1, n.

INDEX

Socialist Party (PSI)—*cont.*
 2, 464 n. 9, n. 14, 465 n. 15, n. 17, 466
 n. 22, n. 29, 467 n. 33, 468 n. 44, 473 n.
 63, n. 64, 474 n. 65, 475 n. 72, 478 n.
 85, n. 91, 484 n. 130, 489 n. 153, n.
 154, 490 n. 155, 495 n. 184, 500 n.
 207, 501 n. 216, n. 221
Social-Revolutionaries (Russia), 139,
 192, 221
Sondrio, 222
Sonnino, Sidney, 79, 451, 457–8, 469 n.
 49, 507 n. 267
South, the; the *Mezzogiorno*, 162, 167,
 202–3, 230, 235, 251, 253, 257, 308,
 316, 330–1, 344–5, 347–8, 351–2,
 354–6, 396–8, 402, 407, 417, 441–61,
 504 n. 240
Spain, 23–4, 321, 409–10, 464 n. 6
Spartacists, 15, 139
Speranzini, Giuseppe, 142, 466 n. 23
Sraffa, Piero, 218, 220, 231–5, 483 n. 127
Stalin, Joseph, 191–2, 327, 428, 487 n.
 148, 497 n. 189
Stampa, La, 6, 8, 41–2, 141, 451–2, 464
 n. 5, 474 n. 69
Stato Operaio, Lo, 189
Stenterello, 53, 422, 467 n. 30, 504 n. 237
Sturzo, Luigi, 266, 499 n. 203
Stuttgart Congress of IInd International
 (1907), 368, 499 n. 207
Switzerland, 137

Tasca, Angelo, 138, 175–6, 177–8, 180,
 188, 219, 241–2, 250, 252, 281, 330,
 336, 338, 470 n. 54, n. 56, 473 n. 63,
 474 n. 66, n. 71, 475 n. 71, 476 n. 80,
 477 n. 82, 484 n. 130, n. 139, 485 n.
 142, n. 143, 500 n. 213, 501 n. 221
Tasca di Cutò, Alessandro, 170
Temps, Le, 38
Terracini, Umberto, 120, 132, 136, 140,
 157, 175, 180, 182, 188, 191–2, 194,
 219–20, 233, 473 n. 63, 474 n. 65, 479
 n. 93, 480 n. 98, n. 104
Thalheimer, August, 192–3
Third-Internationalist Faction; Fusionist-
 maximalists; *Maffisti*, 121, 146, 161,
 222, 301–2, 366, 374, 389, 471 n. 61,

473 n. 63, 475 n. 72, 478 n. 85, 484 n.
 130, 489 n. 153, 491 n. 165
Tilgher, Adriano, 420, 503 n. 235, 504 n.
 235
"Tito": *see* Fortichiari
Togliatti, Palmiro, 49, 173–6, 179–80,
 188, 240, 473 n. 63, 477 n. 83, 479 n.
 93, 486 n. 145, 488 n. 153, 504 n. 239,
 n. 241
Tortona, 222
Tresso, Pietro, 173, 176
Treves, Claudio, 29, 263, 445
Treviso, 59–60, 64, 67, 74
Tribuna, La, 420
Trieste, 35, 135, 219, 447
Triple Alliance, 347, 498 n. 198
Trotsky, Leon, 191–4, 252–3, 284, 297,
 321, 327, 428, 432, 434, 472 n. 63, 481
 n. 110, n. 114, 486 n. 148, 487 n. 148,
 488 n. 149, 492 n. 167, n. 168, 496 n.
 189, 497 n. 189
Turati, Filippo, 37, 74, 129, 220, 232,
 263, 266, 268, 299, 341, 380, 445, 463
 n. 1, 465 n. 20, 473 n. 63, 494 n. 179
Turin, 5–9, 41–2, 48, 50, 59, 68–70, 131,
 138, 142, 169, 187, 188–90, 196,
 207–8, 214, 218–20, 224, 227, 250,
 300–1, 419, 441–9, 452–3, 460
Turin Congress of Popular Party (1923),
 383
Tuscany, 26, 63–4, 393, 457

"Ulenspiegel", 441, 505 n. 245
Umanità Nova, 68–9, 118–19
Umberto: *see* Terracini
Umberto I, 79–80, 164, 469 n. 49
Umbria, 63
Unione Italiana del Lavoro (UIL), 83
Unione Sindacale Italiana (USI) 83, 120,
 164, 471 n. 59, 478 n. 86
Unità, L' (PCI daily), 162, 230, 328, 398,
 477 n. 85, 478 n. 85
Unità, L' (Salvemini's journal), 451, 459,
 506 n. 252
Unitary Socialist Party (PSU);
 Reformists, 152, 185, 221–2, 227, 233,
 258, 262, 265–6, 270, 277, 279,
 287–8, 308, 355, 373–4, 383,

Unitary Socialist Party (PSU)—*cont.*
473 n. 63, n. 64, 475 n. 72, 489 n. 153, n. 154, 495 n. 183, 507 n. 263
United States of America; America, 21, 165, 307–8, 352, 374, 394, 404, 409, 458, 492 n. 168
"Urbani": *see* Terracini

"Valle": *see* Tasca
Vatican, 129, 141, 180, 262–3, 316, 346–9, 352–3, 396, 403, 423, 443, 495 n. 184, 498 n. 199, 499 n. 201, n. 202, n. 203
Vecchi, Nicola, 164, 478 n. 86
Vella, Arturo, 134, 140–1, 144, 146–8, 212, 222
Veneto, 63–4
Venice, 458
Vercelli, 228
Victor Emmanuel III, 273, 276, 490 n. 154
Vie Ouvrière, La, 76

Vita Italiana, La, 420
Viterbo, 59–60, 64
Vittorio Veneto (battle), 3–4, 463 n. 1
Voce, La, 451, 459
Voce della Gioventù, 169, 171
Voce Repubblicana, La, 422, 424
Volpi, Giuseppe, 403, 405

War-veterans' Association, 130
West Europe: *see* Europe

Yugoslavia, 156, 477 n. 81, 502 n. 226

Zaniboni, Tito, 52, 495 n. 183
Zankov, Aleksandr, 326, 497 n. 190
Zimmerwald Conference (1915), 233
Zini, Zino, 218, 220, 483 n. 127
Zinoviev, Grigorii, 148, 191–3, 428, 432, 434, 474 n. 65, n. 71, 492 n. 167, 494 n. 181, 497 n. 189, 505 n. 243
Zuccoli, Giuseppe, 405

The index does not contain entries for Italy or Communist Party (PCI), and only more substantive references to the notes are included.